Lecture Notes of the Institute for Computer Sciences, Social Informatics and Telecommunications Engineering

T0092578

Natarajan Meghanathan   Nabendu Chaki
Dhinaharan Nagamalai (Eds.)

Advances in Computer Science and Information Technology

Computer Science and Information Technology

Second International Conference, CCSIT 2012
Bangalore, India, January 2-4, 2012
Proceedings, Part III

 Springer

Volume Editors

Natarajan Meghanathan
Jackson State University, Jackson, MS, USA
E-mail: nmeghanathan@jsums.edu

Nabendu Chaki
University of Calcutta, Calcutta, India
E-mail:nabendu@ieee.org

Dhinaharan Nagamalai
Wireilla Net Solutions PTY Ltd., Melbourne, VIC, Australia
E-mail: dhinthia@yahoo.com

ISSN 1867-8211   e-ISSN 1867-822X
ISBN 978-3-642-27316-2   e-ISBN 978-3-642-27317-9
DOI 10.1007/978-3-642-27317-9
Springer Heidelberg Dordrecht London New York

Library of Congress Control Number: 2011943315

CR Subject Classification (1998): H.4, C.2, I.2, H.3, D.2, I.4, H.5

Typesetting: Camera-ready by author, data conversion by Scientific Publishing Services, Chennai, India

Printed on acid-free paper

Springer is part of Springer Science+Business Media (www.springer.com)

Preface

The Second International Conference on Computer Science and Information Technology (CCSIT-2012) was held in Bangalore, India, during January 2–4, 2012. CCSIT attracted many local and international delegates, presenting a balanced mixture of intellect from the East and from the West. The goal of this conference series is to bring together researchers and practitioners from academia and industry to focus on understanding computer science and information technology and to establish new collaborations in these areas. Authors are invited to contribute to the conference by submitting articles that illustrate research results, projects, survey work and industrial experiences describing significant advances in all areas of computer science and information technology.

The CCSIT-2012 Committees rigorously invited submissions for many months from researchers, scientists, engineers, students and practitioners related to the relevant themes and tracks of the conference. This effort guaranteed submissions from an unparalleled number of internationally recognized top-level researchers. All the submissions underwent a strenuous peer review process which comprised expert reviewers. These reviewers were selected from a talented pool of Technical Committee members and external reviewers on the basis of their expertise. The papers were then reviewed based on their contributions, technical content, originality and clarity. The entire process, which includes the submission, review and acceptance processes, was done electronically. All these efforts undertaken by the Organizing and Technical Committees led to an exciting, rich and high-quality technical conference program, which featured high-impact presentations for all attendees to enjoy, appreciate and expand their expertise in the latest developments in computer network and communications research. In closing, CCSIT-2012 brought together researchers, scientists, engineers, students and practitioners to exchange and share their experiences, new ideas and research results in all aspects of the main workshop themes and tracks, and to discuss the practical challenges encountered and the solutions adopted. We would like to thank the General and Program Chairs, organization staff, the members of the Technical Program Committees and external reviewers for their excellent and tireless work. We sincerely wish that all attendees benefited scientifically from the conference and wish them every success in their research.

It is the humble wish of the conference organizers that the professional dialogue among the researchers, scientists, engineers, students and educators continues beyond the event and that the friendships and collaborations forged will linger and prosper for many years to come.

January 2012
Natarajan Meghanathan
Nabendu Chaki
Dhinaharan Nagamalai

Organization

General Chairs

David C. Wyld   Southeastern Louisiana University, USA
Natarajan Meghanathan   Jackson State University, USA

General Co-chairs

Jae Kwang Lee   Hannam University, South Korea
Michal Wozniak   Wroclaw University of Technology, Poland

Steering Committee

Abdul Kadhir Ozcan   The American University, Cyprus
Brajesh Kumar Kaushik   Indian Institute of Technology - Roorkee, India
Dhinaharan Nagamalai   Wireilla Net Solutions Pty Ltd., Australia
Eric Renault   Institut Telecom-Telecom SudParis, France
John Karamitsos   University of the Aegean, Samos, Greece
Kamalrulnizam Abu Bakar   Universiti Teknologi Malaysia, Malaysia
Khoa N. Le   University of Western Sydney, Australia
Nabendu Chaki   University of Calcutta, India

Program Committee

A.P. Sathish Kumar   PSG Institute of Advanced Studies, India
Abdul Aziz   University of Central Punjab, Pakistan
Abdul Kadir Ozcan   The American University, Cyprus
Andreas Riener Johannes   Kepler University Linz, Austria
Andy Seddon   Asia Pacific Institute of Information
     Technology, Malaysia

Armendariz-Inigo   Universidad Publica de Navarra, Spain
Atilla Elci   Eastern Mediterranean University, Cyprus
B. Srinivasan   Monash University, Australia
Balasubramanian K.   Lefke European University, Cyprus
Boo-Hyung Lee   KongJu National University, South Korea
Brajesh Kumar Kaushik   Indian Institute of Technology, India
Charalampos Z. Patrikakis   National Technical University of Athens,
     Greece

Chih-Lin Hu   National Central University, Taiwan
Chin-Chih Chang   Chung Hua University, Taiwan
Cho Han Jin   Far East University, South Korea
Cynthia Dhinakaran   Hannam University, South Korea

Nabendu Chaki	University of Calcutta, India
Natarajan Meghanathan	Jackson State University, USA
Nicolas Sklavos	Technological Educational Institute of Patras, Greece
Phan Cong Vinh	London South Bank University, UK
Ponpit Wongthongtham	Curtin University of Technology, Australia
Rajendra Akerkar	Technomathematics Research Foundation, India
Rajesh Kumar P.	The Best International, Australia
Ramayah Thurasamy	Universiti Sains Malaysia, Malaysia
Rituparna Chaki	West Bengal University of Technology, India
S. Hariharan	B.S. Abdur Rahman University, India
Sagarmay Deb	Central Queensland University, Australia
Sajid Hussain	Fisk University, USA
Salah S.	Al-Majeed University of Essex, UK
Sanguthevar Rajasekaran	University of Connecticut, USA
Sarmistha Neogyv	Jadavpur University, India
Sattar B. Sadkhan	University of Babylon, Iraq
Sergio Ilarri	University of Zaragoza, Spain
Serguei A. Mokhov	Concordia University, Canada
Shivan Haran	Arkansas State University, USA
Somitra Sanadhya	IIT-Delhi, India
Sriman Narayana Iyengar	VIT University, India
SunYoung Han	Konkuk University, South Korea
Susana Sargento	University of Aveiro, Portugal
Syed Rahman	University of Hawaii-Hilo, USA
Syed Rizvi	University of Bridgeport, USA
Velmurugan Ayyadurai	Center for Communication Systems, UK
Vishal Sharma	Metanoia Inc., USA
Wei Jie	University of Manchester, UK
Yan Luo	University of Massachusetts Lowell, USA
Yannick Le	Moullec Aalborg University, Denmark
Yao-Nan Lien	National Chengchi University, Taiwan
Yeong Deok Kim	Woosong University, South Korea
Yuh-Shyan Chen	National Taipei University, Taiwan
Yung-Fa Huang	Chaoyang University of Technology, Taiwan

External Reviewers

Amit Choudhary	Maharaja Surajmal Institute, India
Abhishek samanta	Jadavpur University, Kolkata, India
Anjan K.	MSRIT, India
Ankit	BITS, Pilani, India
Aravind P.A.	Amrita School of Engineering India
Ashutosh Dubey	NRI Institute of Science and Technology, Bhopal, India

Ashutosh Gupta   MJP Rohilkhand University, Bareilly, India
Babak Khosravifar   Concordia University, Canada
Balaji Sriramulu
Balakannan S.P.   Chonbuk National University, Jeonju, Korea
Bhupendra Suman   IIT Roorkee, India
Cauvery Giri   RVCE, India
Chandra Mohan   Bapatla Engineering College, India
Debdatta Kandar   Sikkim Manipal University, India
Doreswamyh Hosahalli   Mangalore University, India
P. Sheik Abdul Khader   B.S. Abdur Rahman University, India
Durga Toshniwal   Indian Institute of Techniology, India
Gopalakrishnan Kaliaperumal   Anna University, India
Govardhan A.   JNTUH College of Engineering, India
Hameem Shanavas   Vivekananda Institute of Technolgy, India
Hari Chavan   National Institute of Technology, Jamshedpur,
                                India
Kaushik Chakraborty   Jadavpur University, India
Kota Sunitha   G. Narayanamma Institute of Technology and
                                Science, Hyderabad, India
Lavanya   Blekinge Institute of Technology, Sweden
Mahalinga V. Mandi   Dr. Ambedkar Institute of Technology,
                                Bangalore, Karnataka, India
Mohammad Mehdi Farhangia   Universiti Teknologi Malaysia (UTM),
                                Malaysia
Murty Ch.A.S.   JNTU, Hyderabad, India
Mydhili Nair   M.S. Ramaiah Institute of Technology, India
Naga Prasad Bandaru   P.V.P. Siddartha Institute of Technology, India
Nagamanjula Prasad   Padmasri Institute of Technology, India
Nagaraj Aitha   I.T. Kamala Institute of Technology and
                                Science, India
Nana Patil   NIT Surat, Gujrat, India
Omar Almomani   Universiti Utara Malaysia, Malaysia
Osman B. Ghazali   Universiti Utara Malaysia, Malaysia
Padmalochan Bera   Indian Institute of Technology, Kharagpur,
                                India
Pappa Rajan   Anna University, India
Parth Lakhiya
Pradeepini Gera   Jawaharlal Nehru Technological University,
                                India
R.M. Suresh   Mysore University, India
Rabindranath Bera   Sikkim Manipal Institute of Technology, India
Rajashree Biradar   Ballari Institute of Technology and
                                Management, India
Rajesh Kumar Krishnan   Bannari Amman Institute of Technology, India
Ramin Karimi   University Technology Malaysia

Reena Dadhich	Govt. Engineering College Ajmer, India
Reshmi Maulik	University of Calcutta, India
Rituparna Chaki	West Bengal University of Technology, India
S. Bhaskaran	SASTRA University, India
Saleena Ameen	B.S. Abdur Rahman University, India
Salini P.	Pondichery Engineering College, India
Sami Ouali	ENSI, Manouba, Tunisia
Samodar Reddy	India School of Mines, India
Sanjay Singh	Manipal Institute of Technology, India
Sara Najafzadeh	University Technology Malaysia
Sarada Prasad Dakua	IIT-Bombay, India
S.C. Sharma	IIT - Roorkee, India
Seetha Maddala	CBIT, Hyderabad, India
Selvakumar Ramachandran	Blekinge Institute of Technology, Sweden
Shriram Vasudevan	VIT University, India
Soumyabrata Saha	Guru Tegh Bahadur Institute of Technology, India
Srinivasulu Pamidi	V.R. Siddhartha Engineering College Vijayawada, India
Subhabrata Mukherjee	Jadavpur University, India
Subir Sarkar	Jadavpur University, India
Suhaidi B. Hassan	
Sunil Singh	Bharati Vidyapeeth's College of Engineering, India
Suparna DasGupta	
Swarup Mitra	Jadavpur University, Kolkata, India
Tsung Teng Chen	National Taipei University, Taiwan
Valli Kumari Vatsavayi	AU College of Engineering, India
Yedehalli Kumara Swamy	Dayanand Sagar College of Engineering, India

Technically Sponsored by

Software Engineering & Security Community (SESC)
Networks & Communications Community (NCC)
Internet Computing Community (ICC)
Computer Science & Information Technology Community (CSITC)

Organized By

ACADEMY & INDUSTRY RESEARCH COLLABORATION CENTER (AIRCC)
www.airccse.org

Table of Contents – Part III

Advances in Computer Science and Information Technology

Ad Hoc and Ubiquitous Computing

Driving Hazards Message Propagation Using Road Side Infrastructure in VANETs

M.A. Berlin[1] and Sheila Anand[2]

[1] Department of Computer Science and Engineering,
R.M.D Engineering College Chennai, India
[2] Computer Studies,
Rajalakshmi Engineering College Chennai, India
berlinrajin@yahoo.com, sheila.anand@gmail.com

Abstract. VANET is a special form of Mobile Ad hoc Network (MANET) where the moving nodes are vehicles. Vehicles on the highway can encounter hazardous driving condition like slippery road, road blocks, hairpin curves and other unexpected obstacles. Speedy delivery of such information to other vehicles can help to prevent road accidents and improve passenger safety. The traffic on the highways may not be dense and hence vehicle-to-vehicle communication will not satisfy the requirements. In this paper, we propose the use of Road Side InfrastrUcture (RSU) for propagating the safety message to nearby vehicles travelling in the direction of the road hazard. Vehicles coming across such dangerous road condition will communicate the information to the nearest RSUs. RSUs will selectively forward these messages to other relevant RSUs which in turn will propagate the message to vehicles approaching the unsafe road areas. RSUs use aggregation strategy in order to reduce redundancy, and network overhead. As vehicles would normally travel at high speed on the highways, propagation over a longer distance is required to avoid accidents, ensure passenger safety and prevent vehicular damage.

Keywords: Safety Message Dissemination, Road Hazard, Road Side Infrastructure, Selective Transmission, Aggregation.

1 Introduction

Vehicular Ad hoc Network (VANET) is a key component of Intelligent Transport System (ITS). Each vehicle is equipped with wireless communication devices capable of communicating with each other along with GPS receivers to map the location. VANET is a self organizing network and provides an infrastructure to enhance passenger safety and travelling comfort [1]. VANET provides two types of communication: Vehicle to Vehicle (V2V) and Vehicle to Infrastructure (V2I) called Road Side infrastructUres (RSUs). The RSUs are stationary devices which are deployed on roadside capable of exchanging important information such as road condition, accidents and other emergency and safety related messages with the On Board Unit (OBU) equipped on vehicle. The Federal Communications Commission (FCC), USA, allotted

N. Meghanathan et al. (Eds.): CCSIT 2012, Part III, LNICST 86, pp. 1–8, 2012.
© Institute for Computer Sciences, Social Informatics and Telecommunications Engineering 2012

75MHz frequency spectrum between 5.580 and 5.925 GHz band for Dedicated Short Range Communications (DSRC) in VANETs. The DSRC spectrum is developed to support safety and periodic data transfer through Control and Service Channels respectively. The channel 178 of DSRC is primarily used for exchanging safety messages whereas other periodic hello messages are broadcast through service channels [2]. These messages are used to propagate hazardous event which is ahead of the vehicle and hence warn driver to react based on the received information.

There are a number of major differences between VANET and MANET [3]. VANETs have nodes as vehicles such as cars, dumpers, and trucks etc., which have high mobility as compared to nodes in MANET. However, the movement of the vehicles is restricted to fixed roads and highways unlike in MANETs. In VANET, vehicles have adequate power resources for V2I and V2V communication.

VANET applications are broadly classified as safety and comfort (non- safety) applications [4]. Safety applications propagates safety related information such as abnormal road conditions warning, smooth curve warning, accident warning and traffic jam along the travelling path of the vehicles in the network. The comfort applications can be further classified as convenience and commercial applications and are delay-tolerant. Some of the examples of convenience applications are finding gas filling stations, free parking lots, and nearest hotels. Commercial applications are available for road navigation that allows road maps to be downloaded into GPS systems. Remote vehicle diagnosis is another example of this type of applications. Advertisements and internet access would also be classified under commercial applications.

Road safety applications require fast and reliable propagation of safety messages in network. So it is necessary to use suitable messaging in order to propagate hazardous events as early as possible to the vehicles which are approaching the hazardous location. We propose a message dissemination technique that consumes minimum network bandwidth by selectively transmitting the road safety messages only to vehicles approaching the treacherous road locations.

In this paper we assume that pre-installed infrastructure, RSU, are available to disseminate safety message on the highway. In our proposed approach, RSU will not broadcast the safety message to all vehicles but will selectively propagate only to relevant vehicles likely to traverse the hazardous zones. The rest of the paper is organized as follows: In section 2, we discuss the work related to safety message dissemination techniques. In section 3, we discuss our proposed RSU- based safety message propagation and section 4 concludes the paper.

2   Related Work

One of the common techniques used for safety message dissemination is broadcasting or pure flooding. Simple broadcasting techniques cause broadcast storm problem due to duplication of message transmission [5]. There is high bandwidth usage and duplicate reception of the same messages from different vehicles leading to message congestion and degradation in network performance.

We discuss the related work that uses vehicle to vehicle safety message dissemination on highways. Erwin Van de Velde et al have been proposed a new routing algorithm called REACT, to choose a best forwarder for sending packet along a trajectory on highways using vehicle to vehicle communication [6]. Vehicles exchange beacon messages to know the neighbors position. A node will rebroadcast the packet if it can cover large distance than the transmitter. Yao-Tsung et al have been proposed a Position-based Adaptive Broadcast (PAB) algorithm for delivery of emergency messages. This protocol uses vehicle to vehicle communication [7]. The relay nodes are identified based on the position, direction and velocity of receiving vehicle; mostly, farther nodes are identified as relay nodes in order to propagate messages quickly. The messages are ignored by the vehicles which are travelling in opposite direction. The authors also calculated time delay based on the velocity of vehicles to differ the retransmission. The authors also noticed that the PAB algorithm gives enough time to the drivers to react against emergency event. However, they also pointed out that there are many simultaneous transmissions due to chain events leading to data congestion. Vehicular Reactive Routing (VRR) protocol has been designed by Martin Koubek et al for data dissemination on highways in WAVE based VANETs [8]. VRR is designed for the logical link control layer of WAVE stack. The sender node identifies the relay nodes from each direction with respect to the distance between its neighbors and inserts the information about suitable relay node into the packet. VRR protocol maintains neighboring information in its routing table in order to find out suitable forwarding node. The authors pointed out that this protocol will not provide advantage for simple broadcasting but it can give significant benefit on the systems which uses route discovery process. As future extension, the authors mentioned that the delivery ratio for distant nodes to be considered by resending the broadcast data.

All of the above work is based on vehicle to vehicle communication. In sparse networks identifying the next hop would be difficult due to the large distance of vehicles on highways. VANETs tend to be disconnected, consisting of a collection of disjoint clusters of cars. To overcome the limitations imposed by lack of connection, Mahmoud Abuelela et al have been proposed Smart Opportunistic Data dissemination Approach (SODA) to disseminate packets in sparse networks on highways [9]. Though cars find neighbors to transmit packets to a longer distance, it may not deliver through these neighbors. Instead, cars that move very fast will carry packets until destination in order to use bandwidth effectively.

Data aggregation is one of the powerful techniques to collect similar or dissimilar messages from the neighboring vehicles in order to minimize network overhead and to reduce information redundancy. Khaled Ibrahim et al have been presented a new aggregation technique for aggregating vehicles data without losing accuracy [10]. Vehicles form clusters by exchanging location and speed information periodically to create local view of the vehicle and transmits aggregated record to the neighbors to make a local view up to 1.6km. To extend the local view, the aggregated message of the cluster is transmitted to other clusters. The authors pointed out that there must be a mechanism introduced to minimize number of message broadcast and to build an algorithm for increasing security.

Bruno Defude et al have been developed a system called Vehicular Event Sharing with a mobile P2P Architecture (VESPA) to share information among vehicles in order to extract knowledge from neighboring vehicles [11]. The authors have focused on knowledge extraction and how to aggregate data about dangerous hazards such as accidents, emergency braking and other emergency events or to know the available parking lots. Aggregated messages are stored in a matrix and sent to the neighbors.

Martin Koubek et al have presented Event Suppression for Safety Message Dissemination (ESSMD) scheme to reduce simultaneous reception of same event message from the number of neighboring vehicles [12]. The authors have used an aggregation strategy in which the transmitter has to wait for 10ms or 100ms in order to aggregate the messages received during that time and the aggregated message will be transmitted as one packet. ESSMD+ Rep (repetitions) method was introduced to improve the reliability of ESSMD. The authors pointed out that the packet transmission delay of this scheme is increased due to aggregation.

Kai Liu et al have been proposed a RSU-Assisted Multi-channel Coordination (RAMC) MAC protocol to broadcast safety and non-safety information to all the neighboring vehicles [13]. RSUs will monitor the both service and control channels of DSRC in order to collect emergency warning messages from vehicles. RSUs will aggregate the received information and transmit to the vehicles which are in its transmission range in both service and control channel so that vehicles will not miss the information. The focus of the work is on high delivery ratio and low delay for safety messages. The performance analysis showed that the delay of emergency warning messages such as accidents is much less when compared to status safety messages.

Pratibha Tomar et al have been proposed an approach for emergency data dissemination in sparse and dense networks of VANETs [14]. Highways are divided into clusters with respect to RSUs. The emergency messages are propagated using car to car communication in dense networks whereas in sparse networks, RSU is propagating emergency messages. The authors have pointed out RSUs will help to achieve low latency communication of the safety messages. The authors have based their work for two lane highway traffic which needs to be extended to other type of road networks.

3   Proposed Method

In our proposed system, we look at safety message dissemination of hazardous road condition on highways; where such conditions are normally encountered. In urban areas, the civic authorizes would ensure that the city roads are kept clean and safe for smooth transport of vehicles. Hence we focus our research to highways and look at a fast and efficient method of safety message dissemination of status of dangerous road conditions and obstacles. The traffic on the highways may not be dense and hence only vehicle-to-vehicle communication will not satisfy the requirements. So we propose the deployment of RSUs which can be used to propagate all types of safety, emergency, convenience and commercial message to the vehicles travelling on the highways. We also assume that RSUs can communicate directly with each other even in the absence of vehicular traffic to propagate the messages over a longer distance. As vehicles would normally travel at high speed on the highway, propagation over a longer distance is required to avoid accidents, ensure passenger safety and prevent vehicular damage.

In our proposed solution, vehicles traversing a hazardous area will transmit the information to the nearest RSU. We assume that vehicles are equipped with GPS to know the location of the hazardous area. RSUs will periodically send "hello" message to indicate its location. Hence vehicles will know the location of the nearest RSU. This information has to be efficiently disseminated to vehicles approaching the hazardous areas as early as possible to untoward incidents. The same message may be transmitted by many vehicles that have traversed the hazardous area. Fig. 1 shows a sample scenario.

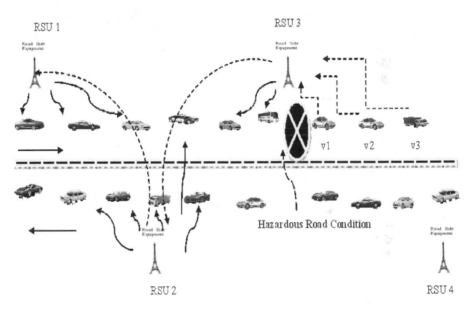

Fig. 1. Hazardous event on travelling path. The dotted line shows safety message delivery to RSUs and solid line shows broadcasting safety message.

Vehicles v1, v2, v3 who have encountered the hazard in the road would send a message to RSU3. RSU3 would receive the messages from the vehicles and send a single message to RSU2 which in turn will forward to RSU1. Since the hazard is before RSU4, message will not be forwarded to RSU4 by RSU3. RSU1, RSU2 and RSU3 will broadcast to vehicles to within the range covered by them. Vehicles in the overlapping zone of the RSUs will receive messages from both RSUs.

We present another scenario depicted in Fig. 2.

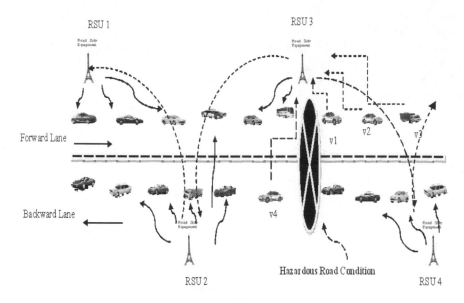

Fig. 2. Hazardous event at both lanes. The dotted line shows safety message delivery to RSUs and solid line shows broadcasting safety message.

Here the hazardous road condition is found on both lanes of the highway. For example, a landslide could have left obstacles on the road. Vehicles travelling on both sides of the road will send the safety message to RSU3. In this case, RSU3 will send the message to both RSU2 and RSU4 for forwarding to other RSU in both directions.

In both the above scenarios, RSU3 will examine and aggregate the messages to avoid duplication of the same message. The message is sent only to the relevant RSUs for re-transmission to the vehicles travelling in the direction of the dangerous area. As such messages will indicate the location of the dangerous area; vehicles can decide to change their travelling route to avoid the hazardous areas. Vehicles can choose to disregard the message if it is not relevant to them. For instance, if a vehicle is planning to turn off the highway before the dangerous area, the message would not be relevant.

RSUs will also aggregate and transmit all hazardous road condition messages to the highway authorities to enable them to rectify such conditions. RSUs will continue to send the message of a particular hazardous location, till it stops getting messages about the concerned location. This would happen if may be the obstacle has been removed or a slippery road condition has been attended by the highway authorities. The highway authorities can also directly communicate with the RSU regarding the rectification of the road condition.

3.1   RSUs "hello" Message

Each of the RSU will broadcast periodic "hello" messages within its transmission range. These messages would include the ID and location of the RSU as given in Fig. 3.

RSU_ID	Date, Time	Location

Fig. 3. RSU periodic message

These messages are captured by the vehicles that are within the transmission range of a particular RSU and enable the vehicle to know the location of the nearest RSUs. Location is expressed as GPS coordinates of latitude and longitude.

3.2   Vehicle to RSU Message

A vehicle detecting any dangerous road condition such as slippery road, road block or any other unsafe zones along its travelling path will generate a safety message with the contents as shown in Fig. 4. This message is sent to the nearest RSU whose location is obtained from the RSUs "hello" message.

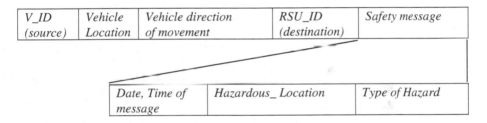

V_ID (source)	Vehicle Location	Vehicle direction of movement	RSU_ID (destination)	Safety message

Date, Time of message	Hazardous_ Location	Type of Hazard

Fig. 4. Vehicle to RSU message

Vehicle location and the hazardous location will be indicated as GPS coordinates. Each message should include the date and time of sending the message. We assume there is an on board clock in every vehicle that would provide the date and time. The hazard type would have to be identified by the vehicle driver; such as slippery road, ice on road, uneven road, obstacle on road etc.

3.3   RSU to RSU Message

RSU will forward the safety message received from RSUs in their near vicinity. RSUs can combine and forward the safety messages received from other RSUs with the safety messages received from vehicles in their zone.

3.4   RSU to Highway Authority

RSUs can deliver the same safety message to the Highway Authorities (HA) to enable them to attend and correct the road problems and hazardous conditions. HA can look at messages received from many RSUs and draw up an appropriate action plan.

4   Conclusion and Future Work

In this paper, we have discussed the use of Road Side infrastrUcture for selectively propagating safety messages about hazardous road condition to enhance passenger safety on highways. We have proposed forwarding of messages to relevant areas in order to warn vehicles approaching the danger zone. As future work, we intend to implement and test the proposed safety message model using SUMO and NS2.

References

1. Rawashdeh, Z.Y., Mahmud, S.M.: Communications in Vehicular Networks,
    http://www.intechopen.com/download/pdf/pdfs_id/12877
2. Kamini, Kumar, R.: VANET Parameters and Applications: A Review. Global Journal of Computer Science and Technology 10(7), Ver. 1.0 (September 2010)
3. Mughal, B.M., Wagan, A.A., Hasbullah, H.: Efficient Congestion Control in VANET for Safety Messaging. In: International Symposium in Information Technology (2010)
4. Bako, B., Weber, M.: Efficient Information Dissemination in VANETs,
    http://www.intechopen.com/download/pdf/pdfs_id/14987
5. Ni, S.-Y., Tseng, Y.-C., Chen, Y.-S., Sheu, J.-P.: The Broadcast Storm Problem in a Mobile Ad Hoc Network. In: Proceeding of ACM International Conference on Mobile Computing and Networking, Seattle, WA, pp. 151–162 (1999)
6. Van de Velde, E., Blondia, C., Campelli, L.: REACT: Routing Protocol for Emergency Applications in Car- to Car Networks using Trajectories. In: Proc. of the 5th Annual Mediterranean Ad Hoc Networking Workshop (2006)
7. Yang, Y.-T., Chou, L.D.: Position based adaptive broadcast for inter-vehicle communications. In: Proc. of ICC Workshop. IEEE (2008)
8. Koubek, M., Rea, S., Pesch, D.: A novel reactive routing protocol for applications in vehicular environments. In: The 11th International Symposium on Wireless Personal Multimedia Communications, WPMC 2008 (2008)
9. Abuelela, M., Olariu, S.: SODA: A Smart Opportunistic Data Dissemination Approach for VANETs. In: Proc. of the 6th International Workshop on Intelligent Transportation (2009)
10. Ibrahim, K., Weigle, M.C.: Poster: accurate data aggregation for VANETs. ACM, Vanet (2007)
11. Defude, B., Delot, T., Ilarri, S., Zechinelli, J., Cenerario, N.: Data aggregation in VANETs: the VESPA approach. In: Proceedings of the 5th Annual International Conference on Mobile and Ubiquitous Systems: Computing, Networking, and Services (2008)
12. Koubek, M., Rea, S., Pessch, D.: Event suppression for safety message dissemination in VANETs. In: 71st Vehicular Technology Conference, pp. 1–5 (2010)
13. Liu, K., Guo, J., Lu, N., Liu, F.: RAMC: a RSU- Assisted Multi-channel Coordination MAC Protocol for VANET. In: GLOBECOM Workshops. IEEE (2009)
14. Tomer, P., Chaurasia, B.K., Tomer, G.S.: State of the art of data dissemination in VANETs. International Journal of Computer Theory and Engineering 2(6) (December 2010)

Policy Based Distributed Run Time Fault Diagnoser Model for Web Services

K. Jayashree[1] and Sheila Anand[2]

[1] Research Scholar
k.jayashri@gmail.com
[2] Dean(Research) Computer studies,
Rajalakshmi Engineering College, Chennai, India
sheila.anand@gmail.com

Abstract. Fault Management is one of the crucial areas in Web Service Management. Tools, methodologies and techniques that support and automate the management efforts have immense commercial application and patentability. In this paper, we present WISDOM (Web Service Diagnoser Model) a generic architecture for detecting faults in Web Services. The focus of WISDOM is on diagnosing problems that occur at run-time. It does not address issues relating to web service testing, debugging, specification or design faults. An independent and external Fault Diagnoser (FD) is used to detect run-time faults during publishing, discovery, composition, binding and execution of web services. We have tested the proposed model by using a sample web service application and present the details.

Keywords: Web Service Faults, Fault Diagnoser, Fault Diagnosis, Fault Diagnosis Model, Web Service Policy.

1 Introduction

Web Services have emerged as the most popular paradigm for distributed computing. The emerging paradigm of Web services opens a new way of quickly designing, developing and deploying web applications by integrating independently published Web services components. Web Service technology is being increasingly used in many practical application domains, such as groupware, electronic commerce, application integration , Transaction processing telecommunications, geographical information systems and digital imagery. Web services are based on XML standards and can be developed in any programming language. It facilitates the delivery of business applications as services accessible to anyone, anytime, at any location, and using any platform.

Managing web services and making them available have become critical issues. Fault Management is one of the crucial areas in Web Service Management. Traditional fault management tools cannot automatically monitor, analyze, and resolve faults in web Services. As Web services are distributed in nature, it is hard to trace the flow of transactions when a large number of services, supplier and

N. Meghanathan et al. (Eds.): CCSIT 2012, Part III, LNICST 86, pp. 9–16, 2012.

technologies collaborate together to perform an activity. This makes monitoring and Fault management of Web Service more difficult then centralized applications. The first step in fault management is to identify and classify the faults that may occur in services. Tools, methodologies and techniques need to be developed to support and automate the fault management efforts.

In this paper, we present WISDOM (Web Service Diagnoser Model) a generic architecture for detecting run-time execution faults in Web Services. The rest of the paper is organized as follows. Section 2 discusses the related work and Section 3 presents the proposed architecture for Web Services Fault Diagnosis. In Section 4, we have discussed the implementation of WISDOM using a sample web service application. Section 5 presents the conclusion and future work.

2   Related Work

In this section we discuss work related to web service monitoring, fault taxonomy and fault detection. There has been considerable work relating to web service testing, debugging and fault tolerance. We however present prior work related to web service monitoring and fault diagnosis.

Avizienis et al [1] discuss basic concepts about the threats to software dependability and security: failures, error and faults. They have classified the different types of software faults that may affect the system during its lifetime. They have presented eight basic viewpoints: phases of creation or occurrence, system boundaries, phenomena logical cause, dimension, objective, intent, capability and persistent. They have examined fault prevention, fault tolerance, fault removal, and fault forecasting. In our proposed work we have used the concepts relating to error detection and recovery explained with respect to fault tolerance to build and implement the Fault Diagnoser model.

Beth A.Schroder et al[2] describes correctness checking as the monitoring of an application to ensure consistency with a formal specification. Monitoring is used as a verification technique to detect runtime errors. The have described the monitoring system as an external observer that monitors a fully functioning application. It can provide increased robustness, security, fault – tolerance and adaptability. In our work we have applied the concept of monitoring and the external observer idea to design the Fault Diagnoser.

Delgado et al [3] have presented a taxonomy for runtime software fault-monitoring approaches for traditional software. Web service characteristics, however, differ considerably from that of traditional software. Web services are loosely coupled and dynamic in nature and monitoring of web services require additional issues to be addressed. Qi yu et al[7] describes web services are autonomous and loosely coupled and they interact dynamically without a priori knowledge of each other. Therefore failures in web service environment are expected to happen frequently. Thus a key step towards such a mechanism is to define what failures are in web service interaction environment and to provide a clear taxonomy for all these kinds of failures.

Stephan Bruing et al [5] have proposed fault taxonomy for possible faults in Service Oriented Architecture (SOA). Faults discussed include Hardware Fault, Software Fault, Network Fault and Operator Fault. They have demonstrated the application of the taxonomy with an example of travel agency. They have not implemented the taxonomy to detect faults in SOA. Farzaneth mahdian et al[15] present an approach to detect faults in the architecture level of service oriented systems which extends the formal SOA core meta model to support fault tolerance. In the fault tolerance architecture presented monitors are used to check the operation of different components of the system.

Benharref et al [4] have presented a web service based architecture for detecting faults in web services using an external Observer. Observers are web services published through Universal Description Discovery and Integration (UDDI). The observer is invoked by a manager which would provide specific information like the location of the service to be observed, its specification and when and what to observe. When the observer finds faults or the observation period expires it returns the result to the manager. This paper deals with only faults relating to inputs and outputs of the web services.

Mahbub and Spanoudakis[11] have developed a framework that monitor requirements for service based systems. The framework is applicable to service based systems whose composition process is specified in BPEL and specifies the requirements to be monitored using event calculus. Event logs are recorded during the execution of a service based system which is then checked against the specifications. Fabio Barbon et al [12] proposed a novel solution to the problem of monitoring web services described as BPEL processes. The approach allows for a clear separation of the service business logic from the monitoring functionality. The monitors they developed can check temporal, Boolean, time related and statics properties

Zheng Li et al [6] has developed a framework for monitoring the run time interactions of web services. Finite state automata are used to represent the service constraints. The framework involves interception of service messages and conformance checking with the service constraints. They have implemented the framework using Java-based open source platform for validating SOAP messages.

3   Proposed Architecture for Web Service Fault Diagnoser

In this paper, we present WISDOM (Web Service Diagnoser Model) a generic architecture for detecting faults in Web Services. The focus of WISDOM is on diagnosing problems that occur at run-time. It does not address issues relating to web service testing, debugging, specification or design faults. An independent and external Fault Diagnoser (FD) is used to detect run-time faults during publishing, discovery, composition, binding and execution of web services. The WISDOM architecture is given in Figure 1.

The Fault Diagnoser (FD) uses policies; a set of rules or guidelines to detect faults that occur during the execution of web services. A service provider will publish their services in the service registry and also provide guidelines for their web service execution. These guidelines are stored as policy in the policy database. For instance, one of the common run-time errors occurs in the specification of input parameters while invoking web services. The service provider would provide in the policy the

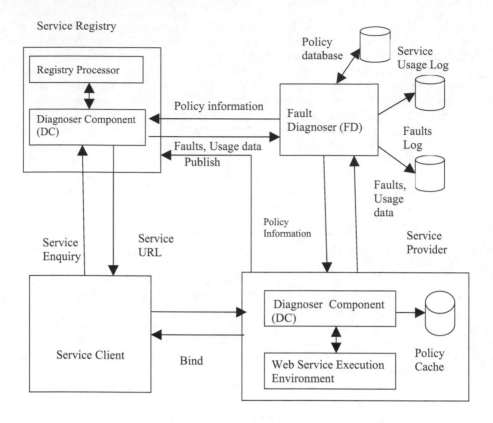

Fig. 1. WISDOM – Architecture for Web Service Fault Diagnosis

details of all run time parameters, their types and constraints. Some sample constraints that can be used to validate the numeric and alphanumeric input parameters could be:

Numeric Constraints:

- Constraint: Fraction Digits- Specifies the maximum number of decimal places allowed. Must be equal to or greater than zero
- Constraint: Maximum Inclusive - Specifies the upper bounds for numeric values (the value must be less than or equal to this value)
- Constraint: Maximum Exclusive- Specifies the upper bounds for numeric values (the value must be less than this value)
- Constraint: Minimum Exclusive- Specifies the lower bounds for numeric values (the value must be greater than this value)
- Constraint: Minimum Inclusive - Specifies the lower bounds for numeric values (the value must be greater than or equal to this value)

Alphanumeric Constraint

- Constraint: Data type – specifies whether the parameter is a string, list or matrix
- Constraint: Size- Specifies the exact number of characters or list items allowed. Must be equal to or greater than zero
- Constraint: Minimum Range - Specifies the minimum number of characters or list items allowed. Must be equal to or greater than zero
- Constraint: Maximum Range - Specifies the maximum number of characters or list items allowed. Must be equal to or greater than zero
- Constraint: Enumeration- Defines a list of acceptable values

Likewise the web service can provide policy information on output parameters that is results of execution of web services. A Diagnoser Component (DC) is present in every service provider to detect such run time faults. When a user invokes a web service, DC will obtain the corresponding policy information from FD. It will use the policy guidelines to monitor the web service execution and give meaningful error messages to the user. We recommend the use of a cache to store frequently accessed web services to improve the performance.

All faults encountered are reported by DC to FD and store in a fault database. The faults can be analyzed to determine common faults that occur during web service execution and try to provide proactive information to users to avoid such errors. The service usage database is used to store the usage of individual web services. An expert system can also be developed to assist in fault diagnosis.

Web services are published in the service registry by the service provider and users access the registry to discover web services. A DC is present in every registry to detect faults in publishing and discovery of web services. A registry listing of web service comprises of three elements, White Pages, Yellow Pages and Green Pages. White Pages is at the highest level and contains basic information about the providing company and its services. Yellow Pages organize services by industry, service type or geography. The Green Pages provide the interface and URL locations to find and execute a Web service. The policy for publishing web services would give details of all elements and constraints for checking the values of these elements. One such constraint could indicate, for instance, whether the element is mandatory or optional. Different policies may be specified for web services based on the type or usage of web services. When a service provider submits a request for publishing a web service, the DC would obtain the corresponding policy information from FD. It will use the policy guidelines to monitor the web service to diagnose faults in publishing.

To discover the service the service user queries the service registry for services by specifying the Business name and Service that meets its criteria. A DC present in the service registry can use policy guidelines to diagnose faults in the submitted query.

Policies are used to specify the accepted behavior of web services and deviations from accepted behavior can be diagnosed as faults. Policies provide a flexible and easy method of specifying the correct behavior of web services. Polices can be changed dynamically to cater to the changing needs of web services.

4   Implementation and Results

We have used IBM Rational Application Developer IDE for the implementation of WISDOM. jUDDI (Java Universal Description Discovery and Integration) is used to configure the web service registry. The web services are published in the jUDDI registry which is implemented using MySQL database.

We have taken a sample web service application from the Railway services domain as an example. Web services have been created for Train Enquiry, Ticket Availability, Reservation and Reservation Status Enquiry. Train Enquiry service allows the users to determine the list of trains to the intended destination. Ticket Enquiry allows users to find out whether seats or berths are available in the train of their choice. They can also obtain information about the number of seats available in the required class. A passenger books tickets using Reservation service by providing details which includes Date of Travel, Train Number, Train Name, Departing station, Destination station, Class, Name, Age etc. Successful ticket bookings will be assigned a unique PNR (Passenger Name Record) number. Reservation Status Enquiry requires the passenger to key-in the PNR number and the reservation status is displayed.

We have simulated different types of publishing, discovery, binding and execution faults which include:

- Publishing faults – incomplete description, described features missing etc.
- Discovery faults – required resource not existing, not listed in the lookup service
- Binding faults – authorization denied
- Execution faults – incorrect input parameter, incorrect results

Policies were used to define the correct behavior of these web services. The policies were implemented as a set of XML tags. The Fault Diagnoser model and Diagnoser components were developed to check the inputs and outputs to registry and web services. We were able to successfully diagnose the above mentioned faults. Policies provided a flexible method to detail the correct behavior of web services. It was easy to modify the policy details to reflect changes in the web service execution.

5   Conclusion and Future Work

Fault Management is one of the crucial areas in Web Service Management. We have presented in this paper a generic architecture for fault diagnosis in the run-time execution of web services. Policies have provided a flexible and simple method to represent the correct behavior of web services. We have tested the proposed model by using a sample web service application. As future work, we intend to extend the model to comprehensively diagnose all types of run-time or execution faults. We also intend to focus on standardizing the representation of the policies and develop a language for representing the policy assertions.

References

[1] Avizienis, A., Radell, B., Ladwehr, C.: Basic Concepts and Taxonomy of Dependable and secure Computing. IEEE Transactions on Dependable and Secure Computing 01(1), 33 (2004)

[2] Schroeder, B.A.: Online Monitoring: a Tutorial. IEEE Computer 28(6), 72–78 (1995)

[3] Delgado, N., Gates, A.Q., Roach, S.: A Taxonomy and Catalog of Runtime Software Fault Monitoring Tools. IEEE Transactions on Software Engineering, TSE-0209-1203

[4] Benharref, A., Clitho, R., Dssouli, R.: A Web Service Based Architecture for Detecting Faults in Web Services, 0-7803-9088-I/05/S20.00©2005 IEEE

[5] Bruning, S., Weibleder, S., Malek, M.: A Fault Taxonomy for Service-Oriented Architecture

[6] Li, Z., Jin, Y., Han, J.: A run time Monitoring and validation Framework for Web Service Interactions. In: Proceedings of the 2006 Australian Software Engineering Conference, ASWEC 2006 (2006)

[7] Yu, Q., Liu, X., Bouguettaya, A., Medjahed, B.: Deploying and managing Web services: issues, solutions, and directions. The VLDB Journal, 537–572 (2008)

[8] Robinson, W.N.: Monitoring Web Service Requirements. In: Proceedings of the 11th International Requirements Engineering Conference 1090-705X/03

[9] Madeira, H., Costa, D., Vieira, M.: On the emulation of software faults by software faults by software fault injection In: Proceedings of the International Conference on Dependable Systems and Networks, pp. 417–426. IEEE (June 2000)

[10] Dingwall-smith, A., Finkelstein, A.: From requirements to monitors by way of aspects

[11] Mahbub, K., Spanousdakis, G.: Run Time Monitoring of Requirements for systems composed of web services: Initial implementation and evaluation experience. In: Proceedings of the IEEE International Conference on Web Services, ICWS 2005 (2005)

[12] Barbon, F., Traverso, P., Pistore, M., Trainotti, M.: Run Time Monitoring of Instances and classes Web Service Compositions IEEE ICWS06 Journal (2008)

[13] Alam, S.: Fault management of Web Services Thesis (August 2009)

[14] Papazoglou, M.P., van den Heuvel, W.-J.: Web Services Managemnet: A survey. IEEE Internet Computing (2005)

[15] Mahdian, F., Rafe, V., Rafeh, R., Zand Miralvand, M.R.: Considering faults in service Oriented Architecture: a graph Transformation based approach. IEEE (2009)

[16] Vierira, M., Laranjeiro, N.: Comparing web Services and Recovery in the Presence of Faults. In: ICWS 2007 (2007)

[17] Degwekar, S., Su, S.Y.W., Lam, H.: Constraint specification and processing in Web Services Publication and Discovery. In: Proceedings of the IEEE International Conference on Web Services (ICWS 2004) (2004)

[18] Console, L., Fugini, M.: WS-DIAMOND: An approach to web services- DIAgnosability. In: MONitoring and DIAgnosis. EDs IOS Press, Amsterdam (2007)

[19] Chen, F., Rosu, G.: Towards Monitoring-Oriented Programming: a Paradigm Combining Specification and Implementation. Elseiver science B.V (2003)

[20] Ardissono, L., Console, L., Goy, A., Petrone, G.: Enhancing Web services with Diagnostic Capabilities. In: Proceedings of the Third European Conference on Web Services. IEEE (2005)

[21] Siblini, R., Mamour, N.: Testing Web services, 0-7803-8735-x-105-2005 IEEE

[22] Papazoglou, M.P.: Web services: Principles and technology. Prentice hall, ISBN 9780321155559

[23] Liu, L., Wu, Z., Ma, Z., Wei, W.: A Fault tolerant framework for Web Services. In: World Congress on Software Engineering. IEEE (2009)

[24] Liu, A., Li, Q., Huang, L., Xiao, M.: FACTS: A Framework for fault–tolerant composition of Transactional Web Services. IEEE Transactions on Services Computing

[25] Plebani, P., Pernici, B.: URBE: Web Service Retrieval Based on similarity Evaluation. IEEE Transactions on Knowledge and Data Engineering (2009)

[26] Arganda, D., Cappielo, C., Fugini, M.G., Mussi, E., Percini, B., Plebani, P.: Faults and recovery Actions for Self-Healing Web Services. In: WWW 2006, Edinburgh, UK, May 22-26 (2006)

[27] HP Openview Web services Management, Business White Paper, Hewlett Packard (November 2002)

[28] Nagappan, R., Skoczylas, R., Sriganesh, R.P.: Developing Java Web services

[29] http://www.apache.org

[30] http://w3schools.com

The Reconstruction Conjecture

Subhashis Banerjee[1], Debajit SenSarma[1], Krishnendu Basuli[1],
Saptarshi Naskar[2], and Samar Sen Sarma[3]

[1]West Bengal State University, West Bengal, India
[2]Sarsuna College, West Bengal, India
[3]University Of Calcutta, West Bengal, India
{mail.sb88,debajit.sensarma2008,
krishnendu.basuli,sapgrin}@gmail.com,
sssarma2001@yahoo.com

Abstract. The Reconstruction Conjecture is one of the most engaging problems under the domain of Graph Theory. The conjecture proposes that every graph with at least three vertices can be uniquely reconstructed given the multiset of subgraphs produced by deleting each vertex of the original graph one by one. This conjecture has been proven true for several infinite classes of graphs, but the general case remains unsolved. In this paper we will outline the problem and give a practical method for reconstructing a graph from its node-deleted.

Keywords: Multiset, Card, Deck, Matching, Perfect matching, K-matching, Matching polynomial, Tree-Decomposition.

1   Introduction

The Reconstruction Conjecture, formulated by Kelly and Ulam in 1942 [11, 16], asserts that every finite, simple, undirected graph on at least three vertices is determined uniquely (up to isomorphism) by its collection of 1-vertex deleted subgraphs.

Harary [7] formulated the Edge-Reconstruction- Conjecture, which states that a finite simple graph with at least four edges can be reconstructed from its collection of one edge deleted sub graphs.

The Reconstruction Conjecture is interesting not only from a mathematical or historical point of view but also due to its applicability in diverse fields. Archaeologists may try to assemble broken fragments of pottery to find the shape and pattern of an ancient vase. Chemists may infer the structure of an organic molecule from knowledge of its decomposition products. In bioinformatics the Multiple Sequence- Alignment problem [1] is to reconstruct a sequence with minimum gap insertion and maximum number of matching symbols, given a list of protein or DNA

N. Meghanathan et al. (Eds.): CCSIT 2012, Part III, LNICST 86, pp. 17–25, 2012.
© Institute for Computer Sciences, Social Informatics and Telecommunications Engineering 2012

sequences. In computer networking, a reconstruction problem can appear in the following scenario: given a collection of sketches depicting partial network connection in a city from different locations, reconstruct the network of the entire city.

In this paper we will give a solution to this problem, using Matching Polynomial of the graph. In general, the reconstruction of graph polynomials can shed some light on the Reconstruction Conjecture itself. For example, reconstruction was investigated by several authors. In particular, Gutman and Cvetkovic [6] investigated the reconstruction of the characteristic polynomial. The existence of a reconstruction for the characteristic polynomial was eventually established by Tutte [15]. Tutte also established the reconstructibility of the rank polynomial and the chromatic polynomial.

Although the reconstruction of several graph polynomials has been established, no practical means of reconstruction exists for any of them. Farrell and Wahid [4] investigated the reconstructibility of matching polynomial and gave a practical method for reconstruction.

Although Farrell and Wahid gave a method for reconstruction of the matching polynomial they did not provide a practical method for generate the matching polynomial for a graph.

In this paper we will first give an algorithm that can generate the matching polynomial of a graph in polynomial time. Then we will give an algorithm for reconstructing a graph from its node deleted sub graphs.

2   Preliminaries

2.1   Some Definitions

Multiset. In mathematics, a Multiset (or bag) is a generalization of a set. While each member of a set has only one membership, a member of a multiset can have more than one membership (meaning that there may be multiple instances of a member in a multiset).

Card. A Card of G is an unlabelled graph formed by deleting 1 vertex and all edges attached to it.

Deck. The Deck of G, D (G), is the collection of all G's cards. Note this is in general a multiset.

Graph Isomorphism. Let V(G) be the vertex set of a simple graph and E(G) its edge set. Then a graph isomorphism from a simple graph G to a simple graph H is a bijection f: V(G) →V(H) such that u v ∈ E(G) iff f(u) f(v) ∈ E(H) (West 2000, p. 7). If there is a graph isomorphism for G to H, then G is said to be isomorphic to H, written G ≈ H.

2.2   Notations

Our alphabet set is $\Sigma=\{0, 1\}$. We use $\{., ., ., \}$ to denote sets and $[::; : : : ; :]$ to denote multiset. We use U to denote set union as well as multiset union. We consider only finite, undirected graphs with no self-loops. Given a graph G, let V(G) denote its vertex set and let E(G) denote its edge set. For notational convenience, we sometimes represent a graph G by (V; E), where V=V(G) and E=E(G). By the order of a graph G we mean | V(G) |, i.e., the cardinality of its vertex set.

3   Matching Polynomial and Reconstruction Conjecture

3.1   Matching Polynomial [4, 5]

Matching. A matching cover (or simply a matching) in a graph G is taken to be a subgraph of G consisting of disjoint (independent) edges of G, together with the remaining nodes of G as (isolated) components.

K–matching. A matching is called a K–matching if it contains exactly K edges.

Matching Polynomial. If G contains P nodes, and if a matching contains K edges, then it will have P–2K component nodes. Now assign weights W_1 and W_2 to each node and edge of G, respectively. Take the weight of a matching to be the product of the weights of all its components. Then the weight of a K–matching will be $W_1^{P-2K}W_2^K$. The matching polynomial of G, denoted by m(G), is the sum of the weights of all the matchings in G. The matching polynomial of G has been defined as $m(G)=\sum akW_1^{P-2K}W_2^K$. ak is the number of matchings in G with k edges.

Example.

$$0 - \text{matching} = 1\ W_1^5\ W_2^0$$
$$1 - \text{matching} = 6\ W_1^3\ W_2^1$$
$$2 - \text{matching} = 6\ W_1^1\ W_2^2$$
$$\text{No 3–matching.}$$

$$m(\ G\ ) = W_1^5 + 6\ W_1^3\ W_2 + 6\ W_1\ W_2$$

Perfect Matching. A perfect matching is a matching of a graph containing n/2 edges, the largest possible. Perfect matchings are therefore only possible on graphs with an even number of vertices. We denote the number of perfect matchings in G by $\delta(G)$. Clearly $\delta(G)$ is the coefficient of the term independent of W_1 in m(G).

3.2   Matching Polynomial Generation Using Tree Decomposition

Algorithm: gen_mpoly(Graph G)

Input: A simple connected graph G.
Output: The Matching Polynomial m(G) of this graph.

Steps:
1. if | V(G) | = 1 then
                   return (create_mpoly("W_1"));
2. else if | V(G) | = 0 then
                   return (create_mpoly("1"));
3. else
           return (create_mpoly(W_1 + gen_mpoly(G –V_i) + $W_2 X \sum$ gen_mpoly(G – e)));
                                                              e : $V_i V_j \in E(G)$
           end if.
4. End

Example.

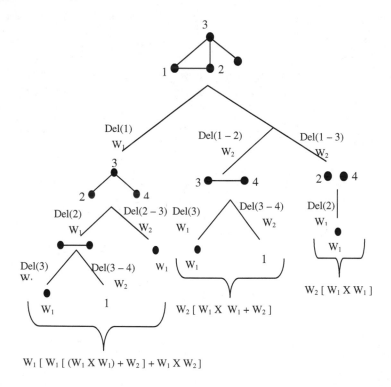

$$m(G) = W_1[W_1[(W_1XW_1)+W_2]+W_1XW_2]+W_2[W_1XW_1+W_2]+W_2[W_1XW_1]$$
$$= W_1^4+4W_1^2 W_2+W_2^2$$

3.3   Reconstruction of Matching Polynomial [4, 6, 7]

In order to establish our main result, we will need the following lemma.

LEMMA 1 : Let G be a graph with n nodes. Then

$$\frac{d}{d\,W_1} m(G) = \sum_{i=1}^{n} m(G - V_i)$$

Proof.

We establish (1) by showing that the two polynomials $A = \frac{d}{d\,W_1} m(G)$ and $B = \sum_{i=1}^{n} m(G - V_i)$ have precisely the same terms with equal coefficients.

Let $W_1^j W_2^k$ be a term of A. Then m(G) has a term in $W_1^{j+1} W_2^k$. It follows that G has a matching S with (j + 1) nodes and k edges. Let $V_r \in V(G)$. Then $G - V_r$ will contain the matching $S - V_r$. Hence B also contains a term in $W_1^j W_2^k$.

Conversely, if B contains a term in $W_1^j W_2^k$, then there exists a node V_r such that $G - V_r$ has a matching with nodes and k edges. Therefore G has a matching with (j+1) nodes and k edges. It follows that m(G) has a term in $W_1^{j+1} W_2^k$. Hence A has a term in $W_1^j W_2^k$. We conclude that A and B have the same kinds of terms.

We will show that the coefficients of like terms are equal. Let $a_k W_1^i W_2^k$ be a term in m(G). Then the corresponding term in A will be $ja_k W_1^{j-1} W_2^k$. Hence the coefficient of $W_1^j W_2^k$ in A will be ja_k. Now, for each matching in G with j nodes, there will be exactly corresponding matchings in the graphs $G - V_r$ with j–1 nodes. Since G contains a_k such matchings, then B will contain the term $W_1^{j-1} W_2^k$ with coefficient ja_k. Therefore the coefficients of like terms are equal. Hence the result follows.

Theorem 1:

$$m(G) = \sum_{i=1}^{n} \int m(G - V_i)\, dW_1 + \delta(G)$$

Proof. This is straightforward from the lemma(1), by integrating with respect to W_1.

4   Node Reconstruction of a Graph

4.1   Algorithm

Input: Deck D=[H_1;H_2;H_3;$\cdots$;H_k] (multiset of subgraphs produced by deleting each vertex of the original graph).

Output: S={G1,G2,G3,$\cdots$,Gn} where n≥1 and G1≈G2≈G3≈$\cdots$≈Gn [≈ : Isomorphic].

Steps:
1. Reconstruct the matching polynomial [m1(G)] of the graph from the given deck D by using Theorem 1.
2. Select any card [vertex deleted sub graph of the original graph] H_i from the deck D.

3. Add a new vertex V_K to H_i and connect it with any vertex of H_i by a tentative edge, obtaining a graph $G_{tentative}$ on K vertices.
4. for i←1 to k – 1 do
   label the tentative edge between i and V_K as X_{iK}.
5. Generate the 2nd matching polynomial[m2(G)] with variable coefficient using the *Tree Decomposition* method [m2(G)=tree_decomposition($G_{tentative}$)].
6. Compare coefficients of m1(G) and m2(G) and generate one or more solutions. Store the solutions in solution vectors $Soln_1$, $Soln_2$, ·········· $Soln_n$. In each solution vector a variable   coefficient X_{ij} can have only two values 0 or 1. 0 means the tentative edge will be deleted from $G_{tentative}$, and 1 means the tentative edge will be converted in to a permanent edge. Also calculate the Perfect Matching by substituting the solutions into m2(G).
7. for every solution [$Soln_{1\ to\ n}$] generate a new graph G_i [i ≤ n] from the $G_{tentative}$ according to step6 and add the generated graph in to the output set S [S=SU{G_i}].

All of the graphs in the set S are isomorphic. So, select any one of them and this is the reconstructed graph isomorphic to the original graph.

4.2   Example

Input:

Deck **D** =

Step 1:[Reconstruct the matching polynomial [m1(G)] of the graph from the given deck D by using Theorem 1.]

$m(H_1) = W_1^4 + 4 W_1^2 W_2 + W_2^2$ $\int m(H_1) = W_1^5 / 5 + 4/3 W_1^3 W_2 + W_1 W_2^2$
$m(H_2) = W_1^4 + 3 W_1^2 W_2 + W_2^2$ $\int m(H_2) = W_1^5 / 5 + 3/3 W_1^3 W_2 + W_1 W_2^2$
$m(H_3) = W_1^4 + 4 W_1^2 W_2 + 2W_2^2$ $\int m(H_3) = W_1^5 / 5 + 4/3 W_1^3 W_2 + 2 W_1 W_2^2$
$m(H_4) = W_1^4 + 4 W_1^2 W_2 + W_2^2$ $\int m(H_4) = W_1^5 / 5 + 4/3 W_1^3 W_2 + W_1 W_2^2$
$m(H_5) = W_1^4 + 3 W_1^2 W_2 + W_2^2$ $\int m(H_5) = W_1^5 / 5 + 3/3 W_1^3 W_2 + W_1 W_2^2$

$m1(G) = W_1^5 + 6 W_1^3 W_2 + 6 W_1 W_2^2 + \delta(G)$ [$\delta(G)$: Perfect Matching]

Step 2: [Select any card (vertex deleted sub graph of the original graph) H_i from the deck D.]
                    Here we select H_5

Step 3: [Add a new vertex V_K to H_i and connect it with any vertex of H_i by a tentative edge, obtaining a graph $G_{tentative}$ on K vertices.]

V_5

1

2   ?

Step 4: [for i ←1 to k – 1 do
    label the tentative edge between i and V_K as X_{iK} .]

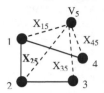

Step 5: [Generate the 2nd matching polynomial [m2(G)] with variable coefficient using the *Tree Decomposition* method [m2(G) = tree_decomposition($G_{tentative}$)].]

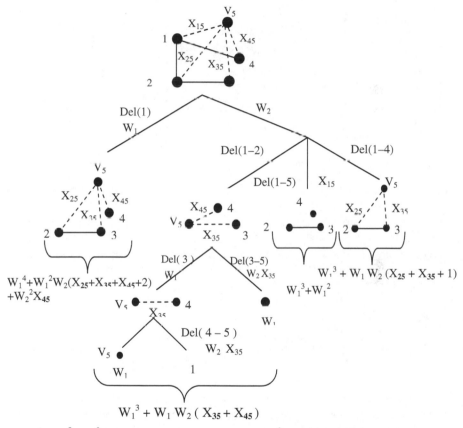

$$m2(G) = W_1{}^5 + W_1{}^3 W_2(X_{15}+X_{25}+X_{35}+X_{45}+3) + W_1 W_2{}^2(X_{15}+X_{25}+2X_{35}+2X_{45}+1)$$

Step 6 : [Compare coefficients of m1(G) and m2(G) and generate one or more solutions. Store the solutions in solution vectors $Soln_1, Soln_2, \cdots, Soln_n$.]
by comparing coefficients of m1(G) and m2(G) we get
    $X_{15} + X_{25} + X_{35} + X_{45} = 3$ $X_{15} + X_{25} + X_{35} + X_{45} = 5$
It is clear that the only solutions to these equations are
    $Soln_1 = [0, 1, 1, 1]$ and $Soln_2 = [1, 0, 1, 1]$
by substituting into m2(G) we get in both cases δ(G) = 0.

Step 7: [for every solution [$Soln_{1 \ to \ n}$] generate a new graph G_i[$i \leq n$] from the $G_{tentative}$ according to step6 and add the generated graph in to the output set S [S=SU{G_i}]].
We can now use $Soln_1$ to constructed a graph G_1 and **Soln₂** to constructed a graph G_2 from $G_{tentative}$.

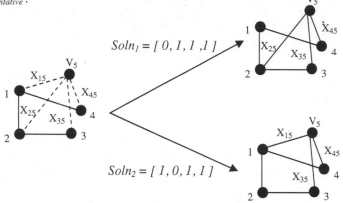

It can be easily confirmed that the mapping defined by φ:G1 → G2 such that
$\phi(1) \equiv 3$; $\phi(2) \equiv 5$; $\phi(3) \equiv 4$; $\phi(4) \equiv 2$ and $\phi(5) \equiv 1$ is an isomorphism. Hence GI≈G2.

4.3   Analysis

On arbitrary graphs or even planar graphs, computing the matching polynomial is #P–Complete(Jerrum 1987)[10].

But using Tree Decomposition we can compute the matching polynomials for all the subgraphs for the given deck in polynomial time.

Tree Decomposition contains recursive calls to itself, its running time can often be described by a recurrence. The recurrence for Tree Decomposition –

$$T(n) = \begin{cases} O(1) & \text{if } n \leq 1 \\[2ex] T(n{-}V_i) + \sum_{V_iV_j \in E(G)} T(n{-}V_iV_j) & \text{otherwise [for } i{\leftarrow}1 \text{ to n-1]} \end{cases}$$

$T(n) = O(n^2)$
Step 1 requires $O(n^2)$ time. Step 2 & 3 require O(1) time. Step 4 requires O(n) times. Step 5 (Tree Decomposition) requires $O(n^2)$ time. Step 6 requires exponential time $O(2^n)$, and Step 7 requires O(n) times.

So, if we can find a polynomial time algorithm for solving this Underdetermined system in Step7 then we can easily reconstruct the original graph in polynomial time.

5   Conclusions

As presented in this paper, if G is a simple undirected graph with at least three vertices then we can use the proposed algorithm for reconstruct G from its vertex deleted subgraphs. Although the proposed algorithm is not tested for all classes of graph, but we can conclude that suppose that a graph G is characterized by a particular matching polynomial and suppose that the matching polynomial is reconstructible, then G is reconstructible.

References

[1] Carrillo, H., Lipman, D.: The multiple sequence alignment problem in biology. SIAM Journal of Applied Mathematics 48, 1073–1082 (1988)

[2] Clark, J., Holton, D.A.: A First Look At Graph Theory. World Scientific Publishing Company (1995)

[3] Cormen, T.H., Leiserson, C.E., Rivest, R.L., Stein, C.: Introduction to Algorithms, 3rd edn. Phi Learning (2010)

[4] Farrell, E.J., Wahid, S.A.: On the reconstruction of the matching polynomial and the reconstruction conjecture. Int. J. Math. Math. Sci. 10, 155–162 (1987)

[5] Farrell, E.J.: Introduction to Matching Polynomials. J. Combinatorial Theory B 27, 75–86 (1979)

[6] Gutman, I., Cvetkovic, D.M.: The Reconstruction Problem for Characteristic Polynomials of Graphs. Univ. Beograd. Publ. Elektrotehn. Fak. Ser. Mat. Fiz. No., 498–541 (1975)

[7] Harary, F.: On the reconstruction of a graph from a collection of subgraphs. In: Fiedler, M. (ed.) Theory of Graphs and its Applications, pp. 47–52. Czechoslovak Academy of Sciences, Prague (1964)

[8] Harary, F.: A Survey of the Reconstruction Conjecture. In: Bari, R., Harary, F. (eds.) Graphs and Combinatorics, pp. 18–28. Springer, New York (1974)

[9] Hemaspaandraa, E., Hemaspaandrab, L.A., Radziszowskia, S.P., Tripathib, R.: Complexity results in graph reconstruction. Discrete Appl. Math. 155, 103–118 (2004)

[10] Jerrum, M.: Two-dimensional monomer-Dimer systems are computationally intractable. Journal of Statistical Physics 48(1), 121–134 (1987)

[11] Kelly, P.J.: On isometric transformations, Ph.D. thesis, University of Wisconsin, USA (1942)

[12] Manvel, B.: Reconstruction of graphs: Progress and prospects. Congressus Numerantium 63, 177–187 (1988)

[13] Nash-Williams, C.S.J.A.: The reconstruction problem. In: Selected Topics in Graph Theory, pp. 205–236. Academic Press (1978)

[14] Ramachandran, S.: Graph Reconstruction - Some New Developments. AKCE J. Graphs. Combin. 1(1), 51–61 (2004)

[15] Tutte, W.T.: All the King's Horses. In: Bondy, J.A., Murty, U.R.S. (eds.) Graph Theory and Related Topics, pp. 15–33. Academic Press (1979)

[16] Ulam, S.: A Collection of Mathematical Problems. Interscience Publishers, New York (1960)

[17] Yongzhi, Y.: The reconstruction conjecture is true if all 2-connected graphs are reconstructible. Journal of Graph Theory 12(2), 237–243 (2006)

Collaborative Framework for Distributed Computing in P2P Network

B. Swsssaminathan[*] and Sheila Anand[**]

Rajalakshmi Engineering College, Chennai, India
{Swamikb,sheila.anand}@gmail.com

Abstract. In this paper, we propose a Collaborative Framework for P2P to enable distribution processing of tasks or application among multiple peers. P2P networks provide a completely decentralized environment wherein each peer can provide services to other peers in the network. Most of the current work on P2P is in the area of data or content sharing. We propose a generic collaborative framework to facilitate distributed processing among peers by enabling provision for job or task scheduling, distributing of a task among multiple peers, messaging between peers, monitoring job execution, follow up and obtain the results of the completed tasks. Peer profiles are maintained to enable peers to discover other willing peers and explore their capacity and capability for distributed processing. Job profiles are proposed to maintain the details of submitted jobs, the job steps or granules and the order of execution of these job granules. A Job Manager component is present in each peer to schedule the jobs and follow up with the participating peers to obtain the result. We have tested the collaboration framework with an example and have presented the results and conclusion.

Keywords: P2P, Collaborative framework, Distributed processing, Distributed computing.

1 Introduction

In P2P system, each computer system or peer node acts as both client and server. As a server, it provides resources to be shared by other peers and as a client it uses or access resources of other peers. P2P networks enable peers to share data and content, communicate through message passing and also distribute the processing and computing. In a pure P2P network, the overlay links between peers are established arbitrarily. [5]. A new peer joining a network of peers can form its own links or copy the existing links of other peers by exchange of messages and route information. When a peer wishes to find a data or other resource, it normally floods the network with its query for the data. Peers having the resource will respond to the query. More than one peer can have the resource and respond to this query. The requesting peer chooses a peer, establishes a direct link with the peer and downloads the data. P2P

---

[*] Associate Professor, Research Scholar.
[**] Dean (Research), Computer Studies.

N. Meghanathan et al. (Eds.): CCSIT 2012, Part III, LNICST 86, pp. 26–35, 2012.
© Institute for Computer Sciences, Social Informatics and Telecommunications Engineering 2012

systems provide a completely decentralized environment wherein each system can provide services to each other systems in the network. The network of peers can thus be easily scaled up to any number and is more reliable. P2P can offer a robust solution that uses optimum bandwidth and network utilization. Some of the popular P2P networks are Napster, Gnutella and Kazaa which were primarily designed to share files and other data resources among multiple peers [15].

Distributed computing involves using many autonomous computer systems that come together to complete a task. One of the common applications of distributed computing is to process large amounts of data in a short span of time. An application or task can be broken up into many discrete and semi-independent parts which can be distributed for processing over multiple computer systems. With Internet as the communicating medium, peers can establish a flexible and reliable computational platform with enormous distributed computing potential. Distribution computing uses message passing whereby objects (code, data) can be exchanged between the computer systems that have come together to perform a large task or application. CORBA and DCOM example of distributed computing that provide a set of standards for object communication.

Many applications like BitTorrent and Limeware have been developed to facilitate sharing of data, music, video etc. There has been less focus on applications for distributed processing or computing. In this paper, we propose a Collaborative framework for P2P networks to enable distributed processing The objective of the framework is to facilitate distributed processing among peers by enabling provision for job or task scheduling, distributing of a task among multiple peers, messaging between peers, monitoring job execution, follow up and obtain the results of the completed tasks. The collaborative framework can also provide to establish the credibility and reliability of peers to enable peers to choose reliable partners for execution of jobs. The rest of the paper is organized as follows. Section 2 provides related work on this area and Section 3 describes the proposed P2P collaborative framework. In Section 4, we have applied the framework for a sample job and present the results. Section 5 concludes the paper.

2   Related Work

In this section, we briefly discuss research work relating to distributed computing. A Distributed computing system [10] consists of a set of independent computers connected by a computer network and operational with distributed system software. Jobs are split into independent small parts and processing of each of the job parts is done on individual PCs and the results are collected on a central server. The central server distributes the job parts among different PCs on the Internet and is also responsible for job coordination and completion. The clients take advantage of inactive periods to perform computation requested by the server.

There are two primary reasons for using distributed systems and distributed computing [1]. The nature of the application may need the use of a communication network to connect many numbers of computers. Data produced at one physical location may be required at another location and the communication network is used to make this possible. Secondly, it may be a case of using in principle a single computer to perform a specific job, but the use of a distributed system is advantageous from the viewpoint of time, efficiency and performance. For example, several low-end computers may together provide a more cost-efficient solution as compared to a single high-end computer.

SETI@home (Search for Extra Terrestrial Intelligence) is an Internet-based volunteer computing system which employs the Berkeley Open Infrastructure for Network Computing (BOINC) platform [13]. Originally, it was designed to search for radio signals emitted in the outer space and thus search for any signs of extra-terrestrial beings. Later, it has branched out into many activities such as parallel and distributed computing. The aim of SETI@home is to demonstrate viability of public-participation distributed scientific computing, and to increase public knowledge and awareness of SETI and radio astronomy. The original design of SETI was centralized with one server and data was distributed to clients using proxy servers. The clients process the job given to them and submit the results to server. As all interactions are with the server, there is a problem of load handling.

Distributed object systems are based on object-oriented programs where objects consisting of code and data are distributed across a network. Remote Method Invocation (RMI) and Common Object Request Broker Architecture (CORBA) are instances of such systems. Client-specific optimization is required for efficient performance thus making such systems difficult to maintain. RMI passes the objects as parameters to remote methods. Remote Procedure Call (RPC) is a dominant technique for constructing distributed, client-server based applications [7]. It is based on extending the notion of conventional or local procedure calls to making remote calls without the need to know the details of network interfaces. RPC tries to isolate the data communication layer from the application layer. RPC makes the client/server model of computing more powerful and easier to program, but the remoteness is not truly transparent to the client.

We have applied the concepts of distributed computing to P2P networks to develop a collaborative framework for distributed processing among many peers.

3   Collaborative Framework for P2P Networssk

In this paper, we propose a P2P collaborative framework to distribute and share the processing load among multiple peers. We propose a generic framework with the use of profiles to stores the details of peers who are willing to collaborate with other peers for job execution. Job profiles are proposed to maintain the details of submitted jobs, the job steps and the order of execution of these job steps.

Peers could be of types: initiator and participating peers. The initiator peer submits jobs to the participating peers which in turn work on the job steps or granules and send the results back to the initiator. The initiator peer collects the response of all the job steps from the participating peer and aggregates the results. The initiator peers can also provide feedback on job execution of the participating peers; thereby providing a method to evaluate the credibility and reliability of peers for collaboration on execution of jobs. The proposed collaborative framework for distributed computing in P2P network is given in Figure 1.

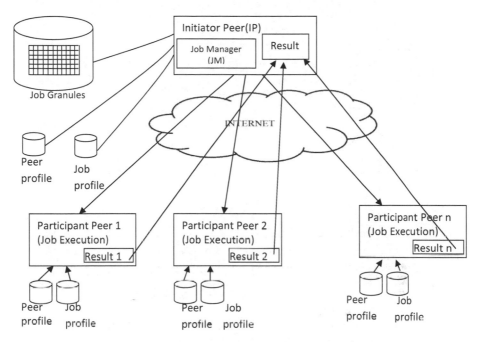

Fig. 1. Collaborative Framework For P2P Network

Peers, who are willing to collaborate with other peers for job execution, advertise their services. Such peer details are maintained as peer profile by each individual peer. The peer profile contains information on the processing capabilities of the peer node; such as CPU specification, memory available for processing, secondary storage space available for temporary storage of data of intermediate steps and final result, operating system, software installed etc. When a job has to be executed, the initiating peer will select the peers based on peer profile and their capacity to execute the job.

The Initiating Peer (IP) which would like to submit a job for distributed processing would first have to break the job into steps or modules which we call as job granules. These job granules are to be executed by the participating peers. Job profile maintains details of each submitted job, the job granules and the order of execution of these job granules. Details of which of the job granules can be executed in parallel and those that have to be executed in sequence and in which order are maintained.

Peers who wish to submit a job would first determine from the peer profile, the peers suitable for execution of the concerned job. The initiating peer will then send a request message to the peers to check their availability and willingness to do the job. Willing peers will respond with an affirmative message while other peers would send back a decline message. No response from peers within a specified time would also be treated as decline message. Based on the response from the peers, a set of peers are selected by the IP as the Participating Peers (PP) for the job execution. A Job Manager (JM) module is present in each peer to schedule the job granules and follow up with the respective peers to obtain the result. JM will send the job granule to the PPs for execution. The participating peers will execute the job granule and send back a successfully completed message and the result. In case of failure of job execution,

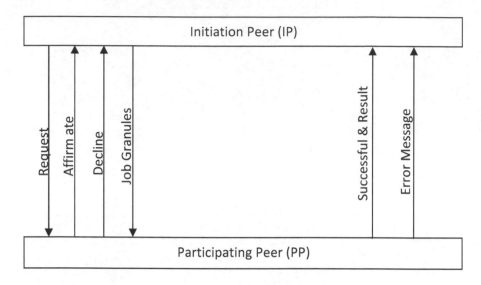

Fig. 2. Interaction among Peers for Job Execution

then an error message would be sent by the PP to the JM. The interactions between IP and PP for job execution are depicted in Figure 2.

JM would ensure that job execution follows the steps and order specified in the job profile. JM would wait for a specified time to obtain the result. If the successful or error message is not obtained within this specified time, then JM would look for another peer to execute the job granule. In case of execution errors, depending on the error type, JM would decide to send the same job granule to another peer. JM would abandon the job in case of serious or critical errors. JM would also abandon the job if required peers are not available for job execution, or there is a delay in obtaining the result. A threshold limit is set for the job execution and if the job is not completed within the threshold, then JM would abandon the job. IP would then examine why the job execution was abandoned. In case of errors in job processing, IP would first need to make necessary corrections before re-submitting the job. If the job was abandoned because of other reasons like network failure, peer non-availability etc, IP could wait and re-submit the job after an interval.

The collaborative framework can also provide feedback mechanisms to establish the credibility and reliability of peers. This would assist peers in choosing reliable partners for execution of jobs

4   Implementation and Results

We have implemented the proposed P2P collaborative framework using JXTA and Windows operating system. We have used JXTA services for peer registration, peer discovery, peer messaging and content communication and management. The nature and details of the job are kept partially hidden from the PP as IP sends only the data and execution module as class file.

As the first step, the peers advertise giving details of their processing capability. The peer details are updated in the Peer Profile which is maintained in XML format and a sample peer profile is given below. The Peer profile has been described using XML tag for Peer Name, Peer ID, Hardware details like Processor, processor details, Memory, etc. Tags have also been provided for installed software and versions. A typical peer profile is given below.

```
<?xml version="1.0" encoding="UTF-8"?>
<!DOCTYPEjxta:Profile>
<jxta:Profile type="jxta: Peer Profile" xmlns:jxta="http://jxta.org">
     <PID>urn:jxta:uuid-
59616261646162614A78746150325033CB4691E17A5E49DB89F0A6CADB9C60
2E03
     </PID>
     <Name>
            peer1
     </Name>
     <Desc>
            Profile of the peer
     </Desc>
     <HWArch>
            X86
     </HWArch>
     <NoCores>
            2
     </NoCores>
     <RAM>
            3 GB
     </RAM>
     <OS>
            Windows
     <OS>
     <OSVer>
            XP
     </OSVer>
</jxta:Profile>
```

The profile can be extended to provide complete and generic details of the peers. The IP uses the peer profile to select PP for execution of jobs.

The Job Profile is also maintained in XML format and we give below a sample format. A job profile has the following specifications about a job, Job ID, Step ID, File Name, Class Name of executable module. The Dependency tag is used to indicate job granules which have to be completed the prior to execution of the concern job granules. For example GranID 2 can be executed only after completion of GranID 1.

```
<?xml version="1.0" encoding="UTF-8"?>
  <!DOCTYPEjxta:JobProfile>
  <jxta:JobProfile type="jxta: Peer Profile" xmlns:jxta="http://jxta.org">
    <JobID>
            1
    </JobID>
    <GranID>
            1
    </GranID>
    <FileName>
            Input.txt
    </FileName>
    <ClassName>
            ExecuteClass2
    </ClassName>
    <Dependency>
            0
    </Dependency>
    < GranID>
            2
    </ GranID >
    <FileName>
            Input.txt
    </FileName>
    <ClassName>
            ExecuteClass2
    </ClassName>
    <Dependency>
            1
    </Dependency>
  </jxta:JobProfile>
```

We explain the job submission and execution process using a standard deviation calculation. A Job Manager (JM) module is present in each peer to schedule the job granules and follow up with the participating peers to obtain the result. We have calculated the time taken by a single peer to execute the job. A threshold limit is set for the complete job execution which is twice the time taken by a single peer to complete the job. We have assumed the same time as threshold limit for each job step as well.

Standard deviation σ is calculated using the formula:

$$\sigma = \sqrt{\frac{\sum_{i=1}^{i=N} (x_i - \bar{x})^2}{N}}$$

Where
$$\bar{x} = \frac{\sum_{i-1}^{i=N} x_i}{N}$$

x is a list of numbers and $\bar{x}$ is the average of the numbers. x_i is the ith number in the list. N is the count of the list of numbers.

The execution of the equation among multiple PP was tested using a range of 10 – 20 lakh numbers. Since the list of numbers is huge, it is a time consuming process when only one peer is doing the calculation. The job is divided into granules and represented as steps below:

Step1: The list of numbers N are divided into sets S of lakh of numbers

Step2: Each set is sent to a different PP for summing up. The count of the numbers in the set can is determined in parallel.

Step3: The total of all the individual sums is determined from the results of the previous step and average is calculated.

Step4: $\sum_{i=1}^{i=n}(x_i - \bar{x})^2$ is calculated in parallel for each of the set of numbers S by PPs

Step5: Final step is to calculate the σ

We have compared the performance for calculating standard deviation using a single peer and multiple peers as shown in Table 1. There was no significant difference in time when the dataset was small, that is, 1 or 2 lakh of data entries. Likewise, when the number of peers (1 - 10) was small, there was an increase in the computation time because of the communication delay. Also when the number of peers was large, there was no significant difference in the total processing time. For a dataset of 10 or 20 lakhs, we obtained optimum result with 20 peers.

Table 1. Dataset for Standard Deviation

no of entries	no of peers	time taken for each peer(in ms)
100000	1	200
200000	1	276
1000000	1	1294
2000000	1	2219
1000000	10	2670
2000000	10	4865
1000000	20	1235
2000000	20	2170
1000000	30	1270
2000000	30	2235
1000000	40	1305
2000000	40	2320
1000000	50	1335
2000000	50	2432

The results are graphically depicted in Figure 3.

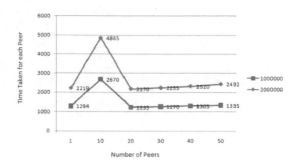

Fig. 3. Graph for the dataset

It can be concluded that for large jobs and datasets, it is significantly faster with multiple peers sharing the processing load. In analyzing the performance benefits of the proposed system, it is clear that as the number of peers in a P2P environment increases, the time taken to process the job modules reduces.

5   Conclusion and Future Work

The proposed collaborative framework for P2P provides a scalable and reliable means for processing large jobs. The proposed framework is a generic one where peer capability and job details are described using peer profile and job profiles. In the given example, execution modules in the form of class files are sent to the participating peers so that the nature of the job is kept hidden from the peers. Likewise, the peers do not have access to the full dataset thereby providing a certain level of data security. As future work, we propose to use well known P2P data distribution protocols and applications like FTP, Bit Torrent, etc. We also aim to develop an efficient scheduler for job execution and management.

References

[1] Berry, K.: Distributed and Grid Computing via the Browser Computing Research. Villanova University, Villanova (2009),
http://www.csc.villanova.edu/~tway/courses/csc3990/f2009/
csrs2009/Kevin_Berry_Grid_Computing_CSRS_2009.pdf
[2] Costa, F., Silva, L., Kelley, I., Fedak, G.: Optimizing Data Distribution layer of BOINC with Bit Torrent. In: IEEE International Symposium on Parallel and Distributed Processing, IPDPS 2008, pp. 1–8 (2008)
[3] Boldrin, F., Taddia, C., Mazzini, G.: Distributed Computing Through Web Browser. In: IEEE 66th Vehicular Technology Conference, VTC-2007, September 30-October 3, pp. 2020–2024. Univ. of Ferrara, Ferrara (2007)
[4] Ho, K., Wu, J., Sum, J.: On the Session Lifetime Distribution of Gnutella. Providence University, Sha-Lu (2007) http://www.citeseerx.ist.psu.edu/

[5] Awan, A., Ferreira, R.A., Jagannathan, S., Grama, A.: Unstructured Peer-to-Peer Networks for Sharing Processor Cycles, vol. 1. Purdue University, USA (2005)

[6] Petrie, D.: A Framework for Session Initiation Protocol User Agent Profile Delivery. PingtelCorp (October 24, 2004)

[7] Tilevich, E., Cook, W.R., Jiao, Y.: Explicit Batching for Distributed Objects, Computer Science Department, Virginia Tech

[8] Milojicic, D.S., Kalogeraki, V., Lukose, R., Nagaraja, K., Pruyne, J., Richard, B., Rollins, S., Xu, Z.: Peer-to-Peer Computing (July 3, 2003),
http://www.hpl.hp.com/techreports/2002/HPL-2002-57R1.html

[9] Brookshier, D., Govoni, D., Krishnan, N., Soto, J.C.: JXTA: Java^{TM} P2P Programming. Sams Publishing (March 22, 2002)

[10] Preliminary Research on Grid-based Remote Sensing Image distributed Processing-2007 IFIP International Conference on Network and Parallel Computing

[11] JXTA Java Standard Edition V2.5: Programmer's Guide

[12] Client-Server Model, http://www.cs.umbc.edu/~mgrass2/cmsc645/

[13] SETI@home, http://www.setiathome.berkeley.edu/

[14] Gnutella, http://www.gnutella.org

[15] JXTA Protocol, https://jxta.dev.java.net/

[16] RPC and RMI,
http://www.careerride.com/
RMI-advantages-and-disadvantages-of-RPC.aspx

[17] ClassLoader,
http://download.oracle.com/javase/1.4.2/docs/
api/java/lang/ClassLoader.html

Minimizing Boolean Sum of Products Functions Using Binary Decision Diagram

Debajit Sensarma[1], Subhashis Banerjee[1], Krishnendu Basuli[1],
Saptarshi Naskar[2], and Samar Sen Sarma[3]

[1] West Bengal State University, West Bengal, India
[2] Sarsuna College, West Bengal, India
[3] University Of Calcutta, West Bengal, India
{mail.sb88,debajit.sensarma2008,
Krishnendu.basuli,sapgrin}@gmail.com,
Sssarma2001@yahoo.com

Abstract. Two-level logic minimization is a central problem in logic synthesis, and has applications in reliability analysis and automated reasoning. This paper represents a method of minimizing Boolean sum of products function with binary decision diagram and with disjoint sum of product minimization. Due to the symbolic representation of cubes for large problem instances, the method is orders of magnitude faster than previous enumerative techniques. But the quality of the approach largely depends on the variable ordering of the underlying BDD. The application of Binary Decision Diagrams (BDDs) as an efficient approach for the minimization of Disjoint Sums-of-Products (DSOPs). DSOPs are a starting point for several applications.

The use of BDDs has the advantage of an implicit representation of terms. Due to this scheme the algorithm is faster than techniques working on explicit representations and the application to large circuits that could not be handled so far becomes possible. Theoretical studies on the influence of the BDDs to the search space are carried out. In experiments the proposed technique is compared to others. The results with respect to the size of the resulting DSOP are as good or better as those of the other techniques.

Keywords and Phrases: Binary Decision Diagram, DSOP, Unate Function, Binate Function.

1 Introduction

A DSOP is a representation of a Boolean function as a sum of disjoint cubes. DSOPs are used in several applications in the area of CAD, e.g. the calculation of spectra of Boolean functions or as a starting point for the minimization of Exclusive-Or-Sum-Of-Products (ESOPs). In some techniques for minimization of DSOPs have been introduced. They are working on explicit representations of the cubes and therefore are only applicable to small instances of the problem.

BDDs in general are an efficient data structure for presenting and manipulating the Boolean functions. They are well-known and widely used in logic synthesis and

N. Meghanathan et al. (Eds.): CCSIT 2012, Part III, LNICST 86, pp. 36–48, 2012.

formal verification of integrated circuits. Due to the canonical representation of Boolean functions they are very suitable for formal verification problems and used in a lot of tools to date [14, 15, 16].BDDs are well-suited for applications in the area of logic synthesis, because the cubes in the ON-set of a Boolean function are implicitly represented in this data structure. A hybrid approach for the minimization of DSOPs relying on BDDs in combination with structural methods has recently been introduced in. It has been shown that BDDs are applicable to the problem of DSOP minimization [5].

Given a BDD of a Boolean function, the DSOP can easily be constructed: each one-path [6], i.e. a path from the root to the terminal 1 vertex, corresponds to a cube in the DSOP, and moreover, different one-paths lead to disjoint cubes. For the construction of the BDD the variables of the Boolean function are considered in a fixed order. The permutation of the variables largely influences the number of one-paths in the BDD and thus the number of cubes in the corresponding DSOP. Additionally, the importance of choosing a good variable order to get a small DSOP has theoretically been supported.

1.1 Motivation

The motivation of this project is to minimize the boolean sum of product function by finding the minimal irridundant expression. Here Binary Decision Diagram(BDD) is used for finding Disjoint cubes first, because BDD is the compact representation of a boolean function, but it highly depends on variable ordering. Then this disjoint cubes are minimizes to get the minimal expression. In Quine McCluskey method, it can be shown that for a function of n variables the upper bound on the number of prime implicantes is $3^n/n$. In this project a heuristic algorihm is used to minimize the upper bound of the prime implicant generation and it gives the near optimal solution.

1.2 Binary Decision Diagrams

A BDD is a directed acyclic graph $G_f = (V, E)$ that represents a Boolean function f: $B^n \rightarrow B^m$. The Shannon decomposition $g = x_i g_{xi} + x_i \cdot g_{xi}$ is carried out in each internal node v labeled with label (v) = x_i of the graph, therefore v has the two successors then (v) and else (v). The leaves are labeled with 0 or 1 and correspond to the constant Boolean functions. The root node root (G_f) corresponds to the function f. In the following, BDD refers to a reduced ordered BDD (as defined in [8]) and the size of a BDD is given by the number of nodes.

Definition: A one-path in a BDD $G_f = (V, E)$ is a path
$p = (v_0 ,\ldots, v_{l-1}, v_l)$;
$v_i \in V; (v_i, v_{i+1}) \in E$
with $v_0 = root(G_f)$ and label(v_l) = 1. p has length l + 1.
$P_1 (G_f)$ denotes the number of all different one-paths in the BDD G_f.

1.3 BDD and DSOP

Consider a BDD Gf representing the Boolean function $f(x_1,\ldots, x_n)$. A one path $p = (v_0 ,\ldots, v_l)$ of length l + 1 in Gf corresponds to an (n - l)-dimensional cube that is a subset of ON(f)[1]. The cube is described by:

$m_p = n \, l_i$ for $i=0\ldots l-1$; where
$l_i = $ label (v_i); if $v_i+1 = $ else (v_i)
       label (v_i); if $v_i+1 = $ then (v_i)

Two paths p1 and p2 in a BDD are different if they differ in at least one edge. Since all paths originate from root (G_f), there is a node v where the paths separate. Let label $(v) = x_i$. Therefore one of the cubes includes xi, the other x_i. Hence, the cubes mp1 and mp2 are disjoint.

Now the DSOP can easily be built by summing up all cubes corresponding to the one-paths.

Remark 1 : Let Gf be a BDD of $f(x_1, \ldots, x_n)$ and M1 be the set of one-paths in G_f. Then G_f represents the DSOP

$$\sum m_p \text{ where p } \epsilon \, M_1$$

where m_p is the cube given above.

From this it is clear that the number of cubes in the DSOP represented by G_f is equal to $P_1(G_f)$. Thus, as opposed to the usual goal of minimizing the number of nodes in a BDD, here the number of one-paths is minimized. Known techniques to minimize the number of nodes can be used to minimize the number of paths by changing the objective function. One such technique is sifting. A variable is chosen and moved to any position of the variable order based on exchange of adjacent variables. Then it is fixed at the best position (i.e. where the smallest BDD results), afterwards another variable is chosen. No variable is chosen twice during this process.

2   Terms Related to Sop Minimization

Unite function: A function that is monotonically increasing or decreasing in each of its variable is called unite function.

Binate function: a function that is not unate. This can also be used to mean a cover of a function that is not unate.

Canonical cover/solution: the SOP cover of a function that contains only minterms, and thus has not at all been reduced.

Cube: a one-dimensional matrix in the form of an implicant. Two cubes are said to be **Disjoint** if their intersection of the set of minterms is null.The intersection is the operation of conjunction (i.e. the Boolean AND operation).

Espresso algorithm: an algorithm that minimizes SOP functions.

Essential prime implicant: a prime implicant that the cover of a function must contain in order to cover the function

Implicant: an ANDed string of literals. It is a term in an SOP function.

Literal: an instance of a boolean variable. It may be the variable complemented, uncomplemented, or ignored (don't-care). In matrix representations or the Q-M algorithm, it may have a value of 0, 1, or 2/X, corresponding to complemented, uncomplemented, and don't-care, respectively.

Matrix representation of a function or implicant: The rows of a two-dimensional matrix representation of a function are the implicants of the function. The columns of a one-dimensional matrix representation of an implicant are the literals of the implicant.

Minterm: an implicant that contains exactly one literal for each variable. It is not at all simplified.

Monotone decreasing: A function is monotone decreasing in a variable if changing the value of the variable from 0 to 1 results in the output of the function being 0.

Monotone increasing: A function is monotone increasing in a variable if changing the value of the variable from 0 to 1 results in the output of the function being 1.

Prime implicant: an implicant that cannot be further reduced by adjacency

Quine-McCluskey (Q-M) algorithms: two algorithms that minimize a boolean function.The first algorithm finds all prime implicants, and the second algorithm eliminates nonessential prime implicants.

3   Proposed Algorithm

In this method at first from the given truth table suitable variable order is chosen based on Shannon entropy measurement, then binary decision diagram is made considering this variable order. After that disjoint cubes are calculated by following the 1-path of the BDD. Then from that the covering matrix is created where columns represent the variables and row represents the applicants or disjoints cubes. Then selecting the most binate variables and by unite simplification the ultimate minimized sop function is obtained.

3.1   Algorithm

Step 1: Generation of truth table.

Step 2:Variable reordering using Shannon entropy measure-ment [2,8] and create Binary Decision Diagram[7,13,14].

Step 3: Finding Disjoint Cubes from Binary decision Diagram [5].

Step 4: Disjoint cube minimization using Binate Covering with Recursion and Unate Simplification Method [11,12].

3.2   Explanation

Step 1:
The truth table is generated from given Boolean expression.
Step2:
Choosing right variable order is very important for constructing Binary Decision Diagram, because if bad variable order is chosen then number of 1-paths can be increased; even number of nodes in the BDD may be increased exponentially.

The measures of a variable's importance are based on information theoretic criteria, and require computation of entropy of a variable. Entropy measures can be quite effective in distinguishing the importance of variables. It is well known that a central problem in using OBDD is the severe memory requirements that result from extremely large OBDD size that arise in many instances.OBDD sizes are unfortunately very sensitive to the order chosen on input variables. Determining the optimal order is a co-NP complete problem [8].Variable ordering heuristics can be classified as either static or dynamic approaches. A static approach , analyzes the given circuit/function and, based on its various properties, determines some variable order which has a high "Probability" of being effective. In dynamic approach to compute variable ordering, one starts with an initial order, which is analyzed and permuted at internal points in the circuit/function, such that some cost function is minimized.

Step 3:
In this step Disjoint Cubes from Binary decision Diagram are found by following the 1-path [5].

Step 4:
Cover matrix is found from the resultant disjoint cubes and this is simplified using Unate Recursive Paradigm [12].

4   Illustration with an Example

f(a,b,c,d)=$\sum$(1,5,6,9,12,13,14,15)

Step1: *Given the truth table.*

a	b	c	d	f
0	0	0	0	0
0	0	0	1	1
0	0	1	0	0
0	0	1	1	0
0	1	0	0	0
0	1	0	1	1
0	1	1	0	1
0	1	1	1	0
1	0	0	0	0
1	0	0	1	1
1	0	1	0	0
1	0	1	1	0
1	1	0	0	1
1	1	0	1	1
1	1	1	0	1
1	1	1	1	1

With this variable order the Binary Decision Diagram is:

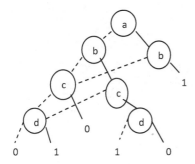

Number of nodes=7

<u>Step 2:</u> *Variable ordering by calculating Entropy and choosing most ambiguous variables.*

I(a,0)=0.954
I(a,1)=0.954
E(a)=0.954
I(b,0)=0.811
I(b,1)=0.811
E(b)=0.811   Select 'b' as the first splitting variable.
I(c,0)=0.954
I(c,1)=0.954
E(c)=0.954
I(d,0)=0.954
I(d,1)=0.954
E(d)=0.954

For b=0 the truth table is:

a	c	d	f
0	0	0	0
0	0	1	1
0	1	0	0
0	1	1	0
1	0	0	0
1	0	1	1
1	1	0	0
1	1	1	0

I(a,0)=0.811
I(a,1)=0.811
E(a)=0.811
I(c,0)=1
I(c,1)=0

E(c)=0.5
I(d,0)=0
I(d,1)=1
E(d)=0.5

For b=1 the truth table is:

a	c	d	f
0	0	0	0
0	0	1	1
0	1	0	1
0	1	1	0
1	0	0	1
1	0	1	1
1	1	0	1
1	1	1	1

I(a,0)=1
I(a,1)=0
E(a)=0.5   Select 'a' as the next splitting variable.
I(c,0)=0.811
I(c,1)=0.811
E(c)=0.811
I(d,0)=0.811
I(d,1)=0.811
E(d)=0.811

If we proceed like this we come up with the variable order->b,a,c,d
   With this variable order the Binary Decision Diagram is:

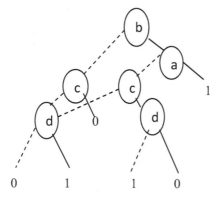

   Number of nodes=6

<u>Step 3</u>: *Finding Disjoint Cubes from Above Binary Decision Diagram.*
   The Disjoint Cubes are: **ab + a'bcd'+ b'c'd + a'bc'd**

<u>Step 4</u>: *Binate Covering with Recursion.*
The Covering Matrix is:

	a	b	c	d
ab	1	1	2	2
a'bcd'	0	1	1	0
b'c'd	2	0	0	1
abc'd	0	1	0	1

<u>Case 1</u>: *Binate Select.*

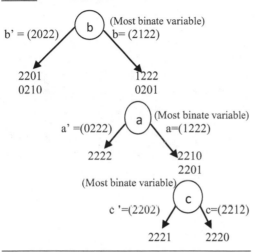

<u>Case 2</u>: *Merge.*

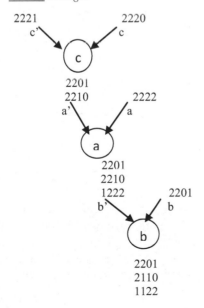

After simplification the expression is:
ab + c'd + bcd'.
<u>Karnaugh Map Representation:</u>

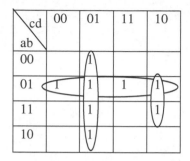

5 Result

This program is done on Intel Pentium 4 CPU, 2.80 GHz and 256 MB of RAM and with Visual c++ 6.0 standard edition. The result is presented here with the following figures.

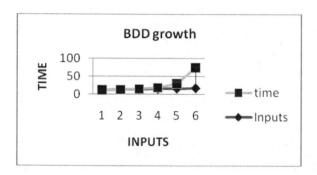

Fig. 1. growth of Binary Decision Diagram. Here X-axis represents the number of inputs and Y-axis represents the required time.

Here growth of the creation of Binary decision diagram with proposed method is shown with respect to 6 variables.

Here comparison of creation of number of disjoint cubes and time taken to create the disjoint cube of Espresso Logic Minimizer and the proposed method is done with respect to 4 variables.

Here number of literals and terms before and after minimizing the given Boolean sum-of-product function is given with respect to 4,5 and 6 variables with the Proposed method.

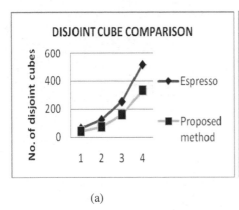
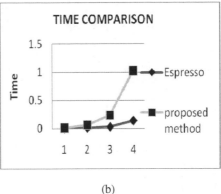

(a)   (b)

Fig. 2. (a) Comparison of number of disjoint cubes generated by ESPRESSO heuristic logic minimizer and the Proposed method. X-axis represents the number of variables and Y-axis represents the number of disjoint cubes. **(b)** Comparison of time taken to generate disjoint cubes by ESPRESSO heuristic logic minimizer and the Proposed method. X-axis represents the number of variables and Y-axis represents the time.

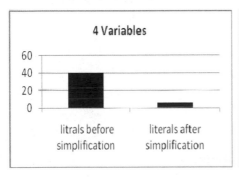
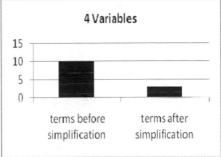

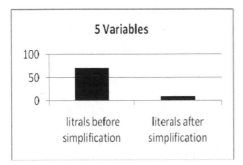
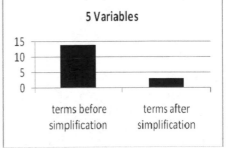

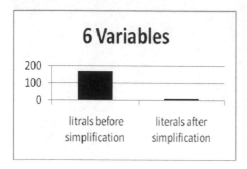 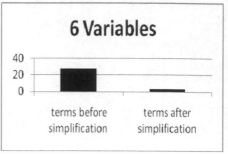

Fig. 3. Comparison of the number of literals and terms before simplification and generated by above program for 4,5 and 6 variables

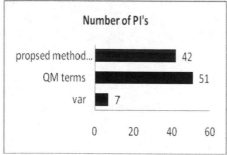 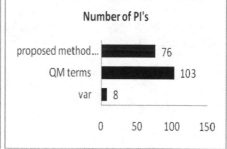

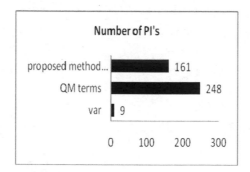

Fig. 4. Comparison of number of Prime implicantes generated by Quine-McCluskey algorithm and the Proposed method for 7, 8 and 9 variables. Here QM stands for Quine-McCluskey

Prime implicants generated by the Quine-McCluskey procedure and the Proposed method is compared here with respect to 7,8 and 9 variables.

5 Conclusions

An approach based on Binary Decision Diagram and Binate covering algorithm to minimize the Boolean SOP function with DSOP representation of a Boolean function was presented. It is completely based on heuristics and gives the near optimum solution. But this procedure will only work for single output and completely specified functions and gives the near optimal solution. Whether it will work for incompletely specified function and multiple-output function is not tested yet.

6 Future Works

1. Generation of all possible minimal covers or minimal expressions.
2. Compare with ESPRESSO logic minimizer.
3. Test whether it will work for incompletely specified function and multiple-output functions.

References

[1] Yang, C., Ciesielski, M.: BDD-Based Logic Optimization System. IEEE Transactions on Computer Aided Design of Integrated Circuits and Systems 21(7), 866–876 (2002)
[2] Popel, D.V.: Towards Efficient Calculation of Informationmeasures for Reordering of Binary Decision Diagrams. Computing Research Repository - CORR, cs AR/0207 (2002)
[3] Knuth, D.E.: The Art of Computer Programming, vol. 4
[4] Swamy, G.M.: An Exact Logic Minimizer Using Implicit Binary Decision Diagram Based Methods. In: ICCAD 1994 Proceedings of the 1994 IEEE/ACM International Conference on Computer-Aided Design (1994)
[5] Fey, G., Drechsler, R.: Utilizing BDDs for Disjoint SOP Minimization. In: 45th IEEE International Midwest Symposium on Circuits and Systems (2002)
[6] Raidl, G.R., Cagnoni, S., Branke, J., Corne, D.W., Drechsler, R., Jin, Y., Johnson, C.G., Machado, P., Marchiori, E., Rothlauf, F., Smith, G.D., Squillero, G. (eds.): EvoWorkshops 2004. LNCS, vol. 3005. Springer, Heidelberg (2004)
[7] Andersen, H.R.: An Introduction to Binary Decision Diagrams. Lecture Notes, Technical University of Denmark (October 1997)
[8] Jain, J., Bitner, J., Moundanos, D., Abraham, J.A., Fussell, D.S.: A new scheme to compute variable orders for binary decision diagrams. In: Proceedings of the Fourth Great Lakes Symposium on, Design Automation of High Performance VLSI Systems, GLSV 1994, March 4-5, pp. 105–108 (1994)
[9] Hilgemeier, M., Drechsler, N., Drechsler, R.: Minimizing the number of one-paths in BDDs by an evolutionary algorithm. In: Congress on Evolutionary Computation (2003)
[10] Nosrati, M., Hariri, M.: An Algorithm for Minimizing of Boolean Functions Based on Graph DS. World Applied Programming 1(3), 209–214 (2011)
[11] Coudert, O.: On solving Covering Problems. In: Proc. of 33rd DAC, Las Vegas (June 1996)

[12] Brayton, R.K.: Logic minimization algorithms for VLSI synthesis

[13] Bryant, R.E.: Graph-based algorithms for Boolean function manipulation. IEEE Transactions on Computers C-35-8, 677–691 (1986)

[14] Bryant, R.E.: Symbolic Boolean Manipulation with Ordered Binary-Decision Diagrams. ACM Computing Surveys (1992)

[15] Bryant, R.E.: Binary decision diagrams and beyond: Enabeling techniques for formal verification. In: Int'l Conf. on CAD, pp. 236–243 (1995)

[16] Drechsler, R., Becker, B.: Binary Decision Diagrams – Theory and Implementation. Kluwer Academic Publishers (1998)

[17] Kohavi, Z.: Switching and Finite Automata Theory

Compression of Gray Scale Images Using Linear Prediction on Wavelet Coefficients

P.S. Arya Devi and M.G. Mini

Dept. of Electronics, Model Engineering College
Kochi, India
aryabinoy@gmail.com, mininair@mec.ac.in

Abstract. Each year, terabytes of image data- both medical and non medical-are generated which substantiates the need of image compression. In this paper, the correlation properties of wavelets are utilised in linear predictive coding to compress images. The image is decomposed using a one dimensional wavelet transform. The highest level approximation and a few coefficients of details in every level are retained. Using linear prediction on these coefficients the image is reconstructed.With less predictors and samples from the original wavelet coefficients compression can be achieved. The results are appraised in objective and subjective manner.

Keywords: Image Compression, bits per pixel (bpp), wavelet transform, linear predictive coding (LPC), correlation.

1 Introduction

Image compression is a key issue to be addressed in the area of transmission and storage of images. The storage and transmission of large volumes of image data is a challenging task owing to limited storage space and bandwidth. With the emerging technologies, there are promises of unlimited bandwidth. But the need and availability for images outgrow the increase in network capacity. The high costs involved in providing large bandwidth and huge storage space further necessitates the need for image compression. Image compression finds its application in various fields ranging from satellite imaging, medical imaging to teleconferencing, HDTV etc. Compressing an image is the process of reducing the size of the image, without degrading the image quality by exploiting its redundancy and irrelevancy. Even as many techniques available and emerging in the field of image compression, the demand for digital image transmission indicate that there is always room for better and novel methods.

Wavelet Transform (WT) is a tool that allows multi resolution analysis of an image. It can extract relevant information from an image and can adapt to human visual characteristics. WT decomposes an image into a set of different resolution sub-images corresponding to the various frequency bands and gives a multi-resolution representation of the image with localization in both spatial and frequency domains.

N. Meghanathan et al. (Eds.): CCSIT 2012, Part III, LNICST 86, pp. 49–58, 2012.
© Institute for Computer Sciences, Social Informatics and Telecommunications Engineering 2012

Images can be modeled using homomorphic systems, in which a logarithmic transformation is used to convert multiplicative superposition to additive superposition of signals. In such systems linear prediction can be compatible [1]. Linear prediction model optimally extract information about a current sample from a neighborhood of samples in its causal past [2]. The process of signal or system modeling removes redundancy, which is the essence of data compression [3].

In our proposed method the image is decomposed into approximation and details at multi-scale. The highest level approximation and details are retained. In addition to that a few coefficients of details in every level are also retained. Using linear prediction on these coefficients the details are reconstructed. The approximation of a lower level is reconstructed from higher level coefficients using inverse wavelet transform (IWT). The predicted coefficients are used here. Finally the original image is reconstructed in this manner.

2   Theory

A brief revision of theory associated with the proposed method is given below. The areas dealt here are image compression fundamentals, wavelet transform, linear prediction and correlation properties of wavelet.

2.1   Image Compression Fundamentals

In most of the images, the neighboring pixels are correlated, and image contains redundant information. By compressing an image we should find a less correlated representation of the image. Image compression relies on reduction of redundancy and irrelevancy. Redundancy reduction removes duplication from image, and irrelevancy reduction omits parts of the signal that will not be noticed by Human Visual System (HVS). The redundancies in an image can be identified as spatial redundancy, coding redundancy and inter pixel redundancy. Image compression aims at reducing the number of bits needed to represent an image by removing the redundancies as much as possible. [4]

Image compression methods can mainly be classified as lossy compression and lossless compression. In lossless compression the decompressed image will be an exact replica of the original image without any loss in data. It offers a compression ratio of around 2 to 4. Lossy compression will not result in exact recovery of original image. Some fine details are sacrificed to obtain better compression ratio. The compression ratio in this case can exceed 100[5]. Wavelet compression methods are one of the most popular compression methods. Due to symmetric impulse response bior9/7 wavelet is suitable from compression perspective [6].

2.2   Wavelet Transform

Discrete dyadic wavelet transforms have been successfully applied to solve different problems in many fields, owing to the good spatial localization and fairly good frequency localization of their bases [7], [8]. They are invertible and efficient. When applied to an image, the image is split into its details at different scales, orientations and positions. The transformed image is de-correlated [9].

One-dimensional wavelet theory defines a function ψ, the wavelet, and its associated scaling function φ, such that the family of functions $\{ \psi^j (x) \}$ j$\in$ Z, are orthonormal , where

$$\psi^j(x) = \sqrt{2^j}\psi(2^j x) \tag{1}$$

The wavelet transform can be implemented by quadrature mirror filters $G = (g(n))$ and $H = (h(n))$, $n \in Z$, where

$$h(n) = 1/2 \langle\phi(x/2), \phi(x - n)\rangle; g(n) = (-1)^n h(n) \tag{2}$$

(< >denotes L^2 inner product). H corresponds to a low-pass filter, and G is an octave wide high-pass filter. The reconstruction filters have impulse responses [10]

$$h^*(n) = h(l - n) ; g^*(n) = g(l - n) \tag{3}$$

A group of transform coefficients resulting from the same sequence of low pass and high pass filtering operations gives approximation and detail coefficients respectively.

Two dimensional wavelet transform is performed by applying a separable filter bank to the image. Applying the one dimensional transform in each row, we get two approximation and details coefficients in each row (L and H subbands). Then applying one dimensional DWT column-wise on these L and H subbands, four subbands LL, LH, HL, and HH are obtained. LL is a coarser version of the original input signal called approximation image. LH, HL, and HH are the high frequency sub-bands containing the detail information (vertical, horizontal and diagonal details images). The number of decompositions performed on original image to obtain sub-bands is called sub-band decomposition [11]. Fig. 1 shows 2-Dimensional DWT (2D DWT) performed in separable form on an image and the two level decomposition of the image.

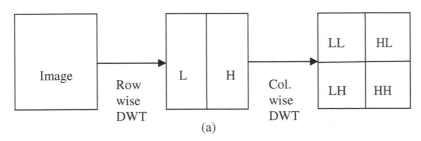

(a)

Fig. 1. 2D DWT performed in separable form on an image a) First level decomposition b) Second level decomposition

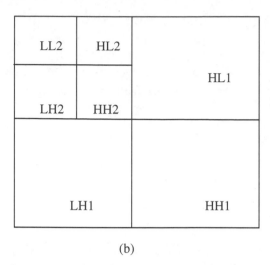

(b)

Fig. 1. *(continued)*

2.3   Linear Prediction

Linear Predictive Coding (LPC) is a popular and efficient technique mainly used in signal compression and speech processing. The signal is modeled as a linear combination of its past values and a hypothetical input to a causal system whose output is the given signal. In the frequency domain, this is equivalent to modeling the signal spectrum by a pole zero model [3]. The sample of the signal is predicted and if the prediction is done from weighted sum of other samples of the signal, the linear predictive model is auto regressive (AR) model [12]. The model parameters are obtained by a least squares analysis in the time domain and frequency domain [3]. The AR model of a process expresses it as finite linear aggregate of its previous values. Let us denote the values of stochastic process at equally spaced times, $n,(n-1),(n-2)...$ by $y(n), y(n-1), y(n-2),.....$

$$y(n) = \alpha_1 y(n-1) + \alpha_2 y(n-2) + .. + \alpha_p y(n-p) \tag{4}$$

Exploiting autocorrelation values the Yule-Walker equations can be arrived at.

$$R_{yy}(k) = \sum_{m=1}^{p} \alpha_k R_{yy}(m-k) \tag{5}$$

Using Levinson- Durbin algorithm [13] the above equations can be solved. Levinson Durbin algorithm is as follows:

1. Initialise the recursion

$$\alpha_0(0) = 1$$

(6)

$$\varepsilon_0 = r_{yy}(0)$$

2. For k=0,1,...M

$$\gamma_{p-1} = r_{yy}(p) + \sum_{k=1}^{p-1} \alpha_p(k) r_{yy}(p-k)$$

(7)

$$\Gamma_p = -\frac{\gamma_{p-1}}{\epsilon_{p-1}}$$

(8)

$$\alpha_p(k) = \alpha_{p-1}(k) + \Gamma_p \alpha_p^*(p-k)$$

(9)

$$\alpha_p(k+1) = \Gamma_p$$

(10)

$$\varepsilon_{p+1} = \varepsilon_p[1 - |\Gamma_p|^2]$$

(11)

Thus we can obtain the predictor coefficients. Using these coefficients, the signal can be predicted using (4).

2.4   Correlational Properties of Wavelet Coefficients

Let $f(t)$ be a signal whose WT is calculated. Let CA_j and CD_j be the approximation and details coefficients at decomposition level j. We assume the signal to be stationary and so transform coefficients also should have same property. The expectation of approximation coefficients at the jth level can be given as

$$E[CA_j] = \sqrt{2^{-j}} \int f(t) E_n[\Phi(2^{-j}t - n)]dt \quad \approx \frac{\sqrt{2^{-j}}}{N} \int f(t)$$

(12)

where E_n is an average operator while N is the length of support range of $[\Phi(2^{-j} t-n)]$. The expectation of approximation coefficients is proportional to the average of the original signal. It can also be found that detail coefficients have zero mean.

$$E[CD_j] = \sqrt{2^{-j}} \int f(t) E_n[\Psi(2^{-j}t - n)]dt = 0 \tag{13}$$

The autocorrelation of CA_j and CD_j are proportional to autocorrelation of original signal. CAj and CDj are decorrelated. The detail coefficients at different levels are also decorrelated. The property of localized WT coefficients is exploited in our method. This property will lead to more correlation of wavelet coefficients in the same prediction channel. The higher the correlation, the more is the scope for redundancy removal in prediction filtering [14]

3   The Proposed Method

In the proposed method one dimensional (1D) DWT is performed on each row of the original image. The decomposition up to four levels is done and the approximation and detail coefficients of fourth level are retained. Predictor coefficients for each row in detail coefficients at $(i-1)^{th}$ level is calculated. Few prediction coefficients and that much detail coefficients, at each level along with retained coefficients from fourth level forms compressed image.

In the decompression, with a few predictor coefficients and that much detail coefficients in the ith level, all the details coefficients in the ith level are reconstructed. Approximation coefficients for i^{th} level is obtained from inverse DWT on $(i+1)^{th}$ level of wavelet coefficients. Using approximation and detail coefficients of ith level approximation of $(i-1)^{th}$ level is obtained. Thus the whole image is reconstructed.

4   Evaluation Criteria

For assessing fidelity of reconstructed image, there are two classes of criteria; objective fidelity criteria and subjective fidelity criteria. In objective fidelity criteria the level of information loss is expressed as a function of input image, compressed image and subsequently decompressed image. Some of the objective fidelity criteria are normalized mean square error (NMSE), normalized absolute error (NAE), and peak signal to nose ratio (PSNR) [11]. The measures like compression ratio (CR) and bit per pixel (bpp) also evaluate a compression method.

Let $x(m,n)$ be the original M×N pixel image and $x^*(m,n)$ be the reconstructed image

$$NMSE = \frac{\sum_{m=1}^{M} \sum_{n=1}^{N}[x(m,n) - x^*(m,n)]^2}{\sum_{m=1}^{M} \sum_{n=1}^{N}[x(m,n)]^2} \tag{14}$$

$$NAE = \frac{\sum_{m=1}^{M} \sum_{n=1}^{N} [x(m,n) - x^*(m,n)]}{\sum_{m=1}^{M} \sum_{n=1}^{N} [x(m,n)]} \tag{15}$$

$$PSNR = 10 \log_{10} \frac{255}{MSE} \tag{16}$$

The subjective fidelity criteria measure the quality of an image by human evaluation using an absolute rating scale. One possible rating scale is as shown below. {-3, -2, -1, 0, 1, 2, 3} which represent {much worse, worse, slightly worse, the same, slightly better, better, much better} [15].

5   Results and Discussions

The images with large dimensions (1024 x 1024) are taken as test images. The test images constitute both medical and natural gray scale images. The wavelet used is bior4.4. The original and reconstructed images are shown in the fig. 2 and fig 3. The magnified versions of original and decompressed images are shown for comparison in fig. 4 and fig. 5.

The subjective assessment of the reconstructed images is also done. The original and decompressed images were shown to different viewers and there were asked to rate the images. As per the feedback this method is found to be effective in compressing the images without losing their vital information.

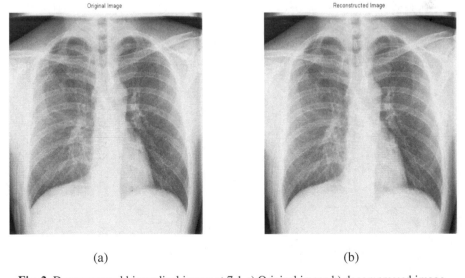

(a)   (b)

Fig. 2. Decompressed biomedical image at 7:1 a) Original image b) decompressed image

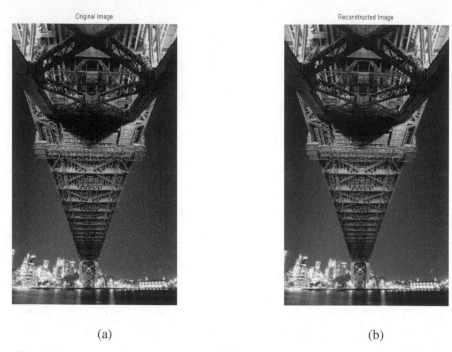

(a)   (b)

Fig. 3. Decompressed natural image at 6.7:1 a) Original image b) decompressed image

The performance of the algorithm is validated using objective criteria like PSNR, NMSE, NAE and BPP and various performance curves are shown in fig. 6. It is found that as compression ratio increases PSNR decreases. At higher compression ratio (CR), PSNR decreases at slower rate. This method gives PSNR higher than 45dB for some images.

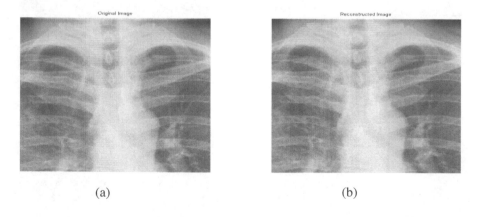

(a)   (b)

Fig. 4. Zoomed medical image -zoomed by 2 Original image b) decompressed image

(a)   (b)

Fig. 5. Zoomed image - zoomed by 4 a) Original image b) decompressed image

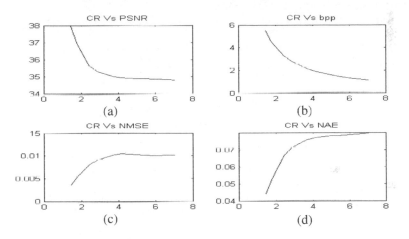

Fig. 6. Performance Curves a) PSNR b) NMSE c) bpp d) NAE

6   Conclusion

The proposed method works well with images of large dimensions. This method gives same compression ratio and bpp on images of same size. Here the correlation of each row in the image with its wavelet coefficients exploited to predict the next wavelet coefficients. The prediction can be done with number of coefficients as small as five. The performance method is evaluated on the basis of subjective criteria and parameters like PSNR, NAE, NMSE and bpp. The experimental results show that the proposed method, in addition to achieving good compression gives a better performance.

References

1. Maragos, P., Schafer, R.W., Mersereau, R.M.: Two-Dimensional Linear Prediction and Its Application to Adaptive Predictive Coding of Images processing in the context of a visual model. IEEE Transactions on Acoustics, Speech and Signal Processing, ASSP 32(6), 1213–1229 (1984)
2. Rajagopalan, R., Orchard, M.T., Ramchandran, K.: Optimal Supports for Linear Predictive Models. IEEE Transactions on Signal Processing 44(12), 3150–3153 (1996)
3. Makhoul, J.: Linear Prediction. Proceedings of IEEE 63(4), 561–579 (1975)
4. Kharate, G.K., Patil, V.H., Bhale, N.L.: Selection of Mother Wavelet for Image Compression on Basis of Nature of Image. Journal of Multimedia, 44–51 (2007)
5. Vidhya, K., Shenbagadevi, S.: Performance Analysis of Medical Image Compression. In: Proceedings of International Conference on Signal Processing Systems, pp. 979–983. IEEE Computer Society, Washington (2009)
6. Masud, S., Canny, J.V.M.: Finding a Suitable Wavelet for Image Compression Applications. In: Proc. IEEE International Conference on Acoustics, Speech and Signal Processing, vol. 5, pp. 2581–2584 (May 1998)
7. Strang, G., Nguyen, T.: Wavelets and Filter Banks. Wellesley Cambridge Press, Wellesley (1996)
8. Mallat, S.: A Wavelet Tour of Signal Processing. Academic Press, London (1999)
9. Ruedin, A.M.C., Acevedo, D.G.: Prediction of coefficients for Lossless Compression of Multispectral Images. In: Satellite Data Compression, Communications, and Archiving. SPIE, vol. 5889, 58890N, pp. 202–211(2005)
10. Lewis, A.S., Knowles, G.: Image Compression Using the 2-D Wavelet Transform. IEEE Transactions on Image Processing 1(2), 244–250 (1992)
11. Shahhoseini, E., Nejad, N.A., Behnam, H., Shahhoseini, A.: A new approach to compression of medical ultrasound images using wavelet transform. In: International Conference on Advances in Circuit, Electronics and Micro-Electronics, pp. 40–44. IEEE Computer Society, Washington (2010)
12. Hu, J.H., Wang, Y., Cahill, P.T.: Multispectral Code Excited Linear Prediction Coding and Its Application in Magnetic Resonance Images. IEEE Transactions on Image Processing 6(11), 1555–1566 (1997)
13. Hayes, M.H.: Statistical Digital Signal Processing and Modeling, pp. 108–116, 188–200. John Wiley, New York (1996)
14. Huang, J.S., Nguyen, D.T., Negnevitsky, M., Philips, C.J.E.: Correlation Properties of Wavelet Transform and Applications in Image Coding. In: Proceedings of Fifth International Symposium on Signal Processing and its Applications, pp. 611–614 (August 1999)
15. Gonzalez, R.C., Woods, R.E.: Digital Image Processing, pp. 419–420. Prentice-Hall, India (2006)

An Innovative Approach to Association Rule Mining Using Graph and Clusters

N. Balaji Raja[1,*] and G. Balakrishnan[2]

[1] Department of Computer Applications,
J.J. College of Engineering & Technology, Tamil Nadu, India
nbalajiraja@yahoo.co.in
[2] Department of Computer Science and Engineering,
Indra Ganesan College of Engineering Tamil Nadu, India
director@igceng.org

Abstract. There is a common belief that the association rule mining has a major stake in data mining research domain. Numerous algorithms are proposed for discovering frequent itemsets. This is the key process in association rule mining. This proposed paper introduces two concepts. First leads to analyze the ability to explore the demographic parameters of the underlying entities and their inter relations using the traditional graph theory approach(vertices and edges). Second is the improved algorithm based on graph and clustering based mining association rules. This improved algorithm is named Graph and Clustering Based Association Rule Mining (GCBARM). The GCBARM algorithm scans the database of transaction only once to generate a cluster table and then clusters the transactions into cluster according to their length. The GCBARM algorithm is used to find frequent itemsets and will be extracted directly by scanning the cluster table. This method reduces memory requirement and time to retrieve the datasets and hence it is scalable for any large size of the database.

Keywords: Association rule mining, Data Mining, Relational, cluster, graph, GCBARM.

1 Introduction

With the rapid development in size and number of available databases in commercial, organizational, administrative and other applications [1, 19], it is the urgent need for new technologies and automated tools to change this wealth of data resources into useful information. The most challenging in database mining is developing fast and efficient algorithms that can deal with large volume of data because several data mining algorithm computation is used to solve diverse data mining problem generally know as associations, clustering, classifications and sequential patterns [2].

---

* Research Scholar, Anna University, Tamil Nadu, India.

N. Meghanathan et al. (Eds.): CCSIT 2012, Part III, LNICST 86, pp. 59–67, 2012.

1.1   Association Rule

Association rule mining is a very important research topic in the data mining field, it's problem in large databases is to generate all association rules [17, 20], of the form X =>Y, that will produce strong association rules which satisfy both minimum support degree (min_sup) and the minimum confidence degree (min_conf) greater then the user defined minimum support and minimum confidence [2, 3.4].

Definition 1. let X={x1,   x2 ..... xn} be a set of items, then $D = \{< T_{id}, T >| T \subseteq X\}$ is a transaction database, where T_{id} is an identifier which be associated with each transaction.

Definition 2. Let $A \subseteq X, B \subseteq X, and A \cap B = \phi$, we call this $A \Rightarrow B$ as association rule.

Most of the algorithm generally is executed in two steps. First, to finding all sets of items that have support above the given minimum, and then generating the desired rules from these item sets. The apriori algorithm is the same as the association rule. The first step is to find all frequent itemsets, the next is to generate strong association rules from frequent item sets during pruning [18].

1.2   Apriori Algorithm

The apriori algorithm is a fast algorithm for mining association rules and is based on [5,20] algorithms for mining association rules, the problem of this algorithm is number of data scans n, where n is the size of large nonempty itemset and number of discovering rules is huge while most of the rules are not interesting. Therefore, after apriori algorithm many improved efficient versions were proposed towards scalability.

This paper introduces an algorithm GCBARM, which is basically different from previous algorithms; the remaining paper is organized as follows: related work is presented in Section 2, Section 3 gives the details of GCBARM algorithm with example, Section 4 show the experimental result and finally the conclusion is given in Section 5.

2   Literature Review on Association Rule and Graph database

Existing studies in data mining have presented efficient algorithm for discovering association rules. But the main drawback of the first algorithm is the need to do multiple passes over the datasets to generate frequent itemsets. The apriori association rule algorithm proposed by Agrawal and Srikant [6] can discover meaningful itemsets, but a large number of the candidate itemsets are generated from single itemsets and level by level in the process of creating association rules. Performance is severely affected because the database is scanned repeatedly to each candidate itemset with the database.

FP – Growth [7] out performs all candidate set generation and test algorithms as it mines frequent patterns without candidate generation. The main problem is no common prefixes within the data items.

Sample algorithm reduces the scanning to the datasets, it's scans single scan, but wastes considerable time on candidate itemsets [8].

The column wise apriori algorithm [9] and the tree based association rule algorithm [10] transformed the storage structure of the data, to reduce the time of scans of the transaction database.

The partition algorithm to improve efficiency and reduce the database scans, but still wasted scans on infrequent candidate itemset [11].

The primitive association rule mining is mining that describe the association among items of the transaction in the database. A uniform frame work was framed to perform association rule of association rules[12].

In the generalized association patterns, one can add all ancestors for each items from concept hierarchy and then apply the algorithm on the extended transactions [13].

The tones of day to day customer transactions stored in a very large database are processed and discovered multiple level of transactions with relevant attributes. Each of these attribute represented certain concept. Combining these attributes later generates multiple level concepts [5].

For frequent patterns in this new graph model which we call taxonomy superimposed graphs, there may be many patterns that are implied by the generalization and specialization hierarchy of the associated node label taxonomy [14]

Graph databases are able to represent as graphs of any kind of information, where naturally accommodated changes in data can be possible [15, 16].

The disadvantage of these algorithms is

- Number of reads the database transaction n time data scans where n is the size of large nonempty itemset,
- It is an incompetent as it requires wastage memory.
- Huge non interesting rules are discovered..

The proposal method GCBARM is a consequence to overcome the above said drawbacks

3   Proposed Methodology

This is a chance to establish that cluster based algorithms are still available by providing a better graph data structure which is used to simplify the process of generating frequent k itemsets, where k>=2. The proposed Graph and Clustering Based Association Rule Mining (GCBARM) algorithm scans the database of transaction only once, which overcome the drawbacks of the previous algorithms.

The process of building the graph is given in sequential numbers, this simplified pre-process is taken in to consideration as an important action before applying our proposed algorithm. The GCBARM algorithm scans the database of transaction only once to generate a cluster table as a two dimensional array where the rows represent transactions' TIDs and the columns represent items. The presence and absence of an item in a transaction indicates that 1 and 0 is content of the table. Here, considering an example, as to predict task whether a person makes ever 50K a year, that person's personal data attributes such as age, work class, fnlwgt, education, educationnum, maritalstatus, occupation, relationship, race, sex, capitalgain, capitalloss, hoursper-week and nativecountry are mainly taken for analysis.

Initially an original database consists of three relations, but it's pre-processed and shown in table 1. Then the three relations are converted into equivalent graph data-basse (GDB) shown in figure 1, using this procrssing to identify the attributes for rule mining. The database consists of three relations, named Adult Personnel Detail, Adult Employment Detail and Qualification. The data structure of the relations is

Adult Personnel Detail (Fnlwgt, Age, marital-status, relationship, race, sex, native-country)

Adult Employment Detail (Work class, fnlwgt, occupation, capital-gain, capital-loss, hours per week, prediction task 50k)

Qualification (Fnlwgt, Education, education num)

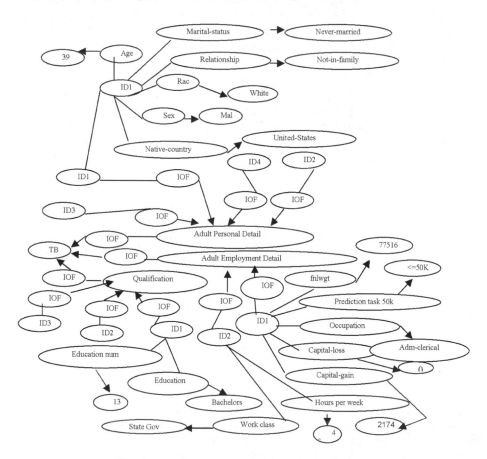

Fig. 1. Mapping of above relation into graph database

Table 1. An example of transaction database

TID	Age	work class	marital-status	native-country	P_task
T1	39	State-gov	Never-married	United-States	<=50K
T2	50	Self-emp-not-inc	Married-civ-spouse	United-States	<=50K
T3	38	Private	Divorced	United-States	<=50K
T4	53	Private	Married-civ-spouse	United-States	<=50K
T5	28	Private	Married-civ-spouse	Cuba	<=50K
T6	37	Private	Married-civ-spouse	United-States	<=50K
T7	49	Private	Married-spouse-absent	Jamaica	<=50K
T8	52	Self-emp-not-inc	Married-civ-spouse	United-States	>50K
T9	31	Private	Never-married	United-States	>50K
T10	42	Private	Married-civ-spouse	United-States	>50K
T11	37	Private	Married-civ-spouse	United-States	>50K
T12	30	State-gov	Married-civ-spouse	India	>50K
T13	23	Private	Never-married	United-States	<=50K
T14	54	Private	Separated	United-States	<=50K
T15	35	Federal-gov	Married-civ-spouse	United-States	<=50K
T16	43	Private	Married-civ-spouse	United-States	<=50K
T17	59	Private	Divorced	United-States	<=50K
T18	56	Local-gov	Married-civ-spouse	United-States	<=50K
T19	19	Private	Never-married	United-States	>50K
T20	23	Local-gov	Never-married	United-States	<=50K

After pre-processing the set minimum support threshold is 50%. There are 20 transactions and five different items named Age, Work class, Marital status, Native country and prediction task in the database. Most of the rule mining algorithms are in lexicographical order. An example of transaction database is shown in Table1.The items name of the transaction database is used rather than numbers to deal with some worst cases. The requirement of numbering system is to first scan the database to identify the length of each transaction, that means length of the numbers to the items in a transaction, and at the same time assigning the numbers to the items: Number 1 is assigned as item Age, Number 2 is assigned as item work class, Number 3 is assigned as marital status, Number 4 is assigned as native country, Number 5 is assigned as prediction task. This conversion process help us in both constructing the cluster table and building the graph, this process help avoid the need to rescan the transaction database. Next move is the clustering table that can easily reside in the main memory. In this example, the maximum transaction length is five, there will be at most five clusters, the total number of clusters is five as shown in table 2, The presence and absence of an item in a transaction is denoted by 1 and 0 in content of the table. After that , the bit vector for each item will be ready and it is an easy process to determine the frequent 1 itemsets by counting the number of 1s in each transaction, the minimum support threshold is not less than counting the number of 1s, but it is considered as a frequent itemset and then building the graph.

Table 2. The cluster table form the database in table 1

Item No. / TID	T7	T8	T9	T10	T14	T17	T19	T2	T3	T4	T5	T11	T12	T13	T16	T18	T1	T6	T20	T15
1	0	0	1	0	0	0	1	0	1	0	1	1	1	1	0	0	1	1	1	1
2	0	0	0	0	0	0	0	0	0	0	0	0	1	0	0	1	1	0	1	1
3	0	1	0	1	0	0	0	1	0	1	1	1	1	0	1	1	0	1	0	1
4	0	1	1	1	1	1	1	1	1	1	0	1	0	1	1	1	1	1	1	1
5	1	0	0	0	1	1	0	1	1	1	1	0	0	1	1	0	1	1	1	1

The bit vectors for the items are:

BV1=00100010101111001111
BV2=00000000000010011011
BV3=01010001011110110101
BV4=01111111110101111111
BV5=10001101111001101111

By counting the number of 1s in each bit vector is determined the support for each candidate itemset of length 1, as follows: support ({1}) = 55%, support ({2}) = 25%, support ({3}) = 55%, support ({4.}) = 85%, support ({5}) = 65%. Thus the frequent 1 itemsets are :{{1}, {3}, {4}, {5}} as their supports are not less than 50%.

The second step starts by reordering frequent 1 itemsets by providing each one with a sequential number to facilitate the process of constructing the graph, which is making logical( ) and operation between each pair of consecutive frequent 1 itemsets<item$_i$,item$_j$>| i<jif the number of 1s in the result is greater than or equal to minimum support threshold, a edge is directed to drawn from item$_i$ to item$_j$, this process is repeated for all frequent 1 itemsets. The simple directed graph to display frequent k – itemsets,k>=2 is shown in figure 2, and by assigning 25% as a new value to the minimum support threshold, the frequent 2 itemsets will be: {{1,3}, {1,4}, {3,5}}as shown in table 3 and the graph is constructed by drawing an edge between each pair of frequent items, as shown in figure 2. By counting the number of 1s in each bit vector is determined the support for each candidate itemset of length 2, as follows: support ({1,3}) = 25%, support ({1,4}) = 45%, support ({3,5}) = 30%. Thus the frequent 2 itemsets are :{{1,3}, {1,4}, {3,5}} as their supports are equal and above 25%.

The traverse of graph as if their path is to determine frequent 3 itemsets among three nodes{i,j} and {j,k} then the set {i,j,k} will be frequent 3 itemsets. Here, in this example, {{1,3,5}} is the only frequent 3 itemsets. As there are no extra edges, by assigning 12.5% as a new value to the minimum support threshold, the frequent 3 itemsets will be: {1,3,5}as shown in table 4 and the support for each candidate itemset of length 3, as follows: support ({1,3,5}) = 15%. Thus the frequent 3 itemsets are :{1,3,5} as their supports are equal and above 25%. Finally the algorithm terminates

Table 3. frequent itemsets 2 from frequent itemsets 1

Item No. / TID	T7	T8	T10	T14	T17	T18	T9	T19	T2	T3	T4	T12	T13	T16	T1	T20	T5	T11	T6	T15
{1,3}	0	0	0	0	0	0	0	0	0	0	0	1	0	0	0	0	1	1	1	1
{1,4}	0	0	0	0	0	0	1	1	0	1	0	0	1	0	1	1	0	1	1	1
{3,5}	0	0	0	0	0	0	0	0	1	0	1	0	0	1	0	0	1	0	1	1

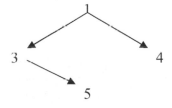

Fig. 2. A simple directed graph to display frequent k-itemsets, k>=2

Table 4. frequent itemsets 3 from frequent itemsets 1

Item No. / TID	T7	T8	T9	T10	T14	T17	T19	T2	T3	T4	T11	T12	T13	T16	T18	T1	T20	T5	T6	T15
{1,3,5}	0	0	0	0	0	0	0	0	0	0	0	0	0	0	0	0	0	1	1	1

In this regard, as the database contains hundreds and thousands of transactions database and different items, constructing only one graph is not suitable for this work: So construct different graphs for each cluster and find from this graph all frequent itemsets, then combine the subsets of frequent itemsets together to get the whole set of frequent itemsets, and this technique is scalable with all transactions databases of different sizes.

4   Experimental Results

In order to appraise the performance of the proposed technique, which was implemented the GCBARM algorithm, along with Apriori algorithm using java programming language. The test databases are collected from UCI standard datasets available to evaluate rule mining algorithms.

Apriori and GCBARM are execute both algorithm at various values of minimum support thresholds, Figure 3 shows the average execution time (seconds) to generate all frequent itemsets using GCBARM and Apriori. The experimental results in figure 3 show the better performance of GCBARM algorithm than Apriori in terms of execution time.

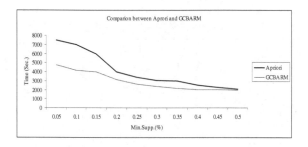

Fig. 3. Comparison between Apriori and GCBARM

5   Conclusion

This paper proposes the use of the graph database for pre-processing, after the hole transaction database is divided into partitions of variable sizes. Each cluster is considered one at a time by loading the first cluster into memory and calculating large itemsets and the corresponding support counts. Then the second cluster is loaded additionally and cumulative support count is then derived for the second clustered large itemsets. This process is continued for the entire set of clusters and finally the whole large itemsets and the corresponding cumulative support counts. This approach reduces main memory requirement since it considers only a small cluster at a time and hence it is scalable for any large size of the database.

References

1. Klosgen, W., Zytkow, J.M.: Hand Book of Data Mining and Knowledge Discovery. Oxford University Press (2002)
2. Kamber, M., Han, J.: Data Mining Concepts and Techniques. Morgan Kauffman Publishers, San Francisco (2001)
3. Imielinski, T., Agrawal, R., Swami, A.N.: Data Mining a Performance Perspective. IEEE Transactions on Knowledge and Data Engineering 5, 914–925 (1993)

4. Agrawal., R., Srikant, R.: Fast Algorithms for Mining Association Rules in Large Databases. In: Proceedings of the Twentieth International Conference on Very Large Databases, Santiago, Chile, pp. 487–499 (1994)
5. Han, J., Fu, Y.: Mining Multiple Level Association Rules in Large Databases. In: Proceeding of 1995 Int'l Conf. on Very Large Data Bases (VLDB 1995), Zurich, Switzerland, pp. 420–431 (1995)
6. Agrawal, R., Imilienski, T., Swami, A.: Mining association rules between sets of items in large databases. In: Proceedings of the ACM SIGMOD Int'l Conf. on Mgt of Data, Washington, DC, pp. 207–216 (1993)
7. Han, J., Pei, J., Yin, Y.: Mining frequent Patterns without Candidate Generation. In: ACM-SIGMOD, Dallas (2000)
8. Berzal, F., Cubero, J.C., Marin, N., Serrano, J.M.: TBAR: An Efficient Method for Association Rule Mining in Relational Databases. In: Elserier Data and Knowledge, Engineering, pp. 47–64 (2001)
9. Cheung, D.W., Han, J., Ng, V.T., Fu, A.W., Fu, Y.: A fast distributed algorithm for mining association rules. In: Proceedings of Int'l Conf. on PDIS 1996, Miami Beach, Florida, USA (1996)
10. Agrawal, R., Srikant, R.: Mining sequential patterns. In: Proceedings of the 11th Int'l Conf. on Data Engineering, ICDE (1995)
11. Franklin, B.: Genealogical Data Mining (2006)
12. Yen, S.-J., Chen, A.L.P.: A Graph based Approach for Discovering Various Types of Association Rules. IEEE Transaction on Knowledge and Data Engineering 13(5), 839–845 (2001)
13. Srikant, R., Agrawal, R.: Mining Generalized Association rules. In: Proc. Of the 21st Int'l Conf. on Very Large Databases, Zurich, Switzerland, pp. 407–419 (1995)
14. Cakmak, A., Ozsoyoglu, G.: Taxonomy superimposed graph mining. In: Proceedings of the 11th Int'l Conf. on Extending Database Technology, Advances in Database Technology. ACM Int'l Conf. Proceeding Series, vol. 261, pp. 217–228 (2008)
15. Silvescu, A., Caragea, D., Atramentov, A.: Graph Databases Artificial Intelligence Research Laboratory. Department of Computer Science Iowa State University Ames, Iowa (2007)
16. Priyadarshini, S., Mishra, D.: A Hybridized Graph Mining Approach. In: Das, V.V., Vijaykumar, R. (eds.) ICT 2010. Communications in Computer and Information Science, vol. 101, pp. 356–361. Springer, Heidelberg (2010)
17. Pan, H., Tan, X., Han, Q., Yin, G.: An Effective Algorithm Based on Association Graph and Matrix for Mining Association Rules. In: Proceeding of IEEE 2010. IEEE PRESS (2010) 978-1-4244-6977-2/10
18. Muthukumar, A., Nadarajan, R.: Efficient and Scalable Partition based Algorithms for Mining Association Rules. Academic Open Internet Journal 19 (2006) ISSN 1311–4360
19. Balaji Raja, N., Balakrishnan, G.: Evaluation of Rule Likeness Measures for a Learning Environment. In: Proceedings of the ICOREM Int'l Conf., pp. 1682–1690. ICOREM (2009)
20. Balaji Raja, N., Balakrishnan, G.: A Model of Algorithmic Approach to Itemsets Using Association Rules. In: Proceedings of IEEE, ICECT 2011, pp. 6–10. IEEE PRESS (2011) 978-1-4244-8677-9

Policy Based Accounting for Web Services

V. MuthuLakshmi[1,*] and Sheila Anand[2]

[1] Information Technology, St. Joseph's college of Engineering,
[2] Computer Studies , RajaLakshmi Engineering College
AnnaUniversity, Chennai, India
{Ajayanish,sheila.anand}@gmail.com

Abstract. In this paper, we propose a Policy based Accounting Architecture to integrate and automate the accounting functions and management for web services. The charging and accounting schemes currently used for web services are relatively simple. Users have either been charged a flat rate or charged based on the Internet connection time. A flexible accounting model is needed to cater to the varying needs of service providers while taking into accounts the user's spending limits and preferences for billing and payment. Policies will enable the service providers to describe the different charging schemes and implement the provisioning of accounting services to allow users to choose schemes that meet their needs. Policies expressed in a standardized way can be used to configure accounting processes to support the collection of information about resource utilization. Policies can also facilitate the distribution of accounting tasks among different entities. We have implemented and tested the proposed model for a on-line book store with web services having different charging schemes like fixed rate and varying rate based on usage of resources.

Keywords: web service, web service accounting, policy based accounting, flexible accounting, accounting architecture.

1 Introduction

Due to the increase in the usage of web services in E-commerce, the methods to provide flexibility in the accounting process have become one of the foremost objectives for the commercial use of web services. Customers need to pay for the usage of web service resources provided by different service providers. Each service provider would like to have a unique charging and pricing methodology. There is the need to provide for metering the web service usage and calculate the payment based on the charging patterns of individual service providers. The charging patterns may also vary depending on the categorization of users and the billing could be on a one-time basis or on a consolidated monthly, annual or periodic basis.

The charging and accounting schemes currently used for web services have been relatively simple. Users have either been charged a flat rate or charged based on the

---

* Corresponding author.

N. Meghanathan et al. (Eds.): CCSIT 2012, Part III, LNICST 86, pp. 68–75, 2012.
© Institute for Computer Sciences, Social Informatics and Telecommunications Engineering 2012

Internet connection time. There is a need to presently integrate charging and accounting with the provisioning of web service by the service providers. The distributed nature of web service components provides challenges for web service accounting. Users may also use composite web services which may comprise of web services offered by different service providers. Hence accounting management systems are required to support a wide range of accounting functionality customized to the needs of the users. Accounting management function should be able to support usage based, content based and/or transaction based charging and accounting facilities.

We propose a Policy based Accounting Architecture to integrate and automate the accounting functions and management. Accounting based on service charging policies will be able to provide flexibility in accounting and enable accounting components to implement the metering and charging as per the service provider's requirements. Policies will enable the service providers to elucidate various types of charging schemes. Such scheme can be provisioned as accounting services that the users can choose based on their requirements. Policies expressed in a standardized way can be used to configure accounting processes to support the collection of information about resource utilization.

In this paper, we have proposed a comprehensive accounting framework which covers all aspects of accounting: metering, charging, accounting, billing and payment. We have presented a policy based approach for web services accounting that can accommodate different pricing schemes and charging based on resource usage. The proposed accounting architecture is given in Section 3. Section 4 outlines the implementation of the proposed framework for an on-line book store with fixed and varying tariffs. Section 5 concludes the paper.

2   Related Work

Authentication, authorization, and accounting (AAA) is a framework that is used to enforce control for access of various computer resources. Accounting policies can be implemented to determine usage of resources and bill the users appropriately. In this paper, we review the work related to the accounting function.

"Accounting, according to the definition of IETF in [1], is the process of collecting the resource usage information for the purpose of billing, trend analysis etc". An Accounting management framework should provide for metering, charging, accounting, billing, payment and auditing. Metering is the function of that collects the information flow regarding the resource usage of a certain service by the consumer and its usage [2]. "Charging is the process of calculating the cost of the services or resources usage according to the pricing strategies" [3]. Accounting is the process of filtering, collecting and aggregating the information of resource usage [2]. Billing is the process of using the accounting information to generate a bill that is delivered to a user. Payment defines a well-defined scheme of money exchange between the users and service providers. The act of verifying the correctness of the accounting process and procedures is termed as auditing [4].

We present the prior work related to web service accounting. A pricing model implemented as a web service focused on accounting for commercial web services [5]. The solution proposed shows how the use of Web services can be metered, and the resulting data used for subsequent accounting and billing processes. The metering and accounting model has been implemented using Service Level Agreements (SLAs). This model remains to be extended to include the other functions of accounting, billing, payment and auditing. Ge Zhang et al have presented Web Service Accounting system architecture and discussed and analyzed the issues and accounting entities related to web services [3]. This paper while very informative and exhaustive does not cover accounting protocols, inter-domain data collection and composite Web Services metering.

In their paper, N. Papatheodoulou, N. Sklavos have introduced the design of a generic AAA architecture for use in modern networks [6]. The authentication architecture is based on EAP (Extended Authentication Protocol), authorization is done by AAA server using X.509 certificates. The duration of a user's session is used to account and bill the network usage. They have proposed the use of the AAA protocol for a web based application scenario but implementation and results have not been discussed. Hasan et al have presented a paper using MobyDick AAAC architecture for Mobile Internet [7]. They have discussed a number of key features such as; tariff announcements, online charge indication, inter-domain support etc., for mobile Internet. These features with appropriate modification and extension could be applied for web service accounting.

Niklas Neumann and Xiaoming Fu have extended the Diameter protocol for web usage and called it the Diameter WebAuth [8]. It presents an AAA-based Identity Management Framework for Web Applications that allows integration of web based services into a Diameter infrastructure for authentication, authorization, credit-control and identity management purposes. This paper focuses on authentication but has suggested that the use of Diameter WebAuth could be extended for accounting also. Ming-Hua Lin et al have presented a flexible time-based pricing policy for charging Internet services [9]. They have discussed different pricing policy such as; duration-based, usage based, volume based etc. A multi-service billing has been developed using Tariff tables.

Igor Ruiz-Agundez et al have presented taxonomy for future Internet Accounting [2]. They have discussed in detail the services of metering, charging, mediation, accounting, pricing, billing and financial clearing [10].They have applied the taxonomy for Cloud Computing using SLAs and discussed various pricing strategies. Sebastien Decugis summarized the fundamentals of AAA architecture, "waaad" and also findings on Diameter limitations such as duplicate requests, hop-by-hop capability exchange mechanism and complexity [11].

3   Policy Based Accounting Architecture

In this paper we present an accounting architecture with mechanism to meter the use of a service's resources and store data generated by this metering activity. We propose the use of an accounting policy to maintain the details of pricing and charging for web service usage. The user can query the policy to determine the pricing details of various web services and then decide on an appropriate web service. The users are charged on basis of the actual usage of the web services. The metered records are aggregated and summarized as accounting records. Bills are prepared from the accounting records and sent to the users for collection of payment.

The basic web service models the interactions between the three roles: the service provider, service registry, and service requestor as shown in Figure 1. The interactions involve publish, find, and bind operations.

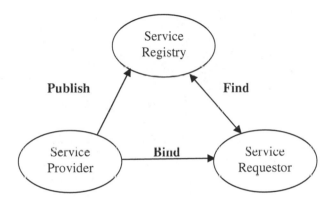

Fig. 1. Web Services Components

The Service registry is a searchable registry of service descriptions where service providers "Publish" their service descriptions. The Service provider defines a service description for the web service and publishes it to a service registry. The service requestor is a user or application looking for a web service that meets their processing requirements. The service requestor is a user or an application searching for a web service that meets their processing requirements. The "Find" operation is used to search the service registry for the required service. The "Bind" operation is used by the service provider to invoke or interact with the web service implementation.

Figure.2.shows the Policy based Accounting Architecture for the web service model. The principal component proposed is the AAA (Authentication Authorization Accounting) server that maintains the service charging policy and manages the usage data records and accounting records. The AAA client component is present at the service provider to collect the usage records and forward it to the AAA server.

The service provider also specifies the methods of charging for the usage of its web services and this policy is maintained at AAA server. The charging details are stored as Service Charging Policy (SCP) at AAA server. The service provider can have different charging policies for different users and can charge is calculated based on the usage time and/or usage of resources. The policy can also indicate a one-time usage charge or monthly and annual charging patterns.

The user, who wishes to access the service, will first send a request to the AAA server for details of pricing and charging of the particular service. The user will study the price details and may then decide to use the service.

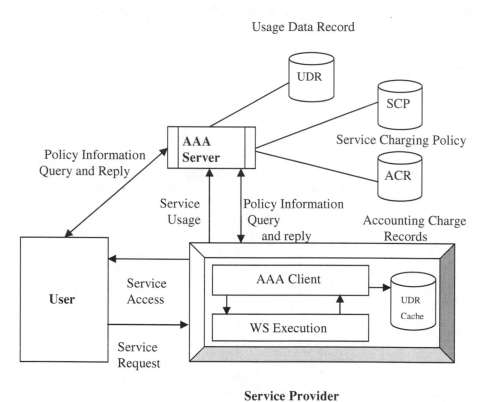

Fig. 2. Policy based Accounting Architecture

The user wishing to access a service will send a service request to the concerned service provider. The service provider will grant access to the requested service. AAA client will measure the service usage and forward the Usage Data Record (UDR) to the AAA server. We propose the use of a UDR cache to temporarily store and aggregate the UDRs before forwarding to the AAA server. In case of any network failure between the Service provider and AAA server, this cache will ensure that usage data is not lost and is maintained in the service provider till it is successfully transmitted to the AAA server.

The charges for usage of web service are calculated using the SCP and UDRs. The charging details are maintained as ACcounting Records (ACR). Bills are produced from the accounting records and sent to the users.

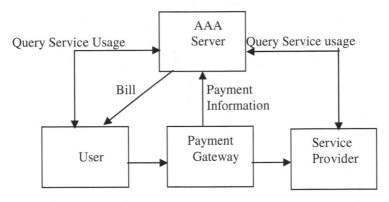

Fig. 3. Payment Process

The user's payments are collected using a third-party payment gateway as shown in Figure 3. The payment is sent to the Service Provider while the payment information is sent to the AAA server and updated in the ACR. The payment gateway provides a secure channel and enables electronic payment of bills. Payments received from users are matched against bills to determine the dues that are outstanding. Users can also query the AAA server and obtain accounting information. Accounting records can also be accessed for auditing and other statutory purposes.

4   Implementation

We implemented and tested the proposed architecture for an on-line book store. The book provides a web service based system that allows the customers to order the books online which will be delivered to their house. We assume that book publishers would register with the book store and provide the available book details. The book store would have links with delivery agencies for delivery of the books within one or two days.The web stores uses three services namely: "Search Book", "Book Enquiry" and "Book Order" services.

The Search Book service allows the user to search based on subject, author, title, publisher and publication year. The Book Enquiry service provides all the details of a particular book such as name, publication, edition, author, price and number of copies of books available. The Book Order service allows the user to place book orders.

Multiple books can be placed in a single order. The cost of individual books and the total amount is displayed. It also provides an option of reduction in price or offer based on their membership. Book delivery options are also displayed to allow the user to choose the mode of delivery and payment is calculated based on the distance between the book store and the destination.

Figure 4 depicts the relationship between the participating entities.

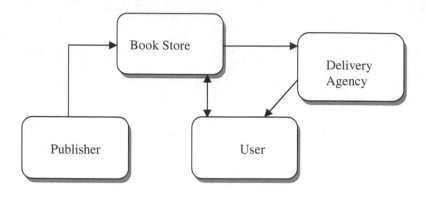

Fig. 4. On line Book Store

The charging pattern for each of the web service was designed as follows:

- The usage of "Search Book" service is charged based on the number of entries that are searched in order to retrieve the results.
- "Book Enquiry" service has a fixed charge as it directly fetches the book details.
- The "Book Order" service is charged on the number of books that are ordered.

There is a fixed charged for each book ordered. A variable charge is also calculated based on the service charge of the delivery agencies. We assume that the various agencies levy   different service charges.

Usage of a particular web service is stored as a UDR. For example, usage of a single search query would be treated as a UDR. To create the accounting records, we categorized users as casual users and registered users. Casual users are billed for every transaction on a transaction-by-transaction basis.

The book store was implemented using ASP.NET. The policy file was maintained in XML format. The UDR and ACR records were maintained in a MS-SQL server. Exchange of policy information and other details was implemented using SOAP protocol. For registered users the transaction charges are aggregated and a single monthly bill is prepared.

The use of a charging policy enabled the implementation of different charges for various web service usages and for different user categories.

5   Conclusion

We have presented a comprehensive policy based accounting architecture for web service metering and charging. Accounting policies offer an easy implementation of different charging patterns offered by various service providers for service differentiation. Service providers can charge for the usage of their resources and manage their pricing policy in a flexible manner. Multiple web usage scenarios can also be implemented in a simple manner. We plan to extend our work in preparing a more complete and extensive charging policy that covers all the different aspects and types of pricing and charging. As future work, we propose to work on standardization of the web usage record and accounting information.

References

1. Aboda, B., Arkko, J., Harrington, D.: Introduction to Accounting Management. RFC2975 (2002)
2. Ruiz-Agundez, I., Penya, Y.K., Bringas, P.G.: Taxonomy of the Future Internet Accounting Process. In: Advcomp 2010 DeustoTech, Deusto Institute of Technology University of Deusto (2010)
3. Zhang, G., Muller, J., Muller, P.: Designing Web Service Accounting System. University of Kaiserslautern, Paul Ehrlich Strasse Geb. 36, 67663 Kaiserslautern, Germany (2004)
4. Rensing, C., Karsten, M., Stiller, B.: AAA: A Survey and a Policy-Based Architecture and Framework (2002)
5. Kuebler, W.E.D.: Metering and accounting for web services (2001)
6. Papatheodoulou, N., Sklavos, N.: Architecture & System Design Of Authorization, & Accounting Services (2009)
7. Hasan, Jahnert, J., Zander, S., Stiller, B.: Authentication, Authorization, Accounting, and Charging for the Mobile Internet (2001)
8. Neumann, N., Fu, X.: Diameter WebAuth: An AAA-based Identity Management Framework for Web Applications. Computer Networks Group, University of Goettingen, Germany (2009)
9. Lin, M.-H., Lo, C.-C., Zhuang, W.: A Flexible Time-based Pricing Policy for Charging Internet Services. Institute of Information Management, National Chiao-Tung University (2003)
10. Ruiz-Agundez, I., Penya, Y.K., Bringas, P.G.: A Flexible Accounting model for Cloud Computing. Deusto Institute of Technology University of Deusto, DeustoTech (Advcomp 2010)
11. Decugis, S.: Towards a global AAA framework for Internet. In: Ninth Annual International Symposium on Applications and the Internet (2009)

Fusion Based Linked Object Web Ranking for Social Networks

Pushpa R. Suri[1] and Harmunish Taneja[2]

[1] Department of Computer Science and Applications, Kurukshetra University
Kurukshetra, Haryana, India, Pin - 136119
[2] Department of Information Technology, M.M. Engineering College,
M.M. University, Mullana, Haryana, India, Pin - 133203
pushpa.suri@yahoo.com, harmunish.taneja@gmail.com

Abstract. Search is no doubt the most critical aspect of information computing over web. Ranking is pivotal for efficient web search as the search performance mainly depends upon the ranking results. The trade-off between the systems costs of extracting a single right web object and a set of potential results continues to be major design issue. Social networks have ensured the expanding disproportion between the face of World Wide Web stored traditionally in search engine repositories and the actual ever changing face of Web. As definition of search is changing, socially-enhanced interactive search methodologies are the need of the hour. In this paper new integrated ranking model based on page rank paradigm for sorting web objects from multiple social forums is proposed. This model identifies relationships between web objects in separate social networks particularly in the light of music search. It can be extended to video and other multimedia forms.

Keywords: Web objects, Ranking, Fusion Based Rank (FBR), Linked Object Web Ranking, Social Networks, Music search.

1   Introduction

Searching from billions of objects, makes it challenging to harness single right result. Also, ranking needs to be redefined beyond the boundaries of query driven search in today's scenario. Traditionally the entities in each search results are similar in sense they are web pages. With the proliferation of social sites there is a big bang explosion of the web users that are not just passive. Enhanced ranking needs to be prepared for selecting and merging heterogeneous results such as videos, images, news and local business listings and not just text features. Web expansion has transformed the "just enter in Google" search approach to the "likes" button of facebook that allows to submit personalized opinion on absolutely any object of interest on web. The "likes" play significant role in increasing or decreasing the popularity of the web object contained in social network. Social networks have paced the wave for involving users at all level of search and creating a raised level of interest in manual indexing [1]. Consequently its impact on the ranking method is imperative. All search engines use some

N. Meghanathan et al. (Eds.): CCSIT 2012, Part III, LNICST 86, pp. 76–86, 2012.

kind of web object link-based ranking in their ranking algorithms. This has been the result of the success of Google, and its PageRank link algorithm [2]. Traditionally from small amount of labeled data to more recently, machine learning technology are exploited to create ranking function. But existing technologies are inadequate for search applications offered by various modern social networks. A new learning framework that could rank related web objects that may be heterogeneous from multiple distinct and or similar social forums is desired. Vertical search engines refer to the search services restricted by specific information, such as music, image, video and academic search [3]. Popular vertical search engines like Academic Search [4], Google Scholar[5], Froogle [6], Movie Search [7], Image Search [8][9], Video Search [7], News Search [10] and many more have become increasingly effective in serving users with specific needs. But social networks reflect real world data sets as heterogeneous, semi-structured and multi-relational. Ranking function is most critical part of the search engine with two key factors viz. relevance and quality [11].

The social network users are the volunteers to actually rate the music which is a development to be noted for enhancing the traditional ranking methodology. If search results for query based on a song are coming from different social networks, then it is not an easy task to rank them because ranking of song in one social network may be higher and in the second it may be less. Motivated by such observation, the proposed framework i.e. FBR (Fusion based Rank) for Social networks fuse the ranking scores of searched web objects (music) from heterogeneous social networks by identifying the relation link between web objects from different social forums. We propose an integrated ranking method in heterogeneous social network by recognizing relatedness among different web objects that could be reflected in the rankings particularly a more famous a singer is, the more likely the songs will receive majority likes. Consequently more famous songs lead to more popularity of singers than those that are less cited. The paper is organised as follows. Section 2 outlines the challenges and choices faced in ranking web objects from multiple social networks and presents the attribute based comparison of popular social networking sites. Section 3 elaborates the framework for fusion based web object ranking in social networks. Section 4 describes the experimental study and results on the effectiveness of the FBR framework on information computing in a simulated music social network and finally in section 5 the paper is concluded.

2   Background

Traditionally search engines have only had access to three major types of data describing web pages, i.e., web page content, link structure and query or click through log data. A not so new entry to this family of document types is the user generated content describing the pages directly is less explored [12]. Networked web pages and their ranking has been noticed at length like PageRank [13], HITS [14]. The theory of PageRank is very simple, i.e, "good pages reference good pages" and are labelled with have higher PageRank. But ranking social network web objects, on the other hand, is employed for exploring links between similar web object from heterogeneous origins. Object-level ranking has been well studied for vertical search engines. But algorithms evolved from PageRank [13], PopRank [3] and LinkFusion [15] proposed to rank objects coming from multiple communities suggests that the ranking is restricted by the unavailability of well-defined graphs of heterogeneous data in some kinds of vertical domains in which objects. The challenge of integrating ranks of web objects from multiple heterogeneous social networks lies in their distinct ranking systems. The ranking interval or scale including the minimal and maximal ratings for each web object is varied from 5 points to 10 points rating scale. Another important issue is the rating criteria of different social forums. Also there may be ambiguity in the quality of the same score [16]. Future of WWW is where individuals are linked together in addition to web pages. The rise of social networks and its hold over common man interest from academician to a naive web surfer indicates the inefficiency of traditional search theories in general. Table 1 presents the comparative elaboration of the top fifteen most popular social networking sites with attributes like monthly visitors and various ranks (as on July 13, 2011) *eBizMBA Rank* [17], *Alexa* Global Traffic Rank [18] and U.S. Traffic Rank from both *Compete* [19] and *Quantcast* [20] that are constantly updated at each website's.

Table 1. Comparisons of the Top 15 Most Popular Social Networking Sites

Name	Logo	Estimated Unique Monthly Visitors	eBizMBA Rank	Compete Rank	Quantcast Rank	Alexa Rank
Facebook	facebook	700000000	2	3	2	2
Twitter	twitter	200000000	15	30	5	9
Linkedin	Linked in	100000000	33	57	26	17
mySpace	my_____	80500000	50	26	44	79
Ning	Ning	60000000	143	180	120	128
Tagged	TAGGED	25000000	255	382	151	141
Orkut	orkut	15500000	401	570	540	93
hi5	hi5	11500000	479	983	392	62
myyearbook	myyearbook YOU'VE GOT FRIENDS!	7450000	617	522	293	1036
Meetup	Meetup	7200000	635	644	732	528
Badoo	badoo	7100000	653	1346	489	125
bebo	b	7000000	655	944	434	588
mylife	mylife	5400000	865	118	688	1789
friendster	friendster	4900000	955	1920	643	301
Multiply	MULTIPLY	4300000	1136	2446	677	285

3   FBR (Fusion Based Rank): Framework

Manually the ranking criterion can be standardized by score normalization and trans-formation if the search involves same song or singer [21]. This section presents an integrated ranking framework FBR to analyse inter- and intra-type links and to sort web objects in different social networks at the same time. The conceptual scheme of proposed integrated ranking framework is shown in figure 1.

Two kinds of links among web objects are defined: intra-type links: which represent the relationship among web objects within a social network, and inter-type links: which represent the relationship among web objects between different social networks.

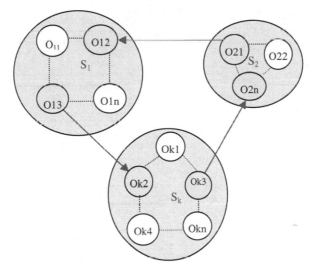

Fig. 1. Integrated social networks for enhanced Fusion based ranks: FBR

FBR exploits the two layer hierarchical approach as shown in Fig. 1 for identifying the inheritance and aggregation relationships between classes by creating super classes that may encapsulate the services or features common to other classes.

There are k graphs $(S_1, S_2,......,S_k)$ where each $S_i = (O_{in}, E_i)$ is the un-weighted un-directed graph (social network) of web objects O_{in} with links as E_i. The classes may belong to different social networks $S_1, S_2,...S_k$. Social Network S_i has a collection of related web objects $(S_i: O_{i1}, O_{i2}, O_{i3}.....O_{in})$ where i varies from 1 to k and k is the social networks integrated. If the web objects of different social networks share such a relationship as "has" or "contains" between them, an aggregation link is identified which is further implemented for rank computation.

The rank computed by each social forum is labelled as the partial rank and the framework add a popularity factor based on this partial rank to each link of the web object relationship graph pointing to the queried object. Different types of relationship are given different popularity factor. The proposed model calculates the rank for web objects with the activity flow of the FBR method as shown in Fig 2. The main components of the proposed framework are as below:

- Query Handler: The Query Handler receives the query terms based user requests and extracts one or more web objects from the entered query.
- Web Object Matching: All the related web objects contribute to the final rank of the search results. This module filters the related objects in various social networks under study.
- Relationship score: Relationships among objects contribute to their popularity factor and this module computes the score of searched web objects in terms of its relationships over other social networks.
- Fused Global Rank: This module computes the final Global rank indicating the actual level of relevancy of the search results.

Algorithm for FBR method (Fig. 2) is as below:

Algorithm: FBR	
Step 1	Rank web objects independently according to the PageRank paradigm [11].
Step 2	Web objects Partial ranks are computed by performing link analysis equipped with user's feedback as manual indexes.
Step 3	Furnish the Partial ranks for each social network S_i by exploiting Intra-type links.
Step 4	The popularity of web object is propagated to other social networks by exploiting inter-type links connected through popularity factor.
Step 5	The popularity factor is combined with the partial ranks to estimate a global rank for the searched web object.

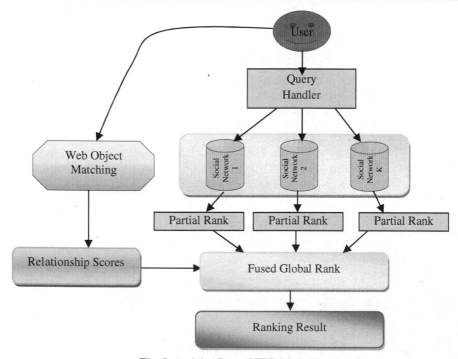

Fig. 2. Activity flow of FBR Method

4   Experimental Study and Results

There exist a number of redundant popular songs between any two social forums, because music web site may submit song to many social forums in order to obtain the feedback or comments. The proposed ranking method FBR emphasizes that although the ranks of duplicate songs in different social forums should be almost equal but practically this is not the case. The rank variation is ruled by the interest of the people connected to the social network. In the proposed work, Object orientation concepts help identifies the relationships of the searched web object within and across social networks. Each social network is viewed as a sub graph where each web object and its relationship with other web objects is reflected in the form of multiple level inheritance.

Fig. 3. Music Object relationship graph

The attribute value of web objects is obtained by iteratively calculating the periodic user's feedback. It is clear that the more popular the web object is, the more likely the user is interested in it. For ranking the most unique feature of the proposed approach is the web object graph with heterogeneous links e.g. a music object song may be searched by a set of other music objects that may be sung by a set of singers object and included in other web object album as shown in Fig. 3.

4.1   Datasets

Our study requires two sets of data: web objects and popular social networks. We explored various options for datasets, and eventually decided not to use data from popular social network services, such as Orkut, Facebook as the datasets in these sites are rich on social networks, but poor on web documents. We used data from YouTube which offers both rich web document data and extensive social network information. We first started with ten internet users randomly chosen with high degree and different interests, and obtained their friends and music interests. Then we used these friends as the new players and fetched the friends and music metadata from these. This process was iterative and stopped until no more options were available or the number of retrieved web users exceeded a pre-defined threshold.

4.1.1 Web Object Data

In the YouTube music dataset, each web object contains rich metadata such as album title, genre, tags, popular artists, description, uploader, rating, etc. These metadata were downloaded with our crawler and stored locally. The music is labelled with 10 main categories (Pop, Rap, Rock, Jazz, Today's hit, Reggae, Country, International, Comedy, and Latin etc.) as provided by YouTube. In this experiment, we defined a user's interest with one of these music categories. If the majority of a user's videos fall into one category, we regard that web object with higher relatedness score. With the metadata of music web objects, the indexes for music documents are built. The values in the fields: title, tags, genre and description were parsed into terms to create an inverted index using, in which each term in a specific field points to a collection of music documents. These indexes can be easily used to generate term document relatedness scores.

4.1.2 Social Network

In YouTube, each user has attributes such as name, gender, location, date of birth, friends, music uploaded, and about-me. Social networks can then be constructed based on the information obtained. An inter-type link was created between two web objects if they exist in similar context. In this experiment, we used two fully connected social networks based on the downloaded music data:

- S_1: Social Network 1: a larger social network that consists of 18,576 different registered users and 39,271 music uploaded by users;
- S_2: Social Network 2: a smaller network that has 2,464 users and 7,978 music uploaded by users.

4.2   Evaluation

To examine the effectiveness of the proposed Fusion based ranking algorithm, we compared following two algorithms:

Baseline: tf-idf [11] was used as the base line method.

Fusion based Rank (FBR): $FBR(Q,O,Rel) = f(S_i\ Rank(Q,\ Web\ object),\ Rel\ (Rel\ Score)\ )$

where Q is the query, Rel score is the similarity value between web objects in social networks. tf-idf values are normalized.

In each category, we choose ten queries that are related to the music category but at the same time could also refer to things that do not belong to the category. Queries in the music category were about album titles, singer etc. The top twenty returned music of each query were mixed and presented to two web surfers for independent evaluation. They evaluated each returned result based on to what extent the returned music was relevant to a query as well as to what extent the music was related to the user's interest. Table 2 shows the scores used to rate the relevance of a return. The highest score of a return is 5 and the lowest score is 0. After a pilot experiment, the inter-rater reliability among two raters was 70%, indicating that they reached a reasonable agreement about the relevance criteria [22].

Table 2. Evaluating Content Relevance

	High	Medium	Low
High	5	3	0
Medium	3	2	0
Low	0	0	0

We used *Normalized Discounted Cumulative Gain (NDCG)* [23] metric to evaluate the ranking algorithms. This method measures the usefulness of the ranking result based on the relationship between the relevance scale of web objects and their position in the ranking. The premise of DCG is that highly relevant documents are more useful when they have higher ranks in the result list. The NDCG at position k is given by:

$$NDCG_k = \frac{DCG^R_K}{DCG^T_K}$$

$$DCG^X_K = Rel_1 (X) + \sum \frac{Rel_i (X)}{\log i}$$
where i goes from 2 to k

$Rel_i(X)$ shows the level of relevancy for the result at position i in rank X.

DCG^T_K is the value for the optimal rank at position k.

4.3   Results

We evaluated the performance of two different ranking approaches. The NDCG values were averaged over all queries without considering the differences in the size of social networks and the degrees. As shown, FBR method performed better than the baseline algorithm. Fig. 4 shows that, for the first 20 search results, the NDCG values of FBR are higher than that of the baseline algorithm.

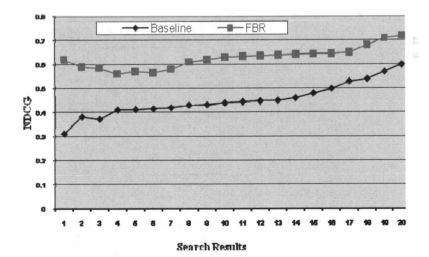

Fig. 4. NDCG: Fusion Based Rank Vs Baseline

The performance of these two algorithms is compared in two social networks with different size. To make the results more comparable, we only used searchers for the music category in both networks. The NDCG results from two social networks are shown in Fig. 5.

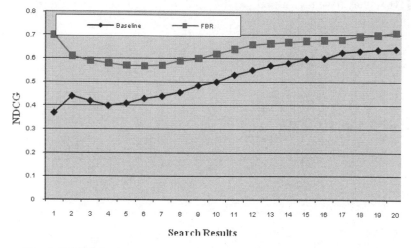

Fig. 5. NDCG: Fusion Based Rank Vs Baseline for Larger Social Network 1

The NDCG scores are averaged over all queries from searchers of music for the two networks. As shown, for the larger social network 1, the FBR method performs better than the baseline algorithm. But the difference in the smaller social network 2 is minimal as shown in Fig.6.

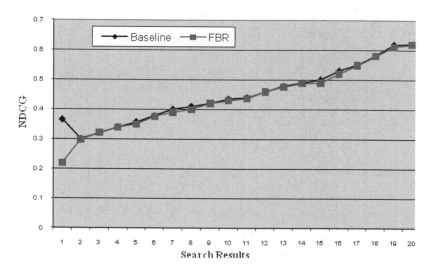

Fig. 6. NDCG: Fusion Based Rank Vs Baseline for Small Social Network 2

5   Conclusion

Social networks facilitate the formation of user generated content in diverse formats. Such networks smooth not only the classification user oriented web objects but also social indexing. Users send comments and feedbacks, likes or dislikes resources, upload and share multimedia contents, communicate online with social contacts, pour in wiki-style knowledge bases, maintain personal bookmarks.

In this paper, the web object ranking problem in case of social networks where traditional ranking algorithms are no longer valid is explored. The fusion based rank (FBR) method integrates many social networks and identifies the aggregation relationship graph highlighting the links among the related or duplicate web objects. The results of our evaluation studies indicate that overall, the FBR framework can return better search results than the traditional tf-idf ranking algorithm in terms of relevance, the ranking effectiveness of returned search results as it considers the global information of a social network. But its performance is appreciable only as the network size reaches a certain magnitude. FBR method is more effective than the baseline approach as it considers the global information of social networks. FBR method benefits more from large social networks than from small networks. The results reflect that the proposed fusion methods are practical and efficient solution to web object ranking in social networks. This framework can be applied with modifications to other multimedia applications.

References

1. Voss, J.: Tagging Folksonomy and Co-Renaissance of Manual Indexing. In: Proceedings of the International Symposium of Information Science, pp. 234–254 (2007)
2. Ding, C., He, X., Husbands, P., Zha, H., Simon, H.: Pagerank, Hits and a Unified framework for link analysis. In: NERSC Division, Lawrence Berkeley National Laboratory, 94720, pp. 1–12. University of California, Berkeley (2001-2002)
3. Nie, Z., Zhang, Y., Wen, J.-R., Ma, W.Y.: Object-level ranking: Bringing order to web objects. In: Proceedings of the 14th International Conference on World Wide Web, Chiba, Japan, pp. 567–574 (2005)
4. Web Site: Microsoft academic search, http://academic.research.microsoft.com/
5. Web Site: Google scholar paper search, http://Scholar.google.com
6. Froogle. Google product search, http://froogle.google.com
7. GoogleVideo. Google video search, http://video.google.com
8. Google. Google image search, http://images.google.com
9. Yahoo. Yahoo image search, http://images.yahoo.com
10. GoogleNews. Google news search, http://news.google.com
11. Page, L., Brin, S., Motwani, R., Winograd, T.: The pagerank citation ranking: Bringing order to the web. Technical report, Stanford Digital Libraries, pp. 1–17 (1998)
12. Paul, H., Georgia, K., Garcia-Molina, H.: Can social bookmarking improve web search? In: First ACM International Conference on Web Search and Data Mining, WSDM, Stanford, pp. 195–206 (2008)
13. Brin, S., Page, L.: The anatomy of a large-scale hyper textual Web search engine. In: 7th WWW Conference, Brisbane, Australia, pp. 107–117 (April 1998)

14. Kleinberg, J.M.: Authoritative sources in a hyperlinked environment. Journal of the ACM 46(5), 604–632 (1999)
15. Xi, W., Zhang, B., Chen, Z., Lu, Y., Yan, S., Ma, W.-Y., Fox, E.A.: Link fusion: A unified link analysis framework for multi-type interrelated data objects. In: Proceedings of the 13th International Conference on World Wide Web, pp. 319–327 (2004)
16. Bao, S., Xue, G.R., Wu, X., Yu, Y., Fei, B., Su, Z.: Optimizing web search using social annotations. In: WWW, pp. 501–510 (2007)
17. http://www.ebizmba.com/articles/social-networking-websites
18. Web Site: http://www.alexa.com/
19. Web Site: http://www.compete.com/
20. Web Site: http://www.quantcast.com/
21. Eck, D., Lamere, P., Bertin-Mahieux, T., Green, S.: Automatic Generation of Social Tags for Music Recommendation. In: Proceedings of Neural Information Processing Systems (NIPS), pp. 1–8 (2007)
22. Landis, R., Koch, G.: The measurement of observer agreement for categorical data. Biometrics 33, 159–174 (1977)
23. Jarvelin, K., Kekalainen, J.: IR evaluation methods for retrieving highly relevant documents. In: Proceedings of the ACM Conference on Information Retrieval (SIGIR 2000), pp. 41–48 (2000)

Comparing Supervised Learning Classifiers to Detect Advanced Fee Fraud Activities on Internet

Abiodun Modupe[1], Oludayo O. Olugbara[2], and Sunday O. Ojo[3]

[1] Department of Information Technology, Tshwane University of Technongy,
Pretoria, South Africa
[2] Department of Information Technology, Durban University of Technongy,
Durban, South Africa
[3] Faculty of Information Technology, Tshwane University of Technongy,
Pretoria, South Africa
{modupea,ojoso}@tut.ac.za, oludayoo@dut.ac.za

Abstract. Due to its inherent vulnerability, internet is frequently abused for various criminal activities such as Advanced Fee Fraud (AFF). At present, it is difficult to accurately detect activities of AFF defrauders on internet. For this purpose, we compare classification accuracies of Binary Logistic Regression (BLR), Back-propagation Neural Network (BNN), Naive Bayesian Classifier (NBC) and Support Vector Machine (SVM) learning methods. The word clustering method (globalCM) is used to create clusters of words present in the training dataset. A Vector Space Model (VSM) is calculated from words in each e-mail in the training set. The WEKA data mining framework is selected as a tool to build supervised learning classifiers from the set of VSMs using the learning methods. Experiments are performed using stratified 10-fold cross-validation method to estimate classification accuracies of the classifiers. Results generally show that SVM utilizing a polynomial kernel gives the best classification accuracy. This study makes a positive contribution to the problem of detecting unwanted e-mails. The comparison of different learning methods is also valuable for a decision maker to consider tradeoffs in method accuracy versus complexity.

Keywords: Advanced Fee Fraud, Word Clustering, Supervised Learning, Cluster Features.

1 Introduction

The objectives of this study are to discover a set of features and an effective learning classifier to accurately detect AFF activities on internet. Despite numerous benefits that internet technology offers to mankind, the information system is open to sabotage. Many crimes, including AFF, identity theft, telemarketing, insurance fraud, cyber squatting, cyber stalking, online gambling, lottery fraud and investment scams are perpetrated on internet. The occurrence of these cybercrimes has negative consequences on security of individuals and compromised security of internet technology.

N. Meghanathan et al. (Eds.): CCSIT 2012, Part III, LNICST 86, pp. 87–100, 2012.
© Institute for Computer Sciences, Social Informatics and Telecommunications Engineering 2012

AFF is a social engineering scheme wherein the defrauder requests a cash advance to facilitate a much greater payoff. This is a variant of the Spanish prisoner scam, which is now known as Nigerian-419. This scam is notoriously based in African countries mostly in Nigeria, Ghana, South Africa and Cameroun [1]. The tactics of defrauders reside in the bulk of email messages to find promising gullible individuals who can be easily tempted by quick financial reward. For instance, AFF emails describe the need under different pretexts to move a huge sum of money across a country. AFF defrauders feel untouchable and secure that they routinely impersonate government authorities and multinational corporations to defraud individuals. AFF activities are malevolence and depressing trades that have constituted a nuisance to national security and prosperity of many individuals. Indeed, sophisticated AFF activities are conducted through the distribution of physical mail, fax and more recently, email messages. The information content is subjected to remote association, inheritance, over-budgeted contract payments, job offers, joint ventures, awards, lotteries and upfront fees for loans.

The US-based Internet Crime Complaint Center (IC3), which is a conglomeration of the National White Collar Crime Center (NW3C), Bureau of Justice Assistance (BJA) and Federal Bureau of Investigation (FBI) received more than three hundred thousand complaints in 2009 [2, 3]. Approximately, 43.56% of these complaints revolved around financial frauds. The total monetary lost for victims is in excess of $559 million. This moves up from $295 million lost reported in 2008. About 9.8% of complaints are reported to be cases of AFF and victims said they were contacted through internet. AFF scam recorded high lost next to FBI scam and non-delivery merchandise [2, 3]. This implies that cost of cybercrimes is constantly increasing and internet facilities are mainly used to facilitate these erroneous crimes. The internet seems to be a safe place for carrying out fraudulent and illegal business. This is because the society of today is heavily dependent on internet technology for different kinds of activities. Criminals are also exploiting numerous opportunities provided by internet technology to perpetrate their malevolence tendencies.

In the light of increasing cybercrimes, a Computer Forensic Competency (CFC) has been established to assist law enforcement agencies in cybercrime investigations [4, 5]. The onus of CFC is to investigate digital scenes by finding relevant facts in form of electronic evidence. These facts are to be presented in a coherent way to prosecute defrauders in law courts. Being able to accurately detect AFF activities on internet can be beneficial in many ways. For example, it would be possible to design intelligent systems to proactively detect and filter out malicious emails to reduce the modus operandi of defrauders. In addition, detecting AFF activities on internet can help to increase confidence and trust levels of individuals to engage in diverse electronic business transactions.

The remainder of this paper is succinctly summarized as follows. In Section 2, we describe related study. In Section 3, we discuss supervised learning classifiers that are compared to detect AFF activities on internet. In Section 4, we discuss methodology of this study. In Section 5, we discuss results of experiments performed. In Section 6, we give a concluding remark.

2 Related Study

The majority of existing techniques for spam message identification differ from one another for several reasons. Spam messages are of diverse forms including AFF, cyber-phishing, drug trafficking, cyber-bullying, sexual harassment and child pornography. As a result, no unified algorithms can accurately detect all of these spam types simultaneously for the following reasons. First, the primary tactic of defrauders is to hide their intent in order to influence an individual of a higher payoff. Second, spam messages are well engineered to read regular emails and successfully pass filters, antivirus, firewalls and scammers tests. Third, diverse messages can originate from the same individual and messages are not equivalent in contents. Fourth, spam messages are not necessarily sent through the same physical path or using the same algorithms.

Chandrasekaran et al [6] develop a technique that detects phishing emails from legitimate emails based on structural attributes such as linguistic properties, vocabulary richness and email subjects. They model 25 features ranked by information gain and tested the model with 200 emails (100 phishing and 100 legitimate). They use SVM to classify phishing emails based on these features. Results of the study show 95% classification accuracy rate with a low false positive prediction. The work reported in [7] uses BLR, SVM, Random Forest (RF), Bayesian Adaptive Regression Tree (BART) and Classification and Regression Tree (CART) learning classifiers to classify phishing emails. They use 43 features to train and test these classifiers. Results of the study show that it is difficult to evaluate prediction accuracy using one evaluation metric when BLR, SVM, RF, BART and CART are used as classifiers.

Fette et al [8] implemented RF learning classifier in a PILFER algorithm to detect phishing email from a corpus of 860 phishing emails and 6950 legitimate emails. Result of the study shows that 96% of phishing emails was correctly predicted with a false positive rate of 0.1%. Airoldi and Malin [9] classify emails into scam, spam and ham by comparing Poisson filter and Spam-Assassin to detect fraudulent hidden scam emails based on words extraction. Hadjidj et al [10] developed a technique to assist forensic investigators to collect clues and evidence in an investigation. Stylometric features such as lexical, syntactic and idiosyncratic were used to identify authors of malicious emails. They used Decision Tree (DT) and SVM learning classifiers coupled with integration of social network algorithm.

In our previous study [11], a model of identifying activities of AFF defrauders was introduced. A training dataset set of 1100 emails of which 680 emails belong to AFF class was used to train BLR and SVM to predict AFF emails. In this current study, we increase dataset size to 2000, add two more classifiers and use more evaluation metrics such as area under receiver operating characteristic curve, cross-validation and cost sensitive analysis with weighted accuracy. This approach is unique because it uses globalCM algorithm [12] to discover a set of cluster features that characterizes AFF activities on internet. Preprocessing of emails using a combination of lemmatization and globalCM algorithms to create clusters of semantically related word is a valuable insight that can be applied to multiple problems in text classification.

3   Supervised Learning Classifiers

A Supervised Learning Classifier (SLC) solves a machine learning task of inferring a function from available example data. The purpose is to predict the desired supervisory signal or output for a valid input vector. A learning or classification task is a famous data mining problem that can be defined as a process of assigning a class label to a data instance, given a set of previously classified data instances. Two basic processes of a SLC are training and testing. During the training phase, parameters associated with the learning model are updated based on inputs received from the environment. During the testing phase, a new input vector whose class is probably unknown is presented to the classifier to predict the appropriate class the input vector belongs. This study experimentally compares BLR, BNN, SVM and NBC learning methods to detect AFF activities on internet.

3.1   Binary Logistic Regression

Binary Logistic Regression (BLR) assumes that a logistic or sigmoid relationship exists between probability of group membership and one or more features [13]. The BLR model is used to relate probabilities of group membership to a linear function of data features. The probability values $p_1(F)$ and $p_2(F)$ that a data instance $F = (F_1 = f_1, F_2 = f_2,..., F_n = f_n)$ of n features belongs to sample groups 1 and 2 respectively is given in terms of logit transform of odds ratio as:

$$\ln\left(\frac{p_1(F)}{p_2(F)}\right) = a_0 + a_1 f_1 + a_2 f_2 + ... + a_n f_n \tag{1}$$

where f_n is the value of nth feature of the data instance, a_n is the coefficient of f_n and $(a_0, a_1, \cdots, a_n)$ are parameters of the logistic model. These parameters are usually estimated during training phase using maximum likehood method.

Equation (1) can be rewritten to directly express the probability that the data instance belongs to group 1 as follows

$$p_1(F) = \frac{1}{1 + \exp(-a_0 - a_1 f_1 - ... - a_n f_n)} \tag{2}$$

The estimated regression coefficients $(a_1,...,a_n)$ and constant a_0 are used to define a logistic model. The constructed model is used during testing to classify a new data instance into one of the two groups. The classification rule is usually based on a probability threshold of 0.5. If $p_1(F) \geq 0.5$, the data instance is classified into group 1 otherwise it is classified into group 2.

3.2   Backpropagation Neural Network

Backpropagation Neural Network (BNN) is a supervised learning classifier that generalizes delta rule and it learns through backward propagation mechanism. The network model provides great flexibility in linear speed so that each element can compare its input value against stored examples [14]. A decision function is usually chosen during network training from a family of functions that are represented by the network architecture. This family of functions is defined by complexity of the network according to the number of neurons in input and hidden layers of the network [15]. The decision function is determined by choosing suitable sets of weights for the network. The training process involves calculation of input and output values, activation and target functions, backward propagation of the associated error, adjustment of weight and biases [16]. The standard BNN model with a single output neuron can be represented as [15]:

$$y = \tilde{g}\left(\sum_{j=1}^{m} w_{1j}^{2} \times g\left(\sum_{i=1}^{d} w_{ji}^{1} \times x_{i} + w_{jo}^{1} \right) + w_{11}^{2} \right) \tag{3}$$

The input function $\tilde{g}$ is usually represented by a linear function. The output function on hidden and output layer units is assumed to be sigmoid or tan-sigmoid. A typical sigmoid transfer function is the following bipolar activation.

$$f(x) = \frac{1 - \exp(-x)}{1 + \exp(-x)} \tag{4}$$

Sets of optimal weights are required to minimize the error function of the network, which represents deviation of predicted values y_k from observed $y(x_k)$ values. The mean absolute error in output layer can be calculated as:

$$E_m = \frac{1}{2} \sum_{i=1}^{n} \sqrt{(y(x_k) - y_k)^2} \tag{5}$$

Where n is the number of training instances. The training of a network is typically performed on variations of gradient descent based algorithm to minimize error function [17]. In order to avoid over-fitting problem, cross-validation method is used to find an earlier point of training [18].

3.3   Support Vector Machine

Support Vector Machine (SVM) [19] is a supervised learning classifier, which is particularly suited for solving binary classification problems. SVM method is widely used because of its ability to handle high-dimensional data through the use of kernels. Given a training dataset $D = \{(x_1, y_1), (x_2, y_2), \ldots, (x_n, y_n)\}$, where each element of the dataset is represent by n-dimensional vector $x_i = (x_1^i, x_2^i, \ldots, x_n^i)$

and $y_i \in \{-1,1\}$. The classifier proceeds to find a separating hyperplane $\{x | w^T x + b = 0\}$ that generates the largest margin between data points in positive and negative classes. This is achieved by solving optimal hyperplane problem, which is the solution of the following minimization problem [20]:

Minimize

$$\frac{1}{2}\|w\|^2 + c\sum_{i=1}^{n}\xi_i \tag{6}$$

Subject to the constraints:

$$\begin{cases} y_i(w^T x_i + b) \geq 1 - \xi_i, \\ \xi_i \geq 0, i = 1, \ldots, n \end{cases} \tag{7}$$

where ξ_i represents a slack-variable that allows misclassification to occur and C is a trade-off parameter for generalization performance.

The basic assumption of SVM is that training dataset is linearly separable. This is not generally the case in reality as training dataset can contain data points that are linearly inseparable. The solution therefore, is to transform non-linear dataset into the one that is linear using kernel functions $K(x_i, x_j)$ such as linear network, polynomial, radial-basis and two-layer perceptions. The ideal of kernels is to enable operations to be performed in the input space instead of the potentially high dimensional feature space [21]. The SVM classification task is a quadratic programming optimization problem that can be solved through kernel based dual formulation to maximize the following performance function.

Maximize

$$J(\alpha) = \sum_{i=1}^{m}\alpha_i - \frac{1}{2}\sum_{i=1}^{m}\sum_{j=1}^{m}y_i y_j \alpha_i \alpha_j K(x_i, x_j) \tag{8}$$

Subject to the constraints:

$$\sum_{i=1}^{m}y_i \alpha_i = 0, (0 \leq \alpha_i \leq C) \tag{9}$$

where $\alpha = \{\alpha_1, \alpha_2, \ldots, \alpha_m\}$ are Lagrangian variables to be optimized and m is the number of training instances. The decision function of the classifier is given by:

$$f(x) = sign(\sum_{i=1}^{n}y_i \alpha_i K(x_i, x_i) + b) \tag{10}$$

where $n \le m$ is number of support vectors $(\alpha_i > 0)$ and b is the bias that satisfied the Karush-Kulu-Tucker optimality constraints of the dual formulation problem.

3.4 Naïve Bayesian Classifier

Naive Bayesian Classifier (NBC) is a probabilistic classifier used extensively to solve text classification problems [21]. During training phase, NBC learns class posterior probabilities $P(F_1 = f_1, F_2 = f_2, ..., F_n = f_n | C = c_j)$ of each data feature F_i given the class label c_j, where $j = 1,2$ is the number of classes and $i = 1, 2, ..., n$ is the number of features. A new data instance of an $n-$dimensional vector of features values $F = (F_1 = f_1, F_2 = f_2, ..., F_n = f_n)$ is classified into one of the two classes by the classifier. Bayesian rule is applied to compute posterior probability of each class c_j as follows.

$$
\begin{aligned}
P(C = c_j | F_1 = f_1, F_2 = f_2, ..., F_n = f_n) = \\
\frac{P(C = c_j)P(F_1 = f_1, F_2 = f_2, ..., F_n = f_n | C = c_j)}{P(F_1 = f_1, F_2 = f_2, ..., F_n = f_n)}
\end{aligned}
\tag{11}
$$

The Bayesian conditional independent assumption of features allows the simplification of class posterior probabilities to be expressed as product of each posterior probability of a feature for the given class. The class posterior probabilities are otherwise impossible to be estimated in reality because of data sparseness problems that can result from large samples. Thus, it follows that:

$$
\begin{aligned}
P(C = c_j | F_1 = f_1, F_2 = f_2, ..., F_n = f_n) = \\
\frac{P(C = c_j) \prod_{i=1}^{n} P(F_i = f_i | C = c_j)}{P(F_1 = f_1, F_2 = f_2, ..., F_n = f_n)}
\end{aligned}
\tag{12}
$$

Class prior probabilities $P(F_1 = f_1, F_2 = f_2, ..., F_n = f_n)$, $P(C = c_j)$ and posterior probability $P(F_i = f_i | C = c_j)$ are easy to estimate from available training dataset as frequency ratios. The law of total probability allows the class posterior probability that an email represented as a feature vector belongs to a class c_j to be expressed as:

$$P(C = c_j | F_1 = f_1, F_2 = f_2, ..., F_n = f_n) =$$

$$\frac{P(C = c_j) \prod_{i=1}^{n} P(F_i = f_i | C = c_j)}{\sum_{c_k \in C} P(C = c_j) \prod_{i=1}^{n} P(F_i = f_i | C = c_k)} \qquad (13)$$

The decision rule of NBC assigns a new data instance to the class $c_k (k = 1, 2)$ with the highest class posterior probability. In order to maximize the class posterior probability, the prior probability $P(F_1 = f_1, F_2 = f_2, ..., F_n = f_n)$ will not be calculated because it serves as a normalizing factor and is constant for both classes. Thus, it follows that:

$$P(C = c_k | F_1 = f_1, F_2 = f_2, ..., F_n = f_n) =$$

$$\arg\max_{c_j} \left\{ P(C = c_j \prod_{i=1}^{n} P(F_i = f_i | C = c_j) \right\} \qquad (14)$$

4   Methodology

The methodology of this study consists of the sequence of actions that must be completed to realize the objectives of the study. In order to meet the objectives, two different essential tasks are to be performed. The tasks are to discover a set of features and an effective learning classifier that can assist to accurately detect AFF activities on internet. Email preprocessing and classification are two important steps of our methodology. Emails considered in this study are assumed to be written in English language.

The email processing procedure strips all attachments to facilitate extraction of contents of header and body from incoming email and its attachment if any. Html tags, video clip and image elements are extracted from email body. The algorithm then performs tokenization to extract words in email body. The process of lemmatization or stemming is performed to group morphological variants of the same words into their canonical form or stem. Porter stemming algorithm [22] is used to remove commoner morphological and inflexional suffixes. For example, stemming algorithm reduces the word forms banks, banking, banker and bankers to their stem bank to improve classification accuracy and AFF vocabularies. A more sophisticated procedure such as concept signatures [23] can also be used, but Porter algorithm is widely used for text stemming. In addition, the preprocessing algorithm removes stopwords and noisy words that often occur in text messages. Precisely 582 English stopwords are removed in this study. The globalCM algorithm [12] is finally used to compute cluster features by partitioning set of distinct words into clusters of semantically related words. This results in a saving of storage space and improves computational time efficiency as cluster features give compact representation of sets of semantically related words.

The email classification procedure implements both training and testing functions to make a Boolean decision on labelled email instances, wherein labels are AFF and not-AFF. We develop training dataset by performing a random selection of 980 AFF emails collected between April 2000 and June 2005 published on polifos[1] and svbizlaw[2] websites. This set of emails covers many of the recent trends in AFF business. For legitimate portion of the dataset, we use 1020 emails selected from Enron corpus [24]. Based on the cluster features discovered, a Vector Space Model (VSM) [25] representation is then calculated from the words in each e-mail in the training set. Precisely 42 cluster features were discovered to characterize AFF activities on internet. As a result, our dataset contains 2000 emails represented by VSM with 42 cluster features as dataset fields. The dataset is given as an input to the classifiers to build classification models that are validated with a set of testing examples.

The WEKA [26] data mining tool is used to build classifiers from our dataset using BLR, BNN, SVM and NBC learning methods. The Java based implementation of our experimentation system has a function to convert a dataset into WEKA compatible Attribute-Relation File Format (ARFF). This provides us with a simple means to interface Java based system with WEKA tool. The integration of an open source specialized machine learning program into our system gives us flavour of reliability and robustness. We used stratified 10-fold cross-validation method to obtain an estimate of the generalized error of all classifiers. K-fold cross-validation method is generally used to estimate performance of a model [27]. The cross-validation method works like this, the dataset is divided into k folds, in our experiment $k = 10$. A single fold is chosen as testing data and the remaining $k-1$ folds are used for training. The process is repeated k times so that each k fold is used exactly once for testing.

5   Results and Discussion

The WEKA tool is used to perform a test to find minimum average error rate for BNN. Different number of units are used in hidden layer with wildcard values 'a' = (attributes + classes)/2, 'i'=attributes, 'o'=classes only and 't'=(attributes + classes), for 2, 22, 42 and 44 units. In addition, we use different weight decays of typical values of 0.1, 0.2, 0.25, 0.3, 0.4 and 0.5 respectively on interconnections. Results of the experiment show that BNN with size 22 and weight decay of 0.3 at epochs 30000 provides the lowest error rate of 0.009. We then use BNN model to establish comparison with other learning methods. Moreover, we obtain minimum average error rate for SVM using all kernel functions in WEKA. Polynomial kernels of degrees 2 and 3 with widths of 0.001, 0.005, 0.01, 0.05, 0.1, 0.5, 1 and 2 give the best performance. This is when compared to other learning methods with maximum optimal that generalized parameter factor of ten in order of $10^{-7} - 10^{3}$ for each

---

[1] http:\\potifos.com/fraud
[2] http:\\www.svbizlaw.com/nigerian.419.letters.htm

kernel. For BLR, we use 10 values of k ranging from 1 to 10 and Euclidean distance weighted as a gain ratio to train the classifier.

Experiments are performed for both regularized and un-regularized classifiers by varying the regularization parameter by factors of 10. The essence of regularization is to reduce over-fitting problems that are often associated with learning methods. The cost sensitive measures of weighted accuracy (WA_{ecc}) and weighted error (WA_{err}) were used to compare classification accuracies of classifiers. Table 1 shows this result with the corresponding standard deviation (STDEV) when $\lambda = 1$ (legitimate and AFF emails are equally weighted) and $\lambda = 9$ (false positives are penalized nine times more than false negatives). The error rate of each classifier is calculated based on average error rate of all 10-fold samples with equivalent STDEV. This result shows that accuracy exceeded 90% for all classifiers when false positive had an equal penalty to false negative, but dropped to below 75% when false positive has a penalty of nine times that of false negative. SVM has the lowest WA of 0.0329 when $\lambda = 1$ and BNN has the lowest WA_{err} of 0.0273 when $\lambda = 9$.

Table 1. WA_{cc} and WA_{err} when $\lambda = 1$ and $\lambda = 9$ for all classifiers\

| Classifier | $\lambda = 1$ | | | | $\lambda = 9$ | | | |
| | WA_{cc} | | WA_{err} | | WA_{cc} | | WA_{err} | |
	AVG	STDEV	AVG	STDEV	AVG	STDEV	AVG	STDEV
BNN	0.9635	0.0025	0.0365	0.0025	0.7271	0.0021	0.273	0.0021
SVM	0.9671	0.0034	0.0329	0.0034	0.7247	0.0010	0.275	0.0010
BLR	0.9635	0.0013	0.0367	0.0013	0.7249	0.0018	0.275	0.0017
NBC	0.9301	0.0008	0.0698	0.0008	0.7197	0.0005	0.280	0.0005

In email classification problem, False Positive (FP) is the set of legitimate emails that is wrongly classified as AFF. Similarly, False Negative (FN) is the set of AFF emails that is wrongly classified as legitimate. Table 2 summarizes the result of calculating FP and FN rates for all classifiers. This result shows that SVM outperforms all classifiers because it has lowest false positive of 0.0435 of legitimate emails being classified as AFF.

Table 2. FP and FN rates for all classifiers

Classifier	FP	FN
BNN	0.0565	0.0282
SVM	0.0435	0.0282
BLR	0.0487	0.0310
NBC	0.0742	0.0679

The precision, recall and F-measure are also determined to compare classification accuracies of the classifiers. Precision measures the validity ratio to distinguish AFF emails predicted as positive. Recall measures the fraction of all AFF emails classified to reflect the performance that AFF emails are successfully distinguished. F-measure is generally defined as the harmonic mean of precision and recall measures. Table 3 summarises this result wherein SVM is seen to have the highest precision of about 98% and F-measure of about 98%.

Table 3. Comparison of Precision, Recall and F-measures for all classifiers

Classifier	Precision	Recall	F-measures
BNN	0.9746	0.9725	0.9736
SVM	0.9803	0.9718	0.9760
BLR	0.9690	0.9780	0.9734
NBC	0.9655	0.9320	0.9485

In this study, we also compare classification accuracies of classifiers. Accuracy is the fraction of emails (AFF and legitimate) correctly predicted by a classifier relative to the size of the dataset. Table 4 summaries this result when cross-validation was used and this shows that SVM has the highest accuracy of about 96.43%.

Table 4. Accuracy rates for all classifiers

Classifier	TP	TN	Accuracy
BNN	0.9725	0.9435	0.9580
SVM	0.9720	0.9565	0.9643
BLR	0.9690	0.9512	0.9601
NBC	0.9320	0.9289	0.9289

Receiver Operating Characteristic (ROC) curve is an important measure used to compare classification accuracies of classifiers. ROC curve is a plot of True Positive Rate (TPR) against False Positive Rate (FPR) for diverse possible cut-points of an accuracy test. We estimate the Area Under ROC Curve (AUC) as a measure of classification accuracy, wherein an area of 1 and 0 represent best and worst accuracies respectively. AUC is defined as isocost gradient chosen as tangent point on the highest isocost line that touches the curve. Table 5 shows AUC computation for all classifiers and SVM is seen to give the best accuracy because it gives the highest AUC of 96.45%. Judging from results presented in Tables 1-5, SVM is nominated as the most effective classifier that can assist to detect AFF activities on internet.

Table 5. Area under the ROC curve (AUC) for all classifiers

Classifier	Cut-point	TPR	FPR	AUC
BNN	100	0.05483	0.03043	0.9573
SVM	100	0.04193	0.02898	0.9645
BLR	100	0.05000	0.03043	0.9597
NBC	100	0.07419	0.06739	0.9292

6   Conclusion

In this study, we compare classification accuracies of four supervised learning classifiers to determine the one that can assist us to accurately detect AFF activities on internet. The natural language processing methodology of removing noisy and stop words, stemming and clustering semantically related words is used. Cross-validation, recall, precision, F-measure, AUC and cost sensitive analysis and weighted accuracy are used to compare classification accuracies of classifiers. The introduction of globalCM algorithm not only reduces dimension, but also overcomes sparseness problems and improves computational efficiency.

The results of experiments conducted in this study to compare classification accuracies of classifiers show that SVM outperforms all other classifiers, making it more appealing to detect AFF activities on internet. Moreover high levels of results (Tables 1-5) obtained for all classifiers give an indication that cluster features give an effective representation that characterizes AFF activities on internet. Consequently, objectives of this study are met. In the current study, cluster size is chosen arbitrary, but in future work it will be varied to determine the effect of cluster sizes on classification accuracies. In future, we also intend to combine social networks analysis to gain more insight on traffic flow of AFF defrauders in all geographical locations. This will provide a better understanding of how to build rich sources of learning about cybercrime activities on internet.

References

1. Grobier, M.: Strategic information security: facing the cyber impact. In: Proceedings of the Workshop on ICT uses in Warfare and Safeguarding of Peace, pp. 12–22. SAICSIT (2010)
2. Internet Crime Complaint Center (IC3). An FBI–NW3C partnership, http://www.ic3.gov/media/annualreports.aspx (accessed July 2011)
3. UAGI. Ultrascan 419unit-419 Advance Fee Fraud Statistics, http://www.ultrascanagi.com/public_html/html/ pdf_files/419_Advance_Fee_Fraud_Statistics_2009.pdf
4. Marcus, K.R., Seigfried, K.: The future of computer forensics:a needs analysis survey. Computer & Security 23(1), 12–16 (2004)
5. Ciardhuáin, O.S.: An extended model of cybercrime investigations. International Journal of Digital Evidence 3(1) (2004)

6. Chandrasekaran, M., Narayanan, K., Upadhyaya, K.S.: Phishing email detection based on structural properties. In: First Annual Symposium on Information Assurance: Intrusion Detection and Prevention, New York, pp. 2–8 (2006)
7. Abu-Nimeh, S., Nappa, D., Wang, X., Nair, S.: A comparison of machine learning techniques for phishing detection. In: Proceedings of the Anti-Phishing Working Groups (APWG), Second Annual eCrime Researchers Summit, Pittsburgh, PA, US, pp. 1–10 (2007)
8. Fette, I., Sadeh, N., Tomasic, A.: Learning to detect phishing emails. In: Proceedings of the 16th International Conference on World Wide Web, pp. 649–656. ACM Press, New York (2007)
9. Airoldi, E., Malin, B.: Data mining challenges for electronic safety: the case of fraudulent intent detection in emails. In: Proceedings of the Workshop on Privacy and Security Aspects of Data Mining, IEEE International Conference on Data Mining, Brighton, England, pp. 1–10 (2004)
10. Hadjidj, R., Debbabi, M., Lounis, H., Iqbal, F.: Towards an Integrated Email Forensic Analysis Framework. Digital Investigation 5, 124–137 (2009)
11. Modupe, A., Olugbara, O.O., Ojo, S.O.: Identifying advanced fee fraud activities on the internet using machine learning algorithms. In: 3rd IEEE International Conference on Computational Intelligence and Industrial Application (PACIIA), Wuhan, China, pp. 240–242 (2010)
12. Wenliang, C., Xingzhi, C., Huizhen, W., Jingbo, Z., Tianshun, Y.: Automatic word clustering for text categorization using global information. In: AIRS, Beijing, China, pp. 1–6. ACM (2004)
13. Worth, A.P., Cronin, M.T.D.: The use of discriminant analysis, logistic regression and classification tree analysis in the development of classification models for human health effects. Journal of Molecular Structure 622, 97–111 (2003)
14. Khan, A., Baharudin, B., Lee, L.H., Khan, K.: A review of machine learning algorithms for text documents classification. Journal of Advanced in Information Technology 1(1), 4–20 (2010)
15. Byvatov, E., Fechner, U., Sadowski, J., Schneider, G.: Comparison of support vector machine and artificial neural network systems for drug/nondrug classification. J. Chem. Inf. Comput. Sci. 43, 1882–1889 (2003)
16. Yu, B., Xu, Z., Li, C.: Latent semantic analysis for text categorization using neural network. Knowledge-Based Systems 24, 900–904 (2008)
17. Bishop, C.M.: Neural networks for pattern recognition. Oxford University Press (1995)
18. Duda, R.O., Hart, P.E., Stork, D.G.: Pattern classification. Wiley-Interscience, New York (2000)
19. Cortes, C., Vapnik, V.: Support vector networks in machine learning, vol. 20, pp. 273–297 (1995)
20. Rios, G., Zhu, H.: Exploring support vector machines and random forests for spam detection. In: Proceedings of CEAS 2004 (2004)
21. Mitra, V., Wang, C., Banerjee, S.: Text classification: a least square support vector machine approach. Applied Soft Computing 7, 908–914 (2007)
22. Porter, M.: An algorithm for suffix stripping. Program 14(3), 130–137 (1980)
23. Kurz, T., Stoffel, K.: Going beyond stemming: creating concept signatures of complex medical terms. Knowledge Based Systems 15, 309–313 (2002)

24. Klimt, B., Yang, Y.: The Enron Corpus: A New Dataset for Email Classification Research. In: Boulicaut, J.-F., Esposito, F., Giannotti, F., Pedreschi, D. (eds.) ECML 2004. LNCS (LNAI), vol. 3201, pp. 217–226. Springer, Heidelberg (2004)
25. Salton, G., Yang, C., Wang, A.: A vector space model for automatic indexing. Communications of the ACM 18(11), 613–620 (1975)
26. Hall, M., Frank, E., Holmes, G., Pfahringer, B., Reutemann, P., Witten, I.H.: The WEKA data mining software. SIGKDD Explorations 11(1) (2009)
27. Wang, T., Chiang, H.: Fuzzy support vector machine for multi-class text categorization. Information Process and Management 43, 914–929 (2007)

Algebra of Geometric Filters Defined over Three Dimenisonal Rectangular Lattice-PartI

Towheed Sultana* and E.G. Rajan**

Pentagram Research Centre Pvt. Ltd.,
Mehidipatnam, Hyderbad, India
tow_sul@yahoo.com, rajan_eg@yahoo.co.in

Abstract. This paper gives a novel concept of what we call as Geometric Filters defined over a 3-D rectangular grid of pixels. These G-Filters have potential applications to processing of volumetric images. In addition, the paper describes in brief the algebra of G-Filters by formulating a lattice of convex polyhedrons constructed in a 3X3X3 grid of pixels. The results are visualized as a distributive lattice. The lattice also contains its proper envelopes as its successors.

Keywords: Geometric Filters, 3-D image processing, Image Algebra, Extended Topology, Topological Filters.

1 Introduction

The processing of digital images, based on well defined mathematical techniques has remained a subject of interest for many years. In particular mathematical theories associated with processing, enhancement, analysis , and recognition[8],[10] of sensed imageries have received significance amount of attention and effort. At present there are methodologies for image processing using rigorous mathematical framework, for example, that of mathematical morphology [1], [7], [8]. In spite of these efforts, the wide variety of existing methodologies associated with image processing operations are yet to be consolidated under one rigorous unifying mathematical structure.

The term mathematical structure refers to 3-tuple <X, O, R>, [2] where X is a set of mathematical objects, O is the set of operations and R is a set of relations. A mathematical structure with binary operations alone would fall under the algebraic structures of monoids, groups, rings, integral domain and fields. Alternatively, a mathematical structure with binary operations alone fall under the category of formal relational structures like that of lattices.

Based on the above said mathematical structures we construct an image algebra either for 2D or 3D images. [2] [4] [5] [9] [11]. The image algebra is defined as a mathematical theory concerned with the transformation and analysis of images. The central idea of image algebra is based, is that of treating an image

---

* Professor, Electronics and Communication Department, Joginpally M.N.Rao Womens Engineering College, Yenkapally, Hyderabad, Andhra Pradesh, India.
** Founder President.

N. Meghanathan et al. (Eds.): CCSIT 2012, Part III, LNICST 86, pp. 101–111, 2012.

as a construct made up of certain convex polygons or polyhedrons according as the image being 2-D or 3-D, and treating an image processing operation as filtering by means of what we call geometric filters (G-filters) .The notion of G-filters has been derived from extended topology, which is a generalization of the traditional mathematical topology [3],[8],[10].There exists a mathematical framework of G-Filters for 2-D images .

The algebra of 2-D filters is discussed in section 2. In this paper we present a mathematical framework of G-Filters and its algebra for 3-D images in section 3, and the corresponding lattice generated from a 256 convex polyhedrons is shown in section 4. The algorithms related to the same work is discussed in [12].

2   2-D Geometric Filters (2-D G-Filters)

The theory of geometric filters has been formulated purely based on the extended topological filters [2],[8],[10].Consider a 3x3 array of cells as shown in Fig.1a. The smallest convex polygon that would be found inside this cell array is also shown in Fig. 1b.

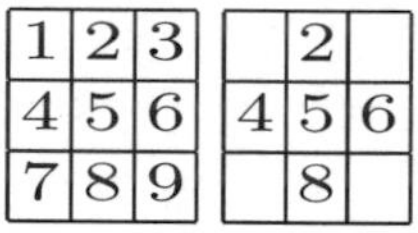

Fig. 1. (a) 3x3 array of cell (b) Smallest Convex Polygon

Note that sixteen such different convex polygons can be formed by dropping indirect neighbour (corner) cells, which are pixels 1, 3, 7 and 9. Fig. 2 shows all 16 convex polygons. The suffixes denote the cells that are dropped.

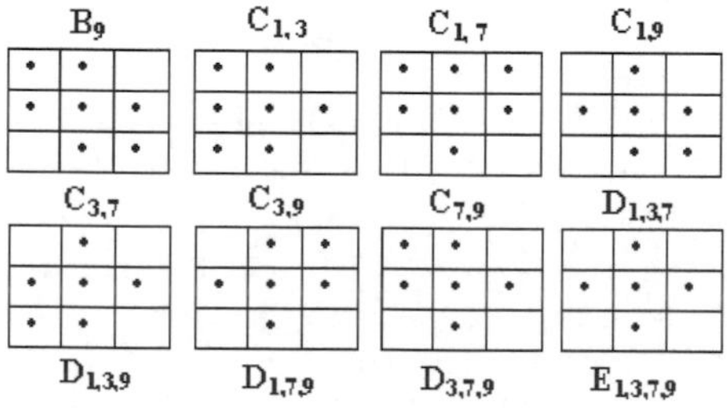

Fig. 2. 16 Convex Polygons

2.1   Algebra Of 2 Dimensional G-Filters

The relational mathematical structure in which the G-filters are studied is a lattice $\phi = < X, \preceq >$ where X is a set of G-filters and $\preceq$ is the partial order relation "finer than". For example, the filter F1 = { A, B_1, B_7, B_9, $C_{1,7}$ } is finer than that of F2 = { A ,B_1, B_7,$C_{1,7}$ }. [2],[4],[5],[6]. All the 2D convex polygons form a lattice with A as their supremum and E as their infimum. Note that there are 5 levels in the lattice Fig. 3. All the elements in a level constitute a group which is viewed as an immediate sub group of the group of elements in the just higher level. We can see from lattice that there are 24 linear chains consisting of proper envelopes starting from E .Each chain exhibits a linear hierarchy of generating A from E.

Theorem 1. *One can construct a total of 95 hierarchical G-filters using 3x3 cell structure.*

Proof. Refer [2]
   we obtain the total number of heirarchical G-filters as

$$2 + 2\sum_{i=1}^{4}{}^4C_i + \sum_{i=1}^{6}{}^6C_i = 95 \tag{1}$$

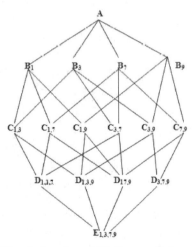

Fig. 3. Lattice of 16 Convex Polygons

3   3-D GEOMETRIC FILTERS (3 D G-Filters)

Consider a 3X3X3 array of 27 cells as shown in Fig. 4. The smallest convex polyhedron that could be formed inside this cell array is also shown in Fig. 5

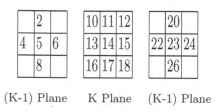

$$
\begin{array}{|c|c|c|} \hline 1 & 2 & 3 \\ \hline 4 & 5 & 6 \\ \hline 7 & 8 & 9 \\ \hline \end{array}
\qquad
\begin{array}{|c|c|c|} \hline 10 & 11 & 12 \\ \hline 13 & 14 & 15 \\ \hline 16 & 17 & 18 \\ \hline \end{array}
\qquad
\begin{array}{|c|c|c|} \hline 19 & 20 & 21 \\ \hline 22 & 23 & 24 \\ \hline 25 & 26 & 27 \\ \hline \end{array}
$$

(K-1) Plane   K Plane   (K-1) Plane

Fig. 4. Cubic array of size 3x3x3

$$
\begin{array}{|c|c|c|} \hline & 2 & \\ \hline 4 & 5 & 6 \\ \hline & 8 & \\ \hline \end{array}
\qquad
\begin{array}{|c|c|c|} \hline 10 & 11 & 12 \\ \hline 13 & 14 & 15 \\ \hline 16 & 17 & 18 \\ \hline \end{array}
\qquad
\begin{array}{|c|c|c|} \hline & 20 & \\ \hline 22 & 23 & 24 \\ \hline & 26 & \\ \hline \end{array}
$$

(K-1) Plane   K Plane   (K-1) Plane

Fig. 5. Smallest 3-D Convex Polyhedron. $I_{1,3,7,9,19,21,25,27}$

The term convex polyhedron refers to a 3-D wire frame contour that could be drawn using certain neighbourhood pixels including a minimum of all 19 neighbourhood pixels shown in figure 5, that is, cells 2, 4, 6, 8, 10, 11, 12, 13, 14, 15, 16, 17, 18 20, 22, 24, 26. The cells 1, 3, 7, 9, 19, 21, 25 and 27 are the corner cells with respect to the central cell 14. For example the pixels (coner pixels) 1, 3, 7, 9,19, 21, 25 and 27 in Fig. 5 form a 3D contour (convex polyhedron) with respect to the central pixel 14. There are 8 corner cells in a 3x3x3 rectangular grid and the main idea is to construct various unique possible convex polyhedrons. 256 convex polyhedrons are obtained using the formula

$$
\sum_{i=0}^{8} {}^{8}C_i = {}^{8}C_0 + {}^{8}C_1 + {}^{8}C_2 + {}^{8}C_3 + {}^{8}C_4 + {}^{8}C_5 + {}^{8}C_6 + {}^{8}C_7 + {}^{8}C_8 = 256 \quad (2)
$$

Starting from, say A which has corner pixels 1, 3, 7, 9,19, 21, 25 and 27 as in Fig .5, the process starts first by eliminating one corner pixel at a time and listing the different possibilities under group B, for set A we are able to find 8, B subsets (B1,B3,B7,B9,B19,B21,B25,B27) which is ${}^{8}C_1$. The process continues, explained in THEOREM 2. The following are the combinations for different sets

$$
A = {}^{8}C_0 = 1, B = {}^{8}C_1 = 8, C = {}^{8}C_2 = 28, D = {}^{8}C_3 = 56, E = {}^{8}C_4 = 70,
$$
$$
F = {}^{8}C_5 = 56, G = {}^{8}C_6 = 28, H = {}^{8}C_7 = 8, I = {}^{8}C_8 = 1.
$$

256 convex polyhedrons are classified under nine groups as A, B, C, D, E, F, G, H, and I as shown in the Table 1.

Table 1. 256 Convex Polyhedrons

A -No Pixel is eliminated we get 1 combination A={1,3,7,9,19,21,25,27}		
Group B - Eliminating one voxel we obtain 8 combinations		
B_1={3,7,9,19,21,25,27}	B_3={1,7,9,19,21,25,27}	B_7={1,3,9,19,21,25,27}
B_9={1,3,7,19,21,25,27}	$B_{1,9}$={1,3,7,9,21,25,27}	B_{21}={1,3,7,9,19,25,27}
B_{25}={1,3,7,9,19,21,27}	B_{27}={1,3,7,9,19,21,25}	
Group C - By Eliminating two voxels we obtain 28 combinations		
$C_{1,3}$={7,9,19,21,25,27}	$C_{1,7}$={3,9,19,21,25,27}	$C_{1,9}$={3,7,19,21,25,27}
$C_{1,19}$={3,7,9,21,25,27}	$C_{1,21}$={3,7,9,19,25,27}	$C_{1,25}$={3,7,9,19,21,27}
$C_{1,27}$={3,7,9,19,21,25}	$C_{3,7}$={1,9,19,21,25,27}	$C_{3,9}$={1,7,19,21,25,27}
$C_{3,19}$={1,7,9,21,25,27}	$C_{3,21}$={1,7,9,19,25,27}	$C_{3,25}$={1,7,9,19,21,27}
$C_{3,27}$={1,7,9,19,21,25}	$C_{7,9}$={1,3,19,21,25,27}	$C_{7,19}$={1,3,9,21,25,27}
$C_{7,21}$={1,3,9,19,25,27}	$C_{7,25}$={1,3,9,19,21,27}	$C_{7,27}$={1,3,9,19,21,25}
$C_{9,19}$={1,3,7,21,25,27}	$C_{9,21}$={1,3,7,19,25,27}	$C_{9,25}$={1,3,7,19,21,27}
$C_{9,27}$={1,3,7,19,21,25}	$C_{19,21}$={1,3,7,9,25,27}	$C_{19,25}$={1,3,7,9,21,27}
$C_{19,27}$={1,3,7,9,21,25}	$C_{21,25}$={1,3,7,9,19,27}	$C_{21,27}$={1,3,7,9,19,25}
$C_{25,27}$={1,3,7,9,19,21}		
Group D - By Eliminating three voxels we obtain 56 combinations		
$D_{1,3,7}$={9,19,21,25,27}	$D_{1,3,9}$={7,19,21,25,27}	$D_{1,3,19}$={7,9,21,25,27}
$D_{1,3,21}$={7,9,19,25,27}	$D_{1,3,25}$={7,9,19,21,27}	$D_{1,3,27}$={7,9,19,21,25}
$D_{1,7,9}$={3,19,21,25,27}	$D_{1,7,19}$={3,9,21,25,27}	$D_{1,7,21}$={3,9,19,25,27}
$D_{1,7,25}$={3,9,19,21,27}	$D_{1,7,27}$={3,9,19,21,25}	$D_{1,9,19}$={3,7,21,25,27}
$D_{1,9,21}$={3,7,19,25,27}	$D_{1,9,25}$={3,7,19,21,27}	$D_{1,9,27}$={3,7,19,21,25}
$D_{1,19,21}$={3,7,9,25,27}	$D_{1,19,25}$={3,7,9,21,27}	$D_{1,19,27}$={3,7,9,21,25}
$D_{1,21,25}$={3,7,9,19,27}	$D_{1,21,27}$={3,7,9,19,25}	$D_{1,25,27}$={3,7,9,19,21}
$D_{3,7,9}$={1,19,21,25,27}	$D_{3,7,19}$={1,9,21,25,27}	$D_{3,7,21}$={1,9,19,25,27}
$D_{3,7,25}$={1,9,19,21,27}	$D_{3,7,27}$={1,9,19,21,25}	$D_{3,9,19}$={1,7,21,25,27}
$D_{3,9,21}$={1,7,19,25,27}	$D_{3,9,25}$={1,7,19,21,27}	$D_{3,9,27}$={1,7,19,21,25}
$D_{3,19,21}$={1,7,9,25,27}	$D_{3,19,25}$={1,7,9,21,27}	$D_{3,19,27}$={1,7,9,21,25}
$D_{3,21,25}$={1,7,9,19,27}	$D_{3,21,27}$={1,7,9,19,25}	$D_{3,25,27}$={1,7,9,19,21}
$D_{7,9,19}$={1,3,21,25,27}	$D_{7,9,21}$={1,3,19,25,27}	$D_{7,9,25}$={1,3,19,21,27}
$D_{7,9,27}$={1,3,19,21,25}	$D_{7,19,21}$={1,3,9,25,27}	$D_{7,19,25}$={1,3,9,21,27}
$D_{7,19,27}$={1,3,9,21,25}	$D_{7,21,25}$={1,3,9,19,27}	$D_{7,21,27}$={1,3,9,19,25}
$D_{7,25,27}$={1,3,9,19,21}	$D_{9,19,21}$={1,3,7,25,27}	$D_{9,19,25}$={1,3,7,21,27}
$D_{9,19,27}$={1,3,7,21,25}	$D_{9,21,25}$={1,3,7,19,27}	$D_{9,21,27}$={1,3,7,19,25}
		continued on next page

$D_{9,25,27}=\{1,3,7,19,21\}$	$D_{19,21,25}=\{1,3,7,9,27\}$	$D_{19,21,27}=\{1,3,7,9,25\}$
$D_{19,25,27}=\{1,3,7,9,21\}$	$D_{21,25,27}=\{1,3,7,9,19\}$	
Group E - Eliminating four voxels we obtain 70 combinations		
$E_{1,3,7,9}=\{19,21,25,27\}$	$E_{1,3,7,19}=\{9,21,25,27\}$	$E_{1,3,7,21}=\{9,19,25,27\}$
$E_{1,3,7,25}=\{9,19,21,27\}$	$E_{1,3,7,27}=\{9,19,21,25\}$	$E_{1,3,9,19}=\{7,21,25,27\}$
$E_{1,3,9,21}=\{7,19,25,27\}$	$E_{1,3,9,25}=\{7,19,21,27\}$	$E_{1,3,9,27}=\{7,19,21,25\}$
$E_{1,3,19,21}=\{7,9,25,27\}$	$E_{1,3,19,25}=\{7,9,21,27\}$	$E_{1,3,19,27}=\{7,9,21,25\}$
$E_{1,3,21,25}=\{7,9,19,27\}$	$E_{1,3,21,27}=\{7,9,19,25\}$	$E_{1,3,25,27}=\{7,9,19,21\}$
$E_{1,7,9,19}=\{3,21,25,27\}$	$E_{1,7,9,21}=\{3,19,25,27\}$	$E_{1,7,9,25}=\{3,19,21,27\}$
$E_{1,7,9,27}=\{3,19,21,25\}$	$E_{1,7,19,21}=\{3,9,25,27\}$	$E_{1,7,19,25}=\{3,9,21,27\}$
$E_{1,7,19,27}=\{3,9,21,25\}$	$E_{1,7,21,25}=\{3,9,19,27\}$	$E_{1,7,21,27}=\{3,9,19,25\}$
$E_{1,7,25,27}=\{3,9,19,21\}$	$E_{1,9,19,21}=\{3,7,25,27\}$	$E_{1,9,19,25}=\{3,7,21,27\}$
$E_{1,9,19,27}=\{3,7,21,25\}$	$E_{1,9,21,25}=\{3,7,19,27\}$	$E_{1,9,21,27}=\{3,7,19,25\}$
$E_{1,9,25,27}=\{3,7,19,21\}$	$E_{1,19,21,25}=\{3,7,9,27\}$	$E_{1,19,21,27}=\{3,7,9,25\}$
$E_{1,19,25,27}=\{3,7,9,21\}$	$E_{1,21,25,27}=\{3,7,9,19\}$	$E_{3,7,9,19}=\{1,21,25,27\}$
$E_{3,7,9,21}=\{1,19,25,27\}$	$E_{3,7,9,25}=\{1,19,21,27\}$	$E_{3,7,9,27}=\{1,19,21,25\}$
$E_{3,7,19,21}=\{1,9,25,27\}$	$E_{3,7,19,25}=\{1,9,21,27\}$	$E_{3,7,19,27}=\{1,9,21,25\}$
$E_{3,7,21,25}=\{1,9,19,27\}$	$E_{3,7,21,27}=\{1,9,19,25\}$	$E_{3,7,25,27}=\{1,9,19,21\}$
$E_{3,9,19,21}=\{1,7,25,27\}$	$E_{3,9,19,25}=\{1,7,21,27\}$	$E_{3,9,19,27}=\{1,7,21,25\}$
$E_{3,9,21,25}=\{1,7,19,27\}$	$E_{3,9,21,27}=\{1,7,19,25\}$	$E_{3,9,25,27}=\{1,7,19,21\}$
$E_{3,19,21,25}=\{1,7,9,27\}$	$E_{3,19,21,27}=\{1,7,9,25\}$	$E_{3,19,25,27}=\{1,7,9,21\}$
$E_{3,21,25,27}=\{1,7,9,19\}$	$E_{7,9,19,21}=\{1,3,25,27\}$	$E_{7,9,19,25}=\{1,3,21,27\}$
$E_{7,9,19,27}=\{1,3,21,25\}$	$E_{7,9,21,25}=\{1,3,19,27\}$	$E_{7,9,21,27}=\{1,3,19,25\}$
$E_{7,9,25,27}=\{1,3,19,21\}$	$E_{7,19,21,25}=\{1,3,9,27\}$	$E_{7,19,21,27}=\{1,3,9,25\}$
$E_{7,19,25,27}=\{1,3,9,21\}$	$E_{7,21,25,27}=\{1,3,9,19\}$	$E_{9,19,21,25}=\{1,3,7,27\}$
$E_{9,19,21,27}=\{1,3,7,25\}$	$E_{9,19,25,27}=\{1,3,7,21\}$	$E_{9,21,25,27}=\{1,3,7,19\}$
$E_{19,21,25,27}=\{1,3,7,9\}$		
Group F - By Eliminating five voxels we obtain 56 combinations		
$F_{1,3,7,9,19}=\{21,25,27\}$	$F_{1,3,7,9,21}=\{19,25,27\}$	$F_{1,3,7,9,25}=\{19,21,27\}$
$F_{1,3,7,9,27}=\{19,21,25\}$	$F_{1,3,7,19,21}=\{9,25,27\}$	$F_{1,3,7,19,25}=\{9,21,27\}$
$F_{1,3,7,19,27}=\{9,21,25\}$	$F_{1,3,7,21,25}=\{9,19,27\}$	$F_{1,3,7,21,27}=\{9,19,25\}$
$F_{1,3,7,25,27}=\{9,19,21\}$	$F_{1,3,9,19,21}=\{7,25,27\}$	$F_{1,3,9,19,25}=\{7,21,27\}$
$F_{1,3,9,19,27}=\{7,21,25\}$	$F_{1,3,9,21,25}=\{7,19,27\}$	$F_{1,3,9,21,27}=\{7,19,25\}$
$F_{1,3,9,25,27}=\{7,19,21\}$	$F_{1,3,19,21,25}=\{7,9,27\}$	$F_{1,3,19,21,27}=\{7,9,25\}$
$F_{1,3,19,25,27}=\{7,9,21\}$	$F_{1,3,21,25,27}=\{7,9,19\}$	$F_{1,7,9,19,21}=\{3,25,27\}$
$F_{1,7,9,19,25}=\{3,21,27\}$	$F_{1,7,9,19,27}=\{3,21,25\}$	$F_{1,7,9,21,25}=\{3,19,27\}$
$F_{1,7,9,21,27}=\{3,19,25\}$	$F_{1,7,9,25,27}=\{3,19,21\}$	$F_{1,7,19,21,25}=\{3,9,27\}$
$F_{1,7,19,21,27}=\{3,9,25\}$	$F_{1,7,19,25,27}=\{3,9,21\}$	$F_{1,7,21,25,27}=\{3,9,19\}$
$F_{1,9,19,21,25}=\{3,7,27\}$	$F_{1,9,19,21,27}=\{3,7,25\}$	$F_{1,9,19,25,27}=\{3,7,21\}$
$F_{1,9,21,25,27}=\{3,7,19\}$	$F_{1,19,21,25,27}=\{3,7,9\}$	$F_{3,7,9,19,21}=\{1,25,27\}$

continued on next page

$F_{3,7,9,19,25}=\{1,21,27\}$	$F_{3,7,9,19,27}=\{1,21,25\}$	$F_{3,7,9,21,25}=\{1,19,27\}$
$F_{3,7,9,21,27}=\{1,19,25\}$	$F_{3,7,9,25,27}=\{1,19,21\}$	$F_{3,7,19,21,25}=\{1,9,27\}$
$F_{3,7,19,21,27}=\{1,9,25\}$	$F_{3,7,19,25,27}=\{1,9,21\}$	$F_{3,7,21,25,27}=\{1,9,19\}$
$F_{3,9,19,21,25}=\{1,7,27\}$	$F_{3,9,19,21,27}=\{1,7,25\}$	$F_{3,9,19,25,27}=\{1,7,21\}$
$F_{3,9,21,25,27}=\{1,7,19\}$	$F_{3,19,21,25,27}=\{1,7,9\}$	$F_{7,9,19,21,25}=\{1,3,27\}$
$F_{7,9,19,21,27}=\{1,3,25\}$	$F_{7,9,19,25,27}=\{1,3,21\}$	$F_{7,9,21,25,27}=\{1,3,19\}$
$F_{7,19,21,25,27}=\{1,3,9\}$	$F_{9,19,21,25,27}=\{1,3,7\}$	
Group G - By Eliminating six voxels we obtain 28 combinations		
$G_{1,3,7,9,19,21}=\{25,27\}$	$G_{1,3,7,9,19,25}=\{21,27\}$	$G_{1,3,7,9,19,27}=\{21,25\}$
$G_{1,3,7,9,21,25}=\{19,27\}$	$G_{1,3,7,9,21,27}=\{19,25\}$	$G_{1,3,7,9,25,27}=\{19,21\}$
$G_{1,3,7,19,21,25}=\{9,27\}$	$G_{1,3,7,19,21,27}=\{9,25\}$	$G_{1,3,7,19,25,27}=\{9,21\}$
$G_{1,3,7,21,25,27}=\{9,19\}$	$G_{1,3,9,19,21,25}=\{7,27\}$	$G_{1,3,9,19,21,27}=\{7,25\}$
$G_{1,3,9,19,25,27}=\{7,21\}$	$G_{1,3,9,21,25,27}=\{7,19\}$	$G_{1,3,19,21,25,27}=\{7,9\}$
$G_{1,7,9,19,21,25}=\{3,27\}$	$G_{1,7,9,19,21,27}=\{3,25\}$	$G_{1,7,9,19,25,27}=\{3,21\}$
$G_{1,7,9,21,25,27}=\{3,19\}$	$G_{1,7,19,21,25,27}=\{3,9\}$	$G_{1,9,19,21,25,27}=\{3,7\}$
$G_{3,7,9,19,21,25}=\{1,27\}$	$G_{3,7,9,19,21,27}=\{1,25\}$	$G_{3,7,9,19,25,27}=\{1,21\}$
$G_{3,7,9,21,25,27}=\{1,19\}$	$G_{3,7,19,21,25,27}=\{1,9\}$	$G_{3,9,19,21,25,27}=\{1,7\}$
$G_{7,9,19,21,25,27}=\{1,3\}$		
Group H - By Eliminating seven voxels we obtain 8 combinations		
$H_{1,3,7,9,19,21,25}=\{27\}$	$H_{1,3,7,9,19,21,27}=\{25\}$	$H_{1,3,7,9,19,25,27}=\{21\}$
$H_{1,3,7,9,21,25,27}=\{19\}$	$H_{1,3,7,19,21,25,27}=\{9\}$	$H_{1,3,9,19,21,25,27}=\{7\}$
$H_{1,7,9,19,21,25,27}=\{3\}$	$H_{3,7,9,19,21,25,27}=\{1\}$	
I Eliminating eight voxels we obtain 1 combination		
$I_{1,3,7,9,19,21,25,27}=\{\}$		

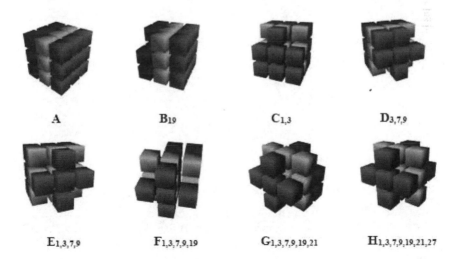

A	B_{19}	$C_{1,3}$	$D_{3,7,9}$

$E_{1,3,7,9}$	$F_{1,3,7,9,19}$	$G_{1,3,7,9,19,21}$	$H_{1,3,7,9,19,21,27}$

Fig. 6. Convex Polyhedrons

Few examples of Convex polyhedrons, constructed in a 3X3X3 grid of pixels as listed in table 1, is shown in Figure 6. An algorithm is developed for constructing the above 256 Convex polyhedrons.The algorithm is not discussed here. Red represents front plane (k-1), Green represents central plane (k), Blue represents rear plane (k+1).

Theorem 2. *One can construct a total of*

$$2 + 2\sum_{i=1}^{8} {}^{8}C_i + 2\sum_{i=1}^{28} {}^{28}C_i + 2\sum_{i=1}^{56} {}^{56}C_i + \sum_{i=1}^{70} {}^{70}C_i \tag{3}$$

hierarchical G-filters[2] in a 3 x3 x3 cell structure.

Proof. Note that there are eight corners cells in a 3x3x3 cell structure and we construct $\sum_{i=1}^{8} {}^{8}C_i$ convex patterns in the following manner. The first group A contains ${}^{8}C_0$ that is , one polyhedron which is 3x3x3 cell structure itself. The group B contains ${}^{8}C_1$ that is, 8 polyhedrons B1 (without cell 1),B2 (without cell 2), B3 , B7 , B9 ,B19, B21, B25 and B27. Similarly the the group C contains ${}^{8}C_2$ that is, 28 polyhedrons C1,3 (without cells 1 and 3), C1,7, C1,9, C3,7, C3,9 and C7,9 C25,27 .In this manner ,the elements of group D, E,F,G,H and I are identified. Now the first G-filter F1 contains the polyhedron I in the set, and as per the definition of G-filter,F1 should contain all of its 256 proper envelopes. It is easy to see the cardinality of the set to be 256. Now, the absence of I in the set would yeild a coarse G-filter F2 with 255 remaining elements. Then by dropping one element at a time from the group H we can generate eight heirarchical G-filters with cardinality 254. Next, in order to get a filter with a cardinality 253,we leave out G and any two elements in group H. We see here ${}^{8}C_2$ such possibilities. subsequently we construct ${}^{8}C_3$ filters with cardinality 252 by dropping I and any three other elements of group D. Lastly we generate one filter with cardinality 251 by dropping I and any four other elements of H.This procedure is repeated for the remaining groups also. Ultimately we obtain the total number of heirarchical G-filters.

$$2 + 2\sum_{i=1}^{8} {}^{8}C_i + 2\sum_{i=1}^{28} {}^{28}C_i + 2\sum_{i=1}^{56} {}^{56}C_i + \sum_{i=1}^{70} {}^{70}C_i$$
$$= 1,180,735,735,908,220,000,000$$

4   Results

The G-Filters for 3 Dimensional rectangular grid is identified and their corresponding convex polyhedrons are listed in the Table 1. All the 256 convex polyhedrons are arranged in 9 levels with A set as root node, I set as leaf node and sets B, C, D, E, F, G, H as intermediate nodes to form a complete distributive lattice, which is shown in the Fig 7. Only connections between A to B and H to I are shown in the Fig 7.,due to the complexity involved in forming

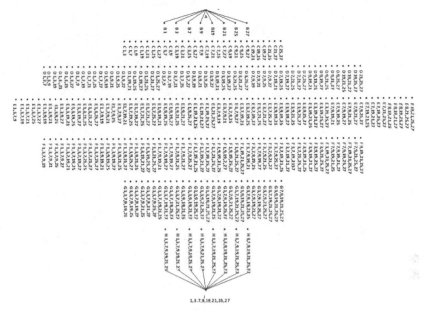

Fig. 7. Lattice Formed By 256 Convex Polyhedrons

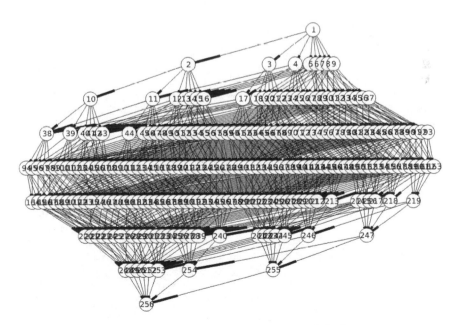

Fig. 8. Lattice Formed By 256 Convex Polyhedrons

the connections of 3D lattice. In the constructed distributive lattice root node A is supremum and leaf node I is infimum. The number of subsets formed from their corresponding sets at each level is identified as 1, 8, 28, 56, 70, 56, 28, 8, 1 at level 0, level 1, level 2, level 3, level 4, level 5, level 6, level 7, level 8, level 9 respectively in the lattice. The hierarchical relationships among the sets and their corresponding sub sets is identified. and visualized by using the hierarchy construction algorithm . Due to the complexity in visualisation the nodes are mentioned in numbers instead of set name. For example, node 1 in Fig 7 is A. Similarly, node 256 corresponds to I1, 3, 7, 9, 19, 21, 25, 27. The number of unique linear chains in the 2-D and 3-D lattices are identified and proved in the Theorem1 and Theorem 2 respectively.

5 Conclusion

In this paper, we have considered three dimensional polyhedrons developed in a 3 X 3 X 3 lattice. These 256 polyhedrons form a lattice with A as the supremum and $I_{1,3,7,9,19,21,25,27}$ as infimum. We developed the notion of 3-D Geometric Filters and showed their potential applications to 3 D image processing.

Acknowledgments. We sincerely thank Mrs. G.Chitra, Managing Director, Pentagram Research Centre Pvt. Ltd.for her support to carry out research work.

References

1. Gonzalez, R.C., Woods, R.E.: Digital Image processing, 2nd edn. PHI
2. Rajan, E.G.: Symolic Computjng Signal & image processing. B.S. Publications, India
3. Choquet, G.: Topology. Academic Press, New York (1966)
4. Rajan, E.G.: The notion of geometric filters and their use in computer vision. In: IEEE International Conference on Systems, Man and Cybernetics, Vancouver, B.C., Canada, pp. 4250–4255 (1995)
5. Rajan, E.G.: On the notion of a geometric filter and its relevance in the neighbourhood processing of digital imagesin hexagonal grids. In: 4th International Conference on Control, Automation, Robotics and Vision, Westim Stamford, Singapore (1996)
6. Vasantha, N., Rajan, E.G.: On the notion of geometric filters. In: National Conference Organized by the the Institution of Engineers, SURGE 1994, India and Annamalai University (1994)
7. Matheron, G.: Random sets and Integral Geometry. Wiley, New York (1975)
8. Serra, J.: Image Analysis and Mathematical Morphology. Acadamic, New York (1982)
9. Maragos, P., Schafer, R.W.: Applications of morphological filtering to image processings and analysis. In: Maragos, P., Schafer, R.W. (eds.) Proc. 1986 IEEE Int. Conf. Acoust., Speech, Signal Processing, Tokyo, Japan, pp. 2067–2070 (April 1986)

10. Sonka, M., Hlavac, V., Boyle, R.: Image Processing, Analysis,and Machine Vision, 2nd edn.
11. Rajan, E.G., Sathya, G., Prashanthi, G.: Theory of Constructive Image Processing-On the notion of a Geometric Filter and Its relevance in the neighborhood Processing of Digital Images. In: 4th IEEE International Conference on Advance Computing and Communication Technologies (ICACCT-2010), pp. 7–15. APIIT, Panipat (2010)
12. Ramesh Chandra, G., Rajan, G.E.: Algorithm for Constructing Complete Distributive Lattice of Polyhedrons Defined Over Three Dimensional Rectangular Grid-Part II. Paper Submitted to This Conference Along with This Paper

Finite State Transducers Framework for Monitors Conflict Detection and Resolution

Soha Hussein

University of Illinois at Urbana-Champaign
soha@illinois.edu

Abstract. Runtime monitoring and verification systems monitor target's events and verify them against specifications during program execution. For such systems the same event might trigger different monitors remedial actions, which can be contradictory in behavior or complementary (with a specific order). This urges the need to have a method to detect and resolve potential conflict between monitors.

In this paper, we present a formal model for modeling monitors based on *Finite State Transducers*. Monitors in the model are transducers with events as their input and output alphabet. Monitors composition is used for those monitors in conflict, where each monitor can add to the output set of events, but it can never remove an event. The output set of events is later evaluated using 2 rewrite rules and resulting in non-conflicting behavior.

1 Introduction

Runtime monitoring and verification has become a widely used methodology for testing and verification of systems. The idea is to encode system's specifications into monitors and observe them during system's operation, not only guaranteeing that the specifications of interests are monitored but issuing a remedial action upon violation that might as well resolve/prevent the problem before actually occurring.

JavaMOP [15,4] is a generic runtime and monitoring verification systems, whose output is an AspectJ file that can later be instrumented on the target program.

JavaMOP, by default, allows multiple specifications to coexist within a given target program. However it makes no guarantees on how they will operate together if they are triggered by the same monitored event. By default, which specification will be triggered first when events interfere is decidable only by the order in which AspectJ [10] files are weaved into the program or by using an aspect precedence declaration, which is part of the AspectJ standard. These are, at best, an incomplete way to allow for policy composition. To ensure proper composition, some sort of coordination and management among different specifications is necessary, in order to allow precedence as well as handlers conflict resolution.

The work in this paper was motivated by resolving conflicts among Java-MOP specifications, although it is not restricted to it. We provide a model that

N. Meghanathan et al. (Eds.): CCSIT 2012, Part III, LNICST 86, pp. 112–123, 2012.
© Institute for Computer Sciences, Social Informatics and Telecommunications Engineering 2012

models monitors as finite state transducers, we define what does it mean to have two monitors in conflict and we provide a methodology using the model to resolve potential conflicts and/or provide little management of monitors over other monitors.

In our model, a monitor receives a set of events and output a set of events. There are no restrictions on the input set of event, but for the set of output events a monitor can output either the same received set of events *or* append either {skip, proceed} events (these are two especial types of events see section 3.1) with possibly some statements to execute. Thus the output set of events keeps growing by visiting each monitor in conflict, or for which coordination is required.

The monitored program (usually we refer to it as just target) is modeled as a special finite state transducer that propagates its events to other transducers in the network. For each target step, an event the network of transducers operate resulting in a set of output events which is later evaluated, using 2 rewrite rules, into an action to be executed by the program.

The paper is organized as follows: the rest of this sections discusses some related work and some properties about conflicting specifications, then in section 2 general definitions used in the paper for finite state transducers are given. Section 3 represents the model, and finally conclusion and future work are in Sections 4.

1.1   Related Work

Policies composition with detecting and resolving potential conflicts are widely addressed in security language specification languages, however they have not received considerable attention in prior research in runtime monitoring systems or execution monitoring systems. For instance, JavaMOP [14] and Tracematches [1] are two runtime monitoring systems that do not specify means to detect and resolve potential conflicts when multiple specifications co-exist together right at the same time, thus causing non-determinism in the final output.

On the other hand, execution monitor systems such as SpoX [8,9], Naccio [7,6] and PoET [5] does not define a means to detect or resolve conflicts between potential specifications, whitelist Polymer [3,2,12,11,13], which defines a number of *Policy Combinators* to enable different compositions of policies. However, there is no formal definition for such combinators.

1.2   Properties about Monitors Conflicts Resolutions

Monitors Conflicts Definition: We say that two monitors are in conflict if they monitor the same event yet each fires a different remedial action.

Types of Conflict: One can define two types of conflicts among monitors:

- *Remedial Action Conflict:* for instance for a file access event that is observed by two monitors; one of the monitors might allow it with a warning while the other prohibit the access. This is a flaw in the design of the policies, and one needs to resolve such conflicts by allowing a single remedial action to take place.

– *Remedial Action Execution Order:* this happens when there is a dependency between the remedial action of both specifications. For example if one specifications writes to a file a certain value while the other reads the old value and outputs a warning message. In that case executing both remedial actions is what one wants but it is the order of execution that should be coordinated.

Typical Procedure: A typical procedure to address such conflicts is usually done in two steps:

1. *Detect Potential Conflicts:* this is the first step that should take place, one needs to detect a conflict. It is better off automating this part, so as to ensure that there are no conflict in the pool of policies that are going to co-exist in the target.
2. *Resolve Potential Conflicts:* once a conflict is detected, resolving it is the next step. There are cases resolving of conflicts can be automated but not always. For instance, the remedial action of a a higher priority can be taken instead of the lower conflicting remedial action (usually the lower bound of the remedial action lattice defined earlier), like if one says Halt, and the other prints out the warning, if one wants to be conservative then Halt should be the dominated remedial action. However if both have the same priority then a different procedure of conflict resolution should be taken, like a precise specification language that manages coordination between specifications based on the user's definition.

2   Finite State Transducers

Finite State transducers are widely used machines in natural language processing. They are also a good candidate to represent monitors, the reason being, one can think of monitors as that machine that, upon receiving an event, moves from one state to another while possibly outputting another event. It thus abstracts what a monitor is doing as a series of transitions on states when receiving events and outputting other events.

In this section we first start by listing some definitions that we are going to use in the model then we will represent out model and show how it can be used to detect potential conflicts and then resolve them.

2.1   Definition of Finite State Transducers (FST)

Finite State Transducers FST [16] can be seen as a Finite State Automata, in which each transition is labeled by a pair of symbols rather than by a single symbol. A Finite State Transducer FST is a 6-tuple $(\Sigma_1, \Sigma_2, Q, i, F, E)$ such that:

– Σ_1: is a finite input alphabet.
– Σ_2: is a finite output alphabet.
– Q is the set of states.

- $i \in Q$ is the initial state.
- $F \subset Q$ is the set of final states.
- $E : Q \times \Sigma_1^* \times \Sigma_2^* \times Q$, is the set of edges.

An alternative definition consists in replacing the set of edges E by the transition function d a mapping from $Q \times \Sigma_1^*$ to 2^Q and an emission function δ a mapping from $Q \times \Sigma_1^* \times Q$ to $2^{\Sigma_2^*}$.

2.2   Sequential Transducers

A *sequential transducer*, is a six-tuple$(\Sigma_1, \Sigma_2, Q, i, \otimes, *)$ such that,

- Σ_1 and Σ_2 are two finite alphabets.
- Q is a finite set of states.
- $i \in Q$ is the initial states.
- $\otimes$ is the partial deterministic transition function mapping $Q \times \Sigma_1$ on Q noted $q \otimes a = q'$.
- $*$ is the partial emission function mapping $Q \times \Sigma_1$ on Σ_2^*, noted $q * a = w$.

Sequential transducers can be seen as a subclass of finite state transducers without final states and with deterministic transition function.

2.3   More about FST

Finite State Transducers are powerful because of the various closure and algorithmic properties. We start by defining *letter transducers* then we represent three closure properties for FST.

Extended Edges: The extended set of edges $\hat{E}$, is the least subset of $Q \times \Sigma_1^* \times \Sigma_2^* \times Q$ such that:

- $\forall q \in Q, (q, \epsilon, \epsilon, q) \in \hat{E}$
- $\forall w_1 \in \Sigma_1^*, \forall w_2 \in \Sigma_2^*$ if $(q_1, w_2, w_2, q) \in \hat{E}$ and $(q_2, a, b, q_3) \in E$ then $(q_1, w_1 a, w_2 b, q_3) \in \hat{E}$.

Transducer Language: The above definition of extended edges us allows us to define a relation $L(T)$ on $\Sigma_1^* \times \Sigma_2^*$ for FST T as:

$$L(T) = \{(w_1, w_2) \in \Sigma_1^* \times \Sigma_2^* \mid \exists (i, w_1, w_2, q) \in \hat{E}\} \text{ with } q \in F$$

$$|T|(u) = \{v \in \Sigma_2^* \mid (u, v) \in L(T)\}$$

Letter Transducers: If $T_1 = (\Sigma_1, \Sigma_2, Q, i.F, E_1)$ is a transducer such that $\epsilon \notin | T_1 | (\epsilon)$ then there is a letter transducer $T_2 = (\Sigma_1, \Sigma_2, Q_2, i_2, F_2, E_2)$ such that:

- $| T_1 | = | T_2 |$
- $E_2 \subseteq (Q_1 \times (\Sigma_1 \cup \{\epsilon\}) \times (\Sigma_2 \cup \{\epsilon\}) \times Q_2)$
- $E_2 \cap (Q_1 \times \{\epsilon\} \times \{\epsilon\} \times Q_2) = \phi$

2.4   Closure Properties of FST

Closure under Union: if T_1 and T_2 are two FST, there exists and FST $T_1 \cup T_2$ such that $|T_1 \cup T_2| = |T_1| \cup |T_2|$, i.e., s.t. $\forall u \in \Sigma^*, |T_1 \cup T_2|(u) = |T_1|(u) \cup |T_2|(u)$.

Closure under Composition: Given two letter transducers FSTs $T_1 = (\Sigma_1, \Sigma_2, Q, i, F, E_1)$ and $T_2 = (\Sigma_2, \Sigma_3, Q_2, i_2, F_2, E_2)$, there exists an FST $T_2 \odot T_1$ such that for each $u \in \Sigma_1^*$, $| T_2 \odot T_1|(u) = |T_2(|T_1|(u))$. Furthermore the transducer
$$T_3 = (\Sigma_1, \Sigma_3, Q_1 \times Q_2, (i_1, i_2), F_1 \times F_2, E_3) \text{ such that}$$

$$E_3 = ((x_1, x_2), a, b, (y_1, y_2)) | \exists c \in \Sigma_2 \cup \{\epsilon\} \text{ s.t.}$$
$$(x_1, a, c, y_1) \in E_1, (x_2, c, b, y_2) \in E_2$$

satisfies

$$| T_3 | = | T_2 \odot T_1 | (u) = | T_2(| T_1 | (u)), \forall u \in \Sigma_1^*$$

3   Modeling of Monitors as FST

3.1   Events Definition

Let ξ be the set of all possible events that can be exhibited by the program or propagated by the transducers. Each member in ξ is defined by $e_{name} < a >$ (we sometimes refer to it as just e_{name}), where $a \in A$ such that A is a set of all system actions and where a is defined by the pair (r, s) such that r is the range or scope of interest, i.e., before or after, and s is the statement(s) enclosed inside the action.

For example, if we want to have a monitor event that monitors just before the creation of files then the monitored event will be in the form of $createFile < before, s >$, where $createFile$ is the monitoring event for the method of file creation, s is the enclosed statement(s) inside the file creation method, and r is the range of the event that can take one of three values: "before" (marking the position before the execution of the action), "after" (marking the position after execution of the action) and "." (this is only used for $result\ events\ R$, see Section 3.1, since their intended meaning does not carry position on their own instead they depends on the action on which they refer to (i.e., follow).)

Events Types: In this model we distinguish between two types of events that can exist mainly:

- **Specification Events:** These are the events that are the monitors want to observe in the target, like the $createFile$ event example above. We refer to this type of events as E_{spec} such that $E_{spec} \subset \xi$.
- **Result Events:** These are exactly two events, that each monitor output to indicate its recommended remedial action for the seen events. Precisely we define the set of result events $R \subset \xi$ as follows:

$$R = \{proceed < (., s_{\rho_m}) >, skip < (., s_{\rho_m}) >\} \tag{1}$$

with the meaning to "*proceed*" or "*skip*" the execution of the previous events while executing statements "*s*" in the environment ρ_m of their monitor "*m*".

Events Matching: We define matching of events and matching of sets of events as follows:

- Two events $e < (r, s) >$ and $e' < (r', s') >$ match *iff* $e = e'$.
- Two ordered sets of event τ_a and τ_b, s.t $\tau_a, \tau_b \in \xi^*$, match *iff* $e_{a_i} = e_{b_i}$, where i is the index of the event in each set.

3.2   Monitors Modeling Architecture

The model is composed of two main layers of transducers, the first is a simple transducer (we call it TM_{pgm}) that models the targets' events and is responsible for propagating them to the next layer of transducers (we call the TM_{net}) which in turn is responsible for enforcing different specifications.

We define a composition function between the two layers of monitor transducers as:

$$comp = TM_{pgm}; TM_{net}; TM_{pgm} \tag{2}$$

The above function specifies how the composition between monitor transducers should take place, such that the output of the TM_{pgm} is read by TM_{net} and the output of the TM_{net} is read by the TM_{pgm}. The TM_{pgm} should only react to the output of final TM in the TM_{net} transducers, thus it should not be able to see any internal events that are used for internal communication between monitors.

We next define the model of TM_{pgm} and TM_{net}.

3.3   Modeling of a Program Monitor TM_{pgm}

We define the program monitor TM_{pgm} $(\Sigma_1, \Sigma_2, Q, i, F, \otimes, *)$ as a letter transducer as follows:

- Q: three states, *Read*, *Wait* and *End*.
- Σ_1: is the set of input events $\{e_{in} : e_{in} \in \xi^*\}$. That is $\Sigma_1 \subseteq \{R \cup E_{spec}\}$.
- Σ_2: is the set of output events $\{e_{out} : e_{out} \in \{\xi \cup \epsilon\}^*\}$. That is $\Sigma_2 \subseteq \{R \cup E_{spec} \cup \epsilon\}$
- i: *Read*
- F: *End*
- $\otimes$ is a deterministic transition function for letter transducers from $Q \times \Sigma_1^*$ to $Q : q \otimes \tau = q'$.
- $*$ is the partial emission function for letter transducers mapping from $Q \times \Sigma_1^*$ to $\Sigma_2 : q * \tau = \tau'$.

Figure 1 shows the Transducer of the program monitor TM_{pgm}, where we write the notation x/y to refer to the input and output events respectively.

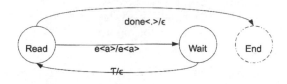

Fig. 1. TM_{pgm}

Semantics for TM_{pgm}:

— *Reading Program Events-Step:*

if $q = $ "Read", then

$$q \otimes e < a >= \text{"Wait"} , q * e < a >= e < a > \tag{3}$$

— *Reading TM_{pgm} Monitor Result-Step:*

if $q = $ "Wait" and $\tau' \in \Sigma_1^*$, then

$$q \otimes \tau = \text{"Read"} , q * \tau = \epsilon \tag{4}$$

— *Stop-Step:*

if $q = $ "Read" & $e < a >= done < . >$,then

$$q \otimes e < a >= \text{"End"}, q * e < a >= \epsilon \tag{5}$$

3.4   Modeling Monitor Transducers in TM_{net} Monitor

Construction of TM monitors (Transducer Monitor) in TM_{net} is simple, it follows the definition of finite state transducer monitors in Section 2.1.

A **TM Monitor** is defined as a variation of a finite state transducer TM, as the tuple $(\Sigma_1, \Sigma_2, Q, 1, \otimes, *)$ such that $\epsilon \notin |TM|(\epsilon)$ and:

— Σ_1: is the the set of input events such that $\Sigma_1 \subseteq \{\xi \cup \epsilon\}$, such that $\Sigma_1 = \{e_{in} : e_{in} \in \{\xi \cup \epsilon\}\}$.
— Σ_2: contains the same alphabet of Σ_1, that is, it is the set of output events, such that $\Sigma_2 \subseteq \xi$, such that $\Sigma_2 = \{e_{out} : e_{out} \in \xi\}$.
— Q is the set of states.
— 1 is the initial state.
— $\otimes$ is a deterministic transition function from $Q \times \Sigma_1^*$ to $Q : q \otimes \tau = q'$, where q and q' are the current and next states of the monitor and $\tau \in \Sigma_1^*$ is the input set of events.
— $*$ is the partial emission function mapping from $Q \times \Sigma_1^*$ to $\Sigma_2^* : q * \tau = \tau'$, where $\tau \in \Sigma_1^*$ and $\tau' \in \Sigma_2^*$ are the set of input and output events respectively.

Informally speaking, each monitor is defined in our model as a variation of finite state transducer which upon receiving a set of events it moves from one state to another (could be the same state) while outputting either the same set of events (thus propagating them)or else appending an element of R to the received set of events, the following specify the restrictions on the emission function:

$$q * \tau = \tau, \text{ where } \tau \in \Sigma_2^* \tag{6}$$

OR

$$q * \tau = \tau; e < a >, \text{ where } e < a > \in R \tag{7}$$

3.5   Identifying Potential Conflicts

Informally speaking, conflicts among monitors happens when the same program event invokes more than one monitor with possibly different remedial actions. Thus conflicts between TM monitors, before composition (i.e., the design of the TM monitor instrumented as a single specification on the program), can simply be identified by using intersection of the input alphabet (excluding R) of the n existing transducers in the system: $\forall_i \bigcap \{\Sigma_{1i} - R\} \neq \emptyset$ for $i - 1..n$.

Or in other words we define conflict between two monitor transducers $TM_x = (\Sigma_{x1}, \Sigma_{x2}, Q_x, 1, Q_x, E_x)$ and $TM_y(\Sigma_{y1}, \Sigma_{y2}, Q_y, 1, Q_y, E_y)$ as:

$$\exists TM_{x_i} - (q_{x_i}, e < a >, e' < a' >, q'_{x_i}) \text{ and } \exists TM_{y_j} = (q_{y_j}, e < u >, e'' < u' >, q'_{y_j}) \tag{8}$$

where $e < a > \notin R$ and $e < a > \neq \epsilon$

3.6   Conflict Resolution with TM Composition

For those monitor transducers that have conflicts as show in Section 3.5, one can distinguish between three types of scenarios to resolve conflicts:

- Allow only a single remedial action.
- Allow both remedial action but in a precise order.
- Allow one monitor to delay its remedial action and base it on the remedial action taken place by the other monitor.

Our model of TM monitors support all the above scenarios, which scenario to be used however should be provided by a monitor specification language that would express which way to go.

Our solution to resolve conflicts among TM monitors is by composing them. The idea behind composition of two or more transducers is that each TM monitor transducer actually gives a distinct output for events that it cares about, while acting as identity function on all other inputs, i.e., propagating other irrelevant events to the next transducer in the chain of conflicting TM monitors. This provides a natural way of composition that does not change almost anything in the original transducers since the identity transition can be easily added as follows:

$$q \otimes \tau = q \text{ and } q * \tau = \tau, \text{ where } \tau \text{ is a set of input events} \tag{9}$$

Transducer Composition: Since our TM monitors are such transducer where $\epsilon \notin |TM|(\epsilon)$, a *letter* conflicting TM monitors TM_x and TM_y can be resolved by finding their composed letter TM monitor. Thus, if

$$TM_x = (\Sigma_{x1}, \Sigma_{x2}, Q_x, 1, Q_x, E_x) \text{ and } TM_y = (\Sigma_{y1}, \Sigma_{y2}, Q_y, 1, Q_y, E_y)$$

Then there exists an $TM_{comp} = TM_y \odot TM_x$ such that for each $\tau \in \Sigma_1^*$,

$$|TM_y \odot TM_x|(\tau) = |TM_y|(|TM_x|(\tau))$$

3.7   Modeling Monitors Not in Conflict

Monitors that do not lay in conflict with others do not need to be in composition, since they potentially have different interests in event. Thus an equivalent union TM can represent those with disjoint interests, even though their composition to the rest of the network is also correct and thus can always be an option.

3.8   Other Composition Usages

As mentioned in Section 3.6 allowing composition of TM monitors can be used for more than just for resolving conflicts. TM monitors up in the chain of composition can be used to alter received events from other transducers (instead of acting as identity function) and thus changing the resulting output for the set of transducers. This change requires user's intervention and it is based on user's definition and the privileges each TM monitor is granted.

With such allowances, the output for the set of transducers will require a different interpretation, since it is going to be the decomposed output for each transition. We now define how to interpret the resulting output for a series of TM monitors.

Interpreting Transducers Results: The output of a composed set of TM monitors is a set of events that keeps growing (element in ξ^*). Suppose we have composition between n TM monitors in the form $TM_1; TM_2; ...; TM_n$, and if $e < a >$ is a the current monitored event generated by the program, and if q_1 to q_n represent the current state for $TM_1, ..TM_n$ respectively then, the generated set of output O of the last TM_n in a composed chain would be:

$$O = \{q_{pgm} * e < a >, q_1 * (q_{pgm} * e < a >), q_2 * (q_1 * (q_{pgm} * e < a >))...\} =$$

$$O = \{e < a >, e' < a' >, e'' < a'' >, ..\}$$

where $\{e < a >, e' < a' >, e'' < a'' >, ..\}$ represents the set of events results from each transition.

The output of the transducers can be evaluated (from left to right) using these two rewrite rules for *skip* and *proceed*. We use the notation $[.., x], [x, ..], [.., x, ..]$

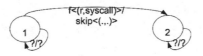

Fig. 2. TM (letter transducer version) for No System Calls Specification

to refer to an open set either from the right side, left side or both sides. Also, in the following rules mi refers to the monitor that generated an event:

$$[...e < (r, S_{\rho_{target}}) >, proceed < (., S_{\rho_{mi}}) >, ...] \xrightarrow{\text{rewrites to}} \\ [e' < (r, S_{\rho_{mi}}; S_{\rho_{target}}) >, ...] \tag{10}$$

$$[...e < (r, S_{\rho_{target}}) >, skip < (., S_{\rho_{mi}}) >, ...] \xrightarrow{\text{rewrites to}} [e < (r, S_{\rho_{mi}}) >, ...] \tag{11}$$

Rule 10 has two versions depending on the scope of the event $e < a >$, the one shown assumes that $r = before$. The rule matches when a *proceed* event is first encountered (since an event can be repeatedly propagated from one TM monitor to another). The rule basically resumes with the action of the event $< r, S_{target} >$ while executing the monitor's statements in the monitor's own environment ρ_{mi}.

Rule 11 also matches when the first *skip* event is encountered. It evaluates to another event that skips the action statement $< S_{target} >$ and executes the statements S in the environment of the monitor ρ_{mi}

Few notes to observe here:

– An *around* scope can be expressed in this model by passing the same $e < a >$ twice, each with a different scope.
– Also, even though skipping of action $e < a >$ that has an after scope, will basically have no effect on the monitored program, since the transducers are skipping an already executed event.
– When a *skip* rule is encountered it actually skips *all* actions of monitors, including skipping the original action of the program. And that actually makes sense since the events and their actions will be wrapped with other *proceed* of *skip*.
– A TM should not have a transition of the form (q, x, y, q') where $y \in R$ unless it has certain privileges on the pervious composed transducer in the chain. This privileges should be defined using the monitoring specification language.

3.9   Example

Shown in figure 2 and figure 3, the TM monitors for composition of the specification of *No System Calls* and *File Network Wall*. We use the notation ? to

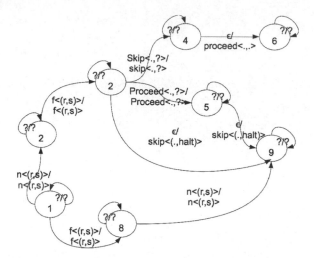

Fig. 3. File Network Wall TM (letter transducer version) after Composition with No System Calls TM

refer to other events (or statements) that are not of concern to the specification, it should generally be taken as *anything*. Also, $f < a >$ is a file access event, $n < a >$ is a network access event and ϵ can be read only when the input events from the pervious TM in the chain are consumed.

The *No System Calls* specification prevents system calls from happening by skipping the event along with its action. while the *File Network Wall* specification halts the program whenever there is a file access after a network access or vise versa.

The two specifications are dependent on each other, since a file access can in fact be a system call invocation, and if the two specifications were composed together in such a way that the *No System Calls* would be checked first, then there would be no violation to the *File Network Wall* specification if the event was already skipped by the previous specification.

4   Conclusion and Future Work

This paper describes a framework for modeling monitors which can be used to resolve conflicts between conflicting monitors. In the model we express monitors as a finite state transducer, where conflicting monitors are composed and other non-conflicting monitors can be grouped with union.

The model gives a little power of control of one monitor on another, by allowing one monitor to change in the output set of events previously received from other monitors.

A future work for the model is to build a specification language on top of the TM framework to define TM monitors and to build the appropriate composition among them.

References

1. Allan, C., Avgustinov, P., Christensen, A.S., Hendren, L.J., Kuzins, S., Lhoták, O., de Moor, O., Sereni, D., Sittampalam, G., Tibble, J.: Adding trace matching with free variables to AspectJ. In: Object-Oriented Programming, Systems, Languages and Applications (OOPSLA 2005), pp. 345–364. ACM (2005)
2. Bauer, L., Ligatti, J., Walker, D.: A language and system for enforcing run-time security policies. Tech. Rep. TR-699-04, Princeton University (2004)
3. Bauer, L., Ligatti, J., Walker, D.: Composing security policies with polymer. SIGPLAN Not. 40, 305–314 (2005)
4. Chen, F., Roşu, G.: MOP: An efficient and generic runtime verification framework. In: Object-Oriented Programming, Systems, Languages and Applications (OOPSLA 2007), pp. 569–588. ACM (2007)
5. Erlingsson, U., Schneider, F.B.: IRM enforcement of java stack inspection. In: IEEE Symposium on Security and Privacy (SOSP 2000), pp. 246–255. IEEE (2000)
6. Evans, D.: Policy-Directed Code Safety. Ph.D. thesis, MIT (2000)
7. Evans, D., Twyman, A.: Flexible policy-directed code safety. In: IEEE Symposium on Security and Privacy (SOSP 1999), pp. 32–45. IEEE (1999)
8. Hamlen, K.W., Jones, M.: Aspect-oriented in-lined reference monitors. In: Workshop on Programming Languages and Analysis for Security (PLAS 2008), pp. 11–20. ACM (2008)
9. Jones, M., Hamlen, K.W.: Enforcing IRM security policies: two case studies. In: Intelligence and Security Informatics (ISI 2009), pp. 214–216. IEEE (2009)
10. Kiczales, G., Hilsdale, E., Hugunin, J., Kersten, M., Palm, J., Griswold, W.G.: An Overview of AspectJ. In: Lee, S.H. (ed.) ECOOP 2001. LNCS, vol. 2072, pp. 327–353. Springer, Heidelberg (2001)
11. Ligatti, J.A.: Policy Enforcement via Program Monitoring. Ph.D. thesis, Princeton University (2006)
12. Ligatti, J., Ligatti, J., Bauer, L., Walker, D.: Edit automata: Enforcement mechanisms for run-time security policies. Journal of Information Security 4, 2–16 (2003)
13. Lomsak, D., Ligatti, J.: PoliSeer: A tool for managing complex security policies. In: International Federation for Information Processing Conference on Trust Management, IFIP-TM (2010)
14. Meredith, P.O., Jin, D., Griffth, D., Chen, F., Roşu, G.: An overview of monitoring oriented programming. Journal on Software Tools for Technology Transfer (to appear, 2011)
15. Meredith, P.O., Jin, D., Griffth, D., Chen, F., Roşu, G.: An overview of the MOP runtime verification framework. Journal on Software Techniques for Technology Transfer (to appear, 2011)
16. Roche, E., Schabes, Y. (eds.): Finite-State Language Processing. Bradford Book, MIT Press, Cambridge, Massachusetts (1997)

Real Time Facial Expression Recognition

Saumil Srivastava

Jaypee Institute of Information Technology, Computer Science Department, Noida India
saumildade@gmail.com

Abstract. This paper discusses Facial Expression Recognition System which performs facial expression analysis in a near real time from a live web cam feed. Primary objectives were to get results in a near real time with light invariant, person independent and pose invariant way. The system is composed of two different entities trainer and evaluator. Each frame of video feed is passed through a series of steps including haar classifiers, skin detection, feature extraction, feature points tracking, creating a learned Support Vector Machine model to classify emotions to achieve a tradeoff between accuracy and result rate. A processing time of 100-120 ms per 10 frames was achieved with accuracy of around 60%. We measure our accuracy in terms of variety of interaction and classification scenarios. We conclude by discussing relevance of our work to human computer interaction and exploring further measures that can be taken.

Keywords: Haar Classifier, SVM, Shi Tomasi Corner Detection, facial expression analysis, affective user interface.

1   Introduction

Major component of human communication are facial expressions which constitute around 55 percent of total communicated message [1]. We use facial expressions not only to express our emotions, but also to provide important communicative cues during social interaction, such as our level of interest, our desire to take a speaking turn and continuous feedback signaling understanding of the information conveyed.

There has been a global rush for facial expression recognition over the last few years. A number of methods have been proposed but no single method which is both efficient in terms of memory and time complexity has yet been found.

In 1978, Paul Ekman and Wallace V. Friesen published the Facial Action Coding System (FACS)[14], which, 30 years later, is still the most widely used method available. Through observational and electromyography study of facial behavior, they determined how the contraction of each facial muscle, both singly and in unison with other muscles, changes the appearance of the face. It talks about six basic emotions (anger, disgust, fear, joy, sorrow, surprise). FACS codes expressions using a combination of 44 facial movements called as action units (AU"s).While lot of work on FACS has been done and also FACS being an efficient, objective method to describe facial expressions, it is not without its drawbacks. Coding a subject's video is

N. Meghanathan et al. (Eds.): CCSIT 2012, Part III, LNICST 86, pp. 124–133, 2012.
© Institute for Computer Sciences, Social Informatics and Telecommunications Engineering 2012

a time- and labor-intensive process that must be performed frame by frame. A trained, certified FACS coder takes on average 2 hours to code 2 minutes of video. In situations where real-time feedback is desired and necessary, manual FACS coding is not a viable option.

This gives rise to our problem statement i.e. to be able to infer emotions in real time using a live video feed with the following challenges

- To be able to provide results in real time
- To be able to make a person independent model
- To be efficient in classifying the emotions into one of the following anger smile, surprise, neutral
- Light Invariant Application
- Pose Invariant

Pantic and Rothkrantz[2] suggested three basic problems for expression analysis, the three steps that can be identified as three separate problems in the whole process i.e. face detection in a facial image or image sequence ,facial expression data extraction and facial expression classification. Face detection methods that have been around mostly assumes frontal face view in image or image sequence being analyzed. Viola & Jones [3] provides competitive face detection in real time, uses the adaboost algorithm to exhaustively pass a search window over the image at various scales for rapid detections. Essa & Pentland[4] perform spatial and temporal filtering together with thresholding to identify the motion blobs from image sequence. To detect face then Eigen face method [5] is used .The PersonSpotter system [6] tracks the bounding box of the head in video using spatio-temporal filtering and disparity in pixels ,thereby selecting the ROI's and then passing through skin detector and convex region detector to check for face.

Second step involves face data extraction, Littleworth et al. [7] used a bank of 40 gabor filters at different scale and orientations to apply convolution on the image and then complex value response was recorded as in [8]. Essa & Pentland [4] use the same face extraction image to find facial feature points using a set of sample images via FFT and local energy computation. Cohn et al. [9] firstly normalize the feature points in first frame of image sequence and then use optical flow to track them .The displacement vectors for each landmark between the initial and peak frame represent the extracted information. Other methods include AAM, T.F.Cootes [10] et al. uses a statistical model of shape and grey-level appearance of object of interest which can generalize to almost any valid example .Match is obtained in a few iterations by changing parameters in accordance to residual of trained and current image.

Third step involves classification of emotions based on a training model constructed on the properties related to feature points for this purpose we have created our learning model using support vector machines[11].

2   Implementation

The overall system has been developed using C/C++ with support of OpenCV, libSVM[11] libraries. The overall process can be shown as follows

Fig. 1. The overall process for facial expression recognition

2.1   Detection of Haar Like Features (Viola & Jones [3])

Viola and Jones in 2001 published their breakthrough work which allowed appearance based methods to run in real time, while keeping the same or improved accuracy.

Rectangle Features
The sums of the pixels which lie within the white rectangles are subtracted from the sum of pixels in the grey rectangles.

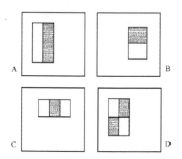

Fig. 2. Examples of Haar-like feature sets

Rectangle Features can be computed very rapidly using an intermediate representation called integral image. The value of the integral image at point (x,y) is the sum of all the pixels above and to the left.

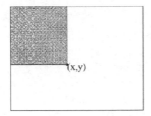

Fig. 3. The value of the integral image at point (x,y) is the sum of all the pixels above and to the left

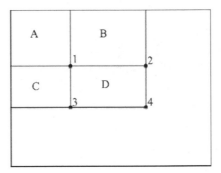

Fig. 4. The sum of pixels within D can be computed as $4+1-(2+3)$

Scan image at multiple positions and scales as in previous approaches. Apply Adaboost strong classifier (which is based on Rectangle Features) to decide whether the search window contains a face or not.

Adaboost Strong Classifier: linear combination of weak classifiers. $H(x) = 1$ if window x has a face and 0 otherwise

$$H(x) = \begin{cases} 1 \text{ if } \sum_{t=1}^{T} \alpha_t h_t(x) \geq \phi & \longrightarrow \text{Threshold} \\ & \longrightarrow \text{Weak Classifier} \\ 0 \text{ otherwise} & \longrightarrow \text{Weights} \end{cases}$$

$$h_j(x) = \begin{cases} 1 \text{ if } p_j f_j(x) < p_j \theta_j & \longrightarrow \text{Threshold} \\ & \longrightarrow \text{Sign} \\ 0 \text{ otherwise} & \longrightarrow \text{Rectangle Feature} \end{cases}$$

Each week classifier corresponds to a single Rectangle Feature

Adaboost ensembles many weak classifiers into one single strong classifier

1. Initialize sample weights
2. For each cycle:
   Find a classifier/rectangle feature that performs well on the weighted samples.
   Increase weights of misclassified examples.
3. Return a weighted combination of classifiers

Attentional Cascade

1. We start with simple classifiers which reject many of the negative subwindows
2. While detecting almost all positive sub-windows
3. Positive results from the first classifier triggers the evaluation of a second (more complex) classifier, and so on
4. A negative outcome at any point leads to the immediate rejection of the subwindow
6. The attentional cascade is based on the assumption that within an image, most sub-images are non-face instances.

2.2   Face Detection

Each frame is processed firstly through Haar classifiers [3] trained for profile faces. To further improve frame rate and compensate for pose variation. We propose to use interleaved Haar Classifiers. Interleaving is done between front and profile classifiers.

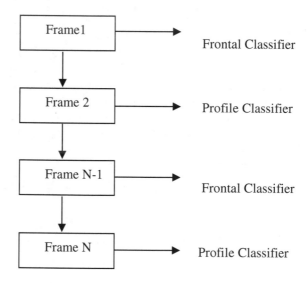

Fig. 5. Interleaved Classifiers

Second to reduce false results produce, output of last step is passed through skin detection algorithm [13].This step makes sure that the region selected is a face. If both profile and frontal faces are not detected and if face has been initialized then Optical Flow [9] is applied to track those feature points which is discussed below.

2.3   Facial Feature Point Extraction

After face has been detected, we narrow our work zone to detected region thereby reducing the search area and improving frame rate. Now face is divided geometrically to find feature points and further confine the search area.

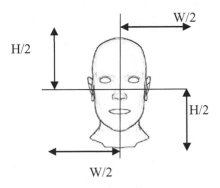

Fig. 6. Geometrically Divided Face

Then classifiers for eyes, nose, and mouth are used in the narrowed output region. After that sobel derivative is applied on the region, The function calculates the image derivative by convolving the image with the appropriate kernel

$$\mathtt{dst}\,(x,y) = \frac{d^{xorder+yorder}\mathtt{src}}{dx^{xorder} \cdot dy^{yorder}}$$

The Sobel operators combine Gaussian smoothing and differentiation so the result is more or less resistant to the noise. Most often, the function is called with (xorder = 1, yorder = 0, apertureSize = 3) or (xorder = 0, yorder = 1, apertureSize = 3) to calculate the first x- or y- image derivative.

After that corners are detected using Shi-Tomasi algorithm[12], The function finds the corners with big eigenvalues in the image. The function first calculates the minimal eigenvalue for every source image pixel and stores them. Then it performs non-maxima suppression (only the local maxima in neighborhood are retained). The next step rejects the corners with the minimal eigenvalue less than quality level of maximum eigen value . Finally, the function ensures that the distance between any two corners is not smaller than minDistance. The weaker corners (with a smaller min eigenvalue) that are too close to the stronger corners are rejected , thus 21 feature points are selected (*Fig 7.b*). If face is not detected by classifier then based on previous 21 feature vector using Optical Flow method[9] (*Fig 7.c*).

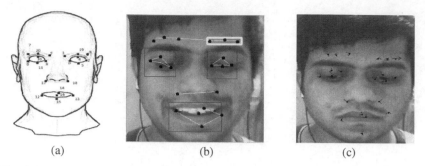

(a)   (b)   (c)

Fig. 7. (a) 21 feature points on face *(b)* When face detected*(c)* When face not detected

Optical Flow states that given a set of points in an image, find those same points in another image. or, given point [ux, uy]T in image I 1 find the point [ux + δx, uy + δy]T in image I 2 that minimizes ε:

$$\varepsilon(\delta_x, \delta_y) = \sum_{x=u_x-w_x}^{u_x+w_x} \sum_{y=u_y-w_y}^{u_y+w_y} \left(I_1(x, y) - I_2(x+\delta_x, y+\delta_y)\right)$$

(the Σ/w's are needed due to the aperture problem)

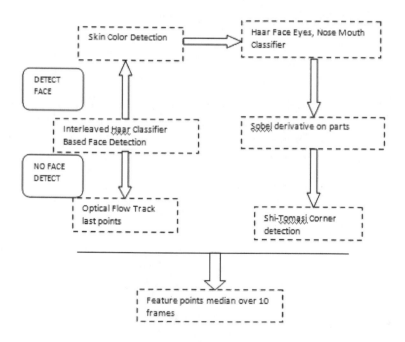

Fig. 8. Over all Feature Extraction Diagram

Median of 21 points over the next ten frames is taken so as to account for any error in calculation that may be occurring like it's not always necessary that we detect all 21 points in which frame, to reduce such error we take median over the 10 frame intervals hence reducing error.

The overall process can be summarized as below

2.4   SVM Classification

Displacements of 21 feature points is used as an input to SVM classifier first a model is created with help of libSVM[11] by training and then Evaluator is used to classify emotions based on the learned model created.

Most computational overhead resides in the training phase. However, due to the fact that the training set is interactively created by the user and hence limited in magnitude and that the individual training examples are of constant and small size, overhead is low for typical training runs.

Training on different individuals lead to model being more of person independent nature. For training purposes 5 subjects 4 expressions (Neutral, Smile, Angry, and Excited) were used.

3   Results

The confusion matrix based on various interaction clips is shown in table below

	Neutral	Smile	Angry	Excited	Over all
Neutral	15	3	12	0	50%
Smile	5	18	5	2	60%
Angry	10	5	13	2	43.3 %
Excited	0	4	0	26	86.6 7%
				Total	59.9 1%

4   Conclusions and Future Work

Average frame processing time 120-150ms per 10 frames. It was observed that result was directly proportional to intensity of training provided. It was also observed that result was robust to pose variations; light intensity changes and is person independent model. Also the result was robust to background changes.

Further work : To minimize the effect of camera distance from user ,also to make database more extensive so as to improve results, link with Paul Ekman's FACS Action Units [14] to increase range of emotions to be tracked and also to be more accurate.

Inclusion of emotions in human computer interface is an emerging field. It provides us with many new opportunities. Development of computationally effective and robust solutions will lead to increased importance of user in the process and set stage for revolutionary interactivity.

Acknowledgments Dr. Krishna Asawa, Associate Professor, Jaypee Institute of Information Technology, Noida mentored me throughout the project and without her project would not have been possible.

References

[1] Mehrabian, A.: Communication without words. Psychology Today 2(4), 53–56 (1968)
[2] Pantic, M., Rothkrantz, L.J.M.: Automatic analysis of facial expressions: The state of the art. IEEE Transactions on Pattern Analysis and Machine Intelligence 22(12), 1424–1445 (2000)
[3] Viola, P., Jones, M.: Robust Real-Time Face Detection. Int'l J. Computer Vision 57(2), 137–154 (2004)
[4] Essa, I., Pentland, A.: Coding, analysis, interpretation and recognition of facial expressions. IEEE Transactions on Pattern Analysis and Machine Intelligence 19(7), 757–763 (1997)
[5] Turk, M., Pentland, A.: Eigenfaces for recognition. Journal of Cognitive Neuroscience 3(1), 71–86 (1991)
[6] Steffens, J., Elagin, E., Neven, H.: Personspotter—fast and robust system for human detection, tracking, and recognition. In: Proceedings International Conference on Automatic Face and Gesture Recognition, pp. 516–521 (1998)
[7] Littlewort, G., Fasel, I., Stewart Bartlett, M., Movellan, J.R.: Fully automatic coding of basic expressions from video. Technical Report, UCSD INC MPLab (March 2002)
[8] Lades, M., Vorbrüggen, J.C., Buhmann, J., Lange, J., von der Malsburg, C., Würtz, R.P., Konen, W.: Distortion invariant object recognition in the dynamic link architecture. IEEE Transactions on Computers 42, 300–311 (1993)
[9] Cohn, J.F., Zlochower, A.J., Lien, J.J., Kanade, T.: Feature-point tracking by optical flow discriminates subtle differences in facial expression. In: Proceedings International Conference on Automatic Face and Gesture Recognition, pp. 396–401 (1998)
[10] Cootes, T.F., Edwards, G.J., Taylor, C.J.: Active Appearance Models. In: Burkhardt, H., Neumann, B. (eds.) ECCV 1998. LNCS, vol. 1407, pp. 484–498. Springer, Heidelberg (1998)
[11] Chang, C.-C., Lin, C.-J.: LIBSVM: a library for support vector machines (2001), Software available at http://www.csie.ntu.edu.tw/~cjlin/libsvm

[12] Shi, J., Tomasi, C.: Good Features To Track. In: Proceedings CVPR 1994, Computer Vision and Pattern Recognition (1994)

[13] Farhad, D., Abdolhossein, S.: An adaptive real-time skin detector based on Hue thresholding: A comparison on two motion tracking methods. Elsevier (2006)

[14] Ryan, A., Cohn, J.F., Lucey, S., Saragih, J., Lucey, P., De la Torre, F., Rossi, A.: Automated Facial Expression Recognition System. In: 43rd Annual 2009 International Carnahan Conference on Security Technology (2009)

[15] Open CV, http://opencv.willowgarage.com/wiki/

Face Recognition System in Cell Phones Based on Text Message Service

Suman Deb, Sourav Biswas, Chinmoy Debnath,
Suddhasatta Dhar, and Priyanka Deb

Department of Computer Science and Engineering. National Institute of Technology Agartala,
Jirania, Tripura - 799 055
{sumandebcs,souravbiswas.cs,suddha14}@gmail.com,
{chinmoy_cse,priyanka_nita.cse07}@ymail.com

Abstract. Face Recognition is a task human performs remarkably easily and successfully. This technology being easy to use, non-intrusive and simple to implement with less hardware requirements has a great advantage over other conventional biometrics. The goal of our work is to present face recognition with the help of sms/text messaging service on mobile platform to enlarge the scope of face recognition in the field of social security. This paper is aimed to help people recognizing any suspects or criminals as well as informing the concerned authorities with the help of sms. The use of mobile based platform gives the portability and versatility to this project. We plan to introduce the sms based face recognition technique which makes the work more scalable and also eliminates the use of GPRS or any other similar services, which is availed by less number of people compared to the total number of cell phone users.

Keywords: SMS, non-invasive, principle component analysis, eigen face.

1   Introduction

Face Recognition has been an emerging technology for last fifteen years or more. The technique is easy to use, non-invasive as well as non-intrusive. As a result it found uses in passport authentications, time attendance systems, control access systems and more.

Despite of all the advantages, this technology has its own limitations. To build up a realistic face recognition system, training sets and a huge database of facial images and large processing power for parsing and other operations is required. This has been the primary obstacle in using this technique in mobile platforms. In this work we provided a cost-effective solution for using face recognition technology on cell phones for the purpose of social security.

1.1   Face Recognition in Cell Phones

The main purpose of this work is the implementation of recognition techniques of human faces in cell phones with a view of enhancing the social security. We have

N. Meghanathan et al. (Eds.): CCSIT 2012, Part III, LNICST 86, pp. 134–141, 2012.

selected Android OS as the mobile OS due to its adequate knowledgebase for developers. The inbuilt face detect class can detect faces efficiently from a given picture which acts as an aid to our face recognition system. A remote centralized database connected with a remote processing has been used to store the personal information related to faces. The processing unit accepts the detected face from the cell phone, processes and recognizes the face and give a relevant feed back to the sender.

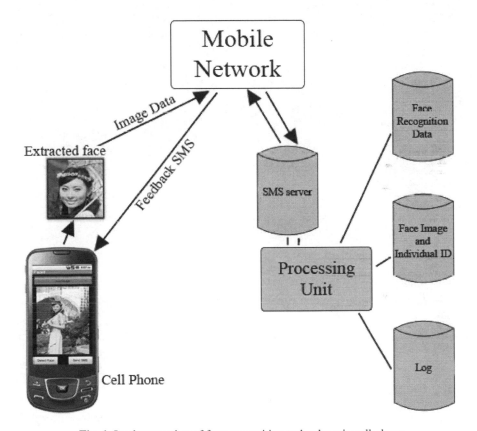

Fig. 1. Implementation of face recognition technology in cell phone

1.2   SMS Based Face Recognition Technology

This technique implies that any type of communication between the cell phone and the remote computer will be through sms/text message service. We have selected text messaging as a data application in this paper, due to its wide range user, its omnipresence and cost effectiveness. About 74% of all mobile phone subscribers use this service as a means to communicate. Text messaging service is available to almost any type of standard GSM network. Compared to any other means of communication available in mobile network, this service is one of the cheapest and fastest ways to communicate. Our remote computer is connected with a sms server to communicate with the mobile phone.

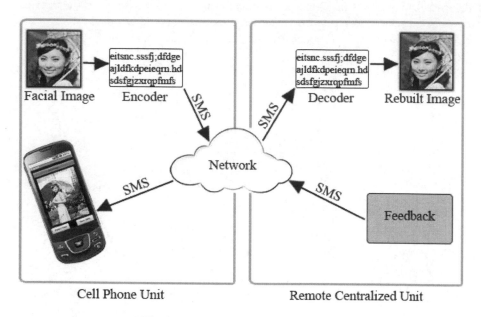

Fig. 2. Communication via text messages

2   Implementation of Face Recognition Technique

The face recognition system in this paper is a modular system. It consists of four primary modules.

2.1   Face Detect

This is the only module installed on the mobile platform. This module processes an image taken by a cell phone camera, to detect a face in the photograph. If a face is detected then the facial image is cropped and resized to 50X50 pixels size for optimized storage.

Fig. 3. Cropped facial images of size 50X50 pixels

The image is then compressed and encoded to a text message and is sent to the remote computer which is connected with a centralized database.

Most of the popular mobile OS has inbuilt Face Detect class/function. We have used the Android's Face Detect class for this module.

2.2   Image Processing

This module on the remote computer, decodes the sms received from the sms server, and rebuilds the facial image. The module adjusts the contrast and brightness of the image to a threshold value for better extraction.

2.3   Face Extraction

OpenCV HaarCascade method is implemented to extract face from the image received from the previous image. A classifier is loaded in this method which scans the image for any region which is likely to be face. The classifier returns "1" if face is found, or else it returns "0".

Next step performs the PCA algorithm on a training set, which has been created from the facial images in the database. Principal Component Analysis algorithm analyses data by performing dimensionality reduction where the projection of the original image onto a lower dimensional space takes place. The PCA subspace is calculated and the training images are converted to points in the subspace. All these data are then stored.

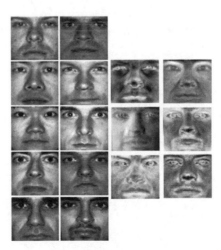

Fig. 4. Face extraction by Eigen's face method using training sets

2.4   Recognition Implementing Eigen's Method

This module loads all the images from the database and projects each image onto the PCA subspace. Then the closest projected training image is located. If the closeness is beyond a threshold value, then the result is taken as a positive match, and a relevant feedback text message is sent to the sender of the image.

3   Image to Text Conversion

In this paper, the two dimensional matrix consisting of the average RGB value of each pixel has been converted to a string array which goes through a proposed lossless string compression algorithm for the sake of reducing the output string size to 160 characters so as to accommodate in a single text message. This will avoid broken sms error, thus ensures data integrity while transmitting. Our proposed data compression algorithm is a combination of Huffman coding and Base 64 coding.

3.1   Encoding

This technique is carried out in the cell phone. Huffman algorithm is first applied to the string array. A binary Huffman tree is built. Then the output string is encoded with Base 64 and the Huffman tree is appended with the output separated by a separator (a special character we used for separating the string from the Huffman tree). Then a character counter checks whether the whole string is under 160 characters. If the check returns negative, then the string is passed to the Huffman function again. This method will iterate until a string with 160 characters or less is produced. The number of iterations will be appended in the end before sending the final string to the remote computer through a sms server.

3.2   Decoding

This algorithm is implemented on the remote computer to rebuild the image from the received text message. The first step is to separate the Huffman tree from the string. Then Base 64 decoding is performed and subsequently Huffman decoding is performed by the separated Huffman tree. In this way after the same number of iterations, the two dimensional pixel matrix can be obtained from which the image can be rebuilt.

4   Testing

We performed black box and white box testing on a database of face image. The efficiency of the recognition is quiet high for frontal faces which decreases gradually on rotating the face.

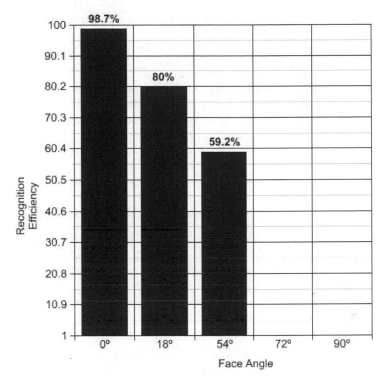

Fig. 5. Face reconition efficiency (under balanced illumination and noiseless background)

The formula of sms compression efficiency is

Efficiency = (Total char in original SMS – Total char in compressed SMS)
                          Total char in original SMS

The image data we used for compression is as in Fig: 6.

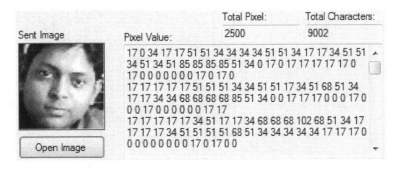

Fig. 6. Extracted pixel value

And the compressed text string with appended header and footer is depicted below.

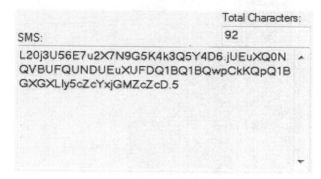

Total Characters:

SMS: 92

L20j3U56E7u2X7N9G5K4k3Q5Y4D6.jUEuXQ0N
QVBUFQUNDUEuXUFDQ1BQ1BQwpCkKQpQ1B
GXGXLly5cZcYxjGMZcZcD.5

Fig. 7. Output text string

Thus efficiency for the above 50X50 pixel image is.

$$(9002\text{-}92)/9002 = 98.97\%$$ (1)

Efficiency for this algorithm is directly proportional to the length of the input string since the number of strings in output of Base 64 will always be within 64 characters. Thus though the compression algorithm is not much efficient for shorter string but for longer strings the algorithm yields more efficiency.

5   Conclusion

In this paper, we have proposed a way in which an individual with a camera phone can easily know the identity of a suspected subject instantly and can help enhance law enforcement. The system extracts the facial image from a photograph and sends it to a remote computer via a sms server. The remote computer then uses the recognition technique to match the face with the database and gives a feedback to the source mobile number. The result of our preliminary experiment shows improved performance in the face detection and the sms compression to the traditionally implemented systems. Current work is focused on the face detection algorithms on mobile platform and the sms compression algorithm. The iterations in the sms compression algorithm add a delay in the process. We propose a threshold value to limit the number of iteration to certain point.

In further work, we intend to improve face recognition effectiveness by implementing other algorithms. On the other hand, the proposed sms compression algorithm can be used in a completely new dimension of text messaging and sending multimedia messages via text messages.

References

1. Huffman, D.A.: A Method for the Construction of Minimum-Redundancy Codes. In: Proceedings of the I.R.E., pp. 1098–1102 (September 1952) Huffman's original article
2. Cormen, T.H., Leiserson, C.E., Rivest, R.L., Stein, C.: Introduction to Algorithms, 2nd edn., Section 16.3, pp. 385–392. MIT Press and McGraw-Hill (2001)
3. Pissarenko, D.: Eigenface-based facial recognition (2003)
4. Acharya, T., Ray, A.: Image Processing: Principles and Applications. Wiley (2005)
5. Nelson, M., Jean, L.G.: The Data Compression Book, 2nd edn. IDG Books Worldwide, Inc., Cambridge (1995)
6. Hashemian, R.: Direct Huffman Code and Decoding Using The Table of Code-Lengths. Northen Illionis University (2005) (unpublished thesis)
7. Bradski, G., Kaehler, A.: O'Reilly Learning OpenCV, 1st edn. (2008)

Requirements Volatility in Software Maintenance

D. Kavitha[1,*] and Ananthi Sheshasaayee[2,**]

[1] Lecturer in Computer Science department,
Nazareth College of Arts and Science,
Chennai, India
d.kavithamoorthy@gmail.com
[2] Computer Science department
Quaid-E-Millath Govt. College for women (Autonomous)
Chennai, India
ananthiseshu@gmail.com

Abstract. Requirements volatility is a common phenomenon present in most software development projects. Change Management dealing with requirement changes is an important function of project managers. If the changes are not handled effectively, then there will be huge difference in efforts, cost, and quality of the Product which results in project delay or project may be failed. Taxonomy of requirements change consists of three components: Change Type, Reason, and Sources. Changes in requirements are additions, deletion or modifications of requirements. These changes to the requirements after the basic set has been agreed to by both clients and maintainers are known as requirement's volatility. Requirements volatility cannot be avoided, but we have to understand the requirements volatility problems to deal with the impact. In this paper we have reviewed the requirement volatility, identified the reasons and sources of changes, and introduced few guidelines to managing changes effectively.

Keywords: Software maintenance, requirement volatility, types of requirement change, reason for requirement change and sources of requirement change.

1 Introduction

Change Management is a set of activities is developed to identify the change, control the change and ensure the change is properly implemented. Changes are indentified and classified into different types under software maintenance.

The requirements change management is concerned with the processes that are used to manage changes to the software requirements. Most of the customers' requirements become clarified during the preliminary study and requirements definition, but it is normal that the requirements change during the project. Therefore, the change management is a very important part of the requirements management.

We have reviewed the requirement volatility, identified the reasons and sources (origin) of changes. Requirement changes are recorded by the change management using the software change request form.

---

* Research Scholar Bharathiyar University.
** GUIDE, HOD & Associate Professor.

N. Meghanathan et al. (Eds.): CCSIT 2012, Part III, LNICST 86, pp. 142–150, 2012.
© Institute for Computer Sciences, Social Informatics and Telecommunications Engineering 2012

1.1   What is Requirements Volatility?

Changes in the requirements after the basic set has been agreed to by both clients and software maintainers are known as requirement volatility.

Requirements volatility is a common fact that is present in most software development projects. Many research published the problems that has been identified in the requirement volatility and also new approaches has been proposed to manage its impact on the software development. If the project managers were not able to manage changes, results in project delay or project may be failed.

When project managers use any tool for documenting requirements and whatever the category of execution model, requirements are bound to change. The only difference is to what extent the change results or impact on project success or failure. If there is a good and effective management mechanism, then there will be success in the project execution.

Requirements are the foundations of the software release process. Requirements provide the basis for estimating costs and schedules as well as developing design and testing specifications. During the execution of the software maintenance, requirement change is agreed by both the client and the software maintainers, which will impacts the cost, schedule, and quality of the resulting product.

Change Requests can be raised by variety of people including users, system operators, maintainers, and external interface teams. Throughout the software release process, the requirements often change in the changing world. During the software release planning, requirements analysis, design, and test reviews, new priorities are established and changes to the release content are requested in the form of change requests being added and/or deleted from the release.

In the maintenance environment, requirements are grouped through change requests that identify feature additions and/or defect corrections. Requirement change is then categorized by requirement type, by the requirement management. A change is one of the important factors that need to be considered in managing requirements change.

Identify the reasons and sources (origin) of requirement changes for review.

2   Review of Literature

The IEEE Standard defines "Software maintenance as the modification of a software product after delivery to correct faults, to improve performance or other attributes, or to adapt the product to a modified environment" [8].

The IEEE Standard for Software configuration management Plans is concerned with the activity of planning for Software configuration management (SCM) [9].

Change Management is also called software configuration management (SCM), is a set of activities are developed to a) identify change b) control change c) ensure that change is being properly implemented , & d) report changes to others who have an interest [16].

Software engineering literature is based on "the assumption of fixed requirements"; this misunderstanding leads managers to believe that they should freeze the requirements before project starts.

However, contrary to this traditional belief most software tends to evolve and requirements change both in the beginning as well as later stages of software development lifecycle.

During the maintenance process of the software projects, Stark has examined the impact of requirements volatility [19]. To deal with the impact of the requirement volatility, we have to identify the requirements volatility problems.

As per Harker and Eason [7] to manage requirements change, we need to classify requirements changes in the proper way. When the software developer classifies the changes, they can easily analyze each type of change and also source for the change and its impact on software development process.

In our maintenance environment a *requirement* is defined as *an approved change request* [19]. According to Stark [19], if we improve the prioritization of requirements during release planning we should be able to reduce the number of releases with added requirements. And also deletions should drop if more accurate staff estimation is there.

Evolution of requirements refers to changes that take place in a set of requirements after initial requirements engineering phase [1]. Thus changes in requirements that may occur in initial elicitation, analysis, specification and validation phases are not evolutionary.

According to Jones [11] more than 70% of large applications (i.e., over 1000 function points) experience requirements volatility.

As per Sommerville, Requirement change is the major root cause of the software project failure [18. Software requirement changes are inevitable and the factors that include software and system requirement, market demand, business goals, work environment and government regulation [2].

Requirements volatility (RV) is generally considered as an unwanted property. It has the possible to produce poor impacts on the software development process [20]. Requirements volatility causes major difficulties during development of the development life cycle. For example, a field study conducted by Curtis et al [5] point out that requirements volatility is one of the major problems faced by most organizations in the software industry. Boehm and Papaccio [4] have stated that requirements volatility is an important reason for software project cost goes beyond the limit.

Pfleeger recommends that "We must find a way to understand and anticipate some of the inevitable change we see during software development" [15].

Literature survey was conducted by McGee and Greer [17] on software requirements change source taxonomy. The authors have provided the information about the requirements change by describing the Change domain, triggers and uncertainties. The change domain can be viewed as the platform of possible classification or broad categorization of changes that occur in requirements.

Triggers are the events that cause the requirements to change whereas the uncertainties are the cause of some event to happen that act as triggers for requirements change. The authors have cumulated a comprehensive list of causes and uncertainties that gives rise to requirements change.

3   Taxanomony of Requirement Change

Taxonomy of requirements change consists of three components: Change Type, Reason, and Origin [13].

a)   Change Type: Changes in requirements are additions, deletion or modifications of requirements. According to Stark, Adding new requirements, deleted or modified to the existing requirements after the basic set of requirements have been agreed upon, is a common problem in software maintenance. These changes to the requirements after the basic set has been agreed to by both clients and maintainers are known as requirement's volatility [19].

Requirement addition – Adding a requirement to make up for the omission or meet the customer's requirement.

Requirement deletion – deleting or removing existing requirements from the business strategy or the requirements redundancy.

Requirement modification – modifying requirement owing to technical restrict or design improvement.

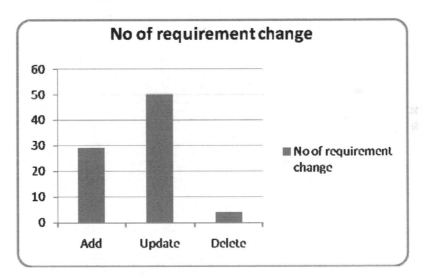

Fig. 1. Distribution of requirement changes by type. [19]

From the above empirical analysis, addition type of requirement changes is taking part the maximum in the software requirement change.

Software Requirement Types are categorized in the below table.

Table 1. Software Requirement Types and Detailed Needs

Requirement Type	Detail Category
Computational	Incorrect Operand in Equation
	Incorrect Use of Parentheses
	Incorrect/Inaccurate Equation
	Rounding or Truncation Error
Logic	Incorrect Operand in Logical Expression
	Logic Out of Sequence
	Wrong Variable Being Checked
	Missing Logic or Condition Test
	Loop Iterated Incorrect Number of Times
Input	Incorrect Format
	Input Read from Incorrect Location
	End-of-File Missing or Encountered Prematurely
Data Handling	Data File Not Available
	Data Referenced Out-of-Bounds
	Data Initialization
	Variable Used as Flag or Index Not Set Properly
	Data Not Properly Defined/Dimensioned
	Subscripting Error
Output	Data Written to Different Location
	Incorrect Format
	Incomplete or Missing Output
	Output Garbled or Misleading
Interface	Software/Hardware Interface
	Software/User Interface
	Software/Database Interface
	Software/Software Interface
Operations	COTS/GOTS SW Change
	Configuration Control
Performance	Time Limit Exceeded
	Storage Limit Exceeded
	Code or Design Inefficient
	Network Efficiency
Specification	System/System Interface Specification Incorrect/Inadequate
	Functional Specification Incorrect/Inadequate
	User Manual/Training Inadequate
Improvement	Improve Existing Function
	Improve Interface

b) Reason for Requirement Change

The identified reasons for change according to Nurmuliani are;

> ➤ Defect Fixing,
> ➤ Missing Requirements,
> ➤ Functionality Enhancement,
> ➤ Product Strategy,
> ➤ Design Improvement,
> ➤ Scope Reduction,
> ➤ Redundant Functionality,
> ➤ Obsolete Functionality,
> ➤ Erroneous Requirements,
> ➤ Resolving Conflicts and Clarifying Requirements. [13] [14] [17].

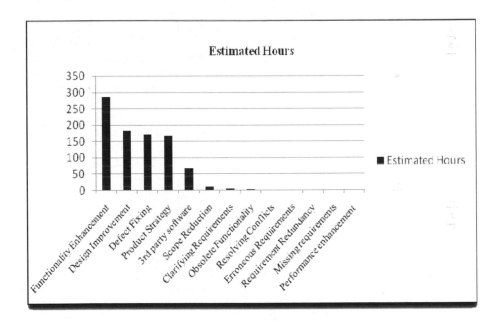

Fig. 2. Reason for Requirement change. [19]

Reason for change has been identified, and the estimated hours have taken from the previous analysis. [19]

It is important to note that these identified reasons for change were mentioned on the basis of previous study, and by no means are inclusive of all the possible reasons for change. Furthermore other reasons have been reported in the literature by other authors such as McGee & Greer et al [17], in their survey on requirements change.

c)   Sources for Requirement Change

Sources of requirement change may be any of the following:

> Defect Reports,
> Engineering's Call,
> Project Management Consideration,
> Marketing Group, Developer's Detailed Analysis,
> Design Review Feedback,
> Technical Team Discussion,
> Functional Specification Review,
> Feature Proposal Review, and
> Customer-Support discussions.

These main causes of requirements change can be viewed as the root causes which influence a change in the requirements.

The connection between these sources of change and the reason for change is the fact that these sources require some change in area of 'what' needs to be changed which is covered by reasons for change which in turn are related to the root causes which were considered or which influenced this change. It is important to note that these origins or sources of change were identified based on a particular case study and it is possible that other cases may reveal other sources of change.

In the technical report, Joost says that size is a factor which determines the flexibility showed either by the software development team or by the organization, while dealing with small requirements changes [10].

Joost [10], has listed out the **source of factors** of requirement volatility,

> Internal and external (with client and users) communication and relationships. Inadequate and poor communication could be one of the reasons causing requirements to change.
> Means of communication. Close face-to-face communication makes that changes in requirements are communicated more clearly.
> Presence and influence of client and users. Having the user and/or client present during the project makes communication and the detection of changes easy.
> Project/product size. The size of the project (in terms of budget and manpower for example) and product (Complexity and KLOC) is an important factor.
> Organization size. The size of the organization (number of employee and annual turnover will gives the size of the organization).
> Development methodology. Some development methodologies inhibit flexibility while others advocate it.
> Outsourcing. Whether (part of) the project is outsourced can influence the way change is managed and communicated.
> Project Management (formalization of documents, tools present, etc.).
> Project team Flexible, self-organizing, small teams with a flat hierarchy and experienced team members tend to cope well with requirements change.

Requirement change is due to changes in government policies, business goals, market demands and work environment. Requirement engineers should get knowledge to classify, whether the requirement change has minor impact or major impact on project before managing it.

There are certain issues that should be kept in mind while changing in requirements like traceability, dependency among requirements, prioritization of requirements and decision making to implement that change [6].

In the thesis Mundlamuri says that, requirement volatility is not a problem, there should be a proper approach while managing the impact of requirement volatility [12].

Chua says that, estimating the cost of effort rework on each change is costly, hence making requirements changes will also be expensive [3].

4   Guidelines to Manage Changes Effectively are Introduced

1. Recognize that change is inevitable, and plan for it: change procedures for the project should be planned.
2. Baseline the requirements: baseline provides a clear concept for identifying the set of requirements, which are used in a design phase. It provides mechanisms for distinguishing which set of requirements is old and which requirements have changed or evolved after the base lining.
3. Establish a single channel to control change: for example, in large systems a Change Control Board (CCB) who share the responsibility about the approval of the change requests. In small systems, the responsibility can be given, for example, to someone who is an owner of the artifact or a person who has an overall understanding of system requirements.
4. Use a change control system to capture changes: a change control system should be used to capture all requested system related changes. Change requests should be transmitted to CCB for the decision making.
5. Manage change hierarchically: changes to the requirements should be managed in a top-down hierarchical fashion. For example, changes to the specification can cause changes to the features or to design, implementation and test.

5   Conclusion

Requirements change is a fact of life. The change management is only found in the software industry background, and getting the company data is very difficult. Change request records and change request forms are the main sources of information in case study. Taxonomies of Software requirement volatility have been reviewed and few guide lines to manage changes effectively are introduced. Analyze the requirements volatility data with respect to the type, reason and source.

An accurate measurement program is useful for preventive and controlling requirement's volatility. Requirements change due to defect fix, product Strategy, missing requirements are considered to be of the expensive change type.

Our future work is to reduce the rework effort related to the requirement change in the software maintenance.

Reference

1. Anton, A.I., Potts, C.: Functional Paleontology: System Evolution as the User Sees It. In: 23rd (IEEE) International Conference on Software Engineering, Toronto, Canada, pp. 421–430 (2001)
2. Barry, E.J., Mukhopadhyay, T., Slaughter, S.A.: Software Project Duration and Effort: An Empirical Study. Information Technology and Management 3(1-2), 113–136 (2002)
3. Chua, B.B., Verner, J.: Examining Requirements Change Rework Effort: A Study. International Journal of Software Engineering & Applications (IJSEA) 1(3) (July 2010)
4. Boehm, B.W., Papaccio, P.N.: Understanding and Controlling Software Cost. IEEE Transactions on Software Engineering 14(10), 1462–1477 (1998)
5. Curtis, B., Krasner, H., Iscoe, N.: A Field Study of the Software Design Process for Large Systems. Communications of the ACM 31(11), 1268–1287 (1988)
6. Gorschek, T.: Requirements Engineering Supporting Technical Product Management. Ph.D. Thesis, Blekinge. Institute Of Technology, Ronneby (2006)
7. Harker, S.D.P., Eason, K.D.: The Change and Evolution of Requirements as a Challenge to the Practice of Software Engineering. In: Presented at Proceeding of IEEE International Symposium on Requirements Engineering (1993)
8. IEEE Standard for Software Maintenance. IEEE std 1219-1998 Software Engineering Standards Committee of the IEEE Computer society (1998)
9. IEEE Standard for Software Configuration management. IEEE STD 1219-1998 Software Engineering Standards Committee of the IEEE Computer society (1998)
10. de Wit, J., Ponisio, M.L.: Technical Report, Faculty of Electrical Engineering, Mathematics and Computer Science, University of Twente (February 8, 2008)
11. Jones, C.: Assessment and Control of Software Risks, pp. 93–98. Prentice-Hall International, Englewood Cliffs (1994)
12. Sudhakar, M.: Managing the Impact of Requirement Volatility. Thesis Department of Computing Science, Umea University, SE-90187 Umea, Sweden (2005)
13. Nurmuliani, N., Zowghi, D., Fowell, S.: Analysis of Requirements Volatility during Software Development Life Cycle. In: IEEE Proceedings of the 2004 Australian Software Engineering Conference (2004)
14. Nurmuliani, N., Zowghi, D., Williams, S.P.: Requirements Volatility and Its Impact on Change Effort: Evidence-based Research in Software Development Projects (2006)
15. Pfleeger, S.L.: Software Metrics: Progress after 25 Years? IEEE Software 25(6) (2008)
16. Pressman, R.S.: Software Engineering A Practitioner's Approach, 6th edn. (2005)
17. McGee, S., Greer, D.: A Software Requirements Change Source Taxonomy (2008)
18. Sommerville, I.: Software Engineering, 6th edn. Addison-Wesley (2001)
19. Stark, G., Oman, P., Skillicorn, A., Ameele, R.: An Examination of the Effects of Requirements Changes on Software Maintenance Releases. Journal of Software Maintenance Research and Practice 11, 293–309 (1999)
20. Zowghi, Offen, R., Nurmuliani, N.: The Impact of Requirements Volatility on Software Development Lifecycle. In: Presented at the International Conference on Software, Theory and Practice (ICS 2000), Beijing, China (2000)

Information Security Measurement and E-Governance

Subhash Chander[1] and Ashwani Kush[2]

[1] Govt PG College Karnal, India
subashjaglan@gmail.com
[2] University College Kurukshetra University, India
akush@kuk.ac.in

Abstract. Security is a buzzword these days. One can hear certain fraud mails, transfer orders, money transfer from bank accounts and many more. Websites are hacked and day by day number of such cases is increasing in whole world. On the other side the number of websites is increasing with huge speed. All the departments whether Government or Private are trying to be online and are in a hurry to provide their more and more services on a mouse click. In such an environment to maintain security of online and digital information is a typical but an important issue. This issue is taken up in this paper and various ways to keep your network/information/website secure are also being discussed. Various existing security metrics their use and hurdles are discussed in the paper. A vulnerability grading scheme has been proposed for the use of novice users. In E-Governance and UID based projects security has to play an important role in their success and failure.

Keywords: EPS, UID, CSC, NeGP, ICT.

1   Introduction

E-Governance means the process of decision making and to implement those processes through electronic means. One can say that Governance is the way those having the power use the power. Governance has social, political, economic and other varied dimensions. E-Government refers to the facilitation of delivery of Government services and main focus is on IT. E-Government uses computing and telecommunication technologies to make radical changes to deliver Government services to its citizens. The major characteristics of governance include participation, Rule of law, Transparency, Responsiveness, equity, inclusiveness, effectiveness efficiency and accountability [1]. In current Indian scenario there is pressure on the political systems and administrators by civil society to share information and make decisions transparent. But such a change can only be possible if there is a change in the minds of the political and permanent executives. Corruption, which is anti poverty, anti-national, anti-economic growth is a major problem faced by India. India ranks 69th out of list of 90 corrupt countries in the world and only 45 paisa out of one rupee is lost in the name of the corruption. Corruption has become a social phenomenon in India. IT can revolutionize the concept of Governance and has the

N. Meghanathan et al. (Eds.): CCSIT 2012, Part III, LNICST 86, pp. 151–159, 2012.
© Institute for Computer Sciences, Social Informatics and Telecommunications Engineering 2012

potential to reduce corruption, enhance functioning of Government and deliver the services in a transparent manner. One of the strong pillars of E-Governance is confidence of service users. Business users are found beneficial to information system security risk management when they participate in the various parts of System analysis and design within a business process. User participation raises organizational awareness of security risks and controls within business processes, which in turn contributes to more effective security control development and performance [8]. Confidence can be built if there is fool proof security embedded in the system. Hence if the users of a system are well convinced about the security of a system then they would not hesitate in using the system. Windows operating system are most prevalent systems in the any network private or public. Hence windows operating system has always been the major target of hackers. It will be much better here to clarify the difference between security and safety. Commonly security is concerned with logical resources e.g. money and whereas safety is concerned with physical (including but not limited to human) resources. There is a relation between security and safety. Security problems (relative harm) can often lead to safety problems (absolute harm) [6]. A military operation information about a proposed offensive reaching the opposing force in time leads to improved defenses. In the commercial sphere one can guess similar information regarding future products. For measuring the security of an information system there are certain security metrics.

2   Electronic Service Delivery

Government will be able to inform and query its people over electronic networks in near future. But there are many obstacles to it like digital divide and most of the information is still on papers till date. Governments by nature are conservative organizations and are very slow to adapt a change. Government is also thought of as foundation of society. E-Government can be more productive if it is well implemented and managed [1]. The challenges in the implementation are resistance from people who do not wish to change the status quo and public distrust. Success of Governance lies in formation of policies according to need of present situations and conditions keeping in mind the future and efficient implementation of these policies. Today to switch from the category of Developing countries to developed countries it is the need of the hour to exploit the full potential of ICT. It may either be the use of Internet for the society and solving problems or providing online services to common man .After looking at the cost saving advantages of Internet services, Government has started thinking on providing many basic services online and diminishing the digital divide by opening Information Kiosks at village level. Government has also started providing Internet connections / broadband connections at lower rates through various schemes of centre Government. One such scheme being utilized by Government colleges in Higher Education Department of Haryana is NME-ICT. This scheme is of centre Government, which provides 10 or more Broadband Internet Connections at very subsidized rate with unlimited downloading facility. These services must be utilized by all the academic institutions in states. Only 25% of the cost is to be borne out by the institution and rest by the centre or state Governments. In a way Government is trying to provide broadband Internet Facility at very low rates so that every common man can take benefit of this electronic world. Infrastructure setup is also being increased by investing a huge amount in purchase of IT apparatus, ensuring electricity and launching satellites in space .Under National E-Governance Plan (NeGP) of Centre Government one lakh Common Service Centers (CSCs) are to opened in the country. From these CSCs basic services (like birth/death certificate, ration card, Income certificate, caste certificate etc.) will be provided at the doorsteps of people.

3   Security Concerns

'Digital Security' gives birth to digital lifestyle and helps to engage confidently in everyday interactions across all digital devices. Digital security affects all aspects of the digital lifestyle, including computers and the internet, telecommunications, financial transactions, and E-Governance applications and their secure access [3]. Internet security means the protection of one's computer's internet account and files from intrusion by an outside user. Internet users of today are very much familiar with internet security products provided by companies like Symantec (Norton Anti-Virus), avast and McAfee. Software provided by these companies helps us to guard against computer viruses, as well as to provide secure firewalls and protection against spyware. For business and e-commerce security organization like CIS (Centre for Internet Security) exists today and is proof of the importance of maintaining adequate internet security [3]. Till date countries power depend on strength of conventional military units for security but in future a country may also depend on how well trained cyber forensic experts and cyber warfare is. In the global world Cyber attacks are increasing day by day and computers control Critical systems that run Power plants, telecommunication infrastructure, air traffic and many more. Security attacks on banks, stock markets and other financial institutions may have a devastating effect on the economy of any country. Economy is the major contributing factor in the development of any country. In case of cyber war there may be break ins in transportation, control systems, financial systems and other utility services being utilized by citizens (may be e-governance services). By keeping in mind the present attacks like 26/11 and the technology being utilized by the terrorists it is the need of the hour have a cyber security cells at various levels in the country. The persons employed in these cells must be of high caliber IT experts and training on latest tools security must be provided so that in future such incidents may be avoided before happening. China is moving ahead in this and is having a cyber warfare army. The core of the attack is that Chinese Cyber Warfare Experts are regularly scanning and mapping India's official networks [5]. More over there is need of proper and strong cyber laws to handle culprits of cyber hacking. There are so many cases of breach of security and online frauds at national and international level. Latest one such a fraud is Speak Asia Online (which asked online people to invest Rs. 11000 and get Rs. 1000 weekly).Proper and strong cyber laws are essential in such cases.

4   Security Measurement

Metrics are the parameters used to ascertain security in the network. In the present digital environment more and more Government activities are going to be online hence one will have to concentrate on various metrics for security of websites and information. Also various penetration loopholes can be taken into consideration before rolling out any online project whether it is related with transaction of online banking or any E-Governance related project involving financial transaction. For any Electronic Payment System (EPS) the major requirements are that it must be secure, flexible and have computational efficiency (support for micro payment & Per transaction cost should be very less).In the modern era there are many risks regarding security in EPS from many angles. From the customer's side, there is danger of stealing payment credentials and passwords. He may also have to face dishonest merchants or financial service providers and there may also be dispute over quality of service or goods. From merchant's viewpoint there may be dishonest or slow financial service providers, there may be forged payment instruments. In case of offline payments there can be danger of insufficient funds in the customer's account. To improve security in such type of EPS one must protect payment credentials with token or smart cards and check for sufficient funds and abnormal spending patterns. Moreover, in the case of Information Technology and Information System security and risk management there is a lack of metrics for years. Having a clear understanding of risk management, in modern IT Environments, gives an important basis for decision making in this area. Such research is clearly necessary, because businesses need tangible figures when provision of security is concerned, not to mention the importance of these elements when an organization is trying to get on the market with a new business model that is focused particularly on security [7]. There are certain myths about the security metrics. Metrics must be objective and tangible. Metrics must have discrete values. One needs absolute measurements. Metrics are costly. It is also essential to measure process outcomes. There is need to handle with numbers [8, 9].

4.1   Related Work

It is commonly known that something can not be managed if it can not be measured and can not be improved if it can not be managed. It also happens in case of security of information systems. Measurements are based on counting whereas metrics are based on analysis. Measuring IT-security is one of the great challenges in modern IT world. Metrics are normally used by industry to gauge performance and evaluate data in areas such as safety, production, efficiency, cost, profitability, and security. A metric is a system of related measures that facilitates the quantification of some particular characteristic. In simpler terms, a metric is a measurement that is compared to a scale or benchmark to produce a meaningful result [11]. Threats in case of information security may be posed by insiders, hackers or crackers, terrorists, organized crime within the nation or states. Insiders, such as staff members, contractor employees, and vendors, may intentionally or unintentionally, damage, or make susceptible an information system. With the efforts of international organizations security measurement using metrics has attracted great interest in recent years. In 2004, Security Metrics Consortium (SECMET) was founded to define quantitative security risk metrics for industry, corporate and vendor adoption by top corporate security officials of the sector. The Metrics work group of International Systems Security Engineering Association (ISSEA) has led another standardization effort in this area. This group developed metrics for SSE-CMM (System Security Engineering – Capability Maturity Model). One model used widely for conveying the vulnerability severity is the CVSS (Common Vulnerability Scoring System) [13]. Metrics are central for measuring the cost and effectiveness of complex security systems. Without widely accepted security metrics, separating promising developments from dead-end approaches would be very difficult [15]. Security improvement begins by identifying metrics that measure various aspects of security for the organization. Network vulnerability assessments collect huge amount of data that is utilized by experts to draw conclusions. A multi-objective evolutionary approach to cluster data of security assessments is available [4]. Clusters hold groups of tested devices with similar vulnerabilities to detect hidden patterns. Clusters group devices with similar operating systems, open ports, and vulnerabilities.

4.2 Metrics

Metrics can be an effective tool for security manager to distinguish the effectiveness of various components of organization. Metrics can also help identify the level of risk in not taking a given action, and in that way provide guidance in prioritizing corrective actions [12]. Metrics can also be used to raise the level of security awareness within the organization. With the help of metrics managers can answer to the management questions related to security of enterprise as compared to earlier one, comparison of security (earlier and now) and need for more security measures .It is difficult to address security issues using technology only. There must be a balance between technology and issues related to people behavior [14]. The types of measures that can realistically be obtained, and that can also be useful for performance improvement, depend on the maturity of the organization's information security program and the information network and system's security control implementation [17]ï

4.3 Impeding Factors in Security Metrics

Information security is a complex area which makes it difficult but not impossible to identify useful metrics. There are certain factors that should be taken into account and suggest a practical approach to design and implementation of a system of measuring, reporting and improving information security. Several factors impede progress in security metrics:

(a) Lack of good estimators of system security.
(b) Well-established reliance on subjective, human, qualitative input.
c) Lengthened and delusive means commonly used to obtain measurements.

(d) Dearth of understanding and insight into the composition of security mechanisms [16].While removing all vulnerabilities is usually not practical; leaving vulnerabilities unattended may cause significant damages to critical resources in a networked environment. It is thus critical to understand and measure the likelihood of sophisticated attacks combining multiple vulnerabilities for reaching the attack Goal [10].

5   Proposed Work Scales for Vulnerability Checks

Self standard metrics may be thought upon while releasing new software for security (Network or System). There are various options to choose a user while installing the software and most of these options become the reason for the breach of security later on. It would be much better to have numerical value in respect of higher level of vulnerability. Higher the value more is the chances of breach of security in network or system. It is proposed to provide particular values between 1 & 10. The values above 7 may be thought as critical, which means system would be more vulnerable if this option is selected. Similarly from 5 to 7 shows vulnerability but less than the earlier cases. The values from 3 to 5 are of less importance as compared to earlier ones. Values from 1 to 3 are of mild security breach and may not be of importance. Thus a scale has been designed for the providing information to the users that if one selects this option having higher value, then you would not be more secure. Depending upon the values grades may be assigned as 8-10 with Grade A, 6 -7 Grade B, 4-5 Grade C and 1-3 Grade D. Means A grade highly vulnerable ,B means vulnerable, C means less vulnerable and D means unnoticeable (secured) . Corresponding to scale more details may be provided (if desired by users) regarding levels of Vulnerability and what can be the loss in terms of monetary values or assets value or image value.

The above mentioned scheme can be applied in various areas of information security. Also if one has entered into secure area by providing user name and password (may be your mail account or bank account). A particular message on the basis of the above grades must be displayed at the time of entering into the area and it must be asked to user to logout from this session otherwise it is highly risk area. Many of the times email accounts remain open when another user occupies the system. One can enjoy the facility of sending & receiving mails from your account if you have not logged it out. In similar cases if you have entered in online banking/purchasing and you forget to log it out. One may imagine the quantity of loss it may occur. This job can be done with above mentioned scale. E-mails and banking transactions come under the highly risk areas to enter. Hence one can easily remember by looking at the message to log it out when job is finished. Conclusively the scales may be adopted by various software vendors and its proper awareness among the users is must. This scaling type categorization of services can be fully utilized for many e-governance services also. The information related with the land records of a farmer may be taken as "A" grade Vulnerability. Whereas services regarding birth/death, caste certificates may be taken as "C" grade vulnerability.

6   Ways to Secure Transactions

It is clear that the people who attack the web application development systems are vicious. Once hackers recognize that particular website is impenetrable then they will move on to someone else which appears to be more vulnerable [2]. In case of websites certain ports are kept to be opened compulsorily otherwise site may not work or may not be visible by the users for which it is designed. One of the most challenging aspects of creating a web application development is that the rogue elements can come from within the industry. They know all the tricks of the trade and will be able to run rings around everybody so that they can access your website and do as they please [2].To maintain security, industry has developed technology that can mix up sensitive information, such as your credit card number, so that it can be read only by the merchant you are dealing with and your credit card issuer. This ensures that your payment information cannot be read by anyone else or changed along the way. Always look for the picture of the unbroken key or closed lock in your browser window. Either one indicates that the security is operative. A broken key or any open lock indicates it is not. Look to see if the web address on the page that asks for your credit card information begins with "https:" instead of "http." Some web sites use the words "Secure Sockets Layer (SSL)" or a pop up box that says you are entering a secure area. The new beta version of the well renowned search engine has started to provide both of these options now. Some web merchants allow you to order online and give your credit card information over the phone. While doing this, make a note of the phone number, company, the date and time of your call, and the name of the person who has recorded your credit card number. One may want to create a special password for particularly sensitive sites, such as your home banking site. Always use a different password for purchase orders and for logging in Network or computer. Some web sites may require creating a password for future orders. Don't write down any password near computer where someone could see it or carry it in your purse or billfold. If you record it somewhere, then reverse the order of the characters or transpose some letters or numbers. In this way, someone finding it won't be able to know the true password. Be careful about responding to an e-mail, phone call, fax, or letter from anyone who asks for your password(s), social security number, birth date, bank account, credit card number, mother's maiden name, or other personal information. Sellers and financial institutions never ask you for such information unless you are entering into a transaction with them. Identity thieves make up emails that look remarkably like real issue. You should only give your password and credit card number in a secure connection on a web site, not in ordinary e-mail while purchasing online. One should not open any attachment file whose name ends in ".exe." Clicking on such files can install / activate a computer virus that may affect the working of the computer and damage the information stored on computer you are working with. Also keep on updating your anti virus programs time to time [18].

7   Conclusion and Future Work

Information Technology (IT), hardware and software related with IT industry are integral part of nearly every major global industry. PC penetration has increased a lot in the past years. In any web based project security has always been a top issue. IT has become most robust industries in the world and has become key driver of global economic growth. Growth of a country can also be increased if proper information is given to right people at right time. For that security of online services is must. There is always a necessity of new security metrics for the proper security of our information systems. Certain tips, regarding use of online services available and would be available, have been discussed. Various existing security metrics and their role in security are explained. This type of grading is better because a novice user will easily understand whether right options for the security of the information system are being selected or not . Otherwise the technical language incorporated in the softwares is not easily understandable and user may be trapped in the net of hackers unknowingly. Because various ports of the server are being scanned time to time by the hackers to find one open so that they can easily penetrate into the target system. If such scale is used the users can be easily told not to download & not to select the option having A grade (vulnerability).Certain new metrics regarding information security will be provided in future work of study.

References

1. Vasu, D.: E-Governance in India – A reality. Commonwealth publishers (2005)
2. Security aspects in web application development, http://www.webdevap.com
3. Digital security, http://www.en.wikipedia.org
4. Corral, G., Garcia-Piquer, A., Orriols-Puig, A., Fornells, A., Golobardes, E.: Multiobjective Evolutionary Clustering Approach to Security Vulnerability Assesments. In: Corchado, E., Wu, X., Oja, E., Herrero, Á., Baruque, B. (eds.) HAIS 2009. LNCS(LNAI), vol. 5572, pp. 597–604. Springer, Heidelberg (2009)
5. Gaurav, K.: Cyber warfare-a global threat. International Journal of Information Technology and Knowledge Management 2(1), 119–122 (2009)
6. Burns, A., Mcdermid, J., Dobson, J.: On the Meaning of Safety and Security. The Computer Journal 35(1) (1992)
7. Trček, D.: Security Metrics Foundations for Computer Security. The Computer Journal 53(7) (2010)
8. Spears, J.L., Barki, H.: User participation in information systems Security risk management. MIS Quarterly 34(3), 503–522 (2010)
9. Gary, H.: Seven myths about information security metrics. ISSA Journal (2006)
10. Lingyu, W., Tania, I., Tao, L., Anoop, S., Sushil, J.: An Attack Graph-Based Probabilistic Security Metric, http://users.encs.concordia.ca
11. http://www.dartmouth.edu
12. Payne Shirley, C.: A Guide to Security Metrics. A paper on SANS Security Essentials GSEC Paractical Assignment Version 1.2 e (June 19, 2006)
13. Sree Ram Kumar, T., Alagarsamy, K.: A Stake Holder Based Model for Software Security Metrics. IJCSI International Journal of Computer Science Issues 8(2) (March 2011)

14. Asheri, C.J., Louise, Y., Stewart, K.: Security metrics and evaluation of information systems security, A paper available at http://www.citeseerx.ist.psu.edu
15. Victor, P.V., Iustin, P., Sebastian, N.: Security metrics for enterprise information systems. Journal of Applied Quantitative Methods (JAQM) 1(2), 151–159 (2006)
16. Deepti, J., Kavita, A., Sonia, D.: Developing security metrics for information security measurement system. International Journal of Enterprise Computing and Business Systems 1(2) (July 2011)
17. Datta, S.P., Pranab, B.: Guideline for Performance Measures of Information Security of IT Network and Systems. International Journal of Research and Reviews in Next Generation Networks 1(1) (March 2011)
18. Security: http://safeshopping.org

Comparison of Efficient and Rand Index Fitness Function for Clustering Gene Expression Data

P.S. Patheja, Akhilesh A. Waoo, and Ragini Sharma

BIST, Bhopal, India
{Pspatheja,raginishrma}@gmail.com,
akhilesh_waoo@rediffmail.com

Abstract. This paper illustrates a comparative study of Efficient Fitness Function and Rand Index Fitness Function, to show how Efficient Fitness Function can give better results when used to cluster gene expression data. Variance which is the main limitation of Rand Index can be improved with Efficient Fitness Function. The results are evaluated by finding the precision value (i.e. sensitivity and specificity) of the dataset. Genetic Weighted K-Mean Algorithm (GWKMA) which is used here is a hybridization of Weighted K-Mean Algorithm (WKMA) and Genetic Algorithm. WKMA is used to perform optimal partition of data. Genetic Algorithm is then applied to get the best fit gene from clusters through the fitness function, on which genetic operators like selection, crossover and mutation are performed.

Keywords: Genetic Algorithm, Fitness Function, Clustering, Gene Expression Data, Variance.

1 Introduction

Clustering is a technique to bring together data having similar characteristics into a group/cluster, so that no two clusters will have similar data. Clustering methods are useful for data reduction, for developing classification schemes and for suggesting or supporting hypothesis about the structure of the data. A generic description of the clustering objective is to maximize homogeneity within each cluster while maximizing heterogeneity among the different clusters.

In this paper we present an Efficient Fitness Function which is implemented in Genetic Algorithm [9] which helps to find the fittest gene which can be transferred next generation. A comparative study of previously implemented Rand Index Fitness Function and proposed Efficient Fitness Function is done here. Both of the functions are applied on GWKMA for the same gene expression dataset [14]. A dataset is a tabular data which gives information about the expression level of genes. The expression level of each gene is calculated with the help of microarray technology by considering the genes (specified in rows) and by samples (specified in columns). The data which we get is known as Gene Expression data. Each value is known as datum. These values may be real numbers or integers. The clustering is performed on Gene Expression data to group the genes with similar characteristics.

N. Meghanathan et al. (Eds.): CCSIT 2012, Part III, LNICST 86, pp. 160–167, 2012.
© Institute for Computer Sciences, Social Informatics and Telecommunications Engineering 2012

To validate our data, synthetic dataset i.e. yeung's et al. dataset is applied. This dataset contains 400 genes and 17 attributes. The reason behind selecting yeung's dataset is that it contains data without repeated measurements and with low noise level. The results are evaluated by finding the precision value (i.e. sensitivity and specificity) of the dataset.

In GWKMA for performing optimal partition of clusters, first Weighted K-Means Algorithm [8] with WKM operator or cost function is used. On these clusters Genetic Algorithm is applied. Genetic algorithm is a heuristic searching algorithm to find fittest gene with the help of the fitness function and performs genetic operations like selection, crossover and mutation on it. Weighted K-Mean Algorithm when merged with Genetic Algorithm not only improves the precision value but also helps the algorithm to converge fast. For our reference, henceforth in this paper we will be refereeing Genetic Weighted K-Mean Algorithm with Rand Index fitness function as GWKMA and Genetic Weighted K-Mean Algorithm with Efficient fitness function as MGWKMA i.e. Modified GWKMA.

2   Related Work

Our purpose is to cluster Gene Expression Data. The Gene Expression Data is formed by calculating the expression level of the Genes using microarray technology. As the gene expression data is a table where rows represents genes and column represents samples, the clustering can be classified as gene based clustering and sample based clustering. Amir Ben-Dor [17] uses appropriate stochastic error model on the input and tries to overcome with the problem of clustering multicondition gene expression pattern, and thus recovers the cluster structure with high probability. K.Y Yeung [15] provides a systematic framework which helps to access the results of various clustering algorithms using one experimental condition. The results analysis is done on simulated Gene Expression data using single link, k-means (with random initialization), CAST and random algorithms. In our paper, the fitness function which we are using is an Efficient Fitness function which is a squared error function used to minimize the variance in the cluster. Erkan Bes.dok [20] has compared various squared error functions as fitness function in improving the camera calibrations. Normalized-Root-Mean-Squared-Error is used by Mohammed Awad [22] as a fitness function to deal with the problem of function approximation from a given set of input/output (I/O) data. The problem consists of analyzing training examples, so that we can predict the output of a model given new inputs, which is solved using Radial Basis Function Neural Networks (RBFNNs) and Genetic Algorithms (GAs). M.K. Deshmukh, C. Balakrishna Moorthy [21] uses squared error function as a fitness function for estimation of wind energy potential at a site using Genetic Algorithm (GA) to Neural Network Mode.

3   Fitness Functions

Fitness biologically can be expressed as a measure of reproductive efficiency of chromosomes. In Genetic Algorithm, fitness acts as some measure of goodness to be maximized. By using fitness function one can state, how fit a specific chromosome is. Better the fitness, more the chances to go to next generation.

3.1   Rand Index Fitness Function

Rand Index [12] is a statistical measure to find similarity between two data clusters. The values of Rand Index can vary from 0 to 1, where the value 0 states that the two clusters do not show any similar characteristics while the value 1 states that the characteristics of two clusters are similar. For understanding the Rand Index Fitness Function equations, let's say that we have a set of n elements E= $\{R_1,....R_n\}$ and two partitions of E to compare P=$\{p_1,....p_r\}$ and Q=$\{q_1,....q_s\}$. We have the equation, with a, b, c and d as the pairs of elements in E.

$$RI = \frac{a+d}{a+b+c+d}$$

Where,

- a- Pairs of elements that are in same sets in P and same sets in Q.
- b- Pairs of elements that are in different sets in P and different sets in Q.
- c- Pairs of elements that are in same set in P & different sets in Q.
- d- Pairs of elements that are in different set in P & in same sets in Q.

3.2   Efficient Fitness Function

Efficient Fitness Function is basically a Squared Error Function to improve the variance of a cluster. Statically it can be represented as a way to measure the difference between the values implied by an estimator and the true values of the quantity being estimated. This difference occurs due to randomness. We have the equation for Squared error function as

$$E=\sum_{N=1}^{N} \sum_{x \in C_n} ||x-mn||^2$$

Where N being the number of clusters, mn the centre of clusters Cn and x represents the data.

4   Limitations of Rand Index Fitness Function

Rand Index Fitness Function is an existing function which is used in GWKMA for clustering large scale gene expression data. Efficient fitness function is the proposed function for the same GWKMA. Efficient fitness function not only gives precise results but also overcomes the limitations of Rand Index. The limitations of Rand Index Fitness Function are:

4.1   Variance

Variance is the means of measurement for the scattered data in clusters, which specifies to minimize the internal feature variation in a cluster or to maximize the variation between different clusters. The cluster variance needs to be taken care when the data is selected randomly. In this paper we are creating clusters using Weighted K-Mean Algorithm, which creates the cluster randomly. In this case there are chances of scattering of data among various clusters. On these clusters when Rand Index fitness function is applied, it is seen that Rand Index fitness function does not give precise results, it's index is quite low when more data is scattered among the cluster i.e. when inter cluster variance is more, as specified in [4]. To overcome this limitation, we use Efficient Fitness Function instead of Rand Index. As the error is squared in Efficient Fitness Function, it neutralizes the appearance of opposite (polarity) internal features in a cluster and hence is able to improve the variance (by minimizing the internal feature variance in a cluster or maximizing the variance between different clusters).

4.2   Equally Weighted Type I and Type II Errors

As Rand Index is also considered as a measure of percentage of correct decision made by an algorithm, it can be computed with the equation

$$RI = \frac{TP+TN}{TP+FP+FN+TN}$$

Where,

o   True positive (TP)- Equation with hit
o   True negative (TN)- Equation with correct rejection
o   False positive (FP)- Equation with false alarm, Type I error
o   False negative (FN)- Equation with miss, Type II error

One issue with Rand Index is that in this False Positive and False Negative is equally weighted, which may be undesirable for some clustering algorithms. As False Positive and False Negative represents Type I and Type II errors, it is not desirable to provide equal weights to both of them.

4.3   Fuzzy and Non-fuzzy Partition

Rand Index can be used for both fuzzy and non-fuzzy partitions, but it has been seen that it is properly defined only for the comparison of a fuzzy partition with a non-fuzzy reference partition, which is not the basic requirement of GWKMA.

5   Experimental Setup

For the implementation of Genetic Weighted k-Means Algorithm with the fitness functions, the experimental setup includes both hardware and software requirements. The algorithm is implemented with MATLAB and Simulink software on LINUX platform using Fedora-9 (Sulphur) as operating system with (2.6.25 – 14.fc9.i686) kernel and Red Hat Nash version. The algorithm can be implemented using the MATLAB software in Windows family to avoid the changes in the resulted data from the virus problem we are using MATLAB in Linux platform. The hardware support required for the implementation includes, at least 60 GB of the Hard disk as even though the capacity of MATLAB software is 3.5 GB while installing it will extract or decompress the compressed files and retrieve the capacity of the hard disk about 45 GB. The memory requirement is1GB RAM, Intel Core TM 2 Duo Processor. The gene expression dataset used for implementation is Yeung's synthetic dataset as these dataset contains values without repeated measurements and with low noise levels. For the implementation the dataset is stored in the form of a text file and then used. The Software System Attribute includes portability. The algorithm is written using Matlab, therefore it can be ported to any Operating System running Matlab.

6   Results

The results are evaluated by implementing both Efficient and Rand Index fitness functions on same Genetic Weighted K-mean Algorithm one by one for the same Yeung's synthetic dataset, by varying the size of population (the number of chromosomes used for clustering) and generation (the number of iteration). The results are evaluated on the basis of precision values obtained by calculating the sensitivity and specificity of the algorithm by implementing both fitness functions one by one. The sensitivity is proportion of actual positives which are correctly identified as such, while specificity represents the proportion of negatives which are correctly identified. According to the results obtained by the precision values evaluated for sensitivity and specificity, comparison graphs are plotted to show how the algorithm (MGWKMA) implementing Efficient fitness function gives better results than the algorithm (GWKMA) implementing Rand Index fitness function.

6.1   Comparison Graphs for MGWKMA and GWKMA

Fig.1 Shows a comparison graph between MGWKMA and GWKMA with Population size=10 and Generation =10. It can be clearly seen from the graph that MGWKMA gives good results than GWKMA.

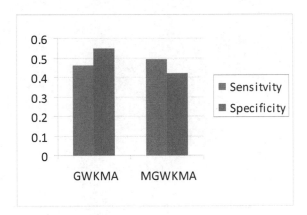

Fig. 1. Comparison graph for Sensitivity & Specificity for P=10, G=10

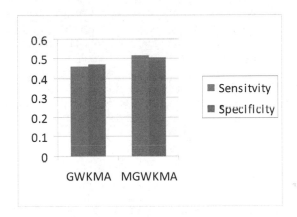

Fig. 2. Comparison graph for Sensitivity & Specificity for P=10, G=20

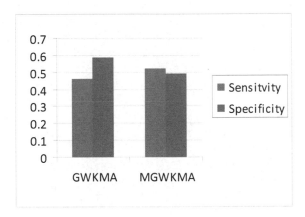

Fig. 3. Comparison graph for Sensitivity & Specificity for P=20, G=10

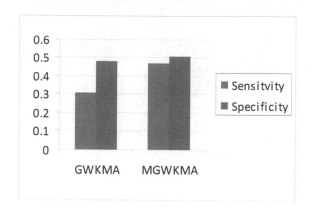

Fig. 4. Comparison graph for Sensitivity & Specificity for P=20, G=20

Fig 2 Shows a comparison graph between MGWKMA and GWKMA with Population size=10 & Generation =20. It is clear from the graph that MGWKMA performs better than GWKMA even though the number of iterations increases.

Fig 3 Shows a comparison graph between MGWKMA and GWKMA with Population size=20 and Generation =10. It is clear from the graph that MGWKMA performs better than GWKMA even though the size of population is increased.

Fig 4 Shows a comparison graph between MGWKMA and GWKMA with Population size=20 and Generation =20. It can be seen from the graph that MGWKMA gives better performance than GWKMA, at high population and generation.

7   Conclusion

In this paper a comparison of Efficient Fitness Function and Rand index fitness function is done for Genetic Weighted K-Means Algorithm used to cluster Gene Expression Data. The dataset used for both is Yeung's Synthetic dataset. An Efficient Fitness Function gives better results in clustering gene expression data than Rand Index fitness function. The limitations of Rand Index Function is learnt and it is shown that Variance (which is a main limitation of Rand Index Function) can be improved using Efficient Fitness Function (as this is a Squared Error Function). A Graphical comparison has been done using Efficient Fitness Function vis-à-vis Rand Index Function in Algorithms for different sets of Population (P) & Generation (G). The comparisons are done by evaluating the precision value by calculating Specificity & Sensitivity. From the comparison it can be concluded that the Algorithm when implemented with Efficient Fitness Function improves the variance in the cluster and gives better results for clustering gene expression data as compared to Genetic Weighted K-Means Algorithm (GWKMA) with Rand Index fitness function.

References

[1] Hartigan, J.: Clustering Algorithms. Wiley, New York (1975)
[2] Obitko, M.: Introduction to Genetic Algorithms (1998)

[3] Krishna, K.K., Murty, M.M.: Genetic K-means algorithm. IEEE Transactions on Systems, Man, and Cybernetics–Part B: Cybernetics 29, 1083-4419(99)00770-0

[4] Wehrens, R., Buydens, M.C., Fraley, C., Raftery, A.C.: Model-Based Clustering for Image Segmentation and Large Datasets Via Sampling. Journal Of Classification 21, doi:10.1007/s00357-004-001-8

[5] Maulik, U., Bandyopadhyay, S.: Genetic algorithm-based clustering technique. Pattern Recognition 33, 1455–1456 (2000)

[6] Wu, F.X., Zhang, W.Z., Kusalik, A.J.: A genetic k-means clustering algorithm applied to gene expression data. In: Proceedings of The Sixteenth Canadian Conference on Artificial Intelligence, Halifax, Canada, pp. 520–526 (June 2003)

[7] Kerdprasop, K., Kerdprasop, N., Sattayatham, P.: Weighted K-Means for Density-Biased Clustering

[8] Tho, D.X.: Genetic Algorithms and Application in Examination Scheduling. In: Scholarly Research Paper (2009), doi:10.3239/9783640636723

[9] Srivastava, P.R., Kim, T.H.: Application of Genetic Algorithm in Software Testing. IJSE (2009)

[10] Dudoit, S., Fridlyland, J.: A prediction-based resampling method for estimating the number of clustering in a dataset. BMC Genome Biology 3, research 0036.1- 0036.2 (2002)

[11] Santos, J.M., Embrechts, M.: On the use of the Adjusted Rand Index as a Metric for Evaluating Supervised Classification

[12] Jeevanand, E.S., Abdul-Sathar, E.I.: Estimation of residual entropy function for exponential distribution from censored samples. ProbStat Forum (2009) ISSN 0974-3235

[13] Sherlock, G., Boussard, T.H., Kasarskis, A., Binkley, G., Matese, J.C., Dwight, S.S., Kaloper, M., Weng, S., Jin, H., Ball, C.A., Eisen, M.B., Spellman, P.T., Brown, P.O., Botstein, D., Cherry, J.M.: The Stanford Microarray Database. Nucleic Acids Research 29, 152–155 (2001)

[14] Jiang, D., Tang, C., Zhang, A.: Cluster Analysis for Gene Expression Data: A Survey. IEEE Transactions on Knowledge and Data Engineering 16(11)

[15] Yeung, K.Y., Fraley, C., Murua, A., Raftery, A.E., Ruzzo, W.L.: Model-based clustering and data transformations for gene expression data. Bioinformatics (2001)

[16] Belacel, N., Wang, Q., Cuperlovic-Culf, M.: Clustering Methods for Microarray Gene Expression Data. OMICS 10(4) (2006)

[17] Ben-Dor, A., Shamir, R., Yakhini, Z.: Clustering Gene Expression Patterns. Journal of Computational Biology 6, 281–297

[18] Suresh, R.M., Dinakaran, K., Valarmathie, P.: Model based modified k-means clustering for microarray data. In: International Conference on Information Management and Engineering, vol. 13, pp. 271–273. IEEE (2009)

[19] Sarmah, S., Bhattacharyya, D.K.: An Effective Technique for Clustering Incremental Gene Expression data. IJCSI International Journal of Computer Science Issues 7(3(3)) (2010) ISSN (Online): 1694-0784

[20] Beşdok, E.: 3D Vision by Using Calibration Pattern with Inertial Sensor and RBF Neural Networks Sensors, vol. 9, pp. 4572–4585 (2009), doi: 10.3390/s90604572

[21] Deshmukh, M.K., Moorthy, C.B.: Application Of Genetic Algorithm To Neural Network Model For Estimation Of Wind Power Potential. Journal of Engineering, Science and Management Education 2, 42–48 (2010)

[22] Awad, M.: Optimization RBFNNs Parameters Using Genetic Algorithms: Applied on Function Approximation. International Journal of Computer Science and Security (IJCSS) 4(3)

A Novel Hybrid Fuzzy Multi-Objective Evolutionary Algorithm: HFMOEA

Amit Saraswat[*] and Ashish Saini

Department of Electrical Engineering,
Dayalbagh Educational Institute, Agra 282110, Uttar Pradesh, India
amitsaras@gmail.com, ashish_711@rediffmail.com

Abstract. This paper presents a development of a new hybrid fuzzy multi-objective evolutionary algorithm (HFMOEA) for solving complex multi-objective optimization problems. In this proposed algorithm, two significant parameters such as crossover probability (P_C) and mutation probability (P_M) are dynamically varied during optimization based on the output of a fuzzy controller for improving its convergence performance by guiding the direction of stochastic search to reach near the true pareto-optimal solution effectively. The performance of HFMOEA is examined and compared with NSGA-II on three benchmark test problems such as ZDT1, ZDT2 and ZDT3.

Keywords: Multi-objective evolutionary algorithms, fuzzy logic controller, global optimal solution, pareto-optimal front.

1 Introduction

In last couple of decades, a number of multi-objective evolutionary algorithms (MOEAs) have been suggested for solving complex multi-objective problems [1]-[3]. The main purpose behind the development of the MOEA approach is that it has ability to find multiple Pareto-optimal solutions in one single simulation run. The non-dominated sorting genetic algorithm (NSGA) proposed in [1] was one of the first such EAs. Over the years, NSGA was criticized in [2] on the basis of some aspects such as high computational complexity of non-dominated sorting, lack of elitism and need for specifying the sharing parameter. In reference [3], an improved version of NSGA called as NSGA-II. Two other contemporary MOEAs: Pareto-archived evolution strategy (PAES) [4] and strength Pareto EA (SPEA) [5] were also reported in the literature. In reference [6], a survey of different multi-objective evolutionary and real coded genetic algorithms is presented.

In present paper, a new Hybrid Fuzzy Multi-Objective Evolutionary Algorithm (HFMOEA) has been proposed for solving complex multi-objective problems. In proposed HFMOEA, a fuzzy logic controller (*FLC_HMOEA*) is developed, which would cause variation in two HFMOEA parameters such as crossover probability (P_C) and mutation probability (P_M) dynamically during optimization process after each k

---

[*] Corresponding author.

N. Meghanathan et al. (Eds.): CCSIT 2012, Part III, LNICST 86, pp. 168–177, 2012.

number of iterations. These parameter variations provide HFMOEA a kind of adaptability to the nature of targeted optimization problem and help to reach the near global optimal solutions and hence arrive near to *true pareto-optimal front*. The performance of HFMOEA is examined on three benchmark test problems such as ZDT1, ZDT2 and ZDT3.

2   Proposed HFMOEA for Solving Multi-Objective Problems

The flowchart of proposed HFMOEA for solution of complex multi-objective problems is outlined in Fig.1. Details of proposed algorithm are discussed as below:

Initialization: HFMOEA based optimization starts with initialization of various input parameters of HFMOEA such as population size (*popsize*), maximum numbers of iterations (*max_iteration*), number of control variables, system constraints limits, crossover probability (P_C), mutation probability (P_M) etc.

Generation of Initial population: it is generated randomly according to following procedural steps:

Step 1:   Generate a string of real valued random numbers within their given variable limits to form a single individual;

Step 2:   Place the individual as valid individual in initial population;

Step 3:   Evaluate fitness value for valid individual;

Step 4:   Check if the initial population has not completed then go to step 1;

Non-Domination Sorting: The generated initial population is sorted on the basis on non-domination sorting algorithm proposed by Deb [2].

For producing the new population for next iteration, the following operators are applied to parent population:

Selection: The Binary Tournament selection as proposed in reference [2] is used as a selection operator for reproducing the mating pool of parent individuals for crossover and mutation operations.

Crossover: The BLX-α crossover as proposed in reference is applied on randomly selected pairs of parent individuals $\left(x_i^{(1,t)}, x_i^{(2,t)}\right)$ with a crossover probability $\left(P_C\right)$ which is a combination of an extrapolation/interpolation method.

Mutation: The PCA based Mutation as proposed in reference [7] with mutation probability $\left(P_m\right)$ is applied to generate the offspring population.

Criterion to prepare population for next iteration: After the execution of above genetic operators, offspring population is checked to prepare new population for next iteration by going through following procedural step:

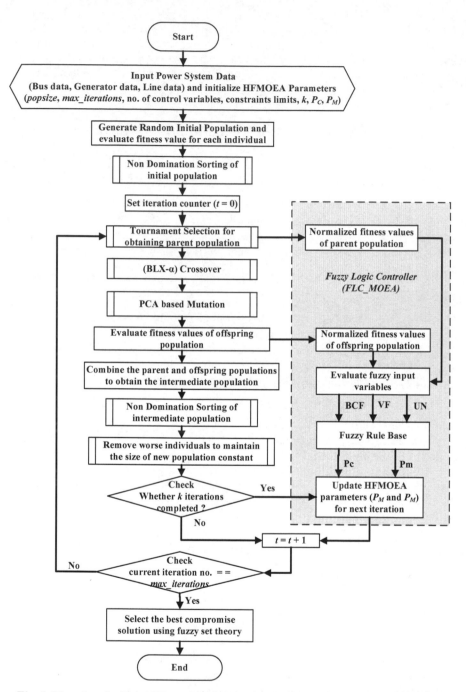

Fig. 1. Flowchart for Hybrid Fuzzy Multi-Objective Evolutionary Algorithm (HFMOEA)

Step 1:   Evaluate the fitness values for each individual in offspring population;

Step 2:   Combine the parent and offspring population to obtain the intermediate population;

Step 3:   Perform the non-domination sorting algorithm on intermediate population;

Step 4:   Remove the worse individuals to maintain the new population size constant. Here the new population for next iteration is prepared;

Step 5:   Check if k^{th} iterations (let k = 10) has completed go to next step 6 otherwise go to step 7.

Step 6:   Update HFMOEA parameters (i.e. P_C and P_M) by using fuzzy logic controller (*FLC_HMOEA*).

Step 7:   Check the termination condition of HFMOEA. i.e. if the current iteration number is equal to *max_iterations*, terminate the iteration process otherwise go to next iteration.

Step 8:   Select the best compromise solution using fuzzy set theory.

Best compromise solution: Upon having the Pareto-optimal set of non-dominated solution using proposed HFMOEA, an approach proposed in [8] selects one solution to the decision maker as the best compromise solution [9]. This approach suggests that due to imprecise nature of the decision maker's judgment, the ith objective function F_i is represented by a membership function μ_i defined as in reference [8]:

$$\mu_i = \begin{cases} 1 & F_i \leq F_i^{\min} \\ \dfrac{F_i^{\max} - F_i}{F_i^{\max} - F_i^{\min}} & F_i^{\min} < F_i < F_i^{\max} \\ 0 & F_i \geq F_i^{\min} \end{cases} \tag{1}$$

Where $F_i^{\min}$ and $F_i^{\max}$ are the minimum and maximum values of the ith objective function among all non-dominated solutions, respectively. For each jth non-dominated solution, the normalized membership function μ^j is calculated as:

$$\mu^j = \frac{\sum\limits_{i=1}^{N_{obj}} \mu_i^j}{\sum\limits_{j=1}^{N_{dom}} \sum\limits_{i=1}^{N_{obj}} \mu_i^j} \tag{2}$$

Where N_{dom} is the number of non-dominated solutions. The best compromise solution is that having the maximum value of μ^j.

Fitness function: The fitness function corresponding to each individual in the population is assigned based on their respective generalized augmented functions as evaluated in equation (3). Thus the fitness function (H_m) for m^{th} objective is evaluated as:

$$H_m = \frac{K_m}{1+f_{obj,m}}; \qquad \forall m = 1 : N_{obj}$$

(3)

Where N_{obj} is the total number of objectives and K_m is the appropriate constant corresponding to m^{th} objective, in this paper.

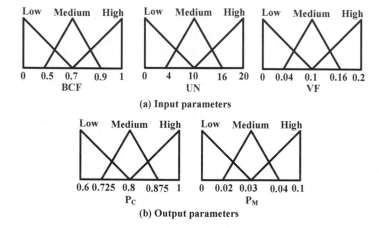

(a) Input parameters

(b) Output parameters

Fig. 2. Input and Output membership functions for Fuzzy Logic Controller

Fuzzy logic controller: It has been experienced that after few iterations, the fitness values of each of the individuals are becoming equal to other individuals in same population and hence the effect of crossover operator beyond that stage becomes insignificant due to lack of diversity. Therefore, the increased mutation probability (P_M) remains the only alternative to produce the better offspring for achieving a more diversified population. A fuzzy logic controller (*FLC_HMOEA*) is designed to vary P_C and P_M dynamically during the optimization process. These parameters (P_C and P_M) are varied based on the fitness function values as per following logic given in reference [10]:

- Ideally the best compromized fitness (BCF) using (1)-(3) should change for each iteration, but if no significant change take places over a number of iterations (UN) then the values of both P_C and P_M must be modified.
- In multi-objecteive problems, the diversity in population supports the stochastic search to reach the perato-optimal fronts. The variance of the fitness values of objective function (VF) of a population is a measure of diversity in population. Hence, it is considered as another factor on which both P_C and P_M may be changed.

Thus the ranges of three input fuzzy parameters such BCF, UN and VF and also two output fuzzy parameters such as P_C and P_M are repersented by three lingustic terms as LOW, MEDIUM and HIGH. The details of membership functions for input and output variables of *FLC_HMOEA* are shown in Fig. 2.

Fuzzy Rule Base for HFMOEA

1. If (BCF is Low) then (Pc is High) (Pm is Low) (1)
2. If (BCF is Medium) and (UN is Low) then (Pc is High) (Pm is Low) (1)
3. If (BCF is High) and (UN is Low) then (Pc is High) (Pm is Low) (1)
4. If (BCF is Medium) and (UN is Medium) then (Pc is Medium) (Pm is Medium) (1)
5. If (BCF is High) and (UN is Medium) then (Pc is Medium) (1)
6. If (UN is High) and (VF is Low) then (Pc is Low) (Pm is High) (1)
7. If (UN is High) and (VF is Medium) then (Pc is Low) (1)
8. If (UN is High) and (VF is High) then (Pc is Medium) (1)
9. If (BCF is High) and (VF is Medium) then (Pm is Low) (1)
10. If (BCF is High) and (VF is High) then (Pm is Low) (1)
11. If (VF is High) then (Pc is High) (Pm is Low) (1)
12. If (VF is Medium) then (Pc is High) (Pm is Low) (1)
13. If (BCF is High) and (VF is Low) then (Pc is High) (Pm is Low) (1)
14. If (BCF is Medium) and (VF is Medium) then (Pc is Low) (Pm is High) (1)
15. If (BCF is Low) and (UN is Low) and (VF is Low) then (Pc is High) (Pm is Low)

3   Simulation Results

The proposed HFMOEA is implemented according to the procedure explained in previous sections and all the simulations are carried out in MATLAB 7.0 programming environment on Pentium IV 2.27 GHz, 2.0 GB RAM computer system. In present case study, the proposed HFMOEA is examined and compared with a popular multi-objective evolutionary algorithm i.e. NSGA-II presented in reference [2]. The detailed specifications of both NSGA-II and HFMOEA are summarized in Table 1. The NSGA-II comprises a simulated binary crossover (SBX) operator and a polynomial mutation [11] like real coded GAs. For real-coded NSGA-II, distribution indexes [11] as $\eta_c = 20, and \ \eta_m = 20$ are used for crossover and mutation operators respectively (see Table 1). Whereas in HFMOEA, a BLX-α crossover and PCA-mutation [7] operators are used with dynamically varying after each 10 iterations with probabilities· (P_C and P_M) based on fuzzy logic controller (*FLC_HMOEA*) as described in section 2.

Three benchmark test problems such as ZDT1, ZDT2 and ZDT3 out of six as suggested by Zitzler, Deb and Thiele [12] are taken for testing and comparison of proposed HFMOEA. In this paper, the whole simulation is divided into four cases such that in each case, both the algorithms (NSGA-II and HFMOEA) are evaluated for deferent population sizes and number of maximum iterations. Thus, the Population size and number of maximum iterations are taken as (100 and 300), (100 and 500), (200 and 500) and (300 and 500) in Case: 1, Case: 2, Case: 3 and Case: 4 respectively (see Table 2). For all three test problems, the best compromised solutions obtained after optimization using NSGA-II and HFMOEA are summarized in Table 2. The best compromised solution is calculated according to (1) and (2) described in previous section.

The pareto-optimal fronts obtained by NSGA-II and HFMOEA for ZDT1 test problem in all four cases are depicted in Fig.3. It has been observed that NSGA-II could not be fully converged in case 1 and Case: 2 when the population size is 100 and maximum numbers of iterations are 300 and 500 respectively. While, proposed HFMOEA has been converged and able to achieve near global pareto-optimal front even in case: 1 (see Fig.3). Similar investigations are conducted on other to benchmark test problems such as ZDT2 and ZDT3 for Case: 1, Case: 2 and Case: 3, the pareto-optimal fronts are obtained shown in Fig.4 and Fig.5, respectively. During the execution of optimization based on proposed HFMOEA, it's two parameters such as crossover probability (P_C) and mutation probability (P_M) are varied dynamically after each ten iterations. These variations are taken place based on the output of fuzzy controller (FLC_HMOEA) as described in section 2. The variations in P_C and P_M for all three test problems (ZDT1, ZDT2 and ZDT3) in Case: 3 are shown in Fig.6. It has been observed that the variations in crossover and mutation probabilities are such that if P_C is going to reduce, P_M will increase (see Fig.6.). These variations in parameters are helping the HFMOEA in searching the global optimal solutions. Therefore, this property will enhance the capability of HFMOEA to achieve the near global pareto-optimal front.

Table 1. Specifications of optimization algorithms

Algorithm Parameters	NSGA-II	HFMOEA
Selection operator	Tournament	Tournament
Crossover operator	Simulated Binary (SBX)	BLX-α crossover
Mutation operator	polynomial mutation	PCA mutation
Crossover probability (P_C)	0.9	varying based on FLC output
Mutation probability (P_M)	$\eta_c = 20$, and $\eta_m = 20$	varying based on FLC output

Table 2. Best Compromised solutions obtained by NSGA-II and HFMOEA

Test Case	Pop. Size	Max. Iterations	optimization Algorithm	Best Compromised Solution after optimization					
				Test Problem : ZDT1		Test Problem : ZDT2		Test Problem : ZDT3	
				f1(x)	f2(x)	f1(x)	f2(x)	f1(x)	f2(x)
Case:1	100	300	NSGA-II	0.1557	0.9129	0	1.2949	0.2505	0.6376
			HFMOEA	0.2838	0.4693	1	0.002	0.2507	0.2579
Case:2	100	500	NSGA-II	0.2593	0.6503	1	0.2403	0.2503	0.4431
			HFMOEA	0.2543	0.4967	1	0.0011	0.2485	0.2565
Case:3	200	500	NSGA-II	0.2236	0.5951	0	1.053	0.2485	0.3706
			HFMOEA	0.259	0.4921	1	0.0007	0.2507	0.2519
Case:4	300	500	NSGA-II	0.2354	0.5543	1	0.0803	0.2498	0.3071
			HFMOEA	0.2614	0.4893	0	1.0001	0.2495	0.2529

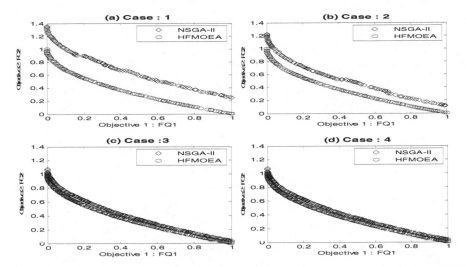

Fig. 3. Comparison of Pareto-optimal fronts obtained using NSGA-II and HFMOEA for ZDT1 test problem for different population sizes after various iterations

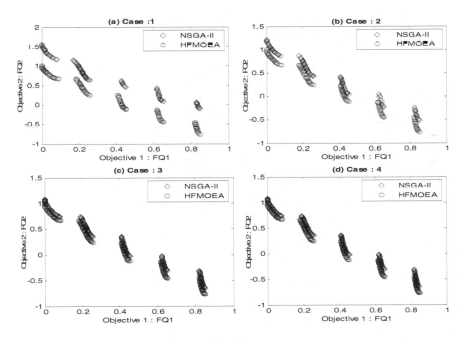

Fig. 4. Comparison of Pareto-optimal fronts obtained using NSGA-II and HFMOEA for ZDT2 test problem for different population sizes after various iterations

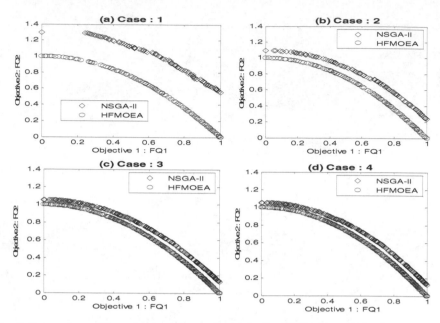

Fig. 5. Comparison of Pareto-optimal fronts obtained using NSGA-II and HFMOEA for ZDT3 test problem for different population sizes after various iterations

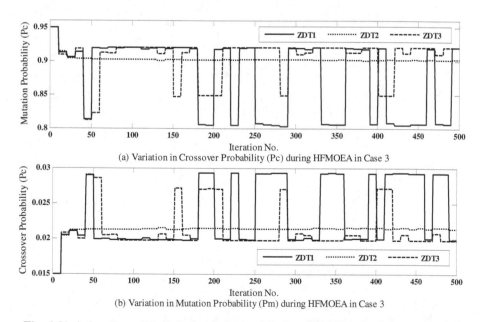

Fig. 6. Variations P_C and P_M during optimization based on HFMOEA for three test problems

4   Conclusion

A fuzzy logic controller called as FLC_HMOEA has been developed and successfully applied in a proposed multi-objective optimization algorithm i.e. HFMOEA. This implementation returns the advantage in terms of improvement in the performance of HFMOEA i.e. good convergence with better quality of the pareto-optimal solutions and consequently arrives to a near pareto-optimal front. FLC_HMOEA helps in guiding the direction of stochastic search to reach the near global optimal solution effectively. HFMOEA has been tested on three benchmark test problems such as ZDT1, ZDT2 and ZDT3 and compared with NSGA-II. The simulation results revealed the effectiveness of HFMOEA for solving multi-objective problems.

References

1. Srinivas, N., Deb, K.: Multi-objective Optimization Using Non-dominated Sorting in Genetic Algorithms. Evolutionary Computation 2(3), 221–248 (1994)
2. Deb, K., Pratap, A., Agarwal, S., Meyarivan, T.: A Fast Elitist Multi-objective Genetic Algorithm: NSGA-II. IEEE Transactions on Evolutionary Computation 6(2), 182–197 (2002)
3. Zitzler, E., Thiele, L.: Multiobjective Optimization Using Evolutionary Algorithms - A Comparative Case Study. In: Eiben, A.E., Bäck, T., Schoenauer, M., Schwefel, H.-P. (eds.) PPSN 1998. LNCS, vol. 1498, pp. 292–301. Springer, Heidelberg (1998)
4. Knowles, J., Corne, D.: The Pareto archived evolution strategy: A new baseline algorithm for multi-objective optimization. In: Proceedings of the 1999 Congress on Evolutionary Computation, pp. 98–105. IEEE Press, Piscataway (1999)
5. Zitzler, E.: Evolutionary algorithms for multiobjective optimization: Methods and applications, Doctoral dissertation ETH 13398. Swiss Federal Institute of Technology (ETH), Zurich, Switzerland (1999)
6. Raghuwanshi, M.M., Kakde, O.G.: Survey on multi-objective evolutionary and real coded genetic algorithms. In: Proceedings of the 8th Asia Pacific Symposium on Intelligent and Evolutionary Systems, pp. 150–161 (2004)
7. Saraswat, A., Saini, A.: Optimal reactive power dispatch by an improved real coded genetic algorithm with PCA mutation. In: Proceedings of Second International Conference on Sustainable Energy and Intelligent System (IET SEISCON 2011), vol. 2, pp. 310–315 (2011)
8. Dhillon, J.S., Parti, S.C., Kothari, D.P.: Stochastic economic emission load dispatch. Electric Power Systems Research 26, 179–186 (1993)
9. Abido, M.A., Bakhashwain, J.M.: Optimal VAR dispatch using a multi-objective evolutionary algorithm. Electric Power and Energy Systems 27(1), 13–20 (2005)
10. Saini, A., Chaturvedi, D.K., Saxena, A.K.: Optimal power flow solution: a GA-Fuzzy system approach. International Journal of Emerging Electric Power Systems 5(2) (2006)
11. Deb, K., Agarwal, R.B.: Simulated Binary Crossover for Continuous Search Space. Complex Systems 9, 115–148 (1995)
12. Zitzler, E., Deb, K., Thiele, L.: Comparison of multi-objective evolutionary algorithms: Empirical results. Evolutionary Computing 8(2), 173–195 (2000)

Testability Estimation Model (TEM^{OOD})

Mohd Nazir and Raees A. Khan

{Mohd Nazir,Raees A. Khan}@Springer.com

Abstract. Testability analysis early in the development process is a criterion of crucial importance to software developers, designers and the managers. Early estimation of testability, exclusively at design phase assists designers to improve their designs before the coding starts. Consequently, it significantly reduces rework during and after implementation, as well as designing effective test plans, better project and resource planning. An effort has been put forth in this paper to identify the major factors contributing in testability estimation at design phase. Further, a model is developed to quantify software testability in design phase. Furthermore, the correlation of Testability with these factors has been tested and justified with the help of statistical measures.

Keywords: Testability, OO Design Constructs, Testability Factors, Testability Estimation.

1   Introduction

Software industry now exists in an environment more turbulent than ever before. It is essential for the companies to develop the processes smart enough to be easily adapted in the fast changing business requirement and then to be able to compete in the highly complex market environments. Software Engineering today needs best practices and tools to support developers to develop software that is as fault free as possible. Many tools and methods exist today, but the question is, if and how they are used and more importantly in which circumstances they are used and why [1]. Testability has been identified as one of the major issues in the field of Software Engineering. It provides insights that are found to be very much valuable during design, coding, testing and quality assurance [2][13].

Testability analysis early in the development process is a criterion of crucial importance to software developers, designers and the managers. However, most of the mechanisms available for testability estimation may be used in the later phases of system development life cycle [5][10]. It is a well understood fact that a decision to change the design at a later stage in order to improve testability proves to be very expensive and error-prone. On the other hand, early estimation of testability, exclusively at design phase assists designers to improve their designs before the coding starts. It may significantly reduce rework during and after implementation, as well as designing effective test plans, better project and resource planning.

The framework can estimate testability of object oriented software early in design phase, and it has been validated with a sound theoretical basis [2]. An effort has been

N. Meghanathan et al. (Eds.): CCSIT 2012, Part III, LNICST 86, pp. 178–187, 2012.

put forth to identify the major factors contributing in testability estimation at design phase. It has been concluded that Understandability and Complexity are the two factors affecting software testability estimation in design phase. Taking into account the significance of their contribution, a model has been developed to quantify software testability in design phase. Furthermore, test is performed to justify the statistical correlation of Testability with Understandability and Complexity.

2   OO Design Constructs

Object-oriented analysis and design have become the popular concepts in software development. These methodologies focus on objects as the primary agents involved in a computation. The process of early analysis and design provides the information needed to assess the quality of a design's classes, structure, and the relationships before they are committed to an implementation. A good object oriented design needs design rules and practices that must be known and used. Their violation will eventually have a strong impact on the quality attributes. Object oriented principles guide the designers what to support and what to avoid.

Several measures have been defined so far to estimate object oriented design. Cohesion, coupling, encapsulation and inheritance are the essential themes of object orientation that are commonly known to be the basis of internal quality of object oriented design and support in the context of measurement. Cohesion is related to the internal consistency of the parts in the design; it can be used to identify the poorly designed classes. Coupling indicates the relationship among the modules. Inheritance is the sharing of attributes and operations among classes based on a hierarchical relationship; it occurs at all levels in the hierarchy. Encapsulation is a mechanism that realizes the concept of abstraction and information hiding; it hides internal specification of an object and shows only the external interface.

3   Testability Factors

Testability is now established to be a distinct software quality characteristic. The notion of software testability has been a subject to a number of different interpretations by the experts. However, testability has always been an elusive concept and its correct measurement is a difficult exercise [10]. Further, there is little consensus among practitioners about 'what aspects are actually related to software testability'. Hence, it is difficult to get a clear view on all the potential factors that can affect testability and the dominant degree of these factors under different testing contexts [14]. Researchers and Practitioners have made significant amount of contributions in the direction of exploring testability factors in general and of object oriented software in particular [12][15][16][17][18][19]. It appears quite conclusive from the available literature that there is a conflict among practitioners in considering the factors while estimating testability in general and exclusively at design level.

An accurate measure of software quality depends on testability measurement, which in turn depends on the factors that can affect testability. Foregoing description shows that there is a conflict among practitioners about considering the factors while estimating testability. Therefore, it seems highly desirable and significant to identify the factors that facilitate or hinder testability in order to get the reliable and correct measure of testability. Though, getting a universally accepted set of testability factor is only probable, an effort has been made to collect a commonly accepted set of factors that can affect testability. However, without any loss of generality, it appears reasonable to include the factors namely, complexity, controllability, Observability, understandability, traceability, built-test as testability factors.

4   Mapping between Design Constructs to Testability Factors

In order to establish a contextual impact-relationship between OO software characteristics and testability factors, the influence of OO characteristic on each factor of testability was examined by several researchers. Most of the studies focused their attempt to examine the impact of object oriented characteristics and have successfully established relationships with quality factors.   However, researcher examined and assessed their impact on the particular aspect of study i.e. testability and by associatively and congruence perspective, concluded on identifying testability factors affected by object characteristics. It was observed that each of these characteristics, either have positive or negative impact on the factors that affect testability of object oriented software.

After an exhaustive review of available literature on the topic [6] [10] [11] [12] [15] 18], the relation between OO software characteristics and testability factors, shown in Figure 1 has been established.   Based on this relationship, models are to be developed for getting the quantitative value of testability factors. Further, the relative significance of individual design properties that influence software testability is weighted proportionally.

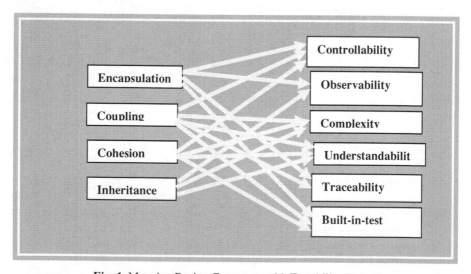

Fig. 1. Mapping Design Constructs with Testability Factors

Using the concept of multiple linear regressions, the relationship between dependent variables and multiple independent variables has been established and coefficients are determined.

5   Major Contributors

From the foregoing discussion it is revealed that the set of factors contributing testability estimation varies with the different school of thoughts. There is no universal set of testability factors to be addressed while computing testability. However, in section 3, it was established that 'a commonly accepted set of six factors of software testability include Complexity, Controllability, Observability, Understandability, Traceability and Built-in-Test'. It is further observed that each of the factors has its own contribution in making software testable. Out of these six factors, some of them have their positive impact in improving testability of object oriented software, while others have negative or negligible impact.

The only reason to establish a set of testability factors is to make the developer understand the factors to be addressed while considering testability. Therefore, it is equally mandatory to address the identified set of testability factors to integrate testability during development. But, it is also very important to know the weightage of the factor to be addressed and its contribution in developing testable software. A factor with low weightage need not be addressed because of its negligible contribution in testability estimation at design phase. Therefore, it is essential to know the contribution of each factor in order to accurately measure testability of software. Understandability and Complexity are the factors affecting software testability estimation in design phase. Therefore, these factors must be addressed well in advance while integrating testability in design phase. Models for these factors are developed in the following section.

6   Model Development

The generic quality models, [8][9] have been considered as a basis to develop the Testability Estimation Model for Object Oriented Design (TEM^{OOD}) shown in Figure 2, which involves the following steps:

  i.   Identification of Factors of Object Oriented Software that influences testability at Design phase.

  ii. Identification of Object Oriented Design Characteristics.

  iii. A means of linking of them

Based upon the relationship of the factors and testability, the relative significance of individual factors that has major impact on testability at design phase is weighed proportionally. A multiple linear regression technique has been used to get the coefficients. This technique establishes a relationship between dependent variable and multiple independent variables. The MR equation takes the following form:

$$Y = \alpha_0 + \beta_1 X_1 + \beta_2 X_2 + \beta_3 X_3 + \ldots\ldots\ldots\ldots\ldots \beta_n X_n \tag{1}$$

Where

- Y is dependent variable,

- The X_1, X_2, X_3.........X_n are independent variables related to Y and are expected to explain the variance in Y.

- The β_1, β_2, β_3,........β_n are the coefficients of the respective independent variables. Regression coefficient is the average amount of dependent increase/decrease when the independents are held constants.

- And α_0 is the intercept.

Using this technique, Understandability Model [3], Complexity Model [4] have been developed that are given below in equation (2) and (3) respectively.

$$\text{Understandability} = 1.33515 + 0.129*\text{CPM} + .0463*\text{COM} + .03405*\text{INM} \tag{2}$$

$$\text{Complexity} = 90.8488 + 10.5849*\text{CPM} - 102.7527*\text{COM} + 128.0856*\text{INM} \tag{3}$$

It has been extensively reviewed and discussed in section 3.0 and 5.0 that Understandability and Complexity are the major factors affecting software testability estimation in design phase. Therefore, these factors must be addressed well in advance while integrating testability in design phase. Furthermore, the model of Understandability [3] and Complexity [4] forms the strong basis for development of Testability Model. Metrics of the design constructs namely Coupling (CPM), Cohesion (COM) and Inheritance (INM) are used to address the major testability factors namely Understandability and Complexity. These two factors are further used to control testability of object oriented software design. Below is the Figure 2, which gives an overview of the main idea.

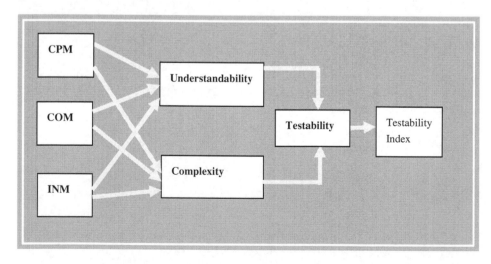

Fig. 2. Mapping Design Constructs with Major Contributors of Testability

In order to establish a model for Testability, a multiple linear regression technique discussed above in equation (1) has been used. Taking into account the impact of Coupling, Cohesion and Inheritance on testability contributors 'Understandability and Complexity', following MR equation has been formulated that can quantify Testability of object oriented design:

$$\text{Testability} = \alpha_0 + \beta_1 *\text{Understandability} + \beta_2 *\text{Complexity} \tag{4}$$

The data used for developing model given in equation (4) has been taken from [20], which consist of six industrial projects with around 10 to 20 classes. The values of 'Coupling Metrics (CPM), Cohesion Metrics (COM) and Inheritance Metrics (INM)' and the values of 'Understandability and Complexity' have been used. Using MATLAB, correlation coefficients are computed and model of Testability estimation is thus formulated as given below in equation (5).

$$\text{Testability} = -483.65 + 300.92*\text{Understandability} - .86*\text{Complexity} \tag{5}$$

The applications that are used in validating the multivariate linear regression model for computation of Testability have been taken from [7]. We labeled the applications as: System A, System B, System C and System D. All the systems are commercial software implemented in C++ with the number of classes as shown in table 6.0 (a).

Table 1. (a): Projects and Classes

Projects	Classes
System A	6
System B	5
System C	6
System D	10

The descriptive statistics and correlations between the design constructs and Understandability are given in Tables 1 (b)-(i).

Table 1. (b): Descriptive Statistics for System A

	Min	Max	Mean
Understandability	1.65	2.39	2.02
Complexity	-823.34	-309.57	-566.45
Testability	-248245	-93643	-170944

Table 1. (c): Correlation Analysis for System A

	Testability	Understandability	Complexity
Testability	1	.71	.99
Understandability		1	.71
Complexity			1

Table 1. (d): Descriptive Statistics for System B

	Min	Max	Mean
Understandability	1.87	2.55	2.21
Complexity	-1726.95	-504.49	-1115.72
Testability	-520158	-152299	-336228.5

Table 1. (e): Correlation Analysis for System B

	Testability	Understandability	Complexity
Testability	1	.94	.99
Understandability		1	.93
Complexity			1

Table 1. (f): Descriptive Statistics for System C

	Min	Max	Mean
Understandability	2.43	5.54	3.98
Complexity	-3862.72	-577.75	-2220.23
Testability	-1162865	-174344	-668604.50

Table 1. (g): Correlation Analysis for System C

	Testability	Understandability	Complexity
Testability	1	.95	.99
Understandability		1	.94
Complexity			1

Table 1. (h): Descriptive Statistics for System D

	Min	Max	Mean
Understandability	3.10	6.83	4.96
Complexity	-5023.94	-2447.64	-3235.79
Testability	2726.41	5894.61	4310.51

Table 1. (i): Correlation Analysis for System D

	Testability	Understandability	Complexity
Testability	1	.81	.84
Understandability		1	.75
Complexity			1

Table 1. (j): Correlation Analysis Summary

	Testability X Understandability	Testability X Complexity
System A	.71	.99
System B	.94	.99
System C	.95	.99
System D	.81	.84

Table 1.(j) summarizes the results of the correlation analysis for Testability model, which shows that for all the Systems, both Understandability and Complexity are highly correlated with Testability.

7   Hypothesis Testing of Coefficient of Correlation

An observed coefficient of correlation of Understandability and Complexity with Testability strongly indicates the higher significance of considering both the factors (Understandability and Complexity) for making a prediction of software testability in design phase. Further to justify the claim, a test to determine the statistical significance of the correlation coefficient observed may be appropriate. For the purpose, Hypothesis testing is performed to test the significance of r (Correlation Coefficient) using the following formula:

$$t_r = \frac{r\sqrt{N-2}}{\sqrt{1-r^2}}$$

With $N-2$ degree of freedom, a coefficient of correlation is judged as statistically significant when the t value equals or exceeds the t critical value in the t distribution table.

$H_{0(T \wedge U)}$: Testability and Understandability are not highly correlated.

Table 2. (a): Correlation Coefficient Test for Testability and Understandability

	System A	System B	System C	System D
Testability ^ Understandability	.71	.94	.95	.81
t_r	2.01	4.77	6.08	3.90
$t_{r\text{-Critical Value}}$	2.447	2.571	2.447	2.228
$t_r > t_{r\text{-Critical Value}}$	x	√	√	√
$H_{0(T \wedge U)}$	Accept	Reject	Reject	Reject

$H_{0(T \wedge C)}$: Testability and Complexity are not highly correlated.

Table 2. (b): Correlation Coefficient Test for Testability and Complexity

	System A	System B	System C	System D
Testability ^ Complexity	.99	.99	.99	.84
t_r	14.03	12.15	14.03	4.37
$t_{r\text{-Critical Value}}$	2.447	2.571	2.447	2.228
$t_r > 2.44$	√	√	√	√
$H_{0(T \wedge C)}$	Reject	Reject	Reject	Reject

Using two-tailed test at the .05 level with different degrees of freedom, it is evident from the tables 2(a) and (b), the null hypothesis is rejected (except for System 'A' of Testability and Understandability). Therefore, the researcher's claim of correlating Testability with Understandability and Complexity at design phase is statistically justified.

8   Conclusion

Software testability factors are identified and their impact on testability has been analyzed in this paper. Two of the major factors affecting software testability in design phase have been taken into account. Considering both the major factors, 'Understandability and Complexity' a model to quantify testability of object oriented design has been formulated (TEM^{OOD}) and the statistical inferences are validated for better acceptability. Hypothesis testing is performed to test the significance of r (Correlation Coefficient). The proposed model to quantify testability of object oriented software design is highly significant and correlated with software design constructs. Though the model has been validated using try-out data, but its utility may be analyzed for larger set of data. An empirical validation of the model TEM^{OOD} will be carried out as a future work.

References

1. Richard, T.: Towards Automated Software Testing: Techniques, Classification and Frameworks, Ph.D. Thesis, Blekinge Institute of Technology, Sweden (2006)
2. Nazir, M., Khan, R.A., Mustafa, K.: Testability Estimation Framework. Internaional Journal Of Computer Applications (June 2010) (accepted for publication)
3. Nazir, M., Khan, R.A., Mustafa, K.: A Metrics Based Model for Understandability Quantification. International Journal of Computing 2(4) (April 2010)
4. Nazir, M., Khan, R.A., Mustafa, K.: Complexity Quantification Model: A Metric-Based Approach. In: 4th IEEE International Conference on Advanced Computing & Communication Technologies, Panipat (October 30, 2010)
5. Nazir, M., Khan, R.A.: Testability Estimation of Object Oriented Software: A Critical Review. In: The Proceeding of International Conference on Information and Communication Technologies, Dehradun, pp. 960–962 (2007)
6. Jungmayr, S.: Identifying Test-Critical Dependencies. In: The Proceedings IEEE International Conference on Software Maintenance, pp. 404–413 (2002)
7. Genero, M., Olivas, J., Piattini, M., Romero, F.: A Controlled Experiment for Corroborating the Usefulness of Class Diagram Metrics at the Early Phases of Object Oriented Developments. In: Proceedings of ADIS 2001, Workshop on Decision Support in Software Engineering (2001)
8. Khan, R.A., Mustafa, K.: A Model for Object Oriented Design Quality Assessment. In: Process Technology Symposium, Kusadasi, Izmir, Turkey, June 28-July 2 (2004)
9. Dromey, R.G.: A Model for Software Product Quality. IEEE Transaction on Software Engineering 21(2), 146–162 (1995)
10. Mouchawrab, S., Briand, L.C., Labiche, Y.: A Measurement Framework for Object-Oriented Software Testability. Info. and Software Technology 47(15), 979–997 (2005)

11. Bruntink, M., Deursen, A.V.: Predicting class Estability using Object-Oriented Metrics. In: Proc. IEEE International Workshop on Source Code Analysis and Manipulation, pp. 136–145 (2004)
12. Lo, B.W.N., Shi, H.: A Preliminary Testability Model for Object-Oriented Software. In: Proc. International Conf. on Software Engineering, Education, Practice, pp. 330–337. IEEE (1998)
13. Voas, Miller: Improving the Software Development Process using Testability Research. IEEE Software, 114–121 (1992)
14. Zhao, L.: A New Approach for Software Testability Analysis. In: Proceeding of the 28th International Conference on Software Engineering, Shanghai, pp. 985–988 (2006)
15. Binder, R.V.: Design for Testability in Object-Oriented Systems. Communications of the ACM 37(9), 87–101 (1994)
16. Gao, J., Shih, M.-C.: A Component Testability Model for Verification and Measurement. In: Proc. of the 29th Annual International Computer Software and Applications Conference, pp. 211–218. IEEE Comp. Society (2005)
17. James, B.: Heuristics of software Testability (1999)
18. Jungmayr, S.: Testability during Design, Software Technik-Trends. In: Proceedings of the GI Working Group Test, Analysis and Verification of Software, Potsdam, pp. 10–11 (2002)
19. Mulo, E.: Design for Testability in Software Systems, Master's Thesis (2007), http://swerl.tudelft.nl/twiki/pub/Main/ResearchAssignment/RA-Emmanuel-Mulo.pdf
20. Khan, R.A., Mustafa, K.: Metric based Testability Model for Object Oriented Design (MTMOOD). SIGSOFT Software Engineering Notes 34(2) (March 2009)

Generation of All Spanning Trees in the Limelight

Saptarshi Naskar[1], Krishnendu Basuli[2], and Samar Sen Sarma[3]

[1] Department of Computer Science, Sarsuna College, India
sapgrin@gmail.com
[2] Department of Computer Science, WBSU, India
krishnendu.basuli@gmail.com
[3] Department of Computer Science and Engineering, University of Calcutta
92, A. P. C. Road, Kolkata – 700 009, India
sssarma2001@yahoo.com

Abstract. Many problems in science and engineering [1, 3, 8, 10] can be formulated in terms of graphs. There are problems where spanning trees are necessary to be computed from the given graphs. Connected subgraph with all the n vertices of the graph $G(V,E)$, where $|V|=n$, having exactly of $n-1$ edges called the spanning tree of the given graph. The major bottleneck of any tree generation algorithm is the prohibitively large cost of testing whether a newly born tree is twin of a previously generated one and also there is a problem that without checking for circuit generated subgraph is tree or non-tree. This problem increases the time complexity of the existing algorithms. The present approach avoids this problem with a simple but efficient procedure and at the same time ensures that a large number of non-tree subgraphs are not generated at all.

Keywords: Spanning Tree, Vertex Connectivity, KMTT, PRIES, SPRIES.

There are three distinct classes of existing tree generation algorithms, viz., (a) Trees by examination of all ${}^eC_{n-1}$ sets of edges, where e and n are number of edges and number of vertices of a simple, connected graph, respectively [2, 11] (b) Trees by cyclic interchange method [3, 6, 10] and (c) Trees by decomposition method [3]. Generation of trees involves three basic questions: (a) What percent of ${}^eC_{n-1}$ edge combinations turns out to be tree? (b) How efficient is the tree-testing algorithm? and (c) How much storage is required?

In this context, the algorithm proposed in this paper generates a very small number of non-trees; its storage requirement is independent of the number of trees and the associated testing procedure is simpler and efficient. The works of Peikarski [7] and Sen Sarma [1] contain the idea of the present method. The major achievements include rejection of non-trees prior to testing and the removal of storage limitations and a part of generated subgraph is tree without checking for circuit.

An undirected graph $G=(V,E,F)$ consists of a set of vertices V, a set of edges E and a function F that maps each edge $e \in E$ onto an unordered pair of vertices. Here G is a simple, symmetric and connected graph, i.e., G has no self-loops, parallel edges and edge orientations. A tree T of a graph G of V vertices is a loop free subgraph encompassing all the vertices of G [3, 8].

N. Meghanathan et al. (Eds.): CCSIT 2012, Part III, LNICST 86, pp. 188–192, 2012.
© Institute for Computer Sciences, Social Informatics and Telecommunications Engineering 2012

Kirchhoff's Matrix Tree Theorem (KMTT): For a given a graph G with no self-loops, parallel edges and edge orientations, let B_0 be its incidence matrix with one row removed, and B_0^t be the transpose of B_0, then determinant $| B_0.B_0^t |$ gives the number of spanning trees of G [5].

Since a tree T of G with n vertices has $n-1$ edges, one can generate all $(n-1)$ edge combinations and filter a subset of them by a testing sieve that allows only trees to pass. A preferable algorithm will be that generates only trees. The present algorithm though generates non-tree edge combinations, but the number of such combinations relative to the number of trees is drastically reduced. For this we generate a set of convenient data structures, namely *PRIES* and *SPRIES* of a graph, at the outset from the incidence matrix of the given graph. Now the proposed algorithms are given below:

Algorithm 1. *Generation of SPRIES Matrix.*

Input: The incidence matrix A of the given graph G.
Output: The *SPRIES* matrix.

Step 1: From the incidence matrix A find the maximum degree vertex, delete the row and hence obtain *PRIES* [1].
Step 2: $i \leftarrow 2$; maxlim $\leftarrow \lfloor 2e/n \rfloor$
Step 3: Choose next highest degree vertex.
Step 4: Keep all the edges in the ith column, leaving the edges already chosen and shift other edges to the right.
Step 5: $i \leftarrow i+1$
Step 6: Repeat through Step 3 while $i \leq$ maxlim.
Step 7: For i=1 to n-1
Step 8:   For j=1 to maxlim
Step 9:   If A[i][j] != null
Step 10:   arr[i]=A[i][j]
Step 11:   break;
Step 12:   End If
Step 13   j←j+1
Step 13: End For
Step 14   i←i+1
Step 15: End For
Step 16: For i=1 to n-1
Step 17:   If arr[i] = null
Step 18:   Insert all edges that are incident to the priority vertices of A[i] into the priority columns.
Step 19:   End If
Step 20:   i←i+1
Step 21: End For
Step 22: Stop.

Algorithm 2. *Combination Generation for Trees only from Privileged Columns.*

Input: The *SPRIES* matrix *A* (derived from Algorithm 1).
Output: The trees one at a time.

Step 1: Choose elements from *SPRIES* in such a way that (i) at least one element from 1st column, (ii) exactly one element from each row.
Step 2: If all elements are selected from privileged columns, then go to Step 3 otherwise go to Step 1.
Step 3: If all the selected elements are unique then output the combination as tree.
Step 4: Repeat through Step 1, while all privileged columns are exhausted.
Step 5: Stop.

Algorithm 3. *Combination Generation for Trees from Non-Privileged Columns.*

Input: The *SPRIES* matrix.
Output: The trees one at a time.

Step 1: Choose elements from *SPRIES* in such a way that (i) at least one element from 1st column, (ii) exactly one element from each row.
Step 2: If chosen elements are taken from non-privileged columns, go to Step 3 else go to Step 1.
Step 3: If all the chosen elements or just subset of the elements are present in the privileged columns and also they are present in the same row or the combination are not distinct do not choose the combination as a tree.
Step 4: Repeat through Step 1, while all privileged columns are exhausted.
Step 5: Stop.

Algorithm 4. *Tree Testing Algorithm* [3]
Input: The adjacency matrix *M* of the given graph *G*.
Output: Checking whether an (*n*–1)-edge combination of *G* is a tree.

Step 1: Read *G* initialize subgraph *g* by *G*.
Step 2: Select vertex *i* in *g*.
Step 3: Fuse all vertices adjacent to *i* with *i*, and call the new vertex *i*.
Step 4: Is the number of vertices nonadjacent to *i* same as before fusion? If no, repeat through Step 3.
Step 5: Delete from *g*, vertex *i* (along with all vertices fused with *i*) call the remaining subgraph as *g*.
Step 6: Is any vertex left in *g*? If yes, do not take the combination as tree, else call the combination as tree of the graph *G*.
Step 7: Stop.

In the present method the algorithms presented, graphs are represented by the adjacency list, hence the storage requirement i.e. space complexity is proportional to

en, where e is number of edges and n is the number of vertices of the graph G. Hence, the space complexity is $O(en)$. The time complexity is given below:

For Algorithm 1: In worst case $\lfloor 2e/n \rfloor$ is $(n-1)$, and choosing the highest degree vertex then need to search total $n^2(n-1)/2$ elements . So the time complexity is $O(n^3)$.

For Algorithm 2: In this algorithm the time complexity is $O(n)$. Since $n-1$ combination is required for individual tree generation.

For Algorithm 3: In this algorithm the time complexity is $O(n)$. Since $n-1$ combination is required for individual tree generation.

For Algorithm 4: In worst case all $n-1$ columns are fused with i^{th} column and in each fusion one perform at most n logical addition. Hence the time complexity is $O(n^2)$.

Since exponential trees are the output of the algorithm, physical time measurement is of no concern here. However we have noted that, for a large graph the computation time is of the order of several minutes using a Pentium IV based Personal Computer.

| V | E | C | | | T | % of Tree | | |
		No of Combinations				(T/C)*100		
No. of vertices	No. of edges	Brute-Force	PRIES	SPRIES	Trees	Brute-Force	PRIES	SPRIES
4	6	20	16	16	16	80	100	100
5	8	70	42	40	40	56	95	100
5	9	126	79	75	75	60	95	100
6	12	792	348	336	300	38	86	89
7	17	12376	3934	4025	3024	25	76	75
7	19	27132	10320	8575	8232	30	80	96

In this paper an algorithm is proposed for computing all possible spanning trees of a simple, connected, non-oriented graph. This algorithm, in general, outperforms the algorithm for computing the same in [1], where a large number of non-tree combinations are generated. This algorithm is also generating such undesired non-tree combinations, but the number of generating such combinations is much less here. In every case of the experimental results, it is been verified that results computed by present algorithm and by the method developed in [1] with the results computed using *KMTT* [5]. The immediate objective is to enrich the algorithm so that no non-tree combinations are obtained.

As the number n of vertices of a simple, connected, non-oriented graph increases, the procedure predominantly surpasses the *PRIES* technique [1]. Observed that, for the graphs with much less number of vertices of degree much higher than the rest, the percentage of non-tree generation becomes negligibly small. Since the time required in computing the trees is proportional to the number of combinations of edges to be tested for trees, a little extrapolation shows how efficient the present algorithm is. The efficiency criterion is still far behind the ideal situation, where no testing for trees is necessary.

References

[1] Sen Sarma, S., Rakshit, A., Sen, R.K., Choudhury, A.K.: An Efficient Tree Generation Algorithm. Journal of the Institution of Electronics and Telecommunications Engineers (IETE) 27(3), 105–109 (1981)

[2] Rao, B., Murti, V.G.K.: Enumeration of All Trees a Graph Computer Program. Electronics Letters 6(4) (1970)

[3] Deo, N.: Graph Theory with Applications to Engineering and Computer Science. Prentice-Hall of India Private Limited, New Delhi (2003)

[4] Sen Sarma, S., Rakshit, A., Sen, R.K., Choudhury, A.K.: An Efficient Tree Generation Algorithm. Journal of the Institution of Electronics and Telecommunications Engineers (IETE) 27(3), 109 (1981)

[5] Bollobas, B.: Modern Graph Theory – Kirchhoff's Matrix Tree Theorem, p. 54. Springer International Edition, New York (2002)

[6] Hakimi, S.L.: On the Trees of a Graph and Their Generation. J. Franklin Inst. 270, 347–359 (1961)

[7] Peikarski, M.: Listing of All Possible Trees of a Linear Graph, lbid, CT-12, Correspondence, pp. 124–125 (1965)

[8] Sen Sarma, S., Rakshit, A., Sen, R.K., Choudhury, A.K.: An Efficient Tree Generation Algorithm. Journal of the Institution of Electronics and Telecommunications Engineers (IETE) 27(3), 109 (1981)

[9] Pak, I., Postnikov, A.: Enumeration of Spanning Trees of Graphs. Harvard University, Massachusetts Institute of Technology (1994)

[10] Mayeda, W.: Graph Theory. Wiley Inter-science (1972)

[11] Mayeda, W., Seshu, S.: Generation of Trees without Duplications. IEEE Trans. CT-12, 181–185 (1965)

A New Encryption Method for Secured Message Passing by Sorting Technique

S. Muthusundari[1] and S. Santhosh Baboo[2]

[1] Sathyabama University
Chennai, India
[2] Department of Computer Science
D.G.Vaishnav College, Chennai, India
nellailath@yahoo.co.in, santhos2001@sify.com

Abstract. Generally, in encryption or decryption process some of the characters are inter changed by using some encryption and decryption algorithms with key. This paper puts focusing a safe mechanism for secured message passing to tackle the security problem of information. We propose a new technique to encrypt the text message by sorting technique. In our method, the encryption process which is carried out by the plain text is arranged in to alphabetical order by sorting procedure and produces the cipher text. The proposed encryption technique needs the ASCII value of the characters. This technique has two advantages over traditional schemes. First, the encryption and decryption procedures are very simple, and subsequently, much faster. Second, the security level is very high due to the ASCII value substitutions of alphabetic characters. In this paper, the encryption and decryption procedures are explained.

Keywords: Encryption, Decryption, Plain text, Cipher text, ASCII value, sorting technique.

1 Introduction

Encryption is a mechanism by which a message is translated into another form so that only the sender and receiver can see. When a message is *encrypted*, that means that it is transformed into a form when the data is passed through some substitute technique, shifting technique, table references or mathematical operations. All those processes generate a different form of that data and that is not readable. When a message is *decrypted*, it will get the original sent message. Encryption can provide strong security for data in the transmission. In general, cryptography concept is for maintaining the secured message passing system. Encryption, a cryptographic implementation, is the conversion of data into mixture of characters that, when viewed, cannot be read as simple text. Simple text is defined as standard written text, by the sender. The encrypt data is called a cipher, or cipher text which is in the other form of given data [1], while unencrypted data is called plaintext. Decryption is the process of converting encrypted data (cipher text) back into its original form (plaintext), so it can be readable.

N. Meghanathan et al. (Eds.): CCSIT 2012, Part III, LNICST 86, pp. 193–201, 2012.

The Network security is concerned with the security of information. [Good security means that the system and users are protected from attacks originating from inside the network just as well as they from outside attacks.] Security – guarding against interference by entities external to a system. The main aim is to protect the information, which is sent from one system to another through network. The information security is defined as follows.

Information security = Confidentiality + integrity + availability+ authentication. There can be no information security without confidentiality. Confidentiality ensures the unauthorized users do not intercept copy or replicate the information. The integrity is necessary so that the accurate information can flow over the network. The information security is also required during the retrial of the data. The users should be authenticated to retrieve data and the information is not secure without authentication. There is no such thing as a completely secure computer network. Fig 1: shows the basic cryptographic system which uses the encryption and the decryption process based on the key.

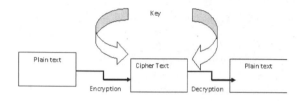

Fig. 1. Basic cryptographic system

2   Existing Techniques

All the encryption algorithms are based on two methods: the first one is   substitution, in which each element in the plaintext (bit, letter and group of bits or letters) is associated with   another element and the second is transposition, the elements of the plaintext have simply been re-arranged in another form; their position   have been changed.[2]

2.1   Transposition Cipher

These ciphers are block ciphers, which changes the position of particular characters or bits of the input block. For the encryption, the plaintext is broken into n symbols and a key specifies one of (n!-1) possible permutations. The deciphering is accomplished by using an inverse permutation which restores the original sequence. [3] Transposition ciphers preserve the frequency distribution of single letters destroy the diagram and higher-order distributions. These techniques are also combined with other ciphers to produce a more secure product cipher. The simplest such cipher is thee rail fence technique, in which the plain text is written down as a sequence of diagonals and then read off as a sequence of rows. For example, to encipher the message——we are discovered flee at once —with a rail fence of depth 3, we write the following

```
W . . . E . . . C . . . R . . . L . . . T . . . . E
. E . R . D . S . O . E . E . F . E . A . O . . C .
. . A . . . I . . . V . . . D . . . E . . . . N . .
```

The encrypted message: WECRLTEERDSOEEFEAOCAIVDEN

2.2 Substitution Ciphers

A substitution technique is one in which the letters of plain text are replaced by other letters or by numbers or symbols. The well known substitution cipher was invented by Julius Caesar. The Caesar cipher involves replacing each letter of the alphabet with three positions. [4]For example: Plaintext: task completed

Cipher text: wdvn frpsohwhg. In this technique alphabet are wrapped around for the alphabets x, y and z so that the letter following Z is A. We can define the transformation as follows Plain: a b c d e f g h i j k l m n o p q r s t u v w x y z

Cipher: D E F G H I J K L M N O P Q R S T U V W X Y Z A B C

3 Proposed Methodology

The system deals with security by using sorting technique for encryption and decryption.

3.1 Encryption Algorithm

The encryption process of C= E (K, P) using the proposed algorithm consists of three steps.

Steps
1. Assign the ASCII numeric values for the alphabets from the figure 2.
2. Arrange the numeric values by ascending order by any other sorting technique.
3. Substitute the alphabets for the ordered set.

ASCII	Hex	Symbol	ASCII	Hex	Symbol	ASCII	Hex	Symbol	ASCII	Hex	Symbol
64	40	@	80	50	P	96	60	`	112	70	
65	41	A	81	51	Q	97	61	a	113	71	p
66	42	B	82	52	R	98	62	b	114	72	q
67	43	C	83	53	S	99	63	c	115	73	r
68	44	D	84	54	T	100	64	d	116	74	s
69	45	E	85	55	U	101	65	e	117	75	t
70	46	F	86	56	V	102	66	f	118	76	u
71	47	G	87	57	W	103	67	g	119	77	v
72	48	H	88	58	X	104	68	h	120	78	w
73	49	I	89	59	Y	105	69	i	121	79	x
74	4A	J	90	5A	Z	106	6A	j	122	7A	y
75	4B	K	91	5B	[	107	6B	k	123	7B	z
76	4C	L	92	5C	\	108	6C	l	124	7C	{
77	4D	M	93	5D	]	109	6D	m	125	7D	|
78	4E	N	94	5E	^	110	6E	n	126	7E	}
79	4F	O	95	5F	_	111	6F	o	127	7F	~

Fig. 2. ASCII value for the characters

3.2   Working Principle of Encryption

Step 1:

The encryption process involves taking each character of data and comparing it against a key. For example, one could encrypt the string "GOD IS GREAT" of data in any number of ways, for example, one may use a simple letter-number method. In this method, each in the alp number encryption (i.e.,ASCII(A)=   65,ASCII (B)=66,ASCII(C)=67, and so on), this data is translated into the following numbers: 71 79 68 73 83 71 82 69 65 84 .

Step 2:

Arrange the series of step 1 with ascending order by using with any sorting technique.
    In this method we are applying the basic bubble sort technique to arrange the series.
    Input of step 1 series: 71 79 68 73 83 71 82 69 65 84
    Output after the bubble sort: 65 68 69 71 71 73 79 82 83 84

Step 3:

Now the output of step 2 is substituted with the corresponding alphabets.
    Substitution of alphabets: ADEGGIORST.

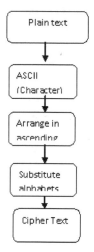

Fig. 3. Encryption Block Diagram

B   Decryption Algorithm

The decryption algorithm performs the reverse operations of encryption such that P = D (K, C). It is done in three steps. The steps are as follows,

    1. Reverse the cipher text. Then substitute the ASCII value.
    2. Arrange the step 1 result by ascending order by using any sorting technique.

3. Match with the cipher text, if it is match with cipher text then it will display the plain text, otherwise it will give us error report. i.e the plain text will not be identified by the receiver.

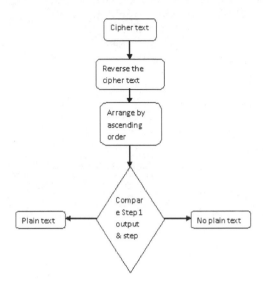

Fig. 4. Decryption Block Diagram

3.3   Working Principle of Decryption

Step 1: Reverse the cipher text from the encryption process.

Cipher Text: ADEGGIORST
Reverse the cipher text: TSROIGGEDA

Step 2: Arrange the reverse of the cipher text in ascending order by using with bubble sort technique.

Now the output is as: ADEGGIORST

Step 3: Compare the output of step 1 and step 2. It is matches then the plain text will be displayed from the file. Otherwise it will not display the plain text. The receiver will not identify the plain text. Once he knows the key process only he can decrypt the message.

Step 1 output   = step 2 output
ADEGGIORST =   ADEGGIORST   hence the receiver can decrypt the text message and he can get the plain text.
Decrypt message: GOD IS GREAT

3.4   Case Study of Encryption Process and Decryption Process

Case 1: Encryption Process

Consider the plain text as a single word: MILITARY
Step 1: Assign the ASCII Value of each alphabet in the plain text. Now we get,
ASCII (M) = 77   ASCII (I) = 73   ASCII (L) = 76
ASCII (I) = 73   ASCII (T) = 84   ASCII (A) = 65
ASCII (R) = 82   ASCII (Y) = 89
PLAIN TEXT   M I   L   I   T   A   R   Y
ASCII VALUE   77 73   76   73 84   65 82   89
STEP 2: Arrange the ASCII value by bubble sort technique
ASCII value   :   77   73 76 73 84 65 82 89
Ascending Order: 65   73 73 76 77 82 84 89
Step 3: Substitute the alphabets for the ascending order.
Ascending Order: 65   73   73   76   77   82   84   89
Cipher Text   : A   I   I   L   M   R   T   Y
PLAIN TEXT: M I L I T A R Y
CIPHER TEXT: A I I L M R T Y

Case 1: Decryption Process

Step 1: Get the cipher text from the encryption process and reverse the cipher text.
CIPHER TEXT: A I I L M R T Y
Reverse Cipher Text: Y T R M L I I A

Step 2: Arrange the output of reverse the cipher text in ascending order by bubble sort
technique.
Reverse Cipher Text: Y T R M L I I A
Ascending order: A I I L M R T Y

Step 3: Match the cipher text and step 2 output. If both are match then the receiver
will get the plain text from the index file, otherwise he will not get the plain text . The
cipher text will not decrypted by the receiver. Hence security provides by the algorithm.

CIPHER TEXT: A I I L M R T Y   is equal to

Ascending order: A I I L M R T Y   Hence the receiver will get the plain text.

PLAIN TEXT: M I L I T A R Y

Case Study of Encryption Process and Decryption Process:

Case 2: Encryption Process

Consider the plain text as a single sentence: WELCOME TO THE STAGE
Step 1: Assign the ASCII Value of each alphabet in the plain text. Now we get,
ASCII (W) =   87   ASCII (E)   = 69   ASCII (L)   =   76
ASCII (C)   = 6   ASCII (O)   = 79   ASCII (M)   =   77

ASCII (E)   = 69   ASCII (T)   = 84   ASCII (O)   =   79
ASCII (T)   = 84   ASCII (H) = 72   ASCII (E)   =   69
ASCII (S)   = 83   ASCII (T)   = 84   ASCII (A) =   65
ASCII (G) = 71   ASCII (E)   = 69
PLAIN TEXT: W E L C O M E T O T   H E   S   T A G   E
ASCII VALUE: 87 69 76 67 79 77 69   84 79   84 72   69   83 84 65 71   69

Step 2: Arrange the ASCII value by bubble sort technique

ASCII VALUE: 87 69 76 67 79 77 69   84 79   84 72   69   83 84 65 71   69
Ascending order: 65 67 69 69 69 69 71   72 76   77 79   79   83 84 84 84   87
Step 3: Substitute the alphabets for the ascending order.
Ascending order: 65 67 69 69 69 69 71   72 76   77 79   79   83 84 84 84   87
Cipher Text: A C E E E E   G H L M O O   S   T   T   T   W
PLAIN TEXT: W E L C O M   E   T O T   H   E   S   T A G   E
Cipher Text: A C   E   E   E E G H L   M O   O   S T   T   T   W

Case 2: Decryption Process

Step 1: Get the cipher text from the encryption process and reverse the cipher text.
CIPHER TEXT: A   C   E   E   E   G   H LM O   O S T   T T W
Reverse Cipher Text W T   T   T S O   O   M LH G E   E   E   E C A

Step 2: Arrange the output of reverse the cipher text in ascending order by bubble sort technique.
Reverse Cipher Text W T   T   T S   O   O   M L   H G   E E   E   E   A
Ascending order: A C   E   E E E G H L M O   O S T   T T   W

Step 3: Match the cipher text   and step 2 output. If both are match then the receiver will get the plain text from the index file, otherwise he will not get the plain text . The cipher text will not decrypted by the receiver. Hence security provides by the algorithm.
CIPHER TEXT: A   C   E   E   E E G   H L M O O   S TT   T W
is equal to
Ascending order: A C EE EE G H L M   O O S T   T   T   W
    Hence the receiver will get the plain text.
PLAIN TEXT: W   E   L   C   O   M   E   TO T H E S   T   A G   E

4   Simulation and Experimental Results

We present here results generated from practical implementation of our algorithm. A plain text is taken as the input to the algorithm. The various steps involved in the encryption algorithm are carried out.

The sample test data is given below from the implementation of C program.

4.1 Implementation Procedure

The plain text which is transformed in to its ASCII value and then ASCII value will be arranged in to ascending order by using Bubble sort technique, then for the value the corresponding characters will replace and hence produce the Cipher text.

The Cipher text are given as input to the receiver than the receiver decrypt by reverse the cipher text and again by the same reverse process of encryption it is substitutes its ASCII value then arrange in ascending order by using Bubble sort technique. Then it match with cipher text and the ascending order substitutes data, if both are match then it takes the plain text from the file and display. On any other way it will not decrypt the plain text. Hence security is higher than any other encryption methods. Even though we know the key for the decryption process also the receiver cannot able to attain the plain text. If receiver cannot then definitely no one can attain the plain text. So 100% security message passing is produced.

The results shown here are implemented by using bubble sort technique. Hence the system is implemented successfully

5   Conclusion and Future Work

The Encryption algorithm, presented above, is a simple, direct substitution algorithm using sorting technique. Consequently, it is very fast and suitable for high speed encryption applications. The ASCII value translations give strength to this encryption algorithm. The combination of alphabetic substitution, sorting makes the decryption process very simple.

In future work, to improve the performance of the encryption and decryption process by using a novel sorting technique D-Shuffle method is going to be proposed , in place of Bubble sort. The performance and the efficiency of our proposed algorithm will be more benefited for secure message passing system.

References

1. Wikipedia, "Encryption",
   http://en.wikipedia.org/wiki/Encryption
   (modified on December 13, 2006)
2. Lee, M.H.: Bounds on Substitution Ciphers. IEEE Information Theory 6, 2294–2296 (2007)
3. Stinson, D.R.: Cryptogrphy Theory and Practice, 2nd edn.
4. Kaufman, C., et al.: Network Security Private Communication in a Public World. Prentice Hall of India Private Limited (2003)
5. Information Technology Journal 4(3), 204–221 (2005)
6. Information Technology Journal 4(3), 204–221 (2005)
7. Shannon's, C.: Communication Theory of Secrecy Systems
8. Yang, K.-H., Niu, S.-J.: Data Safe Transmission Mechanism Based on Integrated Encryption Algorithm. Staffordshire University
9. Chen Tao, X.Y.: Design and implementation of encryption algorithm based on dimension magic cube. Journal of Information 2, 13–14 (2005)

Algorithm for Constructing Complete Distributive Lattice of Polyhedrons Defined over Three Dimensional Rectangular Grid- Part II

G. Ramesh Chandra* and E.G. Rajan

Pentagram Research Centre Pvt. Ltd.,
Mehdipatnam, Hyderbad, India
rameshchandra_g@vnrvjiet.in, rajan_eg@yahoo.co.in

Abstract. This paper initially discusses how Geometric Filters (G-Filters) are useful as an efficient shape filter when compared to other shape filter such as mathematical morphology. The algorithm for constructing complete distributive lattice of polyhedrons for three dimensional rectangular grid is divided in to two algorithms. The first algorithm proposes a new way automatic construction of 256 convex polygons by removing the duplicate subsets. The second algorithm proposes a way for hierarchical path enumeration in visualizing the relationships between convex polyhedron sets and their corresponding subsets. The final lattice is generated based on the information provided by these two algorithms.

Keywords: Geometric Filters, Automatic Convex Polyhedron Construction, lattice, 3D rectangular grid, Hierarchical Path Enumeration, 3-D image processing.

1   Introduction

In very broad set-theoretic terms, a system is a filter which has a separate, to partition a given set of entities in to disjoint subsets, based on whether they have or do not have a stipulated property. One does, in principle, conceive of a procedure for such a partitioning, one that is a function of time and space, and which depends for its realization on physical device, be it a sieve, or on electronic circuit, or a computer.

In the study and design of such filtering procedures for signals, one crucial underlying principle seems to be the following: *System models of signal processing operations and those of sources from which signals originate should belong to the same class.* This principle was introduced by Rajan and Sinha , and is referred here as R-S Principle(RSP). It is implied here that signals are to be thought of as outputs of sources, and that their description is not really complete unless we specify source models.

---

* AssociateProfessor, Computer Science Department, V.N.R. Vignana Jyothi Institute of Engineering and Technology, Bachupally, Hyderabad, Andhra Pradesh, India.

N. Meghanathan et al. (Eds.): CCSIT 2012, Part III, LNICST 86, pp. 202–210, 2012.

The existing time invariant systems which can serve as filters, are governed by differential equations do not serve as canonical models. These systems of filter theory cannot be able to serve the purpose of efficient image processing operations. In general, complex systems that are traditionally modelled in terms of differential equations and partial differential equations could be ideally modelled and studied in the framework of cellular automata[2].

Alternatively, one can create generalized spatial domain techniques for processing images and pictures, which make use of shape based filters. Morphological image processing is one such technique[1][7][8][9][10], which deals with processing of form and structure of digital images. Yet this technique does not measure up to fulfil the requirements of shape based filtering similar to traditional frequency based filtering. The question that arises now is whether it is possible to develop a technique or at least set a trend which leads to the formulation of a theory for shape based filtering. The theoretical foundations for such shape based filters are studied in the framework of Geometric filters also called G-Filters[2][4][5][6]. The G-Filters are practically implemented in the processing of 2-D images to effectively and efficiently identifying the shape features such as corners, curves, lines, dots and skeleton[2][4][5]. The Logical Image processing system (LIPS) version 3.0 implemented these G-Filters for efficient shape feature detection for 2-D images.

There are no such techniques formulated till now for the 3-D images under the rectangular grid. The algebraic intricacies and algorithms development to simulate these theoretical foundations of 3D G-filters are separated in to two papers.

The paper (Part I) [11] discusses the theoretical foundations of 2-D and 3-D G-Filters over the rectangular grid. The same paper initially discusses the 2-D Geometrical filters, and then proposes the 3-D Geometrical filters (3-D G-Filters) and their algebra.

In this paper we deal with the implementation and algorithms related to 3-D G-Filters. The algorithm in the section 2 discusses automatic construction of 255 convex polyhedrons used for constructing complete distributive lattice[3] of polyhedrons for rectangular grid. In Section 3, we discuss the algorithm for hieararchical path enumeration of convex polyhedron set and their relationships formed in hierarchical fashion. Section 4 discusses the results.

2 Algorithm for Automatic Construction of Convex Polyhedron Sets and Their Corresponding Subsets over Rectangular Grid

Consider a 3x3x3 rectangular grid, in which there are 27 neighbourhood elements including central pixel. The central idea is to construct 256 unique convex polyhedrons in a 3-D rectangular grid(3x3x3 array of cells), by dropping one corner, two corners, three corners, four corners, fiver corners, six corners, seven corners and eight corners at a time with different probable combinations. The initial set A contains all the eight different corner voxels of the 3x3x3 voxel grid. (for more details on numbering the corner voxels refer the paper [11] published in the same conference) i.e.

A= {1, 3, 7, 9, 19, 21, 25, 27}
By dropping one voxel at a time we can construct 8 different subsets as follows:
B1= {3, 7, 9, 19, 21, 25, 27}
B3= {1, 7, 9, 19, 21, 25, 27}
B7= {1, 3, 9, 19, 21, 25, 27}
B9= {1, 3, 7, 19, 21, 25, 27}
B19= {1, 3, 7, 9, 21, 25, 27}
B21= {1, 3, 7, 9, 19, 25, 27}
B25= {1, 3, 7, 9, 19, 21, 27}
B27= {1, 3, 7, 9, 19, 21, 25}

The dropped voxel can be easily identified by looking at the subset index. For example, the voxel 1 is dropped from the set of corners i.e. A and formed a subset B1, here one can observe that the dropped voxel is considered as a index of the new subset B. For complete list of the 256 convex polyhedrons refer to Paper (Part I)[11].

For reducing complexity in finding subsets from the set, only one element is removed from the set at each level. For example by removing one element from the set A (level 1) we found subsets B1, B3, B7, B9, B19, B21, B25, B27 (level 2). In the similar way by removing one element from B1 we found C1,3, C1,7, C1,9, C1,19, C1,21, C1,25, C1,27 (level 3). In the level 3 we found 28 such unique C subsets. In the similar way we have 56 D subsets in level 4 by discarding one element from C sets, 70 E subsets in level 5 by discarding one element from D sets, 56 F subsets in level 6 by discarding one element from E sets, 28 G subsets in level 7 by discarding one element from F sets, 8 H subsets in level 8 by discarding one element from G sets, and 1 E subset in level 9 by discarding one element from H sets. When all the subsets are properly arranged we get a complete distributive lattice structure as shown in Figure 3. The total number of convex polyhedrons is calculated by adding all the subsets i.e. 256. The list of all the subsets and their corresponding elements are discussed in Paper (Part I)[11].

So this section discusses the algorithm for automatic generation of convex polyhedron subsets from the set A.

Algorithm 1: Automatic Generation of Convex Polyhedrons

```
Input: Set A. i.e. A= {1, 3, 7, 9, 19, 21, 25, 27}
Output: 255 subsets
Steps:
Step1: Declare a array a[ ] and initialize it with
     {1, 3, 7, 9, 19, 21, 25, 27}

Step 2:
```

```
For Subset Group B:
for ( int i = 0; i <8; i++)
  {
    for (int j = 0; j <8; j++)
      {  Print B+ a[i]+{=
          if ((j == i) )
          {
              //Dont do anything
          }
        else
          {
              Print a[j] + ,
          }
} print }\n
}
Group C:
for(int i=0;i<=7;i++)
{
  for (int j = i + 1; j <= 7; j++)
  {
    Print C+a[i]+a[j]+{=
    for (int d - 0; d <- 7; d++)
    {
      if (d == i || d == j)
      { //Dont do anything
      }
          else
          {
              Print a[d]+,
          }
    }
  } print }\n
}
```

Similarly the group D subset can be generated with four for
loops. Expect out for loop and inner most for loop every for
loop is intialized to its previous for loop variable+1.
For Group E 5 Nested for loops
     Group F 6 Nested for loops
     Group G 7 Nested for loops
     Group H 8 Nested for loops
     Group I 9 Nested for loops

The output of the above said algorithm is discussed in the results section i.e. Section 4

3   Algorithm for Constructing Hierarchical Relationships among Convex Polyhedron Sets and Their Corresponding Subsets

The purpose of this algorithm is to make hierarchical path enumeration among convex polyhedron sets and their subsets. As discussed in the previous section the sets C1,3, C1,7, C1,9, C1,19, C1,21, C1,25, C1,27 are subsets of B1. This algorithm will construct a tree view of the relationships mention above such sets. The algorithm present in this section will form a hierarchical relationship among sets and subsets.

Algorithm 2: Hierarchical Path Enumeration

```
Input: Set A. i.e. A= {1, 3, 7, 9, 19, 21, 25, 27}
Output: Tree view of convex polyhedron sets and their
        corresponding polyhedron subsets
Steps:
Step1: Declare a array a[ ] and initialise it with
    {1, 3, 7, 9, 19, 21, 25, 27}
Step 2:
For Subset Group B:
Create Empty tree
Add set A as root node to the tree
for ( int i = 0; i <8; i++)
{
    Create Empty BNode
    Name node as  "B" + a[i];
    Add the node generated to the
        Root node i.e. A.
    for (int j = 0; j <8; j++)
    {
        // Logic for Subset Creation
    }
}
Group C:
for(int i=0;i<=7;i++)
{
  for (int j = i + 1; j <= 7; j++)
  {
    Create Empty CNode
    Name node as  C+a[i]+,+a[j]
    Add the node generated to the
    Parent node as follows:
    mainNode.Nodes[i].Nodes.Add(CNode);
    for (int d = 0; d <= 7; d++)
```

```
    {
    // Logic for Subset Creation
    }
  }
}
Group D:
for (int i = 0; i <= 7; i++)
{
   for (int k = i + 1; k <= 7; k++)
   {
     for (int j = k + 1; j <= 7; j++)
     {
      Create Empty Node
      Name node as D+a[i]+a[k]+a[j]
      Add the node generated to the
      Parent node as follows:
        m = ((k - 1) - i);
      mainNode.Nodes[i].Nodes[m].
      Nodes.Add(DNode);
      for (int d = 0; d <= 7; d++)
      {
    // Logic for Subset Creation
      }
     }
   }
}
```

Similarly the group E subset can be generated with five for loops.
For Group F 6 Nested for loops
    Group G 7 Nested for loops
    Group H 8 Nested for loops
    Group I 9 Nested for loops

The output of the above said algorithm is discussed in the results section i.e. Section 4

4   Results

The algorithms discussed in the section 2 and 3 are implemented in C#.NET language. The results of the convex polyhedron construction are shown in the Fig 1. The Fig 1(a) shows results of some of the convex polyhedrons. The other subsets ending with F, G, H and I are shown in the Fig 1(b). The algorithm discussed in the section 2 is able to generate all 255 convex polyhedrons. The complete list of convex polyhedrons can not be listed here as output. So the partial list is shown in the Fig 1(a) & 1(b). The results of algorithm discussed in the section 3 is shown in Fig 2. This figure shows the relationships among polyhedron sets and their corresponding subsets. The Fig 2(b) shows the lower part of the some more results of the algorithm for hierarchical subset construction. By looking at the output one can clearly understand that H is subset of

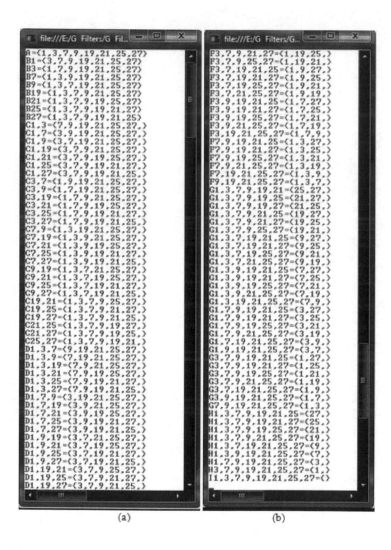

Fig. 1. (a) Results window showing subsets from A to D1, 19, 27(b) Results of subsets showing F, G, H and I

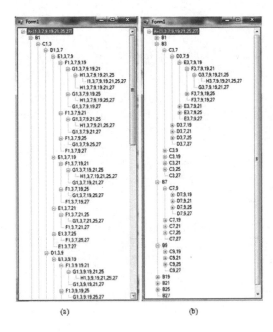

(a)   (b)

Fig. 2. (a)The hierarchical relationships showing upper part of the results(b)The hierarchical relationships showing lower part of the results

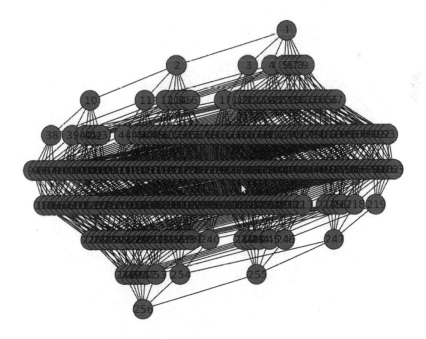

Fig. 3. Lattice Formed By 256 Convex Polyhedrons

G, G is subset of F, F is subset of E, E is subset of D, D is subset of C, C is subset of B and finally B is subset of A. The final lattice generated by using these hierarchical relations, including ambiguous relations is shown in figure 3.

5 Conclusion

Manual construction of 256 convex polyhedrons in a 3X3X3 rectangular grid is cumbersome and highly error prone. One may end up with constructing subsets repeatedly and above all it has been empirically verified that constructing all 256 convex polyhedrons does consume 48 man hours. To overcome this problem, we proposed a new algorithm automatic construction of convex polyhedrons. This algorithm is discussed in the section 2, which generates 255 polyhedron subsets in a fraction of a second.

Secondly, manual construction of paths in the lattice from supremum to infimum is almost impossible task. Each path defines a GE(Evolutionary G-Filter) filter. Each GE filter is of some use in processing 3-D images. So, one comes across the usual problem of enumerating potentially very large GE filters defined over a finite set. To overcome this problem, we proposed in this paper a novel algorithm for Hierarchical Path Enumeration of 256 convex polyhedrons.

Acknowledgments. We sincerely thank Mrs. G.Chitra, Managing Director, Pentagram Research Centre Pvt. Ltd.for her support to carry out research work.

References

1. Gonzalez, R.C., Woods, R.E.: Digital Image processing, 2nd edn. PHI
2. Rajan, E.G.: Symolic Computjng Signal & image processing. B.S. Publications, India
3. Choquet, G.: Topology. Academic Press, New York (1966)
4. Rajan, E.G.: The notion of geometric filters and their use in computer vision. In: IEEE International Conference on Systems, Man and Cybernetics, Vancouver, B.C., Canada, pp. 4250–4255 (1995)
5. Rajan, E.G.: On the notion of a geometric filter and its relevance in the neighbourhood processing of digital imagesin hexagonal grids. In: 4th International Conference on Control, Automation, Robotics and Vision, Westim Stamford, Singapore (1996)
6. Vasantha, N., Rajan, E.G.: On the notion of geometric filters. National Conference organized by the Institution of Engineers, India and Annamalai University, SURGE 1994 (1994)
7. Matheron, G.: Random sets and Integral Geometry. Wiley, New York (1975)
8. Serra, J.: Image Analysis and Mathematical Morphology. Acadamic, New York (1982)
9. Maragos, P., Schafer, R.W.: Applications of morphological filtering to image processings and analysis. In: Proc. 1986 IEEE Int. Conf. Acoust., Speech, Signal Processing, Tokyo, Japan, pp. 2067–2070 (April 1986)
10. Sonka, M., Hlavac, V., Boyle, R.: Image Processing, Analysis and Machine Vision, 2nd edn.
11. Sultana, T., Rajan, E G.: Algebra of Geometric Filters Defined over Three Dimensional Rectangular Lattice-Part I. In: Paper Submitted to This Conference Along with This Paper

Enhancing the Network Security
Using Lexicographic Game

T.P. Anithaashri[1] and R. Baskaran[2]

[1] Anna University, Chennai / VEC – Chennai
thiruani@yahoo.com
[2] Anna University, Chennai
basski@annauniv.edu

Abstract. This paper presents a new modeling method to enhance the network security using game theory. Reconnaissance is applied as a game strategy to obtain more information about the enemy's strategic intentions.Indefinite Event Nets method is used to model the framework and analyze to defend the network attacks. The game issues are solved with the help of Indefinite Key Nets. The course of action for a player in multi-player game environment is also determined. Finally, the Nash equilibrium is computed and best-response strategies for the players (administrator and attacker) are found. It proves how the strategies are realistic and how the administrators can use these results to enhance the security of their network.

Keywords: Repeated game, Reconnaissance, Indefinite Event Nets, Indefinite Key Nets, Game Theory, Lexicographic game, Nash Equilibrium, Network Security.

1 Introduction

Now a days, schools, retailers, banks, Government agencies and a growing number of goods and service providers use the Internet as their integral way of conducting daily business. As an access to the Internet, the individuals either good or bad, can easily connect to the Internet. Due to the ubiquity of the Internet, computer security has now become more important than ever to organizations such as governments, banks, and businesses. Security specialists have long been interested in knowing what an intruder can do to a computer network, and what can be done to prevent or counteract attacks. In this paper, how the game theory can be used to find strategies for both an attacker and the administrator. Let us consider an example of a local network connected to the Internet and consider the interactions between an attacker and the administrator and treating it as a general-sum stochastic game.

The proposed system can find the strategy between the attacker and the administrator with the help of a finite repeated game or infinite repeated game. It also help us to know more information about the attacker's strategic intensions through the concepts of reconnaissance, which is the best strategy among all other game strategies. It can be coded with NLP-1 in MATLAB, that is mathematical computation software package by The Math Works, Inc. and thus the Nash equilibrium solution can be obtained.

N. Meghanathan et al. (Eds.): CCSIT 2012, Part III, LNICST 86, pp. 211–224, 2012.

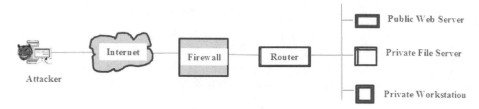

Fig. 1. Network Example (Attacker & Administrator)

2   Related Work

The concept of game technique has been invited to the field of network security and computer security. The literature [1] addresses the problems of false report injection and DoS attacks in wireless networks. This scheme can drop false reports much earlier even with a smaller size of memory. In literature [2], the new framework to detect malicious nodes using zero-sum-game approach and selective node acknowledgements in the forward data path. It proposes a new protocol for preventing malicious bandwidth consumption and demonstrates how game techniques can be successfully used to verify availability-related security properties of network protocols. The network is scanned and mapped for all access points and WLAN nodes in paper [3]. It was focused on many countermeasures and less in feasibility. The literature[4] analyzed the risk assessment of network security and design the new framework by using network prototype. The Stackelberggame technique was used to analyse the payoff functions and Nash equilibrium strategies with payoffs for the malicious users has been adopted in the paper [6]. To analyze the intrusion detection in Mobile Adhoc-Networks , the two-player non-cooperative game technique has been used in the literature [7]. Performance of intrusion detection has been examined for Unix based host machines with Solaris operating system using Markov chain model in the paper [8]. The continuous markov chain model for a homogenous finite state has been utilized to evaluate the system security in the literature [9]. In literature [11], the method of game technique to analyze the security of computer networks was presented. The interactions between an attacker and the administrator are modeled as a two player game for which best-response strategies were computed.

3   Networks as an Indefinite Event

In this section we introduce formal model of anindefinite event . A two-player model is described by a 5-tuple vector as $I=(Z, A^k, H, F^k, \delta)$ where $Z=\{\alpha_1, \alpha_2, ..., \alpha_N\}$ is a finite set of states, $P^k=\{a_1^k, a_2^k, ..., a_M^k\}$, $k=1,2$, $I^k=|P^k|$ is the action set of player k. The action set for player k at state s is a subset of P^k. i.e., P_s^k is contained in or equal to P^k and $\cup_{i=1,...,N} P\alpha_i^k = P^k$. $Q: Z \times P^1 \times P^2 \times Z \to [0,1]$ is the state transition function. $F^k: Z \times P^1 \times P^2 \to F$, $k=1,2$ is reward function of player k. $0 \leq \delta \leq 1$ is a discount factor for discounting future rewards. At the current state the reward worth its full value, but the reward for the transition from the next state is worth δ times its value at the current state.

The event is played as follows : at a discrete time instant t, the event is in state $z_t \in$ Z. Player 1 chooses an action p_t^1 from P^1 and player 2 chooses an action p_t^2 from P^2. Player 1 then receive a reward $f_t^1 = F^1(z_t, p_t^1, p_t^2)$, and Player 2 gets a reward $f_t^2 = F^2(z_t, p_t^1, p_t^2)$. The game then moves to a new state z_{t+1} with conditional probability $G(z_{t+1} | z_t, a_t^1, a_t^2)$ according to $H(z_t, p_t^1, p_t^2, z_{t+1})$.

We are interested in determining a course of action for a player in multi-players environment. Specifically we want to learn a stationary though possibly stochastic strategy that maps states to a probability distribution over its actions. The goal is to find such a strategy that maximizes the player's discounted future reward. For this reconnaissance is used as a game of strategy.

3.1   Reconnaissance

The reconnaissance is used to obtain information about the enemy's strategic targets. The advisability of reconnaissance before attack can be investigated by considering the problem as a game of strategy. Let us consider that the attacker and defender has two strategies. Assuming that the attacker, wishes to seize a defended enemy position. For simplicity, let us assume that he has two courses of action, namely

1. Attack with his entire force;
2. Attack with part of his force, leaving the remainder as reserves and a rear guard in case the enemy "outflanks" him.

The defender, is assumed to have two possible courses of action, namely :
i.   Defend with his entire force the objective of the attacker;
ii. Defend with part of his force, and send the remainder to "outflank" the enemy and attack the enemy from the rear.

There are four possible outcomes of the above courses of action. They can be summarized by the following 2x2 matrix :

$$
A = \begin{matrix} & & \text{i.} & \text{ii.} \\ & 1. & \begin{pmatrix} a_{11} & a_{12} \\ a_{21} & a_{22} \end{pmatrix} \\ & 2. & \end{matrix}
$$

a_{21} represents the value to attacker if he attacks with part of his force and defender defends with his entire force. Suppose the outcomes are such that if defender uses strategy (i), then attacker would prefer to use strategy (1), and i.e, $a_{11} > a_{21}$ and if defender uses strategy (ii), then attacker would prefer to use strategy (2). Clearly the attacker could benefit from a knowledge of the defender's intentions. Thus the attacker might find it profitable to send out a detachment of men to reconnoiter in an attempt to discover the plans of the defender. In order to defend himself against such possible action the defender may take countermeasures. Now if the attacker decides to reconnoiter he must sacrifice some of his attacking forces. If the defender decides to take countermeasures he must sacrifice some of his defensive forces. A strategy for the attacker will be a set of instructions which tell him how to act taking into account the information he may receive. Thus by using reconnaissance the information relevant to the enemy's strategic objective can be obtained.

A strategy is also called a mixed or randomized strategy, which means that the player chooses an action in random manner. The set of mixed strategies includes the pure strategies, when the player chooses the actions in a deterministic way. A pure strategy is a special case of mixed strategy such that probability one is assigned to one action and zero to all other actions. A stationary strategy π^k is a strategy that is independent of time and history. A mixed or randomized stationary strategy is one where $\pi^k (s,a)>0$, $s \in S$ and $a \in A^k$ and a pure strategy is one where $\pi^k (s,a_i) = 1$ for some $a_i \in A^k$. Indefinite games can be classified according to the structure of their payoff functions. Two common classes of games are purely collaborative and purely competitive games. Purely collaborative games are ones where all the players have the same reward function. Purely competitive, or zero-sum, games are two-player games where one player's reward is always the negative of the other's. Like matrix games, zero-sum stochastic games [5] have a unique Nash-equilibrium, although finding this equilibrium is not so easy.

Nash equilibrium is a steady state of the play of a strategic game in which each player holds the correct expectation about the other player's behavior and act rationally. It does not attempt to examine the process by which a steady state is reached.

Since a set of strategy is used in Nash equilibrium, no player has incentive to unilaterally change her action. In equilibrium state , a change in strategies by any one of them would lead that player to earn less than if she remained with her current strategy. For games in which players randomize (mixed strategies), the expected or average cost must be at least as large as that obtainable by any other strategy.

3.2   Indefinite Key Nets

Indefinite Key Nets are augmented with the set of average transition rates for the exponentially distributed transition firing times. A transition represents a class of possible changes of markings. Such a change, also called transition firing, consists of removing tokens from the input places of the transition and adding tokens to the output places of the transition according to the expressions labeled on the arcs. A transition may be associated with an enabling predicate which can be expressed in terms of the place marking expressions. If the predicate of a transition evaluates to be false, the transition is disabled. In this model, transitions can be categorized into two classes: transitions of Class One are used to represent logical relations or determine if some conditions are satisfied [3].This class of transitions is called immediate transition with zero triggering time.

Transitions of class two are used to represent the operations on the tasks or information processing. This class of transitions is called timed transition with exponential distributed firing time. A marking in this model represents a distribution of tokens in the model. The state space of a model consists of the set of all markings reachable from the initial marking through the occurrence of transition firing. An Indefinite Event net is homomorphism to a continuous time Markov Chain (MC), and there is a one-to-one relationship between markings of the key net and states of the MC [3] and [4].

Indefinite Key Net is a quadruple (S, T, F, λ) where
> (1) S is a finite set of states
> (2) M is a finite set of moves (S∩M≠Φ)
> (3) F Contained in or equal to (S x M) U(MxS) is a set of arcs
> (4) $\mu = (\mu_1, \mu_2, .., \mu_n)$ is a set of triggering states of transitions.

As an extension of Indefinite Key Nets, Indefinite Incentive Net is a powerful graphical and mathematical tool, which not only is able to model concurrent, asynchronous and nondeterministic events, but also provide transition enabling function and firing probability that can be used to model various algorithms and strategies.

From a structural point of view, both net formalisms are equivalent to Turing machines. But the incentive net provide enabling functions, marking dependent arc cardinalities, a more general approach to the specification of priorities, and the ability to decide in a marking-dependent fashion whether the triggering time of a transition is exponentially distributed or null, often resulting in more compact nets. Perhaps more important, though, are the differences from an indefinite modeling point of view. The incentive net formalism considers the measure specification as an integral part of the model. Underlying this net is an independent semi Markov process with incentive rates associated to the states and incentive impulses associated to the transitions between states [5].

3.3   Indefinite Event Nets

An Indefinite Event Net is the 9-tuple vector (P,S,M,π, A,I, μ, δ, I_0) where

1. P= 1,2,…,n denotes a finite set of players;
2. S is a   finite set of states;
3. M= M_1 UM_2 U…U M_n is a finite set of moves, where M_k is the set of transitions with respect to player k, for k∈P;
4. π:M→ [0,1] is a routing policy representing probability of choosing a particular transition;
5. A⊆ J U O is a set of arcs where J⊆(P x M) and O ⊆(M x S), such that S ∩ M=Φ and S U M ≠ Φ;
6. I: M→ ($I^{(1)};I^{(2)},....,I^{(n)}$) is an incentive function for the player taking each action;
7. $\mu = (\mu_1, \mu_2, ..., \mu_k)$ is a set of triggering rates of transitions in transition set, where k is the number of transitions;
8. $\delta(s^k_i)$ is the utility function, when player k in the condition s_i. Accordingly, the player can choose the best transition;
9. I_0 is the initial marking.

The Indefinite Event Net structure will represent all possible strategies existing within the game.

3.4   Triggering Rule

The Triggering rule of an Indefinite Event Net is given as follows. A marking m represents a distribution of the tokens in indefinite event. Each token s is related with a reward vector $b(s) = (b_1(s), b_2(s), \ldots, b_n(s))$ as its properties. Each element of M represents a class of possible changes of markings. Such a change of t, also called transition triggering, consists of removing tokens from a subset of places and adding them to other subsets according to the expressions labeling the arcs. A transition t is enabled under a marking I_0 whenever, for all $s \epsilon S$ and $(s,m) \epsilon A$, $I(s) \neq \Phi$. Each player gets the reward I(m) through the transition and the reward is recorded in the reward vector b of each token.

Following are the two steps to solve the Indefinite Event Net to find the Nash equilibrium. The Nash equilibrium corresponds to the optimized strategy[3] of each player. We first build the reachability tree according to the Indefinite Event Net, and then find out the Nash equilibrium.

3.5   Procedure to Build a Reachability Tree for Indefinite Event Net

A reachability tree is consists of nodes, which are denoted by all the reachable markings of the Indefinite Net, and the arcs among the nodes. From a Indefinite Net the initial marking I_0, the reachability tree can drawn with the following steps.

(i) Make I_0 the root r of the tree. No dex marked by I is a leaf if and only if there is no transition $m \epsilon M$ which is enabling under I, or there is a node $y \neq x$ along the road from r to x, which has a similar mark I' as I. Define I_1 and I_2 are the null set such that for all $s \epsilon S$.

(ii) If a node x marked by I is not a leaf, trigger a move m, $(s,m) \epsilon A$ to construct a new node in the reachability tree marked as I'.

Following the above steps, we can build the reachability tree from the Indefinite Net. The procedure is similar with that in Indefinite Key Nets.

3.6   Procedure to Find out the Nash Equilibrium

The algorithm is to find the Nash Equilibrium of an action sequence with π^* for all the players. For every leaf node x_i identified by I_i in the reachability tree and a token s such that there is a state s, $_{Ii}(s) = s_i$, $1 \leq i \leq n$ in the reachability tree.

Generally, there are multiple paths from the initial state to a leaf node. Assume x_i is a leaf node, and there are w_i separate paths from the root to xi. Let $t_1^{(i,w)}, t_2^{(i,w)}, \ldots, t_K^{(i,w)}$, $K = k^{(i,w)}$ be the wth path from root node to leaf node x_i. We define a leaf probability for the leaf node x_i of the wth path as

$$f^{(w)}(x_i) = \pi(t_1^{(i,w)}) \, \pi(t_2^{(i,w)}) \, ,..,\pi(t_K^{(i,w)}) \tag{1}$$

Then the final utility vector for the system is

$$(U1, U2, \ldots, Un) = \quad \sum_{(i=1\ldots m)} [\sum_{a=1\ldots wi} a^{(v)}(x_i) * (b^{(v)}(s_i))] \tag{2}$$

Where m is the number of leaves in the reachability tree. Note that $b^{(v)}(s_i)$ of size n x 1 is the reward vector of the token in leaf node x_i on the vth path, and n is the number of players as in the definition of Indefinite Event Net.

According to the state of Nash equilibrium, every player has achieved his best, when others don't change their strategies. Thus, the problem is to find such π that $(U_1,U_2,...,U_n)$ is a Nash equilibrium for each player, which could be given as:

$$\max \pi\ U = (U_1,U_2,...,U_n) \tag{3}$$

Note that, the above equation is a multi-objective optimization, which can be solved using the mathematical programming methods.

4   Usages in Network Security

In this section, we will apply the Indefinite Event Nets to model the attack and defense actions, and investigate the security properties based on both reconnaissance and Nash equilibrium, and propose the optimum strategy for the computers at each stage to minimise the loss during computer attacks. More information about the enemy's (attacker's) strategic intentions is obtained using reconnaissance [4].By applying the indefinite event net to the basic attack and defend case the structure of sequence can be shown. The following steps are used to apply the Indefinite Event Nets and doing the security analysis.

Step 1: Determine the players in the game N; Present the targets of each player k, and construct each player's action set P^k;

Step 2: Define the incentive function If or each transition and then construct the Indefinite Event Net model;

Step 3: Find the Nash equilibrium with respect to the Indefinite Net model and propose optimum strategy by computing probability;

4.1   Basic Attack-Defend Case

The attack-defend[2] system is the most general form among all the network attacks. In a basic attack-defense cast, there are two players, the defender and the attacker. For easy to illustrate, we choose a simple attack case in this subsection. Here an attacker will try to intrude a computer system, and the computer takes actions to defend. Assume attacker as Player 1 and the defender Player 2. The transition[6] set of the Player 1, the attacker, is given in the following table 1.

Table 1.

m_1	m_2	m_5	m_6	m_7
http attack	ftp attack	web attack	continue attack	web server sniffer

The transition set of the Player 2, the defender, is also given in the following table.

Table 2.

m_3	m_4	m_8	m_9
defend of http attack	Tolerant	defend of web attack	Tolerant attack

By using the above steps the reachability tree can be drawn. Thus the Nash equilibrium can be obtained through equation (3).

5   The Proposed Lexicographic Game for Multi-player Environment

Here we apply Indefinite Event Net to multi player game, which is a typical repeated game in a common defense system. Now a days, more and more systems and agents are trying to cooperate to get a more powerful system. However, each contender in the combined system requires an individual security strategy to satisfy its own target, and these strategies are actually inconsistent at most of times. Therefore, the contender would come to either a finite repeated game or an infinite repeated game for the security strategy.

Let G = {N,(A$_i$), (~i)} be a strategic game, Let A = X$_i \epsilon$NA$_i$. An infinitely repeated game of strategy is an extensive game with perfect information and simultaneous moves {N,H,P,~i} in which H = U$_{t=0...\infty}$A^t (where A^0={Φ} is the initial history). P(h) = N for each non terminal history hϵH. ~i is preference relation on the set A$^\infty$ of infinite sequences (a^t)$_{t=0...\infty}$ of action profiles in G that extends the preference relation ~I in the sense that it satisfies the following condition of weak separability : if (a^t) ϵA$^\infty$, aϵA, a'ϵA and a ~i a' then (a^1,...,a^{t-1},a,a^{t+1},...)~i then (a^1,...,a^{t-1},a',a^{t+1},...) for all values of t.   A history is terminal if and only if it is infinite. After any non-terminal history every player iϵN chooses an action in Ai. Thus strategy of player I is a function that assigns an action in Ai to every finite sequence of outcomes in G.

5.1   Discount Factor

There is some number $\delta \epsilon(0,1)$ called discount factor such that the sequence v$_i^t$ if and only if

$$\sum_{t=0}^{\infty} \delta_t (v_i^t - w_i^t) \geq 0 \qquad (4)$$

According to this criterion a player evaluates a sequence (v_i^t) of payoffs by

$$\sum_{t=0}^{\infty} \delta^t v_i^{t-1} \qquad (5)$$

For some discount factor $\delta\epsilon(0,1)$. When the players' preferences take this form, we refer to the profile

$$(1-\delta)\lim_{T\to\infty}\sum_{t=1}^{T}\delta^{t-1}v_i^t \qquad (6)$$

as the payoff profile in the repeated game associated with the sequence $(v^t)_{t=1}^\infty$ of payoff profiles in the constituent game.

5.2   Limit of Means

The limit of means states that the sequence (v_i^t) of real numbers is preferred to the sequence (w_i^t) if and only if

$$\text{Lim inf}\sum_{t-1}^{T}\frac{v_i^t-w_i^t}{T} > 0 \qquad (7)$$

That is, if and only if there exists $\epsilon > 0$ such that $\sum_{t=1}^{T}\frac{v_i^t-w_i^t}{T} > \epsilon$ for all but a finite number of periods T.When the players' preferences take this form we refer to the profile for $i\epsilon$N,

$$\lim_{T\to\infty}\sum_{t=1}^{T}v_i^t/T \qquad (8)$$

if it exists as the payoff profile in the repeated game associated with the sequence $(v^t)_{t=1}^\infty$ of payoff profiles in the constituent game.

5.3   Overtaking

By the definition of overtaking, the sequence (v_i^t) is preferred to the sequence (w_i^t) if and only if

$$\text{liminf}\sum_{t=1}^{T}(v_i^t - w_i^t) > 0 \qquad (9)$$

The following two Lemmas shows that the set of Nash equilibrium payoff profiles of an infinitely repeated game in which the players evaluate streams of payoffs by the limit of means is the set of all feasible enforceable payoff profiles of the constituent game.

5.3.1   Lemma
Every Nash equilibrium payoff profile of the limit of means infinitely repeated game of G = {N, (A$_i$), (u$_i$)}is an enforceable payoff profile of G. The same is true for any $\delta\epsilon(0,1)$ of every Nash equilibrium payoff profile of the δ-discounted infinitely repeated game of G.

5.3.2   Lemma
Every feasible enforceable payoff profile of G={N,(A$_i$),(u$_i$)}is a Nash equilibrium payoff of the limit of means infinitely repeated game of G.
    The next lemma shows that the set of Nash equilibrium payoff profiles of an infinitely repeated game in which the players evaluate streams of payoffs by the discount criterion factor.

5.3.3   Lemma

Let w be a strictly enforceable feasible payoff profile of G={N,(A$_i$),(u$_i$)}. For all ϵ>0 there exists $\delta \in$ (0,1) large enough and a payoff profile w' of G for which |w'-w|<ϵ, such that w' is a Nash equilibrium payoff profile of δ-discounted infinitely repeated game of G.

The following lemma shows that the set of Nash equilibrium payoff profiles of an finitely repeated game in which the players evaluate streams of payoffs by the set of all feasible enforceable payoff profiles of the constituent game.

5.3.4   Lemma

If the payoff profile in every Nash equilibrium of the strategic game G is profile (v$_i$) of min max payoffs in G then for any value of T the outcome (a^1,...a^T) of every Nash equilibrium of the T-Period repeated game of G has the property that a^{t}is a Nash equilibrium of G for all t=1,...,T.

5.4   Lexicographic Game

Let us assume that the players preferences are lexicographic[18] and restrict the attention to the case in which the repeated component game is Prisoner's Dilemma. Trade of in each player's preferences between the payoffs in the repeated game and the complexity of the network is needed to limit the set of equilibria further.

The set of outcomes that occurs on an equilibrium path is any subset of the given problem. Hence, we obtain the optimal Nash equilibrium for the given network problem.

5.5   Example

If the two individuals repeatedly play the prisoner's dilemma game, then this game has a unique Nash equilibrium, in which each player chooses the action D, which strictly dominates the action C, so that the rationale behind the outcomes (D,D) is very strong. In a repeated game, the desirable outcome in which (C,C) occurs in every period is stable, if each player believes that a defection will terminate the cooperation resulting in a subsequent loss for him that outweighs the short term gain. In this game the focus is to isolate types of strategies which support desirable outcomes in any game. The repeated game has two versions namely finite and infinite. In the finite repeated game, the only Nash equilibrium outcome is that in which the players choose (D,D) in every period and in infinite repeated game, the set of sub game perfect equilibrium payoff profiles is huge.

The objective of this game strategies discernments into the structure of behavior when players interact repeatedly. By defining a machine, which is intended as an abstraction of the process by which a player implements a strategy in a repeated game. A machine for player i, in an infinitely repeated game has the following components namely a set (Q$_i$) of states, the initial state q_i^0, an output function and transition function. This needs a strategy which specifies an action for all possible histories, including those that are consistent with the player's own strategy. The machine of player P1, shown in figure 3 plays C as long as player P2 plays C; it plays

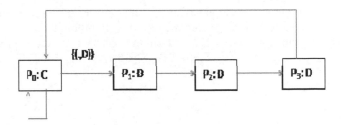

Fig. 2. Strategy of a machine

D for three periods and then reverts back to C, if player p2 plays D when he should play C. Here, we use $\{(.,X)\}$ is to denote the set of all outcomes in which player 2's action is X.

In the bargain of secure strategy, one player take turns to propose a solution, one at each round. When the two players namely (P1) and (P2) agree on a strategy, the game ends. In the kth moment(k=1,3,5,…,2m+1), where m∈N, (P1) shall propose a security strategy S_k. If (P2)agrees with S_k, then (P1) gets a utility of x. and (P2) gets $(1-x).\delta_2^{k-1}$, otherwise the game continues. By equation (4), $\delta1,\delta2$ ∈[0,1] are discount factors for (P1) and (P2) respectively, which measures the bargaining cost on time scale, as defined in the game theory. In the kth (k=2,4,6,…,2m) moment, which is P2's turn to propose his security strategy S_k. If (P1) agrees with S_k, then (P2) gets utility of y. δ_1^{k-1} and (P1)gets $(1-y).\delta_2^{k-1}$ by equation (5) and (6) or the game continues. The Indefinite Event Net model of this multi-round game is as follows :

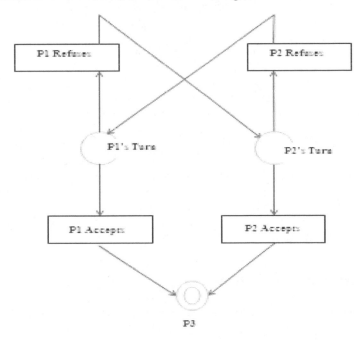

Fig. 3. Indefinite Event Net Model
(Here, D:Accepts, C:Refuses)

In the above Figure-2, each player has two actions, namely accept the strategy and refuse the strategy. The initial marking Io=(1,0,0) and there the reward vector of the initial token is written as b(s₁) = (0,0). Then the reachability tree is given in the Figure-3 below where s1=(1,0,0), s2=(0,0,1), s3=(0,1,0) and T1,T2,T3 are respective actions:

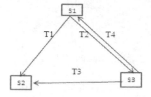

Fig. 4. Reachability Tree

According to a sub-game perfect equilibrium, P1 would always propose x= (1-δ_2)/(1-$\delta_1\delta_2$) and P2 would propose y=(1-δ_1)/(1-$\delta_1\delta_2$). Now at the kth round of P1's turn, the utility function of the two players is :

$$U^{(k,1)} = (\frac{(1-\delta_2)\delta_1^{k-1}}{1-\delta_1\delta_2}, \frac{(1-\delta_1)\delta_2\delta_2^{k-1}}{1-\delta_1\delta_2})$$

(10)

Similarly, at the kth round of P2's turn, the utility function of the two players is written as

$$U^{(k,2)} = (\frac{(1-\delta_2)\delta_1\delta_1^{k-1}}{1-\delta_1\delta_2}, \frac{(1-\delta_1)\delta_2^{k-1}}{1-\delta_1\delta_2})$$

(11)

In the reach ability tree, there is only one leaf node and we have the following constraints :

$$\pi_1+\pi_2=1$$
$$\pi_3+\pi_4=1$$

Thus, we have the following utility function to find the Nash equilibrium

$$\max_\pi U = (U_1, U_2)$$

(12)

Hence, we can find out that π_1=1 is the Nash Equilibrium. In contrast, π_3=1 would be the Nash Equilibrium while P2 gets the first chance to propose the security strategy.If the problem is a repeated game with finite or infinite state, then the lexicographic game method can be appliedby using either discount factor or limits of means according to the requirements, to obtain the best strategy and thus the optimal Nash equilibrium state can be reached.

6   Conclusions and Future Work

This paper presents a lexicographic game to analyse the problems of network security. These applications demonstrate the soundness and efficiency of the game theory. However, the design described is just a beginning. Reconnaissance as game of strategy is used to know more information about the strategies of players. By using lexicographic game technique, we compute the Nash equilibrium of the game issue. Since this proposes a more flexible formulation for the game issue, there may be more than one Nash equilibrium in the solution. Thus, finite repeated game and infinite repeated game theory concept is applied to obtain the multiple solutions of Nash equilibrium and a try is made to propose a bound for the multiple Nash equilibriums. In future we can use the Markov decision process to decompose the large models and our lexicographic method allows us to perform complete analysis for the set of attack scenario states. Moreover, in terms of the modeling and analyzing approach, some simplification and approximation methods of indefinite key net could be well conduced indefinite event net with the repeated game theory lemmas which we believe would be promising in handling the complex game issues and provide a better solution. Thus, estimation of the performance measure of the system with the best-response strategies are chosen, including availability, survivability, measures related to security in wireless sensor network, cloud computing and so on.

References

1. Yu, Z., Guan, Y.: A dynamic en-route filtering scheme for data reporting in wire-less sensor networks. IEEE/ACM Transactions on Networking 18(1) (February 2010)
2. Reddy, Y.B., Srivathsan, S.: Game Theory Model for selective forward attacks in wireless sensor networks. In: 17th Mediterranean Conference on Control and Automation Makedonia Palace, Thessaloniki, Greece, June 24-26. Grambling State University, Lousiana State University (2009)
3. Min-kyu-Choi, Robles, R.J., Hong, C.-H., Kim, T.-H.: Wireless Network Security: Vulnerabilities, Threats and Counter measures. International Journal of Multimedia and Ubiquitous Engineering 3(3) (July 2008)
4. Chunhe, W.H., Zhang, X.C., Ma, Y.J.: A Network Security Risk Assessment framework based on Game Theory. School of Computer Science and Engg. IEEE, Beihang University (2008), doi:10.11.09/FGCN 2008–IEEE & CSI Jnl.
5. Mahimkar, A., Shmatikov, V.: On the advantage of network coding for improving network through-put. In: Proceedings of 18th IEEE Computer Society Foundations Workshop (2005)
6. Theodorakopoulos, G., Baras, J.S.: Game Theoretic modeling of Malicious users in collaborative Networks. IEEE Jnl. (2004)
7. Patcha, A., Jung-Min-Park: A game theoretic approach to modeling Intrusion detection in Mobile-Ad-hoc- Networks. IEEE (2004)
8. Nong, Y., Zhan, Y., Borror, C.M.: Robustness of the Markov-Chain Model for Cyber-Attack Detection. IEEE Transactions on Reliability 53(1) (March 2004)
9. Nicol, D.M., Sanders, W.H., Trivedi, K.S.: Model-based evaluation: From dependability to security. IEEE Transactions on Dependability and Secure Computing 1(1) (2004)
10. Wang, X., Reiter, M.: Defending against denial-of-service attacks with puzzle auctions. In: Proceedings of IEEE Security and Privacy (2003)
11. Lye, K., Wing, J.M.: Game strategies in network security. In: Proceedings of the 15th IEEE Computer Security Foundations Workshop (2002)
12. Sheyner, O., Jha, S., Wing, J.: Automated generation and analysis of attack graphs. In: Proceedings of the IEEE Symposium on Security and Privacy, Oakland, CA (2002)

13. Browne, R.: C41 defensive infrastructure for survivability against multi-mode attacks. In: Proceedings 21st Century Military Communications. Architectures and Technologies for Information Superiority, vol. 1, pp. 417–424 (2000)
14. Shan, Z., Lin, C., Ren, F., Wei, Y.: Modeling and performance analysis of a multi server multi queue system on the grid. In: Proceedings of the 9th International Workshop on Future Trends of Distributed Computing Systems, pp. 337–343 (2000)
15. Howard, R.A.: Dynamic Probabilistic Systems. Semi-Markov and Decision Processes, vol. II. John Wiley and Sons, New York (1971)
16. Liu, P., Zang, W., Yu, M.: Incentive-based modeling and inference of attacker intent, objectives, and strategies. ACM Transactions on Information and System Security 8(1), 1–41
17. Stinson, D.R.: Crypography – Theory and Practice, 2nd edn. Chapman & Hall/CRC (2002) ISN:I-58488-206-9
18. Fudenberg, Tirole, J.: Game Theory. The MIT Press (1991)

Spectral Characterization of Rank Filters Based Directional Textures of Digital Images Using Rajan Transform

Naveed Farhana and Nisar Hundewale

College of Computers and Information Technology, Taif University,
Taif, Kingdom of Saudi Arabia
{n.farhana,n.hundewale}@tu.edu.sa

Abstract. Tissue characterization with the help of ultrasound images has remained an unsolvable problem to clinicians till date. Many techniques have been suggested to solve this issue. Yet a complete solution has not been arrived at so far. This paper gives a new technique which would indeed lead to the formulation of a robust method for characterizing tissues from ultrasound images. Any given image is processed using what we call as rank filters which would detect textures in four different directions. Various spatial features of these textures such as corners, curves, dots and lines are detected independently using the spectral domain pattern recognizing capabilities of Rajan Transform, which is a homomorphic transform developed on the lines of Hadamard Transform. The histogram analysis of these features would finally lead to spectral characterization of tissue textures. Clinicians would be able to resolve then the problem of tissue characterization.

Keywords: Ultrasound, Texture analysis, Rank Filter, Rajan Transform.

1 Introduction

Ultrasound imaging [1],[2],[3] can be performed by emitting a pulse, which is partially reflected from a boundary between two tissue structures, and partly transmitted. The reflection depends on the , difference between the impedance of the two tissues. Basic imaging by ultrasound does merely use the amplitude information in the reflected signal. One pulse is emitted, the reflected signal, however, is sampled somewhat continuously. As the velocity of sound in tissue is almost invariant, the time between the emission of a pulse and the reception of a reflected signal is dependent on the distance; that is, the depth of the reflecting structure. Different structures will reflect with different amount of the emitted energy. Thus the reflected signal from different depths will have variant amplitudes. The time before a new pulse is sent out depends on the maximum desired depth that is desired to image. This works more or less on the principles of a radar. Also, the apparent density of the tissue on the ultrasound image depends on the fiber direction. For example, a part of the heart where the fibers run mainly in a direction across the ultrasound beams will

N. Meghanathan et al. (Eds.): CCSIT 2012, Part III, LNICST 86, pp. 225–238, 2012.
© Institute for Computer Sciences, Social Informatics and Telecommunications Engineering 2012

appear much denser. Variations in amplitude do not necessarily mean differences in density, but may also mean variations in reflectivity due to variation in the incident and reflected angles. Thus, integrated   backscattering   can be used for analysis of cyclicity, but it is not much useful for tissue characterization.

Tissue characterization [4], [5] ,[6]could be carried out using texture analysis[5][6] of the tissues from the acquired image. Spectral characterization [7],[8],[9],[10] of the textures would finally lead to tissue characterization. This paper introduces a novel technique of 'Spectral Characterization of Rank Filters Based Directional Textures of Ultrasound Images[11],[12] ,[13] Using Rajan Transform[14].

Let us briefly review the basics of Rajan Transform and then proceed to study as to how to use this transform for pattern recognition.

1.1   Rajan Transform

Rajan Transform (RT) is a fast transform which is a variant of **Hadamard Transform** (HT) structurally similar to the Decimation-In-Frequency Fast Fourier Transform algorithm. RT is applicable to any arbitrary number sequence of length of power of 2. The two basic operations involved in this fast transform are (i) addition and (ii) difference. Given a number sequence x(n) of length a power of 2, first it is divided into the first half and the second half each consisting of (N/2) points so that the following hold good.

$$g(i) = x(i) + x(i + (N / 2)); \ 0 \leq j \leq N/2 \ ; \ 0 \leq i \leq N/2$$

$$h(i) = |x(i) - x(i - (N / 2))|; \ 0 \leq j \leq N/2 \ ; \ N/2 \leq i \leq N$$

Now each (N/2)–point segment is further divided into two halves each consisting of (N/4) points so that the following hold good.

$$g1(k) = g(j) + g(j + (N / 4)); \ 0 \leq k \leq N/4 \ ; \ 0 \leq j \leq N/4$$

$$g2(k) = |g(j) - g(j - (N/4))|; \ 0 \leq k \leq N/4 \ ; \ N/4 \leq j \leq N/2$$

$$h1(k) = h(j) + h(j + (N/4)); 0 \leq k \leq N/4; \ 0 \leq j \leq N/4$$

$$h2(k) = |h(j) - h(j - (N/4))|; 0 \leq k \leq N/4 \ ; \ N/4 \leq j \leq N/2$$

This process is continued till no more division is possible. The total number of stages thus turns out to be $\log_2 N$ .Let us denote the sum and difference operators respectively as + and ~. If x(n) is a number sequence of length $N = 2^k$; K>0, then its Rajan Transform is denoted as X(k). X (k) is also called 'Rajan Spectrum'. The signal flow graph of RT for an 8-point sequence is shown below.

The forward transform can be obtained by operating the input sequence using a matrix called R matrix, recursively by dividing input sequence as well as by partitioning the R matrix in the following manner.

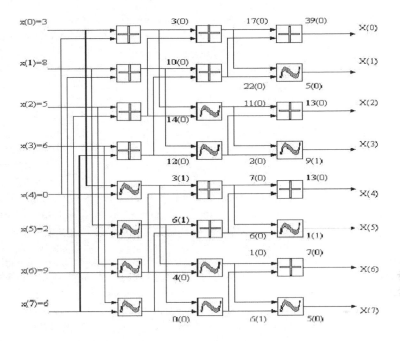

Fig. 1. Signal flow diagram of RT for a 8- point sequence

$$A_{N \times 1} = R_N \times X_{N \times 1}$$

$$\text{where } R_N = \begin{bmatrix} I_{N/2} & I_{N/2} \\ -e_k I_{N/2} & e_k I_{N/2} \end{bmatrix} \text{ of size } N \times N$$

X is the column matrix having input sequence of length N. $I_{N/2}$ is the identity matrix of size N/2, that is, half the size of the input sequence matrix $X_{N \times 1}$. Basic identity matrix $I_1 = 1$; and e_k is the encryption function with k as encryption value which is defined as.

$$e_k = (-1)K \qquad \text{Such that}$$

$$k = 1; \text{ for } x(i+N/2) \leq x(i); \ 0 \leq i \leq N/2.$$

$$k = 0; \text{ otherwise.}$$

And x(i) is the ith element of matrix $X_{N \times 1}$. Now divide the matrix $X_{N \times 1}$ into two column matrices, namely. A_{00} and A_{01} of size N/2 and treating these matrices as two input sequences, compute the two new A_{10} and A_{11} matrices by using the operator $R_{N/2}$ for both sequences.   Note the size of the R matrices used is one half of the original R_N matrix. Continue the above procedure iteratively till the size of the sub matrices is reduced to two. So, we have $N=2^{n-p}$, for p^{th} iteration stage, p=1,2,...,n. All the encryption binary values, that k values thus generated during the process of computation per iteration are to be associated with the final spectrum, to recover the original sequence through inverse transformation technique. Note that this closed form expression precisely defines the algorithms stated in the beginning of this section.

1.2   Inverse Rajan Transform

Now, in order to work with sequences containing negative sample values, we proceed as usual in the case of forward transform. But, the inverse transform is calculated just by adding a constant value $N(2^M-1)$ to the CPI value of the spectrum. M is the bit length required to represent the maximum quantization level of the samples and N is the length of the sequence. This constant factor $k=(2^M-1)$ is chosen such that all the maximum possible negative values of the sequence $x(n)$ are level shifted to 0 or above. This DC shift is required, because we hide the sign of the negative values that are generated while computing the forward RT. As mentioned earlier, RT induces an isomorphism between the domain set consisting of the Inverse, Cyclic, Dyadic and Dual class permutations of a sequence on to a range set consisting of sequences of the form $X(k)E(r)$ where $X(k)$ denotes the permutation invariant RT and E(r) an encryption code corresponding to an element in the domain set. This map is a one-to-one and on-to correspondence and an inverse map also exists. Thus RT is viewed as a transform. Now we provide a technique for obtaining the inverse of Rajan Transform.

Inverse Rajan Transform is a recursive algorithm and it transforms a RT code $X(k)E(r)$ of length $N(1+m)$ where $N=2^m$ and m is the number of stages of computation, into one of its original sequences belonging to its permutation class depending on the encryption code E(r). The computation of IRT is carried out in the following manner. First the input sequence is divided into segments each consisting of two points so that either

$$g(2j+1) = (X(2k) + X(2k+1))/2$$

$$g(2j) = \max(X(2k), X(2k+1)) - g(2j+1)$$

$$\text{if } E_1(2r)=0 \text{ and } E_1(2r+1) = 0; \ 0 \leq j \leq N; \ 0 \leq k \leq N; \ 0 \leq r \leq N$$

or

$$g(2j) = (X(2k) + X(2k+1))/2$$

$$g(2j+1) = \max(X(2k), X(2k+1) - g(2j))$$

$$\text{if } E_1(2r) = 1 \text{ or } E_1(2r+1) = 1; \quad 0 \leq j \leq N; \ 0 \leq k \leq N; \ 0 \leq r \leq N$$

The resulting sequence is divided into segments each consisting of four points. Each 4-point segment is synthesized as per the above procedure. The resulting sequence is further divided into segments each consisting of eight points and the same procedure is carried out. This process is continued till no more division is possible.

Consider X(k)=39,5,13,9,13,1,7,5. The inverse x(n) is obtained from the given X(k)E(r) as shown is Fig 3.2.1.1 The symbols '^', '>' and '~' respectively denote the operators average of two, maximum of two and difference of two. Note that IRT will work only in the presence of encryption sequence E(r) and for every member of the permutation class there would be a unique encryption sequence. Study of the class of encryption sequences corresponding input sequences itself is a field of active research. As already out lined that RT hides negative signs and so it is important to add $N(2^M-1)$ to X(0) in order to get back the original sequence.

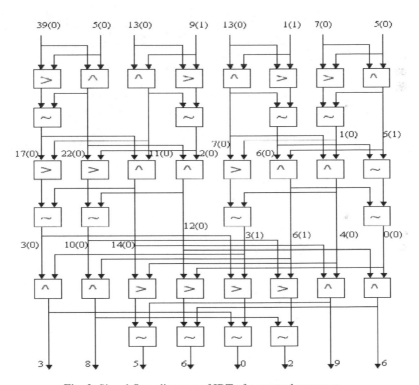

Fig. 2. Signal flow diagram of IRT of a spectral sequence

Let X_{Nx1} be the column matrix of the RT coefficients of length N, and the associated encryption values generated per iteration are orderly arranged in the form of column matrices $E^1, E^2, ..., E^{n+1}$, of length N/2, Where $n=\log_2 N$. For N=8, we have E^1 and E^2, two encryption matrices of size 4X1 with binary encryption values as elements. Here X_{NX1} is the RT coefficient matrix. R_{NX1} is the intermediate matrix. A_{Nx1} is matrix with the elements positioned in their appropriate positions using the encryption matrix E^r corresponding to the current iteration. E^r is the matrix obtained by element wise complementing the E^r matrix, where r=n-1,n-2,.....,1. Since we trace back the forward algorithm, we start initially with $N=2^p$, where p=1, 2, 3,...,n. Hence, we use initially the encryption matrix that is generated at the last stage of forward RT computation and further use the remaining matrices in the reverse order for IRT computation. Each encryption matrix is to be partitioned as per the requirement.

$$[R_{N\times1}] = \begin{bmatrix} max(x_1, x_{1+N/2}) \\ \cdot \\ max(x_{N/2}, x_N) \\ 0 \\ \cdot \\ upto \dfrac{N}{2} (zeros) \end{bmatrix} - \frac{1}{2}\begin{bmatrix} I_{N/2} & I_{N/2} \\ -I_{N/2} & -I_{N/2} \end{bmatrix}[X_{N\times1}]$$

$$[A_{N\times1}] = \begin{bmatrix} I_{N/2} & I_{N/2} \\ I_{N/2} & I_{N/2} \end{bmatrix}[R_{N\times1}] - \begin{bmatrix} [E^r_{N/2}][I_{N/2}] & \overline{[E^r_{N/2}]}_{L-N/2} \\ \overline{[E^r_{N/2}]}[I_{N/2}] & [E^r_{N/2}][I_{N/2}] \end{bmatrix}[R_{N\times1}]$$

The closed form expression shown as equation above represents the Inverse Rajan Transform. For example, let us consider a sequence x(n) which has a maximum sample value of 15. The RT of this sequence is X(k). No one can assume the value of M to be 4 so that the maximum negative sample value in sequence is -15. Addition of +15 to each sample value in a 8-point input sequence x(n) will lead to the sequence,

$$x_1(k)=x(0)+15, x(1)+15, ..., x(7)+15$$

Which is level shifted to 0 and above. Now the spectrum of this level shifted sequence $x_1(n)$ would be

$$X_1(k)=X_1(0), X_1(1), ..., X_1(7),$$

$$\text{where } X_1(0) = X(0)+120, X_1(1)=X(1), ..., X_1(7) = X(7).$$

One can use RT for developing various pattern recognition algorithms like (i) corner detection, (ii) curves detection, (iii) dots detection and (iv) lines detection [15],[16]. In addition, algorithms for classifying textures and for computing volume fraction are also provided in the sequel with suitable example images.

2   RT Based Pattern Recognition Algorithms

2.1   Corners Detection

Please On every move of the 3X3 window, the RT spectral sequence, say, X(0), X(1), X(2), X(3), X(4), X(5), X(6), and X(7) corresponding to the sequence of the numbered cell values is checked for the following:

(i) Corners due to pairs of lines subtending an angle of 45° or its integral multiples:

1. The number of RT elements that are less than T must be 4.
2. RT elements X[0], X[2], X[4], X[6] must be greater than T.

(ii) Corners due to pairs of lines subtending 90° or its integral multiples:

1) The number of RT elements that are less than T must be 4.
2) RT elements X[0], X[1], X[4],X[5] must be greater than T.

The above procedure is repeated till the entire image is scanned. The overall effect is that the resulting image would consist only of corner points.

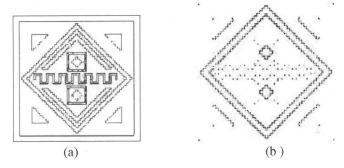

(a)   (b)

Fig. 3. (a) sample pattern of the image (b) corner detection of the sample pattern of the image

2.2 Lines Detection

On every move of the 3X3 window, the RT of each boundary values sequence is checked for the following conditions: (a) the number of RT elements that are less than T must be 4. (b) The first four RT elements including the CPI should be greater than T. In such a case, the central pixel has to be a midpoint of a line and so is chosen.

The overall effect is that the resulting image would consist only of straight lines.

2.3 Curves Detection

A curve is not a straight line. Hence, the algorithm for detecting curves advocates the invalidity of the conditions for detecting lines.

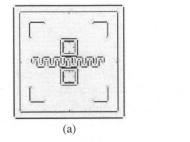
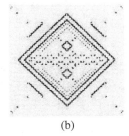

(a)   (b)

Fig. 4. (a) Lines detected from the sample pattern of the image (b) Corners detected from the sample pattern of the image

2.4   Dot Detection

Dots are isolated points. If most of the RT elements are below the average value then the central pixel value is treated as an isolated point.

3   Textures Classification

The term 'texture' refers to 'repeated patterns' in an image [17], [18]. Many applications do require detection of textures in a given image [19], [20]. One can choose four different algorithms Rank1, Rank2, Rank3 and Rank4to detect textures present in an image in four different directions like North-South, East-West, North West-South East and North East-South West.

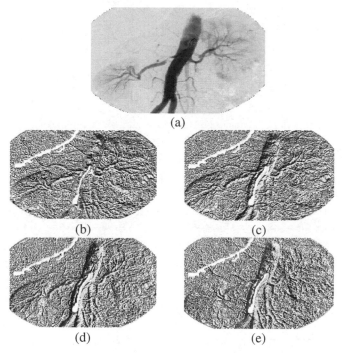

Fig. 5. (a) Example image (b) Rank 1 texturized image (c) Rank 2 texturized image (d) Rank 3 texturized image (e) Rank 4 texturized image

The given image is scanned by a 3X3 window. Each of the image values $x(0)$, $x(1)$, $x(2)$, $x(3)$, $x(4)$, $x(5)$, $x(6)$, $x(7)$is compared with the central image pixel value. If $x(i)$: $0 \leq i \leq 7$ is less than or equal to the central pixel value, then $x(i)$ is replaced by 0, otherwise by a 1. This yields a binary word of length 8. The decimal equivalent of this word is stored as the central image pixel value. The entire image is scanned in this manner and thus the resulting image would turn out to be the textured image.

The algorithm for texturizing an image remains same for all four cases with the exception that Rank 1 algorithm uses the sequence x(0), x(1), x(2), x(3), x(4), x(5), x(6), x(7);Rank 2 algorithm uses the sequence x(1), x(2), x(3), x(4), x(5), x(6), x(7), x(0) ; Rank 3 algorithm uses the sequence x(2), x(3), x(4), x(5), x(6), x(7), x(0), x(1) and Rank 4 algorithm uses the sequence x(3), x(4), x(5), x(6), x(7), x(0), x(1), x(2). The original ultra scanned image of a human artery and all the four textured versions of the image using Rank1, Rank2, Rank3 and Rank4 algorithms are given in the right column. Textures in a specific orientation need not be the same as those in another orientation. Refer to the images shown in Fig.5 to verify this fact.

Now the Rajan Transform is used to de detect various features of textures. The various features such as corners, curves, dots and lines are detected and their negative images are shown in Fig.6, Fig 7 , Fig 8 and Fig.9.

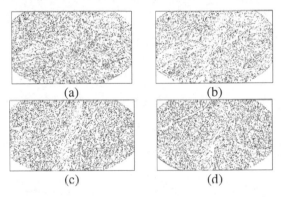

(a)   (b)

(c)   (d)

Fig. 6. (a) Detected corner feature of the texture using rank1 filter (b) Detected corner feature of the texture using rank2 filter (c) Detected corner feature of the texture using rank3 filter (b) Detected corner feature of the texture using rank4 filter

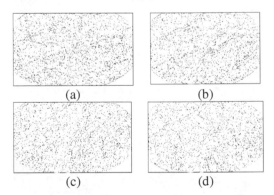

(a)   (b)

(c)   (d)

Fig. 7. (a)Detected curve feature of the texture using rank1 filter (b) Detected curve feature of the texture using rank2 filter :(a)Detected curve feature of the texture using rank3 filter (b) Detected curve feature of the texture using rank4 filter

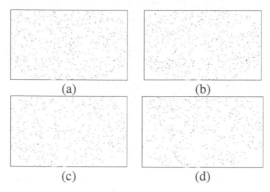

(a)   (b)

(c)   (d)

Fig. 8. (a)Detected dot feature of the texture using rank1 filter (b) Detected dot feature of the texture using rank2 filter :(a)Detected dot feature of the texture using rank3 filter (b) Detected curve feature of the texture using rank4 filter

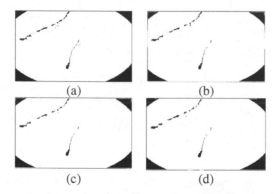

(a)   (b)

(c)   (d)

Fig. 9. (a)Detected line feature of the texture using rank1 filter (b) Detected line feature of the texture using rank2 filter :(a)Detected line feature of the texture using rank3 filter (b) Detected line feature of the texture using rank4 filter

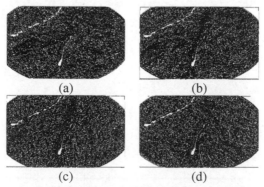

(a)   (b)

(c)   (d)

Fig.10. (a) rank1 features of ultrasound image (b) rank2 feature of ultrasound image (c) rank3 features of ultrasound image (d) rank4 features of ultrasound image

All the features superimposed to yield what we call as feature images. In what follows, we provide the feature images of the example ultrasound image used in this paper.

Low pass filtering is carried out on all the feature images of the example which reduces the entropy of the images to obtain the Fig11.

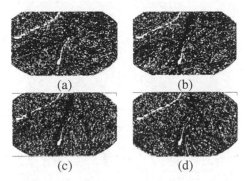

Fig. 11. (a) rank1 features of ultrasound image after low pass filtering (b)rank2 feature of ultrasound image after low pass filtering (c)rank3 features of ultrasound image after low pass filtering (d)rank4 features of ultrasound image after low pass filtering

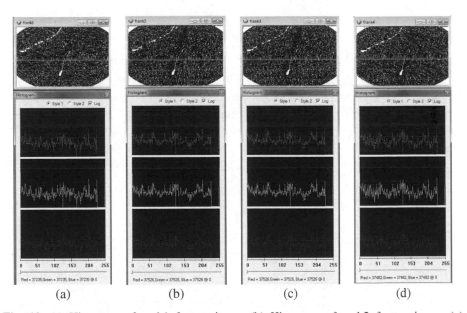

Fig. 12. (a) Histogram of rank1 feature image (b) Histogram of rank2 feature image (c) Histogram of rank3 feature image (d)Histogram of rank4 feature image

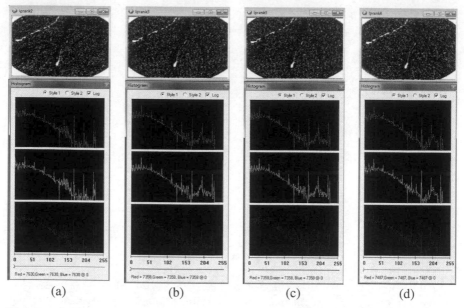

Fig. 13. (a) Histogram of rank1 low pass filtered feature image (b) Histogram of rank2 low pass filtered feature image (c) Histogram of rank3 low pass filtered feature image (d) Histogram of rank4 low pass filtered feature image.

4   Experimental Setup and Results

The image which is shown in the above example has been used as a test image. Logical image processing system Software 3.0 is used for analysis. A desktop PC with 280GB   and 4GB RAM was used to process the images. All the features have dots ,curves , corners and lines have been independently detected using RT based pattern recognition algorithms. The corresponding histograms have also been evaluated for visualize the image which is hidden in the original image.

5   Related Work

Texture analysis has played a prominent role to solve tissue characterization problems in medical imaging [21].Several researchers have been working to develop methods to obtain the tissue characterization of the ultrasound image and in this context many methods have been developed. In [22] ,the authors evolved a technique for reducing the noise of the image in order to have a clear representation of the tissue. The noise reduction is achieved by verging sets of images when the least variance in diameter of the image occurs. At the end, a fuzzy logic based expert system has been used to discriminate the tissues. In [23] .the authors proposed the use of co-occurrence matrices texture analysis and fractal texture analysis to characterize tissues. Thirteen features plus fractal dimension derived from Brownian motion were used for this purpose. In [24], use co-occurrence matrices and discriminate analysis were used to evaluate   different kind of tissues in the ultrasound images.

Further work has been done with the idea of using texture feature extractors for processing the   ultrasound images, though not specifically centered on tissue characterization . In [25] , so many methods derivatives of Gaussian, wavelets, co-occurrence matrices, Gabor filters have been used for finding local moments so as to discriminate blood. This last line of investigation overcomes one of the most significant drawbacks of the texture based tissue characterization systems, the speed. Hence we proposed a novel method for tissue characterization, which uses the pattern recognition capabilities of the Rajan Transform.

6   Conclusions

In this paper, we have proposed a novel technique for tissue characterization   in ultrasound images. This paper uses Spectral characterization of Rank Filters Based Directional Textures of Digital Images Using Rajan Transform, this transform is homomorphic transform and hence it can be to used to classify various features of an image. Texture is a spatially repeated pattern. So , this transform is very much useful for tissue characterization and thus clinicians would benefit to great extend in the form of diagnostic tool analysis the image and hence to diagnose the problem. The present method can also perform effective feature extraction, and also characterize the tissues of images precisely. Future work rests on the application of the present method to different kinds of medical images for classification purposes.

Acknowledgments. The authors sincerely thank the administration of Pentagram Research Centre Pvt Limited, Hyderabad, India for the permitting us to use their software Logical Image Processing System and for the unparallel support extended to the authors in developing the technology introduced in this paper. We also thank Dr. E.G Rajan for his invaluable suggestions and feedback while preparing the contents of this paper.

References

1. Hill, C.R., Bamber, J.C., Ter haar, G.R.: Physical principles of medical Ultrasonics, 2nd edn. John Wiley, Chichester (2004)
2. Saniie, J., Nagle, D.T.: Pattern recognition in the ultrasonic imaging of reverberant multilayered structures. IEEE Trans. Ultrasound, Ferroelectric, Frequency Contr. 36, 80–92 (1989)
3. Fenster, A., Surry, K., Smith, W., Gill, J., Downey, D.: 3D ultrasound imaging: applications in image-guided therapy and biopsy. Computer Graphics, 557–568 (2002)
4. Schmitz, G., Ermert, H., Senge, T.: Tissue-characterization of the prostate using radio frequency ultrasonic signals. IEEE Transactions on Ultrasound Ferroelectrics & Frequency Control 46(1), 126–138 (1999)
5. Materka, A., Strzelecki, M.: Texture Analysis Methods – A Review, A Review, Technical University of Lodz, Institute of Electronics, COST B11 report, Brussels (1998)

6. Grigorescu, S.E., Petkov, N., Kruizinga, P.: Comparison of Texture Features Based on Gabor Filters. IEEE Transactions on Image Processing 11(10), 1160–1167 (2002)

7. Noble, J.A.: Ultrasound image segmentation and tissue characterization. Part H: J. Engineering in Medicine 223, 1–10 (2009)

8. Noble, J., Boukerroui, D.: Ultrasound image segmentation: a survey. IEEE Transaction in Med. Imaging 25(8), 987–1010 (2006)

9. Yang, C., Zhu, H., Wu, S., Bai, Y., Gao, H.: Correlations Between B-Mode Ultrasonic Image Texture Features and Tissue temperature in Microwave Ablation by the American Institute of Ultrasound in Medicine. J. Ultrasound Medicine, 1787–1799 (2010)

10. Prager, R.W., Gee, A.H., Treece, G.M., Kingsbury, N.G., Lindop, J.E., Gomersall, H., Shin, H.-C.: Deconvolution and Elastography based on three-dimensional ultrasound. In: Proceedings of the IEEE International Ultrasonics Symposium (IUS 2008), Beijing, People's republic of China, November 2-5, pp. 548–557 (2008)

11. Fenster, A., Surry, K., Smith, W., Gill, J., Downey, D.: 3D Ultrasound imaging: applications in image guided therapy and biopsy. Computer Graphics, 557–568 (2002)

12. Fitzpatrick, J.M., Reinhardt, J.M.: Prostate ultrasound image segmentation using level set-based region flow with shape guidance. SPIE (2005)

13. Kubota, R., Kunihiro, M., Suetake, N., Uchino, E., Hashimoto, G., Hiro, T., Matsuzaki, M.: An Intravascular Ultrasound-based Tissue Characterization Using Shift-invariant Features Extracted by Adaptive Subspace SOM. International Journal of Biology and Biomedical Engineering (2008)

14. Rajan, E.G.: Symbolic Computing - Signal and image processing. Anshan Publications, Kent (2003)

15. Mandalapu, E.N., Rajan, E.G.: Rajan Transform and its Uses in Pattern Recognition. Informatica 33, 213–220 (2009)

16. Mandalapu, E.N., Rajan, E.G.: Two Dimensional Object Recognition Using Rajan Transform. Engineering Letters 13, 3, EL_13_3_7 Advance online publication (2006)

17. Randen, T.R., Husoy, J.H.: Filtering for texture classification: a comparative study. IEEE Trans. Pattern Anal. Machine Intelligent 21, 291–310 (1999)

18. Noble, J.A.: Ultrasound image segmentation and tissue characterization. Journal of Engineering in Medicine (2010)

19. Landini, L., Verrazzani, L.: Spectral characterization of tissues microstructure by ultrasounds: a stochastic approach. IEEE Transactions Ultrasonics, Ferroelectrics and Frequency Control (1990)

20. Lizzi, F.L., Feleppa, E.J., Kaisar Alam, S., Deng, C.X.: Ultrasonic spectrum analysis for tissue evaluation. Pattern Recognition Letters (2003)

21. Hill, C.R., Bamber, J.C., ter Haar, G.R.: Physical principles of medical ultrasonics, 2nd edn. (2004)

22. Vandenberg, J.: Arterial imaging techniques and tissue characterization using fuzzylogic. In: Proceedings of the 1994 Second Australian and New Zealand Conference on Intelligent Information Systems, 239–243 (1994)

23. Nailon, W., McLaughlin, S.: Intravascular ultrasound image interpretation. In: Proceeding Of the International Conference on Pattern Recognition. IEEE Computer Society, Austria (1997)

24. Dixon, K.: Characterization of coronary plaque in intravascular ultrasound histological Correlation. In: IEEE Conference (1997)

25. Pujol, O., Radeva, P.: Automatic segmentation of lumen in intravascular ultrasound images: An evaluation of texture feature extractors. In: Proceedings for IBERAMIA (2002)

Enlargement of Clinical Stemmer in Hindi Language for Homoeopathy Province

Pramod P. Sukhadeve and Sanjay K. Dwivedi

Department of Computer Science
Babasaheb Bhimrao Ambedkar University, Lucknow, India
sukhadeve.pramod@gmail.com, skd200@yahoo.com

Abstract. Stemming is an evolution that integrates morphologically corresponding stipulations into a single term devoid of doing inclusive morphological scrutiny. Stemming is utilized in information retrieval systems to acquire enhanced performance. Moreover, this process diminished the number of terms in the information retrieval system. This paper presents and discusses rule-based Hindi language clinical stemmer, which incorporates terms manually extracted affix stripping rules. The proposed stemmer is not domain reliant but we use this stemmer in Homoeopathy language. It converse the well-organized technique in which the affix list was developed, and in attendance the linguistic grounds subsequently including various affixes in the inventory. Analogous performance can be tattered to build stemmer for auxiliary fields such as story books, news articles, etc.

Keywords: Homoeopathy, Hindi Stemmer, prefix, suffix, root words, Grammar, clinical words.

1   Introduction

Stemming is the pre-processing step of collapsing words into their morphological root. For example, the terms दवाइ, दवाइयाँ, दवाइवाला, दवाख़ाना, दवात might be conflated to their stem nok - The first paper on the stemmer was published in 1968. It was written by Julie Beth Lovins [1] it is a rule based stemmer. This is a single pass context-sensitive, longest match stemmer which make use of a list of about 250 unusual suffixes, and removes the longest suffix attached to the word, that the stem after the suffix has been removed is always at least 3 characters long. Another popular rule based stemmer developed was by Porter in 1980, popularly called as Porter's stemming algorithm [2].

This stemmer was very extensively used and became the genuine standard algorithm used for English stemming. The procedure of stemming is also called conflation. It is also used in indexing and search system. These will handle automatic removal of word endings. Stemming is usually done by removing any attached suffixes and prefixes from words stemmer uses number of techniques like Brute force

N. Meghanathan et al. (Eds.): CCSIT 2012, Part III, LNICST 86, pp. 239–248, 2012.

algorithm, suffix stripping algorithm, lemmatization algorithm, stochastic algorithm, N gram analysis, hybrid approaches. These stemming algorithms are different in performance and accuracy. These all techniques have different approaches and methods to stem words.

2   Approaches to Stemming

The stemmer for other languages like English, Nepali, Bengali and Hindi are present. Mostly the word is done on English language. Algorithm for suffix stripping is used in 1980 by M. F. Porter. In this it uses a list of suffixes by which it matches an inflected word and removes the suffix, stemming algorithm is used for German languages, and in this stemmer firstly it removes a suffix from the word the word and then checks the validity of word. If the word found to be illogical then it substitutes the suffix with the other words [3]. In the Dutch stemmer it uses a suffix stripping algorithm and dictionary lookup rule based methods [4]. In the Nepali Stemming it uses a morphological analyzer which determines the given inflected word. In this it also tells about the Dawson stemming algorithm, Krowertz algorithm [5]. Lightweight stemmer for Bengali also exists. In which it just strips the affix from the word without doing the complete morphological analysis. It removes suffixes as well as prefixes. This type of approach that is used for stemming is also called affix removal approach [6]. In the lightweight stemmer for Hindi it uses a look up table approach in which word is matched with the words present in the table. Light weight stemmer approach uses affix removal algorithm and n gram stemming algorithm. It also shows the over stemming errors and the under stemming errors [7]. There is a hybrid approach which is used for stemming of Arabic text. In this approach it uses a dictionary technique, morphological analysis, affix removal, statistical and translation technique. It also shows the accuracy of this hybrid approach on various areas like economics, science, medical and sport [8].

3   Language and Grammar

Hindi is a direct descendant of Sanskrit through Prakrit and Apabhramsha. It has been influenced and enriched by Dravidian, Turkish, Farsi, Arabic, Portugese and English. It is a very expressive language. Throughout the world more than hundreds of universities having Hindi as subject in syllabus. Most of the famous composition of Hindi has been translated into foreign languages. In India Delhi, Haryana, Bihar, Uttar Pradesh, Madhya Pradesh, Himachal Pradesh are Hindi heart lands, but non Hindi states like Kerala, Andhra Pradesh, Assam, Manipur, Maharashtra, Gujrat, Calcutta, Nagaland, Tripura etc., are also accumulating Hindi. Today's in India Hindi is using in terms of communicating language, State language, Mother tongue, official language etc. In India most of the states using Hindi and also in News papers, School books, Advertisements, etc. so Hindi language is India's dignity.

In Hindi some of the characters and words prevailing two type of forms like;-

Table 1. Two type of forms of words

(शब्द) Words	
गये	गए
नयी	नई
गयी	गई
चाहिये	चाहिए
जायेंग	जाएँगे
अन्त	टंत
सम्बन्ध	संबंध

There are 13 vowels in Hindi which are shown below in table 2.

Table 2. Hindi Vowels

Vowel (मात्रा)

अ	आ	औ	ऋ	अं	इ
ए	अः	ई	ऐ	उ	ओ

There are certain consonents (व्यजंन) in hindi which are shown in table 3.

Table 3. Hindi Consonants

Consonant (व्यजंन)

क	ख	ग	घ	ड	च	छ	ज	झ
त्र	ट	ठ	ड	ढ	ण	त	थ	द
ध	ऩ	प	फ	ब	भ	म	य	र
ल	ऌ	श	ष	स	ह	क्ष	त्र	ज्ञ

4 Stemmer Characteristics of Hindi Language

A Hindi is morphologically very rich. A single root word may have different morphological variants, for example, words like डॉक्टरों, डॉक्टरी are morphological variants of the word डॉक्टर.

4.1 Prefix

The variants in Hindi are usually formed by adding prefixes to the stem or root word. We can categories the Prefixes found in Hindi language.

Syllable which is added in front of the word and then influenced the meaning of the word, those syllables is called prefix.

Ex. अंगघात   =   अंग + घात
    अंगघाती   =   अंग + घाती
    अंगघातग्रस्त   =   अंग + घात + ग्रस्त
    अंगच्छेदक   =   अंग + च्छेदक

syllables are Prefixes :- In feasible examples "अंग, आ, उप, प्र, वि, स" are syllables. Prefixes are applied only in the form of syllable.

Prefixes are added in front of words: - most of the time peoples remove syllable to obtain the prefix.

Ex. अकरण = अ + करण
    कुशल = कु + शल
    बोध = ब + ओध

In the above examples prefixes are correct and have syllables but they are not concert with any words. In the above examples where prefixes are added to the improper words, hence these types of separations are not true.

Prefix influenced the meaning of words: - Prefixes are used to get the new meaning of the words, when prefixes added to the words, then the meaning of the root words are changed. In the above example "आ, उप, प्र, वि, and सं" are prefixes, they changed the meaning of the root word "अंग".

Hindi Prefixes are shown below in the Table 4.

Table 4. Types of Hindi Prefixes

Prefix	Meaning of prefix	new words
अ	अभाव	अकाल अमर
अन	के बिना	अनजान अनहोनी
अध	आधा	अधमरा अधपका
कु	बुरा	कुपुत्र कुकर्म
भर	पुरा	भरपेट भरमार

Sometimes more than one prefixes are attached with the word examples are shown below in the table 5.

Table 5. Words append with the Prefixes

Prefix	Prefix	Root word	Words
सम्	टा	लेचना	समालोचना
निर्	अभि	मान	निरभिमान
प्रति	डप	कार	प्रत्युकार
सु	सम्	गठित	सुसंगठित

4.2   Suffix

Syllables which are added at the end of the word and then manipulate the meaning of word, those syllables is called suffix.

Ex. धार्मिक = धर्म + इक
    पशुता = पशु + ता
    लिखावट = लिख + आवट

In Hindi there are certain types of suffixes, some suffixes used in verbs, some are used in Noun, Pronoun and Adjectives. Reversal in the gender form by using some of the suffixes, and some consumed in the separation form. In this way there are certain types of suffixes in Hindi. So, for the purpose of perusal it is divided into three main parts.

I) Secondary suffix (तद्धित प्रत्ययद्वरू Suffixes used at the end of the Noun, Pronoun and Adjective are called Secondary suffix

पशुत्व = पशु + त्व
अपनापन = अपना + पन
बुध्दिमान् = बुध्दि + मान्

a) The vibrant (कर्तृवाचक) secondary suffix: Suffix that makes the realization of a task is called the vibrant suffix.

Table 6. Vibrant suffix

Suffix	Words	Suffix	Words
आर	ट्ठुहार	इया	दुखिया
ई	शराबी	एरा	सपेरा
अक	लेखक	कार	कलाकार
आर	छुकानदार	वान	धनवान
वाला	गाड़ीवाला	गर	जादूगर

b) Abstract (भाववाचक) suffix: Suffix that makes the realization of an abstract is called an abstract suffix.

Table 7. Abstract suffix

Suffix	Words	Suffix	Words
आहट	गरमाहट	आई	भलाई
आ	ड्लावा	ई	सर्दी
आस	मिठास	त्व	देवत्व
पा	बुढापा	पन	बालपन

c) Relational (संबंध.वाचक) suffix: Suffix that makes the realization of an relation is called an relational suffix.

Table 8. Relational suffix

Suffix	Words	Suffix	Words
आल	स्सुराल	इक	धार्मिक
एरा	च्चेरा	आ	भतीजा

d) Adjectival (विशेषण) suffix: Suffix that makes the realization of a quality is called an adjectival suffix.

Table 9. Adjectival suffix

Suffix	Words	Suffix	Words
आ	अंडा	ई	क्रोधी
ईय	दयनीय	इत	थ्यंतित
ईला	च्मकीला	इल	जटिल

II) Feminine (स्त्रीवाचक) suffix: - suffixes that are used to convert words into feminine are called feminine suffix.

Table 10. List of Feminine Words

Suffix	Words	Suffix	Words	Suffix	Words
ई	लड़की	आ	शिष्या	इन	सुनारिन
नी	मोरनी	आनी	नौकरानी	आइन	ठकुराइन
इया	बिटिया	इका	अध्यापिका	मती	भगवती

III) Krit (कृत्) suffix: suffix using at the end of the things for making noun, adjective and indeclinable is called Krit suffix.

Ex. लिखावट = लिखना + आवट
  खिलाड़ी = खेलना + आड़ी

a) Virant (कर्तृ) Krit (कृत्) suffix:- Suffix that makes the realization of a verb and Subject is called an vibrant Krit suffix.

Table 11. Virant Krit

Suffix	Words	Suffix	Words
टक	सहायक	आक	तैराक
आड़ी	अनाड़ी	आलू	दयालु
एरा	लुटेरा	वाला	जानेवाला

b) Object (कर्मवाचक) Krit (कृत्) suffix:- Suffix that makes the realization of verb and object is called objective suffix.

Table 12. Object Krit

Suffix	Words	Suffix	Words
औना	खिलौना	नी	ओढ़नी
आना	खाना	आवना	डरावना

c) Abstract (भावाचक) Krit (कृत्) Suffix:- Suffix that makes the realization of verb and abstract is called objective suffix.

Table 13. Abstract Krit

Suffix	Words	Suffix	Words
आई	लिखाई	आन	उड़ान
टाप	थमलाप	आवट	लिखावट
आहट	घबराहट	आव	चढ़ाव

d) Past and Present Krit Suffix:- Suffix that makes the realization of Noun, Indeclinable, and special meaning verbs is called Verbal suffix.

Table 14. Past and Present Krit Suffix

Suffix	Words	Suffix	Words
आ	सूखा	ता	चढ़ता

5   Combination of Suffix and Prefix

Most of the words are made by using prefix and suffix both, for example.

Words	Prefix	+	Root Word	+	Suffix
उपकारक =	उप	+	कार	+	आक
अभिमानी =	अभि	+	मान	+	ई
अपमानित =	अप	+	मान	+	इत
बदचलनी =	बद	+	चलन	+	ई
दुस्साहसी =	दुस	+	साहस	+	ई
शिरट्टी	शिर	+	ट्टा	+	ई

6   Pattern of Hindi Words

The variants in Hindi are usually formed by adding prefixes and suffixes to the stem or root word. We can categories the prefixes and suffixes found in Hindi into three types:

I) Plain Prefixes and Suffixes: when prefixes added to the words, then the meaning of the root words are changed. Plain suffixes are also called dependent vowel signs ा, ि, ी, ो, ु , ॄ are some of the suffixes which combine with the root word to produce its morphological variants.
For Example, लडका, लडकि, लडके, लडकियाँ.
II) Join word Prefixes and suffixes: Join word prefixes are those which are produced by adding उन, उप, नि, वि, and सु.
उनचास = उन + चास
उपहार = उप + हार

Join word suffixes are those suffixes which are formed by merging two or more consonants and vowels. These join words are formed by merging any of the consonants with the morphological variant

गाड़ीवाला = गाड़ी + वाला
कारीगर = कारी + गर
दुकानदार = दुकान + दार

III) Complex suffixes: Complex Prefixes are formed by adding more than one prefixes to the root word. Like

समालोचना = सम् + आ + लोचना
निरभिमान = निर् + अभि + मान
प्रत्युकार = प्रति + उप + कार

Complex suffixes are formed by combining two or more consonants with the plain suffixes. For example,

भुलक्कड़ = भुल + अक्कड़
मनुष्यत्व = मनुष्य + त्व
नैतिक = नैत + इक
are some of the complex suffixes.

IV) Words follow a specific pattern: Unlike other Indian languages it is found that words in Hindi language follow a specific pattern. The words in the Hindi can be expressed as:

Token = Prefix + Root Word   for Prefix
Token = Root Word + Suffix   for Suffix
Token = Prefix + Root Word + Suffix

7   Our Approach towards Affix Stripping

The rule-based stemmer extract affix stripping rules based on the morphological characteristics of Hindi. The common stemming patterns found in Hindi are:

{Original word}:= {Plain Prefix} + {SW}
e.g प्रहार = प्र + हार
{Original word} :={ Complex Prefix} + {Root word}
e.g निर्दय = निर् + दय
{Original word} :={ Plain Prefix + join word + Complex prefix}+ {Root word}
e.g. सुसंगठित = स + उ + सम् + गठित
{Original word} :={ SW} + {Plain suffixes}
e.g, पशुता = पशु + ता

{Original word} :={ Root word} + {complex suffixes}

e.g, पशुत्व = पशु + त्व

{Original word} :={ Root word} + { join word + Complex suffixes+ Join Word}

e.g, भुलक्कड़+ = भुल + अक् + कड़

The affix (prefix and suffix) stripping rules for the rule-based stemmer are based on these patterns. Fig. 1 depicts steps in the algorithm.

Step 1: Input list of words

उपकारक

Step 2: Eliminate all the complex affixes

e.g, {उप} + {कार} + {अक}

Step 3A: Eliminate the join word suffixes i.e. Eliminate the inflections of consonants like क, द, फ, व, with र

e.g, {क} = {क}+{र}

Step 3B: Eliminate the join word prefixes i.e. Eliminate the inflections of consonants like प्र, क, उ, प

e.g, {प्रहार} = {प्र}+{हार}

Step 3C:- Eliminate the inflections for consonant j

Step 4A: Eliminate the inflections for consonant y

Step 4B: Eliminate the inflections involving plain affixes.

Fig. 1. Algorithm developed for Hindi Stemmer

8   Conclusion

In this paper we have presented a stemming methodology that is based on a hand crafted rule based system. The rule based system models phenomena of inflectional languages in a linguistic and consistent way. We discussed different approaches of stemming and detailed depiction of Prefix and Suffix. The proposed clinical stemmer incorporates terms manually extracted affixes stripping rules and algorithm, it is not domain relevant. It converse the well categorized technique in which the affixes are detached.

References

1. Lovins, J.B.: Development of a stemming algorithm. Mechanical Translation and Comp. Linguistics 11, 22–31 (1968)
2. Porter, M.F.: An algorithm for suffix stripping Program, vol. 14(3), pp. 130–137 (1980)
3. Caumanns, J.: A fast and simple stemming Algorithm for German Words1, pp. 1–10. Alg. is published in Dept. of comp. sci. at the free univ. of Berlin (1998)
4. Gaustad, T., Bauma, G.: Accurate Stemming of Dutch for Text Classification. Language Computing 45(1), 104–117 (2000)
5. Bal, B.K., Shrestha, P.: A Morphological Analyzer and a Stemmer for Nepali. In: PAN Localization, Working Papers 2004-2007, pp. 324–331 (2004)

6. Zahurul Islam, M., Nizam Uddin, M., Khan, M.: A Light Weight Stemmer for Bengali and Its Use in Spelling Checker. In: Proceedings of 1st International Conference on Digital Communications and Computer Applications (DCCA 2007), Irbid, Jordan, pp. 87–93 (2004)

7. Ramanathan, A., Rao, D.D.: A Lightweight Stemmer for Hindi. In: Proceedings of the 10th Conference of the European Chapter of the Association for Computational Linguistics (EACL), Workshop on Computatinal Linguistics for South Asian Languages, Budapest, pp. 42–48 (April)

8. Goweder, A.M., Alhammi, H.A., Rashed, T., Musrati, A.: A Hybrid Method for Stemming Arabic Text. Journal of Computer Science,
   http://eref.uqu.edu.sa/files/eref2/folder6/f181.pdf

Fuzziness in Text Classification Using Different Similarity Metrics

M.A. Wajeed[1] and T. Adilakshmi[2]

[1] SCSI, Sreenidhi Institute of Science & Technology,
Ghatkesar, Hyderabad, AP, India
wajeed.mtech@gmail.com
[2] Dept., of CSE, Vasavi College of Engineering,
Ibrahimbagh, Hyderabad, AP, India
t_adilakshmi@gmail.com

Abstract. We are living in the information era where vast amount of data is generated at the end of the day, which can also be in textual form. To cater the further needs and to make decisions effective we need to classify the generated data and store it in the classified repository, so that later it can efficiently be retrieved with minimum effort. The paper attempts to mix the concepts of supervised learning and unsupervised learning techniques, by forming clusters which could act as features so that feature reduction can be made possible. Clusters are formed based on the word patterns, soft, hard and mixed clustering is also considered in the processes of text classification. We employee different similarity measures like Euclidean, square Euclidean, Manhattan, chebyshev, bray-Curtis etc., in the processing of finding the category of the document. The results obtained were encouraging.

Keywords: Text classification, data Clusters, soft-hard-mixed clusters, eucledean, chebyshev, manhattan,bray-curtis, canberra similarity measures.

1   Introduction

To lead a comfortable life man today has stepped in to the era of information technology, where on daily basis huge amount of data is generated which needs to be stored in a proper fashion so as to make it useful in future. The generated data can also be in textual format, so the need of classification of documents based on its contents become inevitable. In this process we have supervised classification and unsupervised classification. In case of supervised classification based on the training data which has a set of independent attribute, with its corresponding decision attribute, a function which can learn how the decision attribute is dependent on the independent attributes is made to learn. But in case of unsupervised learning as we don't have the training data, the given data is split into clusters such that the inter-similarity among the clusters is maximized and intra-similarity among the clusters is reduced. The paper explores the construction of the clusters in case of supervised learning to reduce the no: of features involved in the learning process of the classification function, as in case of text classification large no of features are involved. Different similarity measures are explored in the process of learning.

N. Meghanathan et al. (Eds.): CCSIT 2012, Part III, LNICST 86, pp. 249–260, 2012.

The paper is organized in the following manner, in section 2 basic concepts are furnished in section 3 proposed method is explored. In section 4 diferent similarity measures are discussed and in section 5 implementation details and results are furnished and finally in section 6 conclusion and future enhancements are given.

2   Related Work

Without feature selection text categorization (TC) is almost not possible as in TC naturally large no: of features exists. Need for feature reduction becomes inevitable step. Feature reduction generally can be done either by feature selection or feature reduction. In Feature selection we attempt to find a subset of the original features that can be obtained by the process of either filtering technique or by using wrapper technique. The other possibility to reduce features is to transform the relevant features from a high-dimension space to a space of fewer dimensions such a transformation may be either linear as in case of principal component analysis (PCA), or can be through other nonlinear technique.

In supervised classification Information Gain, Gain Ratio, Odds Ratio, Gini-index, Chi-Square etc techniques are very popular as feature selection measures. On the other hand document frequency, term frequency, and inverse-document frequency are considered as feature selection in unsupervised learning. A brief discussion of few supervised feature selection techniques are given below.

Given a set of categories C_m, where m is the no: of classes the information gain of term t is given by

$$IG(t) = -\sum_{i=1}^{m} P(c_i) \log P(c_i) + P(t) \sum_{i=1}^{m} P(c_i \mid t)$$
$$\log P(c_i \mid t) + P(\bar{t}) \sum_{i=1}^{m} P(c_i \mid \bar{t}) \log P(c_i \mid \bar{t})$$

(1)

Feature reduction can be made possible using the values obtained by the equation (1). The features whose IG is less compared to the other features are discarded.

Chi-Square another supervised feature selection technique for feature reduction which is given by

$$\chi^2 = N \cdot \frac{P(t_k, c_i)P(\bar{t}_k, \bar{c}_i) - P(t_k, \bar{c}_i)P(\bar{t}_k, c_i)}{P(t_k)P(\bar{t}_k) - P(c_i)P(\bar{c}_i)}$$

(2)

Odds Ratio yet another supervised feature selection method which is given by

$$OR = \frac{P(t_k \mid c_i) \cdot P(t_k \mid \bar{c}_k)}{(1 - P(t_k \mid c_i)) \cdot P(t_k \mid \bar{c}_k)}$$

(3)

Based on the values obtained in the above equations, which determines the relationship between the terms and the class label, feature selection can be made.

Definitions: - We are provided with the training document set T_s whose class label is given along with the documents. We are also given a set of document set T_t termed as test data set whose class label is to be determined by the classifier.

In the process of obtaining the class label of the test document lexicon set £, which is a set which contains all words, that have appeared in the training document set T_s is built.

We obtain the word-patterns for each word which appears in the documents, which is the conditional probability of the class given the terms appearance in the document. We find the probability of the terms appearance for all the classes and for all the terms, we denote such a set as W_p. Once we obtain the word patterns then we find the self constructive clusters based on the word patterns using the Gaussian functions.

3   Fuzzy Classifier

[1] gives the detailed steps of pre-processing the training set. Preprocessing is needed so as to remove the noise in the training data. We obtain the lexicon set which is a set of all words which appeared in the training documents. [6] gives the procedure for generating word pattern, we obtain the clusters once word-pattern for all the words in the lexicon set. In the process of generating the cluster we proceed with the given 'n' no: of documents in the training data, that are spread across 'm' no: of classes. Using the lexicon we generate the word patterns for each member of the lexicon set $X_i = <x_{i1}, x_{i2}, x_{i3}, ...x_{in}>$ the elements of the set are defined as

$$P(c_m \mid t_i) = \frac{\sum\limits_{r=1}^{n} d_{ri} * \varepsilon_{rm}}{\sum\limits_{r=1}^{n} d_{ri}} \tag{4}$$

where d_{ri} is the no: of times the term t_i occurs in the document d_r, ε_{rm} is 1 if the document d_r belongs to the class c_m, otherwise it is 0.

Clusters have the property that the inter-similarity among clusters is minimized and intra-similarity is maximized. In order to achieve optimal clusters, they are characterized by the product of m – one dimensional Gaussian function. Let ζ be a cluster containing q word patterns $x_1, x_2, ... x_q$. Let $x_j = <x_{j1}, x_{j2}, ... x_{jm}> i \leq j \leq q$ the mean $\bar{x} = <\bar{x}_1, \bar{x}_2, ... \bar{x}_m>$, the mean is defined as

$$\bar{x}_i = \frac{1}{|\zeta|} \sum\limits_{i=1}^{n} x_i \tag{5}$$

where $|\zeta|$ gives the no: of elements in the ith clusters. The deviation $\sigma = <\sigma_1, \sigma_2, ...\sigma_m>$ of ζ are given by

$$\sigma_i = \sqrt{\frac{1}{|\zeta|} \sum\limits_{i=1}^{n} (x_{ji} - \bar{x}_i) * (x_{ji} - \bar{x}_i)} \tag{6}$$

The fuzzy similarity of a word pattern to cluster ζ is defined by gaussian membership function

$$\zeta_j(x) = \prod\limits_{i=1}^{m} \exp\left[\frac{-(x_i - \bar{x}_i)^2}{\sigma_i}\right] \tag{7}$$

The values of the $\zeta_j(x)$ are bounded in the interval [0, 1], where $1 \le j \le k$. A word pattern close to the mean of a cluster is regarded to be very similar to the cluster i.e. $\zeta(x) \approx 1$, on the other hand a word pattern far distant from a cluster is hardly similar to the cluster so $\zeta(x) \approx 0$. On the basis of $\zeta(x)$ and on the threshold value ς, which is provided by the user one can control the formation of no: of clusters. If we wish to have many clusters then smaller value of the threshold ς is considered otherwise larger value of the threshold is taken.

If $\zeta_j(x_i) \ge \varsigma$, then the word pattern x_i can be added to the cluster ζ_i, and the no: of elements in the cluster ζ_i is increased by 1, corresponding values of the cluster also are updated, i,e the mean $\bar{x_i}$ of the cluster and deviation of the cluster σ_i. In case if $\zeta_j(x_i) < \varsigma$, then a new cluster is created with its mean as $\bar{x} = x_i$, the deviation of the newly formed cluster as $\sigma = 1$ and the no: of clusters so far formed is also incremented. Once all the word patterns are constructed we have 'k' no: of clusters with updated mean values of each of the cluster in the form of the vector $\bar{x} = <\bar{x}_1, \bar{x}_2, \ldots\ldots, \bar{x}_k>$ and updated deviation values of the cluster in the form of the vector $\sigma = <\sigma_1, \sigma_2, \ldots\ldots \sigma_k>$.

We deviate from [6] in the process of text classification based on fuzzy measures. Once we obtain all the updated values of cluster deviation, mean and no: of clusters, we proceed in the following manner.

As explained in section 3 word pattern for all the words which are members of the lexicon are obtained, the no: of clusters, each of the cluster size is also obtained. From the training documents words frequency is obtained as described in [7]. We then find for each word, the membership of it in the clusters. We create soft, hard and mixed mapping based on the membership of the word in the clusters. We create 14,822 vectors with 'k' no: of elements in each, where 'k' is the no: of clusters formed. In case of hard classification based on the equation 9 a word is allowed in a single cluster. But in case of soft classification single word can be considered in more than a single cluster, based on the equation 7. We generate the mixed classification based on the equation 10.

The same steps are repeated for the test documents too. In the case of test data we have 2189, so we get 2189 vectors with k elements in each. Now for each of the test document we find the euclidean distance similarity measure, which is given by the sum of square of the difference of the individual elements [8] of test and train data.

4   Similarity Measures

The sum of the squares of the difference of the individual elements gives the Euclidean similarity [7]. The same can be expresses mathematically as

$$Dist(X,Y) = \sqrt{(x_2 - x_1)*(x_2 - x_1) + (y_2 - y_1)*(y_2 - y_1) + \ldots} \qquad (8)$$

Figure-1 shows the results obtained for different k values varying from 1 to 10, and figure-2 gives the results for different values of k varying through 10 to 100.

- Squared Euclidean Distance is similar to the Euclidean distance, but does not have the square-root over the summation. Figure-3 shows the results obtained for k values varying from 1 to 10, figure-4 gives the results for different values of k varying through 10 to 100. Mathematically square Euclidean distance is expressed as

$$Dist(X,Y) = (x_2 - x_1)*(x_2 - x_1) + (y_2 - y_1)*(y_2 - y_1) + ... \tag{9}$$

- Manhattan Distance is a simple similarity measure when compared to the Euclidean and square-Euclidean distance measure; it takes the summation of the absolute difference among the individual elements of the vector. Figure-5 shows the results obtained for k value varying from 1 to 10, and figure-6 gives the results for different values of k varying through 10 to 100. Mathematical expression of Manhattan distance is expressed as

$$Dist(X,Y) = |x_2 - x_1| + |y_2 - y_1| + ... \tag{10}$$

- Chessboard distance is also called as Chebyshev distance, Tchebychev distance), Maximum metric, it is a metric defined on a vector space where the distance between two vectors the greatest of their differences along any coordinate dimension is. It is named after Pafnuty. Figure-7 shows the results obtained for k value varying from 1 to 10, and figure-8 gives the results for different values of k varying through 10 to 100. Mathematically the same can be expressed as

$$Dist(X,Y) = Max(|x_1 - y_1|, |x_2 - y_2|, ...) \tag{11}$$

- Bray Curtis Distance is also called as Sorenson. It is defined as the fraction of absolute difference in the individual elements of the vector to the sum of the individual elements of the two vectors. The same can be expressed mathematically as

$$Dist(X,Y) = \frac{(|x_1 - y_1| + |x_2 - y_2|, ...)}{(|x_1 + y_1| + |x_2 + y_2|, ...)} \tag{12}$$

- The ratio of the sum of the absolute difference in the individual elements to the sum of the absolute values of the individual elements in the two vectors gives the canberra similarity measure. Figure-9 shows the results obtained for k value varying from 1 to 10, and figure-10 gives the results for different values of k varying through 10 to 100. This is mathematically expressed as

$$Dist(X,Y) = \sum_{k=1}^{n} \frac{|x_{ik} - x_{jk}|}{|x_{ik}| + |x_{kj}|} \tag{13}$$

5   Implementation

[5] has the text categorization corpus, which has 5485 documents across 8 classes. [1] gives the details of the lexicon construction phase; we had 14833 words in the lexicon. We assume that the corpus has no noise, though we found noise in the corpus, but no effort was put to remove the noise. We had vector, with 8 columns representing 8 different classes and 14833 rows for the lexicon entries; the elements in the vector are the word patterns. Using these word patterns, we build the clusters, and the goodness of the clustering algorithm is that we don't need to provide to the algorithm the input stating, the no: of clusters to be build, but no: of clusters are defined on the basis of input value of the similarity threshold ç. By varying the threshold value the no: of clusters obtained can be controlled, for more clusters the threshold value has to be smaller, and for less no: of clusters the value of the threshold has to be larger.

Table 1. showing different threshold values and clusters obtained

Threshold value (ç)	Clusters
0.5	14
0.6	12
0.7	10

We tried with 3 different values of the threshold, table 1 gives the details of the threshold value and the clusters obtained. Once the no: of clusters are formed, we implement the KNN algorithm for the text categorization.

All documents belonging to the training data are processed first. We perform stemming on the training data, and the words obtained after stemming with respect to word patterns are grouped to form clusters. The no: of elements for each of the clusters for each of the document was obtained, thus the training documents were mapped to the numeric values. As the no: of clusters obtained for different values of the threshold is different so the experiment was repeated 3 times and we obtained different clusters.

We take 3 types of clusters into consideration, a word is considered to belong to a single cluster only we refer such a clusters as hard cluster, using the given below equation we obtain the membership of the hard clusters.

$$t_{ij} = \begin{cases} 1 \text{ if } j= \arg \max_{1<=\alpha<=k} (\zeta(x_i)) \\ 0 \text{ otherwise} \end{cases} \qquad .(14)$$

But in case of soft-weighting approach we allow the word pattern to belong to more than a single cluster so rather than considering the maximum value of the function ($\mu G_\alpha(x_i)$) we take its direct value for all the clusters. In case of the soft, hard mixed-weighting cluster we employ the below equation where γ is the constant which dictates domination of the cluster type.

$$t_{ij} = (\gamma) * t_{ij}^{H} + (1 - \gamma) * t_{ij}^{S} \tag{15}$$

where t_{ij}^{H} is hard-weighting clustering approach and t_{ij}^{S} is the soft-weighting clustering membership function. The value of γ can be between 0 and 1. If it is very near to 0 then the hard and mixed weighting equation coincides with the soft-clustering approach and if its value is 1 then the hard and mixed weighting coincides with hard-clustering approach. Taking γ value as 0.1 we have performed the experiment.

In figures 1 through 10 soft1, hard1 and mixed1 refers to the threshold(ς) value as 0.5 which formed 14 clusters, soft2, hard2 and mixed2 refers to the threshold(ς) value as 0.6 which formed 12 clusters, and soft3, hard3 and mixed3 refers to the threshold(ς) value as 0.7 which formed 10 clusters. For 5485 documents in the training data we have 5485 vectors with the no: of elements in the vector equals to the no: of clusters. We have 2189 vectors for the same no: of elements in the vector as equal to the no: of clusters as part of the test data.

The procedure for test data is repeated as that of training, so all the test documents are too converted into vectors. Once we obtain the vectors of the training and test data we apply the KNN algorithm for the vectors. We use the Euclidean measure and obtain the similarity between the training data and the test data. For different values of K we obtain the confusion matrix, in table 2 we give the confusion matrix for k=1 for Euclidean similarity measure.

K-Nearest Neighbour algorithm is also called as instance based learning algorithm. It is a classifier which is based on learning by analogy. It computes the similarity between a given test tuple with training tuples that are similar to it [10]. The training tuples are described by 'n' attributes, in our case attributes are words which are in the lexicon set. Each tuple represents a point in an n-dimension pattern space. When given an unseen tuple, a k-nearest neighbor classifier searches the pattern space for different values of k (which can take any value 1 through some arbitrary number) the training tuples that are closest to the unseen tuple. Depending on the value of k, k training tuples are used which are near to the unseen tuple. Different similarity measures would be applied between two points or tuples say X1 and X2 which have 'n' component elements. It is used to find the similarity (closeness) between the tuples.

For different k tuples, the majority class label is taken, and the unseen tuple class label is declared to be the same as the majority class labels. In case of a tie, arbitrary the tie is resolved. In other words, the test data consists of 2189 documents, the distance between the training and a particular test documents is measured, the class with the nearest training data is taken as the class of the test data, as here K value in K-NN is 1. In case of k value 2 we take two smallest distances, and if both belong to same class than the test tuple also belongs to the same class as it is the nearest distance of the training data class, in case of tie an arbitrary consensus is used to resolve the conflict. Based on the similarity between the training and test tuples we obtain confusion matrix which is a good tool for analyzing, how well the classifier can classify the tuples of different classes. A confusion matrix can be treated as a tool which could be helpful in determining the performance of a classifier in supervised learning. It is a matrix plot of the classifier predicted versus the actual classes of the tuples.

For a dataset that has m different classes, a confusion matrix is a table which has m rows with m columns in each. An entry CMi,j in the first m rows and m columns indicates the number of tuples of class i that are labeled by the classifier as class j. For a classifier to have good accuracy, i,e to be an ideal classifier tuples along the diagonal of the confusion matrix must have non-zero values and rest of the elements, very close to zero. Table 1 gives the confusion matrix obtained, in the experiment for different values of k. The table has an additional row and columns to provide totals and recognition rates per class

In figure 1 we draw a graph showing the accuracy of the classifier, on X-axis we take different value of K, in K-NN algorithm, and on Y-axis we take the accuracy of the classifier, for the 3 types of clusters soft, hard and mixed results for $\varsigma = 0.5$ are shown. Similarly in figure 2 classifier accuracy for k values varying from 10 to 100 are provided for $\varsigma = 0.5$

In figure 3 for $\varsigma=0.6$ for k values 1 to 10 are provided and in figure 4 for $\varsigma=0.6$ for k values 10 to 100 are provided. In figure 5 for $\varsigma=0.7$ for k values 1 to 10 are provided and in figure 6 for $\varsigma=0.7$ for k values 10 to 100 are provided.

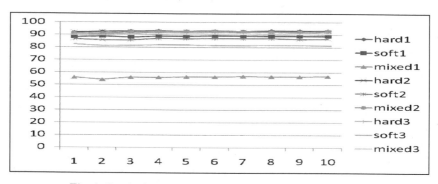

Fig. 1. Graph showing accuracy for Euclidean k values 1 to 10

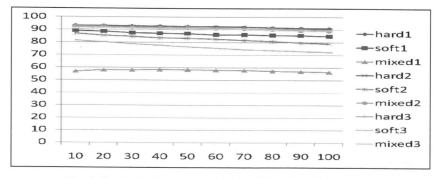

Fig. 2. Graph showing accuracy for Euclidean k values 10 to 100

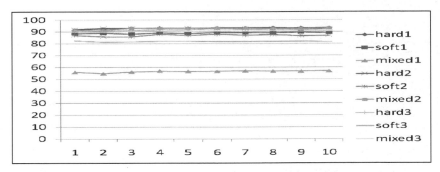

Fig. 3. Graph showing accuracy for Squared Euclidean k values 1 to 10

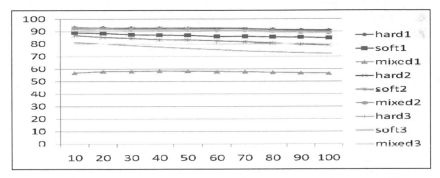

Fig. 4. Graph showing accuracy for Squared Euclidean k values 10 to 100

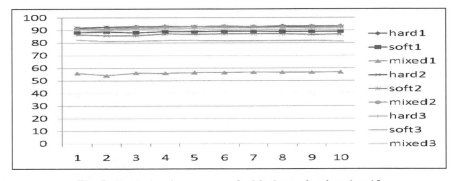

Fig. 5. Graph showing accuracy for Manhattan k values 1 to 10

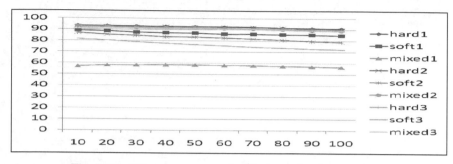

Fig. 6. Graph showing accuracy for Manhattan k values 10 to 100

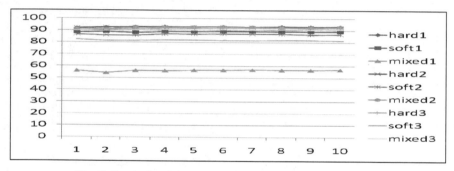

Fig. 7. Graph showing accuracy for Chebyshev k values 1 to 10

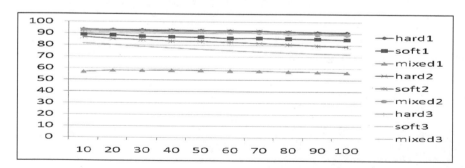

Fig. 8. Graph showing accuracy for chebyshev k values 10 to 100

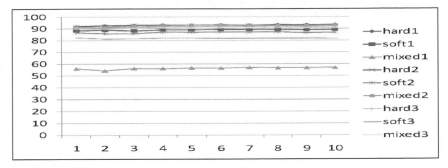

Fig. 9. Graph showing accuracy for Canberra k values 1 to 10

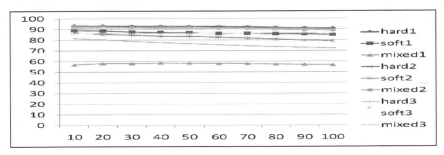

Fig. 10. Graph showing accuracy for Canberra k values 10 to 100

6   Conclusions

Presently bulk data is available which needs to be analyzed, utilizing the data generated decisions making can become effective. The data generated can also be textual form. The paper attempts in achieving learning by building a classifier which has fuzzy capabilities. In the process 3 types of clusters were explored based on the words in the documents occurrence, soft cluster where a word can belong to more than a single cluster at the same time, hard cluster where a word can belong to a single cluster at a time, mixed cluster which is devised using both the soft and hard clusters.

For k values varying from 1 to 10 we find that soft1 is better than soft2, soft2 is better than soft2. As k value increases accuracy also increases. Again decreases in soft2 but in soft3 we get mixed results. Hard is better than soft cluster. Hard also increases with k values, both hard1 and hard2 are the same we find mixed results in hard3. Mixed is the least in case of mixed1 and good in mixed2, mixed3 again decreases.

For k value 10 to 100 soft1, soft2 and soft3 decreases as k value increases. Mixed cluster approach also gives most decreasing accuracy result. Mixed2 is better when compared to mixed1 and mixed3. Hard1 is better than hard2, hard3 and decreases as k value increases. We also find that almost all the similarity measures gave same results giving the choice for the user to choose the similarity measure of his choice.

In future we wish to decrease the size of the lexicon and see how best the classifier can learn from the training data to classify the textual data

References

[1] Wajeed, M.A., Adilakshmi, T.: Text Classification Using Machine Learning. Journal of Theoretical and Applied Information Technology 7(2), 119–123 (2009)
[2] Yen, J., Langari, R.: Fuzzy Logic-Intelligence, Control, and Information. Prentice-Hall (1999)
[3] Wang, J.S., Lee, C.S.G.: Self-Adaptive Neurofuzzy Inference Systems for Classification Applications. IEEE Trans. Fuzzy Systems 10(6), 790–802 (2002)
[4] Correa, R.F., Ludermir, T.B.: Automatic Text Categorization: Case Study. In: Proceedings of the VII Brazilian Symposium on Neural Networks, Pernambuc, Brazil (November 2002)
[5] http://www.daviddlewis.com/resources/testcollections/reuters21578/
[6] Jiang, J.-Y., Liou, R.-J., Lee, S.-J.: Fuzzy Self-Constructing Feature Clustering Algorithm for Text Classification. IEEE Transaction on Knowledge & Data Engineering 23(3) (March 2011)
[7] Wajeed, M.A., Adilakshmi, T.: Different Similarity Measures for Text Classification Using KNN. In: To Be Presented in International Conference on Computer Communication Technology at NIT Allahabad (2011)
[8] Sebastiani, F.: Text classification, automatic. In: Brown, K. (ed.) The Encyclopedia of Language and Linguistics, 2nd edn., vol. 14, Elsevier Science, Amsterdam (2004)
[9] http://tartarus.org/~martin/PorterStemmer
[10] Yeung, C.-M.A., Gibbins, N., Shadbolt, N.: A k-Nearest-Neighbour Method for Classifying Web Search Results with Data in Folksonomies. In: IEEE/WIC/ACM International Conference on Web Intelligence and Intelligent Agent Technology, WI-IAT, vol. 1, pp. 70–76 (2008)
[11] Capdevila Dalmau, M., Márquez Flórez, O.W.: Experimental Results of the Signal Processing Approach to Distributional Clustering of Terms on Shape Reuters-21578 Collection. In: Amati, G., Carpineto, C., Romano, G. (eds.) ECiR 2007. LNCS, vol. 4425, pp. 678–681. Springer, Heidelberg (2007)

Image Compression over Low Channel Bandwidth

S. Anitha and Nagabhushana

Dr Mgr Educational and Research Institute, University, Chennai

anithasd@yahoo.com, bsnaga@gmail.com

Abstract. In recent years, there have been significant advancements in the field of signal processing where various innovative algorithms and architectures are used for the processing of image, video, and audio signals. These advancements have proceeded along several directions. On the algorithmic front, new techniques have led to the development of robust methods to reduce the size of the image, video, or audio data. Such methods are extremely vital in many applications that manipulate and store digital data. Informally, we refer to the process of size reduction as a compression process. On the architecture front, it is now feasible to put sophisticated compression processes on a relatively low-cost single chip; this has spurred a great deal of activity in developing multimedia systems for the large consumer market. One of the exciting prospects of such advancements is that multimedia information comprising image, video, and audio has the potential to become just another data type. This usually implies that multimedia information will be digitally encoded so that it can be manipulated, stored, and transmitted along with other digital data types. For such data usage to be pervasive, it is essential that the data encoding is standard across different platforms and applications. This will foster widespread development of applications and will also promote interoperability among systems from different vendors.

Keywords: Image compression, lossy, lossless, encoder, CD ROM, VHS, DC, CR.

1   Introduction

In recent years, there is a need for algorithms and architectures due to significant advancements for the processing of image, video, and audio signals. These advancements have proceeded along several directions. On the algorithmic front, new techniques have led to the development of robust methods to reduce the size of the image, video, or audio data. Such methods are extremely vital in many applications that manipulate and store digital data. Informally, we refer to the process of size reduction as a compression process.. On the architecture front, it is now feasible to put sophisticated compression processes on a relatively low-cost single chip; this has spurred a great deal of activity in developing multimedia systems for the large consumer market.

N. Meghanathan et al. (Eds.): CCSIT 2012, Part III, LNICST 86, pp. 261–268, 2012.

One of the exciting prospects of such advancements is that multimedia information comprising image, video, and audio has the potential to become just another data type. This usually implies that multimedia information will be digitally encoded so that it can be manipulated, stored, and transmitted along with other digital data types. For such data usage to be pervasive, it is essential that the data encoding is standard across different platforms and applications[1]. This will foster widespread development of applications and will also promote interoperability among systems from different vendors. Furthermore, standardisation can lead to the development of cost-effective implementations, which in turn will promote the widespread use of multimedia information. This is the primary motivation behind the emergence of image and video compression standards.

2   Background

Compression is a process intended to yield a compact digital representation of a signal. The processing of images involves processes such as *source coding, data compression(DC), bandwidth compression,* and *signal compression[2]* . In the cases where the signal is defined as an image, a video stream, or an audio signal, the generic problem of compression is to minimise the bit rate of their digital representation. There are many applications that benefit when image, video, and audio signals are available in compressed form.

Example 1: Let us consider facsimile image transmission. In most facsimile machines, the document is scanned and digitised. Typically, an 8.5x11 inches page is scanned at 200 dpi; thus, resulting in 3.74 Mbits. Transmitting this data over a low-cost 14.4 kbits/s modem would require 5.62 minutes. With compression, the transmission time can be reduced to 17 seconds. This results in substantial savings in transmission costs.

Example 2: Let us consider a video-based CD-ROM application. Full-motion video, at 30 fps and a 720 x 480 resolution, generates data at 20.736 Mbytes/s. At this rate, only 31 seconds of video can be stored on a 650 MByte CD-ROM. Compression technology can increase the storage capacity to 74 minutes, for VHS-grade video quality.

Image, video, and audio signals are amenable to compression due to the factors below.

- There is considerable statistical redundancy in the signal.
  1. Within a single image or a single video frame, there exists significant correlation among neighbour samples[5]. This correlation is referred to as *spatial correlation.*
  2. For data acquired from multiple sensors (such as satellite images), there exists significant correlation amongst samples from these sensors[5]. This correlation is referred to as *spectral correlation.*
  3. For temporal data (such as video), there is significant correlation amongst samples in different segments of time[5]. This is referred to as *temporal correlation.*

- There is considerable information in the signal that is irrelevant from a perceptual point of view.
- Some data tends to have high-level features that are redundant across space and time; that is, the data is of a fractal nature.

For a given application, compression schemes may exploit any one or all of the above factors to achieve the desired compression data rate[3].

There are many applications that benefit from data compression technology. Table 2.1 lists a representative set of such applications for image, video, and audio data, as well as typical data rates of the corresponding compressed bit streams. Typical data rates for the uncompressed bit streams are also shown.

Table 1. Applications for image, video, and audio compression.

Application	Data Rate	
	Uncompressed	**Compressed**
Voice 8 ksamples/s, 8 bits/sample	64 kbps	2-4 kbps
Slow motion video (10fps) framesize 176x120, 8bits/pixel	5.07 Mbps	8-16 kbps
Audio conference 8 ksamples/s, 8 bits/sample	64 kbps	16-64 kbps
Video conference (15fps) framesize 352x240, 8bits/pixel	30.41 Mbps	64-768 kbps
Digital audio 44.1 ksamples/s, 16 bits/sample	1.5 Mbps	1.28-1.5 Mbps
Video file transfer (15fps) framesize 352x240, 8bits/pixel	30.41 Mbps	384 kbps
Digital video on CD-ROM (30fps) framesize 352x240, 8bits/pixel	60.83 Mbps	1.5-4 Mbps
Broadcast video (30fps) framesize 720x480, 8bits/pixel	248.83 Mbps	3-8 Mbps
HDTV (59.94 fps) framesize 1280x720, 8bits/pixel	1.33 Gbps	20 Mbps

In the following figure, a systems view of the compression process is depicted.

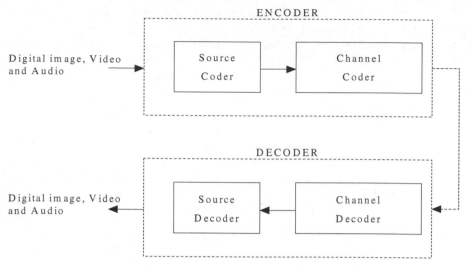

Fig. 1. Generic compression system

The core of the encoder is the source coder. The source coder performs the compression process by reducing the input data rate to a level that can be supported by the storage or transmission medium. The bit rate output of the encoder used in the above compression is measured in bits per sample or bits per second. For image or video data, a pixel is the basic element; thus, bits per sample is also referred to as bits per pixel or bits per pel. In the literature, the term *compression ratio (CR)*, denoted as c_r, is also used instead of *bit rate* to characterise the capability of the compression system. An intuitive definition of c_r is.

$$c_r = \frac{source\ coder\ input\ size}{source\ coder\ output\ size}$$

This definition is somewhat ambiguous and depends on the data type and the specific compression method that is employed. For a still-image the compression ratio is calculated by source coder input represented in terms of pixels to the source coder output. Similarly, for video, more than one frame is present and the compression ratio is calculated accordingly. Many compression methods for video do not process each frame of video, hence, a more commonly used notion for size is the bits needed to represent one second of video.

In a practical system, the source coder is usually followed by a second level of coding: the channel coder (Figure 1). The channel coder is used to develop immunity to noise. In most systems, source coding and channel coding are distinct processes. In recent years, methods to perform combined source and channel coding have also been developed. Note that, in order to reconstruct the image, video, or audio signal, one needs to reverse the processes of channel coding and source coding. This is usually performed at the decoder.

From a system design viewpoint, one can restate the compression problem as a bit rate minimisation problem, where several constraints may have to be met, including the following:

- Specified level of signal quality. This constraint is usually applied at the decoder.
- Implementation complexity. This constraint is often applied at the decoder, and in some instances at both the encoder and the decoder.
- Communication delay. This constraint refers to the end to end delay, and is measured from the start of encoding a sample to the complete decoding of that sample.

Note that, these constraints have different importance in different applications. For example, in a two-way teleconferencing system, the communication delay might be the major constraint, whereas, in a television broadcasting system, signal quality and decoder complexity might be the main constraints.

3   Lossless Versus Lossy Compression

The digital image compression techniques can be broadly classified into lossless and lossy compression techniques.

3.1   Lossless Compression

In many applications, the decoder has to reconstruct without any loss the original data. For a lossless compression process, the reconstructed data and the original data must be identical in value for each and every data sample. The decompression process is in the reverse order of the process of compression. In lossless compression, for a specific application, the choice of a compression method involves a trade-off along the three dimensions depicted in Figure 2; that is, coding efficiency, coding complexity, and coding delay.

3.1.1 Coding Efficiency
This is usually measured in bits per sample or bits per second (bps). Coding efficiency is usually limited by the information content or *entropy* of the source. In intuitive terms, the entropy of a source X provides a measure for the "randomness" of X. From a compression theory point of view, sources with large entropy are more difficult to compress (for example, random noise is very hard to compress).

3.1.2 Coding Complexity
The complexity of a compression process is analogous to the computational effort needed to implement the encoder and decoder functions. The computational effort is usually measured in terms of memory requirements and number of arithmetic operations. The operations count is characterised by the term millions of operations per second and is often referred to as MOPS. Here, by operation, we imply a basic

arithmetic operation that is supported by the computational engine. In the compression literature, the term MIPS (millions of instructions per second) is sometimes used. This is specific to a computational engine's architecture; thus, in this text we refer to coding complexity in terms of MOPS. In some applications, such as portable devices, coding complexity may be characterised by the power requirements of a hardware implementation.

3.1.3 Coding Delay

A complex compression process often leads to increased coding delays at the encoder and the decoder. Coding delays can be alleviated by increasing the processing power of the computational engine; however, this may be impractical in environments where there is a power constraint or when the underlying computational engine cannot be improved. Furthermore, in many applications, coding delays have to be constrained; for example, in interactive communications. The need to constrain the coding delay often forces the compression system designer to use a less sophisticated algorithm for the compression processes.

From this discussion, it can be concluded that these trade-offs in coding complexity, delay, and efficiency are usually limited to a small set of choices along these axes. In a subsequent section, we will briefly describe the trade-offs within the context of specific lossless compression methods.

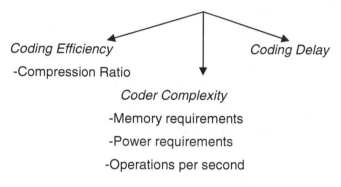

Coding Efficiency

-Compression Ratio

Coding Delay

Coder Complexity

-Memory requirements

-Power requirements

-Operations per second

Fig. 2. Trade-offs in lossless compression

3.2   Lossy Compression

The majority of the applications in image or video data processing do not require that the reconstructed data and the original data are identical in value. Thus, some amount of loss is permitted in the reconstructed data. A compression process that results in an imperfect reconstruction is referred to as a lossy compression process. This compression process is irreversible. In practice, most irreversible compression processes degrade rapidly the signal quality when they are repeatedly applied on previously decompressed data.

The choice of a specific lossy compression method involves trade-offs along the four dimensions shown in Figure 3. Due to the additional degree of freedom, namely, in the signal quality, a lossy compression process can yield higher compression ratios than a lossless compression scheme.

3.2.1 Signal Quality

This term is often used to characterise the signal at the output of the decoder. There is no universally accepted measure for signal quality.

One measure that is often cited is the signal to noise ratio SNR, which can be expressed as

$$SNR = 10\log_{10}\frac{encoder\ input\ signal\ energy}{noise\ signal\ energy}$$

The noise signal energy is defined as the energy measured for a hypothetical signal that is the difference between the encoder input signal and the decoder output signal. Note that, SNR as defined here is given in decibels (dB). In the case of images or video, $PSNR$ (peak signal-to-noise ratio) is used instead of SNR. The calculations are essentially the same as in the case of SNR, however, in the numerator, instead of using the encoder input signal one uses a hypothetical signal with a signal strength of 255 (the maximum decimal value of an unsigned 8-bit number, such as in a pixel). High SNR or $PSNR$ values do not always correspond to signals with perceptually high quality. Another measure of signal quality is the mean opinion score, where the performance of a compression process is characterised by the subjective quality of the decoded signal. For instance, a five point scale such as very annoying, annoying, slightly annoying, perceptible but not annoying, and imperceptible might be used to characterise the impairments in the decoder output[6].

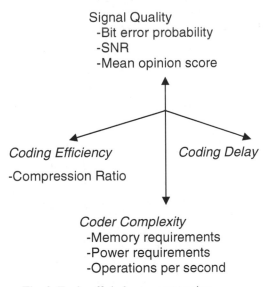

Fig. 3. Trade-offs in lossy compression

In either lossless or lossy compression schemes, the quality of the input data affects the compression ratio. For instance, acquisition noise, data sampling timing errors, and even the analogue-to-digital conversion process affects the signal quality and reduces the spatial and temporal correlation. Some compression schemes are quite sensitive to the loss in correlation and may yield significantly worse compression in the presence of noise.

4   Conclusions

When choosing a specific compression method, one should consider the following issues: Lossless or lossy. This is usually dictated by the coding efficiency requirements. Coding efficiency, even in a lossy compression process, the desirable coding efficiency might not be achievable. This is especially the case when there are specific constraints on output signal quality, variability in coding efficiency. In some applications, large variations in coding efficiency among different data sets may not be acceptable. Resilience to transmission errors. Some compression methods are more robust to transmission errors than others. If retransmissions are not permitted, then this requirement may impact on the overall encoder- decoder design. Complexity trade-offs. In most implementations, it is important to keep the overall encoder-decoder complexity low. However, certain applications may require only a low decoding complexity. Nature of degradations in decoder output. Lossy compression methods introduce artifacts in the decoded signal. The nature of artifacts depends on the compression method that is employed. The degree to which these artifacts are judged also varies from application to application. In communication systems, there is often an interplay between the transmission errors and the coding artifacts introduced by the coder. Thus, it is important to consider all types of error in a system design.

References

1. Woods, G.E.: Digital image processing
2. Jain, A.K.: Digital image processing
3. http://www.wikepedia.com
4. http://www.imagecompression.com
5. http://ce.et.tudelft.nl/~george/students/DCT_FPGA.doc
6. http://www.arehna.di.uoa.gr/thesis/view.php?orderby=Author

Fuzzy Identification of Geometric Shapes

B. Mohammed Imran and M.M. Sufyan Beg

Department of Computer Engineering
Jamia Millia Islamia (A Central University), New Delhi 110025, India
imran.fuz@gmail.com, mbeg@jmi.ac.in

Abstract. The identification of criminals with sketches can no longer sustain using conventional image processing techniques. Since, it behaves mechanistically, that is, a system which behaves as per given set of rules. We propose a humanistic system for identification of sketches of criminals. Certainly, one must be looking forward for a novel approach, which identifies similarity between a photographic image and a transformed fuzzy image i.e., a sketched image. The transformation on images could be anyone among rotation, reflection, translation, scaling or shearing. In this regard, our approach identifies fuzzy geometric shapes, like humans identify any imprecise shape with their cognition. Such fuzzy shapes cannot be left unidentified under crucial conditions. We begin with estimation of f-validity and then the f-similarity for f-geometric objects, which are considered as basics for developing a humanistic identification system. We implement OWA operators for computing f-similarity in fuzzy geometric shapes. Moreover, the results are found to be justified with the extent of fuzziness.

Keywords: f-geometry, f-similarity, fuzzy identification, f-patterns, fuzzy geometry.

1   Introduction

Of Late, the world faces merciless crimes and terrorism leading to a massive loss to the mankind by unidentified wrongdoers. Although the wrongdoers escapes intelligently and does not caught on the surveillance camera either. But, the identification of such persons can only be possible using sketching, which is based on the narrations by spectators in Natural Language. Nevertheless, those sketches do not match with the criminal database using the conventional methods of image processing. Since, there is always a vast difference between a sketched image and the image of database. Therefore, the conventional methodologies can no longer sustain in identification of sketches. The sketches may be in any of the transformation forms such as translation, reflection, rotation, scaling or shearing. Despite all these transformation that remains in sketches, it has to be identified, which is proposed in our approach. Therefore, we assume that the fuzzy geometric shape contains such transformation. Hence, this approaches making inroads to fuzzy face identification, fuzzy feature identification and other fuzzy pattern recognition fields.

N. Meghanathan et al. (Eds.): CCSIT 2012, Part III, LNICST 86, pp. 269–279, 2012.
© Institute for Computer Sciences, Social Informatics and Telecommunications Engineering 2012

This paper is organized as follows. In section 1.1, we look back on previous related work. In section 2, we discuss on the introduction of f-geometry. In section 3, we compute the experimental results of f-triangle, f-rectangle and f-square using f-theorem, followed by estimation using OWA operators. Section 4, we conclude along with future directions.

1.1   Related Work

Many researchers have performed lot of research in face identification through soft computing techniques, including fuzzy face recognition using c-means clustering, neural network based face recognition.

However, the fuzzy identification of geometric shapes has not been discussed in terms of membership functions except in [2]. However, their effort of fuzzy definitions in exponential membership function is resolved using triangular membership function in [9]. Moreover, estimation of f-similarity in f-triangles is performed by Imran.et.al in [11]. Undoubtedly, their work is implemented in perception based image retrieval in [10], which gives rise to many intelligent image retrieval. Nevertheless, there has been a vast literature about fuzzy geometry, which is discussed in [2]. Our work is stepping towards identifying fuzzy geometric shapes. To the best of our knowledge we have not found any such work on identification of fuzzy geometric shapes.

2 f- GEOMETRY

In [1], Zadeh has distinguished geometry in two worlds: the world of fuzzy geometry usually referred as f-geometry, Wfg, and world of Euclidean geometry, Weg. In Weg, drawing instruments such as ruler, ball point pen and compass exist. On the other hand, in Wfg, no such instruments except an unprecisiated spray pen, so the figures in Wfg looks fuzzy in appearances. The transform of Euclidean or crisp geometry, Weg, results in f-point, f-line, f-circle, f-parallel, f-triangle, f-rectangle and f-square are formalized from point, line, circle, parallel, triangle, rectangle and square respectively. The counterpart of crisp concept C in Weg is the fuzzy concept represented as f-concept or f-C or sometimes $*C$ in Wfg. The f-concept is referred as f-transform of crisp concept. But, there are no formal definitions for f-transformation. Nevertheless, it can be applied to the theorems, proofs and axioms. An f-theorem is formalized by Euclidean geometric object to form corresponding fuzzy geometric object (see section 2.1). However, the f-geometry in this sequel is different in both spirit and substance, which is discussed in detail in [1, 2].

2.1   The Concept of f-Theorem

The f-theorem emphasizes on the fuzzification of generic rules of a Euclidean triangle. With reference to the discussion in [2, 9], an f-triangle should have three f-lines and the sum of interior angles of about $180°$. Any form of increase in fuzziness of the previously said aspects result in the decrement of f-validity. So, we need to estimate the fuzziness in three lines and the interior angles in an f-triangle. At first, we apply f-algorithm to estimate the fuzziness in the lines through the f-transformation distance (d) [2, 9]. For f-rectangles, we consider the following basic aspects, such as: i) four straight lines and ii) right angles at the four corners. Similarly, in case of f-squares, we take an additional parameter of four equal sides as pre-requisite along with four lines and four right angles at the corner.

Definition 1:
In *f-geometry*, any polygon is called as *f-triangle*, if its membership value is closer to the membership value of a crisp triangle. Moreover, the membership value decreases with increase in fuzziness. Represented as:

$$\mu(f-triangle) = \mu_D * \mu_{SIA} \quad (or) \quad \mu_{d1} * \mu_{d2} * \mu_{d3} * \mu_{SIA} \tag{1}$$

where μ_D denotes the membership value of D, with $D = d_1 + d_2 + d_3$ and d_1, d_2, d_3 are distance of f-line1, f-line2 and f-line3 from the reference straight line. μ_{SIA} denotes the membership value of sum of internal angles with $\theta - \angle a + \angle b + \angle c$, and $\angle a, \angle b, \angle c$ are the internal angles of a triangle.

The computation of membership function for f-line is same as in Equation (1a) and sum of interior angles in Equation (1b) are represented as

$$\mu(f-line) = \begin{cases} \dfrac{c-D}{c-b} & if \quad b \leq D \leq c \\ 0 & if \quad c \leq D \end{cases} \tag{1a}$$

$$\mu(f-Sum\ of\ Internal\ angle) = \begin{cases} 0 & if \quad \theta \leq a \\ \dfrac{\theta - a}{b-a} & if \quad a \leq \theta \leq b \\ \dfrac{c-\theta}{c-b} & if \quad b \leq \theta \leq c \\ 0 & if \quad c \leq \theta \end{cases} \tag{1b}$$

where D,b and c are the distances in real numbers in Equation 1(a), and θ, a, b and c are the angles in real numbers in Equation 1(b). The Example 2 given below shows the computation of f-validity for a crisp triangle.

Example 1: Any polygon formed with three f-lines of D = 0, makes $\mu_D = 1$ and sum of interior angles $\theta = 180°$ makes $\mu_{SIA} = 1$. By definition.1, $\mu(f-triangle) = 1$, estimates the polygon to be a crisp triangle.

Definition 2:

In *f-geometry*, any quadrilateral is called an *f-rectangle*, if its membership value is closer to the membership value of a crisp rectangle and it decreases with increase in fuzziness. Represented as:

$$\mu(f-rectangle)=\mu_D*\mu_{IA} \text{ or } (\mu_{d1}*\mu_{d2}*\mu_{d3}*\mu_{d4})*(\mu_{IA1}*\mu_{IA2}*\mu_{IA3}*\mu_{IA4}) \tag{2}$$

where $\mu_{d1},\mu_{d2},\mu_{d3},\mu_{d4}$ are the individual membership values of f-line1, f-line2, f-line3 and f-line4 respectively, as depicted in Equation 1(a). $\mu_{IA1},\mu_{IA2},\mu_{IA3},\mu_{IA4}$ are the individual membership values of interior angle1, interior angle2, interior angle3 and interior angle4   respectively. The membership function of each f-line is given as depicted by Equation 1(a), while that of the interior angle are represented as

$$\mu(f-Interior\quad angle)=\begin{cases} 0 & if \quad ia \le a \\ \dfrac{ia-a}{b-a} & if \quad a \le ia \le b \\ \dfrac{c-ia}{c-b} & if \quad b \le ia \le c \\ 0 & if \quad c \le ia \end{cases} \tag{2(a)}$$

where ia, a, b and c are   interior angles in Equation 2(a) in real numbers.

Example 2. Any quadrilateral formed with four f-lines and four f-interior angles having the distances $d_1=d_2=d_3=d_4=0$, makes the membership values $\mu_D=1$ .With interior angles at $90°$ each makes $\mu_{IA}=1$, then from Equation (2), $\mu(f-rectangle)=1$, which estimates the quadrilateral to be a crisp rectangle.

Definition 3:

In *f-geometry*, any quadrilateral is called an *f-square*, if its membership value is closer to the membership value of a crisp square and it decreases with increase in fuzziness. Represented as:

$$\mu(f-square)=\mu_D*\mu_{IA}*\mu_{AS} \tag{3}$$

or

$$=(\mu_{d1}*\mu_{d2}*\mu_{d3}*\mu_{d4})*(\mu_{IA1}*\mu_{IA2}*\mu_{IA3}*\mu_{IA4})*(\mu_{S1/S2}*\mu_{S3/S4})$$

where $\mu_{d1},\mu_{d2},\mu_{d3},\mu_{d4}$ denotes individual membership values of f-line1, f-line2, f-line3 and f-line4 respectively as depicted by Equation 1(a). While interior angles are depicted by Equation 2(a) and $s=\mu_{S1/S2},\mu_{S3/S4}$ denotes the difference in length of adjacent sides. Although, the membership function of an f-square can be computed by taking the product using Equation (3). However, we refer computing

$\mu(f - square)$ using the individual membership function as inputs to Ordered Weighted Averaging operators. The equal sides of an f-square can be represented as:

$$\mu(f - length) = \begin{cases} \dfrac{c-s}{c-b} & \text{if} & b \leq s \leq c \\ 0 & \text{if} & c \leq s \end{cases} \qquad 3(a)$$

where s,b,c are the difference in length of adjacent sides in Equation 3(a).

Example 3: Any quadrilateral formed with four f-lines, four f-interior angles, difference in length of two adjacent sides be zero. Therefore, the distances $d_1 = d_2 = d_3 = d_4 = 0$, makes the membership value $\mu_D = 1$. If all the interior angles at 90° each makes $\mu_{IA} = 1$ and with equal length of all four sides, such that $s = (s1/s2) - (s3/s4) = 0$ makes $\mu_{AS} = 1$. Thus, from Equation (5), $\mu(f - square) = 1$ estimates the quadrilateral to be a crisp square.

3   Computing f-Validity and f-Similarity in f-Geometric Shapes

The computation of f-validity is performed by applying the f-algorithm followed by f-theorem for f-triangles as discussed in [2, 9]. We have inferred a triangle to be crisp triangle in the Example 1. But, the estimation of f-validity in case of fuzzy triangles is shown in the forth coming Example. We have taken three sets of f-triangles for f-validity in this section and f-similarity later in this paper.

Example 4(a): In the first f-triangle shown in Figure 1(a), the f-transformation distance d for three f-lines are (0.4, 0.6, 0.6), which results μ_d as {0.98, 0.96, 0.96}. The sum of interior angles as 179.25° results in $\mu_\Box$ as {0.925}. The f-validity is calculated by taking the product of the above membership function {0.98, 0.96, 0.96 0.925} as 0.8354.

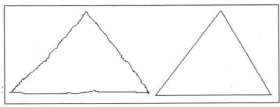

Fig. 1. (a) f-triangle with f-validity as 0.8354 and 1.0

Similarly, we have performed the same method to find the f-validity for the second f-triangle shown in Figure 1a. However, the value of d in f-lines is zero and the sum of interior angles is crisply 180°. Therefore, it is apparent that the membership function for three f-lines and the sum of interior angles are 1.0. Hence, the f-validity is inferred by their product which is computed as 1.0. Let us look into some more examples of f-triangle in Figure 1(b) and Figure 1(c).

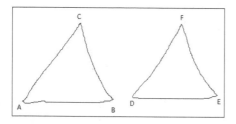   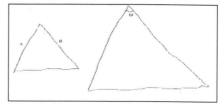

Fig. 1. (b) f- validity as 0.6853 and 0.7757   **Fig. 1.** (c) f- validity as 0.166 and 0.6409

Example 4(b): In the first f-triangle shown in Figure 1(b), the value of d for three f-lines are (0.6, 0.2, 0.8), which results μ_d as {0.94, 0.98, 0.93}. The sum of interior angles as $178.0°$ results $\mu_\square$ as 0.8. The f-validity is calculated by taking the product of the above membership function as 0.6853.

In the second f-triangle shown in Figure 1(b), the value of d for three f-lines are (0.6, 0.7, 0.6), which results μ_d as {0.94, 0.94, 0.94}. The sum of interior angles as $179.34°$ results $\mu_\square$ as 0.934. The f-validity is calculated by taking the product of the above membership function as 0.7757.

In the same way, the f-validity of f-triangles shown in Figure 1(c) is also computed. Their f-validity is 0.166 and 0.6409. The f-validity obtained in this section is a pre-requisite for computing the f-similarity between them, which is discussed in the next section. Since, we have only four parameters involved in the computation of f-validity in f-triangles, we have directly multiplied them. However, we implement Ordered Weighted Averaging for aggregation of multiple criteria as inputs for f-rectangles, f- squares and also for f-similarity in f-triangles. Therefore, we have a brief discussion of the same in this section.

3.1   Ordered Weighted Averaging

Ordered Weighted Averaging (OWA) is the central concept of information aggregation, was originally introduced by Yager [4]. The calculation of weights with example is discussed in detail in [7].

3.2   Computing f-Similarity in f-Triangles

The well known approaches for finding similarity are the AAA, SSS and SAS postulates. However, to estimate the f-similarity among a set of f-triangles, we consider AAA postulate. The parameters are the f-validities of two f-triangles of the set and the difference between the three f-interior angles. In view of the fact that, anyone of the f-triangle can undergo reflection, rotation, translation, scaling or shearing. So, we consider the difference among the closest of any two f- interior angles. Later, the differences of next closer f-interior angles are computed. Finally, the difference of remaining last f-interior angles is computed. Therefore, the mathematical expression for finding f-similarity can be represented as given below.

$$f-similarity = f-val1 * f-val2 * \mu_{diff1} * \mu_{diff2} * \mu_{diff3} \tag{4}$$

where *f-val1*, *f-val2* are the f-validities of triangle1 and triangle2 respectively and $\mu_{diff1}, \mu_{diff2}, \mu_{diff3}$ are the differences of the f-interior angles as discussed before in this section.

For the first set of triangles shown in Figure 1(a), we have got the following values for f-validity as 0.8354 and 1.0. From Figure 1(a), the difference among the closest f-interior angles are found as [1.09, 7.99, 9.83] generates the membership function {0.91, 0.207, 0.01}. Using Equation 4, f-similarity is computed as:

$$f\text{-similarity} = 0.8354*1.0*0.91*0.207*0.01$$

Undoubtedly, the process of aggregation is found better with OWA operator. So, we implement the same here in the forth coming example.

Example 5(a): With the input value m = 5, the fuzzy quantifier 'most' generates the weight vector W [0, 0.2, 0.4, 0.4, 0] (refer [7]). The f-similarity is computed for the ordered inputs X [1.0, 0.91, 0.8354, 0.207, 0.01].

f-similarity = [1.0   0.91   0.8354   0.207   0.01] * [0   0.2   0.4   0.4   0]

$$= [(1.0 * 0) + (0.91 * 0.2) + (0.8354 * 0.4) + (0.207 * 0.4) + (0.01 * 0)]$$

$$= [0 + 0.182 + 0.3341 + 0.0828 + 0]$$

$$= 0.5989$$

By the same method, we compute the f- similarity for other set of f- triangles given below in the following examples.

Similarly, the f-similarity for the f-triangles in Figure 1(b) and 1(c) is computed as 0.461 and 0.656 respectively.

3.3   Computing f-Validity and f-Rectangles

Firstly, we compute the level of f-validity in f-rectangles, here we consider 8 important parameters as inputs, (see Equation 2) i.e., with *m* = 8, the fuzziness in an f-rectangle will be computed using the OWA operator R [4].

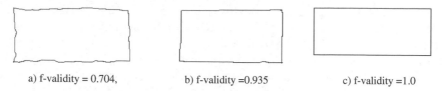

a) f-validity = 0.704,   b) f-validity =0.935   c) f-validity =1.0

Fig. 2. showing the *f*-validity of rectangles in terms of membership values

Example 6(a): The Multiple parameters that necessitate for estimating an f-rectangle are the following 8 inputs in the form of membership values (μ_{d1}, μ_{d2}, μ_{d3}, μ_{d4} μ_{IA1}, μ_{IA2}, μ_{IA3}, μ_{IA4}). Using the *f*-algorithm the following values are computed from the Figure 2(a) as (0.9, 0.88, 0.88, 0.86, 0.852, 0.662, 0.442, 0.232). With the weights being W (0, 0, 0, 0.25, 0.25, 0.25, 0.25, 0), the OWA operator estimates the *f*-validity as 0.704.

In Figure 2(b), the membership values (0.985, 0.98, 0.96, 0.957, 0.95, 0.95, 0.883, 0.879) obtained using *f*-algorithm [2, 9]. With the above weights, the OWA operator estimates the *f*-validity as 0.935.

3.4   Computing f-Similarity in f-Rectangles

To find the f-similarity between two fuzzy rectangles require some of the basic parameters that are described in this section. For a set of two f-rectangles, the f-validity of two rectangles whose f-similarity is need to be found are required. In addition, the difference of any two closest f-interior angles, then the difference of next closer f-interior angles and so on. The method of estimating the angle difference from the minimum is due to reflection, rotation, shearing and translation of anyone of the f-rectangles. Let us consider A, B, C and D are the lengths of sides of an f-rectangle. Then, we assume A/A' *=B/B' *C/C' *=D/D' *= k (fuzzy proportion), where A/A' = $k1$, B/B' = $k2$ C/C' = $k3$ and D/D' = $k4$. Moreover, the differences in the length of fuzzy proportions ($k-k1$, $k-k2$, $k-k3$, and $k-k4$) of the four sides are calculated. The fuzzy proportions $k-k1$ denoted as *fp1* in the equation given below. Therefore, a total of ten parameters constitute as inputs for OWA operators for computing f-similarity as done before.

$$f-similarity = f-val1 * f-val2 * \mu_{diff1} * \mu_{diff2} * \mu_{diff3} * \mu_{diff4} {}_{fp4} * \mu_{fp1} * \mu_{fp2} * \mu_{fp3} * \mu_{fp4}$$

$$(5)$$

where *f-val1* and *f-val2* are the f-validity of two f-rectangles, $\mu_{diff1}, \mu_{diff2}, \mu_{diff3}, \mu_{diff4}$ are the membership function of the difference in f-interior angles and $\mu_{fp1}, \mu_{fp2}, \mu_{fp3}, \mu_{fp4}$ are the membership function of fuzzy proportional difference in four sides of two f-rectangles. Finally, the OWA operator does the computation by aggregating those input values. Let us find f-similarity among two f-rectangles shown in Figure 2(a) and 2(b) in the forth coming example.

Example 7(a): With m = 10, the weight vector W [0 0 0 0.2 0.2 0.2 0.2 0.2 0 0] as computed in [7]. The input vector X [0.99 0.99 0.99 0.99 0.943 0.935 0.757 0.704 0.307 0] is in ordinal position as per the Equation 5. The f-similarity between two f-rectangles shown in Figure 2(a) and   2(b) is found as 0.864. Similarly, the f-similarity in Figure 2(b) and 2(c) is found as 0.945

3.5   Computing f-Validity in f-Squares

In this part, we compute f-validity in f-squares, which reveals the validity index of an f-square. For that, we require membership values of the 10 important parameters of an f-square as inputs $X(x_1, x_2, x_3, ... x_m)$, therefore   m = 10, along with the weights W (0,0,0,0.2,0.2,0.2,0.2,.0.2,0,0).

Example 8(a): The Multiple parameters required for estimating an f-square are the following 10 inputs in the form of membership values (μ_{d1}, μ_{d2}, μ_{d3}, μ_{d4} μ_{IA1}, μ_{IA2}, μ_{IA3}, μ_{IA4}, $\mu_{S1/S2}$, $\mu_{S3/S4}$). These values are computed from the Figure 3(a) as (0.961, 0.868, 0.75, 0.7, 0.691, 0.6, 0.5, 0.464, 0.3, 0.2). The weights W(0,0,0,0.2,0.2,0.2,0.2,0.2,0,0) estimates the OWA that signifies the validity index = 0.591.

In Figure 3(b), the membership values are (0.85, 0.673, 0.51, 0.4, 0.4, 0.2, 0.15, 0, 0, 0). With the above given weight estimates the OWA that signifies the validity index =0.23

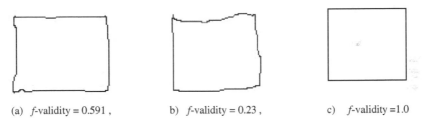

(a) *f*-validity = 0.591 ,   b) *f*-validity = 0.23 ,   c) *f*-validity =1.0

Fig. 3. Showing the *f*-validity of squares in terms of membership values

3.6   Computing f-Similarity in f- Squares Using OWA Operators

To find the f-similarity among a set of f-squares, the following parameters are considered as basics criteria. The parameters required are the f-validity of two f-squares, the difference of the f-interior angles and the difference in the fuzzy proportion of length of the sides. Moreover, the difference among the closest is estimated as performed for the f-rectangles. The mathematical expression for finding f-similarity is the same. Unlike f- rectangles which have two fuzzy propositions in f-similarity of two f-rectangles. But, there is only one common fuzzy proportion k for all the four sides.

Therefore, the difference in fuzzy proportion of lengths *k-k1, k-k2, k-k3* and *k-k4* are calculated. Let us look into some of the examples in this section, in which we compute f-similarity in f-squares.

Example 9(a): With m = 10, the weight vector W [0 0 0 0.2 0.2 0.2 0.2 0.2 0 0]. The input vector X [0.99 0.99 0.99 0.99 0.85 0.715 0.591 0.23 0 0] is as per the Equation 3 and in the ordinal position. The f-similarity between two f-squares shown in Figure 3(a) and 3(b) is found as 0.6752. Similarly, the f-similarity between two f-rectangles shown in Figure 3(b) and 3(c) is found as 0.692. From the above results, the estimated *f*-similarity among f-triangles, f-rectangles and f-squares are evidently true with respect to our perceptions. Moreover, the measure of fuzziness in *f*-geometric objects, such as *f*-circle, *f*-rectangle, *f*-square are estimated as *f*-validity. The *f*-validity in *f*-point, *f*-line, *f*-circle, *f*-parallel is estimated using the *f*-algorithm [2, 9].

4   Conclusions and Future Directions

In this paper, we have estimated the *f*-similarity in *f*-geometric objects of the same class such as rectangle, square and triangle using *f*-theorem. Indeed, we have considered the transformation changes that occur with any geometric shape. Therefore, we find the difference between two closest angles, assuming that the closest angle as the transformed angle from the crisp angle. Additionally, OWA operators are employed to aggregate the membership values of individual features. Undoubtedly, this discussion does not come to an end, instead, it leads to estimate the fuzzy similarity between an image and images of criminal database. Specifically, the features of face like eye, ear, cheek, chin, nose and others in terms of membership values. Therefore, the sketches are estimated by individual membership values of features of a face.   However, the application of *f*-similarity is not restricted to Computational Forensics and fuzzy pattern recognition. But, has wide applications in inexact shape modeling, diabetic retinopathy and other fields of intelligent image retrieval using Computing with Words.

References

1. Zadeh, L.A.: Toward Extended Fuzzy Logic - A First Step, Fuzzy Sets and Systems. Journal of Information Sciences, 3175–3181 (2009)
2. Imran, B.M., Beg, M.M.S.: Elements of Sketching with Words. In: Proc. of IEEE International Conference on Granular Computing (GrC 2010), San Jose, California, USA, August 14-16, pp. 241–246 (2010)
3. Zadeh, L.A.: From Fuzzy Logic to Extended Fuzzy Logic—The Concept of f-Validity and the Impossibility Principle, Plenary session. In: FUZZ-IEEE 2007, Imperial College, London, UK (July 24, 2007)
4. Yager, R.R.: On OWA aggregation operators in multi-criteria decision making. IEEE Transactions on Systems, Man, and Cybernetics 18, 183–190 (1988)
5. Yager, R.R., Filev: Parameterized "andlike" and "orlike" OWA operators. International Journal of General Systems 22, 297–316 (1994)

6. Zadeh, L.A.: The concept of linguistic variable and its Application to Approximate Reasoning-III. Information Sciences (1975)
7. Beg, M.M.S.: User Feedback Based Enhancement in Web Search Quality. International Journal of Information Sciences 170(2-4), 153–172 (2005)
8. Zadeh, L.A.: Fuzzy sets. Inform. and Control, 338–353 (1965)
9. Imran, B.M., Beg, M.M.S.: Elements of Sketching with Words (An Extended paper). International Journal of Granular Computing, Rough Sets and Intelligent Systems (IJGCRSIS) 2(2), 166–178 (2011)
10. Imran, B.M., Beg, M.M.S.: Towards perception based image retrieval. In: Meghanathan, N., et al. (eds.) CCSIT 2012, Part III. LNICST, vol. 86, pp. 280–289. Springer, Heidelberg (2012)
11. Imran, B.M., Beg, M.M.S.: Estimation of f-Similarity in f-Triangles using FIS. In: Meghanathan, N., et al. (eds.) CCSIT 2012, Part III. LNICST, vol. 86, pp. 290–299. Springer, Heidelberg (2012)

Towards Perception Based Image Retrieval

B. Mohammed Imran and M.M. Sufyan Beg

Department of Computer Engineering
Jamia Millia Islamia (A Central University), New Delhi 110025, India
imran.fuz@gmail.com, mbeg@jmi.ac.in

Abstract. To deal with the rising need of perception based image retrieval, we present a novel approach of fuzzy image retrieval. Indeed, with an abrupt increase in crimes, the whole world is looking forward for an intelligent image retrieval system, which retrieves facial features of criminals as input queries. The present work is focused towards retrieving fuzzy images, with features in perceptions as inputs. We begin with retrieving fuzzy geometric shapes by describing its features in natural language propositions as query. Zadeh proposed computing with words (CW) which deals with perceptions, wherein the natural language is a major source of perceptions. That is, the perception based information is the inputs for image retrieval. We devise our image retrieval system with query processing, search module and Lucene. Moreover, the ranking of retrieving fuzzy objects is based on the highest value of query relevance vector. We found that the fuzzy geometric shapes are retrieved correctly based on the perception based query.

Keywords: Extended fuzzy logic, f-image retrieval, f-principle, perception based image retrieval, f-geometry.

1 Introduction

With a sharp increase in crime throughout the world, terrorism in particular is creating nuisance to the whole mankind by some identified miscreants. Such miscreants escape even from the surveillance camera located at the high security zones. However, there are many chances, in which the on-lookers provide some identification about the miscreants. Certainly, such information in natural language mostly in perception contains fuzziness in it. Undoubtedly, the perception based information on features play an important role in retrieving similar facial features from a criminal database. In fact, the criminal database consists of several types of eyes, nose, forehead, ears, lips, cheek, chin, eyebrows, hair style etc are stored along with the descriptions. Nonetheless, this might help a lot in making automated sketches of miscreants in a quicker way. Further, it is possible to retrieve the faces of criminals from the crime database in near future. It is with this idea that this approach of f-image retrieval is being proposed here. f-image retrieval is an image retrieval method in which the objects for image retrieval are perception based query in natural language. Since, the basis of image retrieval is from text retrieval, we implement some of the techniques of text retrieval in our work.

N. Meghanathan et al. (Eds.): CCSIT 2012, Part III, LNICST 86, pp. 280–289, 2012.

This paper is organized as follows, in section 1.1, we discuss about the related work. In section 2, we look into the concept of f-geometry, so that it becomes more noticeable about our work. In section 3, we present a detailed discussion on f-image retrieval system along with the process involved. Section 4, we present some experimental results of retrieved images in snapshots. Finally, we conclude in section 5, along with future directions.

1.1   Related Work

Several researchers and institutes have contributed their research on image retrieval [11]. With Google on top of searching and information retrieval system, but, lacks capabilities of reasoning, deduction and concept of relevance [3, 4]. In [14], work on image retrieval using power law transformation is performed. However, their work is an application of content based image retrieval. In [15], presents an approach of recognizing faces using parallel neural network, in addition to fuzzy clustering and parallel neural networks. In [16], presents their work on information extraction for face recognition using fuzzy logic. In [17], discusses their efforts in a new approach for object tracking system on images in motion [18]. To the best of our knowledge, we have not found any work like f-image retrieval using natural language yet.

2   ƒ-Geometry

In the world of Euclidean geometry (Weg), the instruments for drawing are precisiated pen, rulers and compass. This can be called as the crisp geometry C. In the world of fuzzy geometry (Wfg), the instruments used for drawing are only the unprecisiated spray pen. This can be called as fuzzy geometry f-C or fuzzy version of crisp geometry. Ultimately, the geometric objects drawn in Wfg are irregular in appearance. The formulation of f-definitions for fuzzy geometric shapes is in the seminal paper of f-geometry [1]. Additionally, the extent of validity to a crisp geometric shape called as f-validity is estimated for a set of basic geometric objects in another paper [2]. However, a brief discussion on f-geometry will make a better understanding of our work. The detailed information can be found in [1, 2]. Zadeh's f-geometry belongs to unprecisiated fuzzy logic [6, 13], which is different in both spirit and substance from the earlier fuzzy geometries belonging to precisiated fuzzy logic [1, 2, 5, 10].

3   ƒ- Image Retrieval System

An f-image retrieval system retrieves the f-geometric objects from the image database on querying the features of f-geometric objects. However, the images in the database are stored if it has membership value at least 0.1 and image description. The architecture of f-image retrieval shows the modules and the process that takes place in Figure1.

We have shown the architecture of an f-Image retrieval system with the following modules such as: Query processing, Search module, Creation of relevance matrix and Image Database.

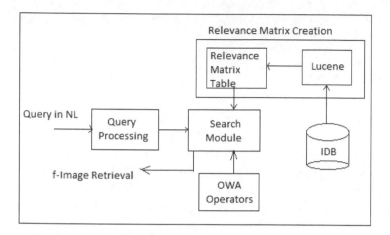

Fig. 1. The architecture of an *f*-image retrieval

3.1   Query Processing

Query Processing (QP) is the first module of our proposed f- image retrieval system. First of all, we begin with QP, which processes the input query by (i) stop word removal and (ii) stemming. The stop word removal eliminates quite often repeated words which may have a very little meaning to play a vital role in the query. Usually, they are articles and prepositions, *like a, an, the, for* etc. But, it has no effect on the semantics of the word. Secondly, stemming is the other process carried out in QP. Ultimately, stemmer increases the performance of searching. Stemmer is required, because, the queries arriving to an image retrieval system is usually not in an artificial language, but, mostly in natural language propositions. So, the stemmer converts a word to its canonical form [19]. Although, it has no major effect on the semantics of the word, like cats, catty, cat like words usually refers to a pet animal cat. At this juncture, we look forward to retrieve fuzzy geometric objects from an image database.

3.2   Search Module

Search module is the combination of several individual units, which includes relevance matrix and Ordered Weighted Averaging operators. The relevance matrix is produced using Lucene, which will be discussed in section 3.3; we discuss the operation of relevance matrix and OWA operators in this section.

3.2.1   Relevance Matrix
The relevance matrix R, created by Lucene, is a two dimensional matrix containing the tf-idf (Term Frequency- Inverse Document Frequency) values for a term in the column and image id in the row. These terms are from the image descriptors

belonging to an image. Let R_{ik} be a variable that takes the values between [0, 1] indicates the relevance of an image i for the associated keyword k and vice versa. The search module we use interacts with an image database that contains f-geometric shapes along with the descriptions of their shapes. The relevance matrix contains the composition values of tf-idf in it. This concept of relevance matrix is very well envisaged by an Example [8].

3.2.2   Term Frequency- Inverse Document Frequency

Term Frequency- Inverse Document Frequency (TF-IDF) is a statistical evaluation to compute the importance of a term in an image description, in a collection of images in a database. Generally, this is used in text mining and information retrieval. Since, we are concerned with image retrieval, so, we have stored a collection of fuzzy valid geometric shapes in the form of images along with their descriptions. The weight of each term in an image increases relatively to the number of occurrences in an image. TF-IDF is higher for the rarely used terms and lower for the more occurrences of the terms in the image description. The various TF-IDF techniques are often used in searching as an important tool for indexing as well as to compute the relevance of a term in a given query.

Term frequency (TF) of a term is computed as the frequency of a term in a given image description. The frequency of a word in a given document is taken as a good measure of importance of that word in the given image description.

$$f_{TF} = \frac{f_w}{f_{w\ max}}$$

Inverse Document Frequency (IDF) is a weighting scheme that makes rare words more important than common words. In other words, it points out the discriminatory power of a given term and is based on the intuition that a term's rareness across the collection is a measure of importance.

$$f_{IDF} = \log \frac{\rho}{\rho_w}$$

where f_w and $f_{w\ max}$ refers to the frequency of keyword w word in the description of image and maximum frequency of any word in the database respectively. ρ_w refers to the number keywords occurs in an image description and ρ is the total number of keywords in image description in the group of images.

3.2.3   Query Formulation Using OWA Operators

The query formulation is needed to resolve the complications that occur in the classification of images. Because, there might be cases where the user uses a set of keywords in query for image retrieval, but, unaware about the preciseness of using AND operator or OR operator to combine these keywords. Use of AND operator may require all the keywords to be present in the image description, therefore, returning a few images. Whereas, usage of OR operator may require any of the keywords present in the image description, returning too many images. In such situations, it is desirable to resolve these complications using OWA operator, described in the next section.

3.2.3.1   Ordered Weighted Averaging (OWA) operators. The OWA operator is the central concept of information aggregation. It was originally introduced by Yager [9]. It facilitates the means of aggregation in solving problems associated with multi criteria decision making. The discussion on calculation of weight is clearly mentioned in [12].

3.2.3.2   OWA operator based queries. We implement linguistic operator so that the user has an option of choosing "most", "at least half", and "as many as possible". In addition, we have provided two more options "AND" and "OR" in addition to the three linguistic operator, along with the user query. For example, if the user selects "most" then, most of the keywords associated with the image description in the database will be retrieved. Let us see common query Q be given as:

$$Q = \text{"linguistic operator"} \ (t_{j1}, t_{j2}, t_{j3}, \ldots, t_{jn})$$

where the linguistic operator "most", "at least half" and "as many as possible" take the parameters a and b as (0.3, 0.8), (0, 0.5) and (0.5, 1) respectively.

The n_{th} element of the Query Relevance (QR) vector will be found as:

$$QR_k = \sum_{j=1}^{n} w_i . x_i$$

where x_i is the ith largest in the set of elements of ($R_{K,j1}$, $R_{K,j2}$, $R_{K,j3}$…$R_{K,jn}$) and w_i are the weights of the OWA operation. However, the ranking of images is based on the highest value of query relevance vector. So, the next rank is for the second highest value QR vector.

3.3   Creation of Relevance Matrix

The relevance matrix is created by Lucene, a text search engine library discussed in this sub-section.

3.3.1   Lucene

Lucene provides search capabilities to various text based information retrieval systems. It indexes and makes searchable any kind of data which is present in a textual format. Moreover, Lucene does not worry about the source, the format and the language, when the data is in text. Nevertheless, Lucene facilitates indexing and searching of data stored in text files, word document files, PDF files, other textual format, web pages, and remote web servers etc. This facilitates full-text search potential, which is normally not available in many databases. The same is performed in our work, wherein the indexing and the searching of image descriptions in the database is carried out. However, the creation of indices and searching is explained in detail in [7].

The process of relevance matrix creation is performed with the help of Lucene. It fetches the image description terms from the image database and indexes them. The Relevance matrix contains the TF-IDF values for each term in each image descriptor as discussed in previous section. The detail discussion of creation of relevance matrix is given below in steps.

3.3.2 Creation of Lucene Index

Step 1: A Lucene index is created which contains details about the terms present in the image descriptors. Later, this index is used to construct the actual Relevant Matrix.

Step 2: Since the no terms can be very large hence a single relevance matrix table is divided into separate relevance matrix viz, t_a, t_b, t_c, t_d,....t_z. Here each table contains tf-idf values of terms beginning with the alphabet that names the table.

3.4   Image Database

We have made a collection of fuzzy geometric objects stored in the database. Each image has undergone fuzzy validity check, wherein each f-geometric object is estimated using f-algorithm. Additionally, some f-geometric objects with multiple attributes like triangle, rectangle and square require f-theorem too. Therefore, we have incorporated two criteria for storing f-images. Firstly, an f-geometric object should have membership value at least 0.1. Secondly, the possible ways in which an f-geometric object can be described in natural language are stored for every image in the image database. Certainly, the terms used in describing the images are perception based, but, not measurement based.

4   Experimental Results

The significance of our work can well be visualized by the inputs and their corresponding outputs. However, we have presented the outputs in terms of snapshots. Moreover, we show some of the process that has taken place in individual modules as snapshots. For example, the relevance matrix table containing the tf-idf values, the image database with fuzzy geometric shapes and their possible descriptions and the query relevance vector.

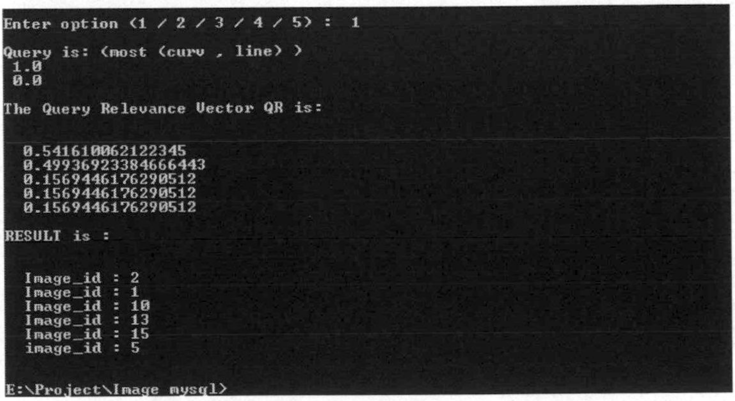

Fig. 2. Snapshot for the linguistic query 'the curved line'.

Figure 2 shows the query relevance vector of the terms used in the input query. For example, we have used a very simple query 'the curved line' manifests the application of stemming and stop word removal in the second line. It means that only the term 'curv' and 'line' are taken as search contents. Additionally, the OWA operator 'most' is applied here. It refers to retrieve the corresponding image, whose description contains the most number of query terms in image description. Moreover, the query relevance vector is the sum of the products of tf-idf and the weights. By this value, the image associated with image id: 2 is retrieved, which is shown in the output snapshots. Nevertheless, the query relevance vector generates its value in a ranking order. The highest value among the ranked order is the optimal output among the relevant images that is found to be as 0.5416. Nevertheless, the ranking of several images could be possible whenever there is a very large corpus of images in our database.

mysql> select image_id,name,image_desc from image;

image_id	name	image_desc
1	Line	exact line, straight line, line, perfect line, line like object, straight object
2	Curved Line	curving line, curved object, concave line, convex line, sinewave like object
3	Zig Zag line	small corner object
4	Circle	circle, circular,round,moon like structure,ball
5	Inexact circle	slightly egg shaped circle, oval shaped circle, elliptical, ellipse
6	Inexact circle	circle with slight outer projection.
7	Triangle	Tricorner shaped, structure with three corners, triangle, eqilateral triangle, good triangle, absolute triangle
8	Improper Triangle	like a triangle, almost a triangle
9	Convex Triangle	Convex triangle ,tri-sided object
10	Concave Triangle	Concave triangle, triangles with bulgy lines,tri-sided
11	Square	Four edged equi-sided four corner, exact square, four sided, right angle
12	Rectangle	Four edged inequal sided proper corner, rectangle, four sided, right angle
13	Inexact square	improper four corner, object with four curvy lines,
14	Right angle triangle	three sided with right angle, right angle triangle
15	Inexact rectangle	improper four corner, object with four curvy lines,

15 rows in set (0.00 sec)

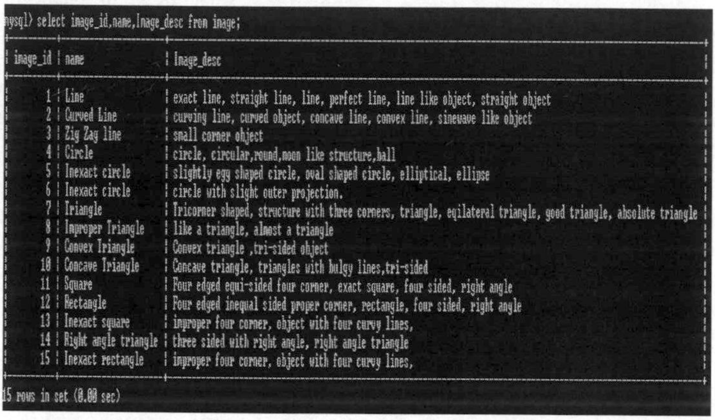

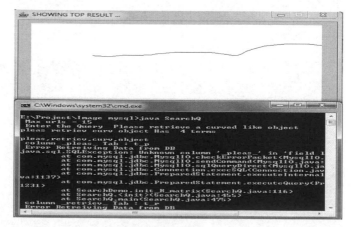

Fig. 3. Snapshot of the image and their descriptors in the database

Fig. 4. Snapshot of the output for the query 'please retrieve a curved like object'

In Figure 3, the image description terms associated with image_id is shown. However, for the sake of identity, we have mentioned the image_id as approximate name of the image in the database as well. For example, we have described the features of an inexact rectangle, which can be formed using four fuzzy lines and four fuzzy right angles. So, we have mentioned four improper corner and four curvy lines. But, there are no such standard terms available for the fuzzy geometric shapes.

Figure 4 shows the output of our f-image retrieval system in an applet. But, we provide the input query in terms of perceptions in the command prompt. In Figure 4, we have entered the input query in natural language containing perceptions, but, not the exact term. For example, we enter the inputs as 'please retrieve a curved like line' which provides us a curvy like line as output. Although, the process of individual modules explained in the architecture is performed for all the types of queries.

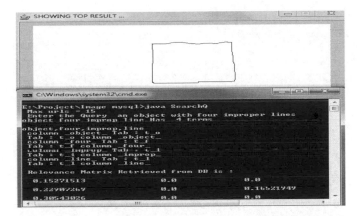

Fig. 5. Snapshot of the output for the query 'an object with four improper lines'

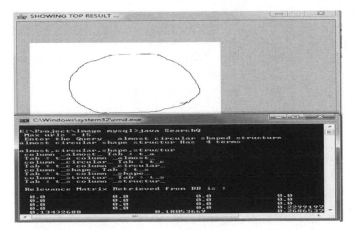

Fig. 6. Snapshot of the output for the query 'almost circular shaped structure'

In Figure 5, the output from f-image retrieval system for the natural language query 'an object with four improper lines' retrieves an improper square like object. For such a query, the stop word removal removes 'an' and 'with', making only four terms as significant terms for searching.

In Figure 6, the output of a perception based query is shown. The query has a vague term 'almost circular' is searched by our search engine, later on application of OWA operators on the terms in the documents fetches an appropriate image. The image retrieved is found to be an improper circle. Similarly, the same process is followed for all the types of queries in this approach. In Figure 7, we have posed a query asking for 'an object which is likely to be a triangle' was our query. This query has much of fuzziness in it, thereby, considering the fuzziness in the term as well as the triangle like structure is retrieved.

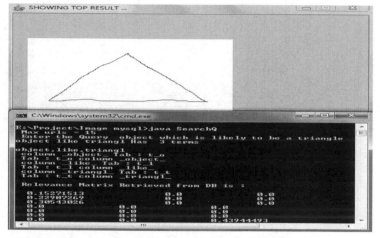

Fig. 7. Snapshot of the output for the query 'object which is likely to be a triangle'

Nevertheless, if the same queries are posed on to image retrieval system like Google, the images retrieved are found to be inappropriate. Moreover, the extension of our work in closed and open domain system will enhance image retrieval for imprecise, vague and fuzzy queries.

5   Conclusion

In this paper, we have presented a novel approach of f-image retrieval using linguistic queries. Since, bivalent logic cannot support the natural language queries in image retrieval systems. So, our work is a model, which reveals the concept of computing with words. Conversely, the approach we have implemented can be extended in retrieving inexact shapes with queries in natural language. Especially, the facial features of different criminals can be retrieved. However, a large database consists of several facial features need to be described in possible ways in natural language. Further, semantic enhancement can be added in query processing and in the search module. In general, our work has wide applications in intelligent image retrieval.

References

1. Imran, B.M., Beg, M.M.S.: Elements of Sketching with Words. In: Proc. of IEEE International Conference on Granular Computing (GrC 2010), San Jose, California, USA, August 14-16, pp. 241–246 (2010)
2. Imran, B.M., Beg, M.M.S.: Towards Computational forensics with f-geometry. In: World Conference on Soft Computing 2011. San Francisco State University, California (2011)
3. Imran, B.M., Beg, M.M.S.: Image Retrieval by Mechanization and f-Principle. In: Proc. Second International Conference on Data Management (ICDM 2009), IMT Ghaziabad, India, February 10-11, pp. 157–165 (2009)
4. Imran, B.M., Beg, M.M.S.: Automation of PNL-based f – Image Retrieval System. In: Proc. of International Conference on Computational Vision and Robotics (ICCVR 2010), Bhubaneswar, India, pp. 291–298 (2010)
5. Imran, B.M., Beg, M.M.S.: Elements of Sketching with Words (An Extended paper). International Journal of Granular Computing, Rough Sets and Intelligent Systems (IJGCRSIS) 2(2), 166–178 (2011)
6. Zadeh, L.A.: Toward Extended Fuzzy Logic - A First Step, Fuzzy Sets and Systems. Journal of Information Sciences, 3175–3181 (2009)
7. Gospodnetic, O., Hatcher, E.: Lucene in Action. Manning (2004)
8. Beg, M.M.S.: User Feedback Based Enhancement in Web Search Quality. International Journal of Information Sciences 170(2-4), 153–172 (2005)
9. Yager, R.R.: On OWA aggregation operators in multi criteria decision making. IEEE Transactions on Systems, Man, and Cybernetics 18, 183–190 (1988)
10. Imran, B.M., Beg, M.M.S.: Fuzzy Identification of Geometric Shapes. In: Meghanathan, N., et al. (eds.) CCSIT 2012, Part III. LNICST, vol. 86, pp. 269–279. Springer, Heidelberg (2012)
11. Salton, G., Buckley, C.: Term weighting approaches in automatic text retrieval. Information Processing and Management 24(5), 513–523 (1988)
12. Beg, M.M.S., Ahmad, N.: Subjective Enhancement and Measurement of Web Search Quality. In: Nikravesh, M., Azvine, B., Yager, R., Zadeh, L.A. (eds.) Enhancing the Power of the Internet, pp. 95–130. Springer, Heidelberg (2004)
13. Zadeh, L.A.: From Fuzzy Logic to Extended Fuzzy Logic—The Concept of f-Validity and the Impossibility Principle, Plenary session. In: FUZZ-IEEE 2007, Imperial College, London, UK (July 24, 2007)
14. Han, Q., Song, C., Zhang, M., Niu, X.: Proc. International Conference on Intelligent Information Hiding and Multimedia Signal Processing, IIHMSP 2008, Harbin, China, pp. 87–90 (August 2008)
15. Lu, J.: A Method of Face Recognition Based on Fuzzy c-Means Clustering and Associated Sub-NNs. IEEE Trans. on Neural Networks 18(1), 150–160 (2007)
16. Vishwakarma, P., Pandey, S.: Fuzzy based Pixel wise Information Extraction for Face Recognition. IACSIT International Journal of Engineering & Technology 2(1), 117–123 (2010)
17. Garcia, J., Monila, J.M., Besada, J.A., Portillo, J.I., Casar, J.R.: Robust Object Tracking with Fuzzy Shape Estimation. In: Proc. of the Fifth International Conference on Information Fusion 2002, Washington, USA, pp. 67–71 (2002)
18. Qi, W., Li, X., Tang, L., Xu, Z.: Shape Recognition by Fuzzy Distance Measure. In: Proc. International Conference Intelligent Computing and Intelligent Systems (ICIS 2010), Xiamen, China, pp. 737–741 (2010)
19. Lovins, J.B.: Development of a stemming algorithm. Mechanical Translation and Computational Linguistics 11, 22–31 (1968)

Estimation of f-Similarity in f-Triangles Using FIS

B. Mohammed Imran and M.M. Sufyan Beg

Department of Computer Engineering
Jamia Millia Islamia (A Central University), New Delhi 110025, India
imran.fuz@gmail.com, mbeg@jmi.ac.in

Abstract. Today, some high profile crimes grab our attention and headlines of the world. But, the core problem underlies is to identify the criminals. However, we acquire the features of miscreants narrated by spectators, the fuzzy patterns of finger prints, shoe prints and sometimes the handwriting found, are the crucial clues to apprehend the criminals. Identifying similarity of fuzzy information with the criminal database is not an easy task; this is what is being investigated in our work. We begin our work with a novel approach of estimating fuzzy similarity call it as f-similarity in fuzzy triangles using the membership values. Undoubtedly, the degrees of similarities persist in figures and hand drawn sketches, but, estimating them is performed here. In this sequel, we have discussed about f-geometry, which are the basics of f-similarity defined in terms of membership values. The membership values generated using three popularly known postulates of similar triangles like AAA, SSS and SAS are applied as inputs to the Fuzzy Inference System (FIS). We have found good results of FIS, which can be applied for any inexact geometric shape evaluation.

Keywords: f-geometry, f-principle, f-similarity, FIS.

1   Introduction

In [1], f-geometry intensifies about the high validity index in similarity that can be very well justified by human cognition as triangle like shape, which is not possible by computer systems. This high validity index in similarity called f-similarity. However, there is no such algorithm or novel approach developed to find the similarity measure between two fuzzy triangles or f-triangles. f-triangles are those triangles drawn in free hand without using rulers or compass. In [4], Zadeh emphasizes that an Impossibility principle is an f-principle, means it may have fuzzy validity or f-validity, which can neither be proved nor be disproved. So, for such f-valid triangles, we have assigned membership values to the different parameters of the postulates of triangle and the values are subjected to FIS to compute the similarity called as f-similarity [1]. This methodology of calculating f-similarity in f-triangles or f-patters can be a base work for irregular pattern recognition, face recognition, inexact modeling and many fields of intelligent image retrieval under uncertainty. We have discussed the basic definitions in our previous paper [3]. Therefore, it can be referred for better understanding of our work.

N. Meghanathan et al. (Eds.): CCSIT 2012, Part III, LNICST 86, pp. 290–299, 2012.
© Institute for Computer Sciences, Social Informatics and Telecommunications Engineering 2012

2   Related Work

Many researchers have contributed their efforts on fuzzy geometry. Nevertheless, the work carried out belongs to the category of Precisiated Fuzzy Logic (FLp). We have discussed about some fuzzy geometry types and previous work related to it in [3]. In [1, 3] discusses about Extended Fuzzy Logic FLe, that is, represented as FLe = FLp + FLu, where FLp is the Fuzzy Logic [11] and FLu is the Unprecisiated FL [1]. Major difference between FLu and FLp is the absence of preciseness in FLu, where the objects of discourse and analysis are imperfect information; in short FLu is an addendum to the existing FLp [5]. FLu facilitates fuzzy validity or f-validity, which emphasizes on high validity index among the collection of f-valid results; this is not allowed in FLp. Whereas FLe permits *f*-valid reasoning for solutions based on perceptions, when there are no provable solutions based on measurements. On similar lines, *f*-geometric shapes of FLu like *f*-line, *f*-point, *f*-circle, *f*-triangle, *f*-proof and *f*-theorem in terms of membership functions were discussed in [3]. To the best of our knowledge, we have not found any intense work on *f*-similarity in *f*-triangles using FIS.

This paper is organized as follows, in Section 1, we have discussed about the introduction of this paper. In section 2, related work which was carried out by various researchers in this domain. In Section 3, computing *f*-similarity in triangles using the postulates is discussed. Section 4 elaborates the Fuzzy Inference System and our method of application with practical results to validate f-similarity between f-triangles. Section 5 sheds light on the future direction in this area and concludes.

3   Computing f-Similarity in Triangles

A key idea in geometry for estimating similarity is that whenever two corresponding angles in two triangles are congruent, then two triangles are called as similar triangles. However, there are three well known postulates AAA, SSS and SAS that proves triangles to be similar. In our work we fuzzify these postulates in terms of membership function, further, computation of f-similar triangles are made using the Fuzzy Inference System. We have taken the data set from hand drawn f-triangles.

3.1   Angle Angle Angle (AAA)

In f-geometry, two triangles are said to be as f-similar if its membership function has high validity index to the property of similar triangles (AAA) and the membership values decreases in difference of the corresponding angles. Mathematically represented as

$$\mu_{AAA}\left(f-Similar\right) = \mu_{A1} * \mu_{A2} * \mu_{A3}$$

$$\mu_{AAA}(f-Similar) = e^{-\left|\theta_1 - \theta_4\right|} * e^{-\left|\theta_2 - \theta_5\right|} * e^{-\left|\theta_3 - \theta_6\right|}$$ ...(1)

where $\mu_{A1}, \mu_{A2}, \mu_{A3}$ - membership functions of angle1, angle2, angle3 are based on the difference in the corresponding angles; Fig 1 shows $\theta_1, \theta_2, \theta_3$ and $\theta_4, \theta_5, \theta_6$ are the f-angles of f-triangle1 and f-triangle2.

3.2   Side Angle Side (SAS)

In f-geometry, two triangles are said to be as f-similar if its membership function has high validity index to the property of similar triangles (SAS) and the membership values decreases in difference in corresponding angle and difference in proportion of two corresponding sides. Mathematically represented as

$$\mu_{SAS}\left(f-Similar\right) = \mu_{S1} * \mu_A * \mu_{S2}$$

$$\mu_{SAS}\left(f-Similar\right) = e^{-\left|k-k_1\right|} * e^{-\left|\theta_1-\theta_2\right|} * e^{-\left|k-k_2\right|} \qquad \text{... (2)}$$

where $\mu_{S1}, \mu_A, \mu_{S2}$ - membership functions of side1, angle, side2 respectively; Fig 2 shows f- proportions of an f-triangle. In case of SAS, we assume that A/A' *=B/B' *= k (A constant) i.e., corresponding sides of the two triangles are in the same ratio as in geometry. Where A/A', B/B' takes the fuzzy proportion values $k1, k2$ respectively, $\theta1$ - $\theta2$ is the difference between angles $\theta1$ and $\theta2$. Point to be noticed is a *=b means a is approximately equals to b, in the sense the fuzzy proportions are approximately equal [1, 2].

3.3   Side Side Side (SSS)

In f-geometry, two triangles are said to be as f-similar if its membership function has high validity index to the property of similar triangles (SSS), with all the three corresponding sides are equal in proportion and the membership values decreases even in slight difference in proportion of the sides. Mathematically represented as

$$\mu_{SSS}\left(f-Similar\right) = \mu_{S1} * \mu_{S2} * \mu_{S3}$$

$$\mu_{SSS}\left(f-Similar\right) = e^{-\left|k-k_1\right|} * e^{-\left|k-k_2\right|} * e^{-\left|k-k_3\right|} \qquad \text{..(3)}$$

where $\mu_{S1}, \mu_{S2}, \mu_{S3}$ - membership functions of side1, side2, side3 respectively; Fig 2 shows an f-triangle. A/A' *=B/B' *= C/C' *= k (A constant), where, A/A', B/B', C/C' takes the fuzzy proportion values k1, k2, k3 respectively, and * denotes that the fuzzy proportions are approximately equal.

4   Fuzzy Inference System

Fuzzy Inference System (FIS) are systems that create the mapping from a given input to an output using Fuzzy Logic. With the mapping in hand, decisions can be done or patterns distinguished. Processes in fuzzy inference are carried by membership functions, fuzzy operators and if-then rules. Inference system has two types of fuzzy toolboxes in general, Mamdani type and Sugeno type was proposed by Ebrahim Mamdani [6] and Takagi Sugeno [7] respectively. FIS is widely used in applications such as expert systems, data classification, control systems and computer vision, but not restricted with the above said applications. Mamdani was amongst the first to propose control system using fuzzy set theory. Much of his work was based on Zadeh's fuzzy algorithms for complex systems and decision processes by [8]. Mamdani's method is extensively used methodology, modelled in conditions where the outputs in membership functions are non-linear. In short Sugeno's method is modelled where the output in membership functions are linear or constant. Even though both these types enhance efficiency of the defuzzification process, the output cannot be expressed in terms of linguistics. We have applied Mamdani's type of fuzzy inference and following steps in our work includes (i) Fuzzification of input variables as angles or sides, (ii) Fuzzy operators are applied to estimate degree of similarity, (iii) Fuzzy outputs are mapped based on similarity, (iv) Aggregation of rules for fuzzy outputs and (v) Defuzzification of aggregated fuzzy output.

Defuzzification is carried on the aggregate output fuzzy set, which consists of range of output values; therefore it has to be defuzzified in order to determine a single output value from the aggregate output. Most widely used defuzzification method is centroid, which returns the centre of area under the curve and we have applied *middle of maximum* method as defuzzification method to estimate the f-similarity between any two f-triangles.

4.1   Compution of f-similarity Using FIS

We have computed f-similarity between two f-similar triangles drawn by free hand. Data sets fed as input for the first postulate AAA, SAS and SSS are given from the metric values given in the table 1, 2 and 3 respectively, are calculated using an *f*-algorithm. We have the following as input to generate the membership values for FIS.

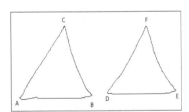

Fig. 1. f-Similarity in triangles based on AAA

Table 1. Values of f-angles for the postulate AAA from Fig 1

Geometric shape I	Angle A	Angle B	Angle C
f-triangle 1	64.65	51.31	66.87
Geometric shape II	**Angle D**	**Angle E**	**Angle F**
f-triangle 2	66.27	53.37	60.87

From (1), Membership values are calculated as,

$$\mu_{AAA}\left(f-Similar\right)=\mu_{A1}*\mu_{A2}*\mu_{A3}$$

$$\mu_{AAA}\left(f-Similar\right)=e^{-\left|\theta_1-\theta_4\right|}*e^{-\left|\theta_2-\theta_5\right|}*e^{-\left|\theta_3-\theta_6\right|}$$

$$\mu_{AAA}\left(f-Similar\right)=e^{-\left|1.62\right|}*e^{-\left|2.06\right|}*e^{-\left|6.0\right|}$$

$$=0.19*0.13*0.002$$

These are the membership values given as inputs to the FIS for AAA postulate.

Table 2. Values to prove SAS postulate from Fig 2 for f-similarity

Geometric shape I	Side A	Angle	Side B
f-triangle 1	16.11	64.18	17.08
Geometric shape II	**Side A'**	**Angle**	**Side B'**
f-triangle 2	28.73	64.18	31.94

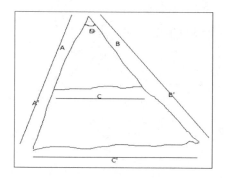

Fig. 2. f-Similarity using SSS and SAS

From (2), Membership values for SAS are calculated as,

$$\mu_{SAS}\left(f-Similar\right)=\mu_{S1}*\mu_A*\mu_{S2}$$

$$\mu_{SAS}\left(f-Similar\right)=e^{-\left|k-k_1\right|}*e^{-\left|\theta_1-\theta_2\right|}*e^{-\left|k-k_2\right|}$$

$$\mu_{SAS}\left(f-Similar\right)=e^{-\left|0.5-0.56\right|}*e^{-\left|0\right|}*e^{-\left|0.5-0.534\right|}$$

$$=0.94*1.0*0.97$$

These are the membership values given as inputs to the FIS for SAS postulate.

Table 3. Values obtained from Fig 2, to prove SSS postulate for f-similarity

Geometric shape I	Side A	Side B	Side C
f-triangle 1	16.11	17.08	13.85
Geometric shape II	**Side A'**	**Side B'**	**Side C'**
f-triangle 2	28.73	31.94	27.04

Membership function of SSS From (3) with k=0.5 as a constant, k1= 0.56, K2=0.534, k3=0.5122 are the fuzzy proportions A/A', B/B' and C/C' respectively. From Equation (3),

$$\mu_{sss}(f\text{-}Similar) = e^{-\left|k\ -k_1\right|} * e^{-\left|k\ -k_2\right|} * e^{-\left|k\ -k_3\right|}$$

$$\mu_{sss}(f\text{-}Similar) = e^{-\left|0.5\ -0.56\right|} * e^{-\left|0.5\ -0.534\right|} * e^{-\left|0.5\ -0.5122\right|}$$

$$\mu_{sss}(f\text{-}Similar) = e^{-\left|0.06\right|} * e^{-\left|0.034\right|} * e^{-\left|0.0122\right|}$$

$$= 0.94 * 0.97 * 0.98$$

These are the membership values given as inputs to the FIS for SSS postulate.

The Fuzzy Inference System for finding the f-similarity between two f-triangles requires three parameters as input, as discussed in these postulates of AAA, SAS and SSS. We have fuzzified each input variable into three linguistic labels, each of which is represented in triangular membership function (trimf), with a range (1-10) angles / centimetres, Exact [-3 0 3], Similar [2 5 8] and Dissimilar [7 10 13]. All the inputs are in the form of angles or sides. Inputs values are substituted for the rules generated in the FIS, input to the three antecedents will determine the fuzzy output for each rule followed by the fuzzy operators. Fuzzy implication operator is applied to determine the area under the membership value curve in output, maximum is applied in aggregation, followed by defuzzification by middle of maximum. Output is categorized based on 27 rules, categorizes into three levels as exact triangle, f-similar triangle and dissimilar triangle as shown in the output snapshots. However, output will be in crisp form after defuzzification.

We have applied 27 rules formed using the three parameters in each of the postulates as discussed in later part of section 3, includes different weights ranging between [0.1, 1]. However, the rules are given in the Table:4. Quiver view in the snapshots depicts the exactness, f- similarity and dissimilarity by small arrows, dots and bigger arrows respectively. Surface view provides a clear vision of similarity in 3D, but it is not possible to represent in snapshots, therefore we have represented in different views as in Fig 4 (b), (c) and (d). Snapshots obtained are the similar in all the three postulates, because, we have applied similar rules all the cases.

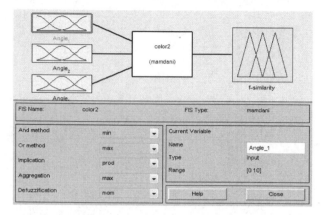

Fig. 3. a) Snapshot of FIS editor for finding f-similarity

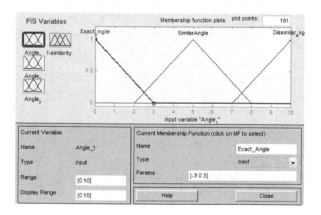

Fig. 3. b) Snapshot of Inputs in triangular membership function

Table 4. Rule base for FIS

S.No	Angle / Side	Angle / Side	Angle / Side	Similarity in triangle
1.	Exact	Exact	Exact	Exact
2.	Exact	Exact	Similar	f-similar
3.	Exact	Dissimilar	Exact	f-similar
4.	Similar	Exact	Exact	f-similar
5.	Exact	Similar	Similar	f-similar
6.	Similar	Exact	Similar	f-similar
7.	Similar	Similar	Exact	f-similar
8.	Similar	Similar	Similar	f-similar
9.	Similar	Similar	Dissimilar	f-similar
10.	Dissimilar	Similar	Similar	f-similar
11.	Similar	Dissimilar	Similar	f-similar
12.	Exact	Similar	Dissimilar	f-similar
13.	Exact	Dissimilar	Similar	f-similar
14.	Dissimilar	Exact	Similar	f-similar
15.	Dissimilar	Similar	Exact	f similar
16.	Similar	Dissimilar	Exact	f-similar
17.	Similar	Exact	Dissimilar	f-similar
18.	Similar	Dissimilar	Dissimilar	f-similar
19.	Dissimilar	Similar	Dissimilar	f-similar
20.	Dissimilar	Dissimilar	Similar	f-similar
21.	Exact	Exact	Dissimilar	f-similar
22.	Dissimilar	Exact	Exact	f-similar
23.	Exact	Dissimilar	Exact	f-similar
24.	Exact	Dissimilar	Dissimilar	f-similar
25.	Dissimilar	Exact	Dissimilar	f-similar
26.	Dissimilar	Dissimilar	Similar	Dissimilar
27.	Dissimilar	Dissimilar	Dissimilar	Dissimilar

4.2   Snapshots

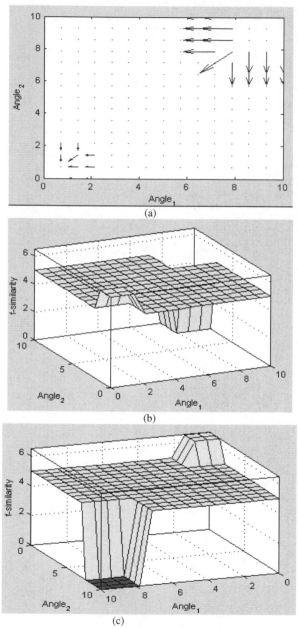

Fig. 4. (a) Quiver view with small arrows depicting exact triangle, dotted for f-triangle and bigger arrows for dissimilar. (a) Surface view shows yellow colour for exactness, green for f-similarity with first 2 parameters. (b) Surface view shows blue colour for dissimilarity at zero for first 2 parameters.(c) Surface view shows exactness and dissimilarity in red, f-similarity in blue colours of last 2 parameters.

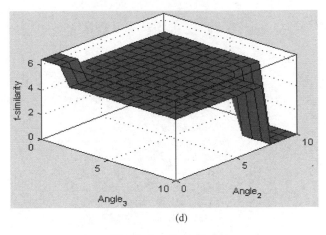

(d)

Fig. 4. *(continued)*

5   Conclusion

In this paper, we have discussed about f-similarity in f-triangles in terms of membership functions. Nevertheless, the number of input parameters can be extended based on the requirements. Our work is not just restricted to fuzzy geometric shapes, but can be implemented for face recognition, inexact modeling, biometrics, many fields where there is possibilities of uncertainty and other areas of intelligent image processing. Further, FIS designed generates good results, without being erroneous. On similar lines we look forward for further work, which can be extended in OWA with multi criteria decision making.

References

[1] Zadeh, L.A.: Toward Extended Fuzzy Logic - A First Step, Fuzzy Sets and Systems. Journal of Information Sciences, 3175–3181 (2009)

[2] Zadeh, L.A.: The concept of linguistic variable and its Application to Approximate Reasoning-III. Information Sciences (1975)

[3] Imran, B.M., Beg, M.M.S.: Elements of Sketching with Words. In: Proc. of IEEE International Conference on Granular Computing (GrC 2010), San Jose, California, USA, August 14-16, pp. 241–246 (2010)

[4] Zadeh, L.A.: From Fuzzy Logic to Extended Fuzzy Logic—The Concept of f-Validity and the Impossibility Principle, Plenary session. In: FUZZ-IEEE 2007, Imperial College, London, UK (July 24, 2007)

[5] Zadeh, L.A.: Fuzzy sets. Inform. and Control, 338–353 (1965)

[6] Mamdani, E.H., Assilian, S.: An experiment in linguistic synthesis with a fuzzy logic controller. International Journal of Man-Machine Studies 7(1) (1975)

[7] Sugeno, M.: Industrial applications of fuzzy control. Elsevier Science Inc., New York (1985)

[8] Zadeh, L.A.: Outline of a new approach to the analysis of complex systems and decision processes. IEEE Trans. on Syst. Man and Cybernetics 3(1), 28–44 (1973)

Survey on Image Compression Techniques: Using CVIP Tools

Sujitha Juliet Devaraj[1], Kirubakaran Ezra[2], and Kenanya kumar Kasaraneni[3]

[1] Karunya University,
Coimbatore, Tamilnadu, India
[2] Bharath Heavy Electricals Limited,
Trichy, Tamilnadu, India
[3] Department of IT, Karunya University,
Coimbatore, Tamilnadu, India
{sujitha_juliet,e_kiru,kenanyakumar}@yahoo.com

Abstract. Due to the heavy increase of network traffic caused by multimedia data, compression and transmission of medical image for telemedicine applications have made the stringent demand on the quality of the reconstructed signal.In this paper, we are comparing different types of image compression techniques using CVIP tools by considering the values of Compression Ratio (CR), Peak Signal to Noise Ratio (PSNR) and Root Mean Square (RMS) error.

Keywords: Image Compression, CR, PSNR, RMS error and CVIP tools.

1   Introduction

The growth in demand for image and video information has made the compression technology at a major task. In telemedicine, medical images generated from hospitals and medical centers with efficient image acquisition devices need to be transmitted conveniently and retrieved efficiently. Thus, efficient data compression is a powerful, technology that plays a vital role in the information age. Image compression is nothing but reducing redundancy of the image to store or transmit data in an efficient form. There are two types of image compression - Lossy and Lossless.

Lossy compression methods used at low bit rates which introduce high compression rates. These methods are especially suitable for natural images where minor amount of loss is acceptable. Lossless compression is mainly used in medical image processing for getting each and every bit of data without loss. These techniques may get the low compression ratio but gives high Signal to Noise Ratio's. This paper compares the different types of image compression techniques using CVIP tools.

CVIP (Computer Vision and Image Processing) tools [46] is a collection of computer imaging tools providing services to the users at four layers: the C function layer, the COM interface layer, the CVIP Image layer and the Graphical User Interface (GUI). The C function layer consists of all image and data processing procedures and functions. The Common Object Module (COM) interface layer implements the COM interface for each higher level CVIP tools function, primarily

N. Meghanathan et al. (Eds.): CCSIT 2012, Part III, LNICST 86, pp. 300–309, 2012.

the Toolbox functions with a few Toolkit functions. The CVIP Image layer encapsulates the COM interface functions and provides an Object Oriented Programming (OOP) approach. The GUI implements the image queue and manages user input and resultant output.

2   Issues Related to Image and Video Compression

The major issues or factors related to image or video compression are shown in Figure 1 which include compression ratio, transmission rate, PSNR, RMS, Compression rate and entropy

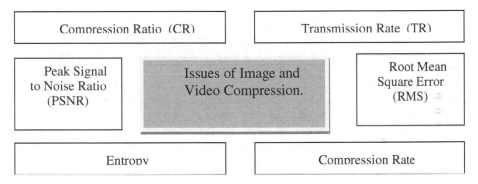

Fig. 1. Issues of image and video compression

2.1   Compression Ratio (CR)

Compression Ratio is the most significant part of the image processing. Getting the maximum CR as well decompressing the data without any loss is the criteria to be focussed. Many researchers have discussed about CR in their research papers.In papers [3], [6], [10], [11], [13], [15], [16], [38], [43] and [45] the authors have used stripe-based SPIHT, 3-D & 4-D integer wavelet transforms, residual approach, Haar wavelet transform, wavelet transforms, evolved wavelets, CREW context model, Advanced video coding (H.264/AVC) and context-based adaptive binary arithmetic coder (CABAC) respectively for the calculation of CR.

In [1], Geetha et al., proposed Embedded Set Partitioning Significant and Zero Block Coding (ESPSZBC) for medical images and gave a conclusion that the proposed method produces a good quality image with excellent compression ratio. In [26], the author used selective image compression scheme in which the ROI is compressed with fuzzy c-means clustering algorithm and wavelets for remaining parts of the image and in [31] different methods have been proposed for analysis of CR and the quality of images. Gloria Menegaz [33] has surveyed different papers and compared the lossless rates of all the traditional compression techniques like JPEG2K, JPEG-LS and EZW (Embedded Zero tree Wavelet Based Coding) and concluded that the compression performance can be improved by combining the real and synthetic data. In [5], the author compared both the state of art and traditional approaches used for Image compression by calculating byte CR.

Using seismic data compression[37] ,Compression ratio of 165:1 can be obtained and also with irreversible compression technique given in [2], highest CR can be obtained. In [42], V. Sanchez et al., proposed a lossless compression technique for 4D medical images and shown the performance evaluations that H.264/AVC significantly outperforms 3D-JPEG2000, with the highest CR of 12.38:1

2.2   Peak Signal to Noise Ratio (PSNR)

PSNR gives how much signal is resistant to the noise. If the PSNR value is high, we can bet the compressed image with less amount of loss of information. So, all the compression techniques try to get the better PSNR values. In the papers [4], [7], [9], [14], [20], [23], [24] and [44] the authors have used Joint Statistical Characteristics in Wavelet Domains, SPIHT, Wavelet techniques, Discrete Wavelet (DW), Adaptive 3D Discrete Cosine Transform (DCT), DFT (Discrete Fourier Transform) & DHT (Discrete Hartley Transform), DCT and 3D SPIHT & 3D QTL (Quad Tree Limited) respectively for the calculation of PSNR. In [29], [22] and [21] , the results are shown with flexible values of PSNR and the authors have used EBCOT spatial, modified SPIHT, DCT with spectral similarity and obtained 40.49, 50.6, 44.98 respectively. Wen Sun et al., in [32] proposed a lossless compression method which utilizes the VOI (value of interest) settings of the medical images, so that only a small part of the coded bit-stream is needed at the decoder to lossless display the original image and obtained the PSNR value as 81.7

2.3   Transmission Rate (TR)

After the compression of image, there is a significant need for efficient transmission of data with greater rate especially in medical image processing. Hence, TR plays a vital role in image processing. In [41], the author has shown TR up to 388 kbps which is very high for remote areas.

2.4   Compression Rate

The rate at which original data is compressed is known as Compression Rate. Along with TR, Compression Rate also plays a major role for fast transmission of the image.
In [17], [18] and [19] they are using Haar transform, wavelet transform and wavelet transform with adaptive prediction for image compression respectively.In [28], [37], [39], [40] and [41] also the authors have mentioned about Compression Rates and suggested few techniques like integer to integer wavelet transforms and high-dimensional wavelet transforms to get high values and especially in [39], J.D.Villasenor used Feed Forward Neural Networks and got the compression rate up to 2.22 and in [27] & [36] the authors have used Region of Interest (ROI) based compression and obtained the compression rate of 2.5

2.5   Entropy

For better processing of an image, the entropy value is expected to be as low as possible. Entropy is the lower bound of bitrate that can represent the source without distortion.So, every compression technique will try to reduce the entropy as low as possible. Here, in [30], the author used Adaptive Lifting Algorithm which can reduce the entropy up to 2.63 whereas [34]and [8] could reduce up to 2.858 and 4.04 which uses Adaptive Predictive Multiplicative Autoregressive Model and Multi-resolution representation for lossy and lossless compression respectively.

2.6   Root Mean Square Error (RMS)

Root Mean Square Error (RMS) gives the difference between the predicted and the observed values of a system. So, it must be as low as possible for getting the lossless image after compression.In [25] and [35], the authors have used perceptual quality metrics and vector quantization method and obtained RMS value as 3.16

3   Our Approach

This section explains the way of our approach about image compression. Table 1 clearly gives the explanation about different image transforms like DCT, FFT, Haar, Hadamard, Walsh and Wavelet.

Table 1. Different Transforms Taken into Consideration

Transform Name	Description
Discrete Cosine Transform (DCT)	It is a technique for converting a signal into elementary frequency components.
Fast Fourier Transform (FFT)	It is a discrete Fourier transform algorithm which reduces the number of computations needed for N points from $2N^2$ to $2N \ln N$, where ln is the base-2 logarithm.
Haar Transform	It is a simplest wavelet transform which cross multiplies a function against the Haar wavelet with various shifts and stretches.
Hadamard Transform	It is a Real, Fast and Simple Transform Based on pulse waveforms: +1 and -1.
Walsh Transform	Walsh and Hadamard use the same transform kernels, or basis images, but with different ordering. The Walsh is sequential-ordered and Hadamard uses natural ordering.
Wavelet Transform	It is a transform based on the tree structure with D levels that can be implemented by using an appropriate bank of filters.

3.1   Lossless and Lossy Compression

Lossless compression is mainly used in medical image processing for getting each and every bit of data without loss. These techniques may gives low compression ratio but produces high Signal to Noise Ratio's. Huffman Coding is variable length entropy encoding algorithm used for lossless data compression. Ziv-Lempel Coding is a variable to fixed length code with limited (practical) and unlimited (theoretical) dictionary sizes. Differential Predictive Coding (DPC) is a common coding scheme for natural images where the predicted pixel value is simply the value of the preceding pixel. Bit plane Run Length Coding (BRLC) is a simple and popular data compression algorithm, which is based on the idea of replacing a long sequence of the same symbol by a shorter sequence.

Lossy compression methods used at low bit rates which introduce high compression rates. These methods are especially suitable for natural images where minor amount of loss is acceptable. Block Truncation Coding (BTC), which works by replacing a sub-image (block) with two gray values (two-level block truncation) and a bit string to identify which pixel in each block gets which gray level. BRLC lossy, is same as that of BRLC (lossless) but it will perform compression for a selected blocks and exclude the remaining blocks. DPC lossy takes advantage of the fact that adjacent pixels in an image are highly correlated. Thus, it helps to predict the next value based on the previous value(s), and then need to compress the error signal. The error signal is the difference between the predicted value and the actual value. The prediction equation used is based on a weighted sum of the previous value and the global mean for the image. DWRLC (Dynamic Window-Based Run Length Coding) finds the gray-level values that lie within a dynamic range and the dynamic window range, and then encode them in the form (C, L). C represents approximations of the pixel gray levels and L the run length. Fractal uses the quadtree scheme to partition the image into sub images and each of the sub images is compared to the domains (which also are sub images) and the mapping equations are stored in the compressed file. Joint Photographic Experts Group (JPEG), which compresses the data in multiple passes of higher detail.

Multilevel Block Truncation Coding (MBTC) is an extension of BTC method which uses a four-level block coding method instead of two level block coding. Predictive Multilevel Block Truncation Coding (PMBTC), which is an extension of MBTC method which uses a predictive algorithm to increase the complexity as well as CR. Transform (PCT), which is designed for experimentation with spectral transform based compression. The color space is Principal Component Transform (PCT) and coding method is Huffman. Transform (RGB), which is designed for experimentation with spectral transform based compression. The color space is RGB and coding method is Huffman. Transform (YCbCr) is designed for experimentation with spectral transform based compression. The color space is YCBCR (Y is the luma component and CB and CR are the blue-difference and red-difference chroma components) and coding method is Huffman. Vector Quantization works by dividing the image into blocks (vectors) and generating a codebook for those vectors. The codebook contains the vectors, which can be as sub-images, which are used to represent the image. The index into the codebook is stored in place of the pixel values. XVQ is designed for compression using vector quantization in the discrete wavelet or discrete cosine transform domains. Zonal is transform domain based compression. After the transform is performed, only selected "zones" in the transform domain are selected for compression, and the other transform coefficients are eliminated. The retained coefficients are linearly quantized to byte-sized data (0-255), and the linear mapping values for each block are retained for the decompression process.

4 Comparison of Experimental Results

Using CVIP tools, an image (Lena Image) which has a size of 256, has been converted to a different image transform techniques, lossless and lossy compression techniques which is shown in Figure 2-4.

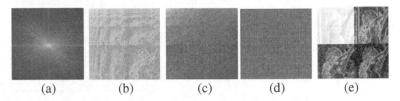

Fig. 2. Image Transform Techniques (a) DCT (b) FFT (c) Haar (d) Hadamard (e) Walsh and (f) Wavelet transforms

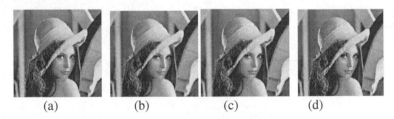

Fig. 3. Lossless Compression Techinques (a) Huffman (b) Ziv-Lempel (c) DPC and (d) BRLC codings

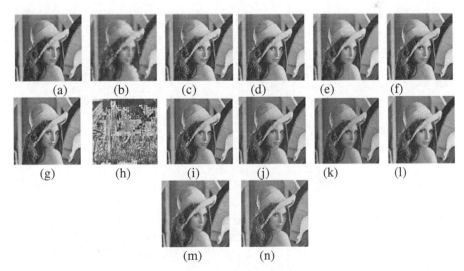

Fig. 4. Lossless Compression Techniques (a) BRLC, (b) BTC, (c) DPC lossy, (d) DWRLC, (e) Fractal, (f) JPEG, (g) MBTC, (h) PMBTC, (i) Transform(PCT), (j) Transform(RGB), (k) Transform(YCbCr), (l) Vector Quantization, (m) XVQ and (n)zonal codings

The comparison of different lossy, lossless compression and image transforms using CVIP tools is listed in Table 2.

Table 2. Comparison using CVIP Tools

Type	Method used	CR (In %)	PSNR			RMS		
			Band 1	Band 2	Band 3	Band 1	Band 2	Band 3
Lossy Codings	BRLC lossy	37	32.491	33.305	31.800	6.053	5.512	6.554
	BTC	**51.15**	24.245	23.483	25.271	15.641	17.075	13.900
	DPC lossy	38	25.296	28.892	29.407	13.859	9.161	8.633
	DWRLC	40	**33.814**	**35.151**	**33.204**	**5.198**	**4.457**	**5.576**
	Fractal	49.5	29.443	29.484	29.312	8.598	8.557	8.729
	JPEG	43	33.635	34.864	32.397	5.307	4.606	6.119
	MBTC	38.5	32.453	32.774	32.123	6.080	5.859	6.316
	PMBTC	-58	9.210	8.202	11.143	88.312	99.183	70.694
	Transform comp- PCT	38	26.380	31.015	31.602	12.233	7.175	6.706
	Transform comp-RGB	40	25.365	30.258	30.716	13.750	7.828	7.425
	Transform comp-YCbCr	44	22.881	22.291	22.840	18.301	19.588	18.389
	Vector Quant.	47.5	26.890	26.779	27.266	11.536	11.685	11.047
	XVQ	40.5	28.779	31.160	31.556	9.281	7.056	6.741
	Zonal	46	27.487	27.385	29.266	10.769	10.896	8.755
Lossless Codings	BRLC	40	34.577	35.934	33.443	4.761	4.072	5.425
	DPC	40	34.588	35.938	33.443	4.755	4.070	5.425
	Huffman	40	34.588	35.938	33.443	4.755	4.070	5.425
	Ziv-Lempel	40	**34.588**	**35.938**	**33.443**	**4.755**	**4.070**	**5.425**
Transforms	DCT	91.80	34.588	35.938	33.433	4.755	4.070	5.425
	Haar	91.80	34.588	35.938	33.443	4.755	4.070	5.425
	Walsh	91.80	34.588	35.938	33.443	4.755	4.070	5.425
	FFT	91.80	34.588	35.938	33.443	4.755	4.070	5.425
	Wavelet	65.45	34.588	35.938	33.443	4.755	4.070	5.425
	Hadamard	**91.85**	**34.588**	**35.938**	**33.443**	**4.755**	**4.070**	**5.425**

* Bold values represent the best results of each type.

By considering the image of resolution 256x256, we calculated the above values using CVIP tools. For the transformation techniques, block size is 256. And for wavelet transform, we have used Haar transform as the base and decomposition size as '1'. In DPC lossless compression technique, we used the correlation factor as 0.9 and the scan direction as horizontal. The table 2 shows that all the compression technique gives the same results of CR, PSNR and RMS errors. For the lossy compression techniques, block size used as '8', except for the zonal compression and for DWRLC, block size as '16' and '10' respectively. Transform compression technique using DCT as transform and Huffman as the coding technique. BTC gives the highest compression ratio but DWRLC gives the maximum PSNR and minimum RMS error.

5   Conclusions

In this paper, we have compared different lossy, lossless and transformation techniques for image compression using CVIP tools. Every technique is having its own pros and corns. Here, we have compared six transforms, four lossless codings and fourteen lossy coding techniques using CVIP tools. In that "Hadamard Transform" is providing the better results for CR, PSNR and RMS error values when compared to all other techniques. In near future, we can work on development of Hadamard Transform by applying some "Truncation" algorithms to get even better results.

References

1. Palanisamy, G., Samukutti, A.: Medical Image Compression Using a Novel Embedded Set Partitioning Significant and Zero Block Coding. The International Arab Journal of Information Technology 5, 132–139 (2008)
2. Bradley, J., Erickson, M.D.: Irreversible Compression of Medical Images. Journal of Digital Imaging 15, 5–14 (2002)
3. Kim, Y., Pearlman, W.A.: Stripe-Based Spiht Lossy Compression of Volumetric Medical Images for Memory Usage and Uniform Reconstruction Quality
4. Buccigrossi, R.W., Simoncelli, E.P.: Image Compression via Joint Statistical Characterization in the Wavelet Domain. IEEE Transactions on Image Processing 8, 1688–1701 (1999)
5. Clunie, D.A.: Lossless Compression of Grayscale Medical Images- Effectiveness of Traditional and State of the Art Approaches. In: Proc. SPIE, vol. 3980, p. 74 (2000)
6. Bilgin, A., Zweig, G., Marcellin, M.W.: Three-dimensional image compression with integer wavelet transforms. Applied Optics 39, 1799–1814 (2000)
7. Kim, B.J., Pearlman, W.A.: An Embedded Wavelet Video Coder Using Three-Dimensional Set Partitioning in Hierarchical Trees (SPIHT). In: Data Compression Conference, pp. 251–260 (1997)
8. Said, A., Pearlman, W.A.: An Image Multi-resolution Representation for Lossless and Lossy Compression. IEEE Transactions on Image Processing 5, 1303–1310 (1996)
9. Bruckmann, Uhl, A.: Selective Medical Image Compression using Wavelet Techniques
10. Kassim, A.A., Yan, P.: Motion Compensated Lossy-to-Lossless Compression of 4-D Medical Images Using Integer Wavelet Transforms. IEEE Transaction on Information Technology in Biomedicine 9, 132–138 (2005)
11. Zukoski, M.J., Boult, T., Lyriboz, T.: A novel approach to medical image compression. Int. J. Bioinformatic Research and Application 2, 89–103 (2006)
12. Lehmann, T.M., Gonner, C., Spitzer, K.: Survey: Interpolation Methods in Medical Image Processing. IEEE Transaction on Medical Imaging 18, 1049–1075 (1999)

13. Mulcahy, C.: Image compression using the Haar wavelet transform
14. Grgic, S., Grgic, M., Zovko-Chilar, B.: Performance Analysis of Image Compression Using Wavelets. IEEE Transaction on Industrial Electronics 48, 682–695 (2001)
15. Lawson, S., Zhu, J.: Image compression using wavelets and JPEG 2000: a tutorial, pp. 1–8 (2003)
16. Grasemann, U., Miikkulainen, R.: Effective Image Compression using Evolved Wavelets. In: Proceedings of the Genetic and Evolutionary Computation Conference (2005)
17. Khashman, A., Dimiller, K.: Image Compression using Neural Networks and Haar Wavelet. WSEAS Transactions on Signal Processing 5, 330–339 (2008)
18. Erickson, B.J., Manduca, A., Palisson, P., Persons, K.P., Earnest IV, F., Savenko, V., Hangiandreoou, N.J.: Wavelet Compression of Medical Images, pp. 599–607 (1998)
19. Chen, Y.-T., Tseng, D.-C.: Wavelet-based medical image compression with adaptive prediction. Computerized Medical Imaging and Graphics 31, 1–8 (2007)
20. Tai, S.-C., Wu, Y.-G., Lin, C.-W.: An Adaptive 3-D Discrete Cosine Transform Coder for Medical Image Compression. IEEE Transactions of Information Technology in Biomedicine 4, 259–263 (2000)
21. Wu, Y.-G., Tai, S.-C.: Medical Image Compression by Discrete Cosine Transform Spectral Similarity Strategy. IEEE Transactions of Information Technology in Biomedicine 5, 236–243 (2001)
22. Tai, S.-C., Chen, Y.-Y., Yan, W.-C.: New high-fidelity medical image compression based on modified set partitioning in hierarchical trees. Optical Engineering 42, 1957–1963 (2003)
23. Villasenor, J.D.: Alternatives to the Discrete Cosine Transform for Irreversible Tomographic Image Compression. IEEE Trans. of Medical Imaging 12, 803–811 (1993)
24. Cosman, P.C., Gray, R.M., Olshen, R.A.: Evaluating Quality of Compressed Medical Images: SNR, Subjective rating, and Diagnostic Accuracy. Proceedings of the IEEE 82, 919–932 (1994)
25. Eckert, M.P., Bradley, A.P.: Perceptual quality metrics applied to still image compression. Signal Processing 70, 177–200 (1998)
26. Karras, D.A., Karkanis, S.A., Maruolis, D.E.: Efficient Image Compression of Medical Images Using the Wavelet Transform and Fuzzy c-means Clustering on Regions of Interest. Euromicro, 2469–2469 (2000)
27. Gokturk, S.B., Tomasi, C., Girod, B., Beaulieu, C.: Medical Image Compression based on region of interest, with application to colon CT images
28. Calderbank, A.R., Daubechies, I., Sweldens, W., Yeo, B.-L. :Lossless image compression using integer to integer wavelet transforms
29. Sudhakar, R., Kathiga, R., Jayaraman, S.: Image Compression using Codin og Wavelet Co efficient - A Survey. ICGST International Journal on Graphics, Vision and Image Processing, 1–12 (2007)
30. Boulgouris, N.V., Tzovaras, D., Strintzix, M.G.: Lossless Image Compression based on optimal prediction, adaptive lifting and conditional arithmetic coding. IEEE Transactions on Image Processing, 1–14 (2001)
31. Mateika, D., Martavicius, R.: Analysis of the compression ratio and quality in medical images. Information Technology and Control 35, 419–423 (2006)
32. Sun, W., Lu, Y., Wu, F., Li, S.: Level embedded medical image compression based on value of interest. In: ICIP, pp. 1769–1772 (2009)
33. Menegaz, G.: Trends in medical image compression. Current Medical Imaging Reviews 2, 1–20 (2006)

34. Chen, Z.-D., Chang, R.F., Kuo, W.-J.: Adaptive predictive multiplicative autoregressive model for medical image compression. IEEE Transactions of Medical Imaging 18, 181–184 (1999)
35. Mishra, J., Parida, S.R., Mohanty, M.N.: An intelligent method based medical image compression. International Journal of Computer & Communication Technology 2, 43–48 (2011)
36. Sumathy, Y.S., Pallavi, A.: Seismic Region of Interest (ROI) based medical image compression and reliable transmission with application to CT images, Liver images (2009)
37. Villasenor, J.D., Ergas, R.A., Donoho, P.L.: Data Compression Using High-Dimensional Wavelet Transforms. In: Data Compression Conference, pp. 396–404 (1996)
38. Gormish, M.J., Schwartz, E.L., Keith, A., Boliek, M., Zandi, A.: Lossless and nearly lossless compression for high quality images
39. Yeo, W.K., David, F.W., Yap, W., Andito, D.P., Suaidi, M.K.: Grayscale medical image compression using feed forward neural networks. Journal of Telecommunication Electronic and Computer Engineering 3, 39–44 (2011)
40. Doukas, C.N., Pliakas, T.A., Magloginiannis, I.: Advanced scalable medical video transmission based on H.264 temporal and spatial compression. In: AFRICON, pp. 1–4 (2007)
41. Kim, Y. H., Lim, I. K., Lee, J. K.: Efficient remote medical support system design on using H.264/AVC. In: Ubiquitous Information Technologies and Applications (CUTE), pp. 1–6 (2010)
42. Sanchez, V., Nasipoulos, P., Abugharbieh, R.: Lossless compression of 4D medical images using H.264/AVC. In: ICASSP II, pp. 1116–1119 (2006)
43. Sanchez, V., Nasiopoulous, P., Abugharbieh, R.: Efficient Lossless Compression of $-D Medical Images Based on the Advanced Video Coding Scheme. IEEE Transaction on Information Technology in Biomedicine 12, 442–446 (2008)
44. Dhouib, D., Nait-Ali, A., Olivier, C., Naceur, M.S.: Comparison of wavelet based coders applied to 3 D Tumor MRI Images. In: 6th International Multi-Conference on Systems, Signal and Devices, pp. 1–6 (2009)
45. Sanchez, V., Nasiopoulos, P., Abugharbieh, R.: Efficient 4D Motion Compensated Lossless Compression of Dynamic Volumetric medical image data. In: ICASSP, pp. 549–552 (2008)
46. CVIP Tools Software,
    http://www.ee.siue.edu/CVIPtools/downloads.php

Developing Hindi POS Tagger for Homoeopathy Clinical Language

Pramod P. Sukhadeve and Sanjay K. Dwivedi

Department of Computer Science
Babasaheb Bhimrao Ambedkar University, Lucknow, India
sukhadeve.pramod@gmail.com, skd200@yahoo.com

Abstract. Part of speech tagging is one of the most basic preprocessing tasks of machine translation in NLP. The problem of tagging in natural language processing is to find a way to tag every word in a text as a meticulous part of speech. In this paper, we first present different approaches and some of the grammatical rules for tagging homoeopathy clinical sentences. Further in the paper we have our approach development of a Hindi tagger by using homoeopathy clinical sentences, for this purpose we have developed a corpus comprising of 250 sentences at present having 20060 words and 3420 tokens. The accuracy of POS tagging is calculated by using standard formula, and achieved the accuracy of 89.55%.

Keywords: POS tagging, Grammar rules, Homoeopathic Corpus, clinical words, POS Approaches.

1 Introduction

Homoeopathy comprises the harmless organism of medicine for treating maladies such as Keloids, Anaemia, Migraine, Rheumatism headache, blood pressure and also for urgent situations. Homoeopathy thus signify an awfully successful way of treatment. Doctors usually write prescriptions and reports in English which is unable to understand by most of the peoples because in India Hindi is widely spoken language. This is the major problem of communication between doctor and patient. So, to remove communication gap between doctor and patient we are endeavor to develop a machine translation system in which part of speech tagging is one of the step.

Part-of-speech tagging is the one of the most indispensable problem of NLP. It is a technique for assigning correct part of speech to each word of a given input sentence depending on the context. The significance of part-of-speech for language processing is the hefty amount of information they give about a word. POS tagging can be used in Text to Speech, Text to Text, Information retrieval, shallow parsing, Information extraction, Linguistic research for corpora [1] and also as an intermediate step for higher level NLP task such as parsing, semantics, translation and many more [2]. Thus POS tagging is a necessary application for advanced NLP application in Hindi or any other languages.

N. Meghanathan et al. (Eds.): CCSIT 2012, Part III, LNICST 86, pp. 310–316, 2012.
© Institute for Computer Sciences, Social Informatics and Telecommunications Engineering 2012

We start this paper by giving an overview of a few POS tagging, different approaches of POS tagging, grammatical rules of POS tagging, and then we describe the proposed POS tagging model with example and results obtained.

2   Approaches to POS Tagging

There have been many implementations of POS tagger using several techniques of machine translation, mainly for Corpus-rich languages like English. Such as, transformation-based error-driven learning based tagger [3] in this paper, E. Brill describe a rule based approach to automated learning of linguistic knowledge, maximum entropy Markov model based tagger [4] this is a new Markovian sequence model which is closely related to HMMs. A POS tagger for English based on probabilistic triclass model was developed [5]. A statistical POS tagger TnT proposed by [6] based on Markov models with a smoothing technique and methods to handle unknown words. POS tagging is typically accomplished by rule-based systems, probabilistic data-driven systems, neural network systems or hybrid systems. For languages like English or French, hybrid taggers [7] have been able to achieve success percentages above 98%. Another tagger for Malayalam was proposed [8] which is based on machine learning approach with Support Vector Machine (SVM) [9]. The objective was to develop a tag set appropriate for Malayalam.

Another approach for POS tagging is based on incorporating a set of linguistic rules in the tagger. A comparison between stochastic tagger and tagger [10] build with handcrafted linguistic rules which explains about the ambiguity, the error rate of the statistical tagger is greater than that of the rule-based. Some implementations combine the statistical approach with the rule-based, to build a hybrid POS tagger. Such a tagger was constructed by [11] for Hungarian, which shares many difficulties such as free word order, with Hindi language.

Due to non-availability of statistical information in Hindi, purely rule-based systems are only able to solve the problem of POS tagging. Such systems will eliminate the large number of definitely wrong tagging which would otherwise be present if no constraints were present. The partial POS tagger for Hindi presented the reduced error rate of possible tagging for a given sentence by imposing some constraints on the sequence of lexical categories that can typically occur in a Hindi sentence.

3   POS Tagging Rules

For the task of Hindi POS tagging, some of the rules are listed below:
I) Noun:
Nouns in Hindi are inflected for gender, number, and case. There are three declensions of nouns;
Declension 1 includes आ [Aa] at the end of masculine nouns.
Declension 2 includes all other masculine nouns, and
Declension 3 includes all feminine nouns.

There are two genders in Hindi: masculine and feminine. The gender of a large number of unresponsive nouns can be predicted by their endings, there are no fixed rules for assigning the genders. We can make some general observations as follows.

i) Most of the आ [*Aa*] ending masculine nouns have their feminine forms ending in ई [*Ee*].

Masculine	Feminine
लड़का [*Larkaa*] (boy)	लड़की [*Larkii*] (girl)
बच्चा [*Baccha*] (child)	बच्ची [*Bacchi*] (child)

in above example suffix of masculine is आ [*Aa*]and suffix of feminine is ई [*Ee*]. The final – आ [*Aa*] in the masculine nouns is replaced by – ई [*Ee*] in their feminine forms.

ii) Most of the –ई [*Ee*] ending animate masculine nouns have their feminine forms ending in –अन [*Aan*].

Masculine	Feminine
धोबी [*dhobee*] (laundress)	धोबन [*dhoban*] (laundress)

iii) Some nouns ending in –आ [*Aa*] form their feminine by replacing –इया [*Eya*].

Masculine	Feminine
डिब्बा [*diibaa*] (Box)	डिब्बियाँ [*dibeeyaan*] (Boxes)

iv) The suffix –नी [*Nee*] is added to the masculine nouns to form the feminine.

Masculine	Feminine
डॉक्टर [*daaktar*] (Doctor)	डॉक्टरनी [*daaktarnee*] (Doctor)
मास्टर [*maaster*] (Sir)	मास्टरनी [*maasternee*] (Madam)

II) Main Verbs

There are three types of main verbs: simple verbs, conjunct verbs, and compound verbs. A simple verb may consist of one main verb and person, gender, number, tense and aspect markers. In the compound verb construction, the person, gender, number and aspect markers are taken by the explicators/operators, and in the conjunct verbal construction they are taken by the verb element. We will classify the verbal constructions as intransitive, transitive, intransitive, causative, dative, conjunct and compound.

i) Intransitive Verbs

Intransitive verbs like आ [*Aa*], जा [*Jaa*], बैठ [*Baith*], do not take a direct object and are not marked by any postposition in the present or future tense. Subjects in such cases are controlled by the verb agreement.

वह जाता है ।   [*wah jaata haai*]   (he goes)

शाम अस्पताल जाएगा।   [*shaam aspataal jaayegaa*] (Shyam will go to hospital)

Besides verb agreement, subjects demonstrate a number of other properties which are explained below. Intransitive verbs in the past tense take their subjects in the direct case.

वह बहुत थक गई।   [*wah bahoot thak gayee*]   (she is very tired).

डॉक्टर समय पर आया।   [*daaktar samay per aaya*]   (Doctor came on time).

Some intransitive verbs, such as खेल [*khel*] (game/play) and पढ़ [*pad*] (study) may sometimes be used as transitives when they take abstract nouns as objects.

डॉक्टर ने किताब पढ़ी ।   [*daaktar ne kitaab padii*]   (Doctor read a book)

डॉक्टर बोला।   [*daaktar*] (doctor said).

ii) Transitive Verbs

Transitive verbs, such as इलाज [*Eelaaj*], दे [*dye*], कर [*kar*], take direct objects and in the past tense they require their subjects with the object in gender and number.

डॉक्टर ने मरीज का इलाज किया । [*daaktar nye mariij ka illaj kiya*] (doctor treated the patient)

4   POS Tagging Model

The proposed tagger for Hindi language has 29 tags where there are 5 tags for Nouns, 1 tag for Pronoun, 7 tags for Verbs, 3 tags for Punctuations, 1 for each adjective, adverb, conjunction, reduplication, intensifier, postposition, emphasize, determiners, complimentizer and question word. The proposed architecture for POS tagging is based on the model of transformation based tagger :

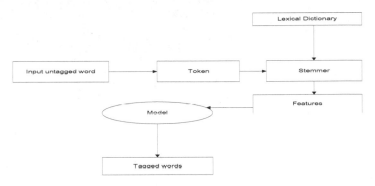

Fig. 1. Proposed model of POS tagger

The POS tagging model consist of different modules which accomplish different functionalities for better accuracy of POS tagger. In this model we first input the untagged text, which is further tokenize and then stemmed by lookup into the lexical dictionary and then with the help of tagging rules, each word is conceded to model where course of action is taken for tagging and in the output we acquire Hindi tagged words.

5   Tagging Example

Part of speech tagging problem is defined as the task of providing the correct grammatical information for words in sentences. We try manually some of the Hindi Language sentences for tagging which are as follows:

Input: राज दवा खा रहा है । [*Raaj dawa kha raha hai*]   (Raj is eating medicine*)*
Output: राज_NP दवा_NP खा_VB रहा_DM है_DM

Whereas, NP- is Proper Noun
       VB- is Verb
       DM-is Determiner

6   Result Analysis

The precision of any part of speech tagger is measured in terms of accuracy i.e. the percentage of words, which are accurately tagged by the tagger. The accuracy has been measured using the following formula [12],

$$Accuracy = \frac{CorrectlyTaggedWords}{TotalNo.ofNumberTagged}$$

For evaluating proposed tagger, a corpus having text from special homoeopathy books, medical reports, symptoms and prescriptions. The outcome was manually appraised to mark the correct and incorrect tag assignments. 123 sentences (2319 words) collected randomly from 20060 words corpus of homoeopathy were manually appraised and are grouped into four different diseases. Only four diseases are to be taken from the complete corpus for tagging.

Table 1. Performance of Part of Speech Tagger

Corpus	Diseases Tagged Words		Total Words
	Incorrect Tag	Correct Tag	
Rheumatism	23	321	344
Anaemia	54	722	776
Migraine	20	110	130
Keloids	118	806	924
Total	215	1959	2174

Table 2. Accuracy of POS tagging

Diseases (from corpus)	Accuracy (%) of Correctly Tagged words
Rheumatism	93.31 %
Anaemia	93.04 %
Migraine	84.62 %
Keloids	87.23 %
Average accuracy	89.55 %

Table 1 shows the performance of part of speech tagger, sentences are collected from the manually built clinical (homoeopathy) corpus. We acquired sentences from some of the diseases like Rheumatism, Anaemia, Migraine, Keloids. Correctly tagged words from Rheumatism are 321 and incorrectly tagged words are 23. From Anaemia 722 words are correctly tagged and 54 words are incorrectly tagged. From Migraine 110 correctly tagged words and 20 incorrectly tagged words. And from Keloids 806 words correctly tagged and 118 words incorrectly tagged. Hence total tagged words are 2174 out of which 1959 are correctly tagged and 215 are incorrectly tagged. The accuracy of POS tagging is revealed in the table 2.

From table 2. Accuracy of correctly tagged words from Rheumatism is 93.31%, Anaemia is 93.04%, Migraine is 84.62%, and Keloids is 87.23%.Total accuracy achieved by the proposed tagger is 89.55%.

7   Conclusion

The proposed Part of Speech tagger of Hindi Language to tagged Homoeopathy was developed manually. The resulting accuracy was computed to 89.55%. We use untagged Homoeopathic corpus of 20060 words, corpus is categories into different diseases. We computed correctly and incorrectly tagged words 1959 and 215 respectively. For tagging we had assembled four diseases (Rheumatism, Anaemia, Migraine, and Keloids). Sentences of each disease were autonomously tagged with accuracy 93.31%, 93.04%, 84.62%, and 87.23%, respectively, and the average percentage is computed to 89.55%. To acquire further accuracy, more data is required. In addition to that, data should be taken from homoeopathy books, patient's medical report and symptoms of different diseases. We plan to broaden the homoeopathy corpus up to 1, 50,000 words to get the better results of tagging.

References

1. Jurafsky, D., Martin, J.H.: Word classes and Part-Of-Speech Tagging. In: Speech and Language Processing, ch. 8. Prentice Hall (2000)
2. Halevi, Y.: Part of Speech Tagging. In: Seminar in Natural Language Processing and Computational Linguistics, School of Computer Science, Tel Aviv University, Israel (April 2006)
3. Brill, E.: Transformation-based error-driven learning and natural language processing: A case study in part-of-speech tagging. Computational Linguistics 21(4), 543–565
4. Ratnaparkhi, A.: A maximum entropy model for part-of-speech tagging. In: Brill, E., Church, K. (eds.) Proceedings of the Conference on Empirical Methods in Natural Language Processing, pp. 133–142. Association for Computational Linguistics, Somerset
5. Merialdo, B.: Tagging English text with a probabilistic model. Computational Linguistics 20(2), 155–171
6. Brants, T.: TnT-a statistical part-of-speech tagger. In: Proceedings of the 6th Applied NLP Conference, ANLP-2000 (April 2000)
7. Schulze, B.M., et al.: Comparitive State-of-the-art Survey and Assessment of General Interest Tools, Technical Report DIB – I, DECIDE Project, Institute for Natural Language Processing, Stuttgart (1994)
8. Antony, P.J., Mohan, S.P., Soman, K.P.: SVM Based Part of Speech Tagger for Malayalam. In: IEEE International Conference on Recent Trends in Information, Telecommunication and Computing, pp. 339–341 (2010)
9. Gim'enez, J., M'arquez, L.: SVMTtool: Technical manual, vol. 3 (August 2006)

10. Samuelsson, C., Voutilainen, A.: Comparing a linguistic and a stochastic tagger. In: Proceedings of the Eighth Conference on European Chapter of the Association for Computational Linguistics, pp. 246–253. Association for Computational Linguistics, Morristown

11. Kuba, A., Hócza, A., Csirik, J.A.: POS Tagging of Hungarian with Combined Statistical and Rule-Based Methods. In: Sojka, P., Kopeček, I., Pala, K. (eds.) TSD 2004. LNCS (LNAI), vol. 3206, pp. 113–120. Springer, Heidelberg (2004)

12. Kumar, D., Josan, G.S.: Part of Speech Taggers for Morphologically Rich Indian Languages: A Survey. International Journal of Computer Applications (0975-8887) 6(5), 1–9 (2010)

Wireless Sensor Network Security

Saurabh Sharma[1], Amit Sahu[2], Ashok Verma[3], and Neeraj Shukla[4]

[1] Computer Science Engineering
Gyan Ganga Institute of Technology & Sciences,
Rajiv Gandhi Proudyogiki Vishwavidyalaya, Madhya Pradesh
[2] Computer Technology & Application
Gyan Ganga College of Technology,
Rajiv Gandhi Proudyogiki Vishwavidyalaya, Madhya Pradesh
[3] Dept. Computer Science Engineering
Gyan Ganga Institute of Technology & Sciences,
Jabalpur, Madhya Pradesh
[4] Computer Technology & Application
Gyan Ganga College of Technology
Jabalpur, Madhya Pradesh
{saurabh.sharma44,kumaramitsahu,neerajshukla28}@gmail.com
ashokverma@ggits.org

Abstract. If sensor networks are to attain their potential, security is one of the most important aspects to be taken care of. The need for security in military applications is obvious, but even more benign uses, such as home health monitoring, habitat monitoring and sub-surface exploration require confidentiality. WSNs are perfect for detecting environmental, biological, or chemical threats over large scale areas, but maliciously induced false alarms could completely negate value of the system. The widespread deployment of sensor networks is directly related to their security strength. These stated facts form the basis for this survey paper. This paper present a brief overview of challenges in designing a security mechanism for WSN, classify different types of attacks and lists available protocols, while laying outline for proposed work.

Keywords: Wireless Sensor Networks, Security Protocols, Network Threats.

1 Introduction

Our previous work pertaining to use of Wireless Sensors in Subsurface exploration proposed novel and efficient deployment strategy [1], routing strategy [2], and information processing using Extended Kalman Filter [3]. Sensor network proponents predict a future in which numerous tiny sensor devices will be used in almost every aspect of life. The goal is to create smart environments capable of collecting massive amounts of information, recognizing significant events automatically, and responding appropriately. Sensor networks facilitate comprehensive, real-time data processing in complex environments. Typical applications of sensors include emergency response information, energy management, medical monitoring, inventory control, and

N. Meghanathan et al. (Eds.): CCSIT 2012, Part III, LNICST 86, pp. 317–326, 2012.

battle-field management. For potential use of sensor networks, secure communication techniques are required so that the system and its users get protected [4].

The need for security in military applications is obvious, but even more benign uses, such as home health monitoring, and sub-surface exploration require confidentiality. WSNs are perfect for detecting environmental, chemical, or biological threats over large scale areas, but maliciously induced false alarms are capable of negating value of the system. Widespread deployment of sensor networks is directly related to their security strength. These stated facts form the basis for this survey paper. Structure of the paper is as follows: Section 2 presents background and throws light on the work of researchers who proposed in-network security mechanisms. Section 3 presents attacks and defenses within WSN, while Section 4 outlines Sensor Security Challenges. Section 5 presents conclusion and proposed future work.

2   Related Work

Re-searchers of WSN have been concentrating on solving a variety of challenges ranging from limited resource capabilities to secure communication. Literature indicates that sensor networks are deployed in public or abandoned areas, over insecure wireless channels [5], [6], [7]. It is therefore alluring for a malicious device / intruder to eavesdrop or inject messages into the network. The traditional solution to this problem has been to take up techniques such as message authentication codes, public key cryptography and symmetric key encryption schemes. However, since there are resource scarcities for motes, the major challenge is to devise these encryption techniques in an efficient way without sacrificing their scarce resources. One method of shielding any network against external attacks is to apply a straightforward key infrastructure. However, it is known that global keys do not provide network resilience and pair wise keys are not robust solution. A more intuitive solution is needed for WSNs.

TinySec [8] introduced security to the link layer of TinyOS suite [9] by incorporating software-based symmetric keying with low operating cost requirements. Not all vulnerabilities present in TinySec could be addressed for example techniques to avoid insider attacks. In contrast, Zigbee or the 802.15.4 standard introduced hardware-based symmetric keying with success. The public key cryptography had been tested out in all development phases to provide complete security . This concept has opened an unheard area for discussion of sensor network cryptographic infrastructure. Wide-spread research is also being carried out on topics such as key storage & key sharing [10], key preservation [11] and shared key pools [12]. Now, since sensor nodes need to cluster aiming to fulfill a particular task, it is desired that the group members' converse securing between each other, in spite of the actuality of global security also present. But contrary to this fact secure grouping has been researched to a very low extent in the past and only a few exhaustive solutions exist.

Further, although, data aggregation (sensor nodes aggregate sensed data from envi-ronment before finally transmitting it to the base station) is one of the promising strate-gies to reduce cost and network traffic but such data is always susceptible to attacks by intruders. A challenger with control over an aggregating node can choose to disregard reports or produce fake reports, affecting reliability of the generated data and at times whole network as well. The main aim in this area is to use flexible functions, which will be able to discover and report forged reports through demonstrating authenticity of the data somehow. Some technique had been established in which aggregator uses hash trees to create proof of its neighbors' data, which in turn is used to verify purity of collected data to the base station. Another approach [13], takes advantage of network density by using the aggregator's neighbors as witnesses. It is also possible to reduce amount of traffic heading to base station by using bloom filters to filter out false aggregations. Latest research trends towards security measures indicate development of Secure Protocols. The main research challenge in this area is to discover new defense techniques to be applied to existing routing protocols, without compromising connectivity, coverage or scalability [14]. Security Protocols in Sensor Networks (SPINS) provide data authentication, semantic security and low overhead, along with replay protection.

Fig 1 elaborates the energy cost of adding security protocols to sensor network. Majority of overhead arises from transmission of extra data rather than any computational costs. SPINS was later used to design a secure cluster based protocols such as LEACH. Karlof and Wagner [5] have provided an extensive analysis on the WSNs routing vulnerabilities and possible countermeasures. According to their study common sensor network protocols are generally vulnerable due to their simplicity and hence security should be incorporated into these protocols right from design time.

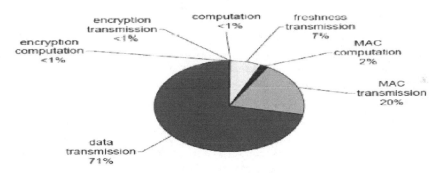

Fig. 1. Energy costs from SPINS [20]

3   Attacks and Defenses

Goals for security sensor networks include the same four primary objectives as conventional networks: availability, secrecy, integrity, and authentication. Though WSN security is characterized by the same properties as compared to traditional network security, but at the same time they are prone to new attacks. Attacks are made at several levels on the network, like Physical Layer, Link Layer or Network Layer.

Attacks at physical level include radio signal jamming as well as tampering with physical devices. One of the most prominent attacks at this layer is Jamming [15], a well-known attack on wireless communication. In jamming, intruder interferes with wireless frequencies on which the transceivers used by a device operates. It represents an attack on the network accessibility. Jamming is different from normal radio transmission in that it is redundant and disorderly, thus creating a denial-of-service condition. The degree of jamming is determined by physical properties such as available power, antenna design, obstacles, and height above ground. Jamming is extremely successful against single channel networks, i.e., when all nodes transmits in small band, single wireless spectrum.

Tampering [16] is the second security issue at physical layer. Sensor nodes are generally deployed in hostile environment, away from personal monitoring. These sensors are available for easy access to intruders, which can potentially harm these devices by tampering, duplicating or even destroying them. One available solution to this problem is manufacturing of tamper-proof sensor nodes. These nodes are smart enough to delete any cryptographic information available within them as soon as they sense some sort of tampering. But these are not economically viable since tamper-proof sensor nodes increase overall cost. Other solutions might be using of multi-key security algorithms. In these security algorithms intruders will not have access to complete data even if one of the key has been compromised upon.

Like the physical layer, link layer is particularly vulnerable to denial of service attacks. The link and media access control (MAC) layer handles neighbor-to-neighbor communication and channel arbitration. The first type of attack at this layer is known as Collision. If a challenger is able to generate a collision of even part of a transmission, one can interrupt the entire packet. A single bit error will cause a Cyclic Redundancy Check (CRC) variance and would require retransmission. In some media access control protocols, a corrupted ACK (acknowledgment) may cause exponential back-off and pointlessly increase latency. Although error-correcting codes guard against some level of packet corruption, intentional corruption can occur at levels which are beyond the encoding scheme's capability to correct. The advantage, to the challenger, of this jamming at MAC level over physical layer jamming is that much less energy is required to achieve the same effect.

Another malicious goal of intruders is Exhaustion [17] of a sensor node's battery power resources. Exhaustion may be initiated by an interrogation attack. A compromised sensor node could repeatedly transmit RTS (Request To Send) packets in order to bring forth CTS (Clear To Send) packets from a uncompromised neighbor, eventually draining the battery power of both nodes. Still more damaging attack on Link Layer is Unfairness. In this type of attack at Link Layer, a compromised node can be misrepresented to sporadically attack the network in such a fashion which induces biasness in the priori-ties for granting of medium access. This fragile form of denial of service attack might, increase latency resulting in real-time protocols miss their deadlines. Another form of this attack generally target one particular flow of data in order to restrain recognition of some event. The use of tokens which avert a compromised node from capturing the channel for a long period of time has been proposed.

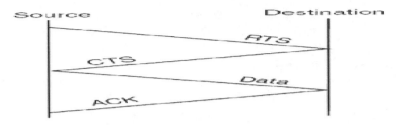

Fig. 2. A Four-Way Handshake ensures collision avoidance in 802.11 networks

Due to the ad-hoc nature of sensor networks, each node eventually at some point of time assumes routing responsibilities. Since every node in a sensor network virtually enact as a router, hence WSN are highly susceptible to routing attacks at network layer. Researchers have identified a variety of routing attacks and have shown them to be effective against major sensor network routing protocol. Various classifications of attacks are summarized below and followed by a general discussion of secure routing techniques.

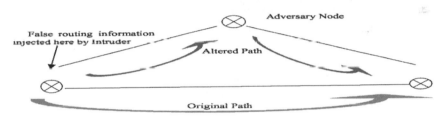

Fig. 3. Redirecting traffic through an adversary node via False Routing Information attack

The most prominent attack on routing is to alter, spoof, or just replay routing information. This type of attack is known as False Routing Information. The false information may allow intruder to attract or repel traffic, create routing loops, shorten or ex-tend route lengths, increase latency, and even partition the network, as shown in Fig 3. Clearly, the distortion of routing information can cripple complete network. The standard solution is to require authentication for routing information, i.e., routers only accept routing information from valid routers encrypted with valid shared key information.

Another attack, known as Selective Forwarding is a more clever attack in which the compromised node is made to transmit forward only some of the packets correctly, while others are silently dropped. Smart networks are capable to routing data along another path, in case of a failure of a particular node. If all packets from a node are dropped, it will be considered as a dead network. Hence only selective packets are being forwarded by compromised node, creating an illusion that it is still active, and that data can be routed via it.

Routing decisions in network are based on distance between nodes. In Sinkhole Attack a compromised node is made to advertise a luring route to the base station or sink. Thus all neighboring nodes are made to route their data towards the compromised node, as shown in Fig 4. The intruder at compromised node thus gains access to major data within its area, and might destroy, manipulate or even modify these packets.

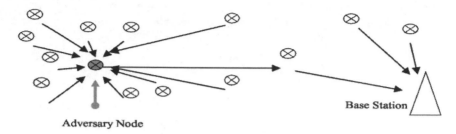

Fig. 4. Model of Sinkhole attack

In Sybil attack , the compromised node spoof neighboring nodes by broadcasting multiple identities. The compromised node claims to be other node present within the network, hence presenting a great threat to overall routing process [Fig 5]. The malicious effect aggravates as other nodes unknowingly further transmit routing data received from compromised node to their neighbors.

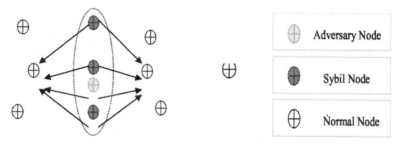

Fig. 5. Model of Sybil attack

In Wormhole Attack [18], two mutually understanding malicious nodes form an out-of-bound channel or transmission tunnel in between them. The end points of this tunnel are called as Start & End point. The compromised node at Start point transmits its data via tunnel to malicious node present at End point, as shown in Fig 6. The End point node then re-transmits the received data packets, hence creating an illusion that these distant nodes are neighbors. This sort of attack is likely to be used in arrangement with selective forwarding or eavesdropping.

Nodes present within a network rely on acknowledgment received from neighboring nodes. In Acknowledgment Spoofing attack [19], a malicious node may respond back to a transmitting node on behest of a weak or a non-active node, and thus deceiving sensor about strength of link. This way sender unknowingly keeps on transmitting to the non-active node and data is eventually lost or captured and destroyed by malicious node. There have been several approaches to defend against network layer attacks. Authentication and encryption may be initial steps, but more proactive techniques such as monitoring, probing, and transmitting redundant packets have also been suggested. Secure routing methods protect against some of previous attacks. Proposed techniques include Authentication & Encryption. Link layer authentication and encryption protect against most outsider attacks on sensor network routing protocol. Even a simple scheme which uses a globally shared key will prevent unauthorized nodes from joining topology of the network. In addition to preventing selective forwarding and sinkhole attacks, authentication and encryption make Sybil attack almost impossible because nodes will not accept even one identity from the malicious node.

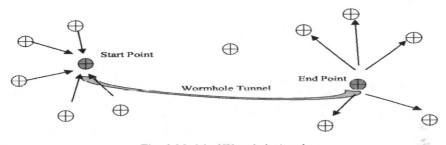

Fig. 6. Model of Wormhole Attack

Another technique is Monitoring, which is a more active strategy for secure routing, where-in nodes monitor their peers and watch for suspicious behavior. In this approach, motes act as "watchdogs" to monitor next hop transmission of the packet. In event that misbehavior is detected, nodes will update routing information in order to avoid the compromised node. Another proactive defense against malicious routers is probing. This method periodically sends probing packets across the network to detect blackout regions. Since geographic routing protocols have knowledge of the physical topology of the network, probing is especially well-suited to their use. Probes must appear to be normal traffic, however, so that compromised nodes do not intentionally route them correctly in order to escape detection. Redundancy is another strategy for secure routing. Redundancy simply transmits a packet multiple times over different routes. Hopefully one of the routes remains uncompromised and will correctly deliver message to the destination. Despite its inefficiency, this method does increase the difficulty for an attacker to stop a data flow.

4   Challenges in Sensor Security

Five of the most looked for challenges in designing security schemes for large wireless sensor networks are Wireless Medium, Ad-Hoc Deployment, Hostile Surroundings, Resource Scarcity and Immense Scale. The deployment scenarios for ad-hoc sensor motes renders use of wired media communication totally infeasible [20]. This leads to more security concerns in WSN, since wireless medium is always prone to security attacks since its method of operation / transmission makes it an easy prey for eavesdropping. Wireless communication can be easily trapped, modified or even replaced by intruders. The wireless media allows intruders to destroy genuine communication packets and inject deceptive data into network, with least of the efforts. Wireless media security problem has been intrinsic to traditional networks too, but enhanced and robust solutions are required for sensor networks, owing to their unpredictable deployment and ad-hoc arrangement.

Another challenge for WSN security is its ad-hoc deployment. Sensors may be required to deploy in deterministic or non-deterministic environments. In both cases no fixed topology can be framed in advance. Even the deployed network may have to change its topology every now and then, subject to addition of new nodes, node failures etc. [21]. Under such conditions, robust security protocols are required which can adapt dynamically as per changing configuration / topology of WSN. Hence in sensor networks traditional security mechanisms based on static configurations cannot be applied.

The environment within which sensor nodes operate, collect and transmit data is hostile. Intruders might have know-about the geographical locations of sensor motes, and subsequently reach them to capture / destroy them. No security protocol can fend WSN against such kind of physical attacks, but these needs to be kept in scenario while designing a security framework, in order to provide self-healing capabilities to network.

Another challenge in WSN is resource scarcity within sensor motes. Due to hostile conditions and non-predictable environment sensor nodes cannot be replenished in terms of battery power. In addition to battery, the memory size and computational powers too are low due to small size of nodes. These factors make efficient but resource extensive security mechanisms totally infeasible for WSN. A representative example of sensor device is Mica mote. It has a 4 MHz Atmel ATMEGA103 CPU with 128 KB of instruction memory, 512 KB of flash memory, and just 4 KB of RAM for data. The radio operates at up to 40 Kbps bandwidth with a transmission range of a few dozen meters. Such constraints on resources demand extremely competent security algorithms in terms of computational complexity, memory as well as bandwidth. While energy is perhaps the most prized resource for sensor networks, earlier research work has given little to no attention to energy efficiency. Transmission is especially expensive in terms of power, as apparent from SPINS [Fig 1] too. The large scale deployment of WSN is its biggest confront. For small area application of WSN there are threats like Sinkhole attack have been overcomed [22]. Traditional networks might be limited to an office or to a bigger geographical location but in a controlled fashion. But in case of sensors, the area being covered may be large and un-predictable. In many cases sensors are even air-dropped and hence their exact geographical location may be different than what might have been thought of. In such cases providing security to all nodes present becomes a challenging task. The develpoment over such Security mechanism which can make available to large number of nodes spread over a large area, and at the same instance maintaining computational and communication efficiency.

5   Conclusion and Future Work

The paper presented known threats and security protocols available for wired and wire-less networks. Works of researchers in this field have been extensively studied. While many frameworks have been devised for WSN, but none were found for robust security mechanisms in subsurface exploration. Keeping in view the extreme harsh conditions prevailing in subsurface, the demand is to devise a novel security mechanism which will make communication within sensors more robust, scalable and efficient.

References

1. Juneja, D., Sharma, A., Kumar, A.: A Novel and Efficient Algorithm for Deploying Mobile Sensors in Subsurface. Computer and Information Science 3(2), 94–105 (2010) ISSN 1913-8989 (Print), ISSN 1913-8997 (Online)
2. Juneja, D., Sharma, A., Kumar, A.: A Query Driven Routing Protocol for Wireless Sensor Nodes in Subsurface. International Journal of Engineering Science and Technology 2(6), 1836–1843, ISSN: 0975-5462
3. Juneja, D., Sharma, A., Kumar, A.: A Novel Application Of Extended Kalman Filter For Efficient Information Processing In Subsurfaces. International Journal of Computer Applications 17(2), 28–32 (2011) ISSN: 0975-8887
4. Pathan, A.-S.K., Lee, H.-W., Hong, C.S.: Security in Wireless Sensor Networks: Issues and Challenges. In: ICACT 2006 (2006)
5. Lu, B., Habetler, T.G., Harley, R.G., Gutiérrez, J.A.: Applying Wireless Sensor Networks in Industrial Plant Energy Management Systems – Part I: A Closed-Loop Scheme. In: Sensors, October 30-November 3, pp. 145–150. IEEE, Los Alamitos (2005)
6. Bokareva, T., Hu, W., Kanhere, S., Ristic, B., Gordon, N., Bessell, T., Rutten, M., Jha, S.: Wireless Sensor Networks for Battlefield Surveillance. In: Land Warfare Conference 2006, Brisbane, Australia (October 2006)
7. Mainwaring, A., Polastre, J., Szewczyk, R., Culler, D., Anderson, J.: Wireless Sensor Networks for Habitat Monitoring. In: ACM WSNA 2002, Atlanta, Georgia, USA, pp. 88–97 (September 28, 2002)
8. Wireless Sensor Networks, http://en.wikipedia.org/wiki/Wireless_Sensor_Networks
9. Tiny Operating System, http://en.wikipedia.org/wiki/TinyOS
10. Chan, H., Perrig, A., Song, D.: Random key predistribution schemes for sensor networks. In: Proceedings of the Symposium Security and Privacy (2003)
11. Du, W., Deng, J., Han, Y., Chen, S., Varshney, P.: A key management scheme for wireless sensor networks using deployment knowledge. In: INFOCOM 2004: Twenty-Third Annual Joint Conference of the IEEE Computer and Communications Societies (2004)
12. Eschenauer, L., Gligor, V.D.: A key-management scheme for distributed sensor networks. In: Proceedings of the 9th ACM Conference on Computer and Communications Security, ACM Press, New York (2002)
13. Du, W., Han, Y.S., Deng, J., Varshney, P.K.: A Pairwise key predistribution scheme for wireless sensor networks. In: Proceedings of the ACM Conference on Computer and Communications Security (2003)

14. Hoger, K., Andreas, W.: Protocols and Architecture for Wireless Sensor Networks. John Wiley & Sons Ltd., Chichester (2005) ISBN: 0-470-09510-5
15. Raymond, D.R., Marchany, R.C., Brownfield, M.I., Midkiff, S.F.: Effects of Denial-of-Sleep Attacks on Wireless Sensor Network MAC Protocols. IEEE Transactions on Vehicular Technology 58(1), 367–380 (2009)
16. Wood, A.D., Stankovic, J.A.: Denial of Service in Sensor Networks. IEEE Computer 35(10), 48–56 (2002)
17. Wood, A.D., Stankovic, J.A.: Denial of Service in Sensor Networks. IEEE Computers, 54–62 (October 2002)
18. Hu, Y.-C., Perrig, A., Johnson, D.B.: Wormhole detection in wireless ad hoc networks. Department of Computer Science, Rice University, Tech. Rep. TR01-384 (June 2002)
19. Tumrongwittayapak, C., Varakulsiripunth, R.: Detecting Sinkhole Attacks In Wireless Sensor Networks. In: Proceedings of the IEEE ICROS-SICE International Joint Conference, pp. 1966–1971 (2009)
20. Feng, Z., Leonidas, G.: Wireless Sensor Networks (An Information Processing Approach). Morgan Kaufmann Publisher under Elsevier, ISBN: 1-55860-914-8
21. Deepak, G., Alberto, C., Wei, Y., Yan, Y., Jerry, Z., Deborah, E.: Networking Issues in Wireless Sensor Networks. Elsevier Science, Amsterdam (2003), CrossBow Technology Inc., http://www.xbow.com/
22. Hsueh, C.-T., Li, Y.-W., Wen, C.-Y., Ouyan, Y.-C.: Secure Adaptive Topology Control forWireless Ad-Hoc Sensor Networks Journal- Sensors 10, 1251–1278 (2010), http://www.mdpi.com/journal/sensors

Recent Developments in Scheduling and Allocation of High Level Synthesis

M. Chinnadurai[1] and M. Joseph[2]

[1] E.G.S. Pillay Engineering College
Nagore, Nagapattinam - 611002, India
chinnaduraimurugan@yahoo.com
[2] Mother Terasa College of Engineering and Technology
Illuppur, Pudukkottai - 622102, India
mjoseph_mich@yahoo.com

Abstract. We survey the recent developments of scheduling and allocation techniques in high level synthesis. Technology driven High-Level Synthesis is a customized high-level synthesis tool to make an optimal hardware generation, it makes the present knowledgeable of the target Field Programmable Gate Array. We then describe the different techniques and applications of different scheduling and allocation concepts in high level synthesis. To maximize the benefits of HLS, this paper describes the scheduling and allocation algorithms using Technology Specific Library (TSL).

Keywords: High Level Synthesis, Scheduling, Allocation, Optimization, Technology Specific Library.

1 Introduction

Todays VLSI technology allows companies to build large, complex systems containing millions of transistors on a single chip. To exploit this technology, designers need sophisticated Computer Aided Design (CAD) tools that enable them to manage millions of transistors efficiently. Rapid increases in chip complexity, increasingly faster clocks, and the proliferation of portable devices have combined to make power dissipation an important design parameter [7]. This paper targets Technology driven High Level Synthesis (THLS) systems, and introduces an exact approach to the scheduling and allocation problem for Technology Specific Library (TSL).

1.1 High-Level Synthesis

High Level Synthesis (HLS) is a sequence of tasks that transforms a behavioral representation into a Register Transfer Level (RTL) design. The input to the high-level synthesis process is given in an algorithmic level specification, such as behavioral VHDL. This type of specification gives the required mapping from sequences of inputs to sequences of outputs [5]. The specification should constrain

N. Meghanathan et al. (Eds.): CCSIT 2012, Part III, LNICST 86, pp. 327–336, 2012.

the internal structure of the system to be designed as little as possible. From the input specification, a synthesis system produces a description of a data path, that is, a network of registers, functional units, multiplexers and buses.

1.2 Technology Driven High Level Synthesis

To retain designers technology knowledge coded into the design, and to exploit the target technology to its potential, HLS tool should be aware of target technology. THLS, is a customized HLS tool for a particular target technology. It infers the hardware rightly, based on the target domain knowledge and generates optimized RTL netlist [1]. All the phases of this tool are knowledgeable of the target technology. In this tool, parses uses AGs (Attribute Grammar), to attach target specific attributes to generate technology attributed parse tree. Elaboration then generates Target Specific Intermediate Representation (TSIR) from that annotated parse tree. Synthesizer converts this TSIR into hardware after optimization. It uses the Technology Specific Library (TSL) not a generic library like Library of Parameterized Modules (LPM).

1.3 Target Technology

At the highest level, FPGAs are reprogrammable silicon chips. Using prebuilt logic blocks and programmable routing resources, you can configure these chips to implement custom hardware functionality without ever having to pick up a breadboard or soldering iron [6]. You develop digital computing tasks in software and compile them down to a configuration file or bitstream that contains information on how the components should be wired together.

2 Related Surveys

There is no paper, which comprehensively survey the scheduling and algorithm techniques in HLS. The scheduling problem will undoubtedly remain an area of research for years to come, so this survey becomes an essential one.

Azeddien M. Sllame et.al. [9] designed the list based efficient algorithms for high level synthesis, it concentrated on the scheduling process because the main design decisions such as the number of hardware resources, clock cycle time, and implementation styles (pipeline, multi-cycle operation, micro-operations, etc.) are made during the scheduling process. The proposed methodology for the proposed schedule exploits some inherent properties of the behavioral flow graphs of Digital Signal Processing systems. It also allows us to incorporate some information extracted from DFG structure to guide the scheduler to find near-optimal/optimal schedules quickly. The method of [12] follows to find a symbolic representation of all minimal latency schedules allowed by a given set of resources. Furthermore, each schedule is (symbolically) associated with all valid subsets of allocated resources, so that the combined space can be explored for efficient allocation purposes. This is achieved by encoding all possible allocations of resources within the given limits. The method also gives target both combinational resource and register minimization. A goal to challenge for crosstalk estimation or optimization at higher abstraction levels is the non-availability of neighborhood details of interconnects until the routing stage in the design flow [14].

3   Basic Techniques

Due to its complexity, high level synthesis is divided into a number of distinct yet inter-dependent tasks:

- **Selection:** What kind of resources are required?
- **Allocation:** How many resources are necessary?
- **Binding:** Which operations have to be performed by a specific resource?
- **Scheduling:** When should specific operations be activated?

A lot of research is done in finding algorithms that solve these tasks satisfactory. The algorithms used, and the order in which they solve the tasks depend on the constraints and objectives given. Scheduling and allocation are the most important tasks in order to synthesize circuits that are efficient in terms of area and performance. They are strongly related and inter-dependent. For example, scheduling attempts to minimize the number of required control steps subject to the amount of available hardware which depends on the results of allocation. Likewise, allocation exploits concurrency among operations to allow sharing of hardware resources, where the degree of concurrency is determined by scheduling. The essentiality of a Control and Data Flow Graph in High Level Synthesis and Hardware/Software Cosynthesis has been highlighted in [10].

3.1   Scheduling

Operation scheduling, or in short scheduling, deals with the assignment of each operation to a time slot corresponding to a clock cycle or time interval. Typically, the input to this task consists of a control and data flow graph (CDFG), a set of available hardware resources and a performance constraint [10]. A schedule will be generated such that the data/control dependency defined by the CDFG will not be violated and the performance constraint is satisfied. Since scheduling determines which operations can be assigned to the same time slot, it affects the degree of concurrency of the resulting design and thus its performance. Further, the maximum number of concurrent operations of a given type in a schedule is a lower bound on the number of required hardware resources for that operation. Therefore, the choice of a schedule affects the cost of the implementation and consequently scheduling plays an important role in high-level synthesis.

3.2   Data Path Allocation

In general, data path allocation and binding deal with the problem of which resources are used to realize in the physical implementation. Such resources include registers, memory units and different functional units as well as their communication channels. The basic principle is to share resources as much as possible provided that the performance and other design criteria can be satisfied. Allocation and binding carry out selection and assignment of hardware resources for a given design. Allocation determines the type and number of hardware resources for a given design. Binding assigns the instance of an allocated hardware resource to a given data path node [2]. Different data path operations can share the same hardware resource if they are not executed at the same time. For example, an adder can be shared by two additions if they are not executed during the same clock cycle.

4   Efficient Scheduling and Allocation Algorithms

Over the years researchers have tried to come up with various kinds of solutions to the scheduling problem. Several algorithms have been put forth and each one has it own advantages and disadvantages. Scheduling algorithms can be broadly classified into time constrained and resource constrained scheduling, based on the goal of the scheduling problem.

4.1   The Basic Scheduling Problem

In more complex behaviors, the CDFG can also represent conditional branches, loops, etc., hence the name "Control/Data Flow Graph"[10]. We give different scheduling algorithms with example.

Time and Resource Constrained Scheduling (TRCS). To find a feasible (or optimal) schedule and also meets resource constraints.

Chaining and Multicycling. Each operation type requires the same amount of time to execute, and that the control step length(i.e. the clock period) is equal to that execution time.

The Hierarchical Conditional Dependency Graph (HCDG) is a powerful internal design representation and can effectively accommodate design descriptions with dataflow-intensive and/or control flow intensive behaviors. Existing HLS heuristics successful for dataflow designs can be easily adapted to HCDG and novel scheduling heuristics for conditional behaviors. The hierarchical control representation, mutual exclusiveness identification capabilities, and formal graph transformations lead to HCDG-based scheduling approach effectively exploiting all of the existing scheduling optimization techniques and enjoying their combined benefits. Both speculative execution and conditional resource sharing are combined in a uniform and consistent framework. Recent work applying a constraint logic programming algorithm on HCDGs [10] indicates that schedules provided by the described heuristic are close to optimal.

4.2   Some Common Scheduling Algorithms

The following is the list of some commonly preferred scheduling algorithms.

- ASAP / ALAP Scheduling
- List Scheduling
- Force Directed Scheduling
- Integer Linear Programming formulation

For a given data path, the minimum execution time is basically equal to the length of the critical path which consists of a sequence of control places which dominating the time needed for a token of variables allocation to flow from the initial place to the final place. This type of method to detect the critical path is based on the reachability tree. When two modules are merged, the operations executed on these modules must be scheduled in different control steps, so that they can share the same component. Similar for registers, the variables stored in these registers must be disjoint and present the rescheduling transformation which is performed by a efficient merge-sort algorithm based on a controllability/observability enhancement strategy [8].

A goal to challenge for crosstalk estimation or optimization at higher abstraction levels is the non-availability of neighborhood details of interconnects until the routing stage in the design flow [14]. In the proposed approach, design by a typical input sequence and synthesize it to an RTL netlist through HLS System. Crosstalk is a function of data correlations as well as physical characteristics. It gives 23.5% of the optimization for bus based designs. To achieve efficient interconnect solutions; data path synthesis approaches in the past have targeted their schedules on to architectures using register files and multiport memories. The proposed approach of [15] is uses the tight packing function for scheduling processing efficiently. The allocation of hardware resources and pipeline processing can be implemented by this approach and also apply this technique to registers, MUXes and Functional units also.

4.3   Efficient Scheduling of Conditional Behaviours for HLS

As hardware designs get increasingly complex and time-to-market constraints get tighter there is strong motivation for High-Level Synthesis (HLS) [10]. HLS must efficiently handle both data flow dominated and control flow dominated designs as well as designs of a mixed nature. In the past efficient tools for the former type have been developed but so far HLS of conditional behaviors lags behind. To bridge this gap an efficient scheduling heuristic for conditional behaviors is presented.

Heuristic and the techniques it utilizes are based on a unifying design representation appropriate for both types of behavioral descriptions, enabling the proposed heuristic to exploit under the same framework several well-established techniques (chaining, multicycling) as well as conditional resource sharing and speculative execution which are essential in efficiently scheduling conditional behaviors.

4.4   Optimization on HLS Scheduling for Conditional Statements

As-Fast-As-Possible (AFAP) is a path-based scheduling algorithm that ensures the minimum number of control steps for all possible sequences of operations in the control flow graph, under given resource constraints. This technique requires scheduling one operation into different states depending on the path. Although the worst case computational complexity is non-polynomial, there are no execution time problems in practice. The Condition Vector List Scheduling (CVLS) algorithm exploits a more "global parallelism" [4].

5   A New Approach to Scheduling and Allocation Algorithms Using TSL

5.1   TSL

Technology Specific Library (TSL) is not a generic library like LPM and it is a library of technology specific devices, defined based on the target technology.

5.2   TSIR

Target Specific Intermediate Representation (TSIR) is a technology details that are embedded into the CDFG to make it technology specific. Elaboration process generates Technology Specific Intermediate Representation (TSIR) from this annotated parse tree. The optimizer then applies compiler optimization techniques on the CDFG, to improve it, keeping speed, silicon area and power as optimization factors.

5.3   Scheduling Strategies Using TSL

In HLS, each segment of register availability in the shift register operation creates register variables with ranges in associates with elaborator. But this solution gives only sub-optimal optimization, since it occupies more silicon area and consumes more power. But, THLS converts [1] the same code segment into a parses by determining the range i.e. register width. Elaboration associates register variable with range. Then it infers a structural shift register object, a TSIR node. The choice between register and shift register is possible based on the width of the identifier. Scheduling strategies to the operation in the TSL for register variables after association with Elaboration. Optimizer then improves this.

In figure 1 shows the range based scheduling and allocation is performed an optimistic binding solutions, which has a minimized the resource usage. So, the minimization of the resources like functional units, registers and MUXes. It is may be based on the better solutions for the scheduling and allocation concepts. In step 1, the creation of feasible solutions of the register variables and ranges are evaluated. In step 3, the different constraints is performed to generate a valid scheduling which improves the performance of the THLS systems.

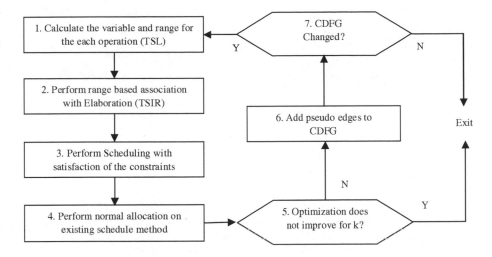

Fig. 1. Scheduling and Allocation design flow using TSL

In the proposed approaches, the merging approach has to be applied for the repeated operations into a single or optimized solution and optimize the operations during scheduling and allocation is mainly concentrated on the design [13]. A unique approach to scheduling and allocation using the above mentioned approaches in the Technology driven High Level Synthesis. M.J.M. Heijiligers, et.al.[11] also described a unique approach to scheduling and allocation problem using genetic algorithm(GA).

Hardware Constraints for the New Approaches. Constraints are restrictions imposed on the implementation stage which are used to guide the scheduling. Constraints are the following:

- Variables can be assigned only once in one control state.
- IO ports can be read or written only once in one control state.
- Functional units can be used only once in a control state.
- The maximal delay within one control state limits the number of operations that can be chained.

Constraints are represented as intervals in the control flow graph. This type of representation allows constraints to be applied on a path basis. A constraint [13] interval involves a sequence of operations and it implies that these operations cannot all be executed in the same cycle step. In other words a new state must start at some point within the interval, for the constraint to be met.

5.4 Allocation Strategies Using TSL

Allocation chooses the type and number of functional units and registers, and thus determines part of the final cost (the interconnection cost still has to be identified) and performance (the clock cycle is affected by this stage). The designer must still explore the design space by defining the acceptable maximum numbers of functional units and registers. Believe that this data path architecture definition is too critical to be left to a tool, and provide the designer with a quick feedback on the effect of his decisions. In TSL, each resources of funcational units and registers is to be allocated efficiently by the new approach.

5.5   New Scheduling Method for Low Power Design

Chi-Co Lin proposed a new scheduling method for low power design is the internal data structure, CDFG, which represents both the control flow and data flow effectively[3], is constructed. The CDFG represents the constraints which limit the hardware design such as conditional branch, sequential operation and time constraints. In order to represent control flow, data dependency and such constraints as resource constraints and timing constraints effectively, the CDFG represents the constraints which limit the hardware design in such a way:

- no variable is assigned more than once in each control step
- no I/O port is accessed more than once in each control step
- the total delay of operations in each control step is not greater than the given control step-length
- all designer imposed constraints for scheduling particular operations in different control steps are satisfied.

In order to satisfy any of the above conditions, the proposed scheduling algorithm generates constraints between two nodes that must be scheduled into different control steps.

6   Power Optimization

Table 1 gives the details of power consumption for the FPA implementation under these three synthesis tools. In this process, the device XC4VLX15 are used in Virtex-IV for this experimentation. Total power consumption is 161 mW for ISE tool and 160 mW for THLS tool. THLS is able to reduce the dynamic power 1 mW and thus optimizes power [1]. It has 0.6% reduction in power consumption over ISE. (*Note: Power consumption is significant for larger volume applications only. On the other hand, power consumption is less and insignificant in low volume applications.*)

Icaurs compiler cannot handle floating-point algorithms. ISE cannot handle floating-point algorithms. THLS customizes the floating-point algorithms into fixed-point and synthesizes. THLS compiler has 26% reduction in silicon usage over the conversion (fixed-point) and compiler methodology (ISE). It has 0.6% reduction in power consumption over ISE.

Table 1. Power Consumption for FPA

No.	Metric	THLS	ISE
1	Quiescent Power	160 mW	160 mW
2	Dynamic Power	000 mW	001 mW
3	Total Power	160 mW	161 mW

6.1 Power Aware High Level Synthesis

High-level synthesis determines which step the operations will be processed in, resources number and the power of resources. They describes three points impact power dissipation in both temporal and spatial aspect. The resources number is the crucial factor of final area of the design [4]. Due to the interaction of two factors, it is essential to make a tradeoff of two objects in the design process.

6.2 Dynamic FU Allocation

As we all know, the behavioral synthesis process consists of three phases: allocation, assignment and scheduling. These processes determine how many instances of each resource are needed (allocation), on what resources a computational operation will be performed (assignment) and when it will be executed (scheduling) [4]. The FU allocation is the vital step to determine the final area and power dissipation. It is widely accepted that the total switching activity (SW) between FUs minimal, the dynamic power dissipation will be lowest with the same other conditions. To achieve dynamic power minimal, the total SW must be smaller. All above we need to do is the proper FU allocation, if the FU allocation is optimal, after applying better scheduling and binding algorithm, the power value will be close to minimal. Since the number of FU is integer, the extremely optimal allocation hardly achieves. The closest integer solution is identified instead, and it is called the proper solution.

7 Summary

This paper presented the detailed survey of different scheduling and allocation techniques in High Level Synthesis. It described the several scheduling algorithms commonly used today in high level synthesis. Then this paper described the technologies used in the Technology driven High Level Synthesis and also presented a new techniques for scheduling and allocation algorithms using TSL to improve the Speed, (silicon)Area and Power.

Acknowledgments. We thank to the anonymous reviewers for their numerous insightful and constructive comments.

References

1. Joseph, M., Bhat, N.B., Chandra Sekaran, K.: Technology driven High-Level Synthesis. In: International Conference on Advanced Computing and Communication - ADCOM 2007. IEEE, Indian Institute of Technology Guwahati, India (2007)
2. Harish Ram, D.S., Bhuvaneswari, M.C., Logesh, S.M.: A Novel Evolutionary Technique for Multi objective Power, Area and Delay Optimization in High Level Synthesis of Datapaths. In: ISVLSI 2011, pp. 290–295 (2011)
3. Lin, C.-C., Yoon, D.-H.: New Efficient High Level Synthesis Methodology for Low Power Design. In: International Conference on New Trends in Information and Service Science (2009)
4. Wu, F., Xu, N., Zheng, F., Mao, F.: Simultaneous Functional Units and Register Allocation Based Power Management for High-level Synthesis of Data-intensive Applications (2010)
5. McFarland, M.C., Parker, A.C., Campasona, R.: Tutorial on High-Level Synthesis. In: 25th ACM IEEE Design Automation Conference (1998)
6. Brown, S.D., Francis, R.J., Rose, J., Vranesic, Z.G.: Field Programmable Gate Arrays. Kluwer Academic Publishers (1992)
7. Gajski, D.D., Dutt, N.D., Wu, A., Lin, S.: High-Level Synthesis: Introduction to Chip and System Design. Kluwer Academic Publishers (1992)
8. Yang, T., Peng, Z.: An efficient algorithm to integrate scheduling and allocation high-level test synthesis. In: Proceedings of Design Automation Test Eur., vol. 81, pp. 74–81 (1998)
9. Sllame, A., Drabek, V.: An Efficient List-Based Scheduling Algorithm for High-Level Synthesis. In: Proceedings Euromicro Symposium on Digital System Design DSD 2002, pp. 316–323. IEEE Computer Society (2002)
10. Kountouris, A., Wolinski, C.: Efficient Scheduling of Conditional behaviors for High Level Synthesis. ACM Transactions on Design Automation of Electronic Systems 7(3), 380–412 (2002)
11. Heijligers, M.J.M., Clutmans, L.J.M., Jess, J.A.G.: High-Level Synthesis Scheduling and Allocation using Genetic Algorithms. In: Proceedings of Asia and Pacific Design Automation Conference, Chiba, Japan, pp. 61–66 (1995)
12. Cabodi, G., Nocco, S., Lazarescu, M., et al.: A Symbolic Approach for the Combined Solution of Scheduling and Allocation. In: Proceedings of ISSS 2002, Kyoto, Japan, pp. 237–242 (2002)
13. Sait Sadique, M., Ali, S., Benten, M.S.: Scheduling and Allocation in High Level Synthesis using Stochastic Techniques. Microelectronics Journal 7 27(8), 693–712 (1991)
14. Sankaran, H., Katkoori, S.: Simultaneous Scheduling, Allocation, Binding, Re Ordering, and Encoding for Crosstalk Pattern Minimization During High Level Synthesis. IEEE Transaction on Very Large Scale Integration (VLSI) Systems 19(2) (2011)
15. Burns, F., Shang, D., Koelmans, A., Yakovlev, A.: Scheduling and allocation using closeness tables. IEE Proceedings - Computers and Digital Techniques 151(5), 332–340 (2004)
16. Free Floating-Point Madness, http://www.hmc.edu/chips
17. Electronic Design Interchange Format, http://www.edif.org
18. FPGA, CPLD, and EPP Solutions, http://www.xilinx.com
19. Icarus Verilog Simulation and Synthesis Tool, http://www.icraus.com

Digital Signature of an Image by Elliptic Curve Cryptosystem

T.N. Shankar[1,*], G. Sahoo[2], and S. Niranjan[3]

[1] Department of Comp.Sc. and Engg., GMR Institute of Technology,
Rajam, Andhra Pradesh, India
tnshankar2003@yahoo.co.in
[2] Dept. of Information Technology, Birla Institute of Technology Mesra,
Ranchi, Jharkhand India
gsahoo@bitmesra.ac.in
[3] Department of Information Technology, PDM College of Engineering,
Bahadurgarh, Haryana, India
niranjan.hig41@gmail.com

Abstract. Digital Images for seamless transmission over mobile network are required to be ensured with authentication and increasing concern for their integrity, originality and non repudiation qualities. In this paper, a novel approach of digital signature scheme of an image is introduced. The proposed scheme consists of three main steps. First, pixel selection, second, pixel values digest through hash function, and finally, creation of digital signature using elliptic curve cryptography based on public key cryptosystem. In this process, the sender uses the private key for hash value encryption, and the recipient uses the public key for signature verification. Instead of directly sending an original image to the recipients, the embedded copy is sent with signed digital signature for authentication.

1   Introduction

With the introduction of mobile devices, smart cards and many other gadgets, it has become an easy task to deal with images over any mobile network. Further improvement in processing power, miniaturization of portable storage media have considerably enhance multimedia transmission capability [6][7]. Despite these technological advances over last few years, users are likely to face situations, where the contents so received may have the possibility of being tampered with, producing copies of, and illegally redistributing digital contents[15][16]. Without solving these security related issues, digital multimedia products and services cannot succeed in the domain of ecommerce. An attempt to work out a tangible solution for achieving image authentication using digital signature [10][11] by Elliptic Curve

---

* Corresponding author.

N. Meghanathan et al. (Eds.): CCSIT 2012, Part III, LNICST 86, pp. 337–346, 2012.

Cryptography(ECC) is introduced. A comparative study of the conventional algorithm and the one that employs ECC justifies our contention.

Images are popular in multimedia with various applications. Each image is composed of pixels. Each pixel can be represented by eight bits [12][18] with its value between 0-255. In the proposed algorithm, a hash function SHA-1 is used to transform some pixels of the image to obtain the digest value followed by encrypting with private key to which ECC is applied for generation of digital signature[8][14]. The image so embedded with digital signature [2][17] received at the destination can be separated by using the method discussed in section 4.3. After separation of digital signature, the hash function SHA-1 is operated upon the selected pixels to generate the message digest. In the end, to assess any undesirable interference, the signature verification on digested message using the public key can be prepared. The security feature attributed to digital signature depends on encryption and verification. Conventional algorithms are not suitable for mobile devices due to more space complexity. Among the non-conventional algorithms, RSA encryption algorithm is not suitable due to large key size. Multimedia files are transmitted as compressed files. If digital signature [8][16] processing will have complexity issues, then its application with the mobile devices is not desirable.

In the following section, there is a brief discussion on background of ECC and point multiplication over GF(p) and $F_2{}^m$ in section 2. In Section 3, we discuss on digital signature. Section 4 describes on proposed algorithm. Section 5 presents a comparative analysis. Finally section 6 concludes the paper.

2   Elliptic Curve

Informally, an elliptic curve is a type of cubic curve defined by an equation of the form

$$y^2 = x^3 + ax + b \tag{1}$$

Where a and b are real numbers.

The definition of elliptic curve also requires that the curve be non-singular. Geometrically, this means that the graph has no cusps, self-intersections, or isolated points. Algebraically, this involves calculating the discriminant

$$D = 4a^3 + 27b^2 \neq 0 \tag{2}$$

The curve is non-singular if and only if the discriminant is not equal to zero. It is not safe to use singular curves for cryptography as they are easy to crack. Due to this reason we generally take non-singular curves for data encryption.

2.1 Elliptic Curves over $F_2{}^m$

The binary finite field implementation is that the elements of $GF(2^m)$ can be represented by m-bit binary code words . This implies that a finite field of form $GF(2^m)$is of characteristic 2. The equation of the elliptic curve on a binary field $F_2{}^m$ is

$$y^2 + xy = x^3 + ax^2 + b \text{ , where } b \neq 0. \tag{3}$$

Here the elements of the finite field are integers of length at most m bits. These numbers can be considered as a binary polynomial of degree $m-1$.In binary polynomial the coefficients can only be 0 or 1.

2.2 Arithmetic in $GF(2^m)$

In this section, we want to introduce briefly the arithmetic operations needed to implement ECC point multiplication over binary polynomial fields $GF(2^m)$. The operations include modular addition, subtraction, multiplication, squaring, division, and inverse, where the operands are polynomials with coefficients of either 0 or 1. We use the polynomial basis representation where a polynomial $a(x) \in GF(2^m)$ in canonical form is written as

$$a(x) = a_{m-1}x^{m-1} + a_{m-2}x^{m-2} + ...+ a_2x^2 + a_1x + a_0 \tag{4}$$

$a_i \in GF(2)$. For computation purposes, an m bit binary vector can be used to represent the coefficients. For example, the polynomial $x^3 + x^2 + 1$ can be written as 1101.

2.3 Point Multiplication Algorithm

Scalar multiplication is the computation of the form $Q = kP$ where P and Q are the elliptic curve points and k is an integer. This is achieved by repeated elliptic curve point addition and doubling operations. Point negation also includes as a miscellaneous operation, which is about to be suggested for fast implementation algorithm of kP.

The integer k is represented as

$$k = x_{m-1}2^{m-1} + x_{m-2}2^{m-2} + ... + x_1 + x_0 \tag{5}$$

where

$x_i \in \{1,0\}$ and $m = 0,1,2, ... , n-1$

The addition of two points on a curve over $F_2{}^m$ is defined as.

Let $P(x_1,y_1)$, and $Q(x_2,y_2)$ be two different points on the curves, when $P \neq Q$ the operation $P + Q = (x_3, y_3)$ can then be derived as shown as shown in

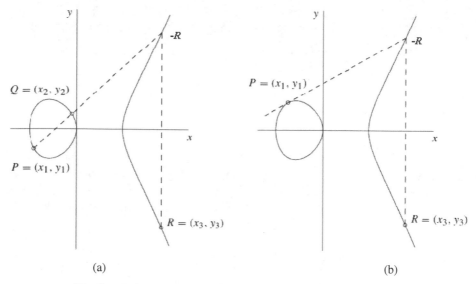

(a)   (b)

Fig. 1. a. Point Addition $P+Q= R$,   b. The operation $P + P = 2P$

Algorithm.1.a

Algebraic Formulae Over Fp

Point addition

$P+ \infty= P$

Case I. If $P \neq Q$, then $((x_1 \neq x_2)$ and $(y_1 \neq y_2))$
Step1. Find $\alpha= (y_2 - y_1) / (x_2 - x_1)$
Step2. $P+Q = (x_3,y_3) = (\alpha^2 - x_1 - x_2 , \alpha(x_1 - x_3) - y_1)$

Point doubling

Case II. If $P = Q$, then $((x_1=x_2)$ and $(y_1=y_2))$
Step1. Find $\alpha= (3x_1^2 + a)/(2y_1)$
Step2. $2P = (x_3,y_3) = (\alpha^2 - x_1 - x_2 , \alpha(x_1 - x_3) - y_1)$

Algorithm.1.b

Algebraic Formulae Over $F_2{}^m$

Point addition

Case I.

Step1.If $P \neq Q$, then $((x_1 \neq x_2)$ and $(y_1 \neq y_2))$

Step2. Find $\alpha = (y_1 + y_2) / (x_1 + x_2)$

Step3. $P+Q = (x_3, y_3) = (\alpha^2 + \alpha + x_1 + x_2 + a , \alpha(x_1 + x_3) + x_3 + y_1)$

Point double

Case II.

Step1. If $P = Q$, then $((x_1 = x_2)$ and $(y_1 = y_2))$,

Step2. Find $\alpha = x_1 + (y_1 / x_1)$

Step3. $2P = (x_3, y_3) = (\alpha^2 + \alpha + a , x_1^2 + (\alpha + 1)x_3)$

Algorithm:1.c

Point negation

Step1. If $Q = (x, y)$ is over $F_2{}^m$ then

$$-Q = (x, x + y) \text{ is over } F_2{}^m$$

3   Digital Signature by ECC

INPUT: Domain parameters = (a, b, P, h, n) private key g, pixel values m.
OUTPUT: Signature (s_1, s_2)

1. Select $k \in R [1, n-1]$
2. Compute $kP = (x_1, y_1)$ and convert x_1 to an integer $\overline{x_1}$.
3. Compute $s_1 = x_1 \mod n$. If $s_1 = 0$ then go to step 1.
4. Compute $d = SHA\text{-}1 (m)$.
5. Compute $s_2 = k^{-1}(d + g s_1) \mod n$. If $s_2 = 0$ then go to step 1.
6. Return(s_1, s_2).

3.1   ECDSA Signature Verification

INPUT: Domain parameters=(q, a, b, P, n) public key Q, pixel values m,
        signature(s_1, s_2).
OUTPUT: Acceptance or rejection of the signature.

1.   Verify that s_1 and s_2 are integers in the interval $[1, n-1]$. If any verification failsthen
     return ("Reject the signature").

2. Compute $d=SHA-1$ (m).

3. Compute $w=s_2-1$ mod n.

4. Compute $v_1=dw$ mod n and $v_2=s_1$ $w$mod n.

5. Compute $X=v_1P+v_2Q$.

6. If $X=\infty$then Invalid the signature";

7. Convert the x-coordinate x_1 of X to an integer x_1; compute $z=x_1$ mod n.

8. If $z=s_1$ then return ("Accept the signature");

9. Else return (" Reject the signature ").

4   Experimental Results

Select the pixels according to desire. More pixels may be assumed for better signature strength. Preparation of digital signature through all the pixels is not so easy and it is too complicated with more time and space complexity. To avoid this situation, select 100 to 1000 number of pixels for preparation of it with best security level will well suit the purpose.

Select the pixels

1. RGB = imread('Litesh.jpg')
2. col = [m ,n, ...]
3. row = [x ,y,...]
4. pixels = im pixel (RGB, col, row)

Assume 4 pixels from Fig.2.a

For testing we have assumed only four pixels of Fig.2, and their representation is as like as the following.

Table 1. Four pixels with the pixel value eight bit each

0	1	1	0	0	0	0	1
0	1	1	0	0	0	1	0
0	1	1	0	0	0	1	1
1	1	0	0	0	1	1	0

Message M =   "01100001   01100010   01100011   11000110"

4.1 Digital Signature by ECC

SHA-1(M) = e364706816aba3e25717850c26c9cd0d89d60e4c

s_1 =   8bac1ab66410435cb7181f95b16ab97c92b341c0

s_2 =   41e2345f1f56df2458f426d155b4ba2db6dcd8c8

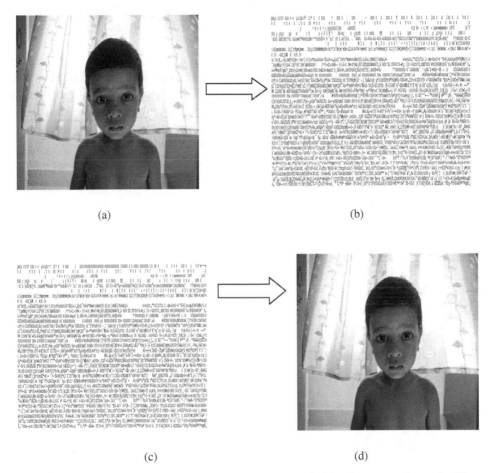

(a)   (b)

(c)   (d)

Fig. 2. a. Litesh.jpg, b. Machine Language Litesh.jpg, c. Machine Language after embedding digital signature(s_1, s_2),   d. Litesh.jpg after embedding digital signature(s_1, s_2)

After creating the digital signature, it's necessary to embed within the image. Fig.2.a to d depict all the processing steps to embed the digital signature with the image.

Here we have illustrated a comparison between before Fig.2.b and after Fig.2.c embedding the digital signature within the image. If we will go after an observation then we can find out the differences amongst the symbols in machine language.

4.2   Embedded Digital Signature Extraction Process

In this process the data embeddable pixels are identified from the embedded image. These pixels are given as input to the next stage i.e., the color of each embeddable pixel and those of its four precedent neighbors are given as input to the color ordering and mapping function. If the output is '1' then the extracted secret bit is taken to be '1' otherwise, '0'. The extracted digital signature is compared with the extracted embedded data for verification.

Recipient will use the same positional pixels which were used by sender as the input to SHA-1 to create the digested message. The image embedded with digital signature can always be robustly verified for authenticity even though the attacker in the transit will attempt to interfere. However, the identical pixel selection at the source and at the destination ends to remain intact lest the authentication and the integrity of the image will be under siege.

4.3   ECDSA Signature Verification

$z = 8bac1ab66410435cb7181f95b16ab97c92b341c0$

$s_1 = z$, So the signature is acceptable

Suppose any tampering is there then there must be impact on "z" and z value must not be matched with s_1.

4.4   Experimental Result after Tampering

Litesh.jpg is tampered on the mid then we can get the output z as

$z = 8b431ab665d1435cb7181f95b16df37c92b341c0$

$s_1 \neq z$, As a consequence signature is not acceptable

5   Comparison between Digital Signature by RSA and ECC

Both the algorithms can be used for preparation of digital signature from an image. We can't use RSA algorithm for mobile devices due to its long key size. Desired level of security can be achieved with ECC using small key size. A comparison between RSA and ECC algorithms is shown in Figure-3. For this occasion Elliptic Curve Cryptography proved to be appropriate for image encryption on mobile devices.

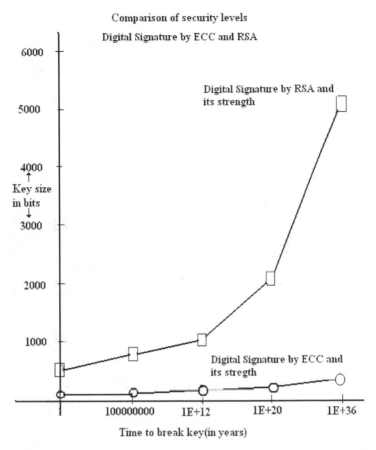

Fig. 3. Comparison between digital signature of an image by RSA and ECC

6 Conclusion

For image authentication, it is desired that the verification method be able to resist content-preserving modifications while being sensitive to content-changing modifications. In this paper, an attempt is made to embed digital signature of an image with ECC for achieving better result. We have assumed only 4 pixels for manual calculation. In the real applications, 100-1000 pixels will cover a secure and strong digital signature. Preparation of digital signature from all pixels requires more time and space that may not be suitable for small devices due to limited space and less processing power. To overcome such type of problem, we propose this technique with limited number of pixels for preparation of digital signature keeping well in view the micro devices with better strength.

References

[1] Koblitz, N., Menezes, A.J., Vanstone, S.A.: The state of elliptic curve cryptography. Design, Codes, and Cryptography 19(2-3), 173–193 (2000)
[2] ElGamal, T.: A public key cryptosystem and a signature scheme based on discrete logarithm. IEEE Trans. Informn, Theory IT-31(4), 469–472 (1985)
[3] Shankar, T.N., Sahoo, G.: Cryptography with ellipitic curves. International Journal of Computer Science And Applications 2(1), 38–42
[4] Shankar, T.N., Sahoo, G.: Cryptography with ASCII codes. International Journal of Secure Digital Age Information 1(2), 141–121
[5] Younes, M.A.B., Jantan, A.: Image Encryption Using Block-Based Transformation Algorithm. IAENG International Journal of Computer Science, IJCS 35(1) (2003)
[6] Shankar, T.N., Sahoo, G., Niranjan, S.: Elliptic Curve Point Multiplication by Using Complementary Recording for Image Encryption. In: INCOCCI 2010, Ieee Xplore, pp. 546–551 (2010)
[7] Shankar, T.N., Sahoo, G., Niranjan, S.: Image Encryption for Mobile Devices. In: ICCCCT 2010, Ieee Xplore, pp. 612–516 (2010)
[8] Johnson, D., Menezes, A., Vanstone, S.: The Elliptic Curve Digital Signature Algorithm (ECDSA). Certicom Research, Canada
[9] Stallings, W.: Cryptography and Network Security: Principles and Practice, 2nd edn. Prentice-Hall (1999)
[10] Chiaraluce, F., Ciccarelli, L., Gambi, E., Pierleoni, P., Reginelli, M.: A New Chaotic Algorithm for Video Encryption. IEEE Trans. Consumer Electron. 48(4), 838–844 (2002)
[11] Sudharsanan, S.: Shared Key Encryption of JPEG Color Images. IEEE Trans. Consumer Electron. 51(4), 1204–1211 (2005)
[12] Dang, P.P., Chau, P.M.: Image Encryption for Secure Internet Multimedia Applications. IEEE Trans. Consumer Electron. 46(3), 395–403 (2000)
[13] Schneider, M., Chang, S.-F.: Robust Content Based Digital Signature for Image Authentication. In: Proceedings of IEEE International Conference on Image Processing (ICIP 1996), vol. 3, pp. 227–230 (1996)
[14] Lou, D.-C., Liu, J.-L.: Fault Resilient and Compression Tolerant Digital signature for Image Authentication. IEEE Transactions on Consumer Electronics 46(1), 31–39 (2000)
[15] Fridrich, J.: Robust Bit Extraction from Images. In: Proceedings of IEEE International Conference on Multimedia Computing and Systems (ICMCS 1999), vol. 2, pp. 536–540 (1999)
[16] Jansirani, A., Rajesh, R., Balasubramanian, R., Eswaran, P.: Hi-Tech Authentication for Palette Images Using Digital Signature and Data Hiding. The International Arab Journal of Information Technology 8(2), 117–123 (2011)
[17] Lu, C.-S., Liao, H.-Y.M.: Structural Digital Signature for Image Authentication, An Incidental Distortion Resistant Scheme. IEEE Transactions on Multimedia 5(2), 161–173 (2003)
[18] Alwan, R.H., Kadhim, F.J., Al-Taani, A.T.: Data Embedding Based on Better Use of Bits in Image Pixels. International Journal of Information and Communication Engineering 2(2), 104–107 (2006)

Mobile-Cloud: A Framework of Cloud Computing for Mobile Application

Jibitesh Mishra[1], Sanjit Kumar Dash[2], and Sweta Dash[3]

[1,2] Department of Information Technology
College of Engineering & Technology
Bhubaneswar, Odisha, India
[3] Synergy Institute of Engineering and Technology
Dhenkanal, Odisha, India
{mishrajibitesh,sanjitkumar303,swetadash123}@gmail.com

Abstract. The proliferation of mobile computing and cloud services is driving a revolutionary change in our information society. We are moving into the Ubiquitous Computing age in which a user utilizes, at the same time, several electronic platforms through which he can access all the required information whenever and wherever needed. The mobile devices provides the easiest solution for ubiquitous access through wireless network. Mobile users can use their cellular phone to check e-mail, browse internet; travelers with portable computers can surf the internet from airports, railway stations etc. The mobile capabilities can be integrated with cloud computing services to give more secure and advanced services to the subscribers. The emerging domain of Mobile Cloud extends the Mobile Computing paradigm to the sharing of cloud resources in distributed computing environment. A Mobile-cloud is the result of the integration of mobile application with the cloud. In this paper we propose a Mobile Cloud Computing architecture to integrate mobile application with various cloud services. Our Paper aims at using cloud computing techniques for storage and processing of data on mobile devices, thereby reducing their limitations.

Keywords: Mobile Subscriber, Cloud Computing, Mobile Cloud Computing, micro browser.

1 Introduction

Cloud Computing means "Internet-based" development, where 'Cloud' is a metaphor for 'Internet' and 'Computing' meaning, the use of "Computer technology". Cloud computing is clearly one of today's most enticing technology areas due to its cost-efficiency and flexibility. But cloud computing's potential doesn't begin and end with the personal computer's transformation into a thin client - the mobile platform is going to be heavily impacted by this technology as well. Cloud computing will dramatically reduce the requirement of advanced handsets for running mobile applications, according to the study. According to the latest study from Juniper Research, the market for cloud-based mobile applications will grow 88% from 2009 to 2014.

N. Meghanathan et al. (Eds.): CCSIT 2012, Part III, LNICST 86, pp. 347–356, 2012.

The market was just over $400 million this past year, says Juniper, but by 2014 it will reach $9.5 billion [1]. In Mobile Cloud Computing both the data storage and the data processing happen outside of the mobile device i.e. when we combined concept of cloud computing in mobile environment, all the computing power and data storage move into the mobile cloud.

The rest of this paper is organized as follows. Section 2 gives an overview of Cloud Computing, Section 3 gives the architecture of Mobile Cloud Computing, Section 4 outlines the working of mobile cloud computing, Section 5 describes an inspiring example "Google Sync" of mobile Cloud Computing, Section 6 discusses various services required by mobile client/server and Section 7 puts forth the Pros and Cons of Mobile Cloud Computing. Finally, Section 8 concludes the paper.

2   Cloud Computing

According to National Institute of Standards and Technology, USA (NIST) Definition of Cloud Computing is[2] :

Definition: Cloud computing is a model for enabling ubiquitous, convenient, on demand network access to a shared pool of configurable computing resources (e.g., networks, servers, storage, applications, and services) that can be rapidly provisioned and released with minimal management effort or service provider interaction.

Cloud computing encompasses a whole range of services can be hosted in a variety of manners, depending on the nature of the service involved and the data/security needs of the mobile subscribers. However, the basic idea behind the cloud model is that anything that could be done in computing from storing data to collaborating on documents or crunching numbers on large data sets can be shifted to the cloud. Certainly, cloud computing enables a new platform and location-independent perspective on how we communicate, collaborate and work So long as you can access the Web, you are able to work when and where you wish. With fast, reliable Internet connectivity , it does not matter where the document, the e-mail or the data the user sees on the screen comes from. With cloud computing for mobile phone user will get benefit in number of ways and help them to ran there business application without large amount of capital investment in infrastructure and services.

For individuals, cloud computing means accessing web-based email, photo sharing and productivity software, much of it for free [3]. For organizations, shifting to the cloud means having the ability to contract for computing services on-demand, rather than having to invest to host all the necessary hardware, software and support personnel necessary to provide a given level of services [4]. And for governments, the value proposition of the cloud is especially appealing, given both changing demands for IT and challenging economic conditions [5]. The delivery model of cloud computing for mobile applications are given below

Fig. 1. Cloud Service Architecture

A. Software as a Service (SaaS)

In this model an application is hosted as a service to customer who accesses it via the Internet [6]. With SaaS the subscriber doesn't own the software, or even have to execute the code, he/she simply pay as he/she uses the software which is hosted elsewhere. For example mobile user can use Google doc and they do not need to install any application for that. Other providers like Amazon provides cloud services and subscriber need to pay only for the amount of services they want to use. Google Apps is also one of the examples which is provided by the service provider to the subscribers as a service. Google Apps aims to provide users with seamless, more secure access to information regardless of location or device. Google Apps supports access to Gmail, Google Calendar, Docs, and Contacts from most common types of mobile devices.

B. Platform as a Service (PaaS)

PaaS services include application design, development, testing, deployment and hosting [6]. In this not only services but server, memory and other platforms can be used and subscriber needs to pay as per terms and conditions. The combination of software and infrastructure services with application development tools so that Web applications and services can be built and hosted. Examples include Google AppEngine and Salesforce.com's AppExchange.

C. Infrastructure-as-a-Service (IaaS)

IaaS is the delivery of computer infrastructure as a service. With Mobile Cloud Computing mobile phone user will get benefit in number of ways and help them to ran there business application without large amount of capital investment in infrastructure and services. The capability provided to the consumer is to provision processing, storage, networks, and other fundamental computing resources where the consumer is able to deploy and run arbitrary software, which can include operating systems and applications. The consumer does not manage or control the underlying cloud infrastructure but has control over operating systems, storage, deployed applications, and possibly limited control of select networking components (e.g., host firewalls).

Network as a Service (NaaS) is a more recent term, originally used in the IT and cloud computing context but now being increasingly applied in the mobile world. The NaaS model is not entirely new for network operators since they have been providing mobile virtual network operator (MVNO) access to their network as a service on a pay per use basis. However, NaaS is really about opening the network to value added subscriber services, created by third party developers, and charging for the use of the service on a pay as you use basis.

3   Architecture for Mobile Cloud Computing

The architecture of mobile Cloud computing mainly consists of three layers

> A. Presentation tier
> B. Application tier
> C. Database tier.

Presentation Tier is used for user interaction to the server and application tier consists of providing various business logic through different service providers. Database tier provides full database and mobile communication functionality. It allows a mobile user to initiate transactions from anywhere and anytime ad guarantees their consistency preserving execution. The Database tier also provide securities, device provisioning etc. The database present in this layer is used for proving backup to the users in case of any loss or damage.

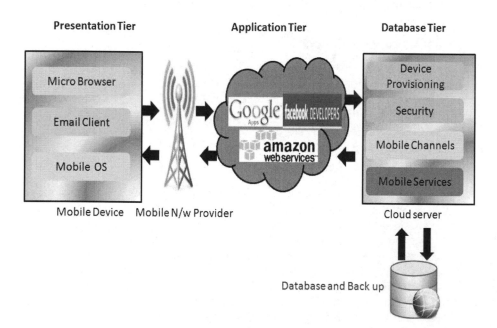

Fig. 2. Mobile Cloud Computing Architecture

A. Presentation Tier

The presentation tier of mobile cloud computing architecture consist of the following components:

Micro-browser: A mobile browser, also called a micro-browser, mini-browser or wireless internet browser (WIB), is a web browser designed for use on a mobile device such as a mobile phone or PDA. Mobile browsers are optimized so as to display Web content most effectively for small screens on portable devices.

Email Client: This is an application which is specifically designed to access remote mail servers, retrieve mail from them, and manipulate that mail. Popular examples of these are Microsoft Outlook, Thunderbird, and Eudora.

Mobile OS: A Mobile operating system, also known as a Mobile OS, a Mobile platform, or a Handheld operating system, is the operating system that controls a mobile device—similar in principle to an operating system such as Linux or Windows that controls a desktop computer or laptop.

B. Application Tier

Application Tier basically focuses on various services provided by a group of service providers . Some of the important cloud service providers are Google Apps, Amazon web services, Facebook developers , IBM, Windows azure etc.

C. Database Tier

In Mobile Cloud Computing both the data storage and the data processing happen outside of the mobile device i.e. when we combined concept of cloud computing in mobile environment. In MCC scenario all the computing power and data storage move into the mobile cloud. MCC will not provide benefits only to the smart phone users but also help a broader range of mobile subscriber. Database not only stores subscribers data but also provides back up facility.

The cloud server is responsible for the following things:

Device Provisioning: Whenever a subscriber signs up for a broadband service, an initial process called device provisioning takes place, as the device used to access a service is "registered" by the provider. On reboot or during troubleshooting some or all of the device provisioning process may be repeated. Three of the most popular technologies used for device provisioning are Session Initiation Protocol(SIP), PacketCable and DOCSIS. SIP is a signaling protocol used for setting up and tearing down real-time communications sessions (voice, instant messaging, etc.). PacketCable is a standards definition maintained by CableLabs, designed for the cable TV industry; it's used for real-time multimedia services delivered using cable networks. DOCSIS, which stands for Data Over Cable Service Interface Specification is also developed by CableLabs, and defines both communications and operation support interface requirement for data over cable systems.

Security: Protecting user privacy and the security of applications and data from those looking for illicit profits or with malicious intent will be key to establishing and maintaining consumer trust in the mobile platform for protection of privacy and data and even more so as a safe means for conducting commercial transactions.

Mobile channel: Mobile Channel Characteristics introduces the principal transmission phenomena of mobile and personal communication - the ones that affect design of modems, channel simulators, smart antennas, and other system components at the physical level.

Mobile Services: Mobile services are provided by different service providers like facebook developer, Amazon Web services, IBM etc.

4   Working of Mobile Cloud Computing

When a mobile subscriber starts using a mobile application the further process depends on whether the application needs a cloud service or not. If the application does not require cloud services then it interact with Mobile Switching Centre (MSC) through various uplink channels for common mobile application like registration, call setup, call termination and SMS etc.

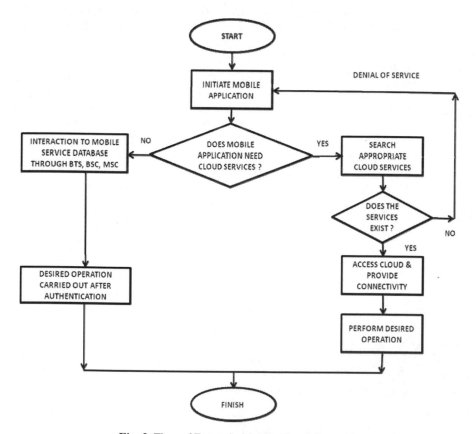

Fig. 3. Flow of Events in Mobile Cloud Computing

But if the application needs cloud services then appropriate cloud service provider is searched according to the mobile user's subscription. If the service requested by the subscriber is existing with the service provider then the connectivity is provided otherwise the service is denied. After the connection is established the cloud can be accessed. The connection can be established many number of times as needed by the subscriber. The payment is variable based on the actual consumption of the resources by the subscriber.

5   An Inspiring Example- Google Sync

One of the best examples of mobile cloud computing using Google is Google sync. Sync is a service provided by Google which allows synchronizing the built -in mobile applications, address book and calendar with users Google account. Once the user set up sync on his mobile it will automatically update phones contacts with contacts from his Gmail account. Sync will also download Google calendar to the user's mobile device. Using sync the mobile phone need not physically connect to laptop to transfer data.

Because sync works by backing up user's information from Google account the data is safe, even if phone is lost or damaged. Google Sync supports the iphone, Blackberry, Windows mobile, Android and Symbian Platform. On most devices, Google Sync uses the Microsoft Exchange ActiveSync Protocol. When setting up a new Exchange ActiveSync account on the mobile device, existing data may be removed from the phone. User should make sure to back up before setting up Google Sync.

Fig. 4. Working of Google Sync

6   Services Needed by Mobile Cloud Client Server

The most essential services required by mobile client includes

1. *Sync:* This service synchronizes all state changes made to the mobile or its applications back with the Cloud Server.
2. *Push:* It manages any state updates being sent as a notifications from the cloud server.
3. *OfflineApp:* It is a service which carries the management capabilities to create smart coordination between low-level services like Sync and Push. It frees the programmer from the burden of writing code to actually perform synchronization as it is this service which decides synchronization management and mechanism which is best for the current state.
4. *Network:* It manages the communication channel needed to receive Push notifications from the server. It carries the ability to establish proper connections automatically.
5. *Database:* It manages the local data storage for the mobile applications. Depending on the platform it uses the corresponding storage facilities.
6. *InterApp Bus:* This service provides low-level coordination/ communication between the suite of applications installed on the device.

The most essential services required by mobile server includes

1. *Sync:* Server Sync service synchronizes device side App state changes with the backend services where the data actually originates. It also must provides a plug-in framework to mobilize the backend data.
2. *Push:* Server Push service monitors data channels for updates. The moment updates are detected, corresponding notifications are sent back to the device.
3. *Secure Socket-Based Data Service:* Depending on the security requirements of the Apps this server side service must provide plain socket server or a SSL-based socket server or both.
4. *Security:* Security component provides authentication and authorization services to make sure mobile devices connecting to the Cloud Server are in fact allowed to access the system.
5. *Management Console:* Every instance of a Cloud Server must have a Command Line application such as the Management Console as it provides user and device provisioning functionalities.

7   PROS and CONS of Using Mobile Cloud Computing Services

Cloud computing actually is not a new term as it has been used since few years ago in services like web-based emails, peer-to-peer networks and other web applications. But with the growth of mobile devices users and the rise of Social Networking sites, the demand of mobile cloud computing services will continue to grow. As an online service, mobile cloud computing also has pros and cons.

Pros

Flexibility: With mobile cloud computing, users can access the applications and data from anywhere and any devices as long as they have internet connections and web browsers.

Availability: Since most of mobile cloud computing services are provided by third party, they usually set a high standard quality of their applications and data availability. Besides, since all data are available on the cloud online, it can be updated in real time and at the same time other people also can access to the same data as well.

Platform support: Unlike native applications which are built specifically for single platform, cloud computing services usually built with broader support of platforms as long as they have compatible browsers.

Cons

Connectivity: Since all mobile cloud computing services are available online, the internet connectivity becomes critical. So when choosing apps or services for your personal or business use, make sure you pay attention on this aspect.

Performance: Like common online services, the performance of mobile cloud computing services is also sometimes questionable compared to native applications. So it becomes important to see the service provider's track record before you decide to use the service.

Security: Some applications which use cloud computing services often deal with sensitive personal information like credit cards, etc. So it could become a serious problem if the service providers can't provide a high level of security.

8   Conclusion

In this paper, we have proposed a three tier framework of Mobile based cloud computing. Here, we have put forward the different components of the framework along with their services. The concept of cloud computing provides a brand new opportunity for the development of mobile applications since it allows the mobile devices to maintain a very thin layer for user applications and shift the computation and processing overhead to the virtual environment. In this day to day changing technology environment, demands of the users also changes. Users demands quality service at anytime and anywhere with speed and accuracy. Hence Mobile Cloud Computing could be a possible solution up to some extent.

References

1. Research Report by ABI Research, Mobile+ Cloud+ Computing (2009),
    http://www.abiresearch.Com/1003385
2. Mell, P., Grance, T.: Draft nist working definition of cloud computing, vol. 15 (August 21, 2005) (2009)

3. O'Gara, M.: Washington itching to take the lead on cloud computing. SOA Journal (July 31, 2009)
4. IDC, Press Release: IDC Finds Cloud Computing Entering Period of Accelerating Adoption and Poised to Capture IT Spending Growth Over the Next Five Years (October 20, 2008)
5. Hamm, S.: How cloud computing will change business. Business Week (June 4, 2009)
6. Velte, T., Velte, A., Elsenpeter, R.C.: Cloud Computing: A Practical Approach. Tata McGraw-Hill Professional (2009)

The Effect of Design Patterns on Aspect Oriented Software Quality–An Empirical Evaluation

Sirbi Kotrappa[1,*] and Kulkarni Jayant Prakash[2]

[1] Department of Computer Science & Engineering,
K L E's College of Engineering & Technology, Belgaum, India
[2] Department of Computer Science & Engineering,
Walchand College of Engineering, Sangli, India
`kotrappa06@gmail.com, pjk_walchand@rediffmail.com`

Abstract. In recent times, software engineers attempted to measure software quality using various approaches and techniques such as metric suites. Aspect oriented programming (AOP) a new technology addressing issues of scattering and tangling of code spread throughout the system. Today, Aspect oriented programming (AOP) is gaining wide attention both in industry and research. OO DPs (design patterns) have difficulties in implementation of crosscutting concerns because of lack of features in OO languages and crosscutting concerns affecting software quality. In this paper, we evaluate metrics of OO Vs AO DPs for separation of concern, size, coupling and cohesion metrics from the C & K metric suite, which was modified to AOP. This empirical evaluation provides a new knowledge about AOP software quality and software developer can adopt in a specific situation. We claim that the AOP has significance effect on design quality than OOP.

Keywords: Aspect oriented programming (AOP), design patterns (DPs), software metrics, quality model.

1 Introduction

When a novel method is planned, this has to provide evidences for its supremacy over presented participants. AOP emerged as a new technology to improve software quality attributes whose implementations would otherwise have been spread throughout the whole application because of the limited abstractions of the underlying programming languages. Since then several studies [3], [6], [7], [8], [9],[10], [11], [12] have suggested that AOP is successful in improving software quality crosscutting concerns. But these studies either provide strong evidences for better software quality offered by AOP or wrongly measure metrics of AO systems. We found in some cases in which an AO implementation was better quality than its OO DPs counterpart.

---

[*] Corresponding author.

N. Meghanathan et al. (Eds.): CCSIT 2012, Part III, LNICST 86, pp. 357–366, 2012.

Many OO DPs methods have been adapted to indicate and employ DPs effectively. But several DPs that impact system quality, when core objects are especially affect by the formation that the DPs needs .AOP AspectJ[24] will help us on separating few of the system's DPs, mentioning and implementing those as a single units of abstraction. Here our objective is to show the OO Vs AO DPs implementation of observer pattern and its effect on software quality [11]. The software developer who wants to apply AOP for implementation of design patterns crosscutting concern will be benefited. Many researchers written at length on the nature of aspect oriented programming [4], [6], [7], [10],[11], [13], [14],[15],[16],[17],[18],[19],[20],[21]. AOP has evolved as a technology for combining separately created software components into working systems. It requires new assessment frameworks specifically tailored to measure the evolution, reusability, security and maintainability of aspect-oriented systems. Our results show that it is possible to use standard Object Oriented Programming (OOP) quality metrics to measure the advantages of AOP, even after adaptation [4]. But very few existing evaluations have been performed at qualitative and quantitative levels in AOP [8]. This paper presents an evaluation of effect of observer pattern OO DPs on AOP quality metrics, which is composed of three components: G-Q-M model, a suite of metrics and a quality model.

2   Measurement Process and a Quality Model

To provide comparison between OO DPs Vs AO DPs of software quality, we can apply the ISO/IEC 9126-1 quality model and Goal-Question-Metric (G-Q-M) [12]. G-Q-M defines a measurement system on three levels (Figure. 1) starting with a goal. The goal is refined in questions that break down the issue into quantifiable components. Each question is associated with metrics that, when measured, will provide information to answer the question. Our goal is to compare AOP and OOP systems with respect to software quality from the viewpoint of the software developer.

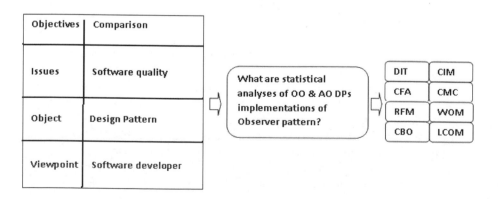

Fig. 1. G-Q-M Model

Our quality model defines a terminology and clarifies the relationships between the reusability, maintainability and the metrics suite. It is a useful tool for guiding software developers in data interpretation. The quality model has been built and refined using Basili's GQM methodology [12] (see Figure 2). The metrics are comparable because they both measure properties of concerns at the class and aspect level (see Table 1 and Figure 2).

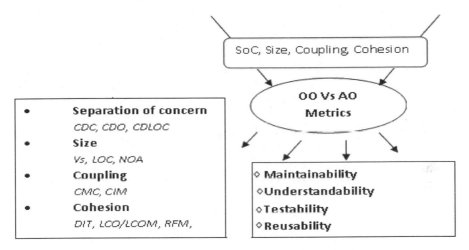

Fig. 2. Association of software quality attributes and their metrics

Table 1. Software quality metrics definitions

Metrics	Definition
RFC/ RFM	Number of methods and advices potentially executed in response to a message received by a given module
WOM/ WMC	Number of weighted operation in a given module
CBO/ CBM	Number of modules or interfaces declaring methods or fields that can be called or accessed by a given module
LCOM/ LCO	Number of pairs of operations working on different class fields minus pairs of operations working on common fields
DIT	Length of the longest path from a given module to the class/aspect hierarchy root
CIM	Number of modules or interfaces explicitly named in the pointcuts of a given aspect
CFA	Number of interfaces or modules declaring fields that are necessary by a given module
CMC	Number of modules or interfaces declaring methods that can be called by a given module

3   Empirical Evaluation

This empirical evaluation uses implementations of the 23 GoF design patterns made freely available by Hannemann & Kiczales [9], [25]. In [9] every pattern explained with an example that uses pattern, which are implemented both in OO DPs (Java) and AO DPs (AspectJ).Observer pattern, known as Model-View is indented to "define a one-to-many dependency between objects so that when one object changes state, all its dependents are notified and updated automatically".OO DPs Observer pattern implementation generally add a field to every Subjects that stores a record of Observers attracted in that exact Subject. Whenever Subject report state change to its Observers, it calls its own *notify* method, which in turn calls an *update* method on all Observers in the record. The sample OO DPs Observer patterns shown in figure 3 and AspectJ [24] AO DPs shown in figure 4 in the perspective of a trivial figure example [9]. In such a system the Observer pattern is used to cause mutating operations to figure elements to update the screen. The code spread across the all classes in this pattern. This method includes code which in important to adopt example of such pattern. Every member i.e., Point and Line has to be familiar with about their responsibility in the pattern and accordingly have pattern code in them. Addition or deletion needs corresponding changes in that particular class [9].Changing the notification mechanism requires changes in all participating classes. In the AspectJ version [9] all code pertaining to the relationship between Observers and Subjects is moved into an aspect, which changes the dependencies between the modules. Subject and Observer roles crosscut classes, and the changes of interest (the *subjectChange* pointcut) crosscuts methods in various classes. In this paper, we have decided to assess the implementation of observer design patterns in both Java and AspectJ. First, we applied the metrics   in Hannemann and Kiczales original code [9]. Afterwards, we changed their implementation to add new participant classes to play pattern roles.

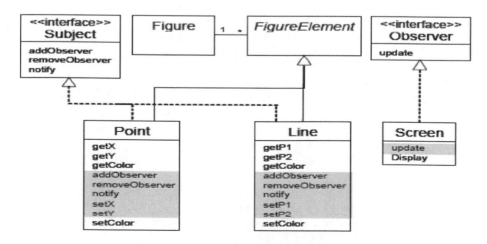

Fig. 3. Observer pattern-Java

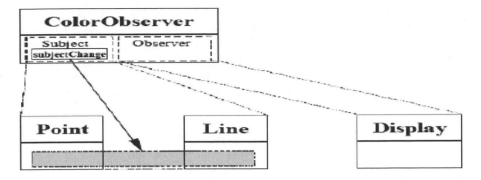

Fig. 4. Observer pattern-AspectJ

These changes were introduced because Hannemann and Kiczales' implementation encompasses few classes per role (in most cases only one) [9]. Hence we have decided to add more participant classes in order to investigate the pattern crosscutting structure. Finally, we have applied the selected metrics to the changed code. We analyzed the results after the changes, comparing with the results gathered from the original code (i.e. before the changes) [9].

4   Software Quality Assessments through OO and AO Metrics

In this paper authors have evaluated the popular C & K metrics [2] on effect of DPs on quality when we change system from OOP to AOP. For an empirical evaluation OO Vs AO metrics, we considered the simple observer patterns DPs to determine the effect of quality attributes on OO Vs AO DPs .In the evaluation of metrics authors have used the AOPMetrics tool [23] to measure the quality metrics related to separation of concern, size, coupling and cohesion. The goal of the AOPMetrics project is to provide a common metrics tool for the object-oriented and the aspect-oriented programming [24]. The project aims to provide CK metrics, Robert Martin's and Henry and Li metrics suite [23]. Table 2 gives total, mean, maximum, and minimum and standard deviation statistical values of OO DPs and AO observer pattern DPs C & K metrics.

5   Descriptive Statistics

Table 2 gives descriptive statistics of OOP and AOP C & K metrics for observer patterns. Also it compares values of total, mean, maximum, standard deviation for both OO and AO observer pattern. Here we present the measurement results for the observer design patterns; we focus on the presentation of results related to RFC, CBM, LCO and WMC from the C&K metric suite and their effects on software quality (see table 2). The relatively high value of standard deviation for CBM and LCO indicates a high variation among the values of these metrics. The results shows that smaller average for number of operations per class (WOM (WMC)), response for class (RFM (RFC)), coupling between objects (CBO (CBM)) and lack of Cohesion (LCO (LCOM)) values for AOP observer patterns. The rest of the metrics shows almost same trends. Additionally, low standard deviation for almost all of the AOP metrics make these averages more meaningful and consistent. At times, mean value of an entity may be misleading particularly when there is a very large variation among the values.

Firstly general observation is that the overall quality of OO and AO metrics values. Table 2 indicates smaller variations of standard deviation for all of AO metrics as compared to their OO version. This is because of the reason that almost all metrics values fall in line a small range with very small outliers.

Table 2. OO Vs AO Observer pattern DPs Software Quality Metrics

	RFC/ RFM		WOM/ WMC		CBO/ CBM		LCOM/ LCO		DIT		CIM/ CAE		CFA		CMC	
	OO	AO	OO	AO	OO	AO	OO	AO	OO	AO	OO	AO	OO	AO	OO	AO
Total	21	28	21	18	5	8	28	19	0	3	0	6	0	0	5	8
Average	4.2	3.1	4.2	2	1	0.9	5.6	2.1	0	0.3	0	0.6	0	0	1	0.8
Max	10	8	10	7	2	5	24	10	0	1	0	1	0	0	2	5
Min	0	0	1	0	0	0	0	0	0	0	0	0	0	0	0	0
Std.Dev	4.2	2.7	3.8	2.4	1	1.6	10	4.2	0	0.5	0	0.5	0	0	1	1.6
Quality Attributes	Understandability	Testability	Testability	Complexity	Main ability	Reusability	Main ability	Complexity	Reusability	Testability	Reusability		Reusability		Testability	Reusability

6   Results and Discussions

6.1   Results

Here we present the empirical results for the observer patterns; we focus on the presentation of results related to quality attributes metrics i.e., separation of concern, size, coupling and cohesion.

6.1.1   SoC: Separation of Concerns

The use of aspects clearly provided better support for separation of observer pattern concerns [4]. This result is supported by all separation of concern metrics. The results shows that CDC measurement identifies each observer pattern concern need many components for their implementation in the OO solution as compared to the AO solution. In addition, all concerns required more operations (methods/advices) in the OO system than in the AO system (CDO metric). Finally, the CDLOC measures also pointed out that the AO solution was more effective in terms of modularizing the observer pattern concerns across the lines of code. The resulting metrics present the gathered data *before* and *after* the changes applied to the pattern implementation. These metrics support an analysis of how the introduction of new classes and aspects affect both solutions with respect to the selected metrics. Those changes also allow us to understand which solution is better to assist the modularization quality of concerns from the application and the pattern points of view. For separation of concerns, we have verified the separation of each role of the patterns on the basis of the three separations of concerns metrics [4], [6].

6.1.2 Coupling, Cohesion and Size

These results show that for the Observer patterns, the AO DPs implementation apparently has much more associated profit. As the changes were accomplished, the AO solution exhibited superior results with respect to DIT, RFC, CBM/CBO, LCO, CIM, CFA, CMC and WMC .The differences were typically higher in favor of the aspect-oriented solution for both OO and AO observer design patterns. The aspect-oriented project produced a more concise system according the number of lines of code. However, the use of aspects produced more complex operations, i.e. advices, than the use of the OO patterns (WOC metric) [4]. The AO system incorporated components with higher coupling (CBC metric). The OO DPs has led to the abuse of the inheritance mechanism, which was fundamental for establishing high inheritance coupling (DIT metric) [4], [6]. The LCOO metric detected some components of the OO system and produced better results in terms of cohesion than the components of the AO system. In the aspect-oriented implementation of this pattern, the major improvements were detected in the LOC, LCOO and NOA measures [4]. The use of aspects led to reduction of LOC in relation to the OO code. Thus aspects solve the problem of code replication related to the implementations of the method notifyObservers().The cohesion in the AO implementation was mostly higher than the OO implementation because the latter incorporates a number of classes that play the Subject and Observer roles and, as a consequence, implement role-specific methods that in turn do not access the attributes of the classes. In the aspect-oriented design, these methods are localized in the aspects that implement the roles, increasing the cohesion of both classes and aspects. The tally of attributes in the OO implementation was respectively higher than in the AO code before and after the introduction of new components into the implementations [4]. In the OO solution, the "subject" classes need attributes to hold references to their "observer" classes; these attributes are not required in the aspect-oriented design [4].

6.2   Discussion

Based on the results, we have observed that the measures relative to quality metrics DIT, RFC, CBM/CBO, LCO, CIM, CFA, CMC and WMC.In general, the AO solutions were superior in terms of quality measures, since the use of AspectJ reduces the overuse of inheritance mechanisms. However, as illustrated in table 2, most measures indicated that AspectJ implementations resulted in higher coupling (CBC) and more lines of code (LOC) than the respective Java implementations. The superiority of AspectJ is CDO, CDC, and CDLOC metrics measures were higher than OO DPs for observer pattern. The AO DPs solutions were better-quality in terms of DIT, RFC, CBM/CBO, LCO, CIM, CFA, CMC and WMC measures. However, in many measurements point to those AspectJ implementations provides in upper coupling (CBC) and extra lines of code (LOC) than particular java implementation. However, a careful analysis of the implementation show that these higher CBC and LOC values for AO solutions in general are related to presence of generic aspects in several AspectJ pattern implementations, which have the intension of making the solution more reusable. We claim that the AOP has significance effect on design quality than OOP.

7   Related Works

As new software development method evolved, it is essential that empirical studies are carried out to provide evidences about benefits to the software developer [10],[22]. Software metrics provide quality indicators of software development. The AOSD community has been developing significant work on quantitative and qualitative analysis of AOP software [22]. Sant'Anna et al. provided one of the exceptional research works on AOP metrics: a suite of metrics for quantifying modularity-related attributes, published in a SBES paper [14], [18], [20]. This metric suite includes coupling, cohesion and size metrics custom-made from existing OO metrics to deal with AOP quality measures [22]. A set of existing metrics has been used to evaluate the quality of different AOP implementations [6], [7], [14].The metric suite also includes novel concern-driven metrics, aimed at quantifying unusual aspect of separation of concerns [22]. Concern-driven metrics endorse the notion of concern as a measurement abstraction. This kind of metric relies on the identification and documentation of the pieces of source code that implement each concern of the system. Experimental studies [14], [15], [16] measured up to the quality of Java and AspectJ solutions of the 23 design patterns from the Gang of Four [22]. One more study methodically examined how AOP degrees up to treaty with modularization of 23 design patterns in the occurrence of pattern interfaces [26]. The investigator completed both qualitative and quantitative evaluation of 62 pair-wise compositions of patterns taken from 3 medium-sized systems implemented in Java and AspectJ programming languages. Kulesza et al. [17] presented an empirical study in which they quantified the effects of AOP in the maintainability of a web-based information system. Figueiredo et al. [13] carry out an experimental study for appraise whether AOP endorse better quality and changeability of product lines than conventional variability mechanisms, such as conditional compilation [22].

8   Concluding Remarks

In this paper, we investigate AOP and DPs effect on software quality. Our evaluation is based on measurements on parameters of software quality attributes of separation of concern, size, coupling and cohesion metrics from the C&K metric suite, which was modified to AOP. An approach to re-implement OO observer pattern DPs by AOP AspectJ is presented in this paper and analyzed for its software quality factors. In this paper, we were focused on the evaluation of OO Vs AO DPs Observer Pattern and software quality. We claim that the AOP has significance effect on design quality than OOP.

Acknowledgments. We place on records and wish to thank the authors Maria Luca Bernardi, Giuseppe Antonio Di Lucca, RCOST Research centre on Software Technology, University of Sannio, Palazzo ex Poste, Benevento, Italy for their valuable contributions to research on design pattern quality using Aspect orientation.

References

1. Fernando, C., Neilo, C., Eduardo, F.: On the modularization and reuse of exception handling with aspects. Softw. Pract. Exper. 39(17), 1377–1417 (2009)
2. Shyam, R.C., Chris, F.K.: A Metrics Suite for Object Oriented Design. IEEE Trans. Softw. Eng. 20(6), 476–493 (1994)
3. Lech, M., Lukasz, S.: Impact of aspect-oriented programming on software development efficiency and design quality: an empirical study. IET Software Journal 1(5), 180–187 (2007)
4. Claudio, N.S.A., Alessandra, F.G., Uira, K.: Design patterns as aspects: a quantitative assessment. Journal of the Brazilian Computer Society 10(2) (November 2004) ISSN 0104-6500
5. Erich, G.: Design Patterns: Elements of Reusable Object-Oriented Software. Addison-Wesley, Reading (1995)
6. Adam, P.: An empirical assessment of the impact of AOP on software modularity. In: 5th International Conference on Evaluation of Novel Approaches to Software Engineering (ENASE 2010), Athens, Greece (2010)
7. Adam, P.: What is wrong with AOP? In: 5th International Conference on Software and Data Technologies (ICSOFT 2010), Athens, Greece (2010)
8. Avadhesh, K., Grover, P.S., Rajesh, K.: A quantitative evaluation of aspect-oriented software quality model AOSQUAMO. ACM SIGSOFT Software (2009); Workshop on Emerging Trends in Software Metrics, WETSoM (2010)
9. Jan, H., Gregor, K.: Design Pattern Implementation in Java and AspectJ. In: Proceedings of OOPSLA 2002, pp. 161–173 (November 2002)
10. Mariano, C., Paolo, T.: Measuring the Effects of Software Aspectization. In: 1st Workshop on Aspect Reverse Engineering, Delft, Netherlands (2004)
11. Mario, L.B., Giuseppe, A.D.L.: Improving Design Pattern Quality Using Aspect Orientation Software Technology and Engineering Practice. In: 13th IEEE International Workshop, September 24-25 (2005)

12. Victor, R.B., Gianluigi, C.H., Dieter, R.: The Goal Question Metric Approach. In: Encyclopedia of Soft. Eng., vol. 2, pp. 528–532. John Wiley & Sons, Inc. (1994)
13. Figueiredo, E., et al.: On the maintainability of aspect-oriented software: A concern-oriented measurement framework. In: CSMR, pp. 183–192 (2008)
14. Sant'Anna, C., et al.: Design Patterns as Aspects: A Quantitative Assessment. In: SBES (2004)
15. Garcia, A., et al.: Modularizing design patterns with aspects: a quantitative study. In: AOSD 2005, pp. 3–14 (2005)
16. Garcia, A., et al.: Modularizing design patterns with aspects: a quantitative study. Trans. on AOSD I, 36–74 (2006)
17. Kulesza, U., et al.: Quantifying the effects of aspect-oriented programming: A maintenance study. In: ICSM, pp. 223–233 (2006)
18. Sant'Anna, C.: On the modularity of aspect-oriented design: A concern-driven measurement approach, Ph.D. dissertation, PUC-Rio (2008)
19. Greenwood, P., Bartolomei, T., Figueiredo, E., Dosea, M., Garcia, A., Cacho, N., Sant'Anna, C., Soares, S., Borba, P., Kulesza, U., Rashid, A.: On the Impact of Aspectual Decompositions on Design Stability: An Empirical Study. In: Bateni, M. (ed.) ECOOP 2007. LNCS, vol. 4609, pp. 176–200. Springer, Heidelberg (2007)
20. Sant'Anna, C., et al.: On the modularity assessment of aspect-oriented multiagent architectures: a quantitative study. IJAOSE 2, 34–61 (2008)
21. Silva, B., et al.: Concern-based cohesion as change proneness indicator: an initial empirical study. In: ICSE WETSoM, pp. 52–58 (2011)
22. Chavez, C., Kuleszay, U., et al.: The AOSD Research Community in Brazil and its Crosscutting Impact, AOSD-BR (2011)
23. AOPMetrics Project home, http://aopmetrics.tigris.org
24. The AspectJ project, http://www.eclipse.org/aspectj
25. Jan, H.: Design Patterns, http://hannemann.pbworks.com/Design-Patterns

A Novel Statistical Fusion Rule for Image Fusion in Non Subsampled Contourlet Transform Domain

V.T. Manu[1] and Philomina Simon[2]

[1] Department of Computer Science, University of Kerala
[2] Kariavattom, Thiruvananthapuram, 695 581, Kerala, India
{manuvt.nitc,philomina.simon}@gmail.com

Abstract. Image fusion provides an efficient way to merge the visual information from different images. A new method for image fusion is proposed based on Weighted Average Merging Method (WAMM) in the Non Subsampled Contourlet Transform domain. A performance analysis on various statistical fusion rules are also analysed. Analysis has been made on medical images, remote sensing images and multi focus images. Experimental results shows that the proposed method, WAMM obtained better results in NSCT domain than the wavelet domain as it preserves more edges and keeps the visual quality intact in the fused image.

Keywords: Non Subsampled Contourlet Transform, Weighted Average Merging Method, Statistical Fusion Rule, Wavelet, Piella Metric.

1 Introduction

Image fusion produces a single fused image from a set of input images. The fused image contains complete information for better human or machine perception and computer-processing tasks, such as segmentation, feature extraction, and object recognition. Image fusion can be done in pixel level, signal level and feature based. The traditional image fusion schemes performed the fusion right on the source images, which often have serious side effects such as reducing the contrast. Later researchers realized the necessity to perform the fusion in the transform domain as mathematical transformations [10] provides further information from the signal that is not readily available in the raw signal.

With the advent of wavelet theory, the concept of wavelet multi-scale decomposition is used in image fusion [9]. The wavelet transform has been used in many image processing applications such as restoration, noise removal, image edge enhancement and feature extraction; wavelets are not very efficient in capturing the two-dimensional data found in images[5]. Several transform have been proposed for image signals that have incorporated directionality and multiresolution and hence, those methods could not efficiently capture edges in natural images. Do and Vetterli proposed contourlet transform[8], an efficient directional multi resolution image representation. The contourlet transform achieves better results than discrete wavelet

N. Meghanathan et al. (Eds.): CCSIT 2012, Part III, LNICST 86, pp. 367–376, 2012.

transform in image processing in geometric transformations. The contourlet transform is shift-variant based on sampling. However, shift invariance is a necessary condition in image processing applications.

The NSCT is a fully shift-invariant, multiscale and multidirection expansion that has a fast implementation[1]. It achieves a similar sub band decomposition as that of contourlets, but without downsamplers and upsamplers in it, thus overcoming the problem of shift variance[2].

2   Non Subsampled Contourlet Transform

The Non Subsampled Contourlet Transform (NSCT) is constructed by combining the Non subsampled Pyramids (NSP) and the Non subsampled Directional Filter Banks (NSDFB)[1]. The former provide multiscale decomposition and the later provide directional decomposition[3]. A Non subsampled Pyramid split the input into a low-pass subband and a high-pass subbands. Then a Non subsampled Directional Filter Banks decomposes the high-pass subband into several directional subbands. The scheme is iterated repeatedly on the low-pass subband [11].

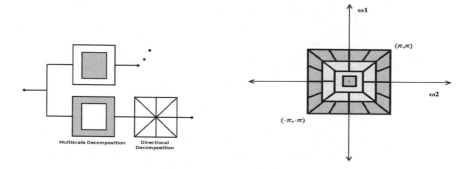

Fig. 1. Block Diagram of NSCT   **Fig. 2.** Block Diagram of Frequency division

3   Image Fusion Scheme and Statistical Fusion Rules

Image fusion scheme in two source images can be considered as a step by step process. First, the source images are divided into coarse scales and fine scales. Coarse scales represent the high frequency components and fine scales represent low frequency components in the source images. Low frequency components contain overall details of the image while the high frequency components contain details about edges and textures. Then, the coefficients of the source images are decomposed. Second, the coarse scales and the fine scales in the source images are separately fused based on statistical fusion rule using NSCT [4][5][6][7]. Separate fusion rules are applied on these fine scales and coarse scales to obtain the fusion coefficients. The fused image is obtained by inverse NSCT from these fusion coefficients.

In this section, two different statistical fusion rules are discussed. These rules are analyzed experimentally thereby examining the performance of the image fusion in both wavelet and NSCT domain.

3.1   Method 1- Fusion Based on Mean

Mean is the representative value of a large dataset that describes the center or middle value. Mean is the measure of the group contributions per contributor which is conceived to be the same as the amount contributed by each n contributor if each were to contribute equal amounts.

$$\bar{x} = \frac{1}{n}\sum_{i=1}^{n} x_i$$

(1)

Mean is calculated on the low frequency components of the input images within a 3-by-3 window and whichever having higher values of mean were selected as the fusion coefficients among the low frequency components. For the high frequency components, regional energy is calculated over a 5-by-5 window using the formula

$$E_k(i, j) = \sum_{m=-2}^{2}\sum_{n=-2}^{2}\sum_{s=-2}^{S}\sum_{d=-2}^{D} W(m+3, n+3) \bullet (C_K^{\{s,d\}}(i+m, j+n))^2$$

(2)

where $C_K^{\{s,d\}}$ is the NSCT coefficient corresponding to scale s and direction d at position (i,j) for the image k.

W is a filter that gives more weightage to the central coefficient and is defined as

$$W = \frac{1}{256}\begin{bmatrix} 4 & 4 & 4 & 4 & 4 \\ 4 & 16 & 16 & 16 & 4 \\ 4 & 16 & 64 & 16 & 4 \\ 4 & 16 & 16 & 16 & 4 \\ 4 & 4 & 4 & 4 & 4 \end{bmatrix}$$

(3)

Then the coefficient is chosen as the fuse coefficient when the region energy of it is larger shown as formula

$$C_F^{\{s,d\}}(i, j) = \begin{cases} C_A^{\{s,d\}}(i, j), & E_A(i, j) \geq E_B(i, j); \\ C_B^{\{s,d\}}(i, j), & otherwise; \end{cases}$$

(4)

Finally the fused image is reconstructed using the fused coefficients, $C_F^{\{s,d\}}$ using the inverse NSCT transform.

3.2   Method 2-Fusion Based on Standard Deviation

Standard Deviation provides a way to determine regions which are clear and vague. It is calculated by the formula

$$s = \sqrt{\frac{1}{n}\sum_{i=1}^{n}(x_i - \tilde{x})^2}$$

(5)

where

$$\tilde{x} = \frac{1}{n}\sum_{i=1}^{n}x_i$$

(6)

Standard Deviation is calculated on the low frequency components of the input images within a 3-by-3 window and whichever having higher values of mean were selected as the fusion coefficients among the low frequency components.

For the high frequency components, regional energy is calculated over a 5-by-5 window using the formula (2) with the help of the window defined in formula (3). Then the coefficient is chosen as the fuse coefficient when the region energy of it is larger, as in formula (4).

Finally the fused image is reconstructed using the fused coefficients, using the inverse NSCT transform.

4   Image Fusion Based on Weighted Average Merging Method (WAMM) – Proposed Approach

In this section, we discuss the fusion based on WAMM in NSCT Domain. WAMM is used in the high frequency components to obtain the fusion coefficient whereas Standard Deviation is calculated on the low frequency components of the input images within a 3-by-3 window. An average of the low frequency components is calculated. Whichever obtains the higher values of average are selected as the fusion coefficients among the low frequency components.

The main features of this new method are that it preserves the image quality and the edge details of the fused image. The visual quality of the fused image is better in NSCT domain.

The Weighted Average Merging Method (WAMM) is formulated as

$$\begin{cases} C_F^{\{s,d\}}(i,j) = w_{max}C_A^{\{s,d\}}(i,j) + w_{min}C_B^{\{s,d\}}(i,j), & E_A(i,j) \geq E_B(i,j); \\ C_F^{\{s,d\}}(i,j) = w_{min}C_A^{\{s,d\}}(i,j) + w_{max}C_B^{\{s,d\}}(i,j), & E_A(i,j) < E_B(i,j); \end{cases}$$

(7)

The weights are estimated as:

$$\begin{cases} W_{min} = 0, W_{max} = 1, & M_{AB}(p) < T; \\ W_{min} = \frac{1}{2} - \frac{1}{2}\left(\frac{1-M_{AB}}{1-T}\right), W_{max} = 1 - W_{min}, & other \end{cases}$$

(8)

where T denote the threshold and $T \in (0, 0.5)$. $M_{AB}(p)$ is the Match Measure which is defined as

$$M_{AB}(p) = \frac{2 \sum_{s \in S, t \in T} w(s,t) C_A^{\{s,d\}}(m+s,n+t) C_B^{\{s,d\}}(m+s,n+t)}{E_A(p) + E_B(p)} \tag{9}$$

Figure 3 represents the steps followed in the Weighted Average Merging Method (WAMM) method.

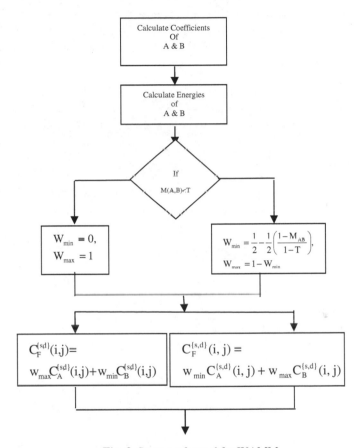

Fig. 3. Steps performed for WAMM

4.1   Performance Measures

The performance of image fusion is analysed and evaluated using Entropy, Similarity and Piella Metric.

Entropy

$$H(S) = -\sum P(X) \log P(X) \tag{10}$$

Similarity

The magnitude of gradient G (m, n) at a point (m, n) of image F is obtained by

$$G(m, n) = \frac{1}{2}\{|F(m,n) - F(m+1, n+1)| + |F(m,n) - F(m+1, n)|\} \quad (11)$$

where G_1, G_2 are the gradient images of input images. Then G_1, G_2 are combined into G'' by taking the maximum gradient value at each position. And G'' can be seen as the gradient image of the ideal fusion image. The gradients of the actual fusion image G are also calculated. The similarity S between the ideal fusion image and the actual fused image is calculated by formula

$$S(G, G') = 1 - \frac{\sqrt{\sum (G(m,n) - G'(m,n))^2}}{\sqrt{\sum (G(m,n))^2} + \sqrt{\sum (G'(m,n))^2}} \quad (12)$$

Piella Metric(PM)

Piella Metric [12] of the fused image f of the input images a and b is defined as

$$Q_E(a,b,f) = Q_W(a,b,f) \cdot Q_W(a',b',f')^t \quad (13)$$

where a', b', f' are the edge images of a, b and f respectively. $Q_W(a,b,f)$ is the *weighted fusion quality index* [13]and is defined as

$$Q_W(a,b,f) = \sum_{w \in W} c(w)(\lambda(w)Q_0(a, f|w) + (1 - \lambda(w))Q_0(b, f|w)) \quad (14)$$

where $\lambda(w)$ is a local weight given by

$$\lambda(w) = \frac{s(a|w)}{s(a|w) + s(b|w)} \quad (15)$$

where $s(a|w)$ is some saliency of image a in window w. The overall saliency of a window is defined as

$$C(w) = \max (s(a|w), s(b|w)) \quad (16)$$

$$c(w) = \frac{C(w)}{\left(\sum_{w' \in I \,w} C(w')\right)} \quad (17)$$

5   Results and Discussion

Image Fusion techniques requires the registered images for testing. Image Registration [14] is the determination of a geometrical transformation that aligns points in one view of an object with corresponding points in another view of that object or another object. The experiments are carried out with the registered images. We have analyzed the various statistical rules and the proposed statistical fusion rule (WAMM) discussed above in both wavelet domain and NSCT domain on medical images, remote sensing images and multi focus images.

5.1   Analysis in Medical Images

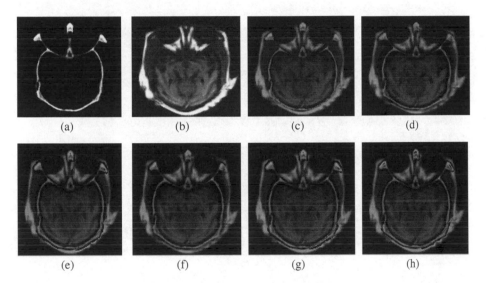

Fig. 4. (a)CT image (b)MR image (c) Wavelet fused image using Method 1(d) NSCT fused image using Method 1(e) Wavelet fused image using Method 2(f) NSCT fused image using Method 2(g) Wavelet fused image using WAMM (g) NSCT fused image using WAMM

Here EN1 and EN2 represent the entropy of the original images to be fused in wavelet and NSCT domain respectively. In the fused image with WAMM in NSCT domain performs better than WAMM in wavelet and it preserves more information content in the fused image. In the above table, it is clearly seen that the fusion with SD, Similarity and PM gives better results.

Here EN1 and EN2 represent the entropy of the original images to be fused in wavelet and NSCT domain respectively. In the fused image with, WAMM performs better than in NSCT than wavelet domain and it preserves more details in the fused image. The artifacts and inconsistencies in wavelet domain is removed in NSCT domain using WAMM method. In the above table, it is seen that the fusion with SD, Similarity and PM gives better results.

Table 1. Performance measures obtained for Medical Image Fusion using different methods

	Domain	EN1	EN2	EN3	S	PM
Method 1 (Mean)	Wavelet	1.7126	5.6561	5.8754	0.5497	0.6782
	NSCT	1.7126	5.6561	5.9090	0.5743	0.7547
Method 2 (standard deviation)	Wavelet	1.7126	5.6561	5.8615	0.4877	0.6174
	NSCT	1.7126	5.6561	5.9090	0.5618	0.6383
WAMM	Wavelet	1.7126	5.6561	5.8595	0.4882	0.6225
	NSCT	1.7126	5.6561	5.9090	0.5625	0.6373

5.2   Fusion in Multi-focus Images

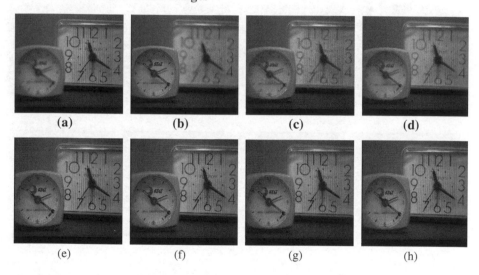

(a)   (b)   (c)   (d)

(e)   (f)   (g)   (h)

Fig. 5. (a)Focus on right clock (b)Focus on left clock (c) Wavelet fused image using Method 1(d) NSCT fused image using Method 1(e) Wavelet fused image using Method 2(f) NSCT fused image using Method 2(g) Wavelet fused image using WAMM (g) NSCT fused image using WAMM

Table 2. Performance measures obtained for Multi-focus image fusion using different methods

	Domain	EN1	EN2	EN3	S	PM
Method 1	Wavelet	6.9803	6.9242	6.9925	0.5039	0.4286
	NSCT	6.9803	6.9242	7.0429	0.6111	0.5258
Method 2	Wavelet	6.9803	6.9242	6.9960	0.5983	0.5508
	NSCT	6.9803	6.9242	7.0386	0.6349	0.5614
WAMM	Wavelet	6.9803	6.9242	6.9980	0.5970	0.5513
	NSCT	6.9803	6.9242	7.0421	0.6379	0.5640

5.3   Fusion in Remote Sensing Images

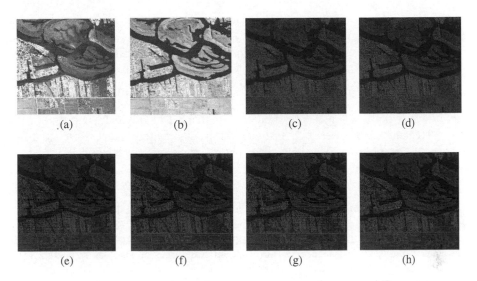

Fig. 6. (a)- (b) Remote sensing images: two bands of a multispectral scanner c) Wavelet fused image using Method 1(d) NSCT fused image using Method 1(e) Wavelet fused image using Method 2(f) NSCT fused image using Method 2(g) Wavelet fused image using WAMM (g) NSCT fused image using WAMM

Table 3. Performance measures obtained for Remote Sensing image fusion using different methods

	Domain	EN1	EN2	EN3	S	PM
Method 1	Wavelet	5.4448	5.4542	5.7905	0.6260	0.4799
	NSCT	5.4448	5.4542	5.8747	0.6947	0.4977
Method 2	Wavelet	5.4448	5.4542	5.8402	0.6168	0.3910
	NSCT	5.4448	5.4542	5.8725	0.6909	0.4074
WAMM	Wavelet	5.4448	5.4542	5.8472	0.6220	0.3963
	NSCT	5.4448	5.4542	5.8879	0.6884	0.4127

Here EN1 and EN2 represent the entropy of the original images to be fused in wavelet and NSCT domain respectively. In the fused image with, WAMM performs better than in NSCT than wavelet domain and it preserves more edges in the fused image. The edges are clearly visible in NSCT domain than wavelet. In the above table, it is seen that the fusion with SD, Similarity and PM gives better results

6   Conclusion

A new statistical fusion rule, WAMM is proposed in NSCT domain is proposed. Experimental results shows that WAMM method for image fusion when tested with performance measures, SD, Similarity and Piella Metric obtained better results in NSCT domain as it preserves the edge details and the visual quality of the fused image. The analysis obtained shows that the proposed WAMM yields better results in NSCT domain.

Acknowledgment. All authors would like to thank Dr. Oliver Rockinger and the TNO Human Factors Research Institute for providing the source IR and visible images that are publicly available online at http://www.imagefusion.org.

References

[1] Cunha, A.L., Zhou, J., Do, M.N.: The Nonsubsampled Contourlet Transform: Theory, Design and Applications. IEEE Trans. Image Processing 15(10), 3089–3101 (2006)

[2] Zhou, J., da Cunha, A.L., Do, M.N.: Nonsubsampled contourlet transform: Construction and Application in Enhancement. In: Proc. of IEEE International Conference on Image Processing (September 2005)

[3] Zhou, J., da Cunha, A.L., Do, M.N.: Nonsubsampled contourlet transform: Filter design and application in image denoising. In: Proc. of IEEE International Conference on Image Processing (September 2005)

[4] Yang, B., Li, S., Sun, F.: Image Fusion Using Nonsubsampled Contourlet Transform. In: IEEE International Conference on Image and Graphics (2007)

[5] Ma, H., Jia, C., Liu, S.: Multisource Image Fusion Based on Wavelet Transform. International Journal of Information Technology 11(7) (2005)

[6] Tang, L., Zhao, F., Zhao, Z.-G.: The Nonsubsampled contourlet transform for image fusion. In: Proc. of the International Conference on Wavelet Analysis and Pattern Recognition (November 2007)

[7] Fu, Q., Ren, F., Chen, L.: Multi-focus Image "Fusion Algorithm Based on Nonsubsampled Contourlet Transform". In: Proc. of IEEE International Conference on Image Processing (2010)

[8] Do, M.N., Vetterli, M.: The contourlet transform: an efficient directional amultiresolution image representation. IEEE Transactions on Image Processing (2005)

[9] Shensa, M.J.: The discrete wavelet transform: Wedding the trous and Mallat algorithms. IEEE Trans. Signal Process. 40(10), 2464–2482 (1992)

[10] Gonzalez, R., Woods, R.: Digital Image Processing, 3rd edn. Prentice-Hall (2009)

[11] Bamberger, R.H., Smith, M.J.T.: A Filter bank for the directional decomposition of images: Theory and design. IEEE Trans. Signal Process. 40(4), 882–893 (1992)

[12] Piella, G., Heijmans, H.: A new quality metric for image fusion. In: Proc. Int. Conf. Image Processing, Barcelona, Spain, pp. 173–176 (2003); World Academy of Science, Engineering and Technology 7 (2005)

[13] Wang, Z., Bovik, A.C.: A universal image quality index. IEEE Signal Processing Letters 9(3), 81–84 (2002)

[14] Zitová, B., Flusser, J.: Image registration methods: a survey. Image and Vision Computing 21, 977–1000 (2003)

Maximizing Lifetime of Wireless Sensor Network through Extended LEACH Algorithm

Indrajit Bhattacharya[1], Saurav Ghosh[2], and Suparna Kundu[3]

[1] Kalyani Govt. Engineering College, Kalyani, Nadia-741235
indra51276@gmail.com
[2] A.K.C.S.I.T., University of Calcutta, Kolkata, India
sgcompu@caluniv.ac.in
[3] A.K.C.S.I.T., University of Calcutta, Kolkata, India
suparnakundu22@gmail.com

Abstract. Wireless Sensor Networks (WSNs) represent a new generation of real-time embedded systems that can be applied to ample of real life applications. LEACH is one of the most popular clustering mechanism in WSN; it elects a cluster head (CH) based on a probability model and rotates the cluster heads periodically to preserve maximum network coverage and lifetime. In our work we extend the LEACH's cluster head selection algorithm in WSN based on different node characteristics like, density, centrality and energy. This paper focuses on increasing the lifetime of wireless sensor networks. Appropriate cluster head selection strategy can enhance the lifetime of the network. In our work we have modified the probability calculation formula for selecting the cluster heads in each round based on three parameters of a node: density, centrality and remaining energy in the network. Simulation results demonstrate that extension of LEACH algorithm can enlarge the lifetime of the Wireless Sensor Network.

Keywords: Wireless Sensor Network, Cluster-head probability, LEACH, lifetime, Last Node Dies (LND).

1   Introduction

A Wireless Sensor Network (WSN) is a wireless network consisting of spatially distributed autonomous devices that use sensors to monitor physical or environmental conditions. In general, the Wireless Sensor Networks [7] consists of a large number of small and cheap sensor nodes with limitations, like their energy resources, dispersed in a region. Sensor networks are the key to gathering the information needed by smart environments [11, 12]. Since a WSN is composed of nodes with non-replenish able energy resources, elongating the network lifetime is the main concern.

For the reason of saving energy, a WSN is broken down into several clusters to reduce communication overhead, and then save energy [8] consumption. A WSN consists of a number of sensor nodes and a sink. Close nodes group themselves into local clusters with one node acting as cluster-head (CH). The cluster-head [4] is responsible

N. Meghanathan et al. (Eds.): CCSIT 2012, Part III, LNICST 86, pp. 377–386, 2012.

for not only the general request but also receiving the sensed data of other sensor nodes in the same cluster and routing these data to the sink. Therefore, the energy consumption of the CH is higher than the other sensor nodes. A CH is responsible for not only the general request but also assisting the general nodes to route the sensed data to the target nodes. Therefore the CH selection will affect the lifetime of a WSN. The main problem is that energy consumption is concentrated on the cluster heads. In order to overcome this demerit, the issue in cluster routing of how to distribute the energy consumption must be solved. The representative solution is LEACH, which is a localized clustering method based on a probability model. In this paper, a modified method based on LEACH is proposed.

2   Related Work

In this section we briefly review the related works.

2.1   LEACH

LEACH, a communication protocol for micro sensor network [1], uses the following clustering-model: Some of the nodes elect themselves as cluster-heads. These cluster-heads collect sensor data from other nodes in the vicinity and transfer the aggregated data to the base station. Since data transfers to the base station dissipate much energy, the nodes take turns with the transmission – the cluster-heads "rotate". This rotation of cluster-heads leads to a balanced energy consumption of all nodes and hence to a longer lifetime of the network. The main idea of LEACH [10] protocol is that all nodes are chosen to be the cluster heads periodically, and each period contains two stages with construction of clusters as the first stage and data communication as the second stage. Each of these rounds consists of a set-up and a steady-state phase. During the set-up phase cluster-heads are determined and the clusters are organized. During the steady-state phase data transfers to the Base Station (BS) [9] occur.

Each node is selected to be the cluster heads according to the probability of optimal cluster heads decided by the networks. In each round, every node gets a random number between 0 and 1. If the number is less than the threshold values-T(n), the node becomes a CH for the current round [3]. T(n) is shown below:

$$T(n) = \frac{P}{1 - P\left(r \bmod \frac{1}{P}\right)} \qquad \text{if } n \in G$$

$$T(n) = 0 \qquad \qquad \text{otherwise} \qquad (1)$$

Where, P is the cluster-head probability, r the number of the current round and G the set of nodes that have not been cluster-heads in the last 1/P rounds. Thus, after (1/P - 1) rounds, $T(n) = 1$ for all nodes that have not been a cluster-head. This algorithm ensures that every node becomes a cluster-head exactly once within 1/P rounds.

The radio model used is similar to[1] with $E_{elec} = 50$ nJ/bit as the energy dissipated by the radio to run the transmitter or receiver circuitry and $\varepsilon_{amp} = 100$ pJ/bit/m^2 as the energy dissipation of the transmission amplifier. The energy expended during transmission and reception for a k-bit message to a distance d between transmitter and receiver node is given by:

$$E_{T_x}(k, d) = E_{elec} * k + \varepsilon_{amp} * k * d^{\lambda} \tag{2}$$

$$E_{R_x}(k) = E_{elec} * k \tag{3}$$

Where, λ is the path loss exponent and $\lambda \geq 2$.

2.2   Modified LEACH Algorithm

Handy et al. [2] proposed an algorithm for reducing the power consumption of the wireless sensor network. The stochastic method of selecting cluster-heads in the LEACH approach was extended by adding a deterministic component. They propose to make it energy efficient by multiplying the factor $\frac{E_{n\_current}}{E_{n\_max}}$ in Eq. (4).Where, $E_{n\_current}$ is the current energy and E_{n_max} is the initialenergy of the node. Hence the new threshold is:

$$T(n) = \frac{P}{1 - P\left(r \bmod \frac{1}{P}\right)} \frac{E_{n\_current}}{E_{n\_max}} \qquad \text{if } n \in G$$

$$T(n) = 0 \qquad\qquad\qquad\qquad\qquad otherwise \tag{4}$$

Their simulations show that such a modification of the cluster-head threshold can increase the lifetime of a LEACH micro sensor network by 30 % for First Node Dies (FND) and more than 20 % for Half Node Alive (HNA).

2.3   LEACH-FL System Model

Ge Ranet al. [5] proposed an algorithm which improves LEACH protocol using Fuzzy Logic. This algorithm takes battery level, distance and node density into consideration. The LEACH-FL system has three parts, four fuzzification functions, an inference engine (conclude 27 rules) and a defuzzification module. The form of the rules is: IF A and B and C THEN D. A, B, C and D represent battery level, node density, distance and probability respectively. The rules are based on the following formula.

$$Probability = batterylevel * 2 + nodedensity + (2 - distance) \tag{5}$$

After aggregating the conclusions obtained by each rule, a defuzzification method is still needed to get the crisp value. They compared LEACH-FL with LEACH and Gupta's method.

Indranil Gupta et al. [3] proposed a new approach for cluster-head election for WSNs. In this paper the cluster-heads are elected by the base station in each round by calculating the chance. Each node has to become the cluster-head by considering three fuzzy descriptors – node concentration, energy level in each node and its centrality with respect to the entire cluster.

3   Proposed Extended LEACH Algorithm

Increasing network lifetime, scalability and load balancing are important factors for Wireless Sensor Networks. Here a new method of clustering algorithm is proposed which prolongs network lifetime by using energy, density and centrality factors [6]. Simulation results demonstrate that using the proposed method offers significant improvement in clustering especially in network lifetime in comparison with the LEACH and Modified Leach methods.

In this proposed algorithm all network nodes are divided into clusters. There are three important factors [6] in the proposed algorithm. Weights can be given to them or use fuzzy logic to count their average amount. These factors are:

1. Density: The density factor of every node reveals the number of nodes around that node such that their distances are less than a threshold Distance. It'll be very good if we choose cluster heads from nodes that have the greatest density factors.
2. Centrality: Sometimes a node has a good density factor meaning that there are lots of near nodes around it but they are all on one side of that node. It is desirable to choose cluster heads from those nodes at the center of their neighbors.
3. Energy: Cluster Heads should be chosen from those nodes with enough remaining energy.

3.1   How Algorithm Works

Setup Phase.

Phase 1
In this phase all nodes should calculate their densities. Each node is aware of its coordinates. After some rounds, some nodes will die and consequently node densities will change. For calculating densities, all nodes send their id and geographical coordinates to other nodes around by broadcasting locally. It is clear that local broadcast doesn't need so much energy. Nodes can broadcast their messages according to geographical coordinates in different time slices to avoid overhead problem. Then they compute density factor (de). Each node can compute its distance from other nodes by knowing its own coordinates and that of the sender node. If the computed distance is less than a range the node increases its density field. At the end of this phase all nodes would know their densities.

Algorithm to calculate the density factor (de):

Step 1: [Initialize] NOOFNODES= NULL.
Step 2: Initialize the no of nodes, N.
Step 3: Initialize the area with in which the Base Station computes
the density for each node, RANGE.
Step 4: Repeat steps (5), (6) and (7) for i= 1 to N.
Step 5: Repeat steps (6) and (7) for j= 1 to N.
Step 6: Calculate distance between two nodes.
DISTANCE = sqrt ((S(i).xd - S(j).xd)^2 + (S(i).yd -S(j).yd)^2);
Step 7: If DISTANCE < RANGE
NOOFNODES = NOOFNODES+1.
[End of If structure]
[End of Step (5) inner loop.]
[End of Step (4) outer loop.]
Step 8: End.

Phase 2
In this phase if the density of node is more than a threshold amount and also if it isn't
a border node, it computes its centrality factor (ce). On the assumption that n is the
number of network nodes and by using the following algorithm the centrality factor
can be computed. Proposed algorithm for computing centrality factor (centrality
algorithm):

Algorithm to calculate the centrality factor (ce) :

Step 1: Initialize the no of nodes, N.
Step 2: Initialize the initialize the area with in which the Base Station
computes the centrality for each node, RANGE.
Step 3: Repeat steps (4), (5), (6) and (7) for i= 1 to N.
Step 4: [Initialize] COUNTLEFT= NULL and
COUNTRIGHT= NULL.
Step 5: Repeat steps (6) and (7) for j= 1 to N.
Step 6: Calculate distance between two nodes.
DISTANCE = sqrt ((S(i).xd - S(j).xd)^2 + (S(i).yd - S(j).yd)^2);
Step 7: if((S(j).xd>=S(i).xd) && (S(j).xd<=S(i).xd+20))
COUNTRIGHT = COUNTRIGHT+1
if((S(j).xd>=S(i).xd-20) && (S(j).xd<=S(i).xd))
COUNTLEFT = COUNTLEFT+1
[End of If structure]
[End of Step (5) inner loop.]
[End of Step (3) outer loop.]
Step 8: S(i).ce=abs(COUNTLEFT- COUNTRIGHT)
Step 9: End.

Phase 3
Now all nodes are aware about their density factors (de), centrality factors (ce) and their energy or remaining energy. In this phase each node calculate their cluster head probability factor using the equation (6)

$$P_{new} = a * de + b * \left(\frac{1}{ce}\right) + c * de \qquad (6)$$

Where, P_{new} is the cluster head probability factor, de is the density factor, ce is the centrality factor and e is the remaining energy of each node. a, b and c are coefficients for giving weights to density factor, centrality factors and energy respectively.

Phase 4
Now, each node knows its probability factor and then calculates threshold value using their cluster head probability factor (Equation (6)). In order to select cluster-heads each node n determines a random number between 0 and 1. If the number is less than a threshold $T_{new}(n)$ the node becomes a cluster-head for the current round. So, the new threshold equation is:

$$T_{new}(n) = \frac{P_{new}}{1 - P_{new}\left(r mod \frac{1}{P_{new}}\right)} \frac{E_{ncurrent}}{E_{nmax}} if n \in G$$

$$T_{new}(n) = 0 \qquad\qquad otherwise \qquad (7)$$

Steady State Phase
In the steady state phase the cluster-heads collect the aggregated data and performs signal processing functions to compress the data into a single signal similar to the steady state phase of LEACH. This composite signal is then sent to the base station.

4   Simulation Result

To test and analyze the algorithm, experimental studies were performed. To compare LEACH, Modified LEACH and Extended LEACH (Proposed) Algorithms, algorithms were simulated and executed in the MATLAB environment. Here energy consumption in WSN is modeled as given in Equations (2, 3). To define the lifetime of the sensor network we used the metric HNA (Half Node Alive) and LND (Last Node Dies). We also use the metric Total no of Node dies at a given round to test for the lifetime of the WSN.

The reference network consists of 100 nodes randomly distributed over an area of 100X100 meters. The Base Station is located at the coordinate 50, 50. The radio model is shown in Table 1. Now three algorithms LEACH, Modified LEACH and Extended LEACH (proposed) algorithm are compared in this network.

Table 1. Radio Model

OPERATION	ENERGY DISSIPATED
Initial Energy	0.02 J
Transmitter Electronics	E_{elec}=50 nJ/bit
Receiver Electronics	E_{elec}=50 nJ/bit
Transmit Amplifier	100 pJ/bit/m^2

Figure 1, shows the density calculation for the network with a random distribution of nodes. Figure 2, shows the centrality calculation for the network with a random distribution of nodes. From Fig.2 it can be observed that many of the nodes have 0 centrality factors. That means those node are in the central position with in a given range.

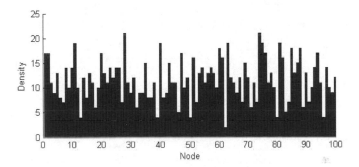

Fig. 1. Calculation of Density for the network cluster

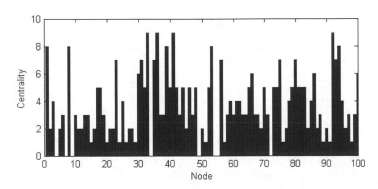

Fig. 2. Calculation of centrality for the network cluster

Simulation shows that modification of the threshold equation can increase the lifetime of a LEACH micro sensor network. In case of LEACH and Modified LEACH probability is chosen as 0.1. But in the proposed algorithm probability factor of cluster head election is depend on three factors. These are Density factor, Centrality factor and node's remaining energy. On the basis of these factors it can be shown that lifetime of the micro sensor network has been increased using our proposed algorithm.

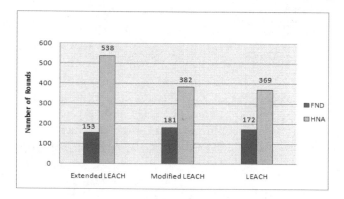

Fig. 3. Simulation Result (FND, HNA) of the Sample Network for 1000 Rounds

Figure 3, 4 and 5 illustrates simulation results of the sample network. In Fig. 3 FND means First Node Dies and HNA means Half Node Alive. The proposed algorithm is compared with the original LEACH and Modified LEACH. From the Figure 3 it can be shown that Proposed Algorithm gives the better result in terms of maximizing network lifetime.

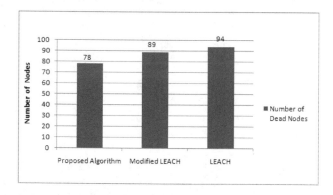

Fig. 4. Simulation Result (No. of Dead Nodes) of the Sample Network for 1000Rounds

Figure 4 shows the total number of node dies after 1000 rounds. In case of LEACH Algorithm total number of node dies after 1000 rounds are 94 and of Modified LEACH the number of node dies is 89. Extended LEACH shows that after 1000 rounds number of node dies are 78. Fig.5 shows the network life time of three algorithms. From figure 5 it can be shown that Extended LEACH Algorithm gives the better network life time of the sensor network in compare to other two algorithms.

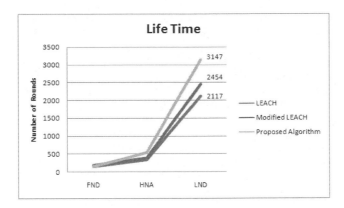

Fig. 5. Network Life time Comparison between LEACH, Modified LEACH and Proposed Algorithm, LND – Last Node Dies

5   Conclusion

In WSN Cluster Head selection is an important issue that must be considered. Objective of this work is to design a routing protocol based on LEACH which increase the network lifetime of the Wireless Sensor Network. This paper discussed a modification of LEACH's probability factor. With this modification increase of lifetime of micro sensor networks can be accomplished. The node themselves calculate their probability factor to become cluster head and using their probability factor, the threshold value is calculated. Though our proposed algorithm performs better than the LEACH algorithm, a considerable computational overhead in the network may occur due to calculation of the probability factor of each node in the network.

References

1. Heinzelman, W., Chandrakasan, A., Balakrishnan, H.: Energy-efficient communication protocol for wireless microsensor networks. In: Proceedings of the 33rd International Conference on System Sciences, HICSS 2000 (January 2000)
2. Handy, M.J., Haase, M., Timmermann, D.: Low energy adaptive clustering hierarchy with deterministic cluster-head selection. In: Proc. 4th International Workshop on Mobile and Wireless Communications Network, pp. 368–372 (September 2002)
3. Indranil Gupta, Denis Riordan and SrinivasSampalli , "Cluster-head Election using Fuzzy Logic for Wireless Sensor networks," in Third Annual Conference on Communication Networks and Services Research (CNSR2005), 2005.
4. Zhu, X., Shen, L.: Near Optimal Cluster-Head Selection For Wireless Sensor Networks. Journal of Electronics (China) 24(6) (November 2007)
5. Ran, G., Zhang, H., Gong, S.: Improving on LEACH Protocol of Wireless Sensor Networks Using Fuzzy Logic. Journal of Information & Computational Science, 767–775 (October 2010)

6. Mehrani, M., Shanbehzadeh, J., Sarrafzadeh, A.: Fault Tolerant, Energy Efficient, Distributed Clustering for WSN. Global Journal of Computer Science and Technology (February 2011)
7. Akyildiz, Su, W., Sankarasubramaniam, Y., Cayirci, E.: A survey on sensor networks. IEEE Communications Magazine 40(8), 102–114 (2002)
8. Zhang, J., Zhao, E., Zhang, Q.: Energy-Balanced Solution for Cluster-Based WirelessSensor Networks with Mixed Communication Modes. In: International Workshop Cross Layer Design, pp. 29–32. IEEE Press, New York (2007)
9. Lindsey, S., Raghavendra, C.: PEGASIS: Power-Efficient Gathering in Sensor Information Systems. In: IEEE Aerospace Conference Proceedings, vol. 3, pp. 1125–1130 (2002)
10. Ibriq, J., Mahgoub, I.: Cluster Based Routing in Wireless sensor Networks: Issues and Challenges. In: Proceedings of the 2004 Symposium on Performance Evaluation of Computer Telecommuincations System (July 2004)
11. Shen, C., Srisathapornphat, C., Jaikaeo, C.: Sensor Information Networking Architecture andapplications. IEEE Personal Communications, 52–59 (August 2001)
12. Hammadi, S., Tahon, C.: Special issue on intelligenttechniques in flexible manufacturing systems. IEEETransactions on Systems, Man and Cybernetics, 157–158 (May 2003)

Intersection Area Based Geocasting Protocol (IBGP) for Vehicular Ad Hoc Networks

Sanjoy Das and D.K. lobiyal

School of Computer and Systems Sciences
Jawaharlal Nehru University, New Delhi-India
{sdas.jnu,lobiyal}@gmail.com

Abstract. Geocasting is a special variant of multicasting, where data packet or message is transmitted to a predefined geographical location i.e., known as geocast region. The applications of geocasting in VANET are to disseminate information like, collision warning, advertising, alerts message, etc. In this paper, we have proposed a model for highway scenario where the highway is divided into number of cells. The intersection area between two successive cells is computed to find the number of common nodes. Therefore, probabilistic analysis of the nodes present and void occurrence in the intersection area is carried out. Further, different forwarding zones are used for data delivery. Number of nodes present and void occurrence in the different forwarding zones have also been analysed to determine the successful delivery of data. Our analytical results show that in a densely populated network, data can be transmitted with low radio transmission range. It also shows that selection of forwarding areas depends on the node density in the network.

Keywords: VANET, Geocast, Forwarding area, Intersection Area, Void.

1 Introduction

VANET is a special class of Mobile Ad hoc Network (MANET).A Mobile Ad hoc network is a dynamically reconfigurable wireless network with no fixed infrastructure. Every node in this network behaves like a router to relay a message from one node to another. In MANET; nodes are laptops, PDAs, palmtops, and other mobile devices whereas in VANET [1] nodes are vehicles. In addition, the other characteristics which differentiate VANET from MANET are mobility of nodes; structure of the geographical areas, delay constraint, privacy, etc. The node movement depends on the structure of road or structure of city or terrain etc. While delivering message from source to destination node, if destination node is not within the transmission range of source node then the source node send the message to the destination node with the help of intermediate nodes. The ad hoc network is multi-hop in nature and message delivery depends on the connectivity among the intermediate nodes. The message delivery from one location to another location is done with the help of intermediate nodes. The aim of Geocast routing

N. Meghanathan et al. (Eds.): CCSIT 2012, Part III, LNICST 86, pp. 387–396, 2012.

protocols is to deliver a message from one location (i.e. sender) to a predefined location known as Geocast region with optimal number of node and time period. It is desirable that protocols should maintain the low end-to-end delay and high success ratio in delivering message.

The rest of paper is organized as follows. Section 2 presents work related to the geocast protocols. In section 3 overview of our proposed mathematical model is presented. In section 4 nodes presence and void occurrences has been analyzed in the intersection area. In section 5 different forwarding areas are discussed. Finally, the work presented in this paper is concluded in section 6.

2   Related Work

Extensive works have been carried out by researchers, academicians and industries for successfully dissemination of messages from source to destination. There are several projects [2], [3], [4], [5] on VANET i.e. CarTalk, FleetNet–Internet on the Road, NoW (Network on Wheel)] are going on for its deployment in the real world. The main focus of all these projects is to provide safety, and timely dissemination of message from one location to another location. One of the message delivery protocols proposed for VANET tries to deliver a message to a geographic region rather than to a node called geocast routing. Many protocols have been developed for geocast routing such as LAR [6], LBM [7], GeoTORA [8],a modified TORA, GeoGRID [9], a modified GRID, GAMER [10], GRUV [11], etc. A Voronoi diagram based geocast protocol has been proposed in [12]. A comprehensive survey of geocasting protocol is presented in [13]. In [6, 7, 10, 11] authors used optimized flooding techniques for data delivery from source node to geocast region. In all these protocols, a forwarding zone is defined. The forwarding zone is a smaller area which includes source node, intermediate nodes and geocast region. The advantage of defining forwarding zone is that it helps in achieving optimized flooding and reduced routing overheads. Further, it also optimizes the network area. The data from source node is routed to geocast region with the help of intermediate nodes present within the forwarding zone. In [7] author's uses two types of forwarding zone LBM-box and LBM-step. The LBM-box is the smallest rectangle that includes source node and geocast region. The LBM-step is adaptive in nature it does not define the forwarding zone explicitly. The intermediate node which is closer to the smallest circle centered at the geometrical centre of the geocast region forwards the message. In [10, 11] authors have used different forwarding zones that are i) CONE ii) CORRIDOR and iii) FLOOD. The GAMER provides mesh of paths between source node and geocast region. The mesh is created within the forwarding zone. As the traffic density in the network vary with time, both the protocols switches among different forwarding zones according to traffic density in the network. Once, a method fails to deliver message to the geocast region it automatically switches to other method. The main advantages of defining a forwarding zone are i) limited flooding in the network. ii) Reduced routing overheads iii) reduced overall network space. Each intermediate node receiving packet from source node will check its position first. If the receiving node falls within the forwarding zone, it only then forwards the packets to its next hop node, otherwise it discards the packet. None of these protocols considered the road structure since they have been primarily designed for MANET. In [14] authors have designed an analytical model for the performance analysis of Contention-based Geographic Forwarding (CGF) protocol with different forwarding areas. Further, they provide procedure for selecting different forwarding area for data transmission. The three forwarding areas named as Maximum Forwarding Area (MFA), Maximum Communication Area (MCA) and 60° Radian Area (DRA).The MFA is the overlapping area of two circular areas and it depends on the transmission radius, distance between the sender and the destination node.

The geocasting is the variant of multicasting, in geocasting source node sends message to a particular geographical area. We divided the geocast method in two phases. In the Phase-I, a source node sends a message to a node inside the geocast region. In the phase-II, the receiving node of the geocast region delivers the message to all the nodes in the geocast region. The node that moves to a geocast region automatically becomes the member of the geocast region. In Phase-II, the message delivery inside the geocast region is done by simple flooding techniques. Here, in this research we have confined our work only on the phase –I. In this work, we have carried out the probabilistic analysis of nodes and effect of various network parameters i.e., transmission range of node, node density on the performance of the network.

3   Proposed Model

We have considered multi-hop environment, because it's very rare that source and destination node fall within each other's transmission range. In case there is no direct connectivity between source and destination node, to route the message, intermediate nodes plays a vital role. The intermediate nodes act as relay or next forwarding node. We have considered highway scenario to deliver message from source to geocast region shown in Fig.1.

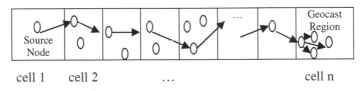

cell 1   cell 2   ...   cell n

Fig. 1. Simple Scenario of Geocast on Highway

Table 1. Symbol notation

Symbols	Description
N	Total number of nodes in network
A	Area of network
R	Radio Transmission Range
A_1 and A_2	Area within the intersection area
S	Source Node
A_{int}	Intersection area between two successive cell
I	Intermediate Node

In our proposed model we have considered a highway scenario. It is divided in to n number cells of rectangular size. The length and width of the rectangular cell is denoted by L, and W, respectively. We assume that each cell is fully covered by a circular region of radius R. According to our assumption two successive cells share some common area that is denoted as intersection area. In Table 1. We have listed different symbols used in our analysis.

3.1   Computation of Intersection Area

In the Fig.1, we have shown a highway model for geocasting. We assume that at the center of each cell one node is present. The connectivity between center nodes depends on the nodes present within intersection area. Here, we compute the intersection area between two successive cells according to Fig.2.

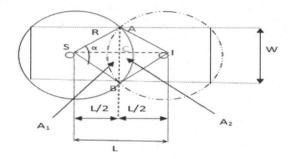

Fig. 2. Shows the intersection area between two cells

The Intersection area is denoted by A_{int}. Where, $A_{int} = A_1 + A_2 = 2\,A_1$, because the area of A_1 and A_2 are equal. The area of A_{int} computed as follows

$$\text{The area of sector ABI=Area of sector SAB} = \frac{\alpha}{360} \times \pi R^2 . \tag{1}$$

The area of triangle SAB and ABI can be calculated as follows. For ΔSAB, SA=SB=R and AB=W and for ΔABI, AI=BI=R and AB=W. According to Heron's area of a triangle it is calculated as

$$\text{The semi-perimeter of } \Delta\text{SAB= } S' = (SA+SB+AB)/2 = (2R+W)/2. \tag{2}$$

$$Area = \sqrt{\frac{(2R+W)}{2} \times \left(\frac{(2R+W)}{2} - R\right) \times \left(\frac{(2R+W)}{2} - R\right) \times \left(\frac{(2R+W)}{2} - W\right)}$$

$$= \frac{W}{4} \times \sqrt{4R^2 - W^2} . \tag{3}$$

$$\text{Now, area of } A_1 = A_2 = \left(\frac{\alpha}{360} \times \pi R^2\right) - \left(\frac{W}{4} \times \sqrt{4R^2 - W^2}\right). \tag{4}$$

$$A_{int} = A_1 + A_2 \qquad = 2 \times \left[\left(\frac{\alpha}{360} \times \pi R^2\right) - \left(\frac{W}{4} \times \sqrt{4R^2 - W^2}\right)\right]. \tag{5}$$

Where, $\tan\left(\frac{\alpha}{2}\right) = \frac{W}{L}$ So,$\alpha = 2 \times \tan^{-1}\left(\frac{W}{L}\right)$. Now compute the value of A_{int} by putting the value of α in eq-(5).

$$A_{int} = 2 \times \left[\left(\frac{2 \times tan^{-1}\left(\frac{W}{L}\right)}{360} \times \pi R^2 \right) - \left(\frac{W}{4} \times \sqrt{4R^2 - W^2} \right) \right]$$

$$= \left(R^2 \times 2 \times tan^{-1}\left(\frac{W}{L}\right) \right) - \left(\frac{W}{2}\sqrt{4R^2 - W^2} \right). \tag{6}$$

4　Analysis of Presence of Nodes in the Intersection Area

We have considered a multi hop network scenario. If source and destination nodes are not in their direct communication range, intermediate nodes act as a relay node to deliver data from source to destination node. According to our model, we have chosen the intermediate node from the intersection area of two successive cells. The availability of node in the intersection area depends on various network parameters such as node density, radio transmission range, size of the cells, area of the network etc. The nodes in the network are distributed according to 2-D poisson point process. The probability of non- availability of nodes (void) in the intersection area can be calculated as follows. The probability of m nodes present within an area A with average node density λ is calculated as

$$p(m) = \frac{(\lambda A)^m \times e^{-\lambda A}}{m!}. \tag{7}$$

The probability of void in the area A_{int} can be calculated as
$p\{A_{int} \text{ (void)}\}$

$$= \frac{\left(\lambda \times \left(R^2 \times 2 \times tan^{-1}\left(\frac{W}{L}\right) \right) - \left(\frac{W}{2}\sqrt{4R^2 - W^2} \right) \right)^0 \times e^{-\lambda \times \left(\left(R^2 \times 2 \times tan^{-1}\left(\frac{W}{L}\right) \right) - \left(\frac{W}{2}\sqrt{4R^2 - W^2} \right) \right)}}{0!}$$

$$= e^{\lambda \times \left(\left(R^2 \times 2 \times tan^{-1}\left(\frac{W}{L}\right) \right) - \left(\frac{W}{2}\sqrt{4R^2 - W^2} \right) \right)}. \tag{8}$$

4.1　Numerical Results

In Fig.3, we have shown probability of void in the intersection area. The data transmission cannot be possible if no node is present in the intersection area. We have considered different number of nodes with varying transmission range from 100 m to 250 m. We have observed that, initially for transmission range of 100 m, as the number of nodes increases from 100 to 500, the probability of occurring void in the intersection area decreases from 0.6420 to 0.1091. For transmission range 150 m, and 500 nodes, the probability of occurring void in the intersection area becomes 0. For the simplicity we have shown the above result only for up to 500 nodes. The overall behavior we observed that as the number of nodes increases probability of occurrence void is almost zero.

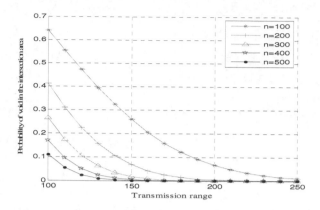

Fig. 3. Shows probability of void in the intersection area with variable number of nodes

Table 2. Probability of occurring void in the intersection region

No of nodes	Transmission Range (m)						
	100	120	150	170	190	200	250
100	0.6420	0.4731	0.2600	0.1590	0.0902	0.0661	0.0105
200	0.4122	0.2238	0.0676	0.0253	0.0081	0.0044	0.0001
300	0.2646	0.1059	0.0338	0.0086	0.0018	0.0007	0.0000
400	0.1699	0.0501	0.0046	0.0006	0.0001	0.0000	0.0000
500	0.1091	0.0237	0.0012	0.0001	0.0000	0.0000	0.0000

In the above we have shown the probabilistic analysis of occurrence of void in intersection area. Now, we will analyze the presence of node in the intersection area by varying different network parameters. Therefore, the probability of m nodes present in A_{int} area can be calculated as

$$p\{A_{int}(m)\} = \frac{\left(\lambda \times \left(R^2 \times 2 \times \tan^{-1}\left(\frac{W}{L}\right)\right) - \left(\frac{W}{2}\sqrt{4R^2 - W^2}\right)\right)^m \times e^{-\lambda \times \left(\left(R^2 \times 2 \times \tan^{-1}\left(\frac{W}{L}\right)\right) - \left(\frac{W}{2}\sqrt{4R^2 - W^2}\right)\right)}}{m!} \qquad (9)$$

Where, λ is the expected number of nodes within a unit area. In Fig.4, we have shown probability of nodes present in the intersection area. We have considered different values of transmission range 150, 200 and 250 m. We have shown only 50 nodes for clarity of graphical representation. For our analysis we have considered number of nodes upto 2000. The probability of getting one node in the intersection area is 1, after 30 and 44 nodes when transmission range is 200 m and 250 m. Further, the probability 0.9988 is constant after 19 nodes onwards when the transmission range is 150 m.

Now from the above analysis we have observed that for the better connectivity of the network intersection area should have one node. In the sparsely populated network the transmission range should be high for better connectivity of network. In the dense network, short transmission ranges results good connectivity in the network.

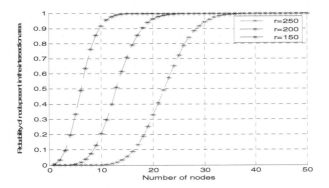

Fig. 4. Shows probability of node present in the intersection area with variable transmission range

5   Forwarding Areas in the IBGP

In our above discussion, we have given analysis of presence and absence of nodes in the intersection area for varying node density, and radio transmission ranges. Now, we have used different forwarding zones based on radian area according to [14]. The advantage of forwarding zone, it reduces the network overheads and network space for data delivery since the nodes that fall outside the forwarding zone do not participate in message delivery. In [14], a fixed radian area considered is of 60^0. In our model we have chosen various value of radian area by varying the value of α shown in Fig.5. The value of radian area is changes with varying value of W and L.

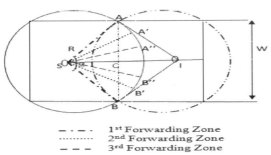

$- \cdot - \cdot$ 1st Forwarding Zone
$\cdots\cdots$ 2nd Forwarding Zone
$- - -$ 3rd Forwarding Zone

Fig. 5. Shows different forwarding zones of IBGP

5.1   Computation of Forwarding Areas

The radian area of angle α, i.e. the area of sector SAB $= \dfrac{\alpha}{360} \times \pi R^2 = \dfrac{2 \times \tan^{-1}\left(\frac{W}{L}\right)}{360} \times \pi R^2 = R^2 \times \tan^{-1}\left(\dfrac{W}{L}\right)$. Now we have defined three different radian forwarding zones according to Eq-(10).

$RadianForwardingarea =$

$$\begin{cases} \alpha_1 \; ; \text{ where } SAB = \tan^{-1}\left(\frac{W}{L}\right) \times R^2, AC = \frac{W}{2} \text{ and } SC = L/2 \\ \alpha_2 \; ; \text{Where } SA'B' = \tan^{-1}\left(\frac{W}{2L}\right) \times R^2, AC = \frac{W}{4} \text{ and } SC = L/2 \;. \\ \alpha_3 \; ; \text{Where } SA''B'' = \tan^{-1}\left(\frac{W}{4L}\right) \times R^2, AC = \frac{W}{8} \text{ and } SC = L/2 \end{cases} \quad (10)$$

Probabilistics analysis of void occurance in the different forwarding area can be calculated as

$$p\{\text{Radian Forwarding area } \alpha_1 \text{ (void)}\} = e^{-\lambda \times \left(\tan^{-1}\left(\frac{W}{L}\right) \times R^2\right)}. \quad (11)$$

$$p\{\text{Radian Forwarding area } \alpha_2 \text{ (void)}\} = e^{-\lambda \times \left(\tan^{-1}\left(\frac{W}{2L}\right) \times R^2\right)}. \quad (12)$$

$$p\{\text{Radian Forwarding area } \alpha_3 \text{ (void)}\} = e^{-\lambda \times \left(\tan^{-1}\left(\frac{W}{4L}\right) \times R^2\right)}. \quad (13)$$

5.2   Numerical Results

In Fig.6 shows the occurrence of void in different forwarding areas. We have fixed the number of nodes as 500 and vary the transmission range from 250 m to 500 m. The probability of occurrence of void in different forwarding areas is clearly shown in Fig 6(a), Fig 6(b) and Fig 6(c). In first forwarding zone the probability of occurrence of void is 0.5099×10^{-7} for transmission range of 250 m. In 2nd and 3rd forwarding area probability of occurrence of void is 0.4865×10^{-22} and 0.4926×10^{-22} respectively for transmission range 250 m. The probability of occurrence of void is zero for 1st forwarding area for transmission range 320 m and for 2nd and 3rd area is zero after transmission range 280 m. In 1st forwarding area to provide better connetcivity in the network data should be transmitted using 320 m transmission range or above and for the other two zones it should be higher than 280 m.

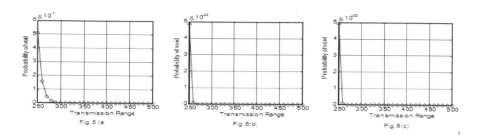

Fig. 6. Shows probability of void in different Forwarding Areas

Probabilistics analysis of presence of nodes in different forwarding areas can be calculated as

$$p\{\text{Radian Forwarding area } \alpha_1 \text{ (m)}\} = \frac{\left(\lambda R^2 \times \tan^{-1}\left(\frac{W}{L}\right)\right)^m \times e^{-\lambda\left(R^2 \times \tan^{-1}\left(\frac{W}{L}\right)\right)}}{m!}. \quad (14)$$

$$p\{\text{Radian Forwarding area } \alpha_2 \text{ (m)}\} = \frac{\left(\lambda R^2 \times tan^{-1}\left(\frac{W}{2L}\right)\right)^m \times e^{-\lambda\left(R^2 \times tan^{-1}\left(\frac{W}{2L}\right)\right)}}{m!}. \quad (15)$$

$$p\{\text{Radian Forwarding area } \alpha_3 \text{ (m)}\} = \frac{\left(\lambda R^2 \times tan^{-1}\left(\frac{W}{4L}\right)\right)^m \times e^{-\lambda\left(R^2 \times tan^{-1}\left(\frac{W}{4L}\right)\right)}}{m!}. \quad (16)$$

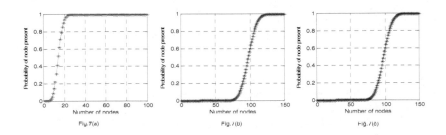

Fig. 7. Shows probability of node presence indifferent Forwarding Areas

In Fig 7 shows the probability of presence of nodes in different Forwarding Areas for a fixed transmission range of 250 m. We have shown the result only for up to 100 nodes. In Fig.7(a), after 30 nodes in the first forwarding zone nodes are always present. In Fig.7(b) and Fig.7(c) till 61 nodes there is no node present but after 139 nodes, there are always nodes present in 2nd and 3rd forwarding zone. Therefore, we can observed that in low density network 1st forwarding zone should be considered and when the number of nodes are above 60 nodes, 2nd and 3rd forwarding zone should be considered.

6   Conclusion

In this paper we have analyzed the impact of node density, transmission range, network size on network connectivity for a highway scenario. In this work we have computed the probability of presence of common nodes between successive cells in a linear route. We have also investigated the impact of three different forwarding zones for data transmission on the network connectivity. From the analysis of simulation results we have that for higher number of nodes and transmission range, the probability of void occurrence in the intersection area is low. But, for better network connectivity and uninterrupted data transmission intersection area should have at least one node. Further, it also suggests that if the number of nodes is small, the probability of void occurrence is high.

References

1. Moustafa, H., Zhang, Y.: Vehicular networks: Techniques, Standards, and Applications. CRC Press, Taylor & Francis Group, Boca Raton, London (2009)
2. The NoW: Network on wheels Project,
   http://www.network-on-wheels.de/about.html

3. CarTalk, http://www.cartalk2000.net/
4. FleetNet–Internet on the Road, http://www.fleetnet.de/
5. http://vanet.info/projects
6. Ko, Y.B., Vaidya, N.: Location-aided routing (LAR) in mobile ad hoc networks. In: Proceedings of the ACM/IEEE International Conference on Mobile Computing and Networking (MOBICOM 1998), pp. 66–75 (1998)
7. Ko, Y.B., Vaidya, N.: Geocasting in Mobile Ad-hoc Networks: Location-Based Multicast Algorithms. In: 2nd IEEE Workshop on Mobile Computing Systems and Applications, New Orleans, Louisiana, pp. 101–110 (February 1999)
8. Ko, Y.B., Vaidya, N.: GeoTORA: A Protocol for Geocasting in Mobile Ad Hoc Networks. In: IEEE International Conference on Network Protocols, Osaka, Japan, pp. 240–250 (2000)
9. Liao, W.H., Tseng, Y.C., Sheu, J.P.: GeoGRID: A Geocasting Protocol for Mobile Ad Hoc Networks Based on GRID. J. Internet Tech. 1(2), 23–32 (2000)
10. Camp, T., Liu, Y.: An adaptive mesh-based protocol for geocast routing. Journal of Parallel and Distributed Computing: Special Issue on Routing in Mobile and Wireless Ad Hoc Networks 62(2), 196–213 (2003)
11. Zhang, G., Chen, W., Xu, Z., Liang, H., Mu, D., Gao, L.: Geocast Routing in Urban Vehicular Ad Hoc Networks. In: Lee, R., Hu, G., Miao, H. (eds.) Computer and Information Science 2009. SCI, vol. 208, pp. 23–31. Springer, Heidelberg (2009)
12. Stojmenovic, I., Ruhil, A.P., Lobiyal, D.K.: Voronoi diagram and convex hull based Geocasting and routing in wireless networks. In: Proc. of the 8th IEEE Symposium on Computers and Communications, ISCC, Antalya, Turkey, pp. 51–56 (2003)
13. Maihofer, C.: A Survey of Geocast Routing Protocols. IEEE Communications Surveys & Tutorials 6(2), 32–42 (2004)
14. Chen, D., Deng, J., Varshney, P.K.: Selection of a Forwarding Area for Contention-Based Geographic Forwarding in Wireless Multi-hop Networks. IEEE Transactions on Vehicular Technology 56(5), 3111–3122 (2007)

Survey on H.264 Standard

R. Vani[1] and M. Sangeetha[2]

[1] Anna University of Technology, Chennai
[2] ECE Dept., Karpaga Vinayaga College of Engineering and Technology, Kanchipuram
{vani_gowtham,sang_gok}@yahoo.com

Abstract. The progress of science and technology demands multimedia applications to be realized on embedded systems as it involves transfer of large amounts of data. Compared with standards such as MPEG-2, MPEG-4 Visual, H.264 can deliver better image quality at the same compressed bit rate or at a lower bit rate. The increase in compression efficiency and flexibility come at the expense of increase in complexity, which is a fact that must be overcome. Therefore, an efficient Co-design methodology is required, where the encoder software application is highly optimized and structured in a very modular and efficient manner, so as to allow its most complex and time consuming operations to be offloaded to dedicated hardware accelerators. This paper provides an overview of the features of H.264 and surveys the emerging studies related to new coding features of the standard.

Keywords: H.264, Motion Estimation, Co-design, Hardware accelerators, Optimization.

1 Introduction

The H.264 Advanced Video Codec is an ITU standard for encoding and decoding video with a target coding efficiency twice that of H.263 and with comparable quality to H.262. MPEG-4 was launched to address a new generation of multimedia applications and services such as interactive TV, internet video etc. An increasing number of services and growing popularity of HDTV are creating much more need for higher coding efficiency. Another name for H.264 is MPEG-4 Advanced Video Coding (AVC) standard. Since the standard is the result of collaborative effort of the VCEG and MPEG standards Committees, it is informally referred to as Joint Video Team (JVT) standard as well [8]. Applications such as internet multimedia, wireless video, personal video recorders,video-on-demand and videoconferencing have an inexhaustible demand for much higher compression to enable best video quality as possible [27]. Ongoing applications range from High Definition Digital Video Disc (HD-DVD) or BluRay for living room entertainment with large screens to Digital Video Broadcasting for Handheld terminals (DVB-H) with small screens [13]. The H.264 standard is a new state of video coding standard that addresses aforementioned applications with higher compression than earlier standards.

N. Meghanathan et al. (Eds.): CCSIT 2012, Part III, LNICST 86, pp. 397–410, 2012.
© Institute for Computer Sciences, Social Informatics and Telecommunications Engineering 2012

It enables PAL 720×576 resolution video to be transmitted at 1Mbit/sec. According to the instruction profiling with HDTV1024P (2048×1024, 30fps) specification, H.264/AVC decoding process requires 83 Giga-Instructions Per Second (GIPS) computation and 70 Giga-Bytes Per Second (GBPS) memory access. As for H.264/AVC encoder, up to 3600 GIPS and 5570 GBPS are required for HDTV 720P (1280×720, 30fps) specification. The increasing video resolutions and the increasing demand for real-time encoding require the use of faster processors. However, power consumption should be kept to a minimum. Therefore, for real-time applications, accelerating by the dedicated hardware is a must. This paper provides an overview and summarizes emerging studies on the coding features of the H.264 standard.

The paper is organized as follows: Section 2 presents an overview of the H.264 standard. It provides details of coding structure of H.264. Following sections highlight some key technical features that enable improved operation of H.264 for broad variety of applications. Section 3 examines new algorithms for variable block size matching algorithm for the Motion Estimation. Section 4 provides information on different scanning methods and search patterns. Section 5 emphasizes co- design and co-simulation approaches. Section 6 elaborates the need for optimization and advance features. Finally, in Section 7 concluding remarks are made.

2   Overview of the H.264 Standard

Video compression efficiency achieved in H.264 standard is not a result of single feature but rather a combination of a number of encoding tools. Figure 1 depicts the structure of H.264/AVC video encoder [24]. The H.264/AVC encoder contains three steps: prediction, transformation/quantization and entropy encoding. In H.264/AVC, Macro block mode decision and Motion Estimation are the most computationally expensive processes. Mode decision is a process such that for each block-size, bit-rate and distortion are calculated by actually encoding and decoding the video. Therefore, the encoder can achieve the best Rate Distortion (RD) performance, at the expense of calculation complexity [27].

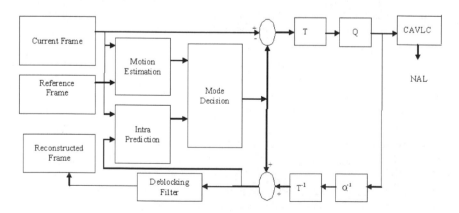

Fig. 1. H.264 Encoder Block Diagram (T-Transform Q-Quantization)

Motion Estimation

An important coding tool of H.264 is the variable block size matching algorithm for the ME (Motion Estimation) [3,18] which is part of the prediction step. In H.264 encoder, the frame is divided in 16×16 pixel macroblocks. The motion estimator has two inputs: a macroblock (MB) from the current frame and a 48×48 pixel search area (SA) from the previous frame. For each MB in the current frame, a search window is defined around a point in the reference frame. A distortion measure is defined to measure the similarity between the candidate MB and the current MB. A search is performed within the search window for the best matched candidate MB with maximum similarity. The displacement of the best matched MB from the current MB is the Motion Vector (MV).

Transformation/Quantization

In [26], H.264 uses three transforms depending on the type of residual data that is to be coded: Hadamard transform for the 4×4 array of luma DC coefficients in Intra-16×16 mode, a Hadamard transform for the 2×2 array of chroma DC coefficients and a DCT-based integer transform for all other 4×4 blocks in the residual data. By using Integer transformation, inverse-transform mismatches are avoided. A quantization parameter (QP) is used in quantization process which can take 52 different values on a macroblock basis. These values are arranged so that an increase of one in QP means an increase of quantization step size by approximately 12%. Rather than constant increment, the step sizes increase at a compounding rate. This feature is not present in prior standards and it is of great importance for compression efficiency.

Entropy Encoding

In H.264, two methods of entropy coding are supported. The first one is Context-Adaptive Variable Length Coding (CAVLC) and the other one is Context-Adaptive Binary Arithmetic Coding (CABAC). In CAVLC,entropy coding performance is superior to the schemes using a single VLC table. CABAC improves the coding efficiency further (approximately 5–15% bit saving) by means of context modeling which is a process that adapts the probability model of arithmetic coding to the changing statistics within a video frame. It is observed from [28] that the encoding time is significantly shorter for CABAC (21s less with a bit-rate of 300 kbps and 43s less with a bit-rate of 1 Mbps) whereas the decoding time is reduced slightly with CAVLC (1.2s less with a bit-rate of 300 kbps and 1.5s less with a bit-rate of 1 Mbps). Concerning the visual quality, the average Y-PSNR is better with CABAC (1.3% better with a bit-rate of 300 kbps and 1.1% better with a bit-rate of 1Mbps).

Inverse Transformation and Quantization

Since residual data exhibits high spatial entropy, H.264 employs a lossy low-pass discrete cosine transform to develop a compact representation of the residual values.

H.264 also allows variable quantization of DCT coefficients to enhance coding density. In [29], the mapping of a two-dimensional inverse discrete cosine transform (2-D IDCT) onto a word-level reconfigurable Montium processor is described. It shows that the IDCT is mapped onto the Montium tile processor (TP) with reasonable effort and presents performance numbers in terms of energy consumption, speed and silicon costs.

Intraprediction

Video frames have a high amount of spatial similarity. Intraprediction use previously decoded, spatially-local macroblocks to predict the next macroblock and it works well for low-detail images [18].

Interprediction

Video frames nearby in time have only small differences.It attempts to capitalize on this similarity by encoding macroblocks in the current frame using a reference to a macroblock in a previous frame and a vector representing the movement that macroblock took to a 1/4 pixel granularity. The decode uses an interpolation process known as motion compensation to generate the prediction value. Fractional motion vectors are interpolated from multiple previous macroblocks.

Deblocking Filter

Lossy compression is used to encode pixel blocks in H.264 and decoding errors appear most visibly at the block boundaries. To remove these visual artifacts, the H.264 CODEC incorporates a smoothing filter into its encoding loop. H.264 also incorporates fine-grained filter control to preserve these edges. With the filter, the blockiness is reduced, while the sharpness of the content is basically unchanged and the subjective quality is significantly improved. The filter reduces bit rate typically by 5-10% compared to the non-filtered video.

3   Motion Estimation Algorithms

Variable Block Size (VBS) ME allows different MVs for different sub-blocks and can achieve better matching for all sub-blocks and higher coding efficiency than Fixed Block Size ME (FFBSME). It is especially useful for MBs containing multiple objects each with possibly different motion and it can also be useful for MBs with rotation and deformation. VBSME has good RD performance compared with FBSME, but it has huge computational requirement and irregular memory access making it hard for efficient hardware implementation. The H.264 in [19] allows a 16×16 MB to be partitioned into seven kinds of sub-blocks as shown in Figure 2.

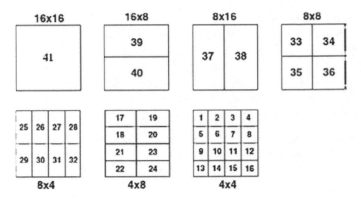

Fig. 2. Variable block size in H.264/AVC

In [9], three key points are observed for deriving an efficient ME algorithm from optimization theory.

1. The initial search point should be as close to optimal solution as possible. This goal can be achieved by exploiting the spatio-temporal correlation of MV fields.
2. An efficient update process is necessary to limit the number of SPs or iterations within an acceptable extent.
3. Multiple update paths induced by multiple initial points prevent local minimal trapping on multimodal error surface.

In an Adaptive Crossed Quarter Polar Pattern Search algorithm [6], an H.264 compatible median vector predictor (MVP) is generated for determining the initial search range. The direction of the pattern is adaptively selected with a shape of the quarter circle. The length (radius) of the search arm is adjusted to improve the search. Procedure of algorithm involves four steps:

1. Get a predicted MV (MVP) for the current block.
2. Find the direction of a search pattern, determine the pattern size "R", choose initial search point (SPs) along the quarter circle and extended predicted MV, together with the point of current block (0, 0) and MVP
3. Check the initial SPs, and get an minimum matching error point (MME) which has the minimum sum of absolute differences (SAD).
4. Refine the initial search by applying the unit-sized square pattern to that MME point and successive MME points iteratively, and find a final MV for the current block, corresponding to the final best matching point is identified.

In Ultra Low-Complexity Fast VBSME fast VBSME algorithm in [31] is described as follows, which adopts the CDS search strategy, and the SAD is replace by the pixel decimated SAD (PDSAD).

1. Cross-search: one cross search pattern with 9 search points is adopted. If the found minimum MV occurs in the cross center, this algorithm stops.
2. Half diamond search: two extra search points which are the nearest to the current minimum are checked. If the found minimum is still located in the middle of the cross pattern, namely $(\pm 1, 0)$ or $(0, \pm 1)$, the algorithm stop.

3. Large diamond search: the current minimum search point is used as the search center and the large diamond pattern with 9 search points is used to trace the motions. This step continues until the found minimum is located in the diamond center.
4. Small diamond search: the minimum search point in previous step is used as the search center, and one small diamond pattern with 4 search points is then adopted to refine the search result. The final minimum is returned as the best MV.

In [30], Multi-pass and frame parallel algorithms are proposed to accelerate various motion estimation (ME) tools in H.264 with the graphics processing unit (GPU), GeForce 7800 GT. Compared to implementations with CPU, about 6 times to 56 times speed-up can be achieved for different ME algorithms.GPU is parallel architecture and it is able to efficiently process motion estimation. First an algorithm is proposed to map motion estimation (ME) on generic GPU to accelerate video encoding. Second, advanced motion estimation algorithms in H.264, such as quarter-pel ME and multiple reference frame ME, are implemented. ME contains mainly two parts: integer ME (IME) and fractional ME. Runtime profiling of H.264 JM encoder reveals that IME consumes close to 60% of total encoder time and up to 90% when fractional ME is included. Thus efficient ME algorithms and hardware architectures for IME are needed. IME architecture in [2] shows high throughput and it's a cost efficient VLSI architecture for integer full-search VBS-ME. In an efficient FME implementation, the trade-off among processing time, memory access data bus and hardware utilization should be balanced. According to [22], IME and FME must be computed in 1025 cycles which will affect the efficiency of the hardware implementation. IME is performed prior to FME in which integer pixel search tries to find the best matching integer position and the best integer pixel motion vectors (MV) are determined by using a performance cost metric. Then, FME performs a half-pixel refinement about the integer search positions and then a quarter-pixel one is performed around the best half-pixel positions. As a result, pipeline architecture is a must to implement IME and FME.The p264 platform [16] is a configurable software application derived from version JM14.0 of the H.264/AVC Reference Software Model that presents a highly modular and flexible structure where all the functional modules of the video encoder are implemented as independent and self-contained software modules. It allows replacing a software realization of any given function of the video encoder by a system call to a hardware accelerator implementing that same function whenever higher performance levels are required. Some algorithms perform best on fine-grain reconfigurable architectures whereas others perform better on coarse-grain reconfigurable or general purpose processing (GPP) tiles [25].

4   Scanning Methods

Different scanning methods and search patterns are discussed in this section. In [3,4,12,31] different Search patterns full search (FS), 3 step search (3SS), 4-step search (4SS), diamond search (DS), cross-diamond search (CDS), and hexagon search (HEXBS) are discussed. In [4,31] 3SS yields better speedup when compared to FS,

DS ME algorithms, by taking a Leon3 uniprocessor video encoding system as the reference platform. The quality of fast ME algorithms have the following relations: DS ≈ CDS > 4SS > HEXBS. It is observed that the diamond pattern in DS and CDS is more accurate than the rectangle pattern in 4SS and the hexagon pattern in HEXBS. It is desirable to employ different search patterns, i.e, adaptive search patterns, for a variety of the estimated motion behaviors. An adaptive search patterns [6] is devised to detect the optimal or sub-optimal search points in the initial stage. The idea is to choose some initial search points (SPs) along the pattern to be checked in the initial search range. To reduce the number of initial SPs and keep the good probability of obtaining best matching point which has the minimum SAD, a fractional (quarter) polar search pattern is designed. The direction of search pattern is defined by the direction of a quarter circles which comes from the predicted motion vector (MV). Figure 3 displays the possible patterns adaptively that employ the directional information of a predicted MV to increase the possibility of acquiring the optimal minimum matching error (MME) point for refined search. The radius of a designed pattern, is defined as

$$R = Max\{|PredMVy|, |PredMVx|\}$$

where R is the radius of quarter circle and PredMVy, PredMVx the vertical and horizontal components of the predicted MV respectively.

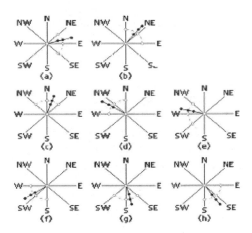

Fig. 3. Possible adaptive search patterns

In Raster Scan, the search locations in the first row are scanned from left to right, followed by the second row from left to right, and so on. Raster Scan is effective in reusing data horizontally with relatively high data re-use ratio but with redundant loading. The data re-usability is improved slightly in some architecture by another scanning order called Snake Scan as shown in Fig. 4(a). Snake Scan processes the first row from left to right, then the second row from right to left, and then the third row from left to right, and so on. In both Raster Scan and Snake Scan, the data re-use ratio and search window size is fixed. A novel scanning order called Smart Snake (SS) is proposed in [1] which can achieve variable data re-use ratios and minimum redundant data loading. Search window is divided into an array of non-overlapping rectangular sub-regions that span the search window which is shown in Fig. 4(b). In each rectangular sub-region, Snake Scan is performed to achieve significantly higher data re-use. After one sub-region is searched, it will move into an adjacent region and Snake Scan will be applied again. In different sub-regions, Snake Scan may be performed from top to bottom (L1), or from bottom to top (L2). It may start from left and end at right (L1, L2, L3), or start from right and end at left (L4, L5, L6). It may be horizontal (L1, L2) or vertical (L3, L4). "Horizontal" to mean the original Snake Scan which processes the search points row-by-row and "vertical" to mean column-by-column Snake Scan. The width (or the height) of each sub-region is restricted to be less than or equal to a parameter M.

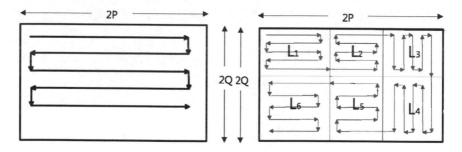

Fig. 4. (a) Snake Scan, (b) Smart Snake Scanning order (SS)

A new scan order for reference datas writing and reading is introduced in [2] to improve the efficiency of memory accessing and to obtain high data-reuse of the search area. The architecture of VBS-ME allows the real-time processing of 1280×720 at 38 fps with FS-BMA in a search range $[-32, +32]$ with 36k gate counts. Processing pipelining of 4×4 SAD Parallel processing and pipelining techniques are used to reduce the latency and increase the data utilization

5   Co-design and Co-simulation Approaches

The emphasizes of Co-Design is on the area of system specification, hardware software partitioning, architectural design, and the iteration in between the software and hardware as the design proceeds to next stage. The hardware and software co design makes it possible. A Multi Core H.264 video encoder is proposed in [4,5,23], by applying a novel hardware software co-design methodology which is suitable for implementing complexity video coding embedded systems. The hardware and the software components of the system are designed together to obtain the intended performance levels. At the hardware level, the designer must select the system CPU, hardware accelerators, peripheral devices, memory and the corresponding interconnection structure. The software component addresses the design of a program to efficiently implement the application algorithms and to support the communications between all the system hardware components. The code is further optimized by taking into consideration the characteristics of the hardware components and by applying the most complex and efficient modes of the software compiler tools. In H.264 video decoder, different blocks can be partitioned into several stages. The implementation of each function under different partitions is shown in Table 1 and it is observed that architecture for partition 4 can achieve more than three times acceleration in performance.

Table 1. Implementation of each function under different partitions

	VLD	IQ	IT	Intra	Inter	Reconst.	DB
Partition 1	SW	SW	SW	HW	HW	SW	SW
Partition 2	SW	SW	SW	HW	HW	HW	SW
Partition 3	HW	HW	HW	HW	HW	HW	SW
Partition 4	SW	HW	HW	HW	HW	HW	HW

Two co-design approaches were identified in [25]. The first co-design approach is shown in figure 5a, to develop both the software and hardware separately. Verification does not take place until the design is deployed to a specific hardware platform which leads to late detection of mistakes in the HW/SW partitioning and implementation. In the second approach, all subsystems are verified in one environment and it becomes a difficult task. One method is to represent all systems in one HDL, which can involve model degradation. The second method is to use a simulator that supports all different HDLs used and the third method is to use different simulators for each system and verify the integrated system using co-simulation. Co-simulation is useful in HW/SW co-design [20,21]. The co-simulation design approach is depicted in figure 5b. Co-simulation can be done by either connecting two simulators known as direct coupling or by the use of a co-simulation backplane. The co-simulation allows for designing in much short iteration while verifying functional behaviour.

Co-design is proposed in [14] as a chip named OR264 with mixed flexibility and it is partitioned that the hardware is used to boost the performance and efficiency of key operations. The chip is fabricated using hardware software architecture to combine performance and 0.1 8-ptm 6-layers metal CMOS process in UMC. It contains 1.5M transistors and 176k bits embedded SRAM and can operate at 100MHz. The die size of the processor is 4.8mm × 4.8mm and the critical path delay is 10ns. Results evidence the low hardware requirements and prove that real-time computation of MVs for QCIF video sequences with only one ME IP core is possible. Data Exchange Mechanism (DEM) controller is the only one master in the architecture used in the co design for H.264 Video Decoder [7] and the other hardware accelerators are all slaves. DEM controller dominates all the I/O access of the hardware accelerators and on the other hand, it will also dispatch the data and the parameters passed by the processor to the corresponding hardware accelerators. As a result, users can add or delete hardware accelerators easily since there is no data dependency among hardware accelerators.

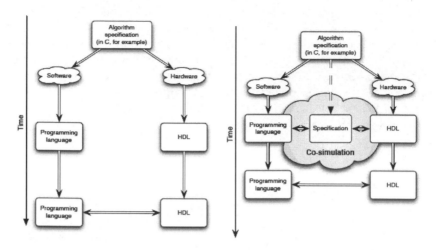

Fig. 5. Co-design approaches (a) Traditional Approach (b) Co-simulation approach

6   Optimization and Other Features

Mismatch measures such as sum of absolute difference (SAD), sum of squared difference (SSD) and sum of absolute transformed difference (SATD) are available and in which SAD is most common due to its simplicity and effectiveness [1]. Most existing hardware ME architectures are based on SAD. In the JM version 15.1 of the H.264 reference software, the ME chooses the best mode by using a Lagrangian mode decision to compute an estimation of the bits required to code MVs. For each subblock of a MB, Langrangian cost (J) defined as

$$J = SAD + \lambda MVcost(MVcur - MVpred)$$

where MVcost represents the number of bits required to code the difference of current MV (MVcur) and motion prediction (MVpred) and λ is the Langrangian multiplier. An alternative measure is called rate-distortion (RD) cost function which is given by

$$RDCost = D + \lambda \cdot R$$

where D is the distortion such as SSD, SATD, or SAD, R is the associated bit rate and λ is the Lagrangian multiplier. Recent ME algorithms tend to use RD cost due to its superior performance. RDOMFS circuit with a small search range can achieve better RD performance with low power consumption than FS-SAD. It is hard to design efficient hardware for RD for at least two reasons. First, RD computation requires floating point operation for the multiplication of and R which is time and resource consuming. If this is to be relieved by using lookup tables, it would require huge chip area for the lookup tables. Second, the data flow in the computation of MVmedian is irregular and requires a large amount of on-chip memory to store the required past MVs. As a result of microarchitectural change, the deblocking filter implementation in [8] decreases area dramatically from 2.74 mm^2 to 0.69 mm^2. Optimized deblocking filter yields 12% increase in throughput of the entire design, and thereby reducing the design critical path by 35%. The 4:1 Haar lter based pixel decimation is adopted to reduce matching costs. In FFSBM proposed in [19], filter reduces bit rate typically by 5–10% compared to the non-filtered video.

In [3,15], it was observed that results obtained with the implementation of a multicore SoC of an H.264/AVC video encoder in a Virtex4 FPGA demonstrated that speedups greater than 15 can be obtained for the ME task and over 3 for the global encoding operation. Huge reduction in the computation time of the ME operation and transfer times for the pixel data (MB and SA) and for the ME results (MVs) are negligible and it's about 0% of the total encoding time. An efficient quarter pel ME hardware [17] is designed for portable applications together with half pel ME This architecture is implemented in VHDL and it was found that code works at 60MHZ in a Xilinx Virtex II FPGA. The performance results [25] shows that FPGA implementation shows a speed-up of 43.6 whereas the Montium implementation shows a speedup of 21.5, both compared to a software-only implementation. The speedup values validate the adopted methodology and hardware software design partitioning.

Adaptivity in search patterns [12], will greatly reduce the dynamic complexities of motion estimation and real time encoding of 1280×720 video can be processed at 30 fps. Reconfigurable architecture for Standards MPEG2, MPEG4, H.263 and H.264 [10] requires more power and silicon area to achieve flexibility Configurable architecture adopting a DEM [7] controller to fit the best tradeoff between performance and cost when realizing H.264 video decoder for different applications. The FPGA implementation can process 34 VGA frames (640×480) per second. It reduces the amount of computation and thereby reducing power consumption. In [24], Montium target platform consists of an ARM946E-S and a Xilinx Virtex XC2V8000 FPGA containing the Montium TP. The clock frequency is 100 MHz, both for the ARM and the Montium. The number of clock cycles needed to process a macroblock is always the same. There are two important observations underlying the main idea of the algorithm of [31] in which the first is direct pixel decimation is not suitable for H.264/AVC because of the small Sub-block sizes. Second is by adopting low-pass lter based pixel decimation, the original SAD operation can be reduced to 25%, reduce the computation to about 0.2% of FFS, average PSNR loss and bit rate increase are 0.12dB and 2.81%, respectively and still maintaining robust image quality. The ACQPPS architecture [6] can yield better performance in terms of average PSNR of −0.05dB, +0.34dB and +0.11dB.

It is observed that under the CBR mode, encoding time using CABAC is superior over CAVLC, whereas the degradation in decoding time is insignificant [28]. The most striking results in the context of VBR, Rate Distortion Optimization (RDO) provides better visual quality but the encoded video is bigger in size and the time needed for encoding is longer. RDO is well suited for broadcasting of prerecorded high quality videos but should be avoided for low delay applications. Testing RDO under CBR is a good means to determine if the improvements in terms of visual quality remain when the sizes of the encoded videos are the same. A second experiment has been carried out to test the performances of RDO under CBR. CBR and RDO can be considered as complementary tools. If the bit-rate is fixed and the QP values are determined by the rate-control algorithm, RDO simply determines the best prediction mode. Particle swarm optimization algorithm (PSO) is presented for multi fusion images in which size of the blocktype regions are optimized. Experiments are conducted on both artificial and natural multi focus images and results show that PSO based method outperforms Laplacian pyramid transform, Discrete Wavelet Transform and Genetic algorithm in terms of quantitative and visual evaluations [26].

VLSI architecture for FME with processing capacity for 1080HD real-time video streams with three different pipelined processors a high throughput and low area cost , which can generate the residual image and the best MVs to be encoded. In [12], better area/throughput is achieved by exactly choosing the Processing Element Array size to reduce the Gate Count and the bandwidth lower bound and upper bound for FS, 3SS, and HS is calculated. To give an accurate comparison, the Gate Count vs Throughput ratio (GCTR) is defined as

$$GCTR = Gate\ Count\ /\ Throughput = (Gate\ Count) * Cycle\ per\ MB$$

and it is found that lower GCTR indicates higher hardware efficiency. With the advent of 3G, Optimization of H.264 codec and improvement of mobile system will have significant improvement [11].

7   Conclusion

H.264/AVC represents a major step in the development of video coding standards in terms of both coding efficiency enhancement and flexibility for effective use over a broad variety of network types and application. Co-Design approaches can be used to explore Motion estimation algorithms to yield better timing and speed optimization by using particle swarm optimization, simulated annealing and other methods. Co-Simulation tools to be used for further enhancing speed and reducing power consumption. Fine grain partitioning may be done for every modules of video codec to reduce the area. Development of the encoder conforming to the standard is still considered to be a challenging issue, particularly for real-time applications. The future design methodologies and associated tools must provide both modular refinement and high-level synthesis.

References

[1] Wen, X., Fang, L., Li, J.: Novel RD-Optimized VBSME with Matching Highly Data Re-Usable Hardware Architecture. IEEE Transactions On Circuits And Systems For Video Technology 21(2), 206–219 (2011)

[2] Gu, M., Yu, N., Zhu, L., Wenhua: High Throughput and Cost Efficient VLSI Architecture of Integer Motion Estimation for H.264/AVC. Journal of Computational Information Systems, 1310–1318 (2011)

[3] Dias, T., Roma, N., Sousa, L.: H.264/AVC framework for multi-core embedded video encoders. In: International Symposium on System on Chip (SoC), pp. 89–92 (2010)

[4] Dias, T., Roma, N., Sousa, L.: Hardware/Software Co-Design Of H.264/AVC Encoders For Multi-Core Embedded Systems. In: Conference on Design and Architectures for Signal and Image Processing (DASIP), pp. 242–249 (2010)

[5] Dias, T., Roma, N., Sousa, L.: Hardware/Software Co-Design Of H.264/AVC Encoders For Multi-Core Embedded Systems: inescid, ISEL (2009)

[6] Qiu, Y., Badawy, W.: The Hardware Architecture Of A Novel Motion Estimator With Adaptive Crossed Quarter Polar Search Patterns For H.264. In: Canadian Conference on Electrical and Computer Engineering, CCECE 2009, pp. 819–822 (2009)

[7] Jian, G.-A., Chu, J.-C., Huang, T.-Y., Chang, T.-C., Guo, J.-I.: A System Architecture Exploration on the Configurable HW/SW Co-design for H.264 Video Decoder. In: IEEE International Symposium on Circuits and Systems, ISCAS 2009, pp. 2237–2240 (2009)

[8] Fleming, K., Lin, C.-C., Dave, N., Arvind, Raghavan, G., Hicks, J.: H.264 Decoder: A Case Study in Multiple Design Points. In: 6th ACM/IEEE International Conference on Formal Methods and Models for Co-Design, MEMOCODE 2008, pp. 165–174 (2008)

[9] Lee, G.G., Wang, M.-J., Lin, H.-Y., Su, D.W.-C., Lin, B.-Y.: Algorithm/Architecture Co-Design of 3-D Spatio-Temporal Motion Estimation for Video Coding. IEEE Transactions on Multimedia 9(3), 455–465 (2007)

[10] Lu, L., McCanny, J.V., Sezer, S.: Reconfigurable ME Architecture for Multi-standard video compression. In: IEEE International Conf. on Application-specific Systems, Architectures and Processors, 2007 ASAP, pp. 253–259 (2007)

[11] Wang, S.-F., Huang, Z.-Q., Hou, Y.-B.: A Design of Low-cost, Low-bandwidth Mobile Video Surveillance System Based on DM6446. In: International Conference on Wireless Communications, Networking and Mobile Computing, WiCom 2007, pp. 3079–3083 (2007)

[12] Zhang, L., Gao, W.: Reusable Architecture and Complexity-Controllable Algorithm for the Integer/Fractional Motion Estimation of H.264. IEEE Transactions on Consumer Electronics, 749–756 (2007)

[13] Chen, T.-C., Lian, C.-J., Chen, L.-G.: Hardware Architecture Design of an H.264/AVC Video Codec. In: Conference on Asia and South Pacific Design Automation, p. 8 (2006)

[14] Yang, K., Zhang, C., Du, G., Xie, J., Wang, Z.: A Hardware-Software Co-design for H.264/AVG Decoder. In: IEEE Asian Solid-State Circuits Conference, pp. 119–122 (2006)

[15] Le, T.M., Tian, X.H., Ho, B.L., Nankoo, J., Lian, Y.: System-on-Chip Design Methodology for a Statistical Coder. In: Seventeenth IEEE International Workshop on Rapid System Prototyping, pp. 82–90 (2006)

[16] Rodrigues, A., Roma, N., Sousa, L.: p264: Open platform for designing parallel H.264/AVC video encoders on multi-core systems. In: International Workshop on Network and Operating Systems Support for Digital Audio and Video, pp. 81–86 (2010)

[17] Lin, C.-C., Lin, Y.-K., Chang, T.-S.: A Fast Algorithm and Its Architecture for Motion Estimation in MPEG-4 AVC/H.264 Video Coding. In: IEEE Asia Pacific Conference on Circuits and Systems, pp. 1248–1251 (2006)

[18] Sayood, K.: Introduction to Data Compression, 3rd edn. Elsevier Publishers (2006)

[19] Zhang, L., Gao, W.: Improved FFSBM Algorithm and its VLSI Architecture For Variable Block Size Motion Estimation Of H.264. In: Proceedings of 2005 International Symposium on Intelligent Signal Processing and Communication Systems, pp. 445–448 (2005)

[20] Hardware/Software Co-design of the H.264/AVC standard. In: Fifth FTW PhD Symposium, Faculty of Engineeering, Ghent University, Paper no.120 (2004)

[21] De Vleeschouwer, C., Nilson, T., Denolf, K., Bormans, J.: Algorithmic and Architectural co-design of a motion-estimation engine for low power devices. IEEE Transactions on Circuits and Systems for Video Technology, 1093–1105 (2002)

[22] Ruiz, G.A., Michell, J.A.: An Efficient VLSI Architecture of Fractional Motion Estimation in H.264 for HDTV. J. Sign. Process. Syst. (2010)

[23] Kalavade, A., Subramanyam, P.A.: Hardware/ Software partitioning for multi function systems. IEEE Transactions on Computer Aided Design of Integrated Circuits and Systems 17(9), 819–837 (1998)

[24] Oktem, S., Hamzaoglu, I.: An efficient Hardware architecture for Quarter Pixel Accurate H.264 Motion Estimation. In: 10th Euromicro Conference on Digital System Design Architectures, Methods and Tools, pp. 444–447 (2007)

[25] Colenbrander, R.R., Damstra, A.S., Korevaar, C.W., Verhaar, C.A., Molderink, A.: Co-design and Implementation of the H.264/AVC Motion Estimation Algorithm using co-simulation. In: 11th EUROMICRO Conference on Digital System Design Architectures, Methods and Tools, pp. 210–215 (2008)

[26] Aslantas, V., Kurban, R.: Extending depth of field of a digital camera using particle swarm optimization based image fusion. In: IEEE 14th International Symposium on Consumer Electronics (ISCE), pp. 1–5 (2010)

[27] Ozbek, N., Tunali, T.: A Survey on the H.264/AVC Standard. Turk. J. Elec. Engin. 13(3) (2005)

[28] Mazataud, C., Bing, B.: A Practical Survey of H.264 Capabilities. In: Seventh Annual Communication Networks and Services Research Conference, pp. 25–32 (2009)

[29] Smit, L., Rauwerda, G., Molderink, A., Wolkotte, P., Smit, G.: Implementation of a 2-D 8 × 8 IDCT on the reconfigurable Montium core. In: International Conference on Field Programmable Logic and Applications, pp. 562–566 (2007)

[30] Lee, C.-Y., Lin, Y.-C., Wu, C.-L., Chang, C.-H., Tsao, Y.-M., Chien, S.-Y.: Multi-Pass and Frame Parallel algorithms of Motion Estimation in H.264/AVC for generic GPU. In: International Conference on Multimedia and Expo., pp. 1603–1606 (2007)

[31] Song, Y., Liu, Z., Ikenaga, T., Goto, S.: Ultra low complexity fast Variable Block Size Motion Estimation algorithm in H.264/AVC. In: IEEE International Conference on Multimedia and Expo., pp. 376–379 (2007)

Self-configurable Processor Schedule Window Algorithm

A. Prasanth Rao[1], A. Govardhan[2], and P.V.V. Prasad Rao[3]

[1] Reasearch Scholar, Dept., of Computer Science and Engineering, JNTUH, Hyderabad
[2] Professor, Dept., of Computer Science and Engineering, JNTUH, Hyderabad
[3] Program Manager, SETU Software Systems Pvt.. Ltd., IIIT Gouchibowli, Hyderabad
adirajupppy@yahoo.com, govardhan_cse@yahoo.co.in,
prasad@setusoftware.com

Abstract. Most periodic tasks are assigned to processors using partition scheduling policy after checking feasibility conditions. A new approach is proposed for scheduling aperiodic tasks with periodic task system on multiprocessor system with less number of preemptions. Our approach is self-configurable and adjusts the periodic tasks to the processor such that different types of tasks are scheduled without violating deadline constraints. The new approach proves that when all different types of tasks are scheduled, it leads to better performance.

Keywords: Scheduling, feasibility, multiprocessor, deadline, synchronous, free slots, sporadic task system.

1 Introduction

Real-Time systems are specifically designed for situations where the correctness of an operation depends not only upon its logical correctness, but also upon the time at which it is performed. Generally real time applications are event driven and the task should complete its execution within the deadline and so it should be completely determinable. Events can be classified according to their arrival pattern. In this context, events can be periodic if their arrival time is a constant or aperiodic when it is not. A task set is said to be synchronous if all offsets are equal to zero and the deadline of the task is equal to or less than its period. The polynomial test has been proposed by Baruah et al [3]. If the deadlines are equal to period, a simple polynomial test has been proposed by Liu and Layland in their seminal work [1]. A task set is asynchronous if the task arrival time is not known in advance and for each asynchronous set a synchronous set is identified. A task set can be categorized as having implicit deadline, constraint deadline or arbitrary deadlines. An asynchronous task is one which has an arbitrary deadline and should be modeled simply as a synchronous set [13].

A task set is said to be have an implicit deadline if $\forall i$, $task_i$, $d_i = p_i$: For constraints deadline the task set has $\forall i$, $task_i$, $d_i \leq p_i$. Finally for a task set with arbitrary deadlines no such relation stated. However, in general there are other types of tasks whose arrival times are not known in advance and these tasks are scheduled together with the periodic tasks set.

N. Meghanathan et al. (Eds.): CCSIT 2012, Part III, LNICST 86, pp. 411–422, 2012.

There are many partitioned scheduling algorithm[2,3,4,5,6,7] which is used to schedule periodic tasks [8,9]. However using partitioned scheduling algorithm, tasks are allocated to processors and each processor is allocated certain fixed number of execution units. The main disadvantage of partitioned scheduling algorithm is that the processor is not fully utilized. This means that there are certain execution time units available and these units are fragmented in the processor. To overcome the disadvantage of partitioned scheduling algorithm, we have to make use of unused cycles properly. So other types of tasks such aperiodic tasks, constrained deadline or arbitrary deadline are scheduled with periodic task sets which improve the overall performance of the system.

There are certain free slots available at different intervals of time and any one of the free slots may accommodate only a few execution time units. The individual fragments may not be large enough, so we can combine all these small fragments to execute a much bigger task. The size of these free slots is configurable with a parameter, which controls the free cycles availability and allocation of dynamic tasks to individual processor.

The main objective of this chapter to develop strategies to schedule aperiodic tasks with periodic tasks and the same model can be extended to schedule a sporadic task system.

This paper is organized as follows. Section 2 describes Theoretical Concepts Configuration Parameter presented in Section 3. Section 4 describes Reserving space for newly created tasks Sections 5 demonstrate Results and Discussions. Finally, the Conclusion and future scope are given in Section 6.

2   Theoretical Concepts

A periodically sampled control system which is modeled on time triggered approach. Time-Triggered tasks (τ) are characterized by a quadruple ($\emptyset$, p, e, d). The periodic task system involves execution of independent task system $\Gamma = \{\tau_1, \tau_2, \tau_3, \tau_4 \dots \tau_n\}$, where each task $\tau_j \in \Gamma$. The period task generates a sequence of jobs at each integral multiple of period p_i. Each job must execute in at most e_i execution units of time and should complete before its relative deadline d_i(equals to period of task). The first job of the given task is released at phase $\emptyset$ (offset). Since periodic task system generates an infinite sequence of jobs with the kth job arriving at an instance $\emptyset_i + (k-1) p_i$ $\forall i=1$, $2, 3,\dots, k$ and each job should complete before $\emptyset_i + (k) p_i$. Before presenting finding free-slots algorithm we need to define Basic Terminology.

2.1   Basic Terminology

In this section we look at definitions which help us to understand the partition parameter and using this parameter we can dynamically configure processor window.

Definition 2.1 (Total Execution Period P_{max}). The total execution time units of a given task system Γ^1 is equal to or less than total execution period (P_{max}), then the task system is feasible on uniprocessor system.

$$P_{max} = \max(p_1, p_2, p_3, \ldots\ldots\ldots, pi, \ldots\ldots p_n) \qquad (2.1)$$

Definition 2.2 (Maximum Execution Units e_{max}). e_{max} is maximum execution units which is defined among a set of n tasks.

$$e_{max} = \max(e_1, e_2, e_3, \ldots, e_m) \qquad (2.2)$$

Definition 2.3. (Configuration Parameter δ). The configuration parameter δ divides the time axis into two windows. One window is used to schedule periodic task sets and the other window is used to schedule aperiodic task sets.

Definition 2.4 (Scheduling Condition). The general scheduling condition given RMCT [2]

$$P_{max} \geq \lfloor P_{max} / p_1 \rfloor e_1 + e_{max(P)} \qquad (2.3)$$

Using the above definitions we can understand partition condition which divides processor window into two parts. Before defining partition condition we need to explain about task execution modeling in next section.

2.2   Task Execution Modeling

A scheduling algorithm provides a set of rules that determine the processor(s) to be used and tasks to be executed at any particular point of time. There many scheduling algorithm were presented in the literature [7,10,11] and also scheduling heuristics [8,13] developed. These entire algorithms are allocating tasks to the processors using partition scheduling policy which results some unused free slots on each processor. Also we configure these unused free slots to schedule different type of tasks together. For further improvement in resource utilization if we make use of these free slots to schedule dynamic tasks.

2.3   Scheduling Conditions

The schedulable condition for task sets scheduled under RM is based on utilization of a processor and period oriented. All scheduling conditions which were mentioned above are oriented towards utilizations i.e. the relative value of task utilization was taken into account. The performance of these algorithms is limited because they fail to consider the relative values of task periods. There are many period oriented scheduling algorithms were developed RMGT [8] RMCT [2] and utilization based algorithms [3][8].

The Rate Monotonic Critical Tasks (RMCT) algorithm is developed based on the maximum execution period (P_{max}) and assumes all tasks in a queue are arranged with decreasing period. The total execution units (T) of all incoming periodic tasks can be computed and the RMCT may allocate maximum possible tasks to given processor till condition 2.4 satisfied. The RMCT Algorithm [2] identifies the number of processors and also total execution time units (T) given to each processor. The δ in the if loop known be configuration parameter.

If $(T > \delta P_{max})$ then
{   increment processor index.   (2.4)
else
    {   allocates to same processor.
    }

In the following section we show how this condition in 2.4 [2] helps to regulate the task being scheduled.

3   Configuration Parameter

Let us consider task system Γ^1 {τ_1, τ_2, τ_3 } and $\tau_1 = (5,2)$, $\tau_2 = (7,1)$, $\tau_3 = (10,4)$. Apply RMCT [2] algorithm, $p_{max} = 10$, $T = 10$ units, so all tasks are allocated to only one processor. In this situation $\delta = 1$ and processor fully loaded with periodic set as shown Figure 1. From figure we conclude that the processor fully loaded and there will be no free slots available and these type of tasks should meet deadline.

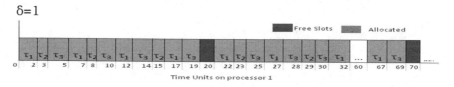

Fig. 1. Task allocation to processor 1

However when we change $\delta = 0.8$, we require two processor to schedule above tasks system as shown in Figure 2. From the figure we conclude that two processor required to schedule above task system and each processor some free slots are available.

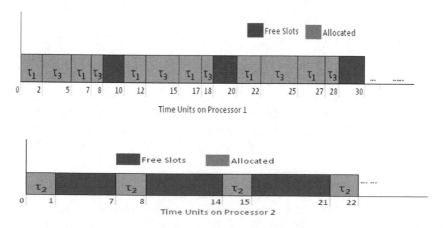

Fig. 2. Tasks allocation two processor system

However we can further increase these free slots by decreasing value of δ. The δ=0.4 as shown in Figure 3.

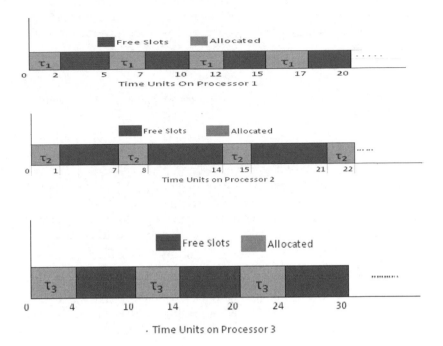

Fig. 3. Task allocation three processor system

In this situation, minimum of three processor required and each processor can allocate one periodic tasks. However it may increase number of processor but there will be more number of free slots are available. This helps us to schedule different type of tasks together and we mix up both high priority and low priority tasks. Not only that an aperiodic tasks whose generation not known in advance can be scheduled with periodic tasks. The configuration parameter dynamically can change depending upon the application. So in order to regulate the proportion of aperiodic tasks we consider a configuration parameter δ and must be selected such that both periodic and aperiodic tasks can be scheduled together. δ is chosen such that at least one periodic task is allocated to an individual processor. δ, the configuration parameter divides the available window into parts ,where one part is reserved for fixed priority algorithm [4]and other part is   dynamic priority algorithm[10]. We observe that for further decreases of δ value, there will be at least one periodic task cannot be allocated any processing element (theorem 4.1).

By choosing an appropriate value of δ, we can use our scheduling algorithm in two different ways. Firstly, it can be used to schedule the task set on an individual processor after checking feasibility analysis. Secondly, it can be used to find free slots on each processor and in turn these are used for allocation of dynamically created tasks. This is called as the Partition Condition which is discussed in the next section.

3.1   Partition Condition

The partition condition divides window into two parts where one window can be used for scheduling periodic tasks and other window is to schedule aperiodic tasks. We propose here the theorem 3.1 states that the window is divided such that at least one periodic task is allocated to each processor.

Theorem 3.1. For given periodic task system Γ^1 the partition condition states that each processor allocates at least one periodic task using configuration parameter δ and its value lies between [δ_{min}, 1].
Where $\delta_{min} = e_{max}/p_{max}$

Proof: Let $\{\tau_1, \tau_2, \tau_3, \tau_4 \dots \tau_n\}$ be n tasks and all tasks are arranged with increasing priorities and first in queue will be given least priority.

Let τ_n, τ_k is two tasks whose maximum periodicity (Def.3.2) and whose maximum execution time (Def.3.7) are (p_{max}) and (e_{max}) respectively.

If $e_i < p_i$ then task$_i$ is schedulable on processor j otherwise the task is infeasible. This implies that there will be a task whose maximum execution units are e_{max} and all other tasks are in a queue below this value. For any given task τ_k i.e. $p_k < p_{max}$ and that implies $e_{max} < p_{max}$. This means minimum δ_{min} equals to e_{max}/p_{max} and its maximum value equals to 1.The configuration parameter value always lies in between [δ_{min}, 1]. So the minimum execution units allocated to each processor equals to e_{max} such that selecting δ value in the range [δ_{min}, 1]. There will be no task allocated to processor if $\delta < \delta_{min}$ and so at least one periodic task allocated to processor if δ lies in the range [δ_{min}, 1].

Hence Proved

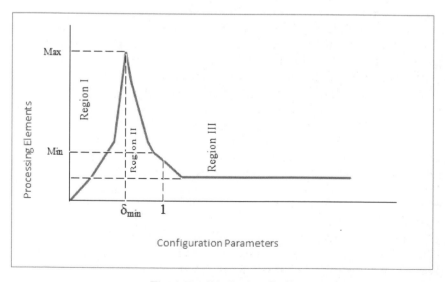

Fig. 4. Feasible Region Graph

The Figure 4 drawn between configuration parameter and processing elements required for computing given load. The observations of three regions from Feasible Region Graph are listed below.

Region I: Configuration parameter value in between $[0, \delta_{min})$. Task allocation cannot done properly and some tasks are unassigned to processing elements. When $\delta = 0$, none of the task assigned.

Region II: Configuration parameter value in between $[\delta_{min}, 1]$. As we move δ_{min} to 1,the number of processing elements required to compute for given task system get decreases. However, more number of free slots available on each processor at δ_{min} and deceases further. In this region all tasks meet deadline and RM schedulable conditions.

Region III: The parameter δ increases further after reaching its value 1, tasks are assigned with lesser number of processing elements. However, they will not meet deadline and also not RM schedulable.

Region II best suitable for scheduling periodic tasks and adjusting parameter δ, we schedule different types of tasks are together.
Depending upon the type of an application we can set the value of δ and based on this value the processor allocates fixed number of periodic tasks and also has few free slots to accommodate aperiodic tasks. The same model can be extended to schedule sporadic task system [13].
When new task arrives at processor m_i, at phase $\emptyset$ with deadline d_i and execution time e_i it is scheduled between the time interval $\emptyset$ and $\emptyset + d_i$. When the new task arrives the algorithm immediately searches for a free slot to schedule the task locally otherwise it is sent to the group scheduler. Few processors are grouped together and allocation of tasks among these processors can be monitored by group scheduler. An integrated procedure is desirable to schedule different types of periodic/aperiodic/sporadic task system. Before presenting an integrated approach we need to find free-slot in given interval and discussed in the next section.

3.2   Availability of Slots at Fixed Interval

Initially, the centralized scheduler allocates a fixed number of execution time units to an individual processor and in each processor available free slots are computed. The total number of processing elements m will be divided into a number of small groups. Each group maintains a group scheduler which contains information about all processing elements within it. The Algorithm 3.1 is used to compute free slots and this information is available at group scheduler. A group scheduler maintains a table which contains information about each processor-ID, total-execution units, planning cycle (M) and size of fixed free slots.

Let the number of tasks allocated by RMCT algorithm $j = n_j$.
Planning cycle or LCM units of periodic tasks allocated to processor $j = M_j$
The number of occurrences $l = M_j/phase$

Initialize first task in priority queue and fixed slots in the interval given by

$$(k.phase_i, K.phase_i + e_{ij}), \forall k = 0, \ldots, 1$$

(3.1)

The rest of tasks which are present in the queue verify availability of free slots and each task from queue is allocated free slots using algorithm 3.1. The fixed allocated slots means that tasks which are assigned to particular processor execute only mentioned slots. The condition which is used in RMCT is said to necessary and sufficient i.e. property of RM algorithm is satisfied. The allocation of fixed time slots means that the execution of the task is predefined in allocated time frame. This results in a very low number of preemptions.

Algorithm 3. 1. Finding Free Slots

```
I for(j=0;j≤m;j++)
Read number of tasks (n_ij ,M,Phase);
for i=0;
//First task only.
Occurrences 1 = M/phase
for (k=0;k≤l; l++)
Slots fixed for task_i= [k*phase_i, K*phase_i + e_ij]
Available slots =[ K*phase_i + e_ij, (K+1)phase)
II for (i=1;i≤n_ij ;i++)
{
Check in available slots.
Occurrences l=M/phase_i
for (k=0; k<=l;k++)
  {
  Pick up one by one available slot
  If (upperbound-lowerbound>=eij)
  Slots fixed = [lower bound, lowerbound+eij]
  Available slot =[lowerbound+eij, upper bound]
  else
  Keep available slot as it is.
  }
  }
```

4   Reserving Space for Newly Created Tasks

On processor p, identify free slots available in the interval $\emptyset$ and $\emptyset + d_i$. If any one of the free slots are sufficient to accommodate newly arrived task then allocate that task to processor otherwise it searches another processor in group scheduler. If one processor not sufficient then task may split into two fragments.

Let the space reserved on processor m_i for one portion of the split-task be $x[m_i]$ and the space reserved for second portion of the split-task on processing element (m_j) be $z[m_j]$.Likewise all the parts of the split-task reserve spaces on processors which are within the group. The dispatching is simple. If processor m_i reserves at time t and other portion of the split task assigned another processor m_j reserve after time t + x $[m_i]$.

Assume S_1, S_2...S_n are the sizes of free slots available on the processor in the interval (0, M).The free slot which has the maximum size, has to be identified and has to be denoted by S_{max}, then splitting of task can be done.

S_{max} = maximum slot size within the interval $\varnothing$ and $\varnothing + d_i$.

S_{max} = max $(S_1, S_2,..S_k)$, where k free slots are available in mentioned Interval.

The space reserved for one portion of task should be equal to S_{max} i.e. $x[m_i] = S_{max}$

Next a suitable processor m_j should be searched for the remaining portion of split-task such that $Z[m_j] = e_{ij} - S_{max}$

The number of processing elements in given system will be m and this number divided smaller groups. Each group contains smaller number of processing elements in order to reduce communication latency. The next section presents an integrated approach to schedule different type of tasks.

4.1   Integrated Procedure to Schedule Different Tasks

The integrated approach integrates all three schedulers (local, global and group) to provide a complete solution to schedule real tasks among different processing elements. This scheme has all the three components and also takes interactions among different processing elements. Each processor has a local scheduler and is allocated a fixed number of execution time units in a given planning cycle. As we know, there will certain free slots available and these intervals were fixed.

The algorithm 4.2 locks those free slots in the given group of processing elements which one optimal by adequate for given tasks taking its phase, periodicity, execution time, deadline. When a dynamic task arrives at time t, the task tries to schedule locally otherwise it searches free slots in that particular processor group. The algorithm 4.1 is used for getting number of free slots in each processor and size of each free slot. The size_free_slots [ ] gives us the size of free slot and no_free_slots [req_size] gives us number of free slots in that particular interval for each and every processing element. The algorithm 4.2 is used for finding optimal size of free slots in the interval θ and $\theta + d$.

Algorithm 4.1. Getting free slots in the interval t and t+d in given group

```
size_free_slots [req_size]
no_free_slots [req_size]
Locked [req_size]
for (i=0;i<req_size; i++)
{
   No_free_slots[i]=available_fslots(i,t,d);
   size_free_slots[i]=available_fssize(i,t,d)
}
```

```
Available_fslots (int i, int t, int d)
{
  get sizes of free slots in the interval t and t+d;
}
```

Algorithm 4.2. Finding optimal free-slot in the interval t and t+d for newly arrived task

```
//optimal allocation:
 optimal_fs_size=size_free_slots
 for (int i=0;i<req_size; i++)
 {
//pick one value greater than min_req and less than
remaining all
    If(size_freeslots[i]•min_req&& locked[i]=0)
    {
       If (optimal_fs_size•size-freeslots[i])
         optima_fs_size = size_freeslots[i];
     }
 }
If (optimal_fs_size<min_req)
 {
   //assign nearest fsize to splitting task
   //find out maximum value so that will get the
nearest value
   Optimal_fssize=Max(availability_fslot[]);
   //lock that processing element;
  Locked[j]=1;
  min_req=min-req-optimal_fssize;
  //repeat optimal allocation block for remaining
 }
 else
 {
   //no need to split task directly lock that
processing element;
   Locked[i]=1;
   Lock-index[j] with request processor[i]
 }
```

In order to use our algorithm, we need to ensure that each task is processed on only one processor at any point of time. Task splitting must therefore address three important challenges (i) Dispatching algorithm to be developed for ensuring that two pieces of a task do not execute simultaneously (ii) Design a schedulable test for the dispatching algorithm. (iii) Order of execution of two pieces is maintained properly.

5   Results and Discussions

The m processor system divides into smaller number of groups and splitting of task can be made within the group. However, we illustrate our results with one example as shown in Figure 3.When δ=.8,The task system requires three processor system and all these processors are grouped together and free slots in each processor as shown table 5.1. Whenever an two aperiodic task1 (4, 4, 6) and aperiodic task2 (5, 5, 7).System invokes finding free slots and also calls finding optimal slots among available free slots in the interval θ and θ + d.

Table 1. Free slots in each processor for given group

Processor-ID	Allocated Blocks	Free Slots	Locked slots
1	(0,2),(5,7),(10,12)…	(2,5),(7,10) (12,15)…..	
2	(0, 1),(7,8),(14,15)…	(1,7),(8,14), (15, 21)….	(5,7),(8,11)
3	(0,4),(10,14),(20,24)…	(4,10),(14,20), (24, 30)……	(4,8)

For first aperiodic task when free slots algorithm invoked in the interval θ and θ + d and it finds suitable slots are (4,10) on processor 3,(4,5),(7,10) on processor 1 and (4,7),(8,10) on processor 2.However (4,8) slot is more suitable and this slot is locked for it. Similarly, the other aperiodic task arrives at phase 5 and again it searches suitable slots in given group. So aperiodic task1 allocated to processor 3 and aperiodic task2 allocated processor 2.We have shown only how our algorithm works with simple example. Simulation works are under progress.

6   Conclusions

This paper provides a solution to make use of unused free-slots on existing processors. Different types of tasks are scheduled with periodic task sets. Initially, the system tries to schedule the newly created dynamic tasks to one of the available processors. However, there are a few cases where CPU cycles are not sufficient to execute a given task. In such scenarios, task splitting can take place between two processors thus improving resource utilization. As a future enhancement, we will group the processing elements using a Maekawa set which reduces communication delay and there is a need develop an integrated scheduler (i.e. local scheduler, group scheduler and centralized scheduler) for real-time task systems.

References

1. C.Liu and J.LayLand, "Scheduling Algorithms for Multiprogramming in Hard Real–Time Environment," JACM 10(1), 1973, pp, 174-189
2. A.Prashanth Rao and A. Govardhan, "An Improved Period Oriented Scheduling Algorithm for Real Time Systems." Ijesce Research Science Press, Vol 3, No.1 January-June 2011.
3. S.Cheng, J.A.Stankovic, and K.Ramamritham, Scheduling Algorithm for Hard Real Time Systems: A   Brief Survey, Tutorial: Hard Real Time Systems, EFF Press, 1988, pp 150-173.
4. J. D Gafford, Rate Monotonic Scheduling, IEE Micro, June 1991, pp 34-39 Real Time Systems by James W.S.Liu Published by Pearson Education, II   Ededition, 1991.
5. D.S Johnson, Near Optimal Bin Packing Algorithms, PhD Thesis, MIT 1973.
6. Giorgio C.Buttazzo, Hard Real-Time Computing Systems Predictable Scheduling Algorithms and   Applications, Kluwer Academic Publishers,1997
7. Edited by Mathai Joseph, Real-time Systems Specification, Verification and Analysis, Tata Research Development & Design Centre, June 2001
8. Almut Burchard, Jorge Liebeherr, Member, Yingfeng Oh, and Sang H. Son,   New Strategies for Assigning Real-Time Tasks to Multimocessor Systems, IEEE Transactions On Computers, Vol.44, No.12, December 1995
9. Sylvain Lauzac, Rami Melhem, Fellow, IEEE, and Daniel Mosse´, Member, IEEE Computer Society An Improved Rate-Monotonic Admission Control and Its Applications, IEEE Transactions On Computers, Vol. 52, No. 3, March 2003
10. C.Siva Ram Murthy and G.Manimaran, Resource Management in Real-Time Systems and Networks, PHI Learning Private Limited, 2009.
11. D. Zmaranda, G. Gabor, D.E. Popescu, C. Vancea, F. Vancea, Using Fixed Priority Pre-emptive Scheduling in Real-Time Systems, International journal of Computers, Communications & Control, Vol.VI (2011), No.1(Marach), pp.187-195.
12. Rodolfo Pellizzoni,Giuseppe Lipari,Feasibility Analysis of Real-Time Periodic Tasks with Offsets, Real-Time Systems,Kluwer Academic Publishers Norwell, Volume 30 Issue 1-2, May 2005
13. Bjorn Anderson, Konstantin's Bletsis, Sanjoy Baruah, Arbitrary-Deadline Scheduling Sporadic Tasks on Multiprocessor, Technical Report HURRAY-TR-080501.

An Authenticated BSS Methodology for Data Security Using Steganography

B. Ravi Kumar[1], P.R.K. Murti[1], and B. Hemanth Kumar[2]

[1] Department of Computer and Information Sciences
University of Hyderabad, P.O. Central University,
Gachibowli, Hyderabad 500 046, Andhra Pradesh, India
[2] Department of IT, R.V.R.& J.C. College of Engineering
Guntur, Andhra Pradesh, India
{ravi_budithi,bhkumar_2000}@yahoo.com,
murti.poolla@gmail.com

Abstract. Within the past several years, there has been an exponential increase in the research community and industry's focus towards information hiding techniques as opposed to the traditional cryptography area. The goal of Steganography is to conceal information, in plain sight. Providing security to the data means the third party cannot interpret the actual information. When providing authentication to the data then only authorized persons can interpret the data. This system deals with secure transmission of data. In computer system to represent a printable character it requires one byte, i.e. 8 bits. So a printable character occupies 7 bits and the last bit value is 0 which is not useful for the character. In BSS method we are stuffing a new bit in the place of unused bit which is shifting from another printable character. To provide authentication a four bit dynamic key is generated for every four characters of the encrypted data and the key is also maintained in the data itself. In this system we implement security using steganography. i.e. hiding large amount of information in an image without disturbing the image clarity and its pixels.

Keywords: Bit Shifting, Steganography, Security, Authentication.

1 Introduction

Steganography is an ancient art that has been reborn in recent years. The word *steganography* comes from Greek roots which literally means covered writing [1], and is usually interpreted to mean hiding information in other information. Markus Kuhn, a steganography researcher has submitted the modern definition of steganography, as "art and science of communicating in a way which hides the existence of the communication" [2]. The goal is to conceal, in plain sight, information inside other innocent information to disallow an outsider or adversary the opportunity to detect that there is a second secret message present One of the primary drivers of the renewed interest in steganography is for mitigating copyright abuses. As audio, video and other works become more readily available in digital forms, the ease

N. Meghanathan et al. (Eds.): CCSIT 2012, Part III, LNICST 86, pp. 423–431, 2012.

with which perfect copies can be made may lead to large-scale unauthorized copying. This type of copying is naturally of great concern to the music, film, book, and software publishing industries. There has been significant recent research into digital watermarks or hidden copyright messages and digital fingerprints or hidden serial numbers. The idea is for file fingerprinting to be used to help identify copyright offenders and then potentially prosecute them with the digital watermark [1].

2   Related Work

The Internet is a vast channel for the mass dissemination of information (e.g. publications and images). Images provide excellent carriers for hidden information. Many different steganographic techniques exist, but most can be grouped into two domains: the image domain and the transform domain. Image domain tools encompass bit-wise methods that implement least significant bit insertion and noise manipulation. These approaches are prevalent in steganographic systems and are characterized as simple systems [2]. The formats (image) used with such steganography methods are lossless; the data can be directly manipulated and recovered easily. The transform domain category of tools includes those that manipulate algorithms and image transforms such as discrete cosine transformation. These methods conceal information in significant areas of the cover and may alter image properties such as luminance. Watermarking tools usually fall in this domain. Typically, these methods are more robust than bit-wise techniques. However, a consideration must be taken as to the benefit of added information to the image versus the extra robustness obtained. Many transform domain methods are unconstrained to image format and may remain persistent for lossless to lossly, or vice versa, conversions. Some techniques share both image and transform domain characteristics. These may employ patchwork, pattern block encoding, spread spectrum methods, and masking which all can add redundancy to the hidden information. These combined approaches may help protect against some image processing techniques such as cropping and rotating. For example, the patchwork method uses a pseudo-random selection technique to mark multiple image sections (or patches). Each patch may include the watermark, so if one section is destroyed or cropped, then others may persist [3].

3   Our Proposed System

In today's Dynamic rich computerized world Steganography has enjoyed resurgence. As computers continue to permeate millions of people's daily routines, their use as steganography instruments makes perfect sense. Steganography's rise in popularity can be attributed. People use steganography as a means to reduce the casual interception of private information. The increase in steganography usage is due to the cover space abundance provided by digital media, particularly within the various computer file formats (e.g. BMP, GIF, JPG, PDF, WAV, HTML, TXT etc). With these almost perfect digital media and the many continuous technology advancements, there has been a rising concern for copyright abuses. This has driven much of the steganography advancements with a immense focus on digital watermarking. This promising technology is proclaimed by industry as an excellent anti-fraud and forgery mechanism. The music and movie industries have invested millions of dollars on techniques to conceal company logos and other proprietary markings in digital images, videos, and music recordings. The interest in creating a robust, tamperproof digital fingerprint has been the focus of much of the academic research in steganography. Although steganography differs from cryptography, many of the techniques and wisdom from the more thoroughly researched discipline can be borrowed. Secure information is not necessarily covert and covert information is not necessarily secure.

Past cryptography history has shown that the adversary usually knows that communication is occurring and is able to intercept it. The adversary is often aware that the information is encrypted and that in most cases will break the encryption algorithm at any cost. Thus, cryptography's underlying security is based on the difficulty of breaking the encryption algorithm. With sufficient time and resources, this decryption task has usually been achieved.

In contrast, steganography assume the adversary can intercept the cover, but cannot perceive any information besides the original cover content. The information is concealed and may have no additional security besides the actual message embedding. However, we combining the two methods for security as shown in Figure 1and 2 can be implemented by using our proposed method. In our proposed system, we have presented new algorithms named Bits Shifting and Stuffing (BSS) methodology [4, 5]. This system is hiding large amount of encrypted and authenticated data irrespective of the size, dimensions of the image and without disturbing the clarity of the image.

4   Methodology

    I.   **Sender**
- Data encryption
- Generating key
- Authentication for encrypted data
- Data hiding in an image

    II.   **Receiver**
- Retrieving data from the image
- Data authentication
- Decryption

The embedded data is the message that one wishes to send secretly. It is usually hidden in an innocuous message referred to as a cover-text, or cover-image or cover-audio as appropriate, producing the stego-text or other stego-object. To restrict detection and/or recovery of the embedded data from the parties who know it (or who know some derived key value) a stego-key is used to control the hiding process.

4.1   Encoding

Architecture for Encryption and constructing stego image.

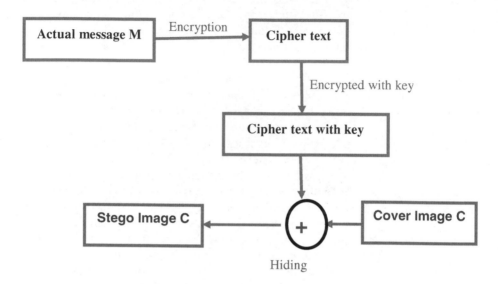

Fig. 1. Encoding steps of Data hiding system in an image

4.2   Data Embedding into the Image

This method deals with identifying the (encrypted data) **cipher text** with key (encr2.) and the image to embed the data before it can be transmitted. Open the given image file in the binary mode and find the size of the original image. This size is maintained in the image itself by using a special signature which is useful to retrieve the data from the image. Now add **cipher text** from the file encrc2.cmp to the image. Now the image is ready to transmit. If the image already contains some data you cannot add some more data for the same image. So before embedding data check whether the image contains data or not.

Algorithm represents that each image contains single message. Embedding multiple times is not acceptable with this algorithm.

1. Open the image file in the binary format
2. Check whether the signature " @!~(= " is existing or not
3. If signature found , the given image has already contains some hidden data, so select another image

4. Else find the size of the image file.

SIZE← size of the image.

5. Open encrypted data with key in the binary mode and append each character to the end of the image.

6. At the end append the signature " @ !~(= "

7. Convert each digit of the size of image into character and append after the signature to the image file.

   Conversion of size into characters.
   a.   TOTAL ← SIZE
   b.   While (TOTAL / 10)
        i.   X ← TOTAL mod 10
        ii.   Char CH← (char) X
        iii.   Append this CH to the end of the image
        iv.   TOTAL ← TOTAL / 10
        v.   End while

8. CH ← (char) TOTAL // last digit.
   a.   Append. this CH to the end of the image.

9. End.

4.3   Decoding

<u>Architecture for Extracing data from Stego Image and Decryption</u>

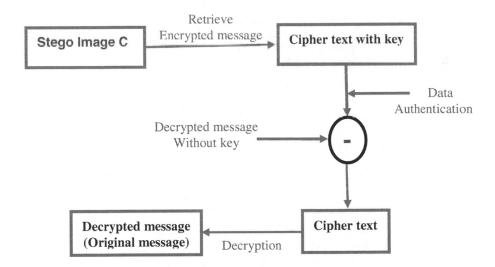

Fig. 2. Decoding steps of Stego image

4.4   Data Retrieve

After receiving the image through some media, the end user also opens the image in the binary mode and checks whether the image contains the special signature or not. If signature found then image contains data. Then   get the original size of the image from that signature. Now except original data of the image extract data from the image up to the special signature. This is encrypted data (cipher text). This data is maintained in a file say decypt2.cmp.For this data check authentication whether data is corrupted or not and then decrypt the data to get the original message.

4.5 Data Retrieving from the Image

First check whether the image contains any hidden data or not. If data found then retrieve the data from the image.

1. Open the image file in the binary format
2. Check whether the signature " @!~(= " is existing or not
3. If signature not found then
    > No hidden data in the image
    > End
4. Else extract each character starting immediately from the signature and converting them in to digits to find the size of image.
    > Conversion of last characters into digits and finding the size of image.
    > a)   N ← number of characters after signature.
    >   Character array TEMP[N]
    > b)   Take the last characters after the signature into the array TEMP
    > c)   Long Integer SIZE , B
    >   Integer A,I
    >   SIZE ← 0, A ← 1, N← N - 1
    > d)   For I 0 to N
    >   B ← (Integer) TEMP[I]
    >   B ← B x A
    >   SIZE ← SIZE + B
    >   A ← A x 10
    >   End For loop.
5. Find position the character SIZE + 1 from the 1st character of the image and mark this position as M
6. Find total size including size of image ,data, signature and last characters after the signature. Let it be TOTAL.
7. Find the position of the last character the data. Let it be D
    > N ← N + 1
    > D ← TOTAL – 5 (size of signature) – N
8. Now extract characters from M to D. This is the embedded data.
    > End.

5   Implementation Results and Discussions

Results

5.1   Encoding

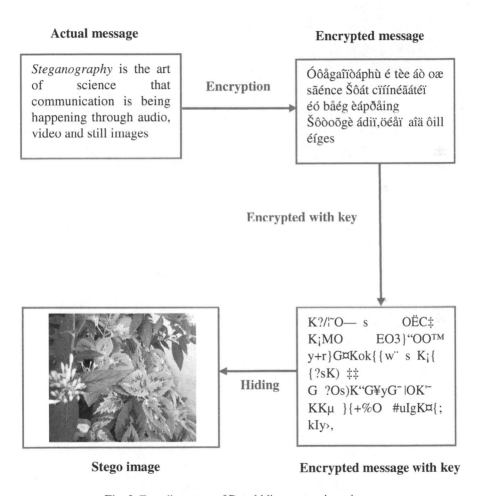

Fig. 3. Encoding steps of Data hiding system in an image

5.2   Decoding

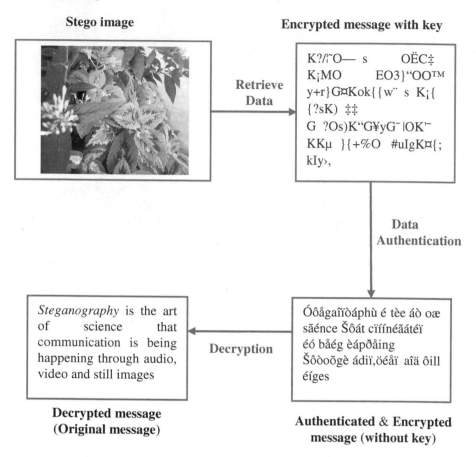

Fig. 4. Decoding steps of Stego image

5.3   Discussions

We have designed a special algorithm to embed the encrypted message into the cover image and assigned a special signature to identify and to locate the information of the message from the stegano image. We have designed special algorithm for decoding process. While decoding the algorithm can identify the data with respect to the signature which is provided in the stegano image. The identified data is authenticated and decrypted. In this system the designed tool deals with providing easy and secure information. The data is encrypted with key and embedded with an Image which is ready to send through communication channels.

References

1. Petitcolas, F.A.P., Anderson, R.J., Kuhn, M.G.: Information Hiding-A Survey. Proceedings of the IEEE, Special Issue on Protection of Multimedia Content 87(7), 1062–1078 (1999)
2. Anderson, R., Petitcolas, F.: On the Limits of Steganography. University of Cambridge, Computer Laboratory, Cambridge (September 1997); Published in IEEE Journal on Special Areas in Communications 16(4), 463–473 (May 1998)
3. Johnson, N.F., Jajodia, S.: Steganalysis of Images Created Using Current Steganography Software. In: Aucsmith, D. (ed.) IH 1998. LNCS, vol. 1525, pp. 273–289. Springer, Heidelberg (1998), http://www.jjtc.com/ihws98/jjgmu.html
4. Ravi Kumar, B., Murti, P.R.K.: Data Encryption and Decryption process Using Bit Shifting and Stuffing (BSS) Methodology. International Journal on Computer Science and Engineering (IJCSE) 3(7), 2818–2827 (2011)
5. Ravi Kumar, B., Murti, P.R.K., Hemanth Kumar, B.: An Authenticated Bit Shifting and Stuffing (BSS) Methodology for Data Security. Computer Engineering and Intelligent Systems 2(3), 94–104 (2011)
6. Johnson, N.F., Jajodia, S.: Exploring Steganography: Seeing the unseen. IEEE Computer 31(2), 26–34 (1998)
7. Marvel, L.M., Boncelet Jr., C.G., Retter, C.: Spread Spectrum Steganography. IEEE Transactions on Image Processing 8, 08 (1999)
8. Johnson, N.F., Jajodia, S.: Steganalysis of Images Created Using Current Steganography Software. In: Aucsmith, D. (ed.) IH 1998. LNCS, vol. 1525, pp. 273–289. Springer, Heidelberg (1998)

A Real Time Multivariate Robust Regression Based Flood Prediction Model Using Polynomial Approximation for Wireless Sensor Network Based Flood Forecasting Systems

Victor Seal[1], Arnab Raha[1], Shovan Maity[1], Souvik Kr. Mitra[1],
Amitava Mukherjee[2], and Mrinal Kanti Naskar[1]

[1] Advanced Digital and Embedded Systems Laboratory, Department of Electronics and
Telecommunication Engineering, Jadavpur University, Kolkata 700032, India
[2] IBM India Private limited, Kolkata 700091, India
{arnabraha1989,shovanju35,souvikmitra.ju}@gmail.com,
{victor.seal,mrinalnaskar}@yahoo.co.in.
amitava.mukherjee@in.ibm.com,

Abstract. The paper introduces a statistical model to be used in wireless sensor network (WSN) for forecasting floods in rivers using simple and uncomplicated calculations and provide a reliable and timely warning to the people who may be affected. The statistical process used for this real time prediction uses linear robust multiple variable regression method to provide simplicity in cost and feature, and yet efficiency is speed, power consumption and prediction accuracy which is the prime goal of any design algorithm. This model is theoretically independent of the number of parameters, which may be varied according to practical needs. When increasing, the water level trend is approximated using a polynomial and its nature is used to predict when the water level may cross the flood line in future. We have simulated the comparison of predicted water level with the actual level in a time interval, around and below the flood line. The accuracy of prediction above flood line is of no value in real life and but a data above flood line is shown in our simulation results for the sake of continuity and logical justification of the algorithm.

Keywords: Flood forecasting, robust regression, WSN, polynomial fitting, multi-square weight minimization, event, query.

1   Introduction

Natural disasters like floods, hurricanes, etc. tremendously affect the lives of the poor and under privileged. A lot of work has been done to develop systems which help to minimize the damage through early disaster predictions. As the network has to be deployed in the rural areas, there is a severe limitation of resources.

Nowadays, WSN based systems are usually used in prediction models. WSNs are low power, low cost, multi-hopping systems, and independent of external service

N. Meghanathan et al. (Eds.): CCSIT 2012, Part III, LNICST 86, pp. 432–441, 2012.

providers that can form an extendable network without line of sight coverage; but have self-healing data paths. WSNs can be deployed more or less homogeneously in a geographical region using a two-tiered approach having clusters of short distance communicating nodes together with some nodes capable of communication over a wider range. WSN nodes communicate only with neighbouring nodes to reduce the transmission power and losses, thus eliminating the need for expensive repeaters and transmitters used in traditional telemetry systems. Every node in a WSN acts as a data acquisition device, a data router and a data aggregator. This architecture maximizes the redundancy and consequently the reliability of the entire flash- flood monitoring system. The independence from 3rd party providers and the absence of infrastructure requirements – as those needed in cellular based telemetry systems allow a WSN to be deployed quickly. They allow online, self-calibration of the prediction model.

Two types of model may be created: First, a centralized model where computation occurs at the central node only. It needs simpler components as terminal nodes don't need any hardware for computational purposes. Second is a distributed model with computations at several levels instead of only one computing node as in the previous model. This model is more immune to errors but cost ineffective. Combining these two to get a get an optimal balance of cost and accuracy is the best idea for a practical system.

2   Related Work

In most of the data-driven statistical flood-prediction models, details of the topography, soil composition, and land cover, along with meteorological conditions and hydro-meteorological quantities such as soil moisture are required [3]. In the development of these rainfall-runoff models, on-going work covers a range of models from lumped to spatially distributed variations [5,6]. Most of the algorithms which come under the same category as our subject requires a set of tests for calibration and require repeated re-calibrations [1,7].Some algorithms even restrict the number of parameters to a fixed quantity thereby making their model a rigid one.

3   Proposed Work

WSN System Architecture
Our proposed model comprises sensors (which sense and collect the data relevant for calculations), some nodes referred to as computational nodes (that have large processing powers and implement our proposed prediction algorithm) and a manned central monitoring office (which verifies the results with the available online information, implements a centralized version of the prediction algorithm as a redundancy mechanism, issues alerts and initiates evacuation procedures). Different types of sensors are required to sense water discharge from dam, rainfall, humidity, temperature, etc. The computational nodes possess powerful CPUs required to implement the algorithm. Computational nodes transmit the prediction results to the monitoring node. Inter-node communication eliminates errors. The work of the

central node is not our concern. However it is important to include a manned central node in this whole process to raise the alarm and co-ordinate evacuation measures if needed.

The next important aspect is to minimize the effect of a node failure while connecting the computational nodes to the central. Intermediate nodes (INs) have to be deployed to ensure this connectivity in case the central does not fall within the communication range of all the nodes. Given below is the entire picture of the WSN at site is given. As we can see the river has been broken into several monitoring zones. In each zone, a sensor node collects data and sends them to its computational node. Data collection and localized prediction takes place at each computational node. The results are then shared between all the computational nodes themselves and also to the central.

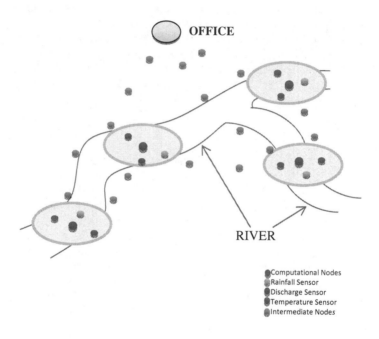

Fig. 1. Wireless Sensor Nodes Deployment Scheme

Our prediction algorithm is compatible with a 2 layered network architecture comprising a number of sensor nodes collecting the data needed for prediction. Data is sent to the single computation node (or administrative office) which bears the responsibility of most of the computations and predictions (online and offline). It has great computational power and processing capability. With data collected online dynamically, forecasts are made using our suggested algorithm and results communicated to the local administrative office which raises alarm if needed.
Sensors take data as decided by one or more of these three parameters:

a)Time- The administrator decides a time interval after which a reading is to be taken, accordingly a sensor takes the time driven data as input.

b)Event-Event refers to sudden change in a parameter affecting the desired output. Suppose the next time driven data is slated to be taken after an hour. But a dam starts discharging water at such a rate that flood may occur within the next 30 minutes. A hardware interrupt has to override the time driven mechanism to get an instant event driven data and make a reliable prediction before the flood occurs.

c)Query-Suppose an administrator wants to see the immediate level and get an instantaneous prediction even when it's not time to take a reading. A hardware interrupt is used get the instant query driven data. It is quite similar to the event driven case, the only difference being that this interrupt is provided by a human unlike natural parameters that trigger the event triggering interrupt.

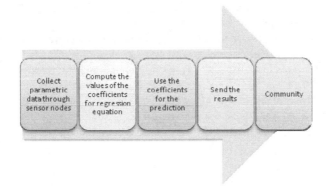

Fig. 2. Block-wise depiction of data sent from sensors to the community

Our algorithm handles all these issues. It operates using a time driven mechanism and checks for hardware interrupt at every instant of wait interval (time before next reading) and forfeits its wait state if there is an interrupt.

The advantage of such a method is that it can incorporate a wide number of parameters upon which the river water-level varies providing us with a more precise prediction and reducing the possibility of false alarms. For simplicity, we, in prior, choose a threshold level for river water such that if the predicted value is more than that level an alarm can be raised. Choosing such a threshold level is very critical and important in our case as it may lead to unnecessary false alarms.

Suppose that the water level is close to the flood line but remains constant, just below it for a long time .instead of sounding a continuous alarm, we suggest reducing the sampling interval then so that the system sensitivity increases and it sounds an alarm only if needed. Even the intensity of flood may be determined based on the predicted value. To make the prediction faster and more accurate, we also need to logically decide the necessity of a parameter in predicting the output.

Our Floodprediction Model
We provide the algorithm of the main program and follow it up with the part wise algorithms of the different functions used in it.

Program Algorithm

Input: Past data tables: Y=water level, R= rainfall, D=Discharge, X_i ,i=1,2...= other parameters affecting water level; Present value of parameters. SC=Storage capacity (in number of readings) of node. S=stored regression coefficient algorithm, W=its weight. P=present coefficient matrix.

Initialise: Set counter=1, weight=0, initialise all matrices to zeroes.

Output: Predicted value of Y.

Step 1. Read past data tables: Y=water level, R= rainfall, D=Discharge, X_i, i=1,2...=other parameters affecting water level.

Step 2. Compute/re-compute linear regression model (i.e. coefficient matrix P) relating Y with the above parameters using the robust fit function.

Step 3. Find the weighted mean of P and S (weight of P=counter value now, weight of S=W).This is our final regression model.

Step 4. Input the present value of parameters and predict corresponding value of Y based on the final regression model.

Step 5. Decide time interval before next reading using the time multiplier function.

Step 6. Maintain a table of water levels v/s time and see if the final trend(most recent reading to back in time) is increasing or not.

Step 7. If water level trend is not increasing, flood is not expected. Go to step 10.

If increasing, use Polynomial Fit function to approximate the trend v/s time (from present value to the 1st local minima reached going back in time) and generate a prediction model for it.

Step 8. Put in values of time in future in progressive order into the prediction model above and predict future values of water level.

Step 9. If water level stays below flood line up to a defined reliability period of our prediction model, predict flood not possible.

If water level exceeds the flood line within the defined reliability period, predict flood possibility.

Step 10. Recalibrate time interval of step 3 based on this prediction.

Step 11. Input present value of water level. Increment counter by 1.

Step 12: If counter value is less than SC, append all present values to the end of their respective tables in step1(Y, D, R, X_i) . Then go to step 2.

Else, store the coefficient matrix and increment its weight (W) by SC. Then clear all the data and output tables, reset counter to one to ready it for taking inputs.

Step 13: Enter a wait state; waiting time= recalibrated time interval (step 10)

Step 14: Check-is the system still in wait state?

If yes, go to step 15.

Else go to step 2.

Step 15: Check- is there any hardware interrupt (event/query driven data acquisition demand) now?

If yes, go to step 2 immediately.

Else go to step 14.

Polynomial Fit function: We approximate the increasing water level by a second order polynomial function to predict future values i.e. $y=a_1x^2+a_2x+a_3$. Where,

x is a time index starting from the moment water level starts rising;

y=corresponding water level at that time.

Tabulating for several values (x_i, y_i), the solution is given in form:
$Y_{nx1} = X_{nx3} A_{3x1}$ (n=no. of readings) where X is the Vandermonde matrix whose elements are given by
$X_{i,j} = x_i^{3-j}$ (i=1,2,3;j=1,2,3) i.e. simply stated, the elements of each row I are $x_i^2, x_i, 1$ respectively.
In Y=XA we know Y,X; solving for A gives the coefficient matrix $[a_1\ a_2\ a_3]'$ above.
To solve,
$X^T Y = X^T X A$
Or, $(X^T X)^{-1} X^T Y = A$.
Now we have the 2nd order polynomial equation $y = a_1 x^2 + a_2 x + a_3$ ready to use.
Going by the present nature of the curve, we predict its future trend and see if it goes over the flood line within the reliability period of our future prediction and predict accordingly.
The 2nd order polynomial function ensures simplicity of calculation over larger polynomial.

Robust Fit function: The main disadvantage of ordinary least-squares fitting is its sensitivity to outliers. Squaring the residuals magnifies the effects of these extreme data points and hence they have a large influence on the fit. To minimize the influence of outliers, we fit our data using robust least-squares regression.

Robust fitting with multi-square weights (explained later) uses an iteratively reweighted least-squares algorithm, and follows this procedure:
1. First, we set the model by weighted least squares using multi-square weight minimization.
2. Then, we calculate the residuals (after adjusting them) and give them a standard value. These residuals are given by
$r_{adjusted} = r_i / (sqrt(i - h_i))$
r_i are the usual least-squares residuals and h_i are *leverages* that adjust the residuals by down-weighting high-leverage data points, which have a large effect on the least-squares fit. The standardized adjusted residuals(r) are given by
$$r = r_{adjusted} / K$$
K is a tuning constant, K=4.685, s=robust variance given by $MaD/0.6745$ where MaD=median absolute deviation of the residuals. Mathematically,
$MaD = median_i (|X_i - median_j(X_j)|)$
1. We find the robust weights as a function of r. The multi-square weights are given by
$$w_i = \begin{cases} (1-(r_i)^2)^2 & \text{if } |r_i| < 1 \\ 0 & \text{if } |r_i| >= 1 \end{cases}$$
2. If the curve converges within a defined tolerable range, our work is done. Otherwise, we perform the next iteration of the fitting procedure by returning to the first step.

Multi-square weight minimization: By extension of definition of a bi-squared number, a multi-square number is the sum of squares of two or more numbers. This method is used to minimize a weighted sum of squares. The weight given to each data point depends on how far it is from the fitted line.

$y=a_1+a_2x_1+a_3x_2+\ldots+a_{m+1}x_m$ is a general form of m variable regression. For n sets of values $\{y(i),x_1(i),x_2(i),\ldots,x_m(i)\}$, $i=1,2,3\ldots n$; we have n equations:
$y(i)=a_1+a_2x_1(i)+a_3x_2(i)+\ldots a_{n-1}x_n(i)$,
which in matrix form is $Y_{nx1}=X_{nxm}A_{mx1}$ where X matrix has 1st column of1s,2nd column of x_1 values (i.e. 1st row of 1st of n readings,...i^{th} row=i^{th} reading of x_1),3rd column of x_2 ,i^{th} column of x_{i-1} and the last column ($m+1^{th}$ column) of x_m values.

The central point of multi-square weight minimization is, unlike simple least square minimization, we do not give same value/weight to the equation $y=a_1+a_2x_1+a_3x_2+\ldots+a_{m+1}x_m$ for every value of i.Let m_y denote mean of y_i .The weight assigned to the ith equation is determined by the value of $(y_i-m_y)^2$. We have used the Andrews function for our procedure but any of the weight assigning functions as suggested in figure2 of [1]may be tried out. For region specific application, the user may try out different functions to decide upon the best predictor for a particular set of data.

In matrix form,
WY=WXA. Where the weight matrix must be nxn, with elements $w_{i,i}$=weight assigned to y_i ;all elements except lead diagonal elements=0.
We have to solve for the coefficient matrix A;
we know W,Y and X.
Solving for A:
$X^TWY=X^TWXA$
Or, $(X^TWX)^{-1}X^TWY=A$.
This coefficient matrix A is used in the next robust approximation.

This method is alterable based on available resources and memory space. We can easily limit the number of iterations to enhance system simplicity by just adding a counter to the algorithm and checking it at the end of every fit. As approximation system improves, the system needed to support it becomes more complicated. For high end systems, non-linear regression models may even be used. For simple sensors, just 2 or 3 iterations of the above algorithm is sufficient to provide a reasonably good approximation over simple least square fit taking the system simplicity into account.

Time Multiplier function: This predicts the time interval in minutes between two successive readings. This is a worst case predictor that tells how soon, or how late the next reading must be taken to predict flood successfully based on two parameters.

a) Difference in water level between subsequent readings-Say the water level has increased by an amount equal to 90% of flood line between two subsequent readings. Our predictor assumes the increase is not uniform over the interval, but may have happened in the last few moments. Thus it asks for another reading in the minimum possible time to see the gradient and make a better prediction. (Note: Flood is not predicted just if the parameter value is high, we only ask for another reading faster for accurate prediction.)
b) Present water level-Say the water level has reached 90% of flood line. A little rain/discharge any moment can trigger a flood. So it is best to take readings as soon as possible and make accurate predictions.

Continuing the thought process, we assign different time intervals for subsequent readings as logical from the measured/calculated values of these parameters.

We define a *time set* containing different time intervals at which the sensor nodes can take readings. Based on the above discussion, the time multiplier function decides which value of the time set is to be taken for a particular calculation.

This function decides the time interval based on a worst case scenario but it doesn't affect prediction of flood. A worst case flood predictor would generate numerous false alarms, hence is undesirable.

Recalibration of time interval: Suppose the next reading is slated to be after 2 hours. But our algorithm predicts a flood within an hour from now. The time interval must be changed to be at least less than the time at which flood is predicted. *If a flood is predicted before the minimum time interval in the time set, an alarm must be issued.*

Consideration for node storage capacity: Our algorithm stores the regression coefficient values and frees the system memory by removing parameter values whenever there is a constraint on system memory. Effectively, nothing is lost as the single coefficient matrix is the result desirable from such enormous amounts of parameter data. A new coefficient matrix is constructed using the new inputs. A resultant coefficient matrix calculated using the weighted mean of these two, each matrix assigned a weight in proportion to the number of readings used in it.

Improvements over [1]:

i) Time adjustment factor- [1] does not talk about forecast time interval for next reading/flood prediction. But we have introduced a logical time predictor to decide the next time for taking a reading. Say flood may occur after a week at the present rate of rainfall. It is impractical to ask for data every 5 minutes now. Our algorithm handles these issues.

ii)Improvement of flood dependency model on its parameters- [1] suggests to incorporate prediction error values as a parameter along with rainfall, etc. (other parameters on which flood level depends) to recalibrate the regression based model and predict a flood level with better accuracy. Treating error as a parameter affecting water level is a poor technique. Also, the parameters will get considerably worsened in presence of any outliers. We append the present input values to our data tables to do the same recalibration using robust techniques quite insensitive to outliers but have nearly same simplicity.

iii) Use of weighted/Robust linear model- [1] suggests smoothing the data using a low pass filter. Arguably, a much better and formal technique is to assign weights to each data and compute accordingly. Its compatibility with low end systems has already been discussed.

iv) Consideration for node storage capacity- As discussed, our algorithm effectively uses all the past data though the actual data is deleted when it exceeds system memory capacity. [1] does not talk about system memory constraints.

v) Independency w.r.t number of parameters- Theoretically, our algorithm can handle any number of parameters and data elements, the only restriction being memory and/or available resources.

4   Simulation Results

Our simulation was conducted in MATLAB. Predicted water-levels were extremely close to actual measurements. Only once the river water level crossed threshold signalling the onset of flood as in Fig. 3. False alarms were not generated in any predicted value proving the reliability of our scheme. We simulated the regression model for water level with reference to two parameters-rainfall and discharge from dam. Fig. 4 denotes the percentage errors in predicted water level at different time instants compared to the actual water level measured at those instants.

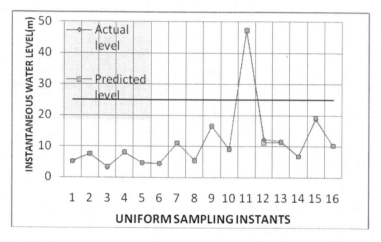

Fig. 3. Plot showing the measured and predicted values of instantaneous water levels at different instants

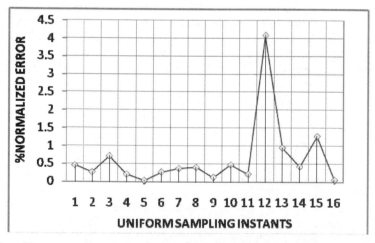

Fig. 4. Plot of Percentage Error in Predicted Instantaneous Water Level w.r.t. Actual Measured Water Level at different time instants (% error normalized with respect to the flood line)

5   Conclusion and Future Work

Our algorithm shows very accurate prediction results in forecasting critical parameters for flood prediction when the data collected are accurate. Even if some data entered may be wrong (due to sensor failure at that instant or loss of data in transmission, etc), the robust fit procedure (or a few iterations of multi-square weighted minimization for very simple nodes) is enough to provide a reasonably accurate data by assigning algorithm outlines a novel way to include the results from those data in calculations though the actual data is deleted. The advantages of our algorithm over present models are evident from the comparison with [1] and simulation results. Although real hardware implementation is going to be the next major step in developing this algorithm further, we can also improve upon accurate time prediction by manipulating the prediction algorithm to suit specific rivers. Future work involves performing field tests to observe the communication process between the nodes and the real-time implementation of the distributed prediction algorithm in situ.

References

1. Basha, E.A., Ravela, S., Rus, D.: Model-Based Monitoring for Early Warning Flood Detection. In: SenSys 2008, Raleigh, North Carolina, USA, November 5-7 (2008)
2. Lawson, C., Keats, J.B., Montgomery, D.C.: Comparison of Robust and Least-Squares Regression in Computer-Generated Probability Plots. IEEE Transactions on Reliability 46(1) (March 1997)
3. Ivanov, Y., Vivoni, E.R., Bras, R.L., Entekhabi, D.: Preserving high-resolution surface and rainfall data in operational-scale basin hydrology: a fully-distributed physically-based approach. Journal of Hydrology 298, 80–111 (2004)
4. Reed, S., Koren, V., Smith, M., Zhang, Z., Moreda, F., Seo, D.-J., Participants, D.: Overall distributed model intercomparison project results. Journal of Hydrology 298, 27–60 (2004)
5. Smith, M.B., Seo, D.-J., Koren, V.I., Reed, S.M., Zhang, Z., Duan, Q., Moreda, F., Cong, S.: The distributed model intercomparison project (DMIP): motivation and experiment design. Journal of Hydrology 298, 4–26 (2004)
6. Box, G.E.P., Jenkins, G.M.: Time series analysis: forecasting and control. Holden-Day, San Francisco (1976)
7. Andrews, D.F.: A Robust Method For Multiple Linear Regression. Technometrics 16, 125–127 (1974)
8. Ramsay, O.: A comparative study of several robust estimates of slope, intercept, and scale in linear regression. J. Amer. Statistical Assoc. 72, 608–615 (1977)
9. MATLAB 7.11.0, Help menu. Copyright 1984-2010. The Mathworks, Inc. (2010b)

AODV Enhancement Based on the Minimization of Route-Request Packets

Puja Rani and G.P. Biswas

Department of Computer Science & Engineering
Indian School of Mines (ISM), Dhanbad – 826004, Jharkhand, India
{puja20.rani,gpbiswas}@gmail.com

Abstract. A MANET is a self-configuring network of mobile devices connected by wireless links. Reactive Routing protocols for MANETs flood RREQ control packets to discover and establish route between the source-destination pairs. This situation becomes worse and degrades the network performance whenever several connections need to be established simultaneously. This paper proposes a mechanism to minimize the route-establishment overhead in AODV by controlling the flooding of RREQ packets. In brief, each intermediate node counts the number of RREQ packets flooded by it and if the count exceeds a threshold, stops further flooding. On the other hand, an intermediate node, after getting a RREP packet within reverse-route-lifetime reduces the counter value; otherwise the reverse link in its cache is removed along with the reduction of the counter value. The proposed scheme has been simulated using ns-2 and compared with the original AODV and it has been found that it enhances network performance.

Keywords: MANETs, Proactive and Reactive or On-demand routing protocol, AODV protocol, M-AODV, Network simulator.

1   Introduction

Mobile Ad hoc Networks (MANET) [3, 6] form a class of dynamic multi-hop network consisting of a set of mobile nodes that intercommunicate on shared wireless channels. Each node in MANET can operate as a host as well as a Router. Design of an efficient routing protocol for MANETs has been proven to be a very challenging task. Routing protocols [10] proposed for ad hoc networks can be classified into two groups: Proactive and Reactive and a short description of them is addressed now.

The Proactive routing was the first attempt for designing routing protocols for MANETs. For instance, the Proactive protocols such as DSDV (Destination-Sequenced Distance Vector) [1] and GSR (Global State Routing) [12] were based on the traditional distance vector and link state algorithms. These protocols periodically maintain and distribute route information to all nodes within the network. The disadvantages of these strategies were their lack of exceedingly large overhead produced due to blind flooding. Blind flooding result in broadcast storm Problem [5] and is thus not efficient. The On-demand or Reactive routing protocols [10], on the

N. Meghanathan et al. (Eds.): CCSIT 2012, Part III, LNICST 86, pp. 442–454, 2012.

other hand, are more efficient for routing in large ad hoc networks because they only maintain that route that is currently needed, initiating a path discovery process whenever a route is needed for message transfer, such as the Lightweight Mobile Routing (LMR) protocol [15], Ad-hoc On Demand Distance Vector Routing (AODV) [2,5], Temporally-Ordered Routing Algorithms (TORA) [14], and Dynamic Source Routing Protocol (DSR) [4] and ABR [13]. In AODV [2,5], the routing table at the nodes caches the next hop router information for a destination and use it as long as the next hop router remains active (originates or relays at least one packet for that destination within a specified time-out period). The DSR [4] is a source-based routing that identifies all the intermediate nodes to be included in the packet header.

When a number of connections need to be established simultaneously, the performance of the On-demand routing protocols is decreased because very few connections get established, due to enormous increase of RREQ/RREP packets. In this paper, we have proposed a technique to enhance the performance of AODV (any other Reactive protocol may be enhanced) by reducing the flooding of the control packets. In this case, each node maintains and updates a counter with respect to a threshold value such that it increases the counter for each flooding of new RREQ packet and stops the same when the counting reaches the *RREQ_Threshold* value, and it decreases the counter when a RREP packet is received or the reverse route entry is deleted from the routing table when the RREP is not received during reverse-route lifetime. The *RREQ_Threshold* value is selected by simulation such that the proposed modification of AODV ensures the establishment of the routes. The proposed scheme allows each node to forward only a limited number of RREQ packets, before getting any RREP packet or within a specified time-out period, thus avoid the network congestion during route discovery phase.

Rest of the paper is organized as follows. The proposed scheme and its implementation are given in section 2. The comparison of the proposed scheme with AODV is presented in section 3. Finally, the conclusion of the paper is given in section 4.

2   Proposed Modification of AODV for Minimization of RREQ/RREP Packets

In this section, a scheme has been proposed for minor modifications of AODV such that a large reduction of the RREQ overhead is possible during route discovery process of AODV if several routes are needed to be established simultaneously. For this, each node in the proposed scheme is allowed to broadcast only a limited number of RREQ packets, and for which each node maintains a counter and a predefined threshold, called *RREQ_Threshold*, beyond which no RREQ packet will be transmitted by a node of the network, before getting any RREP packet or within a specified timeout period. The detail implementation of the proposed modifications is addressed now.

2.1   Route Discovery in Proposed M-AODV

At the beginning the counter of each node is initialized to zero and it is updated as follows:

1)   **Counter Increment:** If the counter value does not exceed *RREQ-threshold*, a node broadcasts the received RREQ packet to its neighboring nodes and increments the counter value. It also sets a timer for the reverse link expiry time, called REV_ROUTE_LIFE and a reverse-link in its routing table to a node from which a RREQ packet is received. Otherwise, instead of broadcasting, it starts dropping the received RREQ packets.

2)   **Counter Decrement:** A node decrements the counter value whenever it receives RREP packet within REV_ROUTE_LIFE corresponding to a RREQ packet forwarded earlier. On the other hand, if it does not receive RREP within REV_ROUTE_LIFE, in addition to the decrement of the counter, the reverse-link entry is deleted from its routing table.

The algorithmic steps of the proposed modification are given below:

Step-1:   Whenever a source node, say *S*, wants to communicate with a destination node, say *D*, it broadcasts the RREQ packet to all of its neighbors, provided the route to *D* is not known to *S* previously.

Step-2:   Upon receiving the RREQ packet, each node checks whether it had received this RREQ packet before. If the RREQ packet is received before, the node discards packet and remains silent, else it executes the following operations:

(a)   The node establishes a reverse link to the node from which the RREQ is received.

(b)   It checks whether the node is the *D* itself or it has a fresh enough route to the *D*. If anyone of the above conditions is true, the node responds by unicasting a RREP back to the source node *S* using the reverse path established, otherwise it compares counter value, say C-Value, with the RREQ-threshold and executes any of the following cases:

Case-1:   If *C-Value >= RREQ_Threshold*, the node rejects the RREQ packet, i.e., the RREQ packet is not broadcasted.

Case 2:   If *C-Value < RREQ_Threshold*, the node increments its counter value, *C-Value* by 1 and broadcasts the RREQ packets to all of its subsequent neighbors.

Step-3:   Upon receiving the RREP packet within REV_ROUTE_LIFE, each node checks whether it has received this RREP before or not and if so, it discards the RREP packet and remains silent, else it continues with functions given below.

(a)   It establishes a forward link to the node from which the RREP is received.

(b) It checks whether it is the *S* itself or not and if so, the node starts sending the data packets using the route just discovered, else it decrements *C-Value* and forwards the RREP towards *S* using the reverse link.

Step-4: If a RREP is not received within REV_ROUTE_LIFE, a node deletes the reverse route from its routing table and decrements the *C-Value*.

2.2   Implementation of the Proposed M-AODV

As stated earlier, our proposed scheme makes some modifications in the route discovery process of AODV that reduce connection establishment overhead when a number of routes need to be established simultaneously. Each node in the proposed scheme keeps following information:

- A **routing table:** Each entry (*rt*) of the routing table has following fields:
  [Destination address (*dst*), Next hop address (*next_hop*), Destination sequence number (*rt_seqno*), Hop count (*hops*), Route type (*rt_type*)], where

$$
rt\_type \ = \ \begin{cases} 1 & \text{for reverse link} \\ 0 & \text{for forward link} \end{cases}
$$

  The *rt_type* is a newly added field in routing table and it is used for decrementing the counter value at a node which forwards the RREQ packet, but does not receive any RREP packet within REV_ROUTE_LIFE.
- A **Counter** (*C-Value*): The *C-Value* counts the number of RREQ packets that are forwarded by a node to its neighboring nodes. *C-value* is initialized to 0 for every node.
- A **RREQ Threshold (RREQ-Threshold***)***:** The RREQ-Threshold is the maximum number of RREQ packets that can be broadcasted by a node, before getting any corresponding RREP or within a specified timeout period.
- A **broadcast id** (*bid*)**:-** it is initialized to 0 for every node.
- A **sequence number** (*seqno*)**:-** it is initialized to 0 for every node.

The pseudo code for the proposed M-AODV (modified AODV) is given in Annexure 1.

2.3   Comparasion of RREQ/RREP Packets Injected in AODV and Proposed M-AODV

Since each node in M-AODV is allowed to broadcast a limited number of RREQ packets, so the total number of RREQ/RREP control packets injected into the network is much less than the RREQ/RREP packets injected in AODV. An estimation of the number of control packets inserted in both AODV and M-AODV for establishing fixed number of connections and their comparison are given below.

According to [9], the average number of RREQ packets, say N_{RREQ1}, needed to be injected into the network to discover a single route in a network of diameter $E\ (h)$ is

$$N_{RREQ1} = E\ (d) + E\ (d)^2 + E\ (d)^3 + \ldots\ldots\ldots\ldots\ldots + E\ (d)^{E\ (h)}$$

where $E\ (d)$ is the average degree of a node.

Thus the total number of RREQ control packets injected into the network to set up $C\ (t)$ routes is

$$N_{TOTAL\text{-}RREQ1} = C\ (t) \times N_{RREQ}$$
$$N_{TOTAL\text{-}RREQ1} = C\ (t) \times [E\ (d) + E\ (d)^2 + E\ (d)^3 + \ldots\ldots\ldots\ldots\ldots + E\ (d)^{E\ (h)}]$$

Although both RREQ and RREP packets create control overhead in the AODV, the major-part of this overhead is due to RREQ packets, because the destination node for each complete path, unicasts a single RREP towards the source node S in the route discovery phase of the protocol. Thus if x number of alternate routes per source-destination pair are identified and all are replied, then the total control overhead in AODV 'contrl-ovhd' is

$$\text{Contrl-ovhd-AODV} = N_{TOTAL\text{-}RREQ1} + C(t) \times x \tag{1}$$

Now the estimation of control packet injected in the network using proposed M-AODV is given below:

The number of RREQ packets broadcasted by the ith node, for $1 \leq i \leq n$, where n is number of nodes present in the network is:

$$N_{RREQ2} = (RREQ\_Threshold + x_i) \times E(d)$$

where x_i is the additional RREQ packets over RREQ-Threshold broadcasted, due to receiving of RREP packets.

Total number of RREQ packets injected into the network is

$$N_{TOTAL-RREQ2} = \sum_{i=1}^{n} (RREQ\_Threshold + x_i) \times E\ (d)$$

$$= E\ (d) \times (n \times RREQ\_Threshold + \sum_{i=1}^{n} x_i)$$

Since $x_i \leq$ RREQ_Threshold, then we have,

$$N_{TOTAL-RREQ2} \leq n \times E(d) \times RREQ\_Threshold + n \times E(d) \times RREQ\_Threshold$$

$$\leq 2n \times E\ (d) \times RREQ\_Threshold$$

If the control overhead due to RREP is included, then the total control overhead in M-AODV is

$$\text{Contrl-ovhd-M-AODV} \leq N_{TOTAL\text{-}RREQ2} + C\ (t) \times x$$

Now the total reduction in the control overhead of the AODV and M-AODV can be calculated as

$N_{RED} = N_{TOTAL-RREQ1} - N_{TOTAL-RREQ2}$

$= (C (t) \times [E (d) + E (d)^2 + \ldots\ldots + E (d)^{E (h)})] - (2n \times E (d) \times$ RREQ_Threshold)

$= C (t) \times E (d) \times [1+ E (d) +\ldots\ldots + E (d)^{E (h)-1}] - 2n \times E (d) \times$ RREQ_Threshold

$$= \frac{C(t) \times E(d) \times [E(d)^{E(h)} - 1]}{E(d) - 1} - 2n \times E(d) \times RREQ\_Threshold$$

$$\cong C(t) \times E(d)^{E(h)} - 2n \times E(d) \times RREQ\_Threshold$$

$$\cong E(d)[C(t) \times E(d)^{E(h)-1} - 2n \times RREQ\_Threshold]$$

Since $E(d)^{E(h)-1} \geq RREQ\_Threshold$, then $N_{RED} > 0$ if $C (t) > 2n$, where n is the number of nodes in the network. Thus, the RREQ/RREQ control packets in AODV can be reduced to a large extent, if the number of connections to be set up is more than $2n$.

3   Simulation and Performance Analysis

Both the AODV and the proposed M-AODV has been simulated using NS-2 network simulator [7, 8] and their performance is reported in this section. The simulation results are measured in terms of two well known comparison metrics, called NRL (normalized routing load) that gives how many control packets are needed to deliver one data packet to the destination, and Percentage of PDF (packet delivery fraction). PDF is defined as the ratio of the total data packets delivered to the destination, to the total data packets sent by the source. The NRL and PDF have been obtained by varying the number of network nodes, number of connections to be established and the RREQ_Threshold used. The following simulation parameters have been considered in our simulation experiments:

Network topology size	:	500 m × 500 m
Number of nodes	:	50, 75 and 100
Simulation time	:	100 sec
Packet rate	:	4 Packets/sec
Packet size	:	512 bytes
RREQ-Threshold	:	45, 90 and 150

The figure 1 and figure 2 show the NRL values required for a network of 50 nodes for different number of connections established in the AODV and the proposed

M-AODV respectively, where three threshold values for RREQ-Threshold = 45, 90 and 150 have been used in M-AODV. It can be seen that the NRL values required in AODV increase very rapidly with the increase of number of connections, whereas the NRL values in M-AODV do not increase with the increase of number of connections, i.e., a large number of connections can be established with almost a constant NRL value. Also the differences of NRL values in AODV and M-AODV are significant.

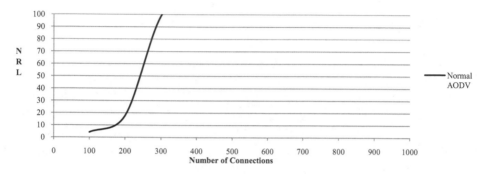

Fig. 1. NRL versus number of connections in AODV (Network with 50 nodes)

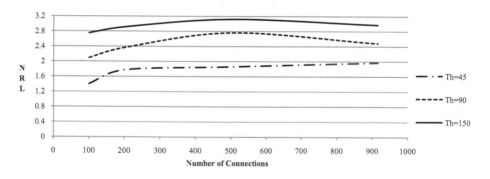

Fig. 2. NRL versus number of connections in M-AODV (Network with 50 nodes)

The PDF values versus number of connections in a network of 50 nodes are given in figure 3, which shows better PDF in M-AODV than the AODV. Also it shows that PDF values in the proposed M-AODV can be further increased by properly adjusting the RREQ-Threshold values.

Similar experiments have been carried out with the networks having 75 and 100 nodes and their results have been shown in figures 4-9. It can be seen that the proposed M-AODV improves both NRL and PDF significantly, and thus performs far better than the original AODV.

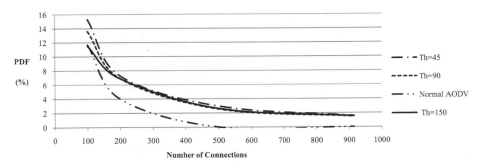

Fig. 3. PDF versus number of connections in AODV and M-AODV (Network with 50 nodes)

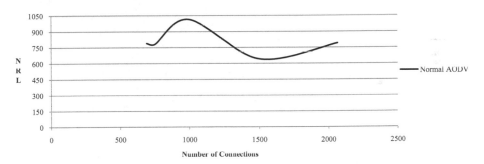

Fig. 4. NRL versus number of connections in AODV (Network with 75 nodes)

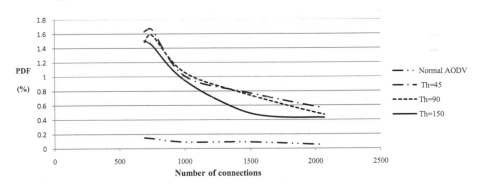

Fig. 5. NRL versus number of connections in M-AODV (Network with 75 nodes)

In summary, our proposed scheme M-AODV achieves more performance when compared to Normal AODV and this achievement can be maximized by critically adjusting the RREQ-Threshold value, otherwise, the network performance is decreased. Because, when we increase the threshold value, the PDF start decreasing and NRL starts increasing and as a result, the control packets injected into the network are increased. These control packets then contend with the data packets to access the shared wireless medium, and thus reduce the data delivery to the destination and hence reduce the network performance. On the other hand, if the threshold value is decreased too much, the injection of control packet into the network is reduced, but the time required to set up the pre-specified number of connections is increased, thus the network is underutilized and reduces the performance.

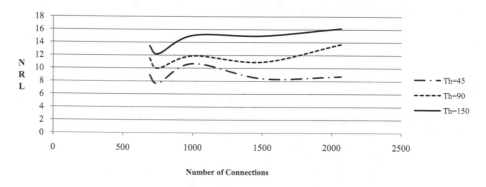

Fig. 6. PDF versus number of connections in AODV and M-AODV (Network with 75 nodes)

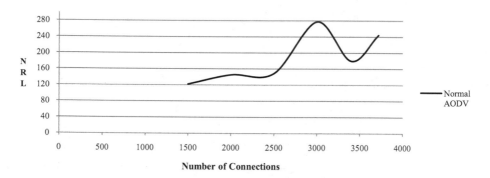

Fig. 7. NRL versus number of connections in AODV (Network with 100 nodes)

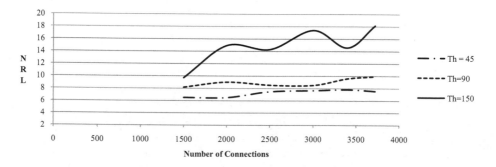

Fig. 8. NRL versus number of connections in M-AODV (Network with 100 nodes)

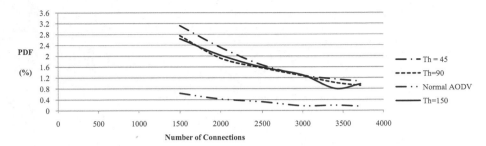

Fig. 9. PDF versus number of connections in AODV and M-AODV (Network with 100 nodes)

4   Conclusion

In this paper, we proposed a scheme for minimizing the routing overhead in the Ad hoc on demand routing protocol (AODV), when a number of connections need to be established simultaneously. In AODV, when a number of connections need to be established simultaneously, then due to the large control overhead, very few data packet gets delivered. Our proposed scheme improves the performance of AODV in such situations. We also simulated our proposal on ns-2.34 and verify that our proposal actually give better result than AODV in worse situation (when a lot of connections need to be established simultaneously).

References

[1] Perkins, C.E., Bhagvat, P.: Highly dynamic destination-sequenced distance-vector routing (DSDV) for mobile computers. In: Proceeding of the Conference on Communications Architectures, Protocols and Applications (SIGCOMM 1994), pp. 234–244 (October 1999)

[2] Perkins, C., Belding-Royer, E., Das, S.: RFC-3561, Ad Hoc on-Demand Distance Vector Routing (July 2003), http://www.faqs.org/rfcs/rfc3561.html

[3] Corson, S., Macker, J.: RFC-2501, Mobile Ad hoc Networking (MANET): Routing Protocol Performance Issues and Evaluation Considerations (January 1999), http://www.ietf.org/rfc/rfc2501.txt, http://www.faqs.org/rfcs/rfc2501.html

[4] Johnson, D., Maltz, D., Hu, Y.: RFC-4728, The dynamic source routing protocol for Mobile ad hoc networks (DSR) (February 2007),

[5] http://www.faqs.org/rfcs/rfc4728.html

[6] Perkins, C.E., Royer, E.M.: Ad-Hoc On Demand Distance Vector Routing. In: Proceedings of the 2nd IEEE Workshop on Mobile Computing Systems and Applications (WMCSA), New Orleans, LA, pp. 90–100 (February 1999)

[7] Spojmenovic, I.: Handbook of wireless network and mobile computing. Publication viley-Interscience

[8] The NS Manual (October 2, 2006), http://www.isi.edu/nsnam/ns

[9] The Network Simulator NS-2 tutorial homepage, http://www.isi.edu/nsnam/ns/tutorial/index.html

[10] Mann, R.P., Arbindi, S., Namuduri, K.: Control Traffic Analysis of On-Demand Routing Protocols in Ad-hoc wireless Networks. In: IEEE 62nd Vehicular Technology Conference, pp. 301–305

[11] Royer, E.M., Toh, C.-K.: A Review of Current Routing Protocols for Ad-hoc Wireless Mobile Networks. IEEE Personal Comn., 46–55 (April 1999)

[12] Chiang, C.C., Gerla, M.: Routing and multicast in multi hop, mobile wireless networks. In: Proceedings of IEEE ICUPC 1997, San Diego, CA, pp. 546–551 (October 1997)

[13] Chen, T.-W., Gerla, M.: Global State Routing: A New Routing Scheme for Ad-hoc Wireless Networks, pp. 171–175 (June 1998)

[14] Toh, C.-K.: Associativity based routing for ad hoc mobile networks. Wireless Personal Communications Journal, Special Issue on Mobile Networking and Computing Systems 4(2), 103–139 (1997)

[15] Park, V., Corson, S.: Temporally-Ordered Routing Algorithms (TORA) Version 1 Functional Specification. IETF, Internet Draft: draft-ietf-manet-tora-spec-01.txt (August 1998)

[16] Corson, M.S., Ephremides, A.: A distributed routing algorithm for mobile wireless Networks. ACM/Baltzer Journal of Wireless Networks 1(1), 61–81 (1995)

ANNEXURE 1: Pseudocode of the Proposed M-AODV

/* Source sends data to destination */

```
Procedure send-data (S, D)      //S: Source node, D: Destination node
    {
        if ( rt == 0)               //rt is a routing table entry for D and
                                        rt=0  means no entry for D
            Send -RREQ (D);
        else
            S sends data to D using the routing table entry rt;
    }


    Procedure Send-RREQ (D)         //S broadcast the RREQ packet to find
route to D
    {
        Broadcast  (P);     //P  is  a  RREQ  packet  that  contains  the
                                fields:hop_count,           RREQ_id,
                                dst_address,               dst_seqno,
                                src_address, src_seqno
    }
```

/* An intermediate node receives a RREQ packet */

```
Procedure Receive-RREQ (Packet P)
    {
        Check the RREQ packet for duplication;
        if (Already_received == 1)
        {
            Print "received duplicate RREQ packet, so discard";
```

```
            Return;
    }

    Receive the packet P;
    Create a reverse link to the source node if it does not exist;

    //check whether the received node is the destination or not
    if ( P.dst_address == myaddress)
    {
        Print "destination sending route reply";
        Update destination sequence number (seqno);
        Sendreply ( P.src_address, 1,  myaddress, seqno);
        Return;
    }

// check whether the received node has a fresh route to D or not,
            where
//dstrt is the routing table entry of the received node that points
            to D
    if ( dstrt != 0 && dstrt.rt_seqno > P.dst_seqno )
    {
        Sendreply ( P.src_address,  dstrt.hops + 1, P.dst_address,
                        dstrt.rt_seqno);
        Return;
    }

    //forward the RREQ packet
    if (C-value > = RREQ-Threshold)
    {
        Print "exceed the limits of forwarding the RREQ packets";
        discard (P);            return;
    }
    C-value++;
    P.hop_count = P.hop_count + 1;
    Broadcast_RREQ (P);
}


/* An intermediate node receives a RREP packet */
Procedure Receive-RREP (Packet P)
    {
    Create a forward link to the destination node if it does not exist;
        //check whether the received node is the original source or not

    if (myaddress == P.src_address)
    {
```

```
        Send all the buffered data packets;
        Return;
}


// otherwise forward the RREP
if (revrt != 0) //revrt is the reverse link routing table entry
{
        P.hop_count = P.hop_count + 1;
        forward the RREP packet P using routing entry revrt;
        C-value--;   return;
}
else                        // backward link to source does not exist.
{
        drop the RREP packet P;   return;
}
}


/* Counter update when a RREP packet is not received in time*/
Procedure Counterupdate ()     //This procedure take care of decrementing
{                       //C-value of a node which does not receive RREP
    // rt and rtn are two variable routing table entries
    for ( rt = routingtable.head; rt; rt = rtn)
    {
        rtn = rt.nextentry();
    if ( current_time >= rt.expiry_time )    // if rt is a stale entry
        {
    If ( rt.rt_flag == 1)             // if rt is a backward link entry
                C-value--;
         routingtable.removeentry (rt); //Remove rt from routing table
        }
    }
}
```

Key Management for Group Based Mobile Ad Hoc Networks

Kamal Kumar Chauhan[1] and Amit Kumar Singh Sanger[2]

[1] Anand Engineering College, Agra, India
[2] Hindustan College of Science and Technology, Mathura, India
{kamalchauhans,sanger.amit}@gmail.com

Abstract. Security of a network depends on reliable key management systems that generate and distribute keys between communicating parties in network. Due to lack of central server and infrastructure in mobile ad hoc networks, this is a major problem to manage the keys in the network. Dynamically changes in network's topology causes weak trust relationship among the nodes in the network. In this paper, we proposed a key management scheme for group based mobile ad hoc networks, where a group leader has responsibility of key management in its group. Proposed key management scheme is a decentralized scheme that does not require any Trusted Third Party (TTP) for key management. Proposed key management system authenticates new node before joining the network and update the keys when a node left the network.

Keywords: MANET, Group, Key management, Authentication.

1   Introduction

A mobile ad hoc network (MANET) is a special type of wireless network in which mobile hosts are connected by wireless interfaces forming a temporary network without any fixed infrastructure. In MANET, nodes communicate each other by forming a multi-hop radio network. Mobile nodes operate as not only end terminal but also as an intermediate router. Data packets sent by a source node can reach to destination node via a number of hops. Thus multi-hop scenario occurs in communication and the success of this communication depends on other nodes' cooperation.

Security of a network is an important factor that must be considered in constructing the network. A network has to achieve security requirements in terms of authentication, confidentiality, integrity, availability and non repudiation. These security requirements rely on the availability of secure key management. Fundamental goal of a key management system is to issue the keys to the nodes in the network to encrypt messages, to manage these keys and to prevent the improper use of legally issued keys. Absence of key management makes a network vulnerable to several attacks [6]. Therefore, key management system is the basic and important need for the security of a network. A key management system normally involves key generation, distribution, updation and revocation of keys in network. The feature of MANETs

N. Meghanathan et al. (Eds.): CCSIT 2012, Part III, LNICST 86, pp. 455–464, 2012.
© Institute for Computer Sciences, Social Informatics and Telecommunications Engineering 2012

such as dynamic topology, lack of centralized authority, resource constrained and node mobility are the major challenge in establishment of key management. Some techniques such as intrusion detection mechanism consume lot of nodes' battery power but cannot account for flexible membership changes. However, an efficient and secure key management system can solve this problem with an affordable cost.

In this paper, we proposed a key management scheme for group based MANET where only group leader can generate, distribute, update and revoke keys in its group. Proposed key management scheme neither depends on a central server nor is it fully distributed. Our key management scheme is decentralized scheme that combines both centralized key management as well as distributed key management so that it can have the merits of both methods. On the other hand, proposed key management scheme is a hybrid key management scheme combining both Symmetric Key Cryptography (SKC) and Public Key Cryptography (PKC).

Rest of the paper is organized as follows. In section 2 some of the related work to key management scheme is discussed. The proposed key management scheme and group formation algorithm are presented in section 3. Security analysis of proposed solution is explained in section 4 and section 5 gives conclusions.

2   Related Work

Many of the key management schemes have been proposed for mobile ad hoc network. Some of the research papers which focus on key management in MANET are discussed below:

L. Zhou and Z. J. Haas [1] presented a secure key management scheme based on (t, n) threshold cryptography. The system can tolerate $t-1$ compromised servers and this scheme does not describe how a node can contact t servers securely when server nodes are scattered in a large area and minimum t number of servers nodes have to present on ground every time, otherwise a new node cannot join network.

R. Blom [7] proposed a distributed symmetric key generation system based on the pre-shared keys and central server. Drawback of this scheme is that a node can derive the future key from the key chain which they have received from the main server and decrypt future traffic, hence lack of backward secrecy. Another problem is single point of failure.

H. N. Nguyen, H. Morino [8] proposed a threshold cryptography based scheme suited for MANET to provide robustness and defense against single point of failure. But main drawback in threshold cryptography is the difficulty in applying the distributive function. Drawback of this scheme is same as key management scheme proposed in [1].

L. Zhu, Y. Zhang, L. Feng [9] proposed a distributed key management scheme based on mobile agent carrying secret key and network state information. Limitation of the scheme is that it requires minimum t nodes must be present always to reconstruct the master private key. Another drawback is that continuously navigation of agent increases traffic and causes congestion in the network.

On the other hand, in the distributed certificate authority [3], [4], and [5] the authoritative power is distributed to several nodes. Since, it addresses the problem of single point failure. However, the major drawback is that the servers have to be chosen and pre-configured by an offline trusted party in advance. Another drawback of DCA is that the sufficient numbers of servers have to be present on ground.

3   Proposed Solution

3.1   System Model

A system model of open MANET is shown in Fig.1. Mobile nodes are divided into several groups in such a way that all the nodes are covered with no groups overlapped. Some of the nodes are selected as group leaders to perform key management and other administrative functions in its group. Aim of constructing the grouped based structure is that grouping in the network preserves the structure of network as much as possible, when nodes moves or topology is slowly changing. On the other hand, grouping reduces the number of keys, required for secure communication in network.

Group based structure divides the functions of a central server into several nodes (group leaders). Therefore, it combines both centralized and distributed approaches of key management providing decentralized solution. Such a structure of networks removes the vulnerability of compromising single central server. In the group based structure, if a group leader is compromised, only nodes of that group will be compromised and rest of the network will remain safe.

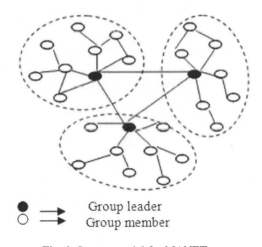

● ⟶   Group leader
○ ⟶   Group member

Fig. 1. System model for MANET

3.2   Group Formation Algorithm

Grouping or clustering is a process that divides the network into interconnected substructure known as groups. Grouping provides a better solution to the problem of key management and routing in MANET. But node mobility is major challenge for grouping in MANET. There is a group leader as coordinator in every group. Each group leader acts as a temporary base station within its zone or group and communicates with other group leader. A good grouping algorithm is one that divides the network into group in such this way that it preserves the structure of network as much as possible.

To select well suited node as group leader, we take into account its mobility, battery power and behavior of node. The following features are considered for grouping:

- Each group leader is capable to only support maximum 'x' number of nodes (a pre-defined value) efficiently. If a group leader is trying to serve more than 'x' number of nodes, the system's efficiency suffers.
- 'Mobility' is the important factor in deciding the group leader. Group leaders are responsible to preserve the structure of group as much as possible when nodes move or topology changing. Moving group leader quickly results detachment of nodes from group leader and also increases the probability of nodes' compromised. Mobility of a node is denoted by 'M' and can be measured as:

$$M = \frac{1}{T} \sum_{t=1}^{T} \sqrt{(Xt - Xt - 1)^2 + (Yt - Yt - 1)^2}$$

Where, (Xt, Yt) and (Xt-1, Yt-1) are the coordinates of a node at time t and t-1.

- 'Battery power' (B) is another important factor to decide a group leader. A group leader consumes more battery power than an ordinary node because a group leader has some extra responsibilities to carry out for its members. A node with maximum battery power should be selected as group leader.
- Another important parameter for electing the group leader is 'behavior of node'. A group leader is responsible for security of whole group. Group Leader monitors the nodes' activities continuously in the group and assigns them a Trust Level (T) on the basis of their behavior.

Finally, group leader is selected on the basis of weight (W), is defined as:

$$W = w_0M + w_1B + w_2T \tag{1}$$

where, w_0, w_1, and w_2 are the weight factor such as:

$$w_0 + w_1 + w_2 = 1 \tag{2}$$

Select a node as group leader with the smallest weight. All the neighbors of the selected group leader are no longer allowed to participate in the election procedure of group leader.

3.3   Key Management Scheme

In this section, proposed key management scheme in group based mobile ad hoc networks is described. Proposed key management scheme includes key generation, distribution and revocation phase. We make following assumptions:

- An offline Trusted Authority is available outside the network which is responsible only to issue a certificate and public/private key pair for the new joining mobile nodes.
- Intergroup communication is done through group leaders.
- Group leaders are trusted.

3.3.1 Key Generation and Distribution

All the group leaders in network are assigned a unique id. Each group leader has a public/private key pair and a secure hash function (e.g. SHA or MD5). We define three types of keys in the network: Group key, this is a common key for all the members in group used to encrypt/decrypt all the traffic communicated in the group. Second key, is a symmetrical key shared between group leader and a member node and third key, is shared among the group leaders in network.

Group leaders generate group key for their groups independently. Group key is updated each time when a node joins or leaves the group to maintain the forward and backward secrecy. Second key (k) shared between group leader and a member node is the function of node_id and a secret number (selected by and known only to group leader).

$$f \text{ (node\_id, Sr)} = k \tag{3}$$

where f is a secure hash function selected by group leader , node_id is the id of node for which key 'k' is being generated and Sr is a secret number randomly selected by group leader and independent of the node_id.

Third key is shared among the group leaders in network. Group leaders can agree on a key to communicate securely using group Diffie-Hellman key agreement protocol [13]. This key is updated when a group leader is changed in any group and new elected group leader starts Diffie-Hellman key agreement to update the key.

3.3.2 Node Addition

Whenever, a new node wants to join the group. It sends a join request to group leader but this request might be captured by a malicious node in between group leader and new node to compromise the new node. On the other hand, a malicious node can also send a join request to group leader to join the group. Therefore, before joining the network it is necessary for both group leader as well as new node to authenticate each other. Upon successfully mutual authentication, a node can join the group and share a key with group leader in a secure manner. A new node can authenticate to group leader using challenge-response protocol. New node sends a challenge to group leader and group leader provide a valid response to be authenticated.

Group leader selects two large prime numbers 'p' and 'q' and calculates:

$$N=p*q$$

Group leader selects a random secret number 'S' and calculates:

$$V=S^2 \bmod N \qquad (1<S<N)$$

'N' and 'V' are publically announced in the group. When group leader has to authenticate itself i.e. it received a challenge from a node, it calculates:

$$X=R^2 \bmod N$$

where 'R' is a random number selected by group leader such that $1<R<N$.

Group leader sends {N, V, X} to new node as well as other members of group. After receiving (N, V, X), new node sends a challenge 'c' to all the members of group including group leader. Group leader calculates $Y=RS^C \bmod N$ and send it to group members and new node. All the group members and the new node calculate XV^C and match with Y^2. If both values are same, group leader is successfully authenticated.

After successful authenticating to group leader, new node can sends its certificate to group leader which is encrypted with the private key of offline certificate issuer. Group leader verifies the certificate using public key of certificate issuer. If nodes' certificate is valid, group leader extracts the public key of new node from its certificate, generate a node_id and sends node_id and its public key to the new node encrypted with public key of new node. To make node_id unique across the network, group leader concatenates its id with node_id. Group leader generates a key using equation (3) and sends it to new node in secure manner. Group leader then update group key and group members list and sends to the members of group encrypting by previous group key and to new node encrypted by key shared between new node and group leader. After joining the network, new node broadcasts its id and public key in the group. When a new node joins the network, the communication between group leader and new node takes place as follows:

A group of mobile nodes with a group leader of MANET is shown in Fig.2, where a new node 'A' wants to join the group. Following are the notations used in communication:

G $\longrightarrow$ Group, {L, M}

M $\longrightarrow$ Set of group members {m_1, m_2, m_3 ...m_n}

L $\longrightarrow$ Group leader

A $\longrightarrow$ New node

ID_A $\longrightarrow$ A's Identity given by group leader

K_{XY} $\longrightarrow$ Session key shared between node X and Y

e_X/d_X $\longrightarrow$ Public key/Private key of node X

DS_X $\longrightarrow$ Digital Signature of node X

T_X $\longrightarrow$ Timestamp added by node X

CERTx $\longrightarrow$ Certificate of node X

S_{LX} $\longrightarrow$ Symmetric key shared between group leader and node X.

X: Y {k(M)} $\longrightarrow$ Node X sends a message M encrypted with key k to node Y

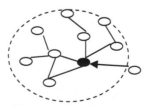

Fig. 2. A Group in MANET

A : L {A, Join_req}

L : A ∪ M {N, V, X}

A : L ∪ M {c}

L : A ∪ M {Y}

A   :   L {CERT$_A$}
L   :   A {e$_A$ (e$_L$, ID$_A$, S$_{LA}$)}
A   :   L {S$_{LA}$ (num}
L   :   A {S$_{LA}$ (num, member_list, group key)}
L   :   M {group_key (new_group_key)}

3.3.3 Key Agreement Protocol

If a node A wishes to communicate securely to node B. Before starting communication, they must agree on a session key. A starts communication by sending message:

$$A : B \{e_B (ID_A, ID_B, T_A, DS_A)\}$$

On receiving this message from A, B decrypts the message and verifies the signature of A using public key of A. If node B does not have A's public key, it sends a message to group leader conveying to send A's public key. Here following two cases are possible:

- A is a genuine node and group leader has pubic key of A. In this case, group leader sends A's public key to B. B then verifies A's signature and share a session key K$_{AB}$.

  B   :   A {e$_A$ (ID$_A$, ID$_B$, T$_A$, T$_B$, DS$_B$)}
  A   :   B {c$_B$ (T$_A$, T$_B$, num1, K$_{AB}$)}
  B   :   A {K$_{AB}$ (num1, num2)}

- In second case, A is malicious node and not affiliated to group leader. In this case, group leader would inform to all the member of group that node A is not a member of group. It might be a malicious node.

3.3.4 Node Deletion

Whenever, a node leaves the group. Group leader removes that node from member list and intimate other member. Group leader regenerates new group key and sends other nodes in group, encrypted by the key shared with individual node. A node can be removed from member list when one of the following events occurs:

- A node can leave the group with prior notification.
- A node can leave the group without any prior notification or node is not forwarding the packets or performing as malicious node. Group leader exclude that node forcefully. In this case, group leader must inform to neighbor leader nodes.

On the other hand, when a group leader leaves the group with or without prior notification, a new group leader must be elected that can coordinate the group. New group leader reconstructs new group key and distributes it using unicast message encrypted with the public key of members and share a new symmetric key with each member in group. New group leader distributes its public key and id to other group leader in network and starts Group Diffie-Hellman key agreement [13] to update key shared among the group leaders.

4   Security Analysis of Proposed Solution

In this section, we discuss the security analysis of proposed solution against different attacks.

4.1   Backward Secrecy

When a node leaves the network either group leader or member node, it should not be able decrypt the future encrypted traffic. In proposed solution, when a member node leaves the group, group leader regenerates new group key and sends to members in group in a secure manner. On the other hand, when a group leader leaves the network, a new group leader is elected and it regenerates group key and distributes in its group in a secure manner. New group leader also starts Group Diffie-Hellman key agreement to update the key shared among group leaders. This ensures that keys are updated securely and backward secrecy is maintained.

4.2   Forward Secrecy

Forward secrecy says that when a new node joins the network, it should not be able to decrypt the past encrypted traffic. On joining of new node, group leader regenerates new group key and sends to members of group encrypted with old group key and unicasts to new node encrypted with key shared between group leader and new node, ensuring forward secrecy.

4.3   Mutual Authentication

In proposed solution, at the time when a new node joins the network both new node and group leader authenticate each other mutually. After successful mutual authentication, a new node can join the network. On the other hand, when two nodes wish to communicate, they also authenticate each other by sending their Digital Signature.

4.4   Man in Middle Attack

In Man in the Middle (MITM) attack, an attacker remains invisible between two nodes say A and B. Attacker splits the connection into two connections, one between node A and attacker and second, between attacker and second node B. Key management scheme proposed in [12] is vulnerable to MITM attack. In their solution, initiator (new joining node) sends its public key to receiver (central node). In response, receiver generates a session key and sends to initiator. This session key is encrypted with initiator's public key. In this scheme, if there is an attacker in between initiator and central node, attacker can capture the public key of new node and send its public key to central node. Then central node would share the session key with attacker and attacker shares session key with initiator. But in proposed solution, when a new joins the network first, it authenticates group leader using challenge-response protocol before sending its certificate. An attacker cannot compromise a new node because challenge value from new node and response of the challenge from group leader are also sent to other members of group. In worst case, attacker can compromise the new node if and only if attacker had compromised all its neighbors already.

5   Conclusions

In this paper, we proposed a group formation algorithm and a key management scheme for group based mobile ad hoc networks. We described a secure key management scheme for group based a mobile ad hoc network that does not rely on a centralized authority for generating and distributing keys. Group leaders generate, maintain, and distribute the keys in their groups in a secure manner. Challenge-response protocol allows a new incoming node to authenticate to group leader, then joins group.

Proposed solution is a decentralized scheme and hybrid solution combining both symmetric and asymmetric cryptography algorithms. Security analysis of proposed solution in section 4 shows that proposed key management maintains forward and backward secrecy and provides security against many attacks such as reply attack, man in the middle attack etc. Limitation of proposed solution is that key management is based on public key cryptography, so it consumes more battery power in comparison of other key management schemes.

References

1. Zhou, L., Haas, Z.J.: Securing ad hoc networks. IEEE Network 13(6), 24–30 (1999)
2. Ge, M., Lam, K.-Y.: Self-healing Key Management Service for Mobile Ad Hoc Networks. In: Proceeding of First International Conference on Ubiquitous and Future Networks (June 2009)
3. Yi, S., Kravets, R.: MOCA: Mobile Certificate Authority for Wireless Ad hoc networks. In: 2nd Annual PKI Research Workshop, PKI 2003 (2003)
4. Luo, H.Y., Kong, J.J., Zerfos, P., Lu, S.W., Zhang, L.X.: Ursa: Ubiquitous and robust access control for mobile ad hoc networks. IEEE/ACM Transactions on Networking 12(6), 1049–1063 (2004)
5. Al-Shurman, M., Yoo, S.-M., Kim, B.: Distributive Key Management for Mobile Ad Hoc Networks. In: International Conference on Multimedia and Ubiquitous Engineering, pp. 533–536 (2008)
6. Kettaf, N., Abouaissa, H., Lorenz, P.: An Efficient Heterogeneous Key Management approach For Secure Multicast Communication in Ad hoc networks. In: Telecommunication System, vol. 37, pp. 29–36. Springer, Heidelberg (2008)
7. Blom, R.: Optimal Class of Symmetric Key Generation Systems. In: Beth, T., Cot, N., Ingemarsson, I. (eds.) EUROCRYPT 1984. LNCS, vol. 209, pp. 335–338. Springer, Heidelberg (1985)
8. Nguyen, H.N., Morino, H.: A Key Management Scheme for Mobile Ad Hoc Networks Based on Threshold Cryptography for Providing Fast Authentication and Low Signaling Load. In: Enokido, T., Yan, L., Xiao, B., Kim, D.Y., Dai, Y.-S., Yang, L.T. (eds.) EUC-WS 2005. LNCS, vol. 3823, pp. 905–915. Springer, Heidelberg (2005)

9. Lina, Z., Yi, Z., Li, F.: Distributed Key Management in Ad hoc Network based on Mobile Agent. In: Proceeding of 2nd IEEE International Symposium on Intelligent Information Technology Application, vol. 1, pp. 600–604 (2008)
10. Safdar, G.A., McGrath, C., McLoone, M.: Limitations of Existing Wireless Networks Authentication and Key Management Techniques for MANETs. In: Proceeding of 7th IEEE International Symposium on Computer Networks, pp. 101–107 (2006)
11. Yang, Y.-T., Zeng, P., Fang, Y., Chi, Y.-P.: A Feasible Key Management Scheme in Ad hoc Network. In: 8th Conference on the International Conference on Software Engineering, Artificial Intelligence, Networking and Parallel/Distributed Computing (SNPD), pp. 300–303 (2007)
12. Boukerche, A., Ren, Y.: The Design of a Secure Key Management System for Mobile Ad Hoc Networks. In: The 33rd IEEE Conference on Local Computer Networks, pp. 302–327 (October 2008)
13. Zou, X., Ramamurthy, B.: A Simple Group Diffie-Hellman Key Agreement Protocol Without Member Serialization. In: Zhang, J., He, J.-H., Fu, Y. (eds.) CIS 2004. LNCS, vol. 3314, pp. 725–731. Springer, Heidelberg (2004)

Optimal Clustering in Zone Based Protocol of Wireless Sensor Network

S. Taruna, Jain Kusum Lata, and G.N. Purohit

Computer Science Department, Banasthali University, India
staruna71@yahoo.com,
kusum_2000@rediffmail.com,
gn_purohitjaipur@yahoo.co.in

Abstract. The placement of base stations in wireless sensor networks affect the coverage of sensor nodes and the energy consumption from communication. In this paper we analyzed the performance of the zone based clustering protocol [2] under varying position of base stations, different zone sizes and the effect on network life time with multiple base stations. While evaluating the communication overhead of various cluster sizes, we observed that the optimal cluster size for a given network is complex, depending on a range of parameters. We show that placing multiple base stations in place of single base station in zone based routing protocol enhance the network life time.

Keywords: Wireless sensor network, clustering protocol, network life time, base stations.

1 Introduction

WSN is an emerging technology that can be deployed in such situation where human interaction is not possible like border area tracking enemy moment or fire detection system. Figure 1 shows an overview of WSN. Sensor are deployed in the environment which can be fire area, border or open environment. These tiny devices sense the area of interest and then communicate with Base Station (BS). On BS the gathered information is analyzed.

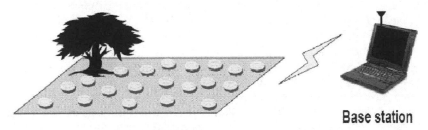

Base station

Fig. 1. Overview of a wireless sensor network

Clustering in wireless sensor networks (WSNs) is the process of dividing the nodes of the WSN into groups, where each group agrees on a central node, called the cluster head, which is responsible for gathering the sensory data of all group members, aggregating it and sending it to the base station(s).

N. Meghanathan et al. (Eds.): CCSIT 2012, Part III, LNICST 86, pp. 465–472, 2012.

Despite the wealth and variety of protocols and their individual evaluations through simulation, experimentation, and comparison to existing approaches, little help is available for the WSN application developer. We define the optimal cluster as the one sized such that routing data from the cluster member to cluster head and subsequently to base stations incurs the minimal communication overhead. We confronted this question of optimal clusters for zone based clustering algorithm ZBCA[2], a low energy, low overhead clustering protocol that divided the area into zone and create a cluster head per zone. While evaluating the communication overhead of various cluster sizes, we observed that the optimal cluster size for a given network is complex, depending on a range of parameters.

Therefore, in this paper, we explore the problem of optimal clustering in detail, through experimentation using MATLAB. Section 2 sketches the current state of the art of clustering algorithms, Section 3 Identifying the optimal cluster, Section 4 Energy model and Simulation parameters, Section 5 Experiments and Simulation Result, Section 6 conclusion.

2   Related Work

Routing is a process of selecting a path in the network between source and destination along which the data can be transmitted. Various protocols are available to route the data from node to base station in WSN in an energy efficient way, enhancing the network survivability. Battery power being limited in the sensor nodes, let the node to expire on its full consumption. The expired node is called the dead node which results in its no contribution in the network further.

Grouping sensor nodes into clusters has been widely pursued by the research community in order to achieve the network scalability objective.[1] Sensors organize themselves into clusters and each cluster has a leader called as cluster head(CH), i.e. sensor nodes form clusters where the low energy nodes called cluster members (CM) are used to perform the sensing in the proximity of the phenomenon. For the cluster based wireless sensor network, the cluster information and cluster head selection are the basic issues. The cluster head coordinates the communication among the cluster members and manages their data.[3]

Low-energy adaptive clustering hierarchy (LEACH) is a popular energy-efficient clustering algorithm for sensor networks. It involves distributed cluster formation. LEACH randomly selects a few sensor nodes as CHs and rotate this role to evenly load among the sensors in the network in each round. In LEACH, the cluster head (CH) nodes compress data arriving from nodes that belong to the respective cluster, and send an aggregated packet to the base station. A predetermined fraction of nodes, p, elect themselves as CHs in the following manner.

Another cluster selection zone based scheme Zone Based Clustering Algorithm (ZBCA)[2,4]. involves dividing the area into rectangle grids called zones. In this algorithm, communication between the sensor nodes for the CH selection is reduced, so that the energy consumption for CH selection can be reduced. . The probability of a node to become CH is p, where p is the maximum number of CHs in network. CHs organize and control the cluster members in their cluster. All nodes have to establish a connection with a CH to join its cluster. The CH of each zone sends the join request to nodes of its neighbouring zones only. On the basis of distance the nodes select one CH, which is most near to it. Sensor nodes send data to CHs and CHs further to base station. Cluster head is responsible for data aggregation and compression that reduces the energy consumed for data transmission.

3   Identifying the Optimal Cluster

Our analysis considers the effect of key clustering parameters on the communication overhead. We follow an experimental approach for two reasons. First, it is hard if not impossible to derive generally valid formulas for the network communication overhead that consider all parameters, especially random topologies. Our motivation is to make our results applicable on a real application and the most relevant scenarios from our experiments directly derive the optimal clustering parameters. We performed our simulations in MATLAB. In the scenario, nodes have uniform random distribution in area. The network area is divided into equal-size zone and each node has a cluster. Results are presented for a variety of cluster sizes that allow the area to be precisely divided into such equal-size zone. The shortest distance in terms of ETX, expected number of transmissions, is computed between each node and its corresponding cluster head and between all cluster heads and the base stations. The energy expenditure is calculated as the sum of ETX and ERX (expected number of receivers) for one round of data gathering. Overhearing costs are included in ERX. Cluster formation energy is used Each of the reported experiments is the mean of 100 independent random topologies with random nodes selected as base stations Our goal is always to identify the optimal cluster size for scenarios, first studying the placement of base stations and then the varying size of zone for the clustering in Zone based routing Algorithm.

4   Energy Model and Simulation Parameters

We use the energy model for simulation as [3,5]. Following simulation parameters is used for the simulation.

Table 1. Simulation Parameters

Parameter	Values
Simulation Round	2000
Topology Size	200 X 200
Number of nodes	100
CH probability	0.5
Initial node power	0.5 Joule
Nodes Distribution	Nodes are uniformly randomly distributed
BS position	Located at (100,250)
Energy for Transmission (ETX)	50*0.000000001
Energy for Reception (ERX)	50*0.000000001
Energy for Data Aggregation (EDA)	5*0.000000001

5   Experiments and Simulation Result

Simulation is performed for two scenarios.

5.1   Multiple Base Stations

In this experiment we change the location of the base station and number of base station. In the first experiment there is a single base station located at the boundary of the wireless sensor area. Table 2 show the distance from the first cluster head to base station. In each round cluster head send the aggregated data to the base station. According to energy model transmission energy depend on the distance. As the distance increases node required the more energy for transmission.

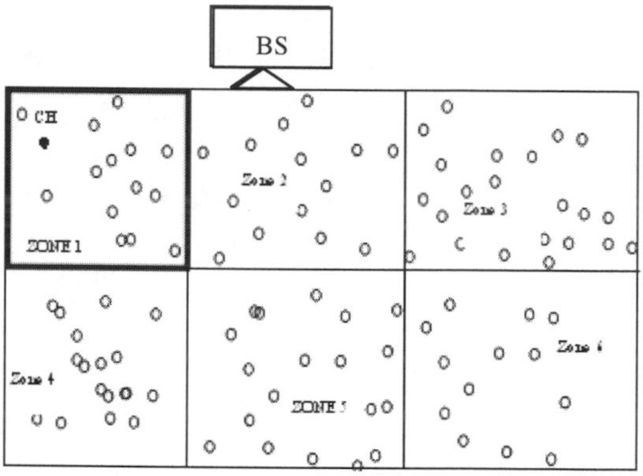

Fig. 2. Zone based clustering with single base station

Table 2. Energy consumption for a single transmission from cluster head to base station in single base station scenario

Zone ID	Distance from cluster to Base Station	Energy consumption for a single transmission
		$E=ETX*PL+Emp*PL*(dist*dist*dist))$
Z1	117.47	5.21073E-05
Z2	100.54	5.13212E-05
Z3	110.89	5.17726E-05
Z4	231.48	6.61244E-05
Z5	226.88	6.51821E-05
Z6	234.09	6.6676E-05

If we use 2 base station located at the boundary of the network area in opposite direction.

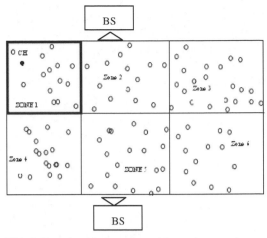

Fig. 3. Zone based clustering with two base station

Following table shows the energy consumption for the single transmission from cluster head to base station.

Table 3. Energy consumption for a single transmission from cluster head to base station in two base station scenarios

Zone ID	Distance from the Cluster head to base station near to it.	Energy consumption for a single transmission
		E=ETX*PL+Emp*PL*(dist*dist*dist))
Z1	182.44	5.78941E-05
Z2	177.13	5.72247E-05
Z3	187.88	5.86215E-05
Z4	176.92	5.7199E-05
Z5	150.36	5.44192E-05
Z6	180.49	5.76437E-05

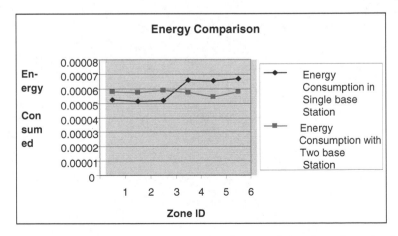

Fig. 4. Comparison in energy consumption for a single transmission from cluster head to base station in one and two base station scenarios

5.1.1 **Network Performance Can Also Be Defined in Terms of Number of Round in Which First Node Dead. In Both above Scenario We Find the Number of Round in Which First Node Dead for 10 Simulation Runs.**

Table 4. Number of round in which first node dead in single base station scenario and two base station scenario

Simulation run	Number of round in which first node dead in case of single Base station located at boundary	Number of round in which first node dead in case of 2 base stations located at boundary in opposite direction
Simulation run 1	667	669
Simulation run 2	682	862
Simulation run 3	754	912
Simulation run 4	860	862
Simulation run 5	594	820
Simulation run 6	822	970
Simulation run 7	710	685
Simulation run 8	781	750
Simulation run 1	745	970
Simulation run 1	611	770

As above the range of first node dead in single base station is from 594 to 860 and in the two base station scenarios it range from 669 to 970. This shows the enhancement in network life time.

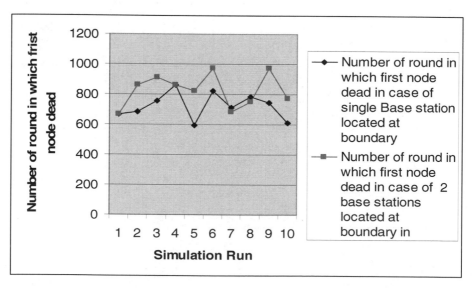

Fig. 5. Number of round in which first node dead in single base station scenario and two base station scenario

5.2   Using Different Zone Size

We also perform simulation with the same simulation parameter but with different zone size. Simulation is done with 6 zone, 16 and 64 zone of network area. Following table shows the number of round in which first node dead.

Table 5. Number of rounds in which first dead node occurs with different zone size

Simulation Run	With 6 zone (100X100m)	with 16 zones (50X50m)	With 64 zone (25X25m)
1	745	1054	1205
2	792	1070	1340
3	683	970	1190
4	782	1140	1423
5	743	1005	1322
6	740	1280	1306
7	692	750	1155
8	699	1153	1465
9	763	1295	1537
10	635	929	1211

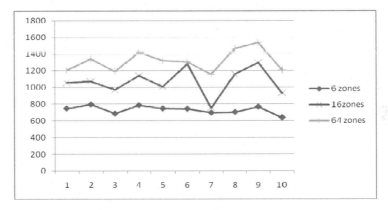

Fig. 6. No. of round in which first dead node occurs with different zone size

As shown in above table as we reduce the area of zone the round number in which the first node dead occur is increased. For a large network area the area can be divided in the smaller zone to increase the network lifetime.

6   Conclusion

In wireless sensor area network clustering is used to increase network lifetime. A zone based algorithm enhance the network life time by reducing the communication cost for cluster selection. As the simulation result show if we increase the number of base station than the energy required for communication will be decrease. Transmission energy depends on the distance and distance for the communication is less in multiple base station scenarios. Placement of the base stations also effect the communication energy. In zone based algorithm the size of the zone will also affect the residual energy of the node. Although this is a theoretical simulation result for homogeneous network, but it can be easily used for the live application.

References

1. Abbasi, A.A., Younis, M.: A survey on clustering algorithms for wireless sensor networks. Computer Communications 30(14-15) (October 15, 2007)
2. Taruna, S., Lata, J.K., Purohit, G.N.: Performance Analysis of Energy Efficient Routing Protocol for Homogeneous Wireless Sensor Network. In: Proceedings of International Conferences on "Trends in Networks and Communication", NeCoM, Chennai, India (July 2011)
3. Al-Karaki, J., Kamal, A.: Routing Technique s in Wireless Sensor Net-works: A Survey. IEEE Communications Magazine 11(6), 6–28 (2004)
4. Taruna, S., Lata, J.K., Purohit, G.N.: Power Efficient Clustering Protocol (PECP)-Heterogeneous Wireless Sensor Network. International Journal of Wireless & Mobile Network (IJWMN) 3(3), 55–67 (2011)
5. Lin, C.R., Gerla, M.: Adaptive Clustering for Mobile Wireless Networks. IEEE Journal on Selected Areas in Communication 15(7), 1265–1275 (1997)
6. Heinzelman, W.R., Chandrakasan, A., Balakrishnan, H.: Energy efficient communication protocol for wireless microsensor networks. In: Proceedings of the Hawaii International Conference on System Sciences (2000)
7. Yu, J.Y., Chong, P.H.J.: A Survey of Clustering Schemes for Mobile Ad Hoc Networks. IEEE Commun. Surv. Tutorials 7, 32–48 (2005)
8. Lin, C.R., Gerla, M.: Adaptive Clustering for Mobile Wireless Networks. IEEE J. Sel. Areas Commun. 15, 1265–1275 (1997)

Optimized FZ-LEACH Using Exponential Weighted Moving Average for Wireless Sensor Network

K. Ramesh[1] and K. Somasundaram[2]

[1] Dept of ECE, Nandha Engineering College, Erode
[2] Dept of CSE, Arupadai Veedu Institute of Technology, Chennai
rameshk.me@gmail.com, soms72@yahoo.com

Abstract. Wireless Sensor Network (WSN), fundamentally opportunistic communication system, where communication links only exist temporally rendering. It is impossible to establish end to end connection for data delivery. In such network, routing is largely based on nodal contact probability. The basic idea of this WSN is to distribute the group mobile node with similar mobility pattern into a cluster. A new energy efficient clustering protocol OFZ-LEACH, which eliminates the above problem by forming Far-Zone. Far-Zone is a group of sensor nodes which are placed at locations where their energies are less than a threshold an Exponentially Weighted Moving Average (EWMA) scheme is employed for on-line updating nodal contact. Based on this, nodal contact probabilities, the set of functions are used. This function is used for clustering formation and gateway selection.

Keywords: Wireless Sensor Network (WSN), Exponential weighted Moving Average (EWMA).

1 Introduction

Wireless Sensor Network (WSN) is an approach to computer network architecture that seeks to address the technical issues in heterogeneous networks that may lack continuous network connectivity. Examples of such networks are those operating in mobile or extreme terrestrial environments, or planned networks in space. WSNs span very challenging application scenarios where nodes (e.g., people and wild animals) move around in environments where infrastructures cannot be installed (e.g., emergency operations, military grounds, and protected environments).

Some solutions to routing have been presented for these cases, starting from the basic epidemic routing, where messages are blindly stored and forwarded to all neighboring nodes, generating a flood of messages. Existing routing protocols (AODV, DSR) are must take to a "store and forward" approach, where data is incrementally moved and stored throughout the network in hopes that it will eventually reach its destination. A common technique used to maximize the probability of a message being successfully transferred is to replicate many copies of the message in the hope that one will succeed in reaching its destination. This is feasible only on networks with large amounts of local storage and internodes

N. Meghanathan et al. (Eds.): CCSIT 2012, Part III, LNICST 86, pp. 473–481, 2012.

bandwidth relative to the expected traffic. The drawbacks that are encountered in Wireless sensor Networks are,

- ✓ Lack of Connectivity.
- ✓ Lack of Instantaneous End-To-End Paths
- ✓ Very High Number of Messages that are needed to obtain a successful delivery to the right recipient.

2   Problem Definitions

Due to the Lack of continuous communication among mobile nodes and possible errors in the estimation of nodal contact probability, convergence and stability becomes a major problem in the Wireless Sensor Network. In non clustered Wireless sensor network any node in the network may not able to get contact with the other neighboring node this is because of the nodes will not be having a correct updating in their nodal contact probability and the gateway information, therefore they lacks in communication. Low-Energy Adaptive Clustering Hierarchy (LEACH) [8] is the most popular cluster-based routing protocols in wireless sensor networks. In LEACH the cluster heads are randomly selected and when the cluster head die then another node will be selected as cluster head. Therefore, the cluster head role keeps on rotating to balance the energy dissipation of the sensor nodes in the networks. The function of cluster head nodes are to fuse and collect data arriving from cluster members and forward the aggregated data to the sink in order to reduce the amount of data and transmission of the duplicated data. The data collection is performed periodically. As a result, the nodes cannot provide end to end delivery of the information. At the same time nodes break up their communication if they move out of the coverage area.

3   FZ-LEACH Clustering Algorithm

The Fair Zone Low-Energy Adaptive Clustering Hierarchy (FZ-LEACH) clustering algorithm used to form a cluster in wireless sensor network. FZ-LEACH is generally divided into two phases the set-up phase and the steady-state phase. In the set-up phase, cluster heads are selected and clusters are organized. In the steady-state phase, the actual data transmissions to the sink take place. In the proposed FZ-LEACH algorithm, few nodes are randomly selected as Cluster Heads (CH). This role is rotated to all nodes to balance the energy dissipation of the sensor nodes in the network. The algorithm is event-driven, where the key part lies on the meeting event between any pair of nodes. The set of functions in the algorithm including Sync, Leave, and Join is outlined below. The Methodology will give an idea about, how the algorithm performs its function

3.1   Methodology

1. The base station (i.e. sink node) is located inside the sensing field.
2. Nodes are location-unaware, i.e. not equipped with GPS capable antennae.

3. Communication within the square area is not subjected to multipath fading.

4. The communication channel is symmetric.

5. Data gathered can be aggregated into single packet by Cluster Heads (CH).

6. Nodes are left unattended after deployment. Therefore battery re-charge is not possible.

7. An Exponentially Weighted Moving Average (EWMA) scheme is employed for on-line updating nodal contact probability.

8. Weighting factors which decrease exponentially. The weighting for each older data point decreases exponentially, giving much more importance to recent observations while still not discarding older observations entirely.

9. True contact probability. Subsequently, a set of functions including *Sync()*, *Leave()*, and *Join()* are devised to form clusters and select gateway nodes based on nodal contact probabilities.

10. The cluster table consists of four fields: Node ID, Contact Probability, Cluster ID, and Time Stamp.

11. Each entry in the table is inserted/ updated upon meeting with another node, by using the aforementioned online updating scheme.

12. The gateway table, used for routing, consists of four fields: Cluster ID, Gateway, Contact Probability, and Time Stamp.

3.2   Nodal Delivery Probability

The delivery probability indicates the likelihood that can deliver data messages to the sink. The delivery probability of a power i, is updated as follows,

$$\xi_i = \begin{cases} (1-\alpha)[\xi_i] + \alpha\xi_k & Transmission \\ \\ (1-\alpha)[\xi_i] & Timeout \end{cases} \tag{1}$$

where ξ_i is the delivery probability of power i before it is updated, ξ_k is the delivery probability of node k (a neighbor of node i), and α is a constant employed to keep partial memory of historic status.

Sync()

The *Sync()* process is invoked when two cluster members meet and both pass the membership check. It is designed to exchange and synchronize two local tables. The synchronization process is necessary because each node separately learns network parameters, which may differ from nodes to nodes. The Time Stamp field is used for the "better" knowledge of the network to deal with any conflict.

Leave

The node with lower stability must leave the cluster. The stability of a node is defined to be its minimum contact probability with cluster members. It indicates the likelihood that the node will be excluded from the cluster due to low contact probability. The leaving node then empties its gateway table and reset its Cluster ID.

Join ()

The *Join ()* procedure is employed for a node to join a "better" cluster or to merge two separate clusters. A node will join the other's cluster if

1. It passes membership check of all current members.
2. Its stability is going to be improved with the new cluster. By joining new cluster, it will copy the gateway table from the other node and update its cluster ID accordingly.
3. Thus the distributed clustering algorithm is used to form a cluster in DTMN [7] (Disruption-Tolerant Mobile Networks).

3.3   Cluster Based Routing

The cluster based routing protocol used to perform a routing in delay tolerant mobile network. We assume that Node i has a data message to Node j then, the types of cluster based routing protocol is given below.

Intra-cluster Routing

If Nodes i and j are in the same cluster, they have high chance to meet each other, thus Node i will transmit the data message to Node j directly upon their meeting. No relay node is necessarily involved, because we considering here the case of intra-cluster communication. Let MinPwri denote the minimum power level required by a node vi, $1 \leq i \leq N$ to communicate with a cluster head u, where N is the number of nodes within the cluster range All cluster members send their *MinPwri* to the CH. CH now computes *Average Minimum Reachability Power* (AMRP) with *MinPwri* values of all sensor nodes. AMRP can be defined as the mean of the minimum power levels required by all *N* nodes within the cluster range to reach

One-Hop Inter-cluster Routing

If they are not in the same cluster, Node i look up gateway information to Node j's cluster in its gateway table. If an entry is found, Node i send the data message to that gateway. Upon receiving the data message, the gateway will forward it to *any* node. e.g. Node *k,* in node j's clusters. Node *k,* which in sum delivers the data message to node j via Intra-cluster Routing. If no gateway entry is found, node i precede the Multi-hop Inter-cluster Routing as to be discussed next.

Multi-hop Intra Cluster Routing

If node i does not have any information about node j, the data transmission needs a multi-cluster routing scheme. Given the low connectivity environment, on-demand routing protocols, with extremely high packet dropping probability, will not work effectively here. However, any table-driven routing algorithm such as the following link-state-like protocol can be employed. In the protocol, every gateway node builds a *Cluster Connectivity Packet (CCP),* and distributes it to other gateways in the network. The CCP of a Gateway comprises its cluster ID and a list of clusters to which it serves as gateway along with corresponding contact probabilities. Such information can be readily obtained from the gateway table.

1. Once a gateway node accumulates a sufficient set of CCP's, it constructs a network graph. Each vertex in the graph stands for a cluster. A link connects two vertices if there are gateways between these two clusters.

2. The weight of the link is the contact probability of the corresponding gateway nodes. Based on the network graph, the shortest path algorithm is employed to establish the routing table. Each entry in the routing table consists of the ID of a destination cluster and the next-hop cluster ID.

3. Once the routing table is obtained, the routing is performed from a cluster to another cluster via one-hop Inter-cluster Routing and Intra cluster Routing. The diagram shows the cluster based routing protocols.

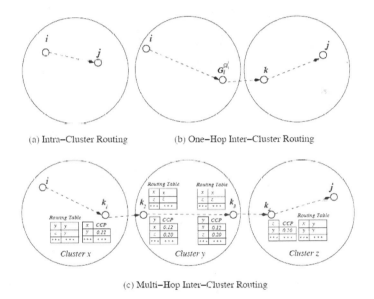

(a) Intra–Cluster Routing   (b) One–Hop Inter–Cluster Routing

(c) Multi–Hop Inter–Cluster Routing

Fig. 1. Cluster based routing protocol

By using the above mentioned[7] concepts with the block diagram in Fig 1 and the flow control the construction of Exponential Weighted Moving Average become simple. Thus the distributed clustering algorithm used to form a cluster in delay tolerant mobile networks and the cluster based routing protocol used to perform routing in delay tolerant mobile networks. We use the AMRP to estimate the communication cost. The AMRP of a node is a measure of the expected intra cluster communication energy consumption for communication to the cluster head. Using AMRP as communication cost, we can find out Far-Zone members. The nodes power levels below the AMRP are considered in Far-Zone. When Far-Zone is formed, any member of the zone is selected as ZH (Zone Head) in pure random basis only for that round may be one with the highest energy. The ZH create TDMA (Time Division

Multiple Access) schedule as LEACH and assign time slots to zone members to transmit the sense data to the ZH. ZH then transmit data to the BS (Base Station). In this way one round is completed.

4   Experimental Setup

The performance of power balanced communication scheme is evaluated using Network simulator-2, which simulate node mobility, realistic physical layer radio network interface and AODV protocol. Evaluation is based on the simulation of 50 nodes located in the area of 1500 x 300 m^2. The traffic simulator is constant bit rate (CBR). The three different scheme non cluster method, EWMA, and power balanced communication are used for comparison.

4.1   Performance Metrics

The performance metric used in this research is throughput packet delivery ratio, bandwidth end to end delay, energy construction and routing overhead. The various measures and details of the all parameters are given below.

Packet Delivery Ratio

It is defined to be the percentage of the ratio of number of packets received to the number of packets sent.

$$PDR = \frac{Number\ of\ packets\ received}{Number\ of\ packet\ sent} x100\ \% \tag{2}$$

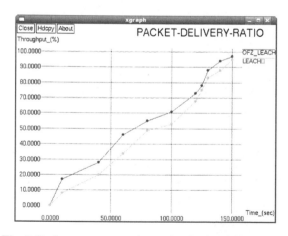

Fig. 2. Performance comparison using Packet delivery ratio

The graph shows in Fig 2 the variation of Packets (bytes) received based on the time when two different routing schemes are implemented.

End to End Delay

The time interval between the first packet and second packet is called End to End Delay. Here the total delay takes 1.3 in non-cluster method and 0.9 in EWMA and power balanced communication have 0.4.

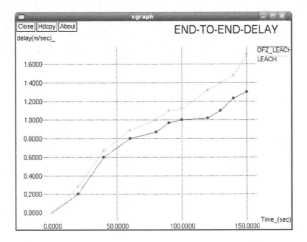

Fig. 3. Performance comparison using end to end latency

From the graph shows in Fig 3 power balance communication system achieves low end to end delay.

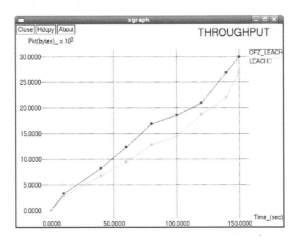

Fig. 4. Performance comparison using Throughput

Throughput

Throughput is the ratio of number of packets received to the time seconds.

$$Throughput = \frac{Number\ of\ packets\ received}{Time(sec)} \tag{3}$$

From the graph shows in Fig 4 throughput high value to the Power balanced communication when compare to other existing methods.

Energy- Consumption

Average energy consumed by node is decreased in our proposed method due to the creation of Fair- Zone Optimization. Fig 5 shows that remaining energy in LEACH & OFZ-LEACH.

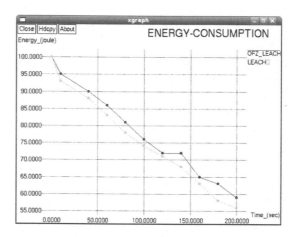

Fig. 5. Performance comparison using Energy- Consumption

5   Conclusions

Establishing end-to-end connections for data delivery among wireless sensor Networks becomes impossible as communication links only exist temporarily. In such networks, routing is largely based on nodal contact probabilities. To solve this problem, an exponentially weighted moving average (EWMA) scheme is employed for on-line updating nodal contact probability. In proposed OFZ-LEACH algorithm, which is based on the original protocol and considers a Far-Zone inside a large cluster. The results proves the improvement in the performance in the original LEACH protocol in terms of energy dissipation rate and network lifetime A set of functions including sync(), leave(), and join() are devised for cluster formation and gateway selection. Finally the gateway nodes exchange network information and perform routing. The results have shown that it achieves higher delivery ratio and significantly lower overhead and end-to-end delay, compared with its non-EWMA.

References

1. Y. Wang, H. Wu, F. Lin, and N.-F. Tzeng, 2008, "Cross-layer protocol design and optimization for delay/fault-tolerant mobile sensor networks," IEEE J. Sel. Areas Commun, vol. 26, no. 5, pp. 809–819.
2. H. Wu, Y. Wang, H. Dang, and F. Lin, 2007, "Analytic, simulation, and empirical evaluation of delay/fault-tolerant mobile sensor networks," IEEE Trans. Wireless Commun., vol. 6, no. 9, pp. 3287–3296.
3. Y. Wang and H. Wu, 2007, "Delay/fault-tolerant mobile sensor network (DFTMSN): a new paradigm for pervasive information gathering," IEEE Trans. Mobile Computing, vol. 6, no. 9, pp. 1021–1034.
4. Y. Wang and H. Wu, 2006, "DFT-MSN: the delay fault tolerant mobile sensor network for pervasive information gathering," in Proc. 26th Annual Joint Conference of the IEEE Computer and Communications Societies (INFOCOM'07), pp. 1235–1243.
5. M. Musolesi, S. Hailes, and C. Mascolo, 2005, "Adaptive routing for intermittently connected mobile ad hoc networks," in Proc. IEEE 6th International Symposium on a World of Wireless, Mobile and Multimedia Networks (WOWMOM), pp. 1–7.
6. T.Small and Z.J. Haas, 2005, "Resource and performance tradeoffs in delay tolerant wireless networks," in Proc. ACM SIGCOMM
7. Ha Dang and Hongyi Wu, 2010, Clustering and Cluster based Routing Protocol for Delay-Tolerant Mobile Networks," in IEEE Transactions On Wireless Communications, Vol. 9, NO. 6, pp.1874-1881
8. W.B. Heinzelman, A.P. Chandrakasan and H. Balakrishnan, "An Application-Specific Protocol Architecture for Wireless Microsensor Networks," IEEE Transactions on Wireless Communications, Vol. 1, No. 4, 2002, pp. 660-670.

IAMKeys: Independent and Adaptive Management of Keys for Security in Wireless Body Area Networks

Raghav V. Sampangi[1], Saurabh Dey[2], Shalini R. Urs[2],
and Srinivas Sampalli[1]

[1] Faculty of Computer Science, Dalhousie University, Canada
[2] International School of Information Management, India
raghav.vs@ieee.org, saurabh@isim.net.in,
shalini@isim.ac.in, srini@cs.dal.ca

Abstract. Wireless Body Area Networks (WBANs) have gained a lot of research attention in recent years since they offer tremendous benefits for remote health monitoring and continuous, real-time patient care. However, as with any wireless communication, data security in WBANs is a challenging design issue. Since such networks consist of small sensors placed on the human body, they impose resource and computational restrictions, thereby making the use of sophisticated and advanced encryption algorithms infeasible. This calls for the design of algorithms with a robust key generation / management scheme, which are reasonably resource optimal. This paper presents IAMKeys, an independent and adaptive key management scheme for improving the security of WBANs. The novelty of this scheme lies in the use of a randomly generated key for encrypting each data frame that is generated independently at both the sender and the receiver, eliminating the need for any key exchange. The simplicity of the encryption scheme, combined with the adaptability in key management makes the scheme simple, yet secure. The proposed algorithm is validated by performance analysis.

Keywords: body area networks, body area network security, wireless network security, key management, encryption.

1 Introduction

Recent advances in wireless communication and sensor technologies have meant that sensors can be used efficiently in human health monitoring. With sedentary lifestyles already having increased the risks of potentially fatal medical conditions such as high blood pressure, cardiac diseases, diabetes, and the like, and given the unpredictable nature of worsening of any such condition in a person, regular and continuous monitoring assumes high priority.

Wireless Body Area Networks (WBANs) [1] are a type of wireless sensor networks, where a group of sensors placed on the human body measure specific physiological parameters of a person and relay it to the monitoring medical center or hospital. This relay happens via the Internet or a cellular network, using

N. Meghanathan et al. (Eds.): CCSIT 2012, Part III, LNICST 86, pp. 482–494, 2012.

personal digital assistants (PDAs) or cellular phones as intermediary devices. Thus, WBANs seem to be a promising solution for the problem of continuous health monitoring. However, with a patient's personal health data travelling in the open, typically in a wireless channel, to reach the intermediary device and then the monitoring station, securing this data becomes critical. This, coupled with the fact that medical decisions are made based on the data received, assumes significant focus in the research on WBANs.

To achieve security in any network, the messages to be transmitted are encrypted using specialized encryption schemes and a special encryption key, and decrypted at the receiver end. Many advanced encryption algorithms, which are used for securing wireless networks, however, cannot be used in WBANs, given that they have severe power constraints and resource constraints since they are small sensor devices residing on a person [1]. Thus, it becomes crucial to design algorithms that are simple in computation and resource utilization, yet achieve the desired security. At the heart of any encryption algorithm is the successful management of the special encryption key. The key generation scheme must also be computationally inexpensive yet secure.

This paper presents a dynamic key generation/management scheme for encryption of data in a WBAN, with focus on security in the part of the network from the central controller node of the WBAN to the receiver at the monitoring station. This scheme makes use of the random nature of the physiological parameters and the simplicity of stream-cipher encryption scheme to achieve efficient encryption of sensor recorded data in the WBAN.

The rest of this paper is organized as follows: Section 2 presents the related work. Section 3 describes the proposed algorithm. Section 4 presents the performance analysis of the algorithm, while Section 5 provides a brief discussion on the scheme and its limitations. In Section 6, we conclude the paper and present a glimpse of the future work.

2   Related Work

A comprehensive description of WBANs, with a detailed description of the system architecture, construction and tested prototypes, is provided in the work by Otto et al [1]. In their work, they present the implementations of an activity sensor that detects an organ's activity, a motion sensor that detects the motion of the person, and a personal server (PS), with a network controller. Though the authors have described in detail the implementation aspects, they have very briefly described a possible security protocol for ZigBee. Data recorded and communicated by WBANs have a direct impact on the decisions made concerning a person's health and well-being. Thus, ensuring the reliability and security of this data assumes a central role in such a system.

Tan et al [2] present an identity-based encryption (IBE) scheme called IBELite for security in WBANs. In this scheme, a sensor generates a public key dynamically using an arbitrary string, but the sensors cannot create secret keys. They, thus, use a trusted third party to ensure security of data in WBAN.

Moving away from the conventional key generation schemes and capitalizing on the inherent random and time variant nature of biometric data, Venkatasubramanian et al [3] present a scheme where the electrocardiogram (EKG) signals of a person are used to generate cryptographic keys between two nodes in a WBAN. The sensors in the network agree upon a common key, generated based on the EKG reading of the patient, to secure inter-sensor communication. Mana et al [4,5] also use EKG signals to secure keys between sensor nodes and the base station, thereby focusing on securing the end-to-end communication, as well as communication among the nodes. On the other hand, Raazi et al [6] propose a scheme where any one of the recorded biometrics is used as the encryption key and is periodically communicated by the personal server to the nodes, as key refreshment schedules.

The proposed algorithm in this paper focuses on exploiting the random nature of physiological data and by introducing additional randomness dynamically. With an underlying distinction of the physiological data between people, this work aims to exploit these characteristics to implement a simple key generation scheme for securing data in a WBAN.

3   The Proposed Algorithm: IAMKeys

We consider the WBAN illustrated in Figure 1 for the purposes of this work. It includes sensors to measure the heart rate (S1), the blood pressure (S2) and the blood glucose (S3) of a patient. The sensors send their recorded data (after basic filtering to remove the noise) to the WBAN Central Controller Node (WCC), which is marked as the sensor node SC in the figure. SC acts as the sink node for receiving the data on the body. The WCC then aggregates the readings in a data frame, along with a sequence number and a timestamp. Figure 2 illustrates the data frame structure. The WCC encrypts the data frame and forwards it to the medical monitoring station, via the intermediate personal device, which in our example is a cellular phone. We consider securing the portion of this WBAN system beginning at the WCC and culminating at the monitoring station.

Resource restriction in WBANs is one of the primary reasons that led us to develop a customized encryption and key management algorithm. Since the network is deployed on the human body, frequent maintenance activities, such as replacement of batteries, would prove highly inconvenient for patients. In case we manage to strike a balance between the computational expense and the algorithm, the next concern to be addressed is that of key exchange. In other proposals, any encryption key that is generated (or refreshed) is exchanged between the sender and the receiver. If an adversary were to eavesdrop on such a conversation, the entire communication between the sender and the receiver will be jeopardized and vulnerable to attacks.

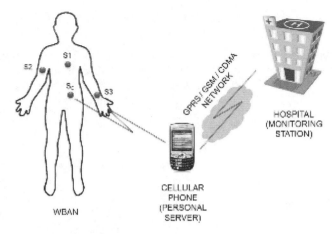

Fig. 1. WBAN used for the purposes of this work

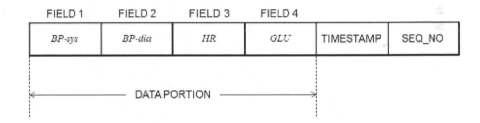

Fig. 2. Data frame format considered in this work

An obvious solution to such an impasse is the use of symmetric cryptography. However, the key being constant in such schemes poses a threat to the system in question. Our work revolves around a scheme that:

- Nullifies the need for key exchange;
- Enables independent generation of keys at both sender and receiver;
- Ensures sender authentication;
- Simplifies the encryption process; and,
- Prioritizes freshness of data

To ensure the successful operation of such a scheme, we make the following assumptions:

- An administrator at the monitoring station (typically, a hospital) deploys the WBAN on the patient.
- At the time of installation, the administrator loads five "dummy" reference frames into both the WCC and the monitoring station data receiver.
- The receiver acknowledges every successful transmission.
- The sender receives the acknowledgement within the transmission of three subsequent frames.

- The study of the effects of radiation of the sensors on the human body has not been considered in this work.

Figure 3 illustrates the proposed scheme in brief. Each data frame is encrypted using a stream cipher based encryption scheme, with a key that is a pseudorandom number. A pseudorandom number generator (PRNG) generates the key using one of the randomly chosen data fields of one of the randomly chosen reference frames as the seed. The encrypted frame is then transmitted.

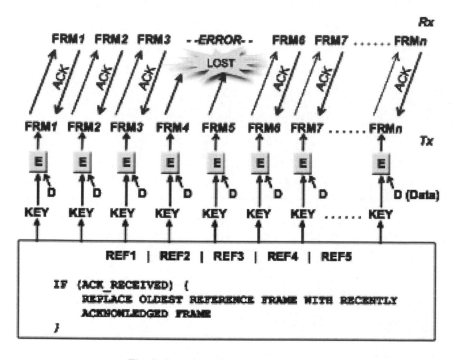

Fig. 3. Overview of the proposed scheme

Upon reception, the receiver verifies the identity of the sender, and on successful authentication, generates the key independently to decrypt the data. Following this, the receiver sends an acknowledgement to the sender (WCC). Upon receiving the acknowledgement, the WCC updates the reference frame list by replacing the oldest reference frame (indicated by the sequence number) with the currently acknowledged data frame. This is a gist of the operation of the presented scheme. In the following sub-sections, we describe the constituents of the scheme in detail.

3.1   Reference Frames

A crucial component of this scheme is the list of five reference frames that are a stored both at the sender and the receiver. During the WBAN deployment, the administrator loads these reference frames with identical dummy values at both the WCC and the monitoring station data receiver. When the receiver successfully receives the sent data frame, it sends an acknowledgement (ACK) to the WCC, along with the sequence number. Then, the receiver waits for one more reception, and updates its reference frame list. Upon reception of the ACK, the WCC proceeds to update its reference frame list. The reference frame list is updated as follows. The sender (or, receiver) checks for the oldest reference frame in its list. This is assumed to be the frame with the oldest sequence number. The system then replaces this reference frame with the acknowledged frame.

3.2   Sender Authentication and Tone

Each encrypted data frame that is transmitted is appended with the sequence number of the reference frame used for generating the key, the field number in this reference frame whose value is used as the seed, a "Tone" value, and a sender authentication code.

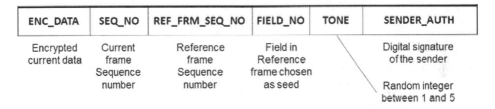

ENC_DATA	SEQ_NO	REF_FRM_SEQ_NO	FIELD_NO	TONE	SENDER_AUTH
Encrypted current data	Current frame Sequence number	Reference frame Sequence number	Field in Reference frame chosen as seed		Digital signature of the sender Random integer between 1 and 5

Fig. 4. Structure of the transmitted frame

The transmitted frame is as illustrated in figure 4. The tone is a random number between 1 and 5, generated for each data frame. To generate the sender authentication code, the reference frame that was chosen to generate the encryption key is hashed the number of times indicated by the Tone value of that frame. This is analogous to generating a digital signature of the sender on the fly for each transmitted frame. The receiver repeats this process by retrieving the reference frame pointed by the reference-frame-sequence-number that was received as part of the transmitted message to authenticate the sender. The value of the tone has a minimum value of 1so as to ensure that the reference frame is hashed at least once, and has a maximum value of 5 to ensure that the hashing process does not become increasingly computationally expensive.

3.3   Key Generation and Management

After aggregating values for the data frame, the WCC proceeds to generate the keys for encrypting the current frame. It begins by randomly choosing one of the five reference frames, and one of the data fields of the chosen frame. The value of this field will be used as the seed for the PRNG, whose output will be the key, K1, which is logically inverted to generate key, K2. To avoid exchange of the keys, the WCC appends the sequence number of the reference frame and the field number in this frame as REF_FRM_SEQ_NO and FIELD_NO, respectively, in the transmitted frame. The receiver, after authenticating the WCC, initiates the key generation process by first retrieving reference frame sequence number, followed by the field number. The receiver then retrieves the value of the particular field from its reference frame list, and uses this value (could be any biometric value in the reference data frame) as the initial seed for the PRNG to generate K1 and inverts it to obtain K2. The key generation operations are summarized in equations (1) and (2). These are the two keys that are used for the encryption and decryption processes, and are independently generated at both the sender and the receiver.

$$K1 = PRNG \text{ (SEED)} \tag{1}$$
$$K2 = INVERT \text{ (K1)} \tag{2}$$

where,

$PRNG$ () = Pseudorandom number generator

SEED = Value of the field pointed by FIELD_NO, in the reference frame pointed by REF_FRM_SEQ_NO

$INVERT$ () = Logical inversion operation

3.4   Data Encryption

Once the keys are generated, the WCC proceeds to encrypt the data. The encryption process is a combination of the concepts of block and stream ciphers, to ensure a simple encryption process that is also slightly complex. This proceeds as follows. At the time of data aggregation, the WCC assembles data as blocks of k bits. This is to avoid the additional computation required to divide the aggregated frame into blocks of the specified size. The k bit blocks of data and the keys, K1 and K2, are then divided into equal halves.

The encryption involves two rounds, one for each key. In the first round, the left half of the data is encrypted (XORed) with the right half of K1 to yield the right half of the intermediate frame, and the right half of the data is encrypted with the left half of K1 to yield the left half of the intermediate frame. The intermediate frame is the output of the first round of encryption. In the second round, the same logic as above is applied to the intermediate frame with K2. The left half of the intermediate frame is XORed with right half of K2 to yield right half of the encrypted frame, and the right half of the intermediate frame and left half of K2 are XORed to yield left half of the encrypted frame. Thus, after two rounds of encryption, the order of the data is preserved, but data is encrypted using a complex mechanism. Figure 5 summarizes the encryption process, and the operations are summarized in equations (3) and (4).

$$E1 = [XOR \text{ (RHD, LHK1)} \mid XOR \text{ (LHD, RHK1)}] \tag{3}$$
$$E2 = [XOR \text{ (RHE1, LHK2)} \mid XOR \text{ (LHE1, RHK1)}] \tag{4}$$

where,

E1, E2 = Encrypted frames after round 1 and round 2, respectively

XOR () = The logical XOR function, that performs exclusive OR operation on its arguments

LHD, RHD = Left and Right halves of the Data frame

LHE1, RHE1 = Left and Right halves of the Intermediate encrypted frame (after round 1)

LHK1, RHK1, LHK2, RHK2 = Left and Right halves of the keys, K1 and K2, respectively.

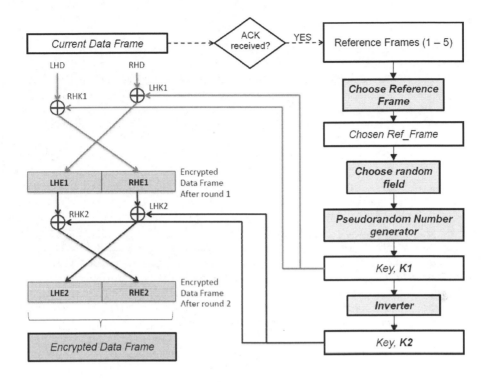

Fig. 5. Illustration of the Encryption process

3.5 Acknowledgements and Data Freshness

In applications that employ WBANs, such as healthcare, freshness (or recentness of data) is of utmost importance. Thus, even if a couple of frames are lost in transmission, and the WCC does not receive the corresponding acknowledgements, it continues to generate keys using the existing reference frames, and transmits the latest data frame encrypted using the keys generated. The concept of re-transmission of a lost data frame is not considered in such a scenario, with data freshness assuming priority. However, one needs to monitor the number of frames, which have not been acknowledged by the receiver. This is to avoid a case of lost connection between the WCC and the monitoring station, when several continuous frames are lost.

To address this, the WCC maintains a count of the number of frames, which have been transmitted since the transmission of a frame, say x1. If the acknowledgement is not received from the receiver within the transmission of 10 subsequent frames, the connection between the WCC and the monitoring station receiver is considered to be lost, and an alarm is raised. Meanwhile, if the receiver does not receive 10 consecutive frames, it considers the connection to be lost. In such a scenario, the administrator has to reset the connection.

4   Performance Analysis

Preliminary analysis of proposed algorithm was done with a java program to emulate the desired operation.

All the values/ sensor readings were randomly generated using predefined mathematical random functions in java packages. In their work, Venkatasubramanian et al [3] present an analysis of randomness, time-variance and distinctiveness characteristics of the keys generated as performance analysis, based on which we present an analysis of our scheme.

Randomness is the unpredictable nature of the keys used. In the proposed scheme, randomness of the keys generated by the PRNG is dependent on the seed, which is a function of three parameters—the chosen reference frame, the field in the reference frame, and the value of the field (physiological data). Since each of these values are randomly chosen for each data frame being encrypted, the randomness property of the seed, and hence the key, is preserved. We generated 100 frames of data, and noted the values of the offsets of randomly chosen reference frames and fields. Figure 6 illustrates the randomness of the reference frames and the field number values that were generated. *Distinctiveness* refers to how different the keys are when compared to different individuals. We observed from our simulation that keys are only identical for a person if the readings are exactly identical and the random reference frame or field values generated are the same, which is highly unlikely.

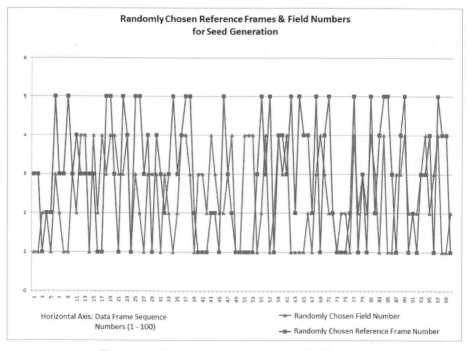

Fig. 6. Simulation of reference frames and field numbers

Time-variance of the keys implies that different instances of time should produce different keys. Not all sensor readings would vary drastically between intervals, and any drastic variation would indicate that the patient might be in distress. The time-variant nature of the keys is a function of the randomness property, and since the keys generated are random, we can say that they are time-variant as well.

We analyze the complexity of the algorithm by determining the number of logical operations performed in the encryption and decryption of one data frame. However, for analysis purposes, we make the following assumptions:

Table 1. Number Of Logical Operations In Key Generation And Encryption / Decryption Of One Frame In IAMKeys

Operation	Encryption [#]	Decryption [#]
Random number generation Encryption: choice of reference frame, field in the reference frame, K1 generation, tone generation Decryption: K1 generation	4	1
Inversion Encryption & Decryption: Generation of K2	1	1
Exclusive OR (XOR) Encryption of each half of data in two rounds; and, Decryption of each half of data in two rounds.	8 x 4	8 x 4
Addition (or, increment) [##] Encryption: Sequence number, ACK monitor counter, addition of data fields in reference frame for hashing Decryption: transmitted frame monitor counter, addition of data fields in reference frame for hashing	$8 \times 5 \times (2 + \alpha)$	$8 \times 5 \times (1 + \alpha)$
Hash operation Encryption & Decryption: dependent on the tone value in the reference frame	β	β
Reference frame refresh Encryption & Decryption: 0, if no ACK 1, if ACK received	γ	Γ
Frame transmission Encrypted frame and Acknowledgement frame transmission	1	1
Total	$118 + 40\alpha + \beta + \gamma$	$75 + 40\alpha + \beta + \gamma$

[#] Addition and XOR operations are multiplied by 8, since they are bitwise operations.
[##] Since 5 logical operations are performed per bit addition, we multiply the factor by 5.

- Data in each field of the frame is 8-bits.
- The PRNG is implemented using 8-bit Linear Feedback Shift Registers (LFSR).
- Reference frame and field numbers are randomly identified by numbers generated using 4-bit LFSRs.
- For addition operation, we consider the use of a *full adder* circuit for adding each bit, which employs 2 XOR gates, 2 AND gates and 1 OR gate. Hence, each bit addition will contribute to 5 logical operations [8].
- For sender authentication, hash operation is performed on the sum of all data values in the reference frame. If $\alpha+1$ is the number of fields in the frame, then, there will be α extra additions during encryption/decryption.
- We have assumed that reference frame list refresh and frame transmission do not count as logical operations, and thus, have not included these numbers in the calculations in table 2.
- Hash operation is assumed to be one-bit circular left shift operation, contributing to one logical operation.

Table 1 highlights the various logical operations in key generation and encryption/decryption of one frame. Table 2 presents the total number of logical operations, with calculations based on assumed values for α, β and γ listed in table 1. The major contributing factor to the total logical operations is the sender authentication, which decides the value of β.

Table 2. Number of logical operations in IAMKeys, with calculations based on assumed values of α, β and γ

Operating Scenarios	Total number of logical operations	
	Encryption	*Decryption*
Best case scenario (4 data fields => $\alpha = 3$; Tone value = $\beta = 1$; ACK received => $\gamma = 1$)	240	197
Average case scenario (4 data fields => $\alpha = 3$; Tone value = $\beta = 3$; ACK received => $\gamma = 1$)	242	199
Worst case scenario (4 data fields => $\alpha = 3$; Tone value = $\beta = 5$; ACK received => $\gamma = 1$)	244	201

5   Discussion

With the primary objective of a WBAN being transmission of patient data with as little delay as possible, and such transmission being fool-proof, security and data freshness assume highest priority. In this algorithm, we focus on data freshness with removing the need for retransmission of a lost frame. Instead of retransmission, the algorithm transmits the frame with the latest data values, hence, maintaining the data fresh. In case more than ten frames are lost or not acknowledged, the sender or the receiver will flag an error, and the administrator will need to check the communication link.

IAMKeys focuses on independently generating keys at both the sender and the receiver. The keys generated will be random for the encryption of each frame, due to the following reasons:

- Randomly, one reference frame out of the five in the list is chosen.
- A random data field is chosen in this reference frame.
- Even though the data may not be very random, the fact that such a data field is chosen randomly from a random reference frame, in addition to refreshing the list of reference frames, induces a sense of randomness in the keys generated.

With security assuming high priority, optimizing resource utilization becomes a challenge. Tables 1 and 2 indicate that the resource utilization varies mainly based on the value of β, which differs for each frame based on the randomly chosen reference frame. However, the actual implementation of hash operation and its complexity will vary the number of operations significantly. This gives the first limitation of this approach, where the complexity is not constant.

One of the important forms of attacks that we need to consider to analyze the security of such a system is man-in-the-middle (MITM). If an adversary were to listen to every conversation occurring in the system and modify the data as required, it would constitute MITM attack. Since randomness of the keys generated in this scheme is a function of three parameters, the proposed scheme has the property of dynamically changing encryption keys, which are not exchanged.

Another important attack that can be considered is the session hijacking, where the adversary initially becomes a part of the network, and gains control of the communication by assuming the role of either of the communicating entities. The decryption of each frame depends on the earlier successfully transmitted frames, which act as reference frames. Further, since reference frames also authenticate the sender, it would be impossible for the adversary to pose as a sender with the absence of the refreshed reference frame list, thereby keeping data secure. However, he may pose as the receiver, since the receiver is not acknowledged in the current implementation. This improves security of such a WBAN system and reduces the probability of an adversary taking control of the conversation.

One of the other limitations of the proposed scheme is relying on humans to ensure the randomness of the dummy (or initial) reference data frames. This can be avoided using an automated program to randomly assign dummy reference frames during the initial set up in the hospital. The second limitation of this scheme is that it if the acknowledgement frame were lost, then, there would be no way for the monitoring station to know if the acknowledgement failed, and no way for the WCC to know that the monitoring station received the transmitted could, however, be avoided if there were two-way acknowledgement, where the transmitted frame would also contain the acknowledgement of the previously acknowledged frame by the receiver. Though the proposed algorithm has some notable limitations, the chaotic nature that it imposes on key generation keeps the algorithm stable and efficient, and less prone to attacks.

6   Conclusion and Future Work

In this paper, we presented a novel algorithm that randomly generates and uses keys for encrypting each data frame in a WBAN. The algorithm randomly picks one of the random frames and one of the random sensor readings from it, and uses this value to generate a pseudorandom number sequence as the key to encrypt the message. The encryption process uses a combination of the concepts of block and stream ciphers, and uses blocks of the data frame being encrypted using simple XOR as in stream ciphers. The division of a data frame into blocks before encryption ensures the security of data by confusion and diffusion, as in block ciphers. The use of XOR encryption as in stream ciphers ensures that single bit errors remain single bit errors and do not propagate. The algorithm exploits the distinct nature of readings among people and the induced randomness of the keys to ensure efficiency. To ensure that the sender is genuine, a hash function-based (or a dynamic digital signature) authentication is employed. As discussed in the previous section, the proposed algorithm achieves confidentiality, integrity, authentication, and non-repudiation, which are a part of the generic security goals of any network.

Future work on this algorithm involves addressing the two limitations listed in the previous section, followed by validation using further simulation exercises. This will be followed by implementation of the algorithm on actual hardware, and the evaluation of the overall system.

References

1. Otto, C., Milenkovic, A., Sanders, C., Jovanov, E.: System Architecture of a Wireless Body Area Sensor Network for Ubiquitous Health Monitoring. Journal of Mobile Multimedia 1(4), 307–326 (2006)
2. Tan, C.C., Wang, H., Zhong, S., Li, Q.: Body Sensor Network Security: An Identity-Based Cryptography Approach. In: Proc. WiSec 2008, March 31-April 02 (2008)
3. Venkatasubramanian, K.K., Banerjee, A., Gupta, S.K.S.: EKG-based Key Agreement in Body Sensor Networks. In: Proceedings of IEEE INFOCOM Workshops 2008, pp. 1–6 (April 2008), doi:10.1109/INFOCOM.2008.4544608
4. Mana, M., Feham, M., Bensaber, B.A.: SEKEBAN (Secure and Efficient Key Exchange for Wireless Body Area Network). International Journal of Advanced Science and Technology 12, 45–60 (2009)
5. Mana, M., Feham, M., Bensaber, B.A.: Trust Key Management Scheme for Wireless Body Area Networks. International Journal of Network Security 12(2), 71–79 (2011)
6. Raazi, S.M.K., Lee, H.: BARI: A Distributed Key Management Approach for Wireless Body Area Networks. In: Proceedings of 2009 International Conference on Computational Intelligence and Security, pp. 324–329 (December 2009), doi:10.1109/CIS.2009.186
7. Robshaw, M.J.B.: Stream Ciphers, in RSA Laboratories Technical Report TR-701, version 2.0 (July 1995)
8. Mano, M.M., Ciletti, M.D.: Combinational Logic. In: Digital Design, 4th edn., pp. 135–196. Pearson Prentice Hall, New Delhi (2008)

A Study on Various Deployment Schemes
for Wireless Sensor Networks

G. Sanjiv Rao[1] and V. Valli Kumari[2]

[1] Associate Professor, Dept of IT, Sri Sai Aditya Institute of Science
and Technology, kakinada, India
[2] Professor, Dept of CS&SE, College of Engineering, Andhra University
Visakhapatnam, India
sanjiv_gsr@yahoo.com,vallikumari@gmail.com

Abstract. The Recent advances in electronics and wireless communication technologies have enabled the development of large-scale wireless sensor networks that consist of many low-powers, low-cost and small-size sensor nodes. Sensor networks hold the promise of facilitating large-scale and real time data processing in complex environments. Some of the application areas are health, military, and home. In military, for example, the rapid deployment, self-organization, and fault tolerance characteristics of sensor networks make them a very promising technique, for military command, control, communications, computing, and the targeting systems. In health, sensor nodes can also be deployed to monitor patients and assist disabled patients and etc. Deployment of nodes in Wireless Sensor Networks (WSNs) is a basic issue to be addressed as it can influence the performance metrics of WSNs connectivity, resilience and storage requirements. Many deployment schemes have been proposed for wireless sensor networks. In this paper we consider the implications of various deployment schemes for the connectivity and resilience of the WSNs. Our approach to deal with the affective trade-offs between resilience, connectivity and storage requirements for each deployment schemes in the literature, we survey four deployment models random, grid, group and grid-group to show which deployment scheme can be used to increase network connectivity, without increasing storage requirements or sacrificing resilience with respect to some factor. Our contribution is we had implemented of WSNs using grid and random deployment Knowledge. WSNs have been simulated with Network Simulator 2.34 for node configuration, sink node configuration, topology creation, with sensing capabilities, temperature and energy by using Mannasim.

Keywords: Wireless Sensor Network, Deployment Knowledge, Grid deployment, Random deployment.

1   Introduction

A wireless sensor network (WSN) is a network formed by a large number of sensor nodes, each equipped with sensor(s) to detect physical phenomena such as heat, light, motion, or sound. Using

N. Meghanathan et al. (Eds.): CCSIT 2012, Part III, LNICST 86, pp. 495–505, 2012.
© Institute for Computer Sciences, Social Informatics and Telecommunications Engineering 2012

different sensors, WSNs can be implemented to support many applications including security, entertainment, automation, industrial monitoring, public utilities, and asset management. However, many WSN devices have severe resource constraints in terms of energy, computation, and memory, caused by a need to limit the cost of the large number of devices required for many applications and by deployment scenarios that prevent easy access to the devices. Such resource limitations lead to many open issues. In a sensor network, many tiny computing nodes called sensors are scattered in an area for the purpose of sensing some data and transmitting data to nearby base stations for further processing. A sensor node, also known as a mote, is a node in a wireless sensor network that is capable of performing some processing, gathering sensory information and communicating with other connected nodes in the network. The transmission between the sensors is done by short range radio communications. The base station is assumed to be computationally well-equipped whereas the sensor nodes are resource- starved. The sensor nodes are usually scattered in a sensor field (i.e., deployment area or target field) as shown in Fig. 1. Each of these scattered sensor nodes has the capabilities to collect data and route data back to the base station. Data are routed back to the base station by a multi-hop infrastructure-less architecture through sensor nodes. The base station may communicate with the task manager node via Internet or Satellite An ad hoc network is a group of mobile, wireless hosts which co-operatively and spontaneously form a network independently of any fixed infrastructure or centralized administration. In particular, an ad hoc network has no base stations, host, also called node, communicates directly with nodes within its wireless range and indirectly with all other destinations using a multi-hop route through other nodes in the network [1].

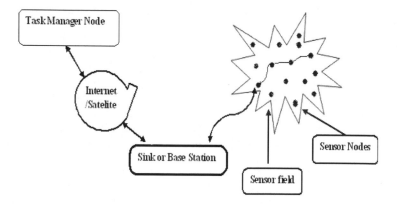

Fig. 1. Sensor nodes scattered in a target field

Many applications require WSNs to exchange sensitive information or contain feedback processes that have high reliability requirements, and they require a high level of security to succeed. Yet, strong security is difficult to achieve with resource-limited sensor nodes, and many well-known approaches become infeasible. In this paper, we explore the node deployment models in WSNs. A WSN can be composed of homogeneous or heterogeneous sensors, which possess the same or different communication and computation capabilities, respectively. [2] However we consider the homogeneous WSNs which can provide less complexity and better manageability.

WSN composed of ten sensor nodes deployed randomly around a base station. Depending on the size of the deployment area, the transmission range of the sensor nodes, and the base station, sensor nodes can communicate with the base station directly or indirectly by computing a hop-by-hop route to it [3].

In WSNs, two specific factors arise: (1) the envisioned applications and the operation of the protocol layers are usually driven by the physical variables measured by the sensors. Therefore, the dynamics of the physical parameters sensed by the network govern the network traffic, and even the topology. (2) The energy is a primary concern in WSN. Usually, nodes run on non-rechargeable batteries. Therefore, the expected node lifetime is a fundamental element that must be taken into account [9]. Recent technological advances have made it possible to have various deployment strategies for wireless sensor networks consisting of a large number of low-cost, low power, and multifunctional sensor nodes that communicate at short distances through wireless links. In our study, we illustrate various node deployment strategies for wireless sensor networks: a random, a grid, a group and a grid-group. We analyze three performance metrics: connectivity, resilience and low memory usage [10].

2   Deployment Schemes for WSNs

In WSNs, the major challenge is the deployment of the nodes in the deployment region to satisfy continuous sensing with extended network lifetime while maintaining uniform coverage. Various architectures and node deployment strategies have been developed for wireless sensor network, depending upon the requirement of application [4] we focus on five deployment schemes for sensor networks environments, random deployment, grid deployment, group-based deployment, and grid-group deployment

2.1   Random Deployment

Random deployment means setting positions of wireless sensor nodes randomly and independently in the target area. On the other hand, in precise deployment, nodes are set at exact positions one by one according to the communication range of the nodes. Usually, the positions are chosen to minimize the number of nodes required to achieve certain deployment goal. However, precise deployment method is time consuming even though costing the least number of nodes. Random deployment method is fast in practice though costs a relatively larger number of nodes to achieve the same deployment goal. When practical application scenarios are considered, random deployment is a feasible and practical method, and sometimes it is the only feasible strategy [5]. Random approach for node deployment is deeply discussed in [6], which has considered as one of the competitors.

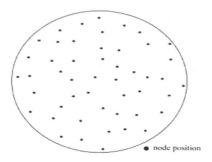

Fig. 2. Random Deployment

In this deployment, as shown in Fig. 2 each of the n sensors has equal probability of being placed at any point inside a given target field. Consequently, the nodes are scattered on locations which are not known with certainty. For example, such a deployment can result from throwing sensor nodes from an airplane. In general, a uniform random deployment is assumed to be easy as well as cost-effective.

2.2   Grid Deployment

So far, we have only considered the non-deterministic deployment scheme, random deployment, in which the sensor nodes are thrown randomly to form a network. However, since excess redundancy is required to overcome uncertainty it could be very expensive. In [4], it has state that grid deployment is an attractive approach for moderate to large-scale coverage-oriented deployment due to its simplicity and scalability. In a grid deployment the amount of connectivity and resilience of the sensor nodes against the adversaries when they are deployed in grid fashion. Grid deployment is conducted by dropping sensors row-by row using a moving carrier. Previously many studies have explored the properties of grid deployment in the ideal circumstance where individual sensors are placed exactly at grid points. However, in practice, it is often infeasible to guarantee exact placement due to various errors, including misalignments and random misplacement.

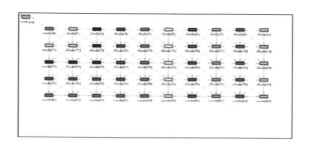

Fig. 3. Grid Deployment

There are three popular grid layouts namely, unit square, an equilateral triangle, a hexagon, etc. Among them, we investigate a square grid because of its natural placement strategy over a unit square. A grid deployment is considered as a good deployment in WSN, especially for the coverage performance. Fig. 3 shows a grid deployment of sensors for a wireless sensor network. The desired distance between consecutive droppings is achieved by controlling the time intervals. However, due to placement errors, this ideal deployment is not realistic. In the unreliable sensor grid model, n nodes are placed on a square grid within a unit area, with a certain probability that a node is active, and a defined transmission range of each node [4].It is a challenging issue to add nodes to ensure wireless connectivity, particularly when there are location constraints in a given environment that dictate where nodes can or cannot be placed. If the number of available nodes is small with respect to the size of the operational area and required coverage, a balance between sensing and routing nodes has to be optimized. Hence we can say that random deployment is more energy efficient than grid deployment.

2.3   Group Based Deployment

We have considered the networks in which sensors are deployed in groups such that sensors from a group are closer together on average than sensors from different groups. They refer to this as group deployment of sensors. we assumed that group deployment may be used in order to improve the coverage of the target region by sensors, as it provides more control over the physical distribution of sensors, and also a convenient way of carrying out the deployment. In the case where several vehicles are available for distributing sensors, they could be used to deliver sensors to different portions of the target area simultaneously. However, the main motivation for considering group deployment from the point of view of key distribution is the fact that the partial location knowledge it provides can be used in order to improve the connectivity of the network.

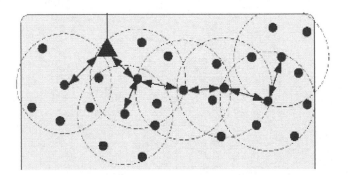

Fig. 4. Group based deployment

In a group-based deployment model [7] to improve key predistribution. In this model, it states that sensor nodes are only required to be deployed in groups. The critical observation that the sensor nodes in the same group are usually close to each other after deployment. This deployment model is practical, it greatly simplifies the deployment of sensor nodes, while still providing an opportunity to improve key predistribution. As Fig. 4 shows a large-scale distributed sensor network composed of a large number of low-power sensor devices. Typically, these networks are installed to collect sensed data from sensors deployed in a large area. Sensor networks often have one or more centralized controllers called base stations or sinks. A base station, usually many orders of magnitude more powerful than a sensor, is typically a gateway to other networks or data centers via high bandwidth communication links. In this scheme, a sensor deployment area is first partitioned into multiple small square areas called zones and then sensors deployed in each zone form a group. This design can restrict the consequence of attacks within a small range.

2.4   Grid Group Deployment

Grid-group deployment scheme for wireless sensor networks is discussed in [8], when nodes are deployed in a region, all nodes need not communicate with all other nodes in the network. Due to limited power, all nodes cannot communicate with all other nodes. So we divide the entire region into equal-sized squares or grids as done in Liu and Ning [2003, 2005], and Huang and Medhi [2007]. In this scheme has the advantage that all nodes within a particular region can communicate with each other directly and nodes which lie in a different region can communicate via special nodes called agents which have more resources than the general nodes as shown in Fig. 5 It is also assumed that it is more difficult to compromise an agent than a sensor node. Whatever the size of the network, the number of agents in a region is always three. This scheme ensures that even if one region is totally disconnected, the regions are not affected.

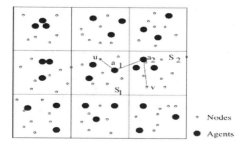

Fig. 5. Grid group deployment

In this we assumed that grid-group deployment provides a very good resiliency in terms of the fraction of nodes disconnected and regions disconnected.

3   Related Work

In this paper WSNs has been simulated with Network Simulator 2.34   for node configuration, sink node configuration, topology creation, and sensor node has been deployment in random and grid models, and sensor node has been configured with sensing, temperature, energy capabilities by using Mannasim.

3.1   Simulation with NS-2.34 and Mannasim

NS-2.34 is a discrete event network simulator that has developed in 1989 as a variant of the REAL network simulator. Initially intended for wired networks, the Monarch Group at CMU has extended NS-2 to support wireless networking. NS-2's code source is split between C++ for its core engine and OTcl, an object oriented version of TCL for configuration and simulation scripts. The combination of the two languages offers an interesting compromise between performance and ease of use. Implementation and simulation under NS-2 consists of 4 steps (1) Implementing the protocol by adding a combination of C++ and OTcl code to NS-2's source base (2) Describing the simulation in an OTcl script (3) Running the simulation and (4) Analyzing the generated trace files.NS-2 is powerful for simulating ad-hoc networks. But to simulate WSN in NS-2, it needs to have additional module to represent the protocols specific to WSN.

MANNASIM is a framework for WSN simulation based on NS-2. It extends NS-2 by introducing new modules for design, development and analysis of different WSN applications. The goal of MANNASIM is to develop a detailed simulation framework, which can accurately model different sensor nodes and applications while providing a versatile test bed for algorithms and protocols The MANNASIM Framework is a module for WSN simulation for development and analysis of different WSN applications.

3.2   Node Configuration

Node-configuration for a wireless, mobile node that runs AODV as its adhoc routing protocol in a hierarchical topology would be as shown below. We decide to turn tracing on at the agent and router level only. Also we assume a topology has been instantiated with "set topo [new Topography]".

Example of a node-config command
$ns_ node-config -addressType hierarchical
-adhocRouting AODV
-llType LL
-macType Mac/802_11
-ifqType Queue/DropTail/PriQueue

-ifqLen 50
-antType Antenna/OmniAntenna
-propType Propagation/TwoRayGround
-phyType Phy/WirelessPhy
-topologyInstance $topo
-channel Channel/WirelessChannel
-agentTrace ON
-routerTrace ON
-macTrace OFF
-movementTrace OFF
-propType Propagation/TwoRayGround

3.3   Sensor Node Configuration

Sensor node can be configured so that an Antenna and physical layer configurations should be set.

Example of an Antenna Setting
Antenna/OmniAntenna set X_ 0
Antenna/OmniAntenna set Y_ 0
Antenna/OmniAntenna set Z_ 1.5
Antenna/OmniAntenna set Gt_ 1.0
Antenna/OmniAntenna set Gr_ 1.0

Example of a Sensor node –config setting
$ns_ node-config -sensorNode ON
-adhocRouting $val(rp)
-adhocRouting $val(rp)
-llType $val(ll)
-macType $val(mac)
-ifqType $val(ifq)
-ifqLen $val(ifqlen)
-antType $val(ant)
-propType $val(prop)
-energyModel $val(en)

Sensor node can be configured so that a specified amount of energy will be deducted from its energy reserve each time it receives a phenomenon broadcast. To set this up, include the following parameters in the sensor node's node-config routine.

Example of sensing capabilities
Node/MobileNode/SensorNode set sensingPower_ 0.015
Node/MobileNode/SensorNode set processingPower_ 0.024
Node/MobileNode/SensorNode set instructionsPerSecond_ 8000000

3.4   Simulation of Random Deployment

Random deployment means setting positions of wireless sensor nodes randomly and independently in the target area. On the other hand, in precise deployment, nodes are set at exact positions one by one according to the communication range of the nodes. In Fig. 6 we visualization of a simulated sensor network with 10 nodes deployed with random deployment scheme.

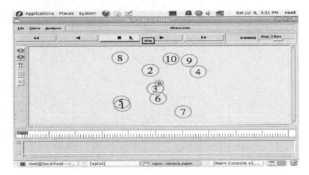

Fig. 6. Simulation output of Random deployment

3.5   Simulation of Grid Deployment

Fig. 7 shows the visualization of a simulated sensor network with 10 nodes deployed with grid deployment scheme, and grid deployment is conducted by dropping sensors row-by row using a moving carrier in the target field.

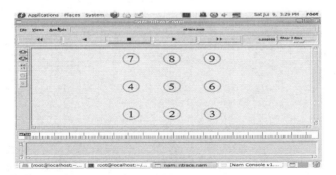

Fig. 7. Simulation output of Grid deployment

Example Grid deployment procedure
proc get_next_x { }

```
{       global val
        set aux [expr int(sqrt($val(nn)))]
        return [expr (($node ) % $aux) * $val(x) / ($aux - 1)] }
        proc get_next_y { } {
        global val
        set aux [expr int(sqrt($val(nn)))]
        return [expr (($node ) / $aux) * $val(y) / ($aux - 1)]       }
```

Fig. 8 shows that wireless sensor network has simulated and sensor nodes have been deployed by grid deployment scheme, hence the sensing capabilities, propagation, processing capability, data generator, setting has configured.

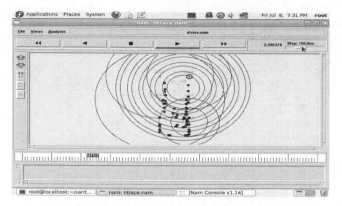

Fig. 8. Data transfer and sensing capabilities of WSNs

3.6   Comparison with Performance Metrics: Connectivity, Storage, Scalability

Thus, so far we have only considered various node deployment schemes for wireless sensor networks .In this we describe the comparative study of these node deployment schemes.

Table 1. Comparison of the Different Schemes with Connectivity, Storage and Scalability

Deployment	Nodes	Connectivity	Storage	Scalability
Random	Homogeneous	Very Poor	$\tau(\lambda+1)$	Scalable
Grid	Homogeneous	Poor	$O(\sqrt{N})$	Not
Group	Homogeneous	Good	$O(\gamma)1$	scalable
			$O(ns)2$	Not
Grid-group	Heterogeneous	Very Good	$O(\log n)1$	scalable
			$O(\log N)2$	Not
				scalable

Table 2. Comparative Study of Deployment Schemes with the Resiliency

Deployment	Random Node Capture Attack	Selective Node Capture Attack
Random	Exists	Exists
Grid	Exists	Exists
Group	Exists	Exists
Grid-group	Exists	Does not exits

4   Conclusion

In this paper, we focus on various node deployment schemes for wireless sensor networks, and our study is based on a network model in which homogeneous nodes distributed in a target area. We also simulated   WSNs with NS-2.34 and Mannasim and sensor nodes has been deployed by random and grid deployment schemes and configured the sensing parameters and also presented the comparative study of those schemes with respect to various performance metrics: connectivity, storage, and resilience. It can be extended for WSNs security requirements, for secure data transmission.

References

1. Akyildiz, I.F., Su, W., Sankarasubramaniam, Y.: A Survey on Sensor Networks. IEEE Communications Magazine (August 2002)
2. Wang, Du, Liu: ShortPK: A Short-Term Public Key Scheme for Broadcast Authentication in Sensor Networks. ACM Transactions on Sensor Networks 6(1), Article 9 (2009)
3. Messai, Aliouat, Seba: Tree Based Protocol for Key Management in Wireless Sensor Networks. Research Article, EURASIP Journal On Wireless Communications and Networking (2010)
4. Monica, Sharma, A.K.: Comparative Study of Energy Consumption for Wireless Networks based on Random and Grid Deployment Strategies. International Journal of Computer Applications (0975-8887) 6(1), (September 2010)
5. Yang, X., Wang, Y., Feng, W., Li, M., Liu, Y.: Random Deployment of wireless sensor Networks: Power of Second chance
6. Poe, W.Y., Schmitt, J.B.: Node Deployment in Large Wireless Sensor Networks: Coverage, Energy Consumption, and Worst-Case Delay. In: AINTEC 2009, Bangkok, Thailand, November 18-20 (2009)
7. Liu, D., Ning, P., Du, W.: Group-based key predistribution for wireless sensor networks. ACM Trans. Sens. Netw. 4(2), Article 11 (March 2008)
8. Huang, D., Medhi, D.: Secure pairwise key establishment in large-scale sensor networks: An area partitioning and multigroup key predistribution approach. ACM Trans. Sens. Netw. 3(3), Article 16 (August 2007)
9. Lopez, Alonso, Sala, Marino, Haro: Simulation Tools for wireless sensor Networks. In: Summer Simulation Multiconference-SPECTS 2005 (2005)
10. Martin, K.M., Paterson, M.B., Stinson, D.R.: Key Predistribution for Homogeneous Wireless Sensor Networks with Group Deployment of Nodes. ACM Trans. Sensor Netw. 7(2), Article 11 (August 2010)

Spanning Tree Based Reliable Data Transmission in LEACH

Neeranjan Chitare[1], Rashmi M[1], Shalini R. Urs[1], and Srinivas Sampalli[2]

[1] International School of Information Management, India
[2] Faculty of Computer Science Dalhousie University, Canada
{neeranjan,rashmi}@isim.net.in, shalini@isim.ac.in,
srini@cs.dal.ca

Abstract. Wireless Sensor Networks are currently finding applications in various upcoming fields such as health care monitoring, environment monitoring, vehicular ad-hoc networks, and many more, even though they have limited power, computational and communication capabilities. Clustering protocols are crucial in wireless sensor networks as they optimize energy consumption. LEACH is a clustering protocol used for minimal consumption of energy. In this paper, we have proposed a scheme to enhance reliability in LEACH by making use of spanning trees generated at base station to achieve multipath and multi-hop data transmission. The assigned paths make use of only cluster heads. This scheme was validated through simulation exercises which highlight the effect of employing spanning trees on the average end to end delay in data transmission and total energy consumed by cluster heads.

Keywords: Wireless sensor networks, clustering protocol, reliability, spanning trees, base station, energy consumed.

1 Introduction

A wireless sensor network (WSN) consists of network of sensors which are used to sense any parameters of interest in the natural or artificial environment. These parameters may be sound, vibration, pollution, moisture, and many more. Accordingly, there are various applications of wireless sensors such as in battle fields, health care systems, and environmental monitoring systems [1].

A plethora of protocols have been proposed and designed for the effective performance of WSNs with respect to time, energy, security, privacy and reliability [2, 3]. Among these, clustering protocols are of great importance in wireless sensor networks as they conserve energy by reducing the amount of energy for message transfer [4].

Low-Energy Adaptive Clustering Hierarchy (LEACH) [5] is a clustering protocol that optimizes energy consumption in wireless sensor networks. LEACH focuses on random selection of cluster heads (CHs) for every round. In every round, data is aggregated at the CH, following which CH sends this data to base station. This data transmission from CH to base station (BS) has to be accomplished in one hop. This is

N. Meghanathan et al. (Eds.): CCSIT 2012, Part III, LNICST 86, pp. 506–514, 2012.
© Institute for Computer Sciences, Social Informatics and Telecommunications Engineering 2012

a limitation since the one hop communication would determine the energy threshold required by the sensor nodes.

In this paper, we propose a novel scheme to enhance the reliability in LEACH. In order to ensure reliability; multiple spanning trees are generated at the base station. The base station is provided with cluster heads and its members for that particular round. These paths involve only cluster heads for multipath and multi-hop data transmission. By incorporating this technique, we overcome the limitation of one hop communication between the cluster head and the base station in the LEACH protocol. We provide simulation results, which shows the effect of incorporating spanning tree in terms of average end to end delay for data transmission and total energy consumed by all cluster heads involved in that particular round.

The rest of the paper is organized as follows. Section 2 surveys the literature in this area. Section 3 describes the proposed scheme. Section 4 provides a brief analysis of the scheme while experimental results are detailed in Section 5. Section concludes the paper.

2   Related Work

Erciyes *et al* [4] provide an excellent overview of different existing clustering algorithms. HEED (Hybrid, Energy Efficient Distributed), a Distributed Clustering protocol in Ad-hoc Sensor Networks proposes a distributed clustering algorithm for sensor networks. The approach used in HEED for electing cluster head is based on the residual energy of a node depending upon neighbors that particular node has. HEED assumes that the network is homogenous in nature, further it assumes the network has information about the node and its neighbors. PEAS (Probing Environment and Adaptive Sleeping) have peculiar feature that if node detects a routing node in its transmission range, the node goes to sleep, that is, node turns off its radio. In GAF (Geographic Adaptive Fidelity), the sensor network is divided into fixed square grid and each grid contains routing node. Routing nodes are responsible for data aggregation at sink. This scheme provides mechanism that ordinary nodes can go to sleep when they have no transmission.

Yeuyang *et al* [7] proposed PEGASIS, an algorithm based on the data chain, where each node aggregates data from downstream node and sends it to upstream node along the chain. PEGASIS has some advantages compared with LEACH; it eliminates the overhead in dynamic formation of cluster. Another problem which PEGASIS addresses is that it provides much shorter distance from nodes to cluster head as compared to LEACH. Consequently, it saves lot of energy. This algorithm constructs chain which result in long distance between a pair of sensors resulting in greater energy consumption. PEGASIS endangers reliability by focusing on aggregation of data at any one node and electing it as a cluster head. Consequently, if this particular node is affected, this may affect entire network.

Chakrabarty and Sengupta [7] in their protocol have suggested an energy efficient scheme which combines and thus enhances the performance of LEACH and PEGASIS (Power-Efficient Gathering in Sensor Information Systems). The protocol provides an optimized solution which is based on minimum cost spanning tree using greedy algorithm to gather the data. This optimized solution is enhanced taking into account the distances between the nodes and the energy dissipation by each node. The protocol increases the system performance as development time is much shorter than using traditional approaches and it is relatively insensitive toward noise.

Wu *et al* [8] in their protocol 'SS-LEACH' provide a modified way of cluster head election. The SS-LEACH algorithm makes use of nodes self-localization technology and keys pre-distribution strategy. It is an extension of LEACH with the pre-distribution of keys and self localization technique. It improves the method of electing cluster heads and forms dynamic stochastic multi-paths cluster-heads chains. SS-LEACH algorithm increases the lifetime of wireless sensor networks effectively. In addition, this protocol also has a mechanism of multi-paths for ensuring reliability. Thus, it also enhances routing security. It is successful in checking for compromised nodes in the network. Although it provides secrecy of packets, it fails to mitigate Sybil and selective forwarding attacks.

3   Proposed Scheme

In this section, we explain how incorporating spanning trees enhances reliable communication in LEACH thereby removing the constraint of one hop communication between CH and BS. Cluster heads will form 5-8% of the total nodes whereas each cluster contains 7-10% nodes as its member [9].

Assumptions:

- Sensor nodes are homogenous.
- Sensor nodes are stationary.
- Data is aggregated at respective CH of that group.
- Base Station has location information of all the nodes prior to computing the spanning tree.
- Base Station has list of all the CH for that particular round.
- CH and nodes are authenticated.
- Packet size is the same for all nodes.

Overview of Steps:

(i)   With the available information, BS computes the multiple Spanning trees for that particular round 'n' for time't'.

(ii)   As per the spanning tree, the BS computes the parent and the child nodes for each CH.

(iii)   BS also computes TD (Time Division) schedule for a CH and unicast it to respective CH.

(iv)   Every CH sends the data to respective parent node as per the schedule provided.

(v)   As the BS receives the data, it also receives the node information from which it is send. Base station will cross check it against the available CH information. After certain time 't', BS validates the source of data and incase data from a CH is missing BS selects the next spanning tree and repeats from step (i).

Let us consider an example.

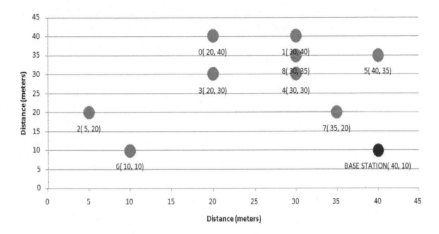

Fig. 1. Deployed sensor nodes along with the base station

As in Fig. 1, each node is a cluster head which is involved in data transmission. BS has the location information of each node and member nodes of cluster head. Based on the location information, BS generates number of spanning trees. For instance, for the nodes in above Fig. 1, we have mentioned four spanning trees possible in TABLE I. Actually, many spanning tree may exist for the given graph, but for explanation we are considering only four spanning trees.

Table 1. Spanning Trees for the network of figure 1

ST1		ST2		ST3		ST4	
S	D	S	D	S	D	S	D
8	7	2	0	2	0	6	2
7	6	1	0	3	0	2	0
2	6	0	3	0	1	0	3
6	3	6	7	1	5	7	3
3	0	7	8	5	4	3	4
4	1	3	4	4	7	1	4
0	1	4	8	6	7	4	8
1	5	5	8	8	7	8	5
5	9	8	9	7	9	5	9

Out of the above spanning trees, BS selects one spanning tree randomly and assigns respective parent node and child node for all cluster heads. These parent and child nodes are allotted taking the location of BS into consideration. When the base station generates a spanning tree, it also keeps record of nodes and the number of hops from the node to the BS. Each node is assigned as parent node and the nodes available within one hop distance are assigned as child node for that particular parent node.

The node with greatest number of hops n from base station is allotted first time slot for data transmission to its parent node. Second time slot is allotted to nodes with $n-1$ hops from base station. if at a particular hop than one nodes are available, the node sequence to transmit data to parent node is random in nature.

This assists in proper aggregation of data at the cluster head. For the spanning trees mentioned in Table 1, the parent and child nodes for all the nodes are mentioned in Table 2.

Table 2. Parent (P) and Child (C) nodes

Node	ST1		ST2		ST3		ST4	
	P	C	P	C	P	C	P	C
0	1	3	3	2,1	1	2,3	3	2
1	5	0,4	0		5	0	4	
2	6		0		0		0	6
3	0	6	4	0	0		4	0,7
4	1		8	3	7	5	8	1,3
5	9	1	8		4	1	9	8
6	3	2,7	7		7		2	
7	6	8	8	6	9	4,6,8	3	
8	7		9	4,5,7	7		5	4
9		5		8		7	0	5

Along with the parent and child node information, it should also allot the time schedule for data transmission for each node. The BS computes the time schedule for each round and accordingly assigns each node with its time slot for communication. Thus each node gets the data from its child node and forwards it to the parent node within the time provided by time schedule.

4   Analysis of Our Approach

In LEACH, if the node fails to communicate with the base station because of any reason the entire process has to be repeated starting from cluster head election, group formation and communication with base station. Our scheme provides more than one spanning tree. Consequently, when cluster heads send data to base station, base station verifies the source. If in case data from any mentioned source is missing, then base station incorporates another spanning tree with same cluster heads. Thus, the scheme provides different paths with each spanning tree and avoids the iteration of entire process.

In our scheme, base station performs number of tasks which involves generation of spanning trees, assigning parent and child nodes to each cluster head, preparing time division schedule for cluster heads involved in that particular round and maintaining record of data received. As base station has more computational and communication capabilities than other nodes, this reduces the workload from other nodes.

The base station has location information of all authenticated nodes, this resists and minimizes the possibility of addition of fake nodes and paths in network. Consequently, the scheme has the potential to mitigate sybil attack and wormhole attack.

5   Performance Evaluations

In this section, we analyzed the effect of incorporating different spanning trees for a given graph with simulation studies. We placed 30 nodes randomly in a terrain of 150 meters x 150 meters. Further we manually generated 10 spanning trees for the given nodes. The layout of the nodes is illustrated in Fig. 2.

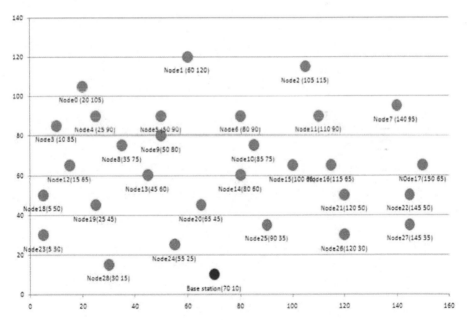

Fig. 2. A sample setup for simulation

For each spanning tree we observed:

- Total energy consumption = Sum of energy consumed at all the nodes
- Average end to end delay = (sum of average end to end delay between pair of nodes)/pair of nodes

We also calculated the same parameters for LEACH and plotted it with the spanning trees.

The simulator used is Glomosim [10], which is an open source simulator and works with PARSEC (Parallel Simulation Environment for Complex Systems). GloMoSim simulates networks consisting of nodes linked by a heterogeneous communications capability that includes multicast, asymmetric communications using direct satellite broadcasts, multi-hop wireless communications using ad-hoc networking, and traditional Internet protocols.

We used constant bit rate [11] for generating time schedule for data communication between nodes. For each spanning tree, we assigned respective parent and child node for all nodes. We simulated the networks for total time of one second. The following parameters were kept constant throughout the simulation:

- Number of items to send: 5
- Size of each item : 100 bit
- Time interval between two transmission of two items: 1 microsecond
- Duration of communication between two nodes: 10 millisecond

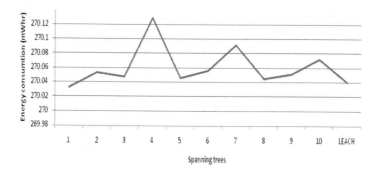

Fig. 3. Total energy consumed

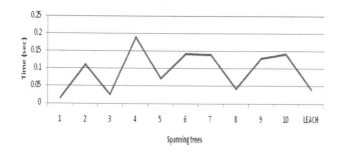

Fig. 4. Average end to end delay

As in the Fig. 3, we can observe that for the spanning tree 1 and spanning tree 4 have total energy consumption less than that of LEACH, whereas remaining spanning trees have comparatively greater energy consumption than LEACH. In terms of average end to end delay (Fig. 4), we observe that spanning tree 1, spanning tree 3 have less average end to end delay compared to LEACH. The rests of the spanning trees have greater average end to end delay.

6   Conclusion and Future Work

In this paper, we have proposed and designed a scheme for enhancing the reliability in the LEACH. The novelty of our approach is the generation of multiple spanning tree paths at the base station to improve the reliability. These paths involve only cluster heads for multipath and multi-hop data transmission. By doing this, we overcome the limitation of one hop communication between the cluster head and the base station as in LEACH protocol. Further, base station performs the task like generation of spanning tree and assigning parent and child nodes for a particular spanning tree for given round. This reduces the workload on the individual sensor nodes. Simulation results show the effect of incorporating spanning tree in LEACH for data aggregation. The proposed scheme adds reliability to the LEACH but the total energy consumption may be greater than or lower than required for LEACH. This also holds true for average end to end delay.

For future work, we intend to provide mechanism where in the base station cross checks the data received with the sender information. This may assist in validating the source of data and furthermore, if information from a particular source is missing then system will be able to detect it. For given layout of the sensor nodes, more than one spanning trees is available. In future, we intend to enhance the protocol to categorize and select the spanning tree based on energy consumed and total time require for unit data transmission.

References

1. Akyildiz, F., Su, W., Sankarasubramaniam, Y., Cayirci, E.: Wireless Sensor Networks: A Survey. Computer Networks, Elsevier Journal 38(4), 393–422 (2002)
2. Perillo, M., Heinzelman, W.: Wireless Sensor Network Protocols. Fundamental Algorithms and Protocols for Wireless and Mobile Networks, 1–35 (2005)
3. Sohrabi, K., Gao, J., Ailawadhi, V., Pottie, G.: Protocols for Self-organization of a Wireless Sensor network. In: 37th Allerton Conference on Communication, Computing and Control, pp. 1–24 (1999)s
4. Erciyes, K., Ozsoyeller, D., Dagdeviren, O.: Distributed Algorithms to Form Cluster based Spanning Trees in Wireless Sensor Networks, pp. 1–10
5. Heinzelman, W., Chandrakasan, A., Balkrishnan, H.: Enery-Efficient Communication Protocol for Wireless Sensor Networks. In: 33rd Hawaii International Conference on System Sciences, pp. 1–10 (2000)
6. Yueyang, L., Hong, J., Guangx, Y.: An Energy-Efficient PEGASIS- Based Enhanced Algorithm in Wireless Sensor Networks. DCN Lab, pp. 1–7. Beijing University of Posts and Telecommunications, Beijing (2006)
7. Chakrabarty, K., Sengupta, A.: An Energy Efficient Data Gathering Scheme in WSN Using Spannig Tree. In: IEMCON, pp. 1–6 (2011)

8. Wu, D., Hu, G., Ni, G.: Research and improve on secure routing protocols in wireless sensor networks. In: Proc. of the 4th IEEE International Conference on Circuits and Systems for Communications, pp. 853–856 (2008)
9. Sharma, S., Jena, S.: SCMRP: Secure Cluster Based Multipath Routing Protocol for Wireless Sensor Networks. Wireless Computing and Networking, 1–6 (2010)
10. GloMoSim, Wireless Sensor Network Simulator,
    http://pcl.cs.ucla.edu/projects/glomosim/
11. Nuevo, J.: A Comprehensible GloMoSim Tutorial, pp. 1–34 (2004)

Image Deblurring Using Bayesian Framework

K. Sitara and S. Remya

Department of Computer Science, University of Kerala
Kariavattom, Thiruvananthapuram, 695 – 581, Kerala, India
{sitarak1987,remyayes}@gmail.com

Abstract. This paper proposes a new method for identifying the blur model and its parameters to restore the image from the blurred image. This is based on the specific distortions caused by the distorting operator in the Fourier spectrum amplitude of an image. Due to the ill-posed nature of image restoration (IR) process, prior knowledge of natural images is used to regularize the IR problem. The Bayesian approach provides the means to incorporate prior knowledge in data analysis. The choice of prior is very important. A comparative analysis using various priors was studied qualitatively. The sparse and redundant prior method gives better results both subjectively and objectively when compared with other priors.

Keywords: Image Restoration, point spread function, image deblurring.

1   Introduction

The goal of image restoration (IR) is to reconstruct the original scene from a degraded observation. Images captured in uncontrolled environments invariably represent a degraded version of an original image due to imperfections in the imaging and capturing process. This degradation can be shift-variant or shift-invariant. This paper focuses on shift-invariant blurs. This degradation may be classified into two major categories: blur and noise. Images may be blurred due to atmospheric turbulence, defocusing of the lens, aberration in the optical systems, relative motion between the imaging system and the original scene. Automatic image deblurring is an objective of great practical interest for the enhancement of images in photo and video cameras, in astronomy, in tomography, in other biomedical imaging techniques, motion tracking applications, etc.

Image deblurring methods can be divided into two classes: *nonblind* and *blind*. In nonblind methods information about the blurring filter are known. Blind deconvolution refers to a class of problems when the original image is estimated from the degraded observations where the exact information about the degradation and noise is not available. The blind deconvolution problem is very challenging since it is hard to infer the original image and the unknown degradation only from the observed image. The method that is described here belongs to the latter class. In most situations of practical interest the blurring filter's impulse response, also called point spread function (PSF), is not known with good accuracy. Since nonblind deblurring methods

N. Meghanathan et al. (Eds.): CCSIT 2012, Part III, LNICST 86, pp. 515–528, 2012.

are very sensitive to mismatches between the PSF used by the method and the true blurring PSF, a poor knowledge of the blurring PSF normally leads to poor deblurring results. In blind image deblurring (BID), not only the degradation operator is ill-conditioned, but the problem also is severely ill-posed as the uniqueness and stability of the solution is not guaranteed: there are infinite number of solutions (original image + blurring filter) that are compatible with the degraded image. An overview of BID methods can be obtained from [1].

In some cases, one has access to more than one degraded image from the same original scene, a fact which can be used to reduce the ill-posedness of the problem [13], [1]. In [13] they presented a novel filtering method for reconstructing an all-in-focus image or an arbitrarily focused image from two images that are focused differently. Karen et. al[14] proposed a novel nonparametric regression method for deblurring noisy images based on the local polynomial approximation (LPA) of the image and the intersecting confidence intervals (ICI) that is applied to define the adaptive varying scales (window sizes) of the LPA estimators. Lokhande, Arya and Gupta [16] proposed a technique for restoring the motion blurred images.

In this work, first the blur model and its parameters are identified from the blurred image to restore the image. Here only Gaussian blur and Uniform blur are considered. A novel method has been proposed for this task. This is based on the specific distortions caused by the distorting operator in the Fourier spectrum amplitude of an image. A template based on several blurred images is constructed for both Gaussian and uniform blur. The Fourier spectrum amplitude of the noisy blurred image is compared with the templates to identify the blur model. The parameters of blur are also determined from the Fourier spectrum amplitude thresholded image. With this estimated blur model and parameter values, the blurring filter PSF is constructed, which is used for obtaining the image estimate (deblurred image) from the blurred image. Due to the ill-posed nature of IR, prior knowledge of natural images can be used to regularize the IR problem. The Bayesian approach [2] provides the means to incorporate prior knowledge in data analysis. The priors used here are Tikhonov (L2), Sobolev, Total Variational (TV) [3], Sparsity [4] and the Sparse and Redundant prior [5].

The system is implemented and experiments were conducted with blur parameter set as 7, 9 and 11 for Uniform blur and parameters 2.5, 2.9 and 3.3 for Gaussian blur. The performance measures used are Peak signal-to-noise ratio (PSNR) and Structural similarity index measure (SSIM). From the results obtained it can be inferred that the sparse and redundant prior (ASDS method) gives better results.

2   Image Deblurring Problem

The image degradation is modeled by

$$y = h * x + w \tag{1}$$

in which y and x are images which represent, respectively, the degraded image, the original image and w is the additive noise (white gaussian noise is taken); h is the PSF of the blurring operator, and $*$ denotes the mathematical operation of convolution.

An alternative way of describing (1) is through its spectral equivalence. By applying discrete Fourier transforms to (2), the following representation is obtained:

$$Y = HX + W \qquad (2)$$

where capitals represent Fourier transforms of y, x, h and w. . In practice the spectral representation is more often used since it leads to efficient implementations of restoration filters in the (discrete) Fourier domain. If deblurring is obtained by dividing the Fourier transform by the blurring filter PSF, this will lead to the explosion of noise.

Prior knowledge of natural images is used to regularize the IR problem. The Bayesian approach [2] provides the means to incorporate prior knowledge in data analysis. Bayesian analysis revolves around the posterior probability, which summarizes the degree of one's certainty concerning a given situation. Bayes's law states that the posterior probability is proportional to the product of the likelihood and the prior probability. The likelihood encompasses the information contained in the new data. The prior expresses the degree of certainty concerning the situation before the data are taken. Inorder to improve the knowledge concerning a parameter x the present state of certainty is characterized by the probability density function $p(x)$. Perform an experiment and take some data d. Bayes's law becomes:

$$p(x \mid d) = \frac{p(d \mid x) p(x)}{p(d)} \qquad (3)$$

$p(x/d)$ is the posterior probability density function, or simply the posterior, because it effectively follows the experiment. It is the conditional probability of x given the new data d. The probability $p(x)$ is called the prior because it represents the state of knowledge before the experiment. The quantity $p(d/x)$ is the likelihood, which expresses the probability of the data d given any particular x. The likelihood is usually derived from a model for predicting the data, given x, as well as a probabilistic model for the noise. The term in the denominator $p(d)$ may be considered necessary only for normalization purposes. As the normalization can be evaluated from the other terms, Bayes's law is often written as a proportionality, leaving out the denominator.

Although the posterior probability completely describes the state of certainty about any possible image, it is often necessary to select a single image as the 'result' or reconstruction. A typical choice is that image that maximizes the posterior probability, which is called the MAP (maximum a posteriori) estimate. Given the data $\mathbf{y}$, the posterior probability of any image $\mathbf{x}$ is given by Bayes's law (3) in terms of the proportionality

$$p(x \mid y) \alpha p(y \mid x) p(x) \qquad (4)$$

where $p(\mathbf{y}/\mathbf{x})$, the probability of the observed data given $\mathbf{x}$, is the likelihood and $p(\mathbf{x})$ is the prior probability of $\mathbf{x}$. The negative logarithm of the posterior probability density function is given by

$$\log[p(x \mid y)] = \phi(x) = \Lambda(x) + \Pi(x) \tag{5}$$

where the first term comes from the likelihood and the second term from the prior probability.

The likelihood is specified by the assumed probability density function of the fluctuations in the measurements about their predicted values (in the absence of noise). For the additive, uncorrelated Gaussian noise assumed, the negative log (likelihood) is just half of chi-squared

$$-\log[p(\mathbf{y} \mid \mathbf{x})] = \Lambda(\mathbf{x}) = \frac{1}{2}\chi^2 = \frac{1}{2\sigma_w^2}\|\mathbf{y} - \mathbf{hx}\|^2 \tag{6}$$

which is quadratic in the residuals. The choice for the likelihood function should be based on the actual statistical characteristics of the measurement noise. The restored image can be obtained from Eq. (7).

$$\hat{\mathbf{x}} = \arg\min_x \frac{1}{2}\|\mathbf{y} - \mathbf{hx}\|_2^2 + \lambda\Pi(\mathbf{x}) \tag{7}$$

where $\hat{\mathbf{x}}$ is the restored image or image estimate and λ is the regularization parameter.

A.   Blur Model

In this paper, only Gaussian and Uniform blurs are considered.

a)   Uniform Blur

The uniform rectangular blur is described by the following function:

$$h(n_1, n_2) = \begin{cases} \frac{1}{l^2}, & |n_1| < \frac{l}{2}, |n_2| < \frac{l}{2}, \\ 0, & elsewhere \end{cases} \tag{8}$$

where parameter l defines the size of smoothing area. The frequency characteristics of Eq. (8) is shown in Fig. 1.

Atmospheric turbulence is a severe limitation in remote sensing. Although the blur introduced by atmospheric turbulence depends on a variety of factors (such as temperature, wind speed, exposure time), for long-term exposures the point-spread function can be described reasonably well by a Gaussian function:

$$h(n_1, n_2) = \frac{1}{2\pi\tau^2}\exp\left(-\frac{n_1^2 + n_2^2}{\tau^2}\right) \tag{9}$$

b)   Atmospheric Turbulence Blur

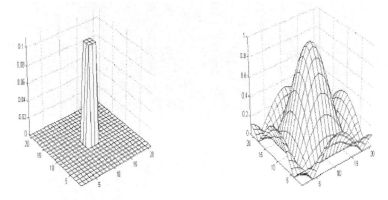

Fig. 1. Uniform blur of size 3 x 3 and its frequency characteristics

where τ^2 is a parameter of the PSF (the variance of the Gaussian function) (Fig. 2). Its Fourier transform is also a Gaussian function and its absolute values are shown in Fig. 2.

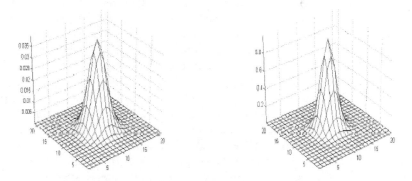

Fig. 2. Gaussian PSF with $\tau = 2$ and its frequency characteristics

B. Estimation of Blurring Filter PSF

A prior knowledge about the distorting operator and its parameters is of crucial importance in blurred image restoration. In this paper, a novel method is proposed for the identification of the type of blur and of its parameters. Only Gaussian and uniform blur can be identified with this method. The Fourier spectrum of an image is influenced by the blur. This is shown in Fig. 3. So here a method to identify the blur from this Fourier amplitude spectrum is proposed. After identifying the type of blur, its parameters are also extracted from the Fourier spectrum thresholded image.

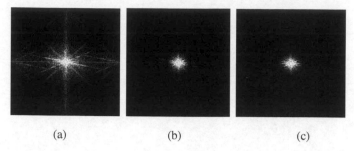

(a)   (b)   (c)

Fig. 3. Influence of blur on Fourier spectrum amplitude: (a) spectrum amplitude of image that is not corrupted (b) spectrum amplitude of the same image corrupted by the uniform blur (c) spectrum amplitude of the same image corrupted by the Gaussian blur

1)   Blur Template

The blur template is constructed from the thresholded Fourier spectrum image of several blurred images. First, the Fourier spectrum amplitude of blurred images are thresholded to reduce the noise effect. After thresholding, a morphological operation [18] is performed on the resultant image. Morphological operations apply a structuring element to an input image, creating an output image of the same size. In morphological operations, the value of each pixel in the output image is based on a comparison of the corresponding pixel in the input image with its neighbors. By choosing the size and shape of the neighborhood, a morphological operation that is sensitive to specific shapes in the input image can be constructed. Here dilation is performed with the disk structuring element. A structuring element is a matrix consisting of only 0's and 1's that can have any arbitrary shape and size. The pixels with values of 1 define the neighborhood. Dilation adds pixels to the boundaries of objects in an image. The number of pixels added or removed from the objects in an image depends on the size and shape of the structuring element used to process the image. The value of the output pixel is the *maximum* value of all the pixels in the input pixel's neighborhood. In a binary image, if any of the pixels is set to the value 1, the output pixel is set to 1. The dilation is performed inorder to set the boundary pixels to connect all the white regions.

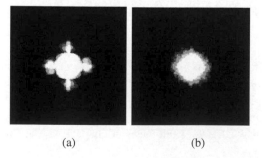

(a)   (b)

Fig. 4. Blur templates: (a) Uniform blur template (b) Gaussian blur template

Several blurred images are created for both Gaussian and Uniform blur. From each of these blurred images, the dilated images are constructed. The mean image of the dilated images of Gaussian blurred images is created and this is taken as the template for identifying Gaussian blur. Similarly the template for uniform blur identification is also constructed. Thus the templates for identifying both the blurs are available (Fig. 4), so by using these templates it can decide to which blur type, a new blurred image belongs.

2) Blur Identification

For deblurring, first the Fourier spectrum amplitude of the blurred image is taken. This image is thresholded and dilated. The resultant image is matched with both of the blur templates shown in Fig. 4. For this, the difference image is computed. i.e., the resultant image is subtracted from each of the blur templates. Now there are two difference images corresponding to the Gaussian and Uniform blur templates. The number of non-zero elements in these difference images is computed. The type of blur template which generates the difference image whose number of non-zero elements is minimum, is identified as the blur type. If the blurred image belongs to some other blur model then the number of non-zero elements in the difference image will be very high. But still there exists a minimum value with the two blur templates. This leads to incorrect blur estimate. So to avoid this, a constraint is made that this minimum value should be less than a constant.

3) Blur Parameter Estimation

For Gaussian blur parameter estimation, the radius of the center white portion of the thresholded and dilated image of the Fourier spectrum amplitude of the blurred image is used. In the case of Gaussian blur, variance is the blur parameter. Variance has influence over the radius of the center white portion of the dilated image. i.e., the radius corresponding to a range of variance values will be different. Once the radius is computed and if it is found less than a specific value, then the variance value corresponding to that will be computed as follows:

$$val = 1 - ((radius - lower\_radius)/(upper\_radius - lower\_radius))$$
$$variance = (0.5 * val) + lower\_variance$$

(10)

The radius and variance range is given in Table 1. For example, if radius > 50, the variance is computed as:

val = 1 - ((radius – 50)/(61 - 50))
variance = (0.5 * val) + 1

For uniform blur, the breadth and height of the center white portion is calculated and minimum of it is taken as length. If length is in the range or less than a specific value, then the kernel size corresponding to that is selected, shown in Table 2. With this estimated blur type and blur parameter, the blurring filter PSF can be constructed as specified in section II.A. This estimated PSF is used for deblurring the image. Image deblurring in Bayesian framework using different priors are explained in the following section.

3   Priors

The choice of prior is very important. Five priors (Tikhonov (L2), Sobolev, Total variational (TV), Sparse, Sparse and redundant prior) are taken here.

A.   *Tikhonov and Sobolev Priors*

The Tikhonov prior is also known as the L2-norm. This prior is based on the fact that the energy present in images is bounded, but this is not the case with noise. The image estimate (deblurred image) can be obtained from the Eq. (11).

$$\hat{x} = \arg\min_{x} \|y - h * x\|_2^2 + \lambda \|x\|_2^2 \tag{11}$$

where $\|x\|_2^2 = \left(\sum_i |x_i|^2 \right)^{\frac{1}{2}}$

Since the filtering is diagonalized over Fourier, the solution is simply computed over the Fourier domain as:

$$\hat{X}(\omega) = \frac{Y(\omega)\hat{H}(\omega)}{\|\hat{H}(\omega)\|^2 + \lambda} \tag{12}$$

where $\hat{X}(\omega)$, $Y(\omega)$, and $H(\omega)$ denotes the Fourier transform of restored image, blurred image and blurring filter PSF. λ is the regularization parameter.

L2 regularization does not perform any denoising. So to remove noise, high frequencies in the blurred image can be penalized using the Sobolev prior. The prior is as follows:

$$\Pi(x) = \sum_i \|\nabla x(i)\|^2 = \sum_\omega S(\omega)\|X(\omega)\|^2. \tag{13}$$

where $S(\omega) = \|\omega\|^2$.

Since this prior can be written over the Fourier domain, the solution to the deblurring with Sobolev prior can be simply computed with the Fourier coefficients:

$$\hat{X}(\omega) = \frac{Y(\omega)\hat{H}(\omega)}{\|\hat{H}(\omega)\|^2 + \lambda S(\omega)} \tag{14}$$

Table 1. Gaussian parameter selection

Radius	Variance range
>= 61	1
>= 50	<= 1.5
>= 41	<= 2
>= 36	<= 2.5
>= 32	<= 3
>= 29	<= 3.5
>= 25	<= 4
>= 23	<= 4.5
>= 21	<= 5
otherwise	>= 5.5

Table 2. Uniform parameter selection

Length	Kernel size taken
> 60	7
Between 49 and 55	9
Otherwise	11

The lena image is blurred using Gaussian blur of variance 2.3. The blurred lena image is deblurred using the L2 and Sobolev priors and the resultant image is shown in Fig. 5. The blur estimated is Gaussian with variance 2.27, the blurring filter constructed using this is used to deblur the image.

B. Total Variation (TV) Prior

Sobolev regularization perform a denoising but also tends to blur the edges. The TV prior [3] is able to better reconstruct sharp edges. It reads:

$$\Pi(x) = \sum_i \left\| \nabla x(i) \right\|$$

(15)

With respect to the Sobolev energy, it simply measure the L1-norm instead of the L2-norm, thus dropping the square in the functional. L1-norm is the summation of absolute values of all the image intensity elements. Unfortunately, the TV functional $\Pi(x)$ is not a smooth function of the image x. It thus requires the use of advanced convex optimization method to be minimized for regularization. An alternative is to replace the absolute value by a smooth absolute value. The smoothed TV norm reads:

$$\Pi(x) = \sum_i \sqrt{\|\nabla x(i)\|^2 + \varepsilon^2} \tag{16}$$

When ε gets close to zero, the smoothed energy becomes closer to the original total variation, but the optimization becomes more difficult. When ε becomes large, the smoothed energy becomes closer to the Sobolev energy, thus blurring the edges. Unfortunately, this prior is non-quadratic, and cannot be expressed over the Fourier domain. So an iterative scheme such as a gradient descent is used to approximate the solution.

For deblurring, initially, the deblurred image denoted by x is initialized with the value of blurred image. By using the gradient descent optimization method, the value of x is updated in each iteration. Gradient descent is implemented in TV with the following equation.

$$x_{(k+1)} = x_{(k)} - \gamma\left(h*\left(h*x_{(k)} - y\right) + \lambda Grad\Pi\left(x_{(k)}\right)\right) \tag{17}$$

where $x_{(k+1)}$ and $x_{(k)}$ denotes the value of x in the current and previous iterations respectively. This process continues until the stopping criteria are met. Here, the number of iterations is fixed which is considered as the stopping criteria. The deblurred image obtained with TV prior of blurred lena image is shown in Fig. 5(e).

C. Sparsity Prior

Sparsity prior[4] considers a synthesis-based regularization, that compute a sparse set of coefficients $(a_m^*)_m$ in a frame $\Psi = (\psi_m)_m$, i.e., wavelet transform [19] is applied over the blurred image. After applying the wavelet transform, the energy will be present in lower number of coefficients (low-low band coefficients are taken). The L1-norm of the sparse set of coefficients is taken as the prior. The deblurred image x can be obtained from

$$x^* = \arg\min_x \frac{1}{2}\|y - h*x\|^2 + \lambda\|\langle x, \psi_m\rangle\|_1 \tag{18}$$

where $\|\langle x, \psi_m\rangle\|_1 = \sum_m |\langle x, \psi_m\rangle|$, y – the blurred image and h – blurring filter PSF.

To solve this non-smooth optimization problem, iterative soft thresholding is used. It computes a series of images $x^{(l)}$ defined as

$$x^{(l+1)} = S_{\tau\lambda}^\psi\left(x^{(l)} - \tau h*\left(h*x^{(l)} - y\right)\right) \tag{19}$$

where λ is a constant which should be adapted to noise. For $x^{(l)}$ to converge to a solution of the problem, the gradient step size should be chosen as

$$\tau < \frac{2}{\|h * h\|}$$

Total number of iterations is set to 1000. Soft thresholding is performed for denoising. The deblurred image of blurred lena image using this sparsity prior is shown in Fig. 5(f).

D. Sparse and Redundant Prior

This prior considers that the contents can vary significantly across different images or different patches in a single image. The adaptive sparse domain selection (ASDS) method [5] uses this prior. This method learns various sets of bases from a pre-collected dataset of example image patches, and then for a given patch to be processed, one set of bases are adaptively selected to characterize the local sparse domain. Consider the Eq (20).

$$x = \Phi \alpha \tag{20}$$

where $\Phi = [\phi_1, \phi_2, ..., \phi_m]$ is a given dictionary of atoms (i.e., code set), α – the set of coefficients where most of coefficients are close to zero and x, the deblurred image. With the sparsity prior, the representation of x over Φ can be estimated from its observation y by solving the following L0-minimization problem:

$$\hat{\alpha} = \arg\min_{\alpha} \left\{ \|y - H\Phi\alpha\|_2^2 + \lambda\|\alpha\|_0 \right\} \tag{21}$$

where the L0-norm counts the number of nonzero coefficients in vector α. Once $\hat{\alpha}$ is obtained, x can then be estimated as $\hat{x} = \Phi\hat{\alpha}$. The L0-minimization is an NP-hard combinatorial search problem, and is usually solved by greedy algorithms. Set of compact sub-dictionaries from high quality example image patches are learned using the principal component analysis (PCA) technique. For an image patch to be coded, the best sub-dictionary that is most relevant to the given patch is selected.

Suppose that $\{\phi_k\}$, $k = 1, 2, ..., K$, is a set of K orthonormal sub-dictionaries. Let x be an image vector, and $x_i = R_i x$, $i=1,2,...,N$, be the ith patch (size: 7×7) vector of x, where R_i is a matrix extracting patch x_i from x. For patch x_i, suppose that a sub-dictionary ϕ_{k_i} is selected for it. Then, x_i can be approximated as $\hat{x}_i = \phi_{k_i}\alpha_i$, $\|\alpha_i\|_0 \leq T$ via sparse coding. The whole image x can be reconstructed by averaging all the reconstructed patches $\hat{x}_i$, which can be mathematically written as:

$$\hat{x} = \left(\sum_{i=1}^{N} R_i^T R_i \right)^{-1} \sum_{i=1}^{N} \left(R_i^T \phi_{k_i} \alpha_i \right) \tag{22}$$

The deblurred image of blurred lena image using the ASDS is shown in Fig. 5(g).

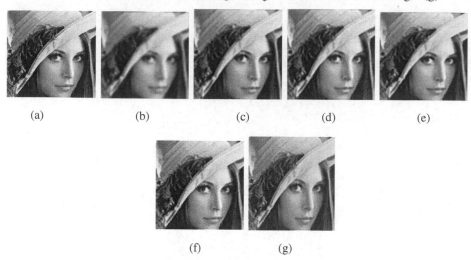

(a)   (b)   (c)   (d)   (e)

(f)   (g)

Fig. 5. L2 & Sobolev Restored images (a) Original Lena image (b) Gaussian blurred image with variance 2.5 (c) L2 (d) Sobolev (e) TV (f) Sparsity (g) ASDS

4   Results and Discussion

Experiments were conducted on gray scale images [20], color images [20] and satellite images. The performance of the restoration process is quantified using Peak Signal-to-Noise Ratio (PSNR) and Structural Similarity Index (SSIM). The PSNR and SSIM values obtained for 6 gray scale images blurred with Uniform blur of length 9are shown in tables 3 - 4. The blur is estimated as Uniform with blur parameter 9. The PSNR and SSIM values obtained for 6 gray scale images blurred with Gaussian blur of variance 2.5 are shown in tables 5 - 6. The blur is estimated as Gaussian. The blur parameter obtained are shown in Table. 5. Naturally blurred satellite image due to atmospheric turbulence is deblurred where the blur type estimated as Gaussian and parameters estimated are 1.3. The deblurred satellite image using various priors is shown in Fig. 6.

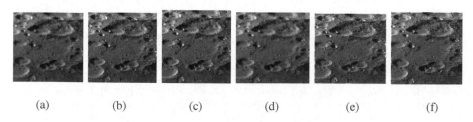

(a)   (b)   (c)   (d)   (e)   (f)

Fig. 6. Restoration performed on blurred raw_moon1 image (a) original blurred raw_moon1 image (b) L2 restored (c) Sobolev restored (d) TV restored (e) Sparsity (f) ASDS

Table 3. Table showing **PSNR** values in dB of the blurred and restored images blurred with Uniform kernel of size 9x9

Name	Blurred	L2	Sobolev	TV	Sparsity	ASDS
boat	20.37	23.91	24.45	24.60	26.02	**29.95**
cameraman	19.34	22.72	23.04	23.45	25.48	**29.26**
lena	21.32	24.12	24.54	24.67	25.79	**29.77**
cactus	20.33	23.51	23.89	23.69	25.08	**26.06**
building	18.56	21.27	21.49	21.36	23.67	**25.32**
animal	21.76	24.63	24.96	24.72	25.84	**27.09**

Table 4. Table showing **SSIM** values of the restored images blurred with Uniform kernel of size 9x9

Name	L2	Sobolev	TV	Sparsity	ASDS
boat	0.575	0.578	0.578	0.582	**0.855**
cameraman	0.604	0.606	0.608	0.612	**0.922**
lena	0.588	0.591	0.591	0.593	**0.822**
cactus	0.572	0.574	0.574	0.577	**0.782**
building	0.574	0.577	0.577	0.583	**0.819**
animal	0.609	0.612	0.612	0.614	**0.770**

Table 5. Table showing **PSNR** values in dB of the blurred and restored images blurred with Gaussian blur of standard deviation 2.5

Name	Blurred	Estimated Variance	L2	Sobolev	TV	Sparsity	ASDS
boat	21.43	2.36	23.53	24.13	24.10	25.78	**26.88**
cameraman	20.39	2.34	22.42	22.92	22.85	25.25	**25.58**
lena	22.24	2.3	24.35	24.69	24.85	25.84	**28.48**
cactus	21.06	2.4	23.39	23.92	23.70	25.29	**25.66**
building	19.33	2.5	20.90	21.34	21.11	23.07	**23.45**
animal	22.54	2.4	24.32	24.85	24.68	26.06	**26.45**

Table 6. Table showing **SSIM** values of the restored images blurred with Gaussian blur of standard deviation 2.5

Name	L2	Sobolev	TV	Sparsity	ASDS
boat	0.574	0.577	0.577	0.579	**0.779**
cameraman	0.603	0.606	0.606	0.608	**0.855**
lena	0.588	0.591	0.591	0.593	**0.797**
cactus	0.572	0.574	0.574	0.576	**0.717**
building	0.574	0.577	0.577	0.581	**0.751**
animal	0.609	0.612	0.612	0.613	**0.727**

5   Conclusion

In this paper, we proposed a new method for estimating the blur type and its parameter. The blurring filter PSF constructed from this estimation is used for deblurring the images. Image restoration is performed in the Bayesian framework where L2, Sobolev, Total variation, sparse, sparse and redundant priors are used. The performance measures used are Peak Signal-to-Noise Ratio (PSNR) and Structural Similarity Index (SSIM). From the deblurred images obtained and performance measured used, it can infer that the sparse and redundant prior gives better result.

References

[1] Kundur, D., Hatzinakos, D.: Blind image deconvolution. IEEE Sig. Process. Mag., 43–64 (May 1996)

[2] Hanson, K.M.: Introduction to Bayesian image analysis. In: SPIE Proceedings in Image Processing, pp. 716–731 (1993)

[3] Radili, J.M., Peyre, G.: Total Variation Projection with First Order Schemes. IEEE Transactions on Image Processing 20, 657–669 (2011)

[4] Donoho, D.L., Raimondo, M.E.: A fast wavelet algorithm for image deblurring. SIAM (August 2004)

[5] Dong, W., Zhang, L., et al.: Image Deblurring and Super-resolution by Adaptive Sparse Domain Selection and Adaptive Regularization. IEEE Transactions on Image Processing (January 2011)

[6] Carasso, A.S.: Direct blind deconvolution. SIAM J. Appl. Math. (2001)

[7] Carasso, A.S.: The APEX method in image sharpening and the use of low exponent Évy stable laws. SIAM J. Appl. Math. 63(2), 593–618 (2002)

[8] You, Y.-L., Kaveh, M.: Blind image restoration by anisotropic regularization. IEEE Trans. Image Process. 8(3), 396–407 (1999)

[9] Molina, R., Mateos, J., Katsaggelos, A.K.: Blind deconvolution using a variational approach to parameter, image, and blur estimation. IEEE Trans. Image Process. 15(12), 3715–3727 (2006)

[10] You, Y.-L., Kaveh, M.: A regularization approach to joint blur identification and image restoration. IEEE Trans. Image Process. 5(3), 416–428 (1996)

[11] Chan, T.F., Wong, C.-K.: Total variation blind deconvolution. IEEE Trans. Image Process. 7(3) (March 1998)

[12] He, L., Marquina, A., Osher, S.J.: Blind deconvolution using TV regularization and bregman iteration. Int. J. Imag. Syst. Technol. 15, 74–83 (2005)

[13] Kubota, A., Aizawa, K.: Reconstructing arbitrarily focused images from two differently focused images using linear filters. IEEE Trans. Image Process. 14(11), 1848–1859 (2005)

[14] Katkovnik, V., Egiazariana, K., Astola, J.: A spatially adaptive nonparametric regression image deblurring. IEEE Trans. Image Process. 14(10), 1469–1478 (2005)

[15] Almeida, M.S.C., Almeida, L.B.: Blind and Semi-Blind Deblurring of Natural Images. IEEE Trans. Image Process. 19(1) (January 2010)

[16] Lokhande, R., Arya, K.V., Gupta, P.: Identification of Parameters and Restoration of Motion Blurred Images. In: ACM SAC 2006 (April 2006)

[17] Gonzalez, R.C., Woods, R.E.: Digital Image Processing. Prentice Hall (2009)

[18] Earl, G., Richard, J.B., Steve, J.: Pattern Recognition and Image Analysis. Prentice Hall of India, NewDelhi (1997)

[19] http://paos.colorado.edu/research/wavelets/

[20] http://www.eecs.berkeley.edu/Research/Projects/CS/vision/grouping/segbench

Taxonomy and Control Measures of SPAM and SPIM

Kamini (Simi) Bajaj and Josef Pieprzyk

Building E6A, Department of Computing,
Macquarie University, North Ryde, Australia
{kamini.bajaj,josef.pieprzyk}@mq.edu.au

Abstract. In this age of electronic money transactions, the opportunities for electronic crime expanded at the same rate as ever expanding rise of on-line services. With world becoming a global village, crime over the internet transcends no boundaries, borders or jurisdictions. This paper critically examines the available literature on spam, and the control measures available to control spam. This study is followed by the literature overview related to mobility of devices and how the application of mobile technologies as communication medium has impacted the handling of spam. The conclusion of this literature review with proposed direction of study is summarized.

Keywords: Spam; Wireless Spam; SPIM; Spam control techniques; Spam Taxonomy.

1   Introduction

With the increase of use of internet, email has become the most popular means of communication. It has gained a lot of popularity as being a very convenient and cost effective means of exchanging messages. The message size in an email may vary from one kilo byte to many megabytes and sending it is very cheap. One of the features of the SMTP protocol is that it allows sending messages to anyone. Consequently, it is easy to send unsolicited email to thousands to recipients with a minimal cost.

1.1   Definition of Spam and Its Impact

The email system may not only be used to circulate messages but also to distribute advertisements in the form of graphics or pictures. The email addresses on the web pages are collected and the virus is appended to emails which then attacks user's personal computers(PCs) for acquiring information [1]. The email addresses are collected in such a way that they are useful for advertisers. However, such emails are called unsolicited emails and hence Spam.

The Word 'SPAM' was originally the brand name for Hormel Foods, maker of the canned "Shoulder Pork and hAM"/"SPiced hAM" luncheon meat. However the term "spam" has today come to mean network abuse, particularly junk E-mail and massive junk postings to USENET. By tracing the history, SPAM originated in 1970's as a

N. Meghanathan et al. (Eds.): CCSIT 2012, Part III, LNICST 86, pp. 529–542, 2012.

repetitive advertising message that was sent to large number of recipients with or without subscribing for the advertising message. SPAM in early 1980's was an innovative way of sending information to large groups of people, however since the last decade it has become a menace.

Spamming is economically viable as the only cost associated is the cost to manage the mailing list [1]. On-line technologies make it relatively simple to disguise one's true identity, to misrepresent one's identity, or to make use of someone else's identity. As a result, even if the user replies to a spam email with disguised identity, it never reaches the sender as the sender address is only temporary.

Recent statistics indicate an increasing problem with spam. The spam numbers have been growing to 45%, 64%, 80%, 92%, 95% for the years 2003, 2004, 2006, 2009 and 2010, respectively ([3,4,5,6,7,8,9]). The most affected countries (with 55% of the total world spam contents) are India, Brazil, Russia, Ukraine, Romania, South Korea, Vietnam, United States, Kazakhstan, Indonesia, Poland, China, Colombia, Israel and Taiwan. The report by MacAfee reveals that in 2008 alone, there were 62 Trillion spam messages sent. They clog the users' inboxes making very difficult to tell apart important messages from spam. They also consume computing and networking resources and are frequently used as a tool for cybercrime activities such as denial of service attack (DoS), distribution of malware, phishing, to name a few.

The abuse of email into spam is done in various ways for example, turning a machine into a relay for spam, a staging ground to attack other systems, or a spy capturing your bank account and credit card information--or all three [2]. According to Ferris Research, the cost of spam mail to organizations in United States was USD 8.9 billion in 2002 with a 12% increase in 2003 to $10 billion and $17 billion in 2005 [3]. They also estimated 40 trillion spam messages sent in 2008, costing businesses more than $140 billion worldwide -- a significant increase from the 18 trillion sent in 2006 and the 30 trillion in 2007 majorly due to employee productivity loss. In Japan, the amount of GDP loss was about 500 billion yen in 2004 [4]. In a press release in 2009, Gartner[1] stated that more than 5 billion US consumers lost money in phishing (type of spam) attacks which was 39.8% more than the year before[5].

1.2   Impact of SPAM (email)

The impact of spam can be shown as:

1. Waste of computing resources - spam consumes bandwidth, introduces delays in routing and unnecessary processing. Some businesses store spam messages to analyze and find a solution.
2. Loss of productivity of users - clearing mail boxes from unwanted email consumes time and can be very frustrating for the recipients.[3]
3. Denial of service - flooding the network with spam can block or create a bottleneck making communication via network impossible [6]

---

[1] http://www.gartner.com/it/page.jsp?id=936913

4. Invasion of Privacy -   collection of email addresses is done without the knowledge of users resulting in the invasion of user's privacy where users receive messages which they do not want to receive.
5. Fraud and Deception - popular kind of spam leading user to a perception of get rich quick schemes for e.g. Nigerian Letter scam. Another case of fraud scam is to lead the user to provide with their confidential access information to their email account or bank details.

2   SPAM in Mobile Devices

The problem of Spam in mobile devices is twofold. While the problem of spam may not bother users so much as on a networked PC, it really affects them on small mobile devices for the reasons of cost, time consumption and inconvenience. If they receive up to 15 spam mails via GPRS or UMTS it does cost real money deleting and getting rid of it on small screen devices. Apart from the usual unsolicited spam messages in inbox, mobile devices also receiving unwanted, unsolicited Instant messages (SMS and MMS). Such Spam in mobile devices is called SPIM (Spam thru Instant Messages). According to report from Adaptive Mobile [7], survey done on smart phone (mobile device) users in UK (1000 participants) in May 2011 reported that 69% received SMS text phishing and 66% SMS spam. In Europe and Asian countries SMS spam is a fashion generating almost half of the total SMS traffic in some countries [8]. The number has been increasing since then [9] reaching 15-25 messages per day . This practice is more common in Asian countries due to poverty and it is easier to lure people to carry out tasks with a lure to make money.

The conversion rate of spam sent compared to products bought is of prime importance in driving the need to reduce spam in mobile devices [10]. Since users of smart phones expose themselves to security risks as reported in [7], 50% would open an SMS text message from someone they don't know, 36% would open an email on their mobile from someone they don't know and 32% save log-in information such as passwords to their mobile, it is crucial to address the problem of spam in mobile devices.

Current mobile devices are offering variety of features for the users such as sending receiving text messages, buying, emailing and many more. Some of the services using these features of mobile devices to carry out their business activities are courier services, Truck GPS systems, and pathology GPS systems. Though these features seem very convenient and useful, attackers are able to take advantage of them [11]. In 2004, Paris Hiltons smart phone was hacked twice and the hackers posted online, intimate photos and personal emails and her address book details causing great deal of embarrassment to all involved [12]. Since 2009 mobile malware threat has been increasing and reports from McAfee labs state that this threat is going to increase even more in 2011 and 2012[13].

2.1   SMS Characteristics

The size of the SMS is generally shorter than the email messages. A typical standard SMS text message contains only 160 characters. It is sent wirelessly using the SMS standard. The user has to open the message to see if it is spam or not since there is no subject. There is a frequent use of abbreviations and acronyms due to the smaller size of the text. The abbreviations and acronyms are not standard for a language; they are dependent upon the user communities such as different age brackets, language, and cultural background. This variability provides sparse representation and variety of features and terms. SMS is a convenient way of communicating when the network or device is busy or unavailable.

2.2   SPIM Characteristics

SMS has become an important medium for mobile advertising due to the nature of use of the device and location specific information availability. Spim has a variety of difference to regular email spam or/and normal message [8, 14-17] .

- Frequent use of abbreviations and acronyms
- Cost per SMS is significant
- Shorter in size, less information to work with
- Community specific varying nature of terms and features
- Additional fields such as attachments, links and images are not commonly used
- The use of topical terms such as 'buy, free, sale, etc' cannot be generalized to identify spim as some of these terms could be included in legitimate SMS
- Transmission mechanism- SMS messages are sent either my mobile device or via email. Mobile originated SMS message go from the device to the SMSC and then it may be directed to the other service provider via mobile, fixed or email network. Email originated SMS messages go to SMS gateway first, which then transmits it to the SMSC for delivery to the receiver. Depending upon the location of the receivers device, the SMS is transmitted to the serving SMSC for that location for delivery.

Spimmers clog mobile devices by sending tones of unwanted SMS or MMS and hence making the devices useless. By using text messaging or email, an attacker could lure user to a malicious site or convince them to install malicious code on your portable device [18]. In any phishing (type of spam- identity theft) attack first few hours are very crucial as many attacks are blocked or the site are taken down after that. The chances that a mobile device user will be hit are much higher than a desktop user, since these spam emails arrive on the mobile users device first and they are 3 times more likely to submit their login details than the desktop users [19].

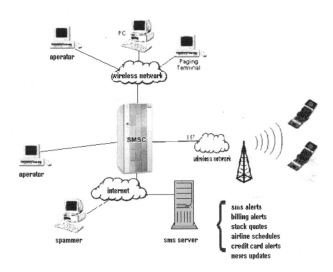

Fig. 1. SMS Network Architecture

The mobile device users receive spam for the three main reasons[17]:

1. Service providers being paid by the third parties to deliver SMS to the user. The providers have an opt out option for the user.
2. Service providers are not aware or paid for the delivery of the SMS to the user. This is a case of fraud as the third parties may use techniques such as online messaging services to send SMS to the user.
3. Users sending the messages to other users (forwarded messages, promotions) with the involvement of service provider.

2.3   Impact of SPAM and SPIM in Mobile Devices

The impact of spam and spim in mobile devices as follows:

1. Abuse of service - Most cell phone plans limit the number of text messages you can send and receive. If an attacker spams the device with text messages, you may be charged additional fees. An attacker may also be able to infect your phone or PDA with malicious code that will allow them to use your service. Because the contract is in your name, you will be responsible for the charges.

2. Luring to a malicious web site - While PDAs and cell phones that give you access to email are targets for standard phishing attacks, attackers are now sending text messages to cell phones. These messages, supposedly from a legitimate company, may try to convince you to visit a malicious site by claiming that there is a problem with your account or stating that you have been subscribed to a service. Once you visit the site, you may be lured into providing personal information or downloading a malicious file.

3. Use of device in an attack - Attackers who can gain control of your service may use your cell phone or PDA to attack others. Not only does this hide the real attacker's identity, it allows the attacker to increase the number of targets.

4. Gain access to account information - In some areas, cell phones is becoming capable of performing certain transactions (from paying for parking or groceries to conducting larger financial transactions). An attacker who can gain access to a phone that is used for these types of transactions may be able to discover your account information and use or sell it.

5. Clogging the device – Once they get access to your device they would send you numerous messages which will clog the device and hence the device will not be able to carry out the service it is intended to do.

3   Taxonomy of Spam

In this section we investigate various categories of spam. Most of these categories are applicable to Networked PCs as well as mobile devices. Many researchers have studied the content of spam messages for developing taxonomies [20-28]. This section focuses on categorizing the content of spam.

Two major Categories of Spam (email as well as SMS and MMS):

3.1   Spam without Attachment

Spam without attachment are mostly text messages with or without clickable URL to a website. Hence can be categorized as:

Content Spam[29]

The content spam contains text messages as means of advertising or scam. For example the Nigerian letters scam. Most of the sender's mail accounts are fake or don't exist. Such emails are limited in number as compared to other categories. In case of text messaging spam in mobile devices as SMS, the spammers target users with lucrative offers and ask them to reply this is at a very high cost.

Link Spam[29, 30]

Contemporary search engines rank web pages by taking into consideration the number of links connected to the pages. A web page to which more links (called in-links) are connected is more likely to be ranked higher. Spammers, therefore, often attempt to manipulate links on the web, for example, add thousands or even millions of links to the pages which they want to promote – a technique referred to as 'link spam'[30]. On mobile devices, link spam on the messages demands the user to click on a link which would take them to another website to complete the task and hence, either generate numerous amounts on the device and clogging the device for its intended use or compromise identity and details.

3.2   Spam with Attachment

This kind of spam contains combination of image, text and URL or a clickable link to a website. The attachments in most of the cases are image files or executable files. The image files are mostly in .gif format.

Image Spam

Image spam is growing and serious problem. The origin of image spam comes from the conventional spam blocking tools relying on the textual analysis of incoming messages which does not work well against image spam. The volumes of image spam has increased dramatically from <4% in 2005 to over 40% in 2007. In a March 200,7 survey conducted by Osterman Research, more than 60% of messaging decision makers cited image spam as a problem for their organizations. There are various combinations of image spam: Image and text as attachment, Image, text and URL and Image and URL [31, 32].

Image spam on mobile device takes the form of MMS. MMS initially introduced as a mean of sharing pictures with family and friends have taken an abusive form where spammers' send numerous MMS and clogs the mobile device.

Executable file (Virus Spam)[33]

The spam with executable file as an attachment are intended to spread virus, trying to establish mail bombs to plan DDoS attack on the mail server and the network. Upon execution of the attachment, the machine acts as a zombie and performs tasks intended by the spammer such as downloading big programs to harm the network, automatic generation of emails to other in the same domain clogging the entire network. [32]

4   Existing Control Measures

4.1   Regulatory Laws and Legislation

Many efforts have been put in by individuals and organizations such as governments, ISPs, anti-spam organizations, consumer protection organizations, organizations providing anti-spam solution at commercial as well as noncommercial end. An article published by Organization for Economic Co-operation and Development, France provides a list of 39 national and international anti-spam organizations where most of them being noncommercial [34].These measures have been set up by a large number of countries and are basically two kinds of approaches – a. existing laws and regulations which though not specifically addressed to spam, may nevertheless be implicated by some aspect of spam, e.g. laws to protect consumers from deceptive marketing or to prevent the distribution of pornographic images and b. amendment of existing laws and regulations or new regulations to address the problem of spam are created. There are various kinds of regulatory approaches such as opt-in, opt-out, ISP rights and responsibilities, scope of spam(for example CAN_SPAM for wireless phones and Mobile Devices), spam ware, disclosure of personal data, EU member states and National Cyber Alert systems and complaint mechanisms. 80% of spam in Europe and North America originates from fewer than 200 spammers operating illegally [35].

The laws and legislation addressing mobile devices are: General guidelines provided by US-CERT for mobile devices such as securing your device, posting your device number and email address carefully, not to follow links sent in email or text messages, careful of downloadable software and applying security settings which is also applicable to networked PCs [18]. US Federal Government's CAN SPAM Act for mobile devices prohibit sending unwanted commercial email messages to wireless devices without prior permission. The Commission found that Short Message Service messages transmitted solely to phone numbers (as opposed to those sent to addresses with references to Internet domains) are not covered by these protections.

Unfortunately, a code of conduct provides only limited protection against "bad" spammers. Spammers easily find methods to avert systems and/or punitive self-regulatory action, e.g. creative use of programming, switching ISPs, falsifying their identities, etc.

4.2   Education and Awareness

Educating spam victims may have an important impact on reducing spam. Awareness could turn those victims who unknowingly post their email addresses on public sites into spam free users. This also would increase the efforts spammers have to put to collect email addresses. Such social approaches cannot eliminate spam however in general increase awareness about spam and how to deal with it. Legal provisions can control the problem to some extent however steps taken by informed user will certainly help reduce the problem if not eliminate. Consumer protection and government organizations have raised public awareness by informing consumers about spamming tactics and providing them with suggestions on how to prevent spam. Examples are National Cyber Alert System by United States Computer Emergency Readiness team published a document on Defending Cell Phones and PDAs Against Attack [18]. The US Federal Trade Commission operates a Web site dedicated to spam awareness.

4.3   Technical Approaches

List Based Techniques
White-lists (set of email addresses of users whose messages are allowed) and blacklists (email or IP addresses known to be used spammers) are used to filter spam

by using the e-mail address, IP address and DNS address. Real-time Blacklist is one kind of application based on this method. [36] Lists are vulnerable to address spoofing and may also include receiving legitimate messages from users who are not in a white list or who are present in a black list by mistake[37].

Digital Signatures

Digital signatures, also known as fingerprints, identify messages. In some cases where secure data is involved, messages without digital signatures are identified as spam. Signatures of messages that have been identified as spam can be put in a database. This database is then used to compare the signature of received e-mail with the list of signatures of spam. If there is a match, the e-mail is spam [38] [39]. For messages coming through an unsecured channel having a digital signature makes the recipient believe that the message was sent by a claimed sender. The signature can be provided by the sender or the service provider.

Spam Filtering Techniques

Collaborative Filtering

Some organizations prefer tagging/identifying large number of messages sent as spam. They are either labeled as spam and sent to inbox or sent to spam mail box.

Content Based Filtering

Spam filtering is performed at 2 levels mail server level and users email program level. This is post acceptance system. Emails are first received before any filtering is performed. Spam filtering is implemented at various classification methods, all using the features of spam email for classification. The techniques have been classified as content, statistical, rule-based, machine learning and many more.

The techniques are Neural Network Algorithm [31, 39],Boosting, Bayesian Statistics [31, 39], Heuristic[40] [39], Signature based analysis, k-Nearest Neighbor, Decision Trees, Support Vector machines [30, 40], Visualization, Instance based Learning (Ming, Yunchun et al. 2007) [39], Ontology based Machine Learning Approach [41], [42] present a Markov Random Field model based approach to filter spam. This approach examines the importance of the neighborhood relationship (MRF cliques) among words in an email message for the purpose of spam classification.[43] propose a multi-agent based collaborative peer-to-peer system to combine content based filter into p2p collaborative filter, in this way, system can response to new spam rapidly as well as take advantage of the spam knowledge learnt before.

Other Techniques Suggested

Another economic solution suggested is where senders have to pay for emails. [35] This kind of spam control is based on increasing cost to spammers, proportional to the volume of email sent [35, 44].

Several methods have been proposed to detect spam email but the volume of those email continue to grow [45] [21]. This imparts a need for further refinement in the approach used for spam control.

The false positives and false negatives are still great problems, especially the false positives. Generally speaking, misclassifying a legitimate mail as spam is much more severe than letting a spam message pass the filter [36].

5   Mobile Devices Are Not Same as PCs

At present legislation has appeared to have very little effect on spam volumes, some argument suggest that it has increased spam by giving bulk advertisers permission to send spam [46].

In general, mobile devices are not the same as networked personal computers.

- There are many differences between mobile devices and personal computers, and it would be a mistake to consider devices as just smaller versions of PCs. In order to deliver rich experiences onto devices, solution architects need to consider a number of constraining factors, much more so than when delivering applications to a personal computer. These constraints include hardware capabilities of the devices themselves, device operating systems and application runtimes, development tools, connectivity choices, and also available services running on the Web[47].
- With increasing connection capabilities such as 3G/4G voice and data network access, Wi-Fi/WLAN, Bluetooth, WiMax, and UpnP, mobile computing has become more pervasive and ad-hoc than ever [48]. Nodes in a wireless network have limited resources compared to the average wired workstation making spam a serious threat and not just a nuisance [49].
- Mobile devices often use a public transmission medium for (wireless) communication, which implies that the physical signal is easily accessible to eavesdroppers and hackers. Wireless security is a challenging problem, perhaps even more so than wired security in many respects that must be addressed by many mobile devices [50].
- The security of mobile device is different as compared to networked personal computers.   Although much has been done to secure networks and devices, a different set of technologies are needed to broker trust among applications running on those devices (and services that they connect to)—technologies for federated identity. These technologies help the user manage multiple digital identities and control how much personal information is shared with other devices and services [47].
- Management of devices does differ in some crucial respects because devices are often much harder to secure: Mobile devices are easy to misplace, and in many cases, access to the devices cannot be restricted [47].

6   Discussion on Control Measures for PCs Verses Mobile Devices

Spam (or spim) on mobile device can be very annoying and inconvenient. Whether it is Blackberry, PDA or Smartphone, it is very frustrating by the lack of built in features to filter spam. There is no software currently available to filter all the spam in mobile devices, although some wireless companies are beginning to place spam filters on their networks to prosecute spammers [35].

Spam Verses SPIM

Although spam and spim have a lot in common there are significant differences between them. Spim like spam mainly consists of commercial advertisements. However, we need to face the fact that spim does not have the same structure and characteristics as spam. Most of the anti-spam techniques are not suitable for spim filtering with accuracy because of the differences in their underlying technology and system infrastructure as well [9]. The characteristics of spim listed in this paper are another major contributing factor among several issues in applying the spam control techniques for wired devices (PCs, wired computers, networks) to mobile devices[8, 14-17]. There would be certain restriction which are as [47]:

- Changes to schema to support mobile extension — there is often little that can be done (or should be done) to change the schema to support mobile applications.
- Data access directly from the database, and update into the tables from the mobile device — often there are several layers of communication to go through and it is not possible to access the database directly from the device.
- Understanding the schema of the data store — schemas for these types of applications are designed to be extended, and as a result can be large and unwieldy.
- Designing a staging area with a schema structure similar to the back end for data to flow to the mobile devices — creating a replica environment for development and staging can be a challenge.

Various authors have suggested techniques to minimize spam in mobile devices [51-54] such as Legal actions, Blacklisting and white listing of the originator, Time- and quota control, limit number of SMS/time interval and per SMSC, Content analysis and filtering, recognition of repetitive text patterns, user data header analysis, block , feature engineering- bag of words, Originating SMSC address prefixes filtering, guards faking, Originator control, IMSI & MSISDN analysis , Challenge response , Blocking the SMS originating from the online SMS generating tools, advanced location analysis, last known location is compared with the calling party, Destination control, IMSI analysis, possible to define different blocking criteria based on the SMS Source and IMSI masking. While a lot of research has happened in the areas of spam control techniques and mobile device/technology, there appears to be dearth of literature and study on the applicability of the control techniques to mobile devices as evident by the statistics of growing amount of losses occurring by obile spam.

This could be attributed to non-applicability of existing spam control techniques to the mobile devices without modifications.

7   Conclusion

It has been 25 years since the first virus was written and since then the security of the devices have been compromised one way or the other, no end seems to be visible [2]. At present Spam and Spim is taking on to become a major problem in mobile devices and before it takes to the heights of spam in networked PCs, this has to be nipped in the bud. The problem of spam in networked PCs is still tacked at some level but the one at mobile devices is a major open issue to be addressed for several reasons: cost, time and inconvenience. Current literature and knowledge shows that security of mobile device is different as compared to networked personal computers.

This research will further investigate into the possibility of adapting the technology in the existing techniques to develop a methodology to minimize spam in mobile devices.

References

1. Takumi, I., et al.: A classification method for spam e-mail by Self-Organizing Map and automatically defined groups. In: IEEE International Conference on Systems, Man and Cybernetics, ISIC (2007)
2. Ford, R., Spattord, E.H.: Happy Birthday, Dear Viruses. Science 317(5835), 210–211 (2007)
3. Ferris_Research Spam Control: The Current Landscape (2007)
4. Takemura, T., Ebara, H.: Spam Mail Reduces Economic Effects. In: Second International Conference on the Digital Society 2008, pp. 20–24. IEEE Computer Society Press, Sainte Luce (2008)
5. Gartner: Gartner Says Number of Phishing Attacks on U.S. Consumers Increased 40 Percent in 2008, 2009 Press Release (April 14, 2009)
6. Nagamalai, D., Dhinakaran, C., Lee, J.K.: Multi Layer Approach to Defend DDoS Attacks Caused by Spam. In: International Conference on Multimedia and Ubiquitous Engineering, MUE 2007 (2007)
7. AdaptiveMobile, Mobile Trust and Security Barometer. Global Security Insight Center (2011)
8. Dixit, S., Gupta, S., Ravishankar, C.V.: LOHIT: An Online Detection & Control System for Cellular SMS Spam. In: Proceedings of the IASTED International Conference, Communication, Network, and Information Security, ACTA Press, Phoenix (2005)
9. Zhijun, L., et al.: Detecting and filtering instant messaging spam - a global and personalized approach. In: 1st IEEE ICNP Workshop on Secure Network Protocols, NPSec (2005)
10. AdaptiveMobile, Global Security Insight for Mobile. Global Security Insight Center (2011)
11. Naraine, R.: iPhone passcode lock bypass vulnerability (again). Security News and Blog (2010)

12. Hong, J.I.: Minimizing security risks in ubicomp systems. Computer 38(12), 118–119 (2005)
13. Security, I.: Mobile Malware on the Rise. News (2011)
14. Yoon, J.W., Kim, H., Huh, J.H.: Hybrid spam filtering for mobile communication. Computers and Security 29(4), 446–459 (2010)
15. De, P.: SMSAssassin - Crowdsourced SMS Spam Filter. Mobile News (2011)
16. Cormack, G.V., et al.: Spam filtering for short messages, Lisboa (2007)
17. Hidalgo, J.M.G., et al.: Content based SMS spam filtering. In: Proceedings of the 2006 ACM Symposium on Document Engineering, pp. 107–114. ACM, Amsterdam (2006)
18. McDowell, M.: Defending Cell Phones and PDAs Against Attack. a.g.o. US-CERT, National Cyber Alert System, USA (2006)
19. Ashford, W.: Mobile users most vulnerable to phishing attacks, study shows. In: IT Management-Security Alerts-News 2011 (2011); Computer Weekly: online
20. Aradhye, H.B., Myers, G.K., Herson, J.A.: Image analysis for efficient categorization of image-based spam e-mail. In: Proceedings of Eighth International Conference on Document Analysis and Recognition (2005)
21. Balakumar, M., Vaidehi, V.: Ontology based classification and categorization of email. In: International Conference on Signal Processing, Communications and Networking, ICSCN 2008 (2008)
22. Chao, X., Yiming, Z.: Transductive Support Vector Machine for Personal Inboxes Spam Categorization. In: International Conference on Computational Intelligence and Security Workshops, CISW 2007 (2007)
23. Chih-Chin, L., Ming-Chi, T.: An empirical performance comparison of machine learning methods for spam e-mail categorization. In: Fourth International Conference on Hybrid Intelligent Systems, HIS 2004 (2004)
24. Drucker, H., Donghui, W., Vapnik, V.N.: Support vector machines for spam categorization. IEEE Transactions on Neural Networks 10(5), 1048–1054 (1999)
25. Islam, M.R., Wanlei, Z., Chowdhury, M.U.: Email Categorization Using (2+1)-Tier Classification Algorithms. In: Seventh IEEE/ACIS International Conference on Computer and Information Science, ICIS 2008 (2008)
26. Islam, R., Wanlei, Z.: Email Categorization Using Multi-stage Classification Technique. In: Eighth International Conference on Parallel and Distributed Computing, Applications and Technologies, PDCAT 2007 (2007)
27. Kun-Lun, L., et al.: Active learning with simplified SVMs for spam categorization. In: Proceedings of International Conference on Machine Learning and Cybernetics (2002)
28. Zhen, Y., et al.: Application of the Character-Level Statistical Method in Text Categorization. In: 2006 International Conference on Computational Intelligence and Security (2006)
29. Jindal, N., Liu, B.: Analyzing and Detecting Review Spam. In: Seventh IEEE International Conference on Data Mining, ICDM 2007 (2007)
30. Guoyang, S., et al.: Detecting Link Spam Using Temporal Information. In: Sixth International Conference on Data Mining, ICDM 2006 (2006)
31. Sirisanyalak, B., Somit, O.: An artificial immunity-based spam detection system. In: IEEE Congress on Evolutionary Computation, CEC 2007 (2007)
32. Dhinakaran, C., Chae, C.-J., Lee, J.-K.: An Empirical Study of Spam and Spam Vulnerable email Accounts. In: Future Generation Communication and Networking, FGCN 2007 (2007)
33. Qiu, X., Hao, J., Chen, M.: Flow-based anti-spam. In: Proceedings IEEE Workshop on IP Operations and Management (2004)

34. Ahn, S.-I.: Background Paper For The OECD Workshop On Spam (2004), doi: DSTI/ICCP(2003)10/FINAL
35. Hoanca, B.: How good are our weapons in the spam wars? IEEE Technology and Society Magazine 25(1), 22–30 (2006)
36. Yang, L., Bin-Xing, F., Li, G.: TTSF: A Novel Two-Tier Spam Filter. In: Seventh International Conference on Parallel and Distributed Computing, Applications and Technologies, PDCAT 2006 (2006)
37. Garg, A., Battiti, R., Cascella, R.G.: "May I borrow your filter?" Exchanging filters to combat spam in a community. In: 20th International Conference on Advanced Information Networking and Applications, AINA 2006 (2006)
38. Pelletier, L., Almhana, J., Choulakian, V.: Adaptive filtering of spam. In: Proceedings of Second Annual Conference on Communication Networks and Services Research (2004)
39. Ali, A.B.M.S., Xiang, Y.: Spam Classification Using Adaptive Boosting Algorithm. In: 6th IEEE/ACIS International Conference on Computer and Information Science, ICIS 2007 (2007)
40. Ming, L., Yunchun, L., Wei, L.: Spam Filtering by Stages. In: International Conference on Convergence Information Technology (2007)
41. Brewer, D., et al.: Towards an Ontology Driven Spam Filter. In: Proceedings of 22nd International Conference on Data Engineering Workshops (2006)
42. Chhabra, S., Yerazunis, W.S., Siefkes, C.: Spam filtering using a Markov random field model with variable weighting schemas. In: Fourth IEEE International Conference on Data Mining, ICDM 2004 (2004)
43. Guoqing, M., et al.: Multi-agent Interaction Based Collaborative P2P System for Fighting Spam. In: IEEE/WIC/ACM International Conference on Intelligent Agent Technology, IAT 2006 (2006)
44. Schryen, G.: Approaches Addressing Spam. In: Proceedings of the HHCCII, Hawaii (2004)
45. Pfleeger, S.L., Bloom, G.: Canning Spam: Proposed Solutions to Unwanted Email. Security and Privacy in IEEE, 40–47 (2005)
46. Hunt, R., Carpinter, J.: Current and New Developments in Spam Filtering. In: 14th IEEE International Conference on Networks, ICON 2006 (2006)
47. Banerjee, A.: Architectural Considerations for a World of Devices. The Architectural Journal 14, 2–7 (2007)
48. Xinwen, Z., Onur, A., Jean-Pierre, S.: A trusted mobile phone reference architecturevia secure kernel. In: Proceedings of the 2007 ACM Workshop on Scalable Trusted Computing. ACM, Alexandria (2007)
49. Gavidia, D., et al.: Canning Spam in Wireless Gossip Networks. In: Proc. 4th IEEE Conference on Wireless On Demand Network Systems and Services (WONS). IEEE, Obergurgl (2007)
50. Anand, R., et al.: Securing Mobile Appliances: New Challenges for the System Designer. In: Proceedings of the Conference on Design, Automation and Test in Europe, vol. 12003. IEEE Computer Society
51. Aggarwal, M.: Does SMS text message pose a security risk? News (2010)
52. LightReading, AdaptiveMobile Fights Off SMS spam. LR Mobile News Feed (2011)
53. Weili, H., et al.: Anti-Phishing by Smart Mobile Device. In: IFIP International Conference on Network and Parallel Computing Workshops, NPC Workshops (2007)
54. De Santis, A., et al.: An Extensible Framework for Efficient Secure SMS. In: 2010 International Conference on Complex, Intelligent and Software Intensive Systems, CISIS (2010)

A Distributed OFDM Polarizing Transmission via Broadcast Switching

Chengrong Huang[1], Ying Guo[1,*], and Moon Ho Lee[2]

[1] School of Information Science & Engineering,
Central South University, Changsha 410083, China
[2] Institute of Information and Communication,
Chonbuk National University, Chonju 561-756, Korea
sdguoying@gmail.com

Abstract. A simple polar-and-forward (PF) relay scheme, with source polar coding and relay polar coding, is proposed to provide an alternative solution for transmitting with high reliability. We analyze the bit error rate (BER) performance behaviors with the switching polar system equipped with four OFDM blocks, which is an idea approach to select OFDM symbols that tend to polarize in terms of the reliability under certain OFDM combining and splitting for the polarizing frequency selective fading (FSF) channels.

Keywords: Frequency selective fading, OFDM, bit error rate, polar codes.

1 Introduction

The channel polarization shows an attractive construction of provably capacity-achieving coding sequences [1, 2, 3, 4]. Recently, MIMO relay communications, together with orthogonal frequency division multiplexing (OFDM) techniques, have proposed an effective way of increasing reliability as well as achievable rates in next generation wireless networks. A usual approach to share information is to tune in the transmitted signals and process the whole (or partial) received information in regenerative [5] or non-regenerative way [6].

The problem with the previous relay system is the data rate loss as the number of relay nodes increases [7, 8]. This leads to the use of polar sequences in the MIMO-OFDM system, where relay nodes are allowed to simultaneously transmit multiple OFDM symbols over the FSF channels. In the light of superiority of these relay strategies with the availability of channel state information (CSI), we consider the relay scheme design for the FSF channels using the polar-and-forward (PF) technique, in which each relay node polarizes and retransmits the partial signals with the fixed power constraint. We consider a simple polar system that achieves the fascinating symmetric capacity of the FSF channels based on OFDM polarizing with a successive interference cancellation (SIC) decoder at

---

* Corresponding author.

N. Meghanathan et al. (Eds.): CCSIT 2012, Part III, LNICST 86, pp. 543–551, 2012.

destination node, which is motivated by Arikan's channel polarization that shows the occurrence of capacity-achieving code sequences for the binary-input discret memoryless channels. It is an extension of work where OFDM combining and splitting are used for recursive code construction with the SIC decoding, which are essential characters of the polar system.

Some notations are defined throughout this paper. $\mathbb{Z}_N$ denotes an integer set $\{0, 1, \cdots, N-1\}$. Superscripts $(\cdot)^{\mathrm{T}}$, $(\cdot)^{\mathrm{H}}$, and $(\cdot)^*$ represent the transpose, complex conjugate transpose, and complex conjugate of a matrix. $\mathrm{diag}(\mathbf{d}_0, \cdots, \mathbf{d}_{N-1})$ is a diagonal matrix with diagonal entries $\mathbf{d}_0, \cdots, \mathbf{d}_{N-1}$.

2   Channel Polarization

We consider the distributed wireless system [7, 8] based on OFDM modulation with N subcarriers. There is one source node S, one destination node D, and two relay nodes $R \triangleq \{R_1, R_2\}$, which are provided with one transmit antenna. The design of the relay scheme that can mitigate relay synchronization errors is considered. The N_s independent OFDM symbols are transmitted simultaneously from source node S to destination node D in two stages. In the first stage the initial OFDM symbols are polarized and transmitted from source node S to each relay node R_k, $\forall\ k \in \{1, 2\}$. In the second stage each relay node R_k polarizes and forwards the (partial) symbols received from source node S to destination node D while source node S keeps silent. We further assume that each single-link between a pair of transmit and receive antenna is frequency selective Rayleigh fading with L independent propagation, which experiences quasi-static and remains unchanged in certain blocks. Denote the fading coefficients from source node S to relay node R_k as $\mathbf{h}_{SR_k} = \phi_k$ and coefficients from relay node R_k to destination node D as $\mathbf{h}_{R_k D} = \kappa_k$. Assume that ϕ_k and κ_k are all independent zero mean complex Gaussian random variables. Channel impulse responses $\phi_k(t)$ from source node S to destination node R are

$$\phi_k(t) = \sum_{l=0}^{L-1} \alpha_{sk}(l)\delta(t - \tau_{l,sk}),$$

where $\alpha_{sk}(l)$ represents the channel coefficient of the lth path of the FSF channels, and $\tau_{l,sk}$ is the corresponding path delay. Each channel coefficient $\alpha_{sk}(l)$ is modelled as zero mean complex Gaussian random variables with variance $\sigma_{l,sk}^2$ such that $\sum_{l=0}^{L-1} \sigma_{l,sk}^2 = 1$. Similarly, other channel impulse responses $\kappa_k(t)$ from R_k to D are

$$\kappa_k(t) = \sum_{l=0}^{L-1} \alpha_{rk}(l)\delta(t - \tau_{l,rk}),$$

where $\alpha_{rk}(l)$ represents the channel coefficient, and $\tau_{l,rk}$ is the corresponding path delay. In addition, we denote the average power of each relay R_k as p_r. The average transmit power at source node S is p_t. The constraint on the total network power is $p = p_t + 2p_r$. We adopt the power allocation strategy suggested in [9], i.e.,

$$p_t = 2p_r = p/2. \tag{1}$$

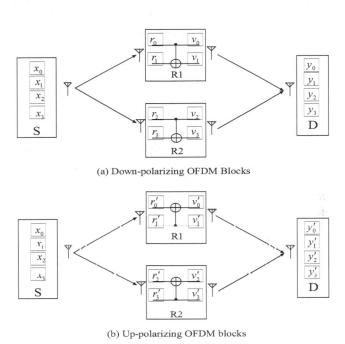

(a) Down-polarizing OFDM Blocks

(b) Up-polarizing OFDM blocks

Fig. 1. The polar MIMO-OFDM relay system based on the OFDM polarizing for the FSF channels

At source node S the transmitted information are modulated into complex symbols x_{ij} and then each N modulated symbols as a block are poured into an OFDM modulator of N subcarriers. Denote four consecutive OFDM symbols by $x_i = (x_{i,0}, \cdots, x_{i,N-1})^{\mathrm{T}}, \forall i \in \mathbb{Z}_4$. We define $x_i + x_j = (x_{i,0} + x_{j,0}, \cdots, x_{i,N-1} + x_{j,N-1})^{\mathrm{T}}, \forall i, j \in \mathbb{Z}_4$, for polarization calculation.

The four consecutive OFDM symbols are processed with the *down-polarizing* 4×4 matrix $\mathbf{Q}_4$ at source node S, i.e., $\mathbf{U} = \mathbf{X}\mathbf{Q}_4$, where $\mathbf{U} = (u_0, u_1, u_2, u_3)$ denotes the polarizing matrix of size $N \times 4$, $\mathbf{X} = (x_0, x_1, x_2, x_3)$ denotes the signal matrix of size $N \times 4$ corresponding to four OFDM blocks, the source polar matrix $\mathbf{Q}_4$ is given by $\mathbf{Q}_4 = \mathbf{I}_2 \otimes \mathbf{Q}_2$, where $\otimes$ denotes the Kronecker product and $\mathbf{Q}_2$ is the Arikan *down-polarizing* matrix [1], i.e., $\mathbf{Q}_2 = \begin{pmatrix} 1 & 1 \\ 0 & 1 \end{pmatrix}$. Namely, we have $u_{2k-2} = x_{2k-2}$ and $u_{2k-1} = x_{2k-2} + x_{2k-1}, \forall k \in \{1, 2\}$.

In the OFDM modulator, the four consecutive blocks are modulated by the N-point FFT. Then each block is precoded by a cyclic prefix (CP) with length

l_{cp}. Thus each OFDM symbol consists of $L_s = N + l_{cp}$ samples, which are broadcasted to two relay nodes. Denote by τ_{sd2} the overall relative delay from source node S to relay node R_2, and then to destination node D, which is relative to relay node R_1. In order to combat against timing errors, we assume that $l_{cp} \geq \max_{l,k}\{\tau_{l,sk}+\tau_{l,rk}+\tau_{sd2}\}$. Denote four consecutive OFDM symbols by $\breve{u}_i$, $\forall i \in \mathbb{Z}_4$, where $\breve{u}_i$ consists of FFT(u_i) and the CP.

At each relay R_k, the received noisy signals will be polarized, processed and forwarded to destination node D. We define two processed vectors $\breve{\mathbf{u}}_1 = (\breve{u}_0^\mathrm{T}, \breve{u}_2^\mathrm{T})^\mathrm{T}$ and $\breve{\mathbf{u}}_2 = (\breve{u}_1^\mathrm{T}, \breve{u}_3^\mathrm{T})^\mathrm{T}$, which are polarized at R_1 and R_2, respectively. Therefore, the received signals at each relay node R_k for four successive OFDM symbol durations can be given by

$$\breve{r}_{k0} = \sqrt{p_t}\breve{u}_0 \circledast \phi_k + \breve{\tilde{n}}_{k0}, \ \breve{r}_{k1} = \sqrt{p_t}\breve{u}_1 \circledast \phi_k + \breve{\tilde{n}}_{k1},$$
$$\breve{r}_{k2} = \sqrt{p_t}\breve{u}_2 \circledast \phi_k + \breve{\tilde{n}}_{k2}, \ \breve{r}_{k3} = \sqrt{p_t}\breve{u}_3 \circledast \phi_k + \breve{\tilde{n}}_{k3}, \tag{2}$$

where ϕ_k is an $L \times 1$ vector defined as $\phi_k = (\alpha_{sk}(0), \cdots, \alpha_{sk}(L-1))$, $\circledast$ denotes the linear convolution, and $\breve{\tilde{n}}_{ki}$, $\forall i \in \mathbb{Z}_4$, denotes the additive white Gaussian noise (AWGN) at R_k with zero-mean and unit-variance.

Table 1. Implementation of the PF scheme for the down-polarized system at relay nodes. OM$_i$ denote the ith OFDM block.

	Polar R_1	Polar R_2	Process R_1	Process R_2
OM$_0$	$\breve{r}_{10}$	$\breve{r}_{20}$	$\zeta(\breve{r}_{10})$	0
OM$_1$	$\breve{r}_{11}$	$\breve{r}_{21}$	0	$\breve{r}_{21}^*$
OM$_2$	$\breve{r}_{10}+\breve{r}_{12}$	$\breve{r}_{22}$	$\zeta(\breve{r}_{10}+\breve{r}_{12})$	0
OM$_3$	$\breve{r}_{13}$	$\breve{r}_{23}+\breve{r}_{21}$	0	$(\breve{r}_{23}+\breve{r}_{21})^*$

Then each relay node R_k polarizes, processes and forwards the received noisy signals as shown in Table I, where $\zeta(\cdot)$ denotes the time-reversal of the signals [5], i.e., $\zeta(\breve{r}_{ki}(\epsilon)) \triangleq \breve{r}_{ki}(L_s - \epsilon)$, $\forall \epsilon \in \mathbb{Z}_{L_s}$, $\forall k \in \{1,2\}$ and $\forall i \in \mathbb{Z}_4$. Denote by $\breve{v}_0 \triangleq \zeta(\breve{r}_{10})$, $\breve{v}_1 \triangleq \zeta(\breve{r}_{10} + \breve{r}_{12})$, $\breve{v}_2 \triangleq \breve{r}_{21}^*$ and $\breve{v}_3 \triangleq (\breve{r}_{21} + \breve{r}_{23})^*$. For the ϵth subcarrier of $\breve{v}_i$ we also take the notations $\breve{v}_{i,\epsilon} \triangleq \breve{v}_i(\epsilon)$, $\forall \epsilon \in \mathbb{Z}_N$.

After the above-mentioned processing, each relay node R_k amplifies the yielded symbols with a scalar $\lambda = \sqrt{p_r/(p_t + 1)}$ while remaining the average transmission power p_r. At destination node D, the CP is removed for each OFDM symbol. We note that relay node R_1 implements the time reversions of the noisy signals including both information symbols and CP. What we need is that after the CP removal, we obtain the time reversal version of only information symbols, i.e., $\zeta(\text{FFT}(u_i))$, $\forall i \in \mathbb{Z}_4$. Then by using some properties of FFT/IFFT, we achieve the feasible definition as follows.

Definition 2.1 [5]: According to the processed four OFDM symbols at relay node R_1 we can obtain $\zeta(\phi_1')\circledast\zeta(\text{FFT}(u_i))$ at destination node D if we remove the CP as in a conventional OFDM system to get an N-point vector and shift the last

$\tau_1' = l_{cp} - \tau_1 + 1$ samples of the N-point vector as the first τ_1' samples. Here ϕ_1' is an equivalent $N \times 1$ channel vector defined as $\phi_1' = (\alpha_{s1}(0), \cdots, \alpha_{s1}(L-1), 0, \cdots, 0)$, and τ_1 denotes the maximum path delay of channel ϕ_1 from source node S to relay node R_1, i.e., $\tau_1 = \max_l\{\tau_{l,s1}\}$. In a similar way, we define another equivalent $N \times 1$ channel vector $\kappa_1' = (\alpha_{r1}(0), \cdots, \alpha_{r1}(L-1), 0, \cdots, 0)$.

At destination node D, after the CP removal the received four successive OFDM symbols can be written as

$$
\begin{aligned}
y_0 &= \lambda(\sqrt{p_t}\zeta(\text{FFT}(u_0))) \circledast \zeta(\phi_1') + \bar{n}_{10}) \circledast \kappa_1' + n_0 \\
y_1 &= \lambda(\sqrt{p_t}\zeta(\text{FFT}(u_0+u_2)) \circledast \zeta(\phi_1') + \bar{n}_{10} + \bar{n}_{12}) \circledast \kappa_1' + n_1 \\
y_2 &= \lambda(\sqrt{p_t}(\text{FFT}(u_1))^* \circledast t_{sd2} \circledast t_1' \circledast \phi_2' + \bar{n}_{21}^*) \circledast \kappa_2' + n_2 \\
y_3 &= \lambda(\sqrt{p_t}(\text{FFT}(u_3+u_1))^* \circledast t_{sd2} \circledast t_1' \circledast \phi_2' + \bar{n}_{21}^* + \bar{n}_{23}^*) \\
&\quad \circledast \kappa_2' + n_3,
\end{aligned}
\tag{3}
$$

where t_{sd2} is an $N \times 1$ vector that represents the timing errors in the time domain denoted as $t_{sd2} = (\mathbf{0}_{\tau,sd2}, 1, 0, \cdots, 0)^{\text{T}}$, and $\mathbf{0}_{\tau_{sd2}}$ is a $1 \times \tau_{sd2}$ vector of all zeros, and t_1' is the shift of τ_1' samples in the time domain defined as $t_1' = (\mathbf{0}_{\tau_1'}, 1, 0, \cdots, 0)^{\text{T}}$. Since the signals transmitted from R_2 will arrive at the destination τ_{sd2} samples later and after the CP removal, the signals are further shifted by τ_1' samples. The total number of shifted samples is denoted by $\tau_2 = \tau_{sd2} + \tau_1'$. Here $\bar{n}_{ki}$ is the AWGN at relay node R_k and n_i denotes the AWGN at destination node D after the CP removal.

After that the received OFDM symbols are transformed by the N-point FFT. As mentioned before, because of timing errors, the OFDM symbols from relay node R_2 arrive at destination node D τ_{sd2} samples later than that of symbols from relay node R_1. Since l_{cp} is long enough, we can still maintain the orthogonality between subcarriers. The delay τ_{sd2} in the time domain corresponds to a phase change in the frequency domain, i.e., $f^{\tau_{sd2}} = (1, e^{-\iota 2\pi\tau_{sd2}/N}, \cdots, e^{-\iota 2\pi\tau_{sd2}(N-1)/N})^{\text{T}}$, where $f = (1, e^{-\iota 2\pi/N}, \cdots, e^{-\iota 2\pi(N-1)/N})^{\text{T}}$ and $\iota = \sqrt{-1}$. Similarly, the shift of τ_1' samples in the time domain also corresponds to a phase change $f^{\tau_1'}$, and hence the total phase change is f^{τ_2}.

Denote by $\check{y}_i = (\check{y}_{i0}, \check{y}_{i1}, \cdots, \check{y}_{i(N-1)})$, $\forall\, i \in \mathbb{Z}_4$, the received four consecutive OFDM symbols at destination node D after the CP removal and the N-point FFT transformations. Therefore, we have

$$
\begin{aligned}
\check{y}_0 &= \lambda[\sqrt{p_t}\text{FFT}(\zeta(\text{FFT}(u_0))) \circ \check{\phi}_1 \circ \check{\kappa}_1 + \check{\bar{n}}_{10} \circ \check{\kappa}_1] + \check{n}_0 \\
\check{y}_1 &= \lambda[\sqrt{p_t}\text{FFT}(\zeta(\text{FFT}(u_0+u_2))) \circ \check{\phi}_1 \circ \check{\kappa}_1 \\
&\quad + (\check{\bar{n}}_{10} + \check{\bar{n}}_{20}) \circ \check{\kappa}_1] + \check{n}_1 \\
\check{y}_2 &= \lambda[\sqrt{p_t}\text{FFT}((\text{FFT}(u_1))^*) \circ f^{\tau_2} \circ \check{\phi}_2 \circ \check{\kappa}_2 + \check{\bar{n}}_{21} \circ \check{\kappa}_2] + \check{n}_2 \\
\check{y}_3 &= \lambda[\sqrt{p_t}\text{FFT}((\text{FFT}(u_3+u_1))^*) \circ f^{\tau_2} \circ \check{\phi}_2 \circ \check{\kappa}_2 \\
&\quad + (\check{\bar{n}}_{21}^* + \check{\bar{n}}_{23}^*) \circ \check{\kappa}_2] + \check{n}_3,
\end{aligned}
\tag{4}
$$

where $\circ$ denotes the Hadamard product, $\check{\phi}_1 = \text{FFT}(\zeta(\phi'_1))$, $\check{\kappa}_1 = \text{FFT}(\kappa'_1)$, $\check{\phi}_2 = \text{FFT}((\phi'_1)^*)$, $\check{\kappa}_2 = \text{FFT}(\kappa'_2)$, $\check{\bar{n}}_{ki} = \text{FFT}(\bar{n}_{ki})$, and $\check{\bar{n}}_i = \text{FFT}(\bar{n}_i)$, $\forall\, k \in \{1,2\}$ and $\forall\, i \in \mathbb{Z}_4$.

According to the properties of the well-known N-point FFT transforms for an $N \times 1$ vector x, we have $(\text{FFT}(x))^* = \text{IFFT}(x^*)$ and $\text{FFT}(\zeta(\text{FFT}(x))) = \text{IFFT}(\text{FFT}(x)) = x$ [5]. Therefore, the formulas in (4) can be written in the polar form for each subcarrier ϵ, $\forall\, \epsilon \in \mathbb{Z}_N$, as follows

$$
\begin{pmatrix} y_{0\epsilon} \\ y_{1\epsilon} \\ y_{2\epsilon} \\ y_{3\epsilon} \end{pmatrix} = \lambda\sqrt{p_t} \begin{pmatrix} \check{\phi}_{1\epsilon}\check{\kappa}_{1\epsilon} & 0 & 0 & 0 \\ \check{\phi}_{1\epsilon}\check{\kappa}_{1\epsilon} & \check{\phi}_{1\epsilon}\check{\kappa}_{1\epsilon} & 0 & 0 \\ 0 & 0 & \Phi_{2\epsilon} & 0 \\ 0 & 0 & \Phi_{2\epsilon} & \Phi_{2\epsilon} \end{pmatrix} \begin{pmatrix} u_{0\epsilon} \\ u_{2\epsilon} \\ u_{1\epsilon}^* \\ u_{3\epsilon}^* \end{pmatrix} + \mathbf{e}_{0\epsilon} \qquad (5)
$$

which can be rewritten as

$$
\begin{pmatrix} y_{0\epsilon} \\ y_{1\epsilon} \\ y_{2\epsilon}^* \\ y_{3\epsilon}^* \end{pmatrix} = \lambda\sqrt{p_t} \left(\begin{array}{cc|cc} \check{\phi}_{1\epsilon}\check{\kappa}_{1\epsilon} & 0 & 0 & 0 \\ \check{\phi}_{1\epsilon}\check{\kappa}_{1\epsilon} & 0 & \check{\phi}_{1\epsilon}\check{\kappa}_{1\epsilon} & 0 \\ \Phi_{2\epsilon}^* & \Phi_{2\epsilon}^* & 0 & 0 \\ \Phi_{2\epsilon}^* & \Phi_{2\epsilon}^* & \Phi_{2\epsilon}^* & \Phi_{2\epsilon}^* \end{array} \right) \begin{pmatrix} x_{0\epsilon} \\ x_{1\epsilon} \\ x_{2\epsilon} \\ x_{3\epsilon} \end{pmatrix} + \mathbf{e}_\epsilon
$$
$$
= \mathcal{H}_I \mathbf{x}_{I\epsilon} + \mathcal{H}_F \mathbf{x}_{F\epsilon} + \mathbf{e}_\epsilon, \qquad (6)
$$

where $\Phi_{2\epsilon} \triangleq f_\epsilon^{\tau 2} \check{\phi}_{2\epsilon} \check{\kappa}_{2\epsilon}$, $\Phi_{2\epsilon}^* \triangleq (f_\epsilon^{\tau 2} \check{\phi}_{2\epsilon} \check{\kappa}_{2\epsilon})^*$, $f_\epsilon^{\tau 2} = \exp(-\iota 2\pi\epsilon\tau/N)$, $\mathbf{x}_{I\epsilon} = (x_{0\epsilon}, x_{1\epsilon})^{\text{T}}$, $\mathbf{x}_{F\epsilon} = (x_{2\epsilon}, x_{3\epsilon})^{\text{T}}$, $x_{i\epsilon}$ is the ϵth element of x_i, $\check{\kappa}_{k\epsilon}$ and $\check{\phi}_{k\epsilon}$ denote the ϵth element of $\check{\kappa}_k$ and $\check{\phi}_k$, $\forall\, k \in \{1,2\}$ and $\forall\, i \in \mathbb{Z}_4$. Two vectors $\mathbf{e}_{0\epsilon}$ and $\mathbf{e}_\epsilon$ denote the corresponding polarized noises.

We note that sub-vector $\mathbf{x}_{I\epsilon}$ serves as the *information* vector while sub-vector $\mathbf{x}_{F\epsilon}$ as the *frozen* vector for the *down-polarizing* MIMO relay system, which can be derived from the Bhattacharyya parameter vector for the derivation of the reliability of the FSF channels calculated in next section.

3   Depolarizing MIMO-OFDM Relay System

So far we have established the polar system based on the OFDM polarizing for the FSF channels. Next, we analyze the reliability of the the FSF channels with transmission probabilities $W_4^{(i)}$ for the ith OFDM symbol based on the Bhattacharyya parameter vector $\mathbf{z}_4 = (z_{4,0}, z_{4,1}, z_{4,2}, z_{4,3})$, which can be calculated from the recursion formula [1], i.e.,

$$
z_{2k,j} = \begin{cases} z_{k,j}^2, & \text{for } 0 \le j \le k-1; \\ 2z_{k,j-k} - z_{k,j-k}^2, & \text{for } k \le j \le 2k-1, \end{cases} \qquad (7)
$$

for $\forall\, k \in \{1,2\}$ starting with $z_{1,0} = 1/2$. From scratch, we form a permutation $\pi_4 = (i_0, i_1, i_2, i_3)$ of $(0,1,2,3)$ corresponding to entries of $\mathbf{x} = (x_0, x_1, x_2, x_3)^{\text{T}}$ so that the inequality $z_{4,i_j} \le z_{4,i_k}$, $\forall\, 0 \le j < k \le 3$, is true. Thus we have the reliability of OFDM splitting for the FSF channels given by

$z_4 = (1/16, 7/16, 9/16, 15/16)$, which creates a permutation $\pi_4 = (0, 1, 2, 3)$. It implies that for each subcarrier of the source OFDM symbols $\mathbf{x}_\epsilon$, the first two signals $\{x_{0,\epsilon}, x_{1,\epsilon}\}$ can be transmitted with higher reliability than that of the last two signals $\{x_{2,\epsilon}, x_{3,\epsilon}\}$. Therefore, for the reliable transmission of signals, we let $\{x_{0,\epsilon}, x_{1,\epsilon}\}$ to be the *information* bits that are required to be transmitted from relay nodes, and $\{x_{2,\epsilon}, x_{3,\epsilon}\}$ to be *frozen* bits that provide assistance for transmissions. In practice, the *frozen* bits $\{x_{2,\epsilon}, x_{3,\epsilon}\}$ are always be set zeros for simplicity, i.e., $\{x_{2,\epsilon} = 0, x_{3,\epsilon} = 0\}$. This property can be utilized for the flexible transmission of signals on the FSF channels with high reliability [1].

In the similar way, we can derive the reliability of *up-splitting* system for the FSF channel $W'^{(i)}_4$ based on the Bhattacharyya parameter vector $\mathbf{z}'_4 = (z'_{4,0}, z'_{4,1}, z'_{4,2}, z'_{4,3})$, which can be calculated from [1], i.e.,

$$z'_{2k,j} = \begin{cases} 2z'_{k,j-k} - z'^2_{k,j-k}, & \text{for } 0 \le j \le k-1; \\ z'^2_{k,j}, & \text{for } k \le j \le 2k-1, \end{cases} \tag{8}$$

The reliability of the FSF channels can be derived as $z_4 = (15/16, 9/16, 7/16, 1/16)$. Therefore, for the reliable transmission of signals over each subcarrier, we select the *information* bits $\{x_{2,\epsilon}, x_{3,\epsilon}\}$ and the *frozen* bits $\{x_{0,\epsilon}, x_{1,\epsilon}\}$.

4 Simulation Results

According to the OFDM depolarizing algorithm with the SIC decoder for the polar system, we present some simulation results and compare their BER performance behaviors. We present the BER performance as functions of the transmit power p_t. We deploy the Alamouti code while implementing the OFDM depolarizing techniques for the FSF channels. We can also use the ML symbol-wise decoding, as well as the OFDM depolarizing in four time slots, where the data symbols in $\mathcal{A}$ are drawn from BPSK constellation.

In Fig. 2, we present the BER curves of the stacked Alamouti code for four OFDM symbols transmitted at source node S. We consider the polar systems provided with transmission power p_t for reference in terms of the fixed power allocation strategy in (1). For the present polar system, it shows that the slope of the BER performance curve of the proposed PF scheme with the stacked Alamouti code for the polar system via the OFDM depolarizing algorithm approaches the direct transmitting system when power p_t increases. It implies that the PF scheme can achieve full diversity with the depolarizing algorithm. Furthermore, the BER performance behavior of the present polar system outperforms that of the direct transmission approach which verifies our analysis of the transmission reliability of the FSF channels. Simulations demonstrate that the proposed PF scheme has a similar performance as that of the Alamouti scheme with the ML decoding when the depolarizing is applied at the receiver.

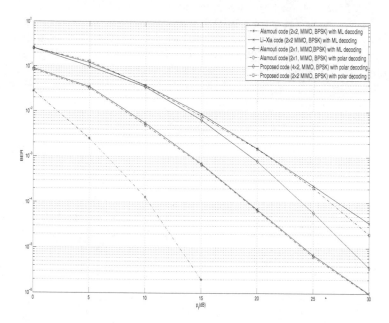

Fig. 2. BER performance behaviors with the depolarizing receiver

5 Conclusion

In this paper, we have presented a simple design of the PF scheme based on the switching polar systems over the FSF channels, i.e., the *down-polarizing* system and the *up-polarizing* system using two polarizing operations $\mathbf{Q}_2$ and $\mathbf{Q}'_2$ first suggested by E. Arikan. The present polar wireless system has a salient recursiveness feature and can be decoded with the SIC decoder, which renders the PF relay scheme analytically tractable and provides a low-complexity coding algorithm while multiple OFDM symbols are equipped and broadcasted from source node S. We analyze the BER performance and diversity of this system based on the Alamouti code with the fixed transmit power using over the FSF channels, which tend to polarize with respect to the increasing reliability under certain OFDM combining and splitting operations. Simulations demonstrate that the proposed polar system has the similar BER performance behaviors as that of the stacked Alamouti code with the ML decoding, but outperforms this direct transmission method in terms of the BER performance for large transmission power p_t when the OFDM depolarizing algorithm is applied at destination node D.

Acknowledgements. This work was supported by the National Natural Science Foundation of China (60902044), and in part by World Class University R32-2010-000-20014-0 NRF, Korea.

References

1. Arikan, E.: Channel Polarization: A Method for Constructing Capacity-Achieving codes for Symmetric Binary-Input Memoryless Channel. IEEE Trans. Inf. Theory 55, 4366–4385 (2009)
2. Korada, S.B., Şaşoğlu, E., Urbanke, R.: Polar Codes: Characterization of Exponent, Bounds, and Constructions. IEEE Trans. Inf. Theory 56, 6253–6264 (2010)
3. Lee, M.H., Arikan, E.: Polar code and Jacket matrix. Seminar at Bilkent University, Turkey (August 2009)
4. Guo, Y., Lee, M.H.: A Novel Channel Polarization on Binary Discrete Memoryless Channels. In: IEEE ICCS, Singapore (November 2010)
5. Li, Z., Xia, X.-G., Lee, M.H.: A Simple Orthogonal Space-Time Coding Scheme for Asynchronous Cooperative Systems for Frequency Selective Fading Channels. IEEE Trans. Commun. 58, 2219–2224 (2010)
6. Muhaidat, S., Cavers, J.K., Ho, P.: Transparent Amplify-and-Forward Relaying in MIMO Relay Channels. IEEE Trans. Wireless Commun. 9, 3144–3154 (2010)
7. Harshan, J., Rajan, B.S.: High rate single-symbol ML decodable precoded DSTBCs for cooperative networks. IEEE Trans. Inf. Theory 55, 2004–2015 (2009)
8. Rajan, G.S., Rajan, B.S.: Multigroup ML Decodable Collocated and Distributed Space-Time Block Codes. IEEE Trans. Inf. Theory 56, 3221–3246 (2010)
9. Jing, Y., Hassibi, B.: Distributed Space-Time Coding in Wireless Relay Networks. IEEE Trans. Wireless Commun. 5, 3524 3536 (2006)
10. Alamouti, S.M.: A simple transmit diversity technique for wireless communications. IEEE J. Sel. Areas Commun. 16, 1451–1458 (1998)

Multipath OLSR with Energy Optimization in Mobile Adhoc NETwork (MANET)

Kirti Aniruddha Adoni[1] and Radhika D. Joshi[2]

[1] Modern College of Engineering, Electronics and Telecommunication
Engg. Department, Shivaji Nagar, Pune 5, India
[2] College of Engineering, University of Pune, India
k_adoni@rediffmail.com, akirti2008@gmail.com,
rdj.extc@coep.ac.in

Abstract. Mobile Adhoc Network (MANET) eliminates the complexity associated with an infrastructure networks. Wireless devices are allowed to communicate on the fly for applications. It does not rely on base station to coordinate the flow of the nodes in the network. This paper introduces an algorithm of multipath OLSR (Optimized Link State Routing) for energy optimization of the nodes in the network. It is concluded that this solution improves the number of nodes alive by about 10 to 25% by always choosing energy optimized paths in the network.

Keywords: OLSR, multipath, energy optimization, nodes alive.

1   Introduction

A Mobile Adhoc NETwork (MANET) is a multi-hop, distributed and self configuration network[1].The communication between two distant nodes is through the number of intermediate nodes which relays the information from one point to another. As nodes can move randomly within the network, routing packets between any pair of nodes become a challenging task. A route that is believed to be optimal for energy utilization at certain time might not be optimal at all, few moments later [4].

Traditional proactive routing protocols [3,5] maintain routes to all nodes. Even if traffic is unchanged, repeated topology interaction happens among nodes. Also, they require periodic control message to maintain routes to every node in the network. Optimized Link State Routing (OLSR) is such a proactive routing protocol. Requirement of bandwidth and energy will increase for higher mobility. The behaviour of routing protocol depends on the network size and node mobility.

OLSR is an optimization of pure link state routing protocol which inherits the stability of a link state algorithm and takes over the advantage of proactive routing nature to provide routes immediately when needed. Here, to achieve energy optimization of all nodes in the network; first OLSR has been modified to multipath OLSR.

N. Meghanathan et al. (Eds.): CCSIT 2012, Part III, LNICST 86, pp. 552–561, 2012.
© Institute for Computer Sciences, Social Informatics and Telecommunications Engineering 2012

Among these multiple paths between the two distant nodes at given time, path containing all intermediate nodes with higher energies are considered.

The remaining of the paper is organized as follows. Section 2 discusses overview of OLSR routing protocol. Section 3 describes algorithm used for multipath and energy optimization in OLSRM by modification made in OLSR. Section 4 describes simulation parameters to analyse performance differences. Section 5 discusses results of the OLSR and OLSRM for parameters like nodes alive and end to end delay, considering the effect of node velocity, node density and pause time. Finally, conclusions are in Section 6.

2   Overview of OLSR Routing Protocol

OLSR, proactive routing protocol exchanges routing information with other nodes in the network. The key concept used in OLSR is of MPRs (Multi Point Relays)[6]. It is optimized to reduce the number of control packets required for the data transmission using MPRs. To forward data traffic, a node selects its one hop symmetric neighbours, termed as MPR set that covers all nodes that are two hops away. In OLSR, only nodes, selected as MPRs are responsible for forwarding control traffic. The selected MPRs forward broadcast messages during the flooding process, contrarily to the classical link state algorithm, where all nodes forward broadcast messages. So mobile nodes can reduce battery consumption in OLSR compared with other link state algorithms.

A. Control Message

There are three types of control messages: HELLO messages, Topology Control (TC) messages, Multiple Interface Declaration MID messages. To achieve energy optimized multipath OLSR, HELLO message and TC message format has been modified.

- The link status and one hop neighbours' information data is given by HELLO message.
- Topology information is received by a node by periodical TC message using Multipoint Relaying (MPR) mechanism.
- MID message is sent on network to announce that if node is running multiple interfaces.

B. Routing Table and Topology Table

As a proactive routing, the routing table has routes for all available nodes in the networks. It has Destination Address, Next Hop Address, Local interface address and number of hops. It is as presented as follows:

Dest	next	iface	dist
0	0	37	1
2	6	37	2
14	20	37	3

From the above table, distance between 37 and 0 is 1 hop, the path is 37-0, distance between 37 and 2 is two hop, the path is 37-6-2, distance between 37 and 14 is 3 hop, the path is 37-20-?-14. If the number of hops are more than two, then intermediated nodes on the path has to find out the next (?), which is not displayed in routing table.

The topology table gives the information about entire network. It informs about one hop. There is no information about Residual energy of the node in topology table format of OLSR.

Its original format is as follows:

Dest	Last	Seq
0	13	2
36	13	2
1	13	2
0	38	6

C. Routing Discovery

To work in distributed manner, OLSR does not depend on any central entity [5]. Each node chooses its as multipoint relays (MPR) which are responsible to forward control traffics by flooding. The nodes maintain the network topology information where MPRs provide a shortest path to a destination with declaration and exchange of the link information periodically for their MPR's selectors. The HELLO messages are broadcast periodically for neighbour's detection and MPR selection process. It contains how often node send HELLO messages. It also includes node's MPR willingness and information about neighbour node. The information of node's is in the form of its link type, interface address and neighbour type.

The neighbour type can be one of: symmetric, MPR or not a neighbour. Link type indicates whether link is symmetric, asymmetric or lost link. A node is chosen as MPR if link to the neighbour is symmetric.

A node builds a one hop routing table with the reception of HELLO message information. It discards duplicate packet with same sequence number. The node updates when there is change in neighbour r node or route to a destination has expired.

OLSR does not require sequenced delivery of messages as each control message contains a sequence number which is incremented for each message.

D. Source Routing

Multiple paths calculated between a pair of source destination are independent, and they have no common nodes. However, because of the characteristic of next hop routing in OLSR, node can forward data based on its own routing table, and it cannot get the correct next node, source will forward, so cross among multiple paths happens. To avoid the problem for the next-hop routing in standard OLSR protocol, we use the source path in our multipath_OLSR algorithm. When a node calculates a path, the information of the path is recorded in its routing table (R_dest, R_next, Rdist, Rbuffer, nexthopO, and nexthopI... nexthopl4}. So, when source send data along the path, it add the source path (nexthopO, nexthopI... nexthopl4) to the IP header in the data. Now the intermediate nodes only need to get the path information from IP header of data to forward the data, need not to query its routing table as in standard OLSR protocol. So, the mechanism of source path added to multipath OLSR can avoid the problem of next hop node.

E. Energy-Efficient Route Selection Metric

There are different Route selection metric based on transmission power, link distance or residual energy of the node.

A brief description of the relevant energy aware metric proposed are given below.

1. MTPR (Minimum Total Transmission Power Routing)[8]

The MTPR mechanism uses a simple energy metric. It repr esents the total energy consumed to forward the information along the route. MTPR uses shortest path routing. It reduces the overall transmission power consumed per packet. It does not take into account available residual energy of the node.

2. MBCR (Minimum Battery Cost Routing)[8]

The MBCR selects the route that minimizes the battery cost function. Battery cost function for a node is the reciprocal of available Residual energy of that node.

$$f(n_i) = \frac{1}{c(n_i)} \tag{1}$$

Where $c(n_i)$ denotes the residual energy of node n_i.

Therefore, the battery cost for a route l, length D, is given by:

$$P_l = \sum_{i=0}^{D-1} f(n_i) \tag{2}$$

The selected route P_k is the one that satisfies the following property,

$$P_k = min\{P_l : l \in A\} \tag{3}$$

Where A is the set of all the possible routes.

The main disadvantage of the MBCR is that selection is based only on the battery cost. In this one node may be overused.

3. MMBCR (Min-Max Battery Cost Routing) [8]

The MMBCR selects the route with the maximum values of the minimum battery cost of the nodes. Therefore, the equation for battery cost is modified to,

$$P_l = \max_{l \,\epsilon\, route\, l} f(n_i) \tag{4}$$

The selected route P_k is the one that satisfies the following property:

$$P_k = min\{P_l : l \in A\} \tag{5}$$

4.   CMMBCR (Conditional Min-Max Battery Cost Routing) [8]

This mechanism considers both the total transmission power consumption of routes and the residual energy of nodes. When all nodes in some possible routes have sufficient remaining battery cost, i.e. above a threshold [criteria for setting the threshold based on application are subjective], MTPR is applied, to find out optimal path.

But, if all routes have nodes with low battery, i.e. below defined threshold, then MMBCR technique is applied. The performance of CMMBCR totally depends on selected threshold value.

5.   MDR (Minimum Drain Rate)[8]

Only the Residual energy cannot be used to establish the best route between source and destination nodes. If a node has higher residual energy, too much traffic load will be injected through it, results in unfair sharp reduction of battery power. To avoid this problem MDR is used.

In this metric, cost function is considering both Residual energy of node and Drain rate of that node. Maximum Lifetime for a given path is determined by minimum value of cost along that path. Finally, MDR selects the optimal path having the highest maximum lifetime value.

6.   LCMMER (Low Cost Min-Max Energy Routing) [9]

The difference between MMBCR and LCMMER is that MMBCR avoids the path with lowest energy nodes, does not consider the cost of the path and may select excessively long paths, whereas LCMMER also tries to avoid least energy nodes.

3   Modified OLSR

OLSR applies shortest hop routing method for the transmission of data. It leads the congestion on specific path, or rise in energy expenditure of particular intermediate nodes.

If multiple paths are available, then congestion can be avoided, and energy expenditure of all nodes would be uniform. To achieve this, following changes are carried out.

Following are the changes made in OLSR protocol:

A. Changes in control messages

The 'reserved' field available in HELLO and TC message format is used to pass residual energy. This residual energy is further used to find out appropriate path.

B. Changes in Routing table and Topology table

As discussed in section II-B, in OLSR, user is not aware of intermediate nodes present on the path and also its residual energies.

The modified Routing Table of Multipath OLSR is as follows- from the modified routing table, information of residual energies of intermediate nodes are obtained.

Dest	next	iface	dist
14	20	37	3
20			
11			
14			

Residual energy of intermediate node1
Residual energy of intermediate node2
....

So from the modified Routing Table, for the given source-destination pair, multiple paths are available.

Now to select one of the available path, energy aware metric is applied.

The energy expenditure (in Joules) needed to transmit a packet p is given by,[7]

$$E(p) = i * v * t_p \tag{6}$$

Where i is the current value,

v is the voltage,
t_p the time taken to transmit the packet p.

For our simulation, the voltage is chosen as 5 V.

Algorithm for modified OLSR

- Maintain all one hop ing nodes for each node using modified HELLO message, with the residual energy of the nodes.
- Based on its one hop table, insert the appropriate entries to its routing table.
- Match the entries with topology set and add to the routing table.
- For each node, see recursively its last address until reached to the destination node, record the complete path information in the routing table using modified TC message (with the residual energy of the nodes).
- Discard the loop entries.
- Get all the paths for given source-destination pair, with the residual energy of each node to the entire network.
- Select all paths, for given source-destination pair
- Find out minimum energy of node, E(min), on each selected paths.
- Find out maximum energy of node, E(max), out of that E(min) values.
- Use this selected path.

4   Simulation Parameters

We use network simulator ns2 [2] to analyse OLSR and OLSRM routing protocols and measure Number of node alive and Average end to end delay with varying Nodes' velocity and node density.

We use a movement pattern of the random waypoint mobility model, obtained from a tool called "setdest", developed by Carneige Mellon University. The performance of ad-hoc routing protocols greatly depends on the mobility model it runs over[10]. For simulation, Two ray ground propagation model is used. The nodes are 40 in the area of 1000 X 1000 square meter. Traffic type used is CBR (Constant Bit Rate), Packet send rate is 20 packets/sec and Packet size is 512 Bytes.

5   Simulation Results

Quality of Services (QoS) Parameters:
We evaluate essential Quality of Service parameters to analyse the performance differences of OLSR and OLSRM. Each node in the network has some constant Initial energy. The QoS parameter, alive nodes are chosen to show that more number of nodes alive for longer time in the network. More number of alive nodes implies the optimization of energy. The parameter Delay is chosen to study the effect of, addition of multipath technique and energy aware metric to the original OLSR

Number of Nodes Alive: This is one of the important metric to evaluate the energy efficiency of the routing protocol. It tells about Network Lifetime,

* The time to the first node failure due to battery outage
* The time to the unavailability of an application functionality[11]

First point gives the failure of first node, whereas second gives the time when only one node is alive (for communication at least two nodes must be alive). Both can be extracted from the trace file and tells about time at which first node died and the information about how alive nodes changes with the simulation time.

Average End to End Delay: This is the time difference between sending of data packets and time at which the same data packet is received.

A. Effect of   Node Mobility, and Node Density on Number of   Nodes Alive

In case of OLSR, the shortest hop path is always chosen; whereas in OLSRM the path for the data delivery is considered with the available energy of nodes (at that instant) on the path, even if the path is long (in terms hop). Therefore OLSRM has more number of nodes alive compared to OLSR. As the node mobility increases, the number of alive nodes in OLSRM increases implies that modified protocol is suitable for dynamic network.

By varying number of nodes, it has been observed that OLSRM has more number of nodes, for high node density. It is obvious, as multiple paths will be more for large number of nodes. So it can be seen from the results, OLSRM is best suitable for dynamic and dense network.

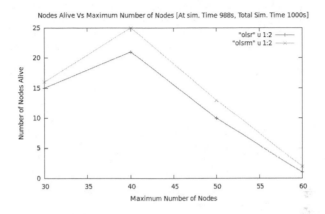

Fig. 1. Effect of node density on nodes alive

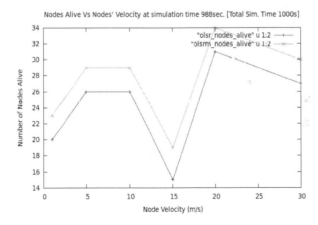

Fig. 2. Effect of node velocity on nodes alive

B. Effect of Node Mobility and Node Density on Average End-to-End Delay:

For various Node's maximum velocity, OLSRM has less end-to-end delay, as multiple paths are available, than that of OLSR.

By varying node density, it has been observed that end-to-end delay is less for OLSRM than that of OLSR.

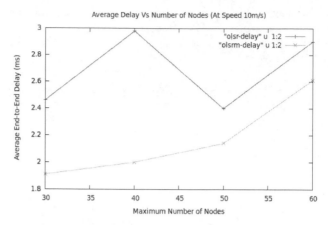

Fig. 3. Effect of node density on average end-to-end delay

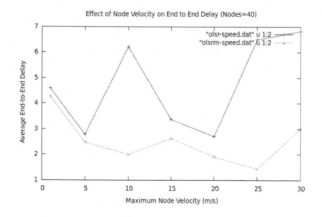

Fig. 4. Effect of node velocity on average end-to-end delay

6   Conclusion

We examine the performance differences of OLSR and OLSRM. We measure Number of alive nodes and average end to end delay as QoS parameters.

OLSR, always uses shortest hop route, so congestion occurs and distribution of load is not considered. Also, OLSR does not consider available node energy of nodes for path selection and communication purposes. In this paper, algorithm for multipath OLSR with the addition of energy aware metric is given and simulation is performed using NS-2. Our simulation results show that OLSRM (modified OLSR with multipath) outperforms OLSR for number of alive nodes by 10 to 25% with considering performance parameters as node velocity and node density.

Thus, congestion of the network disappears and load is transmitted uniformly throughout the network. The modified OLSR also gives the reduction in average end to end delay.

As a future work, we will evaluate optimum paths based on number of hops and available energy. Load will be mainly assigned to the main path, but if the energy of the intermediate nodes is reaching to threshold (given by the user and generally depends on data type), then another path to be considered. This will give the benefit of shortest hop route as well as optimum node energy consideration for longer life span of the network.

Acknowledgments. We are thankful to Mr. Aniruddha B. Adoni as his help was very useful which gave a direction to complete the work by his timely critics and relevant   inputs and suggestions.

References

1. Rashmi: MANET, http://WWW.SACHING.COM
2. Entan, Jimenez, T.: NS Simulator for beginners, Lecture Notes. University of Merida, ESSI, Sophia-Antipolis, France (December 4, 2003)
3. Chiang, C., Wu, H.K., Liu, W., Gerla, M.: Routing in clustered multihop mobile wireless networks with fading channel. In: Proc. IEEE SICON 1997, pp. 197–221 (1997)
4. Do, M.Z., Othman, M.: Performance comparisons of AOMDV and OLSR routing protocols for MANET. In: IEEE 2010. Iccea, vol. 1, pp. 129–133 (2010)
5. Clausen, T., Jacquet, P.: rfc3626.txt, Network working group DRAFT for OLSR protocol (October 2003)
6. De Rango, F., Fotino, M.: Energy Efficient OLSR performance Evaluation under Energy Aware Metrics. In: SPECTS 2009, pp. 193–198. IEEE (2009)
7. Kim, D., Gracia-Luna-Aceves, J.J., Obraczka, K., Cano, J.-C., Manzoni, P.: Power-Aware routing based on the energy Drain Rate for Mobile AdHoc Networks, University of California, U.S.A., Polytechnic University of Valencia, October 14-16, pp. 565–569. IEEE (2002)
8. De Rango, F., Fotino, M., Marano, S.: EE-OLSR: Energy Efficient OLSR routing protocol for Mobile Adhoc Networks. In: MILCOM 2008, D.E.I.S. Department, University of Calabria, Italy, November 16-19, pp. 1–7. IEEE (2008)
9. Vergados, D.J., Patazis, N.A.: Enhanced route selection for energy efficiency in wireless sensor networks. ACM International Conference Proceeding Series, Greece, vol. 329, Article 63 (2007)
10. Chen, B.-R., Hwachang, C.: Mobility Impact on Energy Conservation of Ad-hoc Routing protocols. Tufts University, Medford, USA, NSF Grant #0227879
11. Mahfoudh, S., Minet, P.: An Energy Efficient routing based on OLSR in wireless ad hoc and sensor networks. In: 22nd AINA Workshop 2008, March 25-28, pp. 1253–1259. INRIA, France (2008)

Author Index

564   Author Index